# ISSUES FOR DEBATE
# IN SOCIAL POLICY

# ISSUES FOR DEBATE
# IN SOCIAL POLICY

## SELECTIONS FROM CQ RESEARCHER

# 2ND EDITION

Los Angeles | London | New Delhi
Singapore | Washington DC

Los Angeles | London | New Delhi
Singapore | Washington DC

FOR INFORMATION:

CQ Press

An Imprint of SAGE Publications, Inc.

2455 Teller Road

Thousand Oaks, California 91320

E-mail: order@sagepub.com

SAGE Publications Ltd.

1 Oliver's Yard

55 City Road

London EC1Y 1SP

United Kingdom

SAGE Publications India Pvt. Ltd.

B 1/I 1 Mohan Cooperative Industrial Area

Mathura Road, New Delhi 110 044

India

SAGE Publications Asia-Pacific Pte. Ltd.

3 Church Street

#10-04 Samsung Hub

Singapore 049483

Printed in the United States of America

Library of Congress Control Number: 2014938715

ISBN: 978-1-4833-6597-8

This book is printed on acid-free paper.

Acquisitions Editor:   Kassie Graves

Editorial Assistant:   Carrie Baarns

Production Editor:   Kelly DeRosa

Typesetter:   C&M Digitals (P) Ltd.

Cover Designer:   Candice Harman

Marketing Manager:   Shari Countryman

14 15 16 17 18 10 9 8 7 6 5 4 3 2 1

# Contents

# Preface

Keeping students up to date on timely policy issues can be challenging given the range of issues, changing administrations, and the volatile political economy. Furthermore, finding readings that are student friendly, accessible, and current can be an even greater challenge. Now *CQ Researcher*, CQ Press and SAGE have teamed up to provide a unique selection of articles focused on social policy, specifically for courses in Social Welfare Policy and Social Policy. This collection aims to promote in-depth discussion, facilitate further research, and help students formulate their own positions on crucial issues.

This volume includes eighteen up-to-date reports by *CQ Researcher*, an award-winning weekly policy brief that brings complicated issues down to earth. Each report chronicles and analyzes executive, legislative, and judicial activities at all levels of government. This collection was carefully crafted to cover a range of issues from the mortgage crisis, to women's rights, child welfare reform, aging baby boomers, the Obama Presidency, and much more. All in all, this reader will help your students become better versed on current policy issues and gain a deeper, more critical perspective of timely and important issues.

## CQ RESEARCHER

*CQ Researcher* was founded in 1923 as *Editorial Research Reports* and was sold primarily to newspapers as a research tool. The magazine was renamed and redesigned in 1991 as *CQ Researcher*. Today, students are its primary audience. While still used by hundreds of journalists and newspapers, many of which reprint portions of the reports, the *Researcher's* main subscribers are now high school, college and public libraries. In 2002, *Researcher* won the American Bar Association's coveted Silver Gavel award for magazine excellence for a series of nine reports on civil liberties and other legal issues.

*Researcher* staff writers—all highly experienced journalists—sometimes compare the experience of writing a Researcher report to drafting a college term paper. Indeed, there are many similarities. Each report is as long as many term papers—about 11,000 words—and is written by one person without any significant outside help. One of the key differences is that writers interview leading experts, scholars and government officials for each issue.

Like students, staff writers begin the creative process by choosing a topic. Working with the *Researcher's* editors, the writer identifies a controversial subject that has important public policy implications. After a topic is selected, the writer embarks on one to two weeks of intense research. Newspaper and magazine articles are clipped or downloaded, books are ordered and information is gathered from a wide variety of sources, including interest groups, universities and the government. Once the writers are well informed, they develop a detailed outline, and begin the interview process. Each report requires a minimum of ten to fifteen interviews with academics, officials, lobbyists and people working in the field. Only after all interviews are completed does the writing begin.

## CHAPTER FORMAT

Each issue of *CQ Researcher,* and therefore each selection in this book, is structured in the same way. Each begins with an overview, which briefly summarizes the areas that will be explored in greater detail in the rest of the chapter. The next section chronicles important and current debates on the topic under discussion and is structured around a number of key questions, such as "Does corporate social responsibility really improve society?" or "Does corporate social responsibility restrain U.S. productivity?" These questions are usually the subject of much debate among practitioners and scholars in the field. Hence, the answers presented are never conclusive but detail the range of opinion on the topic.

Next, the "Background" section provides a history of the issue being examined. This retrospective covers important legislative measures, executive actions and court decisions that illustrate how current policy has evolved. Then the "Current Situation" section examines contemporary policy issues, legislation under consideration and legal action being taken. Each selection concludes with an "Outlook" section, which addresses possible regulation, court rulings, and initiatives from Capitol Hill and the White House over the next five to ten years.

Each report contains features that augment the main text: two to three sidebars that examine issues related to the topic at hand, a pro versus con debate between two experts, a chronology of key dates and events and an annotated bibliography detailing major sources used by the writer.

We hope that you will be pleased by this edition of *Issues for Debate in Social Policy.* We welcome your feedback and suggestions for future editions. Please direct comments to Kassie Graves, Publisher, SAGE Publications, 2455 Teller Road, Thousand Oaks, CA 91320, or *kassie.graves@sagepub.com.*

—The Editors of SAGE

# 1

# Women and Work

Michelle Johnson

Sheryl Sandberg, Facebook chief operating officer, argues in her new book that women, in their quest for full workplace equality with men, have limited their own advancement by not being forceful enough. Others blame persistent cultural and economic barriers for women's lack of greater progress.

From *CQ Researcher*, July 26, 2013.

L aura Leigh Oyler decided in seventh grade that education was her ticket to a good life.

"My parents got divorced when I was pretty young," says Oyler, who grew up in Fayetteville, Ark. "And I remember watching the women in my mom's social circle, one by one, go through a divorce. They lost their big, pretty houses. They had to go back to work. A lot of them, and my mom was no exception, started cleaning houses. She did that while going to school and raising three children, and I thought, 'I'm not doing that.'"

Oyler attended law school at the University of Arkansas, where she met her husband. Four years ago she was offered a job in employment law at Reynolds American, the nation's second-largest tobacco company, with a huge pay jump from her salary as a juvenile prosecutor in Arkansas. Although she had no direct experience in employment law, her fiancé (now her husband) encouraged her to make the leap to the Winston-Salem, N.C., firm.

He is now an associate at a local law firm and Oyler — 32, pregnant with the couple's first child — just accepted a promotion to lead Reynolds' youth smoking-prevention efforts.

Having a supportive spouse has been essential for her career says Oyler, the family's primary breadwinner. "He was the first one to say 'you can do anything. I've got your back. Go for it,'" she says.

Although Oyler is reluctant to call herself a feminist, she realizes her generation benefited from the women's movement led by her mother's generation. "I live in a very different America than women even 30 years ago did," she says. "A lot of social change happened in the '60s

## Women Now Earn Most College Degrees

Women are expected to earn more than half of all college degrees in the 2012-13 academic year, a significant increase from four decades earlier. The number of doctoral degrees increased sharply: Women earned 9,553 doctorates in 1972-73 compared with 90,100 in 2012-13 — an 800 percent increase. In 1972-73, women earned fewer than half of all degrees.

### Percentage of Degrees Earned by Women

| | Associate degrees | Bachelor's degrees | Master's degrees | Doctoral degrees |
|---|---|---|---|---|
| 1972-73 | 44.5% | 43.8% | 40.6% | 12% |
| 2012-13 (projected) | 61.6% | 56.7% | 59.9% | 51.6% |

*Source:* "Degrees conferred by degree-granting institutions, by level of degree and sex of students: Selected years, 1869-70 through 2021-22," National Center for Education Statistics, U.S. Department of Education, http://nces.ed.gov/programs/digest/d12/tables/dt12_310.asp

and the '70s, so I think that I benefit every day from that. And it's not just women who changed — it's men, too."

After women won the right to vote in 1920, feminism waned in the mid-20th century, overshadowed by concerns over the need to reintegrate returning veterans into the national economy after World War II. By the early 1960s, however, the "second wave" of the women's movement was quietly gaining momentum. Then, in 1963, labor journalist Betty Friedan's *The Feminine Mystique* landed as a bombshell in the lives of millions of American women.

"The feminine mystique," Friedan said in a 1964 interview, defined "woman solely in terms of her sexual relation to men, as man's sex object, as wife, mother, homemaker and never as a human being herself . . . and has not been good for their marriages, good for women, or good for love or good for men or even good for children."[1]

The feminist movement, which Friedan helped lead for decades before her death in 2006, has led to substantial gains in women's lives over the 50 years since the book was published. Women now make up half the workforce, earn more than half of almost all college degrees and hold half of all professional and management jobs in the United States.[2] They also have risen to the some of the highest levels in politics — including secretary of State and House majority leader — and have run some of the nation's biggest corporations, including Yahoo and Hewlett-Packard.

But despite such gains, women continue to face formidable barriers, from both within and without the movement: Ever since Friedan published her book half a century ago, sharp differences have arisen between those who have seen male oppression as women's primary obstacle and those who rejected sexual politics and pursued their goals within the traditional male-dominated economic and political system. The movement also has fought a tide of external social, cultural, political and economic barriers that continue to make it hard for many women to achieve full equality. American women still earn less than men for similar work, hold far fewer political and corporate leadership positions, shoulder more of family caregiving burdens and benefit from far fewer family-friendly corporate and government policies than women in other industrialized countries.[3]

What's more, some obstacles women face are self-imposed, according to Facebook chief operating officer Sheryl Sandberg, whose 2013 best-seller, *Lean In: Women, Work and the Will to Lead*, laments the dearth of females in leadership positions and urges women to be more assertive in their professional ambitions.

"It is time for us to face the fact that our revolution has stalled," she wrote. "The promise of equality is not the same as true equality. A truly equal world would be one where women ran half our countries and men ran half our homes."[4]

Sandberg's book has drawn both praise and criticism and established her as a new kind of feminist leader — one who acknowledges the social and cultural barriers women face but challenges them to confront certain behaviors that she says keep them from achieving their full potential.

Christina Hoff Sommers, a resident scholar at the conservative American Enterprise Institute (AEI), calls the progress of women in the workplace and economy "a great American success story," since women "are represented in virtually every economic sector and at every level."

However, she would like to see a women's movement "that catches up with where women are," she says. "About 20 percent of women are high-powered careerists. They're just as committed and high octane [as men], and I'm very glad that we have a society that now permits them to flourish. However, they are not the majority of women. There are just about as many who would prefer to stay home and be full-time mothers, and there's a huge group in between. They're adapters, who want to work part time once they have children. It would be nice if we had a women's lobby that understood that and made it possible."

When large numbers of women began entering the workforce in the mid-1970s, nearly half of the country's families with children had stay-at-home moms and breadwinner dads. Today that is true for only one family in five.[5] Women increasingly are choosing nontraditional fields, ranging from natural resources conservation to homeland security and law enforcement. They now earn half of all business administration degrees and more than half of degrees in the biological sciences and health.[6]

Nearly three-quarters of Americans say having more women in the workforce has been a change for the

## Families More Dependent on Mothers' Income

Mothers — married or single — were the sole or main breadwinner in a record 40 percent of households with children under age 18 in 2011, compared with only 11 percent in 1960 (top). Single mothers were the sole provider in a fourth of households with children, up sharply from five decades earlier. Meanwhile, the percentage of dual-income married couples with children rose sharply over the past five decades, reaching 59 percent in 1990 before hitting a plateau (bottom). The share of households in which only fathers were employed plunged from 70 percent in 1960 to 31 percent in 2011.

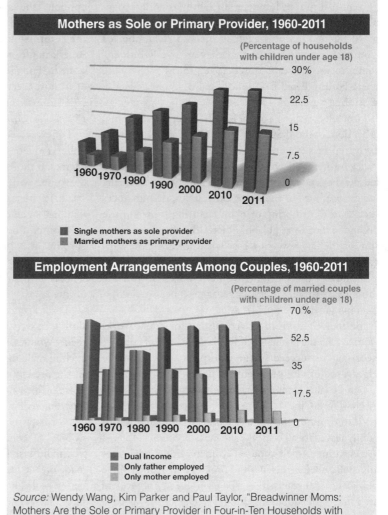

### Mothers as Sole or Primary Provider, 1960-2011

(Percentage of households with children under age 18)

- Single mothers as sole provider
- Married mothers as primary provider

### Employment Arrangements Among Couples, 1960-2011

(Percentage of married couples with children under age 18)

- Dual Income
- Only father employed
- Only mother employed

*Source:* Wendy Wang, Kim Parker and Paul Taylor, "Breadwinner Moms: Mothers Are the Sole or Primary Provider in Four-in-Ten Households with Children; Public Conflicted about the Growing Trend," Pew Research Center, May 29, 2013, pp. 1, 20, www.pewsocialtrends.org/files/2013/05/Breadwinner_moms_final.pdf

better in society and that marriages are more satisfying when men and women share responsibilities of work and children.[7] But workplaces and laws have yet to catch up with the realities of family life, says Joan C. Williams, director of the Center for WorkLife Law at the University of California's Hastings College of the Law. The American workplace is "still perfectly designed for the workplace of the 1960s," Williams says. "It assumes that you have someone else taking care of all your other family obligations, and that just isn't true anymore."

Feminist groups lobbying for family-friendly workplace policies have run into stiff opposition from organized business groups such as the U.S. Chamber of Commerce, which argues that they are overly burdensome for businesses. Conservative groups such as the Eagle Forum, based in Alton, Ill., also oppose federally subsidized daycare.[8]

Women have been a major force in American economic expansion. In the 1980s and '90s, their earnings grew relatively well, says economist Heidi Shierholz of the Economic Policy Institute, a liberal think tank. That growth helped to narrow the gender wage gap, though not entirely. Women's wages continued to rise in the early 2000s, despite forces such as the offshoring of manufacturing jobs and the decline in the power of labor unions. But the severe recession of the last few years has "wreaked havoc on wage growth," for both men and women, she says.

"The key thing driving women's wages is the same thing that's driving everyone's wages — persistent high unemployment," Shierholz says.

Besides fighting to get equal pay for equal work, women face the challenge of finding the kind of support necessary to succeed in the workplace, says Chanelle Hardy, senior vice president for policy at the National Urban League, a national civil rights organization based in New York City.

"From minimum wage to workers' compensation to family leave, are all critical," she says.

As women, their spouses, women's rights advocates and policymakers discuss the progress of women since publication 50 years ago of *The Feminine Mystique*, here are some of the questions being debated:

### Are women better off today than they were 50 years ago?

The idea that women's equality benefits everyone is at the heart of feminism.

The modern women's movement challenged discriminatory laws in education and employment and advocated for stronger laws on spousal rape, domestic violence and reproductive freedom.

The women's movement has worked at the local, state and federal level to change laws, says Eleanor Smeal, president of the Fund for the Feminist Majority and a former president of the National Organization for Women (NOW). "We raised consciousness, but without the change in laws, we could not have influenced public opinion," she says.

Many social and cultural changes brought about by the feminist movement are deeply integrated into American life, but the debate about feminism is far from settled. "For the most part, women are vastly better off on almost every measure than they were 50 years ago," says Hanna Rosin, author of *The End of Men And the Rise of Women*.

For example, in 1960, women earned 35.3 percent of undergraduate degrees and only 10 percent of doctoral degrees in the United States. Since 1968, the percentage of women with at least a college degree has tripled.[9] In the 2012-13 academic year, women earned slightly more than half of all doctorates.[10]

Women now comprise 57 percent of U.S. college enrollment.[11] In fact, women are attending college — and graduating — in such great numbers that some schools have quietly begun practicing affirmative action for men.[12]

The wage gap between men and women is closing, slowly, in part because of women's educational attainment. Women, on average, earn 77 cents for every dollar a white male makes, up from about 61 cents in 1960.[13] At the present rate, women's earnings won't catch up to those of men until 2056. The wage gap is even greater for women of color — black women earn, on average, 68 cents for every dollar a white male makes, Hispanic women, 59 cents.[14]

In the last five years or so, most of the progress made on the wage gap is not because women have done better — it's because men have done worse, Shierholz says. "That is not the kind of equity we want to see," she says. "We want women to see real, rising wages without men seeing declines."

The recession hit men especially hard. Women, Shierholz says, did better as a group because so many of them work in jobs that are less cyclical than more male-dominated fields such as construction and manufacturing.[15]

But for all their progress, women in general today say they are less happy than women were 40 years ago, Rosin says. "That's probably a natural consequence of [having] lots of choices," she says. "Often when you are supposed to compete in many different realms, and when your role is less defined, there are just more opportunities to find yourself wanting."

Economists Betsey Stevenson and Justin Wolfers, both at the University of Michigan, termed the phenomenon "the paradox of declining happiness." Their findings were consistent among women, regardless of their marital status, age, education or income level. The trend also held true for European women.[16]

But, Stevenson says, the decline in reported happiness is not tied to women's participation in the labor force. Perhaps it's due to women's higher expectations, she suggests. "One of the possibilities is that the women's movement changed how people think about and answer these questions," she says.

Stevenson and Wolfers also theorized that declines in family life or social cohesion have hurt women more than men. Or, in an era of greater gender equality, women may be more likely to compare their lives with those of the men around them, they wrote.[17] "It wasn't clear to us why," Stevenson is quick to point out. "What we were trying to do is document the trend and pose it as something that was important but difficult to understand."

Some see the happiness data as evidence that the feminist movement has let women down. "The idea that you can have it all . . . has not proven to be very family friendly," says Janice Shaw Crouse, a senior fellow at the Beverly LaHaye Institute, a Washington, D.C.-based Christian women's organization that is critical of the feminist movement. "It's not a pretty picture in women's personal lives."

She cites the declining U.S. marriage rate — it hit a record low of 51 percent in 2011 — as a sign of trouble, along with the fact that people are marrying later. The current median age for marriage is about 27 for women and 29 for men.[18] In 1960, by contrast, 72 percent of Americans were married, and the median age of marriage was the early 20s for both men and women.[19]

The reasons for delaying marriage vary; many women put it off until they finish school and get established in their careers. And many couples live together before marriage, instead of marrying.[20] Marriage, Crouse says, provides the best environment for raising children, forms an important cornerstone of society and makes women happier.

But the happiness data should be viewed in light of contemporary social and economic conditions, says Stephanie Coontz, a professor of history and family studies at Evergreen State College in Olympia, Wash. "In the 1950s and '60s, people were measuring their lives against World War II and the Depression," she says. "People's standards of happiness change."

Higher expectations — and greater anxiety — about their careers, their family's economic well-being, and their ability to provide for the life's big-ticket items, such as a home and their children's college tuition, may account for a decline in women's feelings of happiness, she says. "It's easy for people to say, 'well, maybe we've opened a Pandora's box here.' In fact, I think that's the wrong way to look at it," she says. "We're facing some new challenges — having overcome much worse ones in the past," she says.

Eagle Forum founder Phyllis Schlafly believes the feminist movement devalued marriage and family, to the detriment of women's happiness. "The ones who have planned their life without husband and children are living alone," she says. "And then when they get to be 38 or 40, they realize that life is passing them by. I think there are just so many who are not happy with the choices that they made."

Women are now the sole or primary breadwinner in 40 percent of households with children under 18. In 1960, that was true for just one in 10 households. Nearly two-thirds of these breadwinners are single mothers, whose median family income was $23,000 in 2011, well below the national median income of $57,000 for all families with children. By comparison, among the 37 percent of families in which women out-earned their husbands, the median family income was nearly $80,000.[21]

"There are groups of women who are in significant distress in our society," says Ellen Bravo, the executive director of Family Values at Work, a coalition of groups pressing for mandatory paid sick leave laws. "To say we're better off doesn't mean that we're anywhere near done. If we want to measure the progress of women, we have to measure all women."

## Are women limiting themselves?

When it comes to advancing in the workplace, are women victims of a "glass ceiling" or a "sticky floor"?

Plenty of evidence suggests that women encounter systemic barriers on their way up the career ladder — and that they also may impose career limits on themselves, sometimes for the sake of juggling family and professional responsibilities.

Women make up about half of the management ranks at American companies, but relatively few are making it into the executive suite.

In 2012, women held executive officer positions at 14.3 percent of *Fortune* 500 companies.[22] Women still face barriers, internal and external, in reaching the highest levels of leadership and achievement in professional life.

As for female behaviors Facebook COO Sandberg sees as self-limiting, women "systematically underestimate themselves," she said. "Why does this matter? Boy, it matters a lot. Because no one gets to the corner office by sitting on the side — not at the table — and no one gets the promotion if they don't think they deserve their own success or they don't even understand their own success."[23]

But women also face stereotypes. In 2003, Francis Flynn, a professor of organizational behavior at the Stanford University Graduate School of Business, and Cameron Anderson, a professor of leadership and communication at the Haas School of Business at the University of California-Berkeley, conducted a study in which their students were presented the real-life business case of venture capitalist Heidi Roizen, who had leveraged her "outgoing personality . . . and vast professional network" to her advantage.[24]

However, one group read about "Heidi Roizen," the other about "Howard Roizen." The students saw Heidi and Howard as equally competent. But when asked which they liked more, the students chose "Howard."[25]

Research into gender stereotypes bears out such findings. Studies show that women are generally expected to be more nurturing, sympathetic and kind and that when they show dominance or self-promotion they may face social or career-related consequences.[26] Even when women adopt the same career-advancement strategies as men — saying what they want in their careers, asking for opportunities, volunteering to work long hours — they advance less and their salaries grow more slowly than those of their male counterparts, the studies have found.[27]

Women also are less likely to negotiate for starting salaries or raises, potentially depriving themselves of hundreds of thousands of dollars in lifetime earnings. A study of graduate students indicated that while 57 percent of the male college graduates negotiated for their starting salary, only 7 percent of the women did.[28] Gender socialization explains some of the difference, said Linda Babcock, a professor of economics at Carnegie Mellon University's Heinz College School of Public Policy & Management and the co-author of *Women Don't Ask: Negotiation and the Gender Divide.* While boys are taught to focus on themselves, girls are taught to pay attention to the needs of others first, she said.[29]

Women also may think — correctly, in some cases — that they'll face a backlash for negotiating. Babcock's research revealed a "negotiation penalty" that was 5.5 times higher for women than for men: Both male and female hiring managers were less likely to hire women who negotiated.[30]

"As for the question 'are women limiting themselves?' I think the answer is definitely yes," says Daria Burke, CEO of Black MBA Women, an organization she founded to support aspiring executives. "But external factors play a significant role in our ability to push past the limits that have been set for us."

Women also hesitate to help themselves, according to a study by the London-based Institute of Leadership and Management. "Women managers are impeded . . . by lower ambitions and expectations [of themselves]," the study said. On average, men's higher expectations of themselves and self-confidence help them land management roles three years earlier than women.[31]

Ambivalence toward leadership also keeps women stuck, said Henna Inam, an Atlanta-based executive coach. She identified several typical self-limiting mindsets.

"If we perceive that leadership involves 'exerting power over others,' we are reluctant to lead," she said. "For many women, social acceptance is much more important than for men." Women also may think that accepting a leadership role is too stressful, she said, or that they need to improve themselves before they take on a new challenge, or that they can make a bigger difference in their current role than they could in the upper ranks of the organization.[32]

A study of 60 corporations by management consultant McKinsey & Co. found that a majority of successful women — 59 percent — don't aspire to the top job. When asked why, they gave answers such as "I'm happy doing what I'm doing."[33]

For a lot of women, ambition to climb the career ladder pales in comparison to wanting a balance between work and home life. According to a *New York Times*/CBS News poll, only one-quarter of mothers with children under 18 said they would work full time if money were no object.

"If it were up to me," said Angie Oler, a University of Wisconsin-Madison researcher who switched to part-time work when her first child was born four years ago, "I would never ever go back to full time. . . . I think the world would be a much happier place if we all worked fewer hours, like if everyone worked just four eight-hour days, and I think we'd all still manage to get all of our work done."[34]

For AEI's Sommers such views show that women's relationship to the workplace is "still more tenuous than men's, and not because of oppression. It's because of women's choice, women's freedom."

But women are frequently making those choices inside systems they didn't create, says Williams, of the Hastings College of the Law. Women — and men, for that matter — who want more flexibility in their working lives often are seen as slackers, even when their workplaces offer such arrangements. Moreover, women who leave the workplace to parent full time often face career penalties in the form of lower salaries when they try to return.[35]

The problem, Williams says, is the pervasive, implicit message in many workplaces that "a high-level professional

## Women Lag in Some Occupations

Women predominate in mostly traditional female jobs; they represent 98.1 percent of kindergarten teachers and 90.6 percent of nurses (top). And while women represent more than a third of U.S. doctors and surgeons, they account for only 19.7 percent of software developers and 4.1 percent of pilots and flight engineers (bottom). Overall, females now comprise 53.5 percent of the labor force.

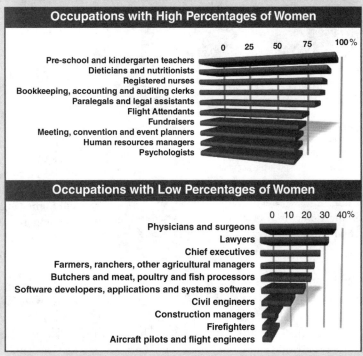

*Source:* "Current Population Survey," U.S. Bureau of Labor Statistics, www.bls.gov/cps/cpsa2012.pdf

is someone who makes work the central commitment of their lives."[36]

"So long as you have workplaces where the work-devotion ideal remains intact, we're never going to be able to address the 'hours problem,'" Williams says. The "hours problem," she says, is the expectation that to get ahead, workers must devote most of their lives to their jobs.

Among college-educated working mothers ages 25 to 44, she says, only 13.9 percent work more than 50 hours a week, compared to 37 percent of their male cohort (men 25-44, with college educations). It's unrealistic to think that more women will advance to the top of

AP Photo/*The Republic*/Andrew Laker

Taylor Baker stops to say hello to her 5-month-old daughter, Graesyn Steinkoenig, at the Cummins Childcare Center, part of Cummins Inc., an engine manufacturer, in Columbus, Ind., on Jan. 26, 2012. Baker, who works in the center's office, returned to work seven weeks after having her daughter. Advocates of family-friendly corporate policies say they are good not only for parents and children but also for the economy.

organizations — much less that the needs of ordinary working women will be addressed — without a fundamental shift in how workplaces approach work-life balance.

## Should workplaces become more accommodating for women?

The discussion about greater work-life balance often begins with the issue of maternity leave. The United States is the world's only high-income country that doesn't offer a legal right to paid time off after the birth of a child. The Family Medical Leave Act (FMLA), passed in 1993, mandates 12 weeks of job-protected leave to qualified workers, but the leave is unpaid, limited to companies with 50 or more employees and only covers employees who worked at least 1,250 hours in the year before requesting leave. As a result, about 40 percent of workers are not eligible for the benefit.[37]

Congressional Democrats, such as Rep. George Miller of California, have called for extending the FMLA to all workers.[38] While a few states have expanded family and medical leave, federal legislation is not expected to be adopted because of strong opposition from Republicans, who believe such measures would constitute onerous government intrusions into private companies' policies.

Only 11 percent of American workers have access to paid family leave, according to the National Partnership for Women & Families.[39]

"Providing 12 weeks of paid leave is expensive. We should not expect employers to pay for that individually," says Ariane Hegewisch, a study director at the Institute for Women's Policy Research, a Washington think tank that examines the impact of pay equity, immigration and education on women. "It really is something we need to do through social insurance."

A few states, such as California and New Jersey, offer family leave insurance, which — like Social Security or Medicare — is usually funded by a special payroll tax.

Most family-friendly policies in Europe are funded through social insurance. Parental leave policies in other countries vary widely — from Sweden's generous 40 weeks of full-time equivalent paid leave to nearly six years of combined job-protected leave for couples in France and Spain, much of it unpaid. A comparative study of "family friendly" policies in the United States and Europe found that most offered some kind of financial support.[40] Some American companies do offer paid maternity leave, and a few, such as Google and Yahoo, have begun offering paid paternity leave. But they are the exception.

"Employers are not filling the hole left by regulations," says Hegewisch. Laws are needed, she said, "to create a basic floor."

The benefits of "family friendly" policies, according to Hegewisch, include gender equality, lower infant mortality, higher fertility rates, better child health, labor force growth and lower poverty rates.[41] Paid maternity leave could also help the U.S. address its declining birth rate.

Still, says Roger Clegg, general counsel for the Center for Equal Opportunity, a conservative public policy institute, employers have no compelling reason to provide paid leave or other family accommodations. "Individuals should have choices about where they work, and companies should have choices about how to structure their jobs and allow the market to work these things out," Clegg says. "I think it would be a bad thing if we started moving toward the European model. This kind of micromanaging is bad for the economy, bad for economic growth."

In fact, some economists cite high labor costs as a factor in many European countries' ongoing economic woes.[42]

The U.S. Chamber of Commerce led the opposition to the FMLA when it passed in 1993 and opposes paid leave. "Employers have constraints on them," said Marc Freedman, the executive director for labor law policy at the Chamber. Even unpaid leave, he said, is too big a burden for many small companies. While larger companies can accommodate FMLA leave for new parents, he said, it can be difficult for them to track employees' medical leave.[43]

The lack of paid parental leave in the United States may partly explain why women's participation in the labor force has stopped growing, says Francine Blau, a labor economist at Cornell University. It has been at a standstill since the mid-1990s and is falling behind its European counterparts. In 1990, 74 percent of working-age women (16-64) were either employed or looking for a job, the sixth-highest rate among 22 economically advanced countries. By 2010, it had risen to just over 75 percent, while women's labor force participation in other advanced economies had increased on average from 67 percent to nearly 80 percent. Blau and her co-author, Lawrence Kahn, found that the expansion of "family friendly" policies in European countries explained nearly 30 percent of the difference between American women's labor force participation and that of their European counterparts.[44]

"These other countries started with much more aggressive policies of parental leave and part-time entitlements, and expanded those policies over the last 20 years," Blau says. Such generous policies appear to help women "handle both their work and their family responsibilities and increase labor force participation."

But more of the jobs available to European women were part-time, and a larger share of U.S. women are professionals or managers than among their European counterparts.

"We think there probably are some unintended consequences of these [parental leave] policies, if they become extremely generous," Blau says. Women may "spend more time out of the labor force than they otherwise would have and be more likely to work in part-time jobs than they otherwise would have."

"The U.S. may be too low, but other countries may have gone overboard in the other direction."[45]

While work-family policies are good for parents and children, they're also good for the economy as a whole, Blau says. "If we do not fully utilize the skills and talents, our output is not as great as it would be, and we're not as prosperous as we could be," she says.

Paid maternity leave also increases the likelihood that women will return to work once the leave is over, studies show.[46] And a study by one of Blau's graduate students at Cornell, Ankita Patnaik, suggests that encouraging men to take paid paternity leave may have long-term effects on how partners share child care and household duties. Patnaik looked at the long-term effects of Quebec's "use it or lose it" paid parental leave and found that dads who took the leave were more likely to shoulder more of the domestic chores than those who didn't.[47]

## BACKGROUND

### The Second Wave

When President John F. Kennedy appointed his Presidential Commission on the Status of Women in 1961, political momentum had been growing to address the issue of women's equality. The 26-member commission, headed by former first lady Eleanor Roosevelt, was charged with investigating discrimination against women.

"I don't think he meant to give birth to the modern women's movement," historian Ruth Rosen, a professor emerita at the University of California-Davis, said of Kennedy, "but in effect that's what he did."[48]

For more than 40 years after women won the vote with ratification of the 19th Amendment in 1920, feminism in America had largely faded from public view. The coalition that had fought for suffrage splintered, as one wing, the National Woman's Party, began pursuing an Equal Rights Amendment (ERA), led by suffragist Alice Paul.[49] Another began pushing for legislative changes more narrowly focused on helping to protect working women through the Women's Bureau at the Department of Labor; a third party sought to carve out a more prominent place for women in political parties.[50]

The Women's Bureau, according to historian Georgia Duerst-Lahti, "nurtured a coalition of groups concerned

## CHRONOLOGY

### 1848-1945 *Women press for voting rights and workplace equality.*

**1848** First women's rights convention takes place in Seneca Falls, N.Y.

**1920** States ratify 19th Amendment, giving women the right to vote. . . . Labor Department's Women's Bureau formed to collect data about working women.

**1923** Equal Rights Amendment (ERA) introduced in Congress.

**1930** Half of single women and 12 percent of wives are in labor force.

**1938** Fair Labor Standards Act establishes rules for a minimum wage, overtime pay and child labor.

**1941-1945** Almost 6 million women enter the workforce during World War II.

### 1960s *Women win landmark victories for equal rights in the workplace.*

**1961** President John F. Kennedy establishes Commission on the Status of Women.

**1963** Kennedy signs Equal Pay Act. . . . Betty Friedan's *The Feminine Mystique* spurs women's rights movement.

**1964** Civil Rights Act outlaws employment discrimination on basis of race, color, religion, sex and national origin.

**1966** National Organization for Women founded.

**1968** Equal Employment Opportunity Commission bans sex-segregated help-wanted ads.

### 1970s *Feminist movement spurs political and social change.*

**1972** Congress passes Equal Rights Amendment (ERA), sends it to states for ratification. . . . Congress passes Title IX, requiring gender equity in educational programs.

**1973** Supreme Court legalizes abortion, energizing women's movement.

**1974** Supreme Court rules employers cannot justify lower wages for women.

**1978** Pregnancy Discrimination Act bans firing pregnant women or denying them jobs. . . . Labor Department acts to increase the number of women in skilled construction trades.

### 1982-2000 *ERA fails; unpaid family leave becomes law.*

**1982** Equal Rights Amendment falls three states short of 38 needed for ratification.

**1986** Supreme Court declares sexual harassment in workplace illegal.

**1993** Family and Medical Leave Act entitles eligible employees to take job-protected leave.

### 2001-Present *Equal-pay fight continues.*

**2001** Female Walmart employees file sex-discrimination claim.

**2004** Morgan Stanley agrees to pay $54 million in sex-discrimination suit.

**2007** Supreme Court throws out woman's pay-discrimination claim because it was not filed within a 180-day deadline from her first paycheck.

**2009** President Obama signs the Lilly Ledbetter Fair Pay Act, invalidating the 2007 Supreme Court ruling. The act allows employees to contest pay discrimination 180 days after any discriminatory paycheck.

**2011** Supreme Court dismisses *Walmart v. Dukes*, saying it cannot determine whether all 1.5 million plaintiffs were victims of discrimination.

**2012** Record number of women elected to Congress — 20 senators and 81 House members.

**2013** Census Bureau finds that women are primary breadwinners in 40 percent of U.S. households with children under 18, up from 10 percent in 1960.

with the plight of working women and favoring protectionist legislation, and in the process it kept a spark of activism alive."[51]

By and large, these groups opposed the Equal Rights Amendment because they believed that women needed labor protections, such as maximum work hours and minimum wages, which they feared would be abolished under the ERA. Paul's group, meanwhile, felt that labor standards did not promote equality. "Labor legislation as a form of sex discrimination," she wrote, "is enacting another handicap for women in the economic struggle."[52]

Women's participation in the labor force had been on the rise before World War II, and the war brought about six million women into the workplace between 1940 and 1944 to replace men called up for military service. By the spring of 1944, nearly one-third of all women and girls over age 14 were working, and their ranks in industrial jobs had increased almost 500 percent.

As the war was winding down in 1945, the government waged an aggressive campaign to encourage women to return to their traditional roles as full-time housewives and mothers, or to take jobs in traditional "feminine" (and lower paying) occupations, such as clerical work. But the women were not keen to do so: Polls showed that more than three-quarters of women employed in wartime occupations said they hoped to keep their jobs when the war ended.[53]

Equal-pay legislation, which would ensure equal pay for women doing work that required comparable skills as their male counterparts was proposed in 1945, mainly as a tribute to female wartime workers. But in a postwar economy focused on reintegrating veterans into the workforce, the legislation languished. Large numbers of American women entered or remained in the workforce after World War II. In 1960, nearly 35 percent of American women over age 16 were working, and public opinion — including organized labor — was rallying around the concept of equal pay for equal work.[54]

But until 1963, opposition from business groups blocked the legislation.[55]

In June of 1963, a few months before his Presidential Commission on the Status of Women published its final report, Kennedy signed the legislation amending the 1938 Fair Labor Standards Act. The Equal Pay Act required employers to pay men and women equally for doing the same work. It also allowed for pay differentials based on seniority, merit, quantity or quality of production or a factor other than gender. (Current legislative efforts such as the Paycheck Fairness Act are aimed at closing some of these loopholes.)

A few months later, the presidential commission's final report documented workplace discrimination and recommended equal employment opportunities for women, affordable child care and paid maternity leave. Both developments came in the same year that *The Feminine Mystique* hit book stores, making 1963 an important year in the birth of the modern feminist movement.

Friedan went on to help found NOW in 1966. In 1970 she led the Strike for Women's Equality, a march on the 50th anniversary of women's suffrage that drew an estimated 50,000 women to the streets of New York City and gave the nation its first sweeping visual of the new feminist movement.

Coontz, who explored the impact of *The Feminine Mystique* in her book, *A Strange Stirring: The Feminine Mystique and American Women at the Dawn of the 1960s*, said Friedan's book struck a nerve among women who had left domestic life during World War II but were expected to return to it once the war was over, along with younger women who had watched the expansion of new jobs and educational opportunities in the postwar era only to be told it was abnormal for a woman to want anything other than a traditional role as wife and mother.

"It was a catalyst for stuff that was already coming," she says. "It inspired and had a tremendous emotional impact on women who had at first thought they were neurotic or even crazy for wanting something more out of life," she says.

The movement also attracted an entire generation of young (mostly white) middle-class women who had been raised with the idea that they would go to college but who aspired to defy the stereotype that Friedan depicted in the book. "They create the noise, they politicize these issues, and in effect create the women's movement," Rosen said. "They create the shock troops."[56]

But they were often made to feel unwelcome in the business world. In a recent commentary for *The Washington Post*, former *Post* restaurant critic Phyllis Richman described the discouraging experience of being asked by a Harvard graduate school professor to spell out exactly

# Women Still Hold a Fraction of Skilled-Trades Jobs

*"There's a big feeling that these are men's jobs."*

In the late 1970s, Connie Ashbrook enrolled in a pre-apprenticeship program to become a dump truck driver, her first job toward a career in the skilled trades.

Eventually she became an elevator installer. Her employer was looking for women because the company had a large federal contract and needed to comply with U.S. Department of Labor affirmative action guidelines calling for federal contractors to make a "good faith effort" to hire female workers.

"I always say that I got my job because of affirmative action and all the organizations that fought for equal opportunity, from the civil rights folks . . . to the feminist policymakers and lawyers fighting for women's equal opportunity," says Ashbrook, now executive director of Oregon Tradeswomen, Inc., which provides training and networking opportunities for women. "I kept my job because I was good at it . . . but the door was opened because of those people that believed in justice and equal opportunity."

Women increasingly are an accepted part of construction workplaces, and more women hold key leadership positions in unions and professional organizations than ever before. Despite such gains, however, they still occupy fewer than 3 percent of the nation's skilled trade jobs and apprenticeships.[1]

The construction industry employed 7.1 million people — 5.1 percent of all jobs — in 2011, but women comprised only 2.3 percent of that workforce, which includes electricians, carpenters, bricklayers and other trades.[2] Moreover, the percentage of female skilled apprentices in 2009 was smaller than in 1992, according to the Department of Labor.[3]

Women can earn significantly higher wages in the trades than in other occupations requiring only a high school education. The median weekly income of a male electrician, for example, is $855, which is 159 percent of the median wages of a woman with a high school diploma.[4]

So why aren't more women working in the skilled trades?

"I think there's a big feeling that these are men's jobs," says Francoise Jacobsohn, program director of the Equality Works project at Legal Momentum, a women's advocacy organization. "It's just entrenched discrimination."

The Department of Labor's Office of Federal Contract Compliance Programs (OFCCP) tracks whether federal contractors follow affirmative action guidelines. OFCCP Director Pat Shiu said in March that investigators have found violation rates in the construction industry are significantly higher than in other industries. The "vast majority" of those occurred because companies failed to take the established steps for

how she planned to balance her studies with her family responsibilities if she were to be accepted at Harvard. She replied, 52 years later, in a letter also published in *The Post*: "Before your letter, it hadn't occurred to me that marriage could hinder my acceptance at Harvard or my career," Richman wrote to the professor, William A. Doebele, Jr.[57]

After the 1972 passage of Title IX, the federal civil rights law prohibiting sex discrimination in education, women began heading to college in record numbers.

Women's access to higher education has been the "big advance" for the feminist movement, Smeal, the former NOW president, says. "Down deep, we thought if we could open the doors women would flood in, but we didn't really know. I have to say, once we got the doors open more, it went faster than we probably thought it would have gone."

## Women At Work

Still, what women choose to study and the professions they select factor into the persistent wage gap between

ensuring equal opportunity. Her office has beefed up enforcement efforts, she said, and long-awaited Labor Department employment goals for women and minorities will be published this fall.[5]

"I believe that the key to getting more women and minorities in the construction trades is strong enforcement," Shiu said.[6]

"You still run into contractors that say, 'Oh, do I have to take a woman?' says Leah Rambo, director of training for the Sheet Metal Workers Local 28 in New York City. "You tell them, 'Yes you do.' You still have a lot of people who need to be educated."

That goes for the public as well, Rambo says. Girls and women generally don't think of the trades as a career possibility, she says, and they also have to deal with sexual harassment and discrimination.

"A lot of women aren't prepared for that," she said.

Jenna Smith thinks sexual harassment is a major reason women drop out of the skilled trades. "They get worn out," says Smith, who works as the apprentice coordinator at Northwest Line Joint Apprenticeship Training Committee, a multistate organization based in Portland, Ore. "It's a really scary thing to stand up."

Smith remembers her own battle to win her journeywoman license after finishing an apprenticeship as an electric-line worker in Eugene, Ore. Smith reported being sexually harassed on the job when she was an apprentice. She was initially denied her journeywoman license, but eventually won an appeal.

Tradeswomen's groups are trying to get more women in the skilled trades, especially in leadership roles, says Carolyn Williams, director of civic and community engagement for the International Brotherhood of Electrical Workers union.

Oregon Tradeswomen Inc.

Trainees in Portland, Ore., learn carpentry in a state-certified pre-apprenticeship career class for women sponsored by the group Oregon Tradeswomen.

"Seeing someone who looks like me sends the message that 'there's a place for me here,' " says Williams.

— *Michelle Johnson*

[1] Timothy Casey, "Still Excluded: There Are Still Virtually No Women in the Federally Created and Supervised Apprenticeship Program for the Skilled Construction Trades," *Legal Momentum*, March 2013, www.legalmomentum.org/sites/default/files/reports/still-excluded.pdf.

[2] "A Databook 2012," U.S. Bureau of Labor Statistics, pp. 29, 38, www.bls.gov/cps/wlf-databook-2012.pdf.

[3] Casey, *op. cit.*, p. 5.

[4] *Legal Momentum* says statistically reliable data on female earnings is unavailable because so few women are employed in the trades.

[5] "Director Shiu Addresses 'Working on Equal Terms' Summit," U.S. Department of Labor Office of Federal Contract Compliance Programs, March 18, 2013, www.dol.gov/ofccp/addresses/Director_address_WETS_March182013.htmp.

[6] *Ibid.*

men and women. Women, especially women of color, are overrepresented in occupations considered "women's work" — child care and elder care, for example.

Much of the gender wage gap can be explained by wage differences in "traditionally male" and "traditionally female" occupations.

"Predominantly male jobs, particularly at the higher educated level, tend to pay much more than the female dominated jobs," says Hegewisch, of the Institute for Women's Policy Research. "I think the solution to this is not just to say, "OK, all women should become engineers now. It's also how we can more equitably fund and pay for the jobs that are done primarily by women. We do need librarians and teachers and psychologists and social workers. So it's not just saying women are wrong to go in for those jobs. Neither is there evidence that as soon as men move in, the wages will go up."

But the differences in chosen careers can't explain the entire gender wage gap, and discriminatory wage practices also persist, despite laws meant to prevent them.

# 'End of Men' Author Charts Women's Growing Power

*"We can't have this fixed idea that men are more dominant."*

*I*n her 2012 book The End of Men: And the Rise of Women, *Hanna Rosin maps what she sees as a seismic cultural shift — one accelerated by the recent recession, in which men lost a disproportionate share of jobs.*

*Women, she says, haven't just pulled even with men in education and social status — they've surpassed them. It's no longer a man's world.*

*Rosin, a senior editor for* The Atlantic, *says the book is "not a triumphalist feminist book that says, 'We won. We have everything.' Things have changed a lot, but the change has mixed results."*

*Here is an edited transcript of* CQ Researcher'*s Michelle Johnson's interview with Rosin.*

**Q: How have feminists responded to your book?**

A: There's been a mixed reaction. I have had to think about why the resistance, why the idea that we are doing well feels to many people like a betrayal of feminism. In an era of feminism in the 1970s, you would cheer at that idea. There was a sense that it was great to be triumphant. Now, as we get closer to more and more power, I think there's a sense that it's dangerous to say we're triumphant. I thought people would say, 'What about CEOs? There are so few women CEOs.' But it was more the mood that surprised me. From more working-class women to middle-class women, the sort of striving women who write me, the response is like, 'Duh, this is completely obvious,' or 'Thank you for laying it out.' And those women would not call themselves feminists. One surprise is that men have reacted pretty positively to the book.

**Q: At the beginning of writing the book, you thought that a world dominated by women would be more gentle or nurturing, but what you saw happening with women didn't seem "the result of fixed values or traits." You note the rise in arrest rates among women for violent crime, particularly among juveniles.**

A: It seems that these traits exist along a continuum, so as women gain more power, they start to show some of the traits of the more powerful. One of the more surprising findings for me was just looking at the violence statistics. We can't have this fixed idea that men are more aggressive, more dominant, more powerful, and women are weaker

In 2009, President Obama signed the Lilly Ledbetter Fair Pay Act, reversing a Supreme Court ruling from two years earlier. Ledbetter, a supervisor at a Goodyear Tire and Rubber Co. plant in Gadsden, Ala., had been paid less than her male counterparts for years but didn't know about the gap until she received an anonymous tip. Her complaint to the Equal Employment Opportunity Commission eventually made its way to the Supreme Court, which said she had failed to file the complaint within 180 days from when the discrimination first occurred. The Ledbetter law extended the statute of limitations for employees to contest pay discrimination to 180 days after any discriminatory paycheck.[58]

But a pay gap persists, even among women who do not choose traditionally female occupations. According to a 2012 study by the American Association of University Women, an inexplicable gap of about 7 percent remained between men and women with identical experience, education and occupational status one year after graduation from college or after obtaining advanced degrees, even after controlling for every known variable.[59]

And the gap has appeared to widen over time, even among high earners. The gap is driven in part by the choices that women often make when trying to balance work and family, experts say. Harvard University economists Claudia Goldin and Lawrence F. Katz examined the "career cost" of having a family among both women and men in business, medicine and law. They found that women pay a higher cost for having a family than men do. For example, while earnings for males and females with an

and more vulnerable. We move along the continuum. We can move a lot further than we think.

**Q: You also write that you had this mental image of an imaginary comic book duo, "Cardboard Man" and "Plastic Woman," but they aren't fixed gender traits.**

A: I think part of the reason that women have been more flexible in responding to changes in the economy is because they've been the underdogs. They've had to hustle. They've had to work twice as hard and fit into the cracks and struggle and struggle. Those two things are connected. Men have had a kind of entitlement to position, so they haven't had to struggle. But there certainly have been periods after World War II when men . . . behaved in ways that I'm describing women behaving now. They came back from war, bought up farms, went to school, got lots of degrees. They were really hustling in that brief period after the war. So no, I don't think those traits are innate.

**Q: Ellen Bravo, executive director of Family Values at Work, talks about "the feminization of work." That is, more jobs are temporary, part-time or on contract — something that has been more common for women — and that it's affecting everyone. Would you use that term?**

A: The fundamental structures of the economy have changed. It's not like a bunch of men lost their jobs and they'll get them back. The way the economy works and what it values has changed drastically, from a manufacturing economy to a service and information economy. Jobs

Hanna Rosin, author *of The End of Men: And the Rise of Women.*

can change at any moment, because technology can make jobs obsolete in a second. But the key element is the ability to adapt, which effectively means go to school and get whatever degree you need for whatever is happening at the moment. And that's something that women are doing much better than men.

*— Michelle Johnson*

MBA were similar immediately after graduation, a substantial wage gap between them existed 10 to 16 years after graduation, when the women's earnings fell to about 55 percent of the men's.[60]

Women with children were much more likely to take time out of the workforce or work part time — 24 percent fewer hours than men or women without children — and MBA moms who dropped out cited family, not career, as the reason, according to Goldin and Katz.[61]

They also found that high-powered career women increasingly are going into specialties that allow greater flexibility, even if it means lower incomes. Many women are choosing specialties that allow them to schedule or control their own hours — such as veterinary medicine, pharmacy and other medical specialties — and slowly are

helping to make those professions more flexible, the Harvard researchers found.[62]

## Sharing the Load

As a group, working dads are doing more around the house. A March report from the Pew Research "Social and Demographic Trends" found that fathers spend twice as much time doing household chores as they did in 1965 — from about four hours to 10 hours a week. Mothers in two-parent families put in about 18 hours a week, down from 32 hours in 1965. But while both parents spend more time with their children than parents did in 1965, moms spend more than dads do.[63]

They also tend to carry more of the emotional weight of running a family, says Kerry Fierke, an assistant professor at the University of Minnesota College of Pharmacy.

"We're the ones who send the birthday cards and keep the house set and take on a lot of responsibilities. I'm always working with women on how to shed some of those responsibilities," Fierke says. She dropped off the management track in corporate health care a few years ago and now focuses on healthcare leadership issues, especially for women.

While she and her husband share housework and child care fairly equally, she says, "I do more of the management part of it."

Men may be doing more, but they're also more likely than women to report work-family conflicts and less likely to take advantage of flexible work options offered by their employers, says Williams, of Hastings College of the Law.[64] "Men who take parental leave, much less go part-time, encounter career penalties because they are seen as more feminine," she says.

Yet many younger men, particularly college-educated couples, are taking a more hands-on approach to fathering. Fatherhood has gone from a "provide, protect scenario to a team effort, especially nowadays with couples raising children where both work full time," said 37-year-old Jeremy Foster, an online creative director and designer in Kansas City, Mo.[65]

In single-parent families, however, the "team effort" often involves a logistical juggling act in which children spend time at day care and with a combination of extended family members and friends.

Full-time day care is too expensive for many families, costing more than half the annual income of a family of three living at the poverty level ($18,530). Single parents are not the only ones who struggle, however. In 40 states (plus the District of Columbia), infant day care costs more than 10 percent of the median income for a married couple.[66]

Child care in the United States is also largely unregulated, often resulting in haphazard conditions and low pay for workers. A 2007 survey by the National Institute of Child Health Development rated the majority of day care centers as "fair" or between "poor and good."[67]

Except for a brief period during World War II, when day care centers were set up for women who worked in wartime factories, the United States has never had a national child care system. In 1965, Congress created Head Start, a federal program that provides early childhood education for low-income families. In 1971, Congress passed the Comprehensive Child Care Act, which would have set up a federally subsidized national day care system with standards for quality and money for training and facilities. President Richard M. Nixon, who initially supported the legislation, ultimately vetoed it, declaring that it would promote "communal approaches to child rearing over the family-centered approach."[68]

Head Start expanded during the Clinton administration and serves more than 1 million children in 50 states, but a comprehensive federal child care system has never gained momentum as a national policy issue. Some blame the feminist movement for focusing more on fighting sex discrimination and promoting abortion rights at the expense of working mothers' needs. Friedan herself echoed that criticism in her 1981 book *The Second Stage*, saying that pushing for family-friendly workplace policies was "the new feminist frontier."[69]

Obama has proposed spending $75 billion over 10 years to create a "universal pre-K" system, in which the federal government would provide states with matching funds to set up programs for 4-year-olds, funded with higher cigarette taxes.[70]

## CURRENT SITUATION

### Leadership Gap

Women such as Facebook's Sandberg and Anne-Marie Slaughter, a former high-ranking State Department official and professor of politics and international affairs at Princeton University, argue that true gender equity won't be possible until a critical mass of women wield power at the highest levels of political and corporate life.

In a widely debated article in *The Atlantic*, "Why Women Still Can't Have It All," Slaughter wrote that the best hope for improving the lot of all women, and for closing what some call "'a new gender gap'" — measured by well-being rather than wages — is to close the leadership gap: to elect a woman president and 50 women senators; to ensure that women are equally represented in the ranks of corporate executives and judicial leaders. Only when women wield power in sufficient numbers will we create a society that genuinely works for all women. That will be a society that works for everyone."[71]

# Are women better off than they were 50 years ago?

## YES

**Eleanor Smeal**
*President, Fund for the Feminist
Majority; Former President,
National Organization for Women*

Written for *CQ Researcher*, July 2013

Of course American women are better off today than 50 years ago! As a proud feminist activist for more than 40 years, I don't claim to be an impartial observer. Although inequities remain and the struggle is far from over, women's advancements are revolutionary.

In education, women have soared, both academically and athletically. In the 1960s women comprised a third of students enrolled in college, and some 60 percent never graduated. When I first began speaking for equality, women made up just 3 percent of the lawyers and 8 percent of the medical doctors. Feminists fought restrictive quotas that limited the number of women entering not only professional schools, but college itself. We were taunted with the ditty, "women don't want to be doctors or lawyers, they want to marry them."

Today such taunts are gone. Women are some 57 percent of college graduates and a majority of medical and law students. Women earn some 60 percent of the master's degrees and 52 percent of the doctorates.

In 1963 women were just 20 percent of the paid workforce; today we are nearly half. Women-owned businesses now employ more people than *Fortune* 500 companies combined. Women did not have equal credit opportunities until 1975, and the Pregnancy Discrimination Act did not pass until 1978. Fifty years ago a woman could be fired if she became pregnant. This was a typical fate for pregnant teachers, flight attendants and many more. Today's laws prohibit this practice.

Advances in birth control and abortion, and access to them, have improved women's health, economic well-being and educational opportunities. Women's longevity and maternal health have increased, while infant mortality and morbidity have decreased.

Fifty years ago domestic violence was treated as a personal problem, not talked about in public. Rape was considered a crime of passion, not a crime of violence. That day is over. Feminists at the state and federal levels have passed and are passing laws to combat such violence. Rates of violence, although still high, have been reduced. Sexual assault in the military and on college campuses is at intolerable levels, but an aware public is insisting on change.

Yes, the world is changing for women. Today the movement is worldwide. The need is still great, but the vision, hope and odds for winning women's equality have never been better.

## NO

**Phyllis Schlafly**
*Founder and President,
Eagle Forum*

Written for *CQ Researcher*, July 2013

Whether women are better off today depends on what the goals in life are: to be rich, to be important, to achieve the aims of feminism, or to be happy. Women will have different answers. But because the trigger for this question is the 50th anniversary of the feminist movement, perhaps we should answer in that context.

The goal of the women's liberation movement, as it labeled itself when it was launched in 1963 by Betty Friedan's book *The Feminine Mystique*, was to move all fulltime homemakers out of their homes and into the labor force. This was not based on any economic argument; the feminist rationale was that the home was a "comfortable concentration camp" to which wives and mothers were confined by the patriarchy. As Supreme Court Associate Justice Ruth Bader Ginsburg wrote in her book *Sex Bias in the U.S. Code*, "the concept of husband-breadwinner and wife-homemaker must be eliminated from the Code to reflect the equality principle."

The separation of marriage from a recognition of the complementary roles of mother and father, plus the easy divorce laws, brought about the unfortunate separation of babies from marriage. So now 41 percent of births in the United States are illegitimate. Generous federal handouts give women an incentive to look to Big Brother for financial support instead of to husbands and fathers.

A National Bureau of Economic Research working paper by University of Pennsylvania economists reported that women's happiness has declined measurably since 1970. One theory advanced by the authors is that the feminist movement "raised women's expectations" (in other words, sold them a bill of goods), making them feel inadequate when they fail to have it all.

Women's unhappiness is better explained by the fact that the feminist movement taught women to see themselves as victims of the patriarchy and that their true worth will never be recognized, so success in life is forever beyond their reach.

It's sad to read feminists' self-psychoanalysis. Their principal problem was that they took women's studies courses in college where they learned to plan a career in the workplace without any space or time for marriage or babies, at least until the women are over age 40 and their window of opportunity has closed. So they don't have the companionship of a husband in their senior years or grandchildren to provide a reach into the future.

At the current rate of growth, however, it would take more than 70 years for women to pull equal with men in leadership roles.[72]

Burke, of Black MBA Women, cites studies that correlate female leadership with better financial performance by companies as proof that the gender leadership gap needs to close.[73] "Organizations run by women perform better, and not just a little bit," she says. "The same thing goes for companies that have diverse leadership. You look at Wall Street and who ran it into the ground, and it was largely middle-aged white men."

For Sandberg, the leadership issue is a feminist issue. She is one of relatively few high-profile business executives to call herself a feminist, and she came in for some withering criticism, some of it from feminists who see her as too elitist to speak to the average woman's experiences. Others applaud her for speaking up.

"The truth is, feminism could use a powerful ally," wrote feminist author Jessica Valenti in an op-ed for *The Washington Post*.[74]

Though Sandberg identifies as a feminist today, she didn't think of herself that way in college. "But I think we need to reclaim the 'F word' if it means supporting equal opportunities for men and women," she said during an interview with *The Harvard Business Review* in April.[75]

Williams, of Hastings College of the Law, says perhaps "executive feminism" is just what the feminist cause needs in order to advance on behalf of other women. "More women in power might well lead to greater success in other arenas," she said in a recent blog post for *The Harvard Business Review*.[76]

Female leaders aren't immune to trouble, however. For example, the board of Hewlett-Packard forced out Carly Fiorina as CEO over her business decisions. Other powerful businesswomen, such as lifestyle maven Martha Stewart and hotel magnate Leona Helmsley, ran into legal trouble for their business practices. Stewart went to prison for insider trading, and Helmsley served time for tax evasion and fraud.

## Legislative Efforts

Many grass-roots feminists today are focusing on policies that they believe would benefit a wide swath of working American families. Bravo's Family Values at Work coalition of groups in 21 states is pushing for state and local measures to provide paid sick leave. Some 44 million Americans lack paid sick leave, and millions of others can't use their sick days to care for others, such as a sick child or parent. Some 60 percent of Latinos, the fastest-growing segment of the American workforce, get no sick leave.[77]

In 2011, Connecticut became the first state to adopt a sick-leave law, and San Francisco, Portland, Chicago and Seattle have adopted similar local measures. A recent New York City ordinance extends sick leave to about 1 million workers, and hundreds of thousands more get job-protected sick leave without pay.

"Many millions of workers are going without the protections they need in terms of sick days and family leave, so the present market hasn't worked, particularly for those at the middle and lower ends of the income ladder," says Vicki Shabo, director of Work and Family Programs for the National Partnership for Women and Families, a Washington, D.C.-based group that advocates for issues including paid family leave, paid sick leave and wage equity.

Shabo's group is working with House and Senate Democrats to push the Healthy Families Act, first introduced in 2004 by the late Sen. Edward M. Kennedy. The measure would allow workers in businesses with at least 15 employees to earn up to seven job-protected, paid sick days a year. The bill was reintroduced in 2013, by Connecticut Rep. Rosa DeLauro in the House and Iowa's Tom Harkin in the Senate. Both bills are stuck in committee and face widespread opposition among Republicans and pro-business advocates, who do not believe in a mandate for paid sick time.

"Republicans want to ensure that working families have the flexibility to get the health care they need, but we don't think the answer is a 'one size fits all' government mandate," said Michael Steel, a spokesman for House Majority Leader John Boehner, R-Ohio.

"It represents the intrusion of the federal government into the benefits policies of millions of companies, large and small," said Republican Rep. Tom Price of Georgia during hearings on the bill in 2009.[78]

Randel K. Johnson, the vice president for labor, immigration and employee benefits at the U.S. Chamber of Commerce, said his group was worried that the legislation could later be expanded. "Some say, 'What's seven days of paid sick leave?' My concern is it would never be just seven days. A year from now it will be 14 days, and then 21," said Johnson.[79]

A 2013 report by the Employment Policies Institute, a conservative think tank, said in places where paid leave laws have gone into effect, such as San Francisco, workers already are losing jobs.[80]

Democrats also would like to update the 1993 Family and Medical Leave Act to provide 12 weeks of paid, job-protected leave for new parents or workers facing family medical emergencies. And they have introduced the Paycheck Fairness Act, which would close loopholes in the 1963 Equal Pay Act. Advocates cite problems with how courts have interpreted the law's provision allowing pay differentials based on factors other than gender as evidence that the law needs to be clarified.[81] But political observers say the measure stands little chance of advancing this year.[82]

In the absence of federal action, some states are taking on the issues of equal pay and workplace flexibility. For example, as part of a larger measure fixing loopholes in Vermont's equal pay law, legislators recently enacted a measure that provides safeguards against retaliation for employees requesting flexible work hours.[83]

## OUTLOOK

### More Jobs

The aging of America is likely to influence the job market for women. The U.S. Bureau of Labor Statistics projects that most of the 30 fastest-growing occupations through 2020 are in female-dominated fields, such as health care, child care and education.[84]

As the baby boom generation ages, the need for home-health and personal-care aides is expected to grow by 70 percent by 2020, creating an estimated 1.3 million additional jobs.[85]

Hegewisch, at the Institute for Women's Policy Research, also expects many women to work beyond the traditional retirement age of 65, in part because they will need to supplement their retirement incomes. Older women are much more likely than older men to be poor: More than 60 percent of women 65 or older have insufficient income to cover basic expenses.[86]

Jobs in post-secondary education also are projected to grow — by 17 percent — but it is unclear whether those will be full-time positions with benefits or follow the current trend of adjunct and part-time instruction, she says.

The National Urban League's Hardy expects significant growth in the number of female entrepreneurs. Passage of the Affordable Care Act, designed to make health insurance available to all, is expected to help boost the ranks of the self-employed by 11 percent once it is fully implemented.[87] The Urban League found that women own nearly half of all black-owned businesses and employ nearly a quarter of all employees at black-owned companies.[88] Women own nearly 35 percent of all Hispanic-owned businesses.[89]

"They are really being employers and job creators," Hardy says. Entrepreneurship is seen as a key way to address unemployment in communities of color, and women are leading the way, she says.

"As we look at barriers to growth, [we] have to start focusing on technology and health care and education," Hardy says.

In the new economy, the best jobs may be the ones that can't be outsourced easily, writes *End of Men* author Rosin, and women are poised to do well.

"The sure bets for the future," she wrote, "are still jobs that cannot be done by a computer or someone overseas. They are the jobs that require human contact, interpersonal skills and creativity, and these are all areas where women excel."[90]

## NOTES

1. "Rewind with Michael Enright," CBC, March 7, 2013, from an interview originally broadcast in 1964 on the CBC program "Take Thirty," www.cbc.ca/rewind/sirius/2013/03/07/betty-friedan/.

2. "Usual Weekly Earnings of Wage and Salary Workers," U.S. Bureau of Labor Statistics, April 2103, www.bls.gov/news.release/pdf/wkyeng.pdf.

3. See "The Gender Wage Gap by Occupation," Institute for Women's Policy Research, April 2013, www.iwpr.org/initiatives/pay-equity-and-discrimination.

4. Sheryl Sandberg, *Lean In: Women, Work, and the Will to Lead* (2013), p. 7.

5. Heather Boushey, Ann O'Leary and Sarah Jane Glynn, "Our Working Nation in 2013: An Updated Agenda for Work and Family Policies," Center for

American Progress, February 2013, www.american progress.org/issues/labor/report/2013/02/05/517 20/our-working-nation-in-2013/.

6. "Bachelor's, master's, and doctor's degrees conferred by degree-granting institutions, by sex of student and discipline division: 2009-10," *U.S. Digest of Education Statistics*, Table 290, National Center for Education Statistics, *U.S. Department of Education*, 2011, http://nces.ed.gov/programs/digest/d11/ tables/dt11_290.asp.

7. Eileen Parker and Kim Patton, "A Gender Reversal on Career Aspirations," Pew Social & Demographic Trends, April 19, 2012, p. 7, www.pewsocialtrends. org/files/2012/04/Women-in-the-Workplace.pdf.

8. Phyllis Schlafly, "Obama's Pre-K Power Grab," Eagle Forum, June 26, 2013, www.eagleforum.org/publi cations/column/obamas-pre-k-power-grab.html. Also see Heather Boushey and Joan C. Williams, "The Three Faces of Work-Family Conflict: The Poor, the Professionals, and the 'Missing Middle,'" Center for American Progress and the Center for WorkLife Law, University of California, Hastings College of the Law, 2010, www.americanprogress. org/wpcontent/uploads/issues/2010/01/pdf/three faces.pdf.

9. "Women in America: Indicators of Social and Economic Well-Being," White House Council on Women and Girls, March 2011, p. 21. National Center for Education Statistics, Table 32. "Degrees Conferred by Institutes of Higher Education, by level of degree and sex of student: 1949-50 to 1993-94," National Center for Education Statistics, http:// nces.ed.gov/pubs98/yi/yi32.pdf.

10. "Degrees conferred by degree-granting institutions by level of degree and sex of student: Selected years, 1869-70 through 2020-21," National Center for Education Statistics, Table 283, http://nces.ed.gov/ programs/digest/d11/tables/dt11_283.asp? referrer=list.

11. See "Projections of Education Statistics to 2021," National Center for Education Statistics, Table 21, p. 60. http://nces.ed.gov/pubs2013/2013008.pdf.

12. See Hanna Rosin, *The End of Men and the Rise of Women* (2012), pp. 145-149.

13. "The Wage Gap Over Time," National Committee on Pay Equity, www.pay-equity.org/info-time.html.

14. "The Simple Truth About the Gender Pay Gap, 2013 Edition," American Association of University Women, www.aauw.org/files/2013/02/The-Simple-Truth-2013.pdf.

15. For more, see Shierholz's presentation at a 2011 Institute for Women's Policy Research roundtable: "Women and Jobs in the Great Recession and its Aftermath," www.iwpr.org/roundtable-on-women-and-economy-files/Shierholz%20IWPR%202011 .pdf.

16. Betsey Stevenson and Justin Wolfers, "The Paradox of Declining Female Happiness," *American Economic Journal: Economic Policy*, August 2009, Vol. 1, Issue 2. A working paper version is available through the National Bureau of Economic Research, www.nber .org/papers/w14969.

17. *Ibid.*

18. D'Vera Cohn, "Love and Marriage," Pew Research Social & Demographic Trends, Feb. 13, 2013, www.pewsocialtrends.org/2013/02/13/love-and-marriage/.

19. D'Vera Cohn, "Marriage Rate Declines and Marriage Age Rises," Pew Research Social & Demographic Trends, Dec. 14, 2011, www.pewso cialtrends.org/2011/12/14/marriage-rate-declines-and-marriage-age-rises/.

20. Casey E. Copen, Kimberly Daniels and William D. Mosher, "First Premarital Cohabitation in the United States: 2006-2010, National Survey of Family Growth," National Center for Health Statistics, April 4, 2013, www.cdc.gov/nchs/data/ nhsr/nhsr064.pdf.

21. Wendy Wang, *et al.*, "Breadwinner Moms," Pew Social & Demographic Trends, May 28, 2013, www .pewsocialtrends.org/files/2013/05/Breadwinner_ moms_final.pdf.

22. "2012 Catalyst Census: Fortune 500 Women Executive Officers and Top Earners," Dec. 11, 2012, www.cata lyst.org/knowledge/2012-catalyst-census-fortune-500-women-executive-officers-and-top-earners.

23. Sheryl Sandberg, "Why We Have Too Few Women Leaders," TEDWomen, December 2010,

www.ted.com/talks/sheryl_sandberg_why_we_have_too_few_women_leaders.html.

24. The case study was conducted by Kathleen McGinn and Nicole Tempest, "Heidi Roizen, Harvard Business School, Case Study #9-800-228" (2009). As cited in Sandberg, p. 39.

25. Sandberg, *Lean In, op. cit.*, p. 39.

26. Madeline E. Heilman and Tyler G. Okimoto, "Why Are Women Penalized for Success at Male Tasks? The Implied Communality Deficit," *Journal of Applied Psychology*, 2007, Vol. 92, No. 1, pp. 81-92. See also L. A. Rudman "Self-promotion as a risk factor for women: The costs and benefits of counterstereo-typical impression management," *Journal of Personality and Social Psychology*, 74, 1998, pp. 629-645; and L. A. Rudman, and P. Glick "Prescriptive gender stereotypes and backlash toward agentic women," *Journal of Social Issues*, 57, 2001, pp. 743-762.

27. Nancy M. Carter and Christine Silva, *The Myth of the Ideal Worker: Does Doing All the Right Things Really Get Women Ahead?* (2011), p. 2.

28. Linda Babcock and Sara Laschever, *Women Don't Ask: Negotiations and the Gender Divide* (2003).

29. "Interview with Linda Babcock and Sara Laschever," *The Woman's Connection*, www.youtube.com/watch?v=RcZn7zYGrp8.

30. Hanna Riley Bowles, Linda Babcock and Lei Lai, "Social incentives for gender differences in the propensity to initiate negotiations: Sometimes it does hurt to ask," *Organizational Behavior and Human Decision Processes*, 103, 2007, pp. 84-103.

31. Helen Mayson, "Ambition and Gender at Work," Institute of Leadership and Management, 2013, https://www.i-l-m.com/Insight/Inspire/2013/May/ambition-gender-key-findings.

32. Henna Inam, "Five Mindsets that Keep Women Ambivalent About Leading," www.transformleaders.tv/why-i-dont-want-to-be-1/.

33. Joanna Barsh and Lareina Yee, "Unlocking the Full Potential of Women at Work," McKinsey & Co., 2012.

34. Catherine Rampell, "Coveting Not a Corner Office, But Time At Home," *The New York Times*, July 7, 2013, www.nytimes.com/2013/07/08/business/coveting-not-a-corner-office-but-time-at-home.html.

35. See Jeremy Staff and Jeylan T. Mortimer, "Explaining the Motherhood Wage Penalty During the Early Occupational Career," *Demography*, Vol. 49, No. 1, February 2012, pp. 1-21.

36. For more, see Mary Blair-Loy, "Cultural Constructions of Family Schemas: The Case of Women Finance Executives," *Gender and Society*, Vol. 15, No. 5, October 2001, pp. 687-709.

37. Tara Siegel Bernard, "In Paid Family Leave, U.S. Trails Much of the Globe," *The New York Times*, Feb. 23, 2013, www.nytimes.com/2013/02/23/your-money/us-trails-much-of-the-world-in-providing-paid-family-leave.html.

38. "Rep. Miller on House Floor: "Extend FMLA Benefits to All Americans," Feb. 13, 2013, http://democrats.edworkforce.house.gov/blog/rep-miller-house-floor-extend-fmla-benefits-all-americans.

39. "Paid Family and Medical Leave: An Overview," National Partnership for Women & Families, April 2012, www.nationalpartnership.org/site/DocServer/PFML_Overview_FINAL.pdf?docID=7847.

40. Ariane Hegewisch and Janet C. Gornick, "The Impact of 'Family Friendly' Policies on Women's Employment Outcomes and the Costs and Benefits of Doing Business," World Bank, June 2010.

41. *Ibid.*

42. For background, see Sarah Glazer, "Social Welfare in Europe," *CQ Global Researcher*, Aug. 1, 2010, pp. 185-210.

43. Jennifer Ludden, "FMLA Not Really Working for Many Employees," NPR, Feb. 5, 2013, www.npr.org/2013/02/05/171078451/fmla-not-really-working-for-many-employees.

44. Francine D. Blau and Lawrence Kahn, "Female Labor Supply: Why is the U.S. Falling Behind?" *The American Economic Review*, American Economic Association, May 2013, p. 251.

45. For background, see Sarah Glazer, "Mothers' Movement," *CQ Researcher*, April 4, 2003, pp. 297-320.

46. Hegewisch and Gornick, *op. cit.*

47. Ankita Patnaik, "Merging Separate Spheres: The Role of Policy in Promoting Dual Earner, Dual Career Households," Working Paper, Social Science Research Network, http://papers.ssrn.com/sol3/papers.cfm?abstract_id=2179070.

48. "Conversations With History: Ruth Rosen," University of California, June 12, 2008, www.youtube.com/watch?v=Bw2Zf1XUPWY.

49. For background, see Sarah Glazer, "Women's Rights," *CQ Global Researcher*, April 3, 2012, pp. 153-180.

50. Cynthia E. Harrison, *On Account of Sex: The Politics of Women's Issues, 1945-1968* (1989), p. 120.

51. Georgia Duerst-Lahti, "The Government's Role in Building the Women's Movement," *Political Science Quarterly*, Vol. 104, No. 2, Summer 1989, pp. 249-268, 251.

52. Harrison, *op. cit.*, p. 122.

53. Union polls found that 85 percent of female union members planned to continue working after the war; Women's Bureau studies found that almost 80 percent of women working in the Detroit area and in Erie County, N.Y., hoped to keep their jobs (CIO News, July 30, 1945, clipping, in folder "S.1178," box H1, Wayne Morse papers, University of Oregon), as cited in Harrison, *op. cit.*

54. George H. Gallup, *The Gallup Poll: Public Opinion, 1935-1971* (1972), Vol. 1, p. 322. Also see Claudia Goldin, "The Female Labor Force and American Economic Growth," in Stanley L. Engerman and Robert E. Gallman, eds., *Long-Term Factors in American Economic Growth* (1986), www.nber.org/chapters/c9688.pdf.

55. Harrison, *op. cit.*, p. 51.

56. "Conversations With History: Ruth Rosen," *op. cit.*

57. Phyllis Richman, "Answering Harvard's Question About My Personal Life, 52 Years Later," *The Washington Post*, June 6, 2013, http://articles.washingtonpost.com/2013-06-06/opinions/39784052_1_graduate-school-letter-52-years.

58. The case is *Ledbetter v. Goodyear Tire & Rubber Co. Inc.*, 550 U.S. __ (May 29, 2007). For background, see Thomas J. Billitteri, "Gender Pay Gap," *CQ Researcher*, March 14, 2008, pp. 241-264.

59. Christianne Corbett and Catherine Hill, "Graduating to a Pay Gap: The Earnings of Men and Women One Year After Graduation," American Association of University Women, 2012, p. 21, www.aauw.org/files/2013/02/graduating-to-a-pay-gap-the-earnings-of-women-and-men-one-year-after-college-graduation.pdf.

60. Claudia Goldin and Lawrence F. Katz, "The Career Cost of Family," paper prepared for the Workplace Flexibility 2010 conference at the Georgetown School of Law, p. 11, http://workplaceflexibility.org/images/uploads/program_papers/goldin_formatted_12-12-10.pdf.

61. *Ibid.*, pp. 11-12.

62. For background, see Sarah Glazer, "Telecommuting," *CQ Researcher*, July 19, 2013, pp. 621-644.

63. Kim Parker and Wendy Wang, "Modern Parenthood: Roles of Moms and Dads Converge as They Balance Work and Family," Pew Research Social & Demographic Trends, March 14, 2013, www.pewsocialtrends.org/2013/03/14/modern-parenthood-roles-of-moms-and-dads-converge-as-they-balance-work-and-family/.

64. Ellen Galinsky, Kerstin Aumann and James T. Bond, "Times Are Changing: Gender and Generation at Work and Home," Families and Work Institute, 2009, http://familiesandwork.org/site/research/reports/Times_Are_Changing.pdf, as cited in "Our Working Nation in 2013," *op. cit.*

65. The Associated Press, "New Dads: Diaper Duty's Just the Start," NPR, June 12, 2013, www.npr.org/templates/story/story.php?storyId=191021263.

66. "Parents and the High Cost of Child Care," Child Care Aware of America, 2012, www.naccrra.org/sites/default/files/default_site_pages/2012/cost_report_2012_final_081012_0.pdf.

67. "The NICHD Study of Early Child Care and Youth Development," National Institute of Child Health and Human Development, National Institutes of Health, 2006, p. 11, https://www.nichd.nih.gov/publications/pubs/documents/seccyd_06.pdf.

68. Abby J. Cohen, "A Brief History of Federal Financing for Child Care in the United States," *Financing Child Care*, Vol. 6, No. 2, Summer/Fall 1996,

http://futureofchildren.org/publications/journals/article/index.xml?journalid=56&articleid=326&sectionid=2177.

69. Betty Friedan, *The Second Stage* (1981), p. 90.

70. Lyndsey Layton, "Paying for preschool with a $1 a pack cigarette tax," *The Washington Post*, April 10, 2013, http://articles.washingtonpost.com/2013-04-10/local/38434932_1_cigarette-tax-r-j-reynolds-tobacco.

71. Anne-Marie Slaughter, "Why Women Still Can't Have It All," *The Atlantic*, July 2012, www.theatlantic.com/magazine/archive/2012/07/why-women-still-cant-have-it-all/309020.

72. Melissa Stanger, "Number of Women Leaders Will Equal Men in 2085," *Business Insider*, Dec. 11, 2012, www.businessinsider.com/number-of-women-leaders-will-equal-men-in-2085-2012-11.

73. For example, see "The Bottom Line: Corporate Performance and Women's Representation on Boards," Catalyst, October 2007, http://catalyst.org/knowledge/bottom-line-corporate-performance-and-womens-representation-boards.

74. Jessica Valenti, "Sheryl Sandberg isn't the perfect feminist: So what?" *The Washington Post*, March 1, 2013, http://articles.washingtonpost.com/2013-03-01/opinions/37366536_1_sheryl-sandberg-jessica-valenti-vanity-project.

75. "Now Is Our Time," *Harvard Business Review*, April 2013, http://hbr.org/2013/04/now-is-our-time/ar/1.

76. Joan C. Williams and Rachel W. Dempsey, "The Rise of Executive Feminism," *Harvard Business Review blog*, March 28, 2013, http://blogs.hbr.org/cs/2013/03/the_rise_of_executive_feminism.html.

77. "Latino Workers and their Families Need Paid Sick Days," National Partnership for Women and Families, April 2013, www.nationalpartnership.org/site/DocServer/Latinos_and_Paid_Sick_Days_Fact_Sheet_English.pdf?docID=8544.

78. "Price Statement: H.R. 2339, the Family Income to Respond to Significant Transitions Act, and H.R. 2460, the Healthy Families Act," http://edworkforce.house.gov/news/documentsingle.aspx?DocumentID=173150.

79. Steven Greenhouse. "Bill Would Guarantee Up to 7 Paid Sick Days," *The New York Times*, May 15, 2009, www.nytimes.com/2009/05/16/health/policy/16sick.html?_r=0.

80. Michael Saltsman, "Mandatory Paid Leave: A Remedy Worse Than the Disease," Employment Policies Institute, April 2013, www.epionline.org/oped/mandatory-paid-leave-a-remedy-worse-than-the-disease/.

81. For more background, see www.nwlc.org/sites/default/files/pdfs/factorotherthan_sexfactsheet_5.29.12_final.pdf.

82. See entries for the House and Senate versions of the Paycheck Fairness Act on GovTrack.us: "Tracking the U.S. Congress": www.govtrack.us/congress/bills/113/s84 and www.govtrack.us/congress/bills/113/hr377.

83. "Gov. Shumlin signs into law equal pay legislation to eliminate pay inequity and create family-friendly workplaces," press release, May 14, 2013, http://governor.vermont.gov/newsroom-gov-peter-shumlin-signs-equal-pay-act.

84. "The 30 occupations with the largest projected employment growth, 2010-20," Bureau of Labor Statistics, U.S. Department of Labor, www.bls.gov/news.release/ecopro.t06.htm.

85. *Ibid.*

86. "Doing Without: Economic Security and Older Americans," Wider Opportunities for Women, No. 2: Gender, March 2012, www.wowonline.org/documents/OlderAmericansGenderbriefFINAL.pdf.

87. Linda J. Blumberg, Kevin Lucia and Sabrina Corlette, "The Affordable Care Act: Improving Incentives for Entrepreneurship and Self-Employment," The Urban Institute Health Policy Center, May 2013.

88. Lucy J. Reuben, "Make Room for the New 'She Eos': An Analysis of Businesses Owned by Black Females," The State of Black America 2008, In the Black Women's Voice, National Urban League, 2008, p. 118.

89. Data is based on a 2007 Census Bureau survey of business owners, the most current data available, www.latinamarketplace.com/index.php?node=316.

90. Rosin, *op. cit.*, pp. 139-140.

# BIBLIOGRAPHY

## Selected Sources

### Books

Coontz, Stephanie, *A Strange Stirring: The Feminine Mystique and American Women at the Dawn of the 1960s*, Basic Books, 2011.
An historian interviews nearly 200 women on Betty Friedan's seminal 1963 work, *The Feminine Mystique*.

Friedan, Betty, *The Feminine Mystique*, W. W. Norton, 1963.
A groundbreaking feminist examines the dissatisfaction of U.S. housewives helping to fuel the modern women's movement.

Rosen, Ruth, *The World Split Open: How the Modern Women's Movement Changed America*, Penguin Books, 2000.
An historian documents the multiple threads of feminism from the early 1960s through the 1990s.

Rosin, Hanna, *The End of Men And the Rise of Women*, Riverhead Books, 2012.
A national correspondent for *The Atlantic* argues that women have surpassed men by almost every measure.

Sandberg, Sheryl, *Lean In: Women, Work, and the Will to Lead*, Alfred A. Knopf, 2013.
Facebook's chief operating officer has drawn both praise and scorn for questioning why so few women are leaders.

### Articles

Burke, Daria, "What Lean In Means for Women of Color," *The Huffington Post*, April 25, 2013, www.huffingtonpost.com/daria-burke/what-lean-in-means-for-wo_b_3150201.html.
The founder and CEO of Black MBA Women reflects on Sheryl Sandberg's core messages in her book *Lean In*.

Cohn, Jonathan, "The Hell of American Day Care," *The New Republic*, April 15, 2013, www.newrepublic.com/article/112892/hell-american-day-care#.
An investigation finds a poorly regulated, expensive daycare system in the United States.

Gunn, Dwyer, "The Flex Time Ruse: Does Working Flexibly Harm Women?" *Slate*, March 28, 2013, www.slate.com/articles/double_x/doublex/2013/03/flex_time_is_not_the_answer.html.
A journalist writes that "family friendly" policies can have unintended consequences on women's long-term career prospects.

Slaughter, Anne-Marie, "Why Women Still Can't Have It All," *The Atlantic*, July 2012, www.theatlantic.com/magazine/archive/2012/07/why-women-still-cant-have-it-all/309020/.
A former high-ranking State Department official ignites a fierce debate about gender equality and women's choices.

### Reports and Studies

"Fifty Years After the Equal Pay Act: Assessing the Past, Taking Stock of the Future," National Equal Pay Task Force, The White House, June 2013, www.whitehouse.gov/sites/default/files/image/image_file/equal_pay-task_force_progress_report_june_10_2013.pdf.
An Obama administration panel analyzes law, policy, economic trends and demographics since President Kennedy signed the Equal Pay Act in 1963.

Barsh, Joanna, and Lareina Lee, "Unlocking the Full Potential of Women At Work," McKinsey & Co., 2012, www.mckinsey.com/client_service/organization/latest_thinking/women_at_work.
An analysis of 60 large corporations reveals that for women to advance, top leadership must demonstrate a commitment to gender diversity in the workplace.

Beninger, Anna, and Nancy M. Carter, "The Great Debate: Flexibility vs. Face Time: Busting the Myths Behind Flexible Work Arrangements," Catalyst, July 8, 2013, www.catalyst.org/knowledge/great-debate-flexibility-vs-face-time-busting-myths-behind-flexible-work-arrangements.
A business think tank finds that flexible work arrangements help recruit and retain top talent, especially women.

Blau, Francine, and Lawrence Kahn, "Female Labor Supply: Why is the U.S. Falling Behind?" National Bureau of Economic Research, Working Paper No. 18702, January 2013, www.nber.org/papers/w18702.

Economists find that the expansion of "family-friendly" policies in other economically advanced countries explains nearly 30 percent of the decrease in U.S. women's labor force participation relative to the other nations.

**Shriver, Maria, "The Shriver Report: A Woman's Nation Changes Everything," Center for American Progress, October 2009, www.americanprogress.org/issues/women/report/2009/10/16/6789/the-shriver-report/.**
A journalist joins forces with a liberal think tank to examine the economic, social and health impacts of women as breadwinners.

**Williams, Joan C., and Heather Boushey, "The Three Faces of Work-Family Conflict: The Poor, the Professionals, and the Missing Middle," Center for American Progress, January 2010, www.americanprogress.org/wp-content/uploads/issues/2010/01/pdf/threefaces.pdf.**
The founding director of the Center for WorkLife at the University of California Hastings College of the Law (Williams) and the chief economist at the Center for American Progress examine the impact of policy on the largest segment of working American families.

# For More Information

**Catalyst**, 120 Wall St., 15th Floor, New York, NY 10005; 212-514-7600; www.catalyst.org. A nonprofit organization that works to expand opportunities for women in business.

**Center for Women and Work**, Rutgers University School of Management and Labor Relations, 50 Labor Center Way, New Brunswick, NJ 08901-8553; http://smlr.rutgers.edu/smlr/CWW. Focuses on policy issues for women's advancement in the workplace.

**Center for WorkLife Law**, Hastings College of the Law, University of California, 200 McAllister St., San Francisco, CA 94102; 415-565-4640; www.worklifelaw.org. Focuses on workplace discrimination against women.

**Concerned Women for America**, 1015 15th St., N.W., Suite 1100, Washington, DC 20005; 202-488-7000; www.cwfa.org. A Christian women's organization focused on policy that supports traditional marriage and opposes abortion.

**Eagle Forum**, P.O. Box 618, Alton, IL 62002; 618-462-5415; www.eagleforum.org. A conservative organization that helped to defeat ratification of the Equal Rights Amendment and continues to oppose feminist causes.

**Economic Policy Institute**, 1333 H St., N.W., Washington, DC 20005-4707; 202-775-8810; www.epi.org. A nonprofit, nonpartisan think tank that focuses on economic policy for low- and middle-income workers.

**Family Values at Work**, 207 E. Buffalo St., Suite 211, Milwaukee, WI 53202; 414-431-0844; www.familyvaluesatwork.org. A coalition of state groups that advocate mandatory paid sick leave.

**Feminist Majority Foundation**, 1600 Wilson Blvd., Suite 801, Arlington, VA 22209; 703-522-2214; www.feminist.org. Works to advance women's equality.

**Institute for Women's Policy Research**, 1200 18th St., N.W., Suite 301, Washington, DC 20036; 202-785-5100; www.iwpr.org. Conducts research on women, including pay equity, immigration and education.

**LeanIn.org**, P.O. Box 1452, Palo Alto, CA 94302-1452; leanin.org. A social network aimed at encouraging women to pursue their ambitions; created by Facebook COO Sheryl Sandberg.

**Legal Momentum**, 395 Hudson St., New York, NY 10014; 212-925-6635; legalmomentum.org. Focuses on workplace rights for women.

**MomsRising**, www.momsrising.org. An online community of more than 700 bloggers who focus on issues such as parental leave, flexible work and daycare.

**National Partnership for Women and Families**, 1875 Connecticut Ave., N.W., Suite 650, Washington, DC 20009; 202-986-2600; www.nationalpartnership.org. Advocates for family leave and other family-friendly policies.

# 2

# International Adoption

Alan Greenblatt

Adoptive parents, Maria Murphy (left) and Maria Alberto, both from Argentina, depart Haiti on Feb.16, 2010, with newly adopted Haitian sisters Samantha (left) and Mora Louis. Haiti temporarily halted foreign adoptions following a devastating 2010 earthquake, when 10 American missionaries tried to take 33 children — some of whom were not orphans — out of Haiti. The Argentinian women were permitted to complete their adoptions because they had begun the process before the quake. Child traffickers sometimes rush into disaster areas seeking orphans.

From *CQ Researcher*, December 6, 2011.

obert Harrington and Fionnuala Creegan never expected to be raising a Mexican child. But after unsuccessful fertilization treatments, the Irish couple decided to look abroad to adopt a child.

Like many prospective adoptive parents in Europe, they looked to the east — first to Russia and then to Ukraine. But in both countries political and diplomatic wrangling had led to a slowdown in foreign adoptions. Then, they heard they wouldn't have to wait so long in Mexico. In 2008, they adopted a baby girl, Calia, and brought her home to Galway, on Ireland's rugged west coast.

"The system in Mexico is private," Creegan told *The Irish Times*. "A baby is placed by the birth mother and not by the government."[1] Since then, the couple has adopted a second Mexican child.

Their story is typical. Many couples turn to adoption after being unable to conceive, but fewer babies are available in wealthy countries — in part because abortion is legal in those countries and the stigma of being a single parent has lessened. As a result, European, Canadian and American would-be parents increasingly looked to other countries to find a healthy baby during the 1990s and early 2000s, causing international adoptions to soar.

Generally speaking, about 30 mostly wealthy, industrialized nations "receive" babies from about 100 "sending" countries, most of them in the developing world, according to Peter Selman, a visiting fellow at Newcastle University in England. A country might open its doors to prospective adoptive parents when it suddenly finds itself with a high number of abandoned babies — due to war, natural disaster or civil strife. Once the doors are open, foreign

## Adoptions Flow from Poor to Rich Countries

In 2010 about 30,000 babies and children from some 100 "sending" countries, most in the developing world, were adopted by people in about 30 mostly wealthy, industrialized nations. International adoptions have been on the decline in recent years, largely because many countries have severely restricted foreign adoptions due to national pride and concerns about bribery, kidnapping and child trafficking. There are nearly 18 million orphans worldwide, about 2 million of whom are still living in orphanages. The rest live in foster homes, with relatives or on the street.

### Countries that Send and Receive the Most Adoptive Children

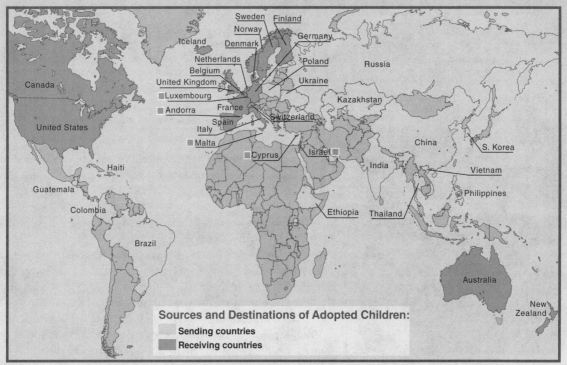

*Source:* Peter Selman, *The Rise and Fall of Intercountry Adoption in the 21st Century: Global Trends From 2001 to 2010,* Ashgate, 2011-2012 (forthcoming); map by Lewis Agrell

adoption agencies and their clients quickly come looking for children.

But in recent years, the numbers have plummeted — down by half in countries such as Belgium, the Netherlands and Spain, as well as the United States. The process of "shopping around" by foreign adopters, such as Harrington and Creegan, is partly to blame, because the adoption systems in some small, poor countries have been overwhelmed by the demand for babies.

Several other factors have contributed to a "boom and bust" cycle in international adoption. As countries discover abuses or fraud in their adoption programs, they respond — some say overreact — by shutting down or severely restricting foreign adoptions. Then another country opens its doors, and foreign adopters rush in. The increase in adoptions — and the vast amount of money foreigners are willing to spend on adoption fees — create a marketplace for middlemen who sometimes turn to fraud, bribery, kidnapping and even trafficking in stolen children to secure candidates for adoption.

"In reality, the demand for children far outstrips the supply of orphans, and the result is kidnapping and fraud — in countries with weak legal systems that can be easily corrupted," writes Rupert Wolfe Murray, a former advisor to the European Union on children's welfare.

Once such problems are exposed, demand then shifts to a new "sending" country, such as Ethiopia, and the cycle repeats itself. "A country becomes fashionable," says Susan Jacobs, the U.S. State Department's special advisor for children's issues. "People go to the countries where it's easiest to adopt, where the rules are lax, and they can do an adoption quickly and perhaps get a baby."

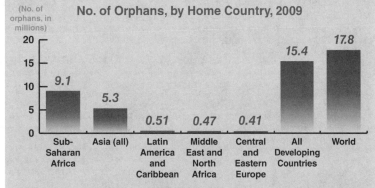

### Nearly 18 Million Children Are Orphans

More than 85 percent of the world's 17.8 million orphans live in developing countries, and 9 million of them live in Sub-Saharan Africa, where the HIV-AIDS epidemic has left behind millions of parentless children. Central and Eastern Europe and the Middle East/North Africa regions have the fewest orphans.

**No. of Orphans, by Home Country, 2009**
(No. of orphans, in millions)

- Sub-Saharan Africa: 9.1
- Asia (all): 5.3
- Latin America and Caribbean: 0.51
- Middle East and North Africa: 0.47
- Central and Eastern Europe: 0.41
- All Developing Countries: 15.4
- World: 17.8

*Source:* "Orphan Estimates," UNICEF, January 2011, www.childinfo.org/hiv_aids_orphanestimates.php.

But the response of many countries, once they are overwhelmed by demand, has been to shut the gates altogether. That leaves millions of kids who might have found good homes trapped in institutions or living on the street. Social-science research indicates that institutionalization of children has negative consequences for their IQ and long-term quality of life and exposes them to disease, malnutrition and neglect.[2] The United Nations Children's Fund, known as UNICEF, estimates that there are 17.8 million orphans worldwide, 2 million of them living in orphanages. In addition, millions of older orphans are living on the street.[3]

"If they're lucky, the kids are stuck in orphanages, and if they're not lucky, they're dead," says Stevan Whitehead, vice president of Overseas Adoption Support and Information Service, or OASIS, which supports British families who have adopted abroad.

Demand for healthy babies is extremely high among American and European parents, who may spend upwards of $50,000 in fees and travel costs. That kind of money — multiplied many thousands of times over — can lead to corruption in some countries. "It's this entrepreneurial thing, where an agency goes looking for children, and there are Canadian and Dutch parents who want children," says David Smolin, a law professor and director of the Center for Biotechnology, Law and Ethics at Samford University in Birmingham, Ala.

In recent decades, China has allowed the most babies to be sent abroad for adoption, mainly because of its one-child limit for most families. In addition, because of a cultural preference for boys, tens of thousands of Chinese girls have been abandoned or put up for adoption.[4]

But China, Russia and South Korea — traditionally the countries sending the most adopted children abroad — have begun restricting foreign adoptions. Sometimes a sending country will halt foreign adoptions if judges and lawyers are alleged to be taking bribes from adoption agencies or other procurers or if gangs are stealing children in order to pair them with foreign adopters. At the other end of the process, U.S. or European nations may stop issuing visas to children adopted from countries where there may be corruption.

In 2008, Guatemala provided 4,123 children for adoption in the United States — more than any other country. Over the past year, the number had plummeted

# Adoptive Families Struggle with Cultural Identity

*Should parents stress assimilation or encourage pride in child's foreign roots?*

Every memoir about the experience of adopting a child from abroad seems to include a moment that shows how perfectly the child, born in a remote village in a poor country, has taken to life in the West.

"I slipped into my American life easily, as if I was always meant to be there," writes Mei-Ling Hopgood, who was adopted from China by a Michigan couple and now lives in Argentina. "I grew up on Gerber baby food . . . my parents read me Dr. Seuss before bed and let me watch 'Sesame Street.'"[1]

Most adopted children assimilate well into their new families and countries. When children struggle, it's often not their racial or cultural backgrounds that cause problems but their age — how old they were when they were adopted and how long they were institutionalized.

"In transracial adoption, children feel very much this is their real family, and they identify with their family," says Rita J. Simon, an adoption expert at American University, in Washington, D.C. "One of the very good things about

adoption is that the people feel loved and secure and comfortable with their racial and ethnic identities. That is just a general theme."

But in recent decades, adoptive parents have felt obliged to expose their foreign-born children not only to the culture in which they're being raised but also to the culture of their home countries. Caucasian parents in the United States, England, Belgium and other Western countries may send their adoptive children to Chinese schools or Korean culture camps in the summer or offer them homeland tours of India. Often, they belong to culture-specific family support groups.

"All adoptive parents are socialized today to think those things are important," says Elizabeth Bartholet, faculty director of the child-advocacy program at Harvard Law School, which studies international adoptions, among other issues.

That represents a "dramatic change" from the way things were done a generation ago, says Victor Groza, a social work professor at Case Western Reserve University.

to 32, as Guatemalan authorities sought to regain control of the country's troubled adoption system.

The combination of concern about corruption and a growing reluctance to send children abroad has been putting downward pressure on international adoption, or "intercountry" adoption, as the experts call it. "It is a tumultuous time right now in the world of intercountry adoption," says Adam Pertman, executive director of the Evan B. Donaldson Adoption Institute in New York, which conducts research on adoptions. "The number of adoptions from abroad into this country, and generally, is plummeting."

Concerns about kidnapping and corruption also have taken some of the humanitarian shine off international adoptions. The problems associated with an unregulated international marketplace were meant to be addressed by the Hague Convention, an international accord drafted by representatives of 55 countries in 1993 and since

adopted by more than 70 countries. But not all countries involved in international adoptions have signed on. Poor nations often lack the resources to enforce it, and there are no clear penalties for violations.

"There are no sanctions," says René Hoksbergen, a social psychologist at Utrecht University in the Netherlands. "No one can be punished."

Some critics say the Hague Convention has had perverse effects. For instance, it slows down the process for legitimate adoptions. And, when problems develop, some countries have simply closed their doors altogether, rather than find ways to fix the system.

"Instead of Hague cleaning up a potentially corrupt situation, everything closes down," Whitehead says.

No one wants to keep children in institutions, but, increasingly, officials believe it's better to try to care for children in their home countries than to send them abroad. Most experts prefer to keep children within their

"Then, the emphasis was on assimilation, almost to forget the kid is different ethnically and culturally and racially. Families are much more engaged now to help kids stay connected to part of who they are."

But not everyone thinks that's a great idea. Some social scientists believe that treating adopted children as if they are somehow essentially or inherently different can leave them feeling caught between two worlds — not fully American or Dutch, but no longer Korean or Chinese, either.

Hannah Pool was an Eritrean baby adopted by an English couple. In her memoir, she writes about feeling "unmoored," uncertain whether her true relations were those she had grown up with or those with whom she shared genes. "One was white and English, the other was black and Eritrean, but which one was my true brother?" she writes.[2]

Discussing adopted children's foreign roots also reminds them that they were, in some sense, abandoned, says Marlène Hofstetter, adoption director for the Terre des Hommes International Federation in Switzerland, a coalition of children's welfare organizations.

"I don't think it's a good thing to remind the child all the time 'you are from China,' or 'you are from Russia,'" she says. "You want the child to be integrated into its community."

It's always a question for immigrants — how much to assimilate and how much to hold onto the culture of one's native land. Often, the adopted children themselves put an end to the effort to inculcate them with the culture of their home countries because they just want to fit in.

"Sometimes parents force their 8-year-old or 10-year-old to go to those summer camps," says René Hoksbergen, a social psychologist at Utrecht University in the Netherlands. "Children want to be the same as the other children. They are American now, they want to be as the other children."

But many adoptive parents say exposing their children to their native cultures is important. "If you're growing up racially different in this country, it's probably helpful to be raised with pride in that group," Bartholet says.

Others point out that while children may feel perfectly at ease growing up within their family group, once they leave home they pay more attention to their racial differences. "My kids are now 13 and 14," says Stevan Whitehead, an English parent of two adopted children from Guatemala. "It's important for them to have kids they have always known — who are also adopted from Guatemala — who are going through the same issues and can talk from a personal experience that I as a parent don't share," he says.

— *Alan Greenblatt*

[1]Mei-Ling Hopgood, *Lucky Girl* (2009), p. 67.
[2]Hannah Pool, *My Father's Daughter* (2005), p. 7.

own families or communities, if possible, or have them adopted domestically. Intercountry adoptions should be a last choice, they say.

But there is a heated debate going on just now about whether — and how often — international adoption should be an option even when there appear to be no good choices at home. Some people say it's criminal to deprive a child of a home because of political boundaries. But others say insisting that children need to be taken out of the country to find a decent home does nothing to alleviate the conditions in their own country that may have led to their abandonment. Support for families and beefed up social services would help more children than international adoption, which allows the home country to avoid investing in domestic services for the poor, they say.

"If this poverty argument comes up, then you should support the family with food stamps or whatever," says Wolfe Murray, a public relations consultant in Romania who has worked on children's issues. "It's not about taking poor kids away and sending them somewhere else. You should only take kids away if there are clear cases of abuse."

But foreign adoption should remain an option, advocates say, because many countries lack a culture of domestic adoption. Sometimes a foreign home is the only chance for children to receive the nurturing they need, says Charles Johnson, president of the National Council for Adoption, an advocacy group in Alexandria, Va. "Stopping international adoption completely ends up harming far more children than do the abuses you're preventing," he says.

At the same time, Johnson recognizes that many countries are embarrassed at appearing unable to care for their own children. "No country, no matter how poor, wants to let go of its own," he says. "There's this cultural pride and nationalistic pride." That seems to be especially true in countries such as Brazil, India and South Korea, formerly poor countries that now have greater means to provide improved social services to their citizens.

As officials and parents consider the possible benefits and drawbacks of international adoption, here are some of the questions they are asking:

### Should international adoptions be promoted?

Twenty-five years ago, pediatrician Dana Johnson opened a pioneering clinic at the University of Minnesota to treat children with medical problems who had been adopted from overseas. Around that time, Johnson adopted a boy from India who was at a facility for children with poor health prospects.

"It's been wonderful watching him grow up," Johnson says. "His future was to be dead, so clearly it was beneficial for him."

Over the years, Johnson has met and consulted with "literally of thousands of families" that have adopted children from other countries. "I know what a positive experience it has been for the children in these families," she says.

Most social scientists say international adoptions have worked well for most children, including those from poor countries. Growing up in a rich country ensures they will be well fed and guarantees them a home where they receive nurturing that might not have been available in orphanages or other institutions, they say.

"There are many people whose lives have been transformed in a very positive way," says Newcastle University's Selman. "The majority of adopters do a remarkable job and offer a great benefit to the children."

Nevertheless, he says, "the healing power of a family life" is an argument for adoption in general, not necessarily for international adoption. And even proponents of foreign adoption, such as pediatrician Johnson, concede it's preferable for children who need homes to be kept within their extended families or adopted domestically.

But not all children can find a home in their native countries. Then the argument turns on whether children would be better off in their home countries or adopted by foreign parents — most often, in the United States or Western Europe.

That process has created its own pitfalls. Because of the amount of money involved, corruption and kidnapping have been associated with international adoptions. "What we saw in Romania time after time was social services wanting to place children locally, but that couldn't compete with people from the U.S. willing to pay up to $50,000 cash for a kid," says Wolfe Murray, who served as a European Union-sponsored adviser to the Romanian government on children's-rights issues.

Romania, which saw thousands of its children adopted abroad during the 1990s, shut down intercountry adoptions — except to biological grandparents — in 2001. Because of the large sums of money involved, many children with living parents were being adopted, Wolfe Murray says, either because they were stolen or because often-illiterate birth mothers were tricked into signing a document saying they were abandoning their child. Similar problems have been encountered in Peru, Ethiopia, Vietnam, Nepal and Cambodia. Even well-meaning groups have sometimes departed with children who were not, in fact, orphans.

For example, after the 2010 earthquake in Haiti, the New Life Children's Refuge, a Christian group from Idaho, tried to take 33 Haitian children — some who were not orphans — to neighboring Dominican Republic without official permission. They had planned to build an orphanage in the Dominican Republic.[5] The 10 American missionaries were arrested and released shortly afterward.

"God wanted us to come here to help children, we are convinced of that," Laura Silsby, one of the 10, said during a jailhouse interview with *The New York Times*. "Our hearts were in the right place."[6]

In addition, an airlift of Haitian children who survived the quake was arranged by Pennsylvania Gov. Ed Rendell. Several of those children also turned out not to be orphans, including the 11-year-old son of Marie Claude Pierre. The impoverished Pierre had signed papers willingly releasing him for adoption. "Tell him bonjour, bonsoir. Tell him to behave and not to make problems. Send him kisses," she told a reporter.[7]

This past June, Haitian President Michel Martelly said he would issue a decree to tighten the country's adoption rules and ensure that all applications go through authorized entities.[8]

"Look what happened in Haiti, with the earthquake, all the shenanigans that went on there," says Howard Altstein, a social work professor at the University of Maryland, Baltimore. "Organizations were trying to get, quote, orphans out of Haiti who were not orphans."

There have been other such cases of well-intentioned organizations not ensuring that the children they were attempting to adopt were in fact orphans or had been abandoned.

Perhaps even more disturbing have been horror stories about children being ripped out of the arms of mothers and taken to other provinces to be presented as "abandoned" orphans ready for foreign adoption.

"Local agents would facilitate statements that the kid is a genuine orphan," Wolfe Murray says, referring to cases in Ethiopia. "In fact, nine times out of 10, the parents are alive and poor and have absolutely no recourse. Everybody gets bribed, and they'll do everything they can to keep the [adoptive] parents in the dark."

Evidence of such practices has led to the adoption process being halted or considerably slowed in poor countries such as Nepal and Guatemala. Some Europeans blame America for continuing to allow adoptions from those countries long after concerns have been raised — and for contributing to the problem in the first place through the largesse of hopeful parents.

In the United States international adoptions are facilitated by lawyers and private, for-profit agencies, which is not allowed in Europe. "The U.S. is a special case because profit-oriented adoptions are allowed, which isn't the case in any other country," says Marlène Hofstetter, adoption director for Terres des Hommes International Federation, a nonprofit organization based in Switzerland that works with disadvantaged children.

In Guatemala, until the past couple of years no government agency was responsible for matching adoptive parents with mothers wishing to give up their children. "A network of private notaries and attorneys sprang up to fill the void, charging adoptive parents $20,000 to $30,000," according to *The Washington Post*.[9]

"As soon as [the Europeans] saw the Guatemalans move to this market system, they got out," says Victor Groza, a professor of parent-child studies at Case Western Reserve University in Cleveland. "What did the U.S. do? We increased our adoptions from Guatemala."

## Foreign Adoptions Follow Boom-Bust Cycles

China and Guatemala sent the most children abroad between 2003 and 2007 but then began restricting overseas adoptions after bribery, kidnapping and child trafficking were discovered in the adoption process. Since then adoptions from other countries, such as Ethiopia, have surged — a boom-bust pattern experts say is common in international adoptions.

### International Adoptions in Select Countries, 2003-2010

Source: Peter Selman, *The Rise and Fall of Intercountry Adoption in the 21st Century: Global Trends From 2001 to 2010*, Ashgate, 2011-2012 *(forthcoming)*

And under the U.S. system, because the same private agencies both assess the suitability of the parents and children and arrange the placements, there are financial incentives for them to push through approvals even if there are questions about individual cases.

"From outside the U.S., looking at intercountry adoption, it's amazing that nothing has changed to stop the illegal, immoral, unethical agencies . . . and practitioners in the U.S. from carrying on their work," says Whitehead, the OASIS vice president.

Whitehead says evidence of greed has made some people worry that the essence of adoption — offering help to children — has been lost in a process that has become too "parent-centric."

Nonetheless, he contends, international adoptions have been enormously beneficial to many thousands of children.

Advocates of international adoption, such as Whitehead, say the rare cases of abuse and relatively isolated examples of corruption have been exaggerated way out of proportion. They should not be used as an excuse to deprive needy children of the care and nurturing of a family, say supporters. And while a handful of American parents have been abusive toward Russian adoptees, the vast majority of the 50,000 Russian children adopted by

Adopted from Liberia, 5-year-old Cynthia Newton (left) and her brother James, 11, proudly show off their new American citizenship certificates during a children's naturalization ceremony in Fairfax, Va., on Nov. 14, 2011. In celebration of National Adoption Month, 25 adopted children from nine countries received their U.S. citizenship during the ceremony.

U.S. parents since 1993 are growing up in secure and supportive homes, they point out.

With Guatemala no longer sending 5,000 children a year to supportive homes in the United States and elsewhere, roughly that number of children will be forced to live in institutions or fend for themselves on the street, says Elizabeth Bartholet, faculty director of the child-advocacy program at Harvard Law School.

"Some mothers who have surrendered their kids got money," she says. "I don't see that as an equivalent evil to condemning kids either to death or a life significantly destroyed by institutionalization. If you look at kids who grow up in institutions, those are the ones who end up seriously trafficked for slavery — sex slavery or other forms of slavery."

"If adoptions were not successful — if most adoptees didn't do pretty well and most adopted parents weren't having success — this would not continue," says Groza, from Case Western. "This has been a very successful legal and emotional relationship for a very long time, but it comes with some baggage."

## Has the Hague Convention improved the international adoption process?

The problems related to intercountry adoptions — primarily, corruption and child trafficking — were the

impetus for an international conference in 1993 to craft a pact aimed at regulating the intercountry adoption process.

"People recognized that an international convention was needed so everyone plays by the rules," says Groza.

The so-called Hague Convention (officially, the Hague Adoption Convention on the Protection of Children and Cooperation in Respect of Inter-Country Adoption) has been more widely adopted than most private-law treaties. More than 70 countries have passed implementing legislation — most recently, Vietnam, in November. The convention took effect in the United States in 2008 — several years after most European countries.

Its main provisions are designed to prevent child trafficking and to ensure that intercountry adoptions serve the best interests of children. It also calls on signatory countries to establish a "central authority" to act as the main source of information and coordination on foreign adoption policies and problems.

In the United States, the State Department acts as the central authority. "We wish every country were a member of Hague," says Jacobs, the State Department's special advisor for children's issues. The treaty tries to ensure that "there won't be a birth parent knocking on somebody's door five years later, saying 'You have my kid.' Each country has a database, so they are able to match the child and the parent."

But the convention, while offering up a framework for regulation, has not created a seamless process nor perfect safeguards. For one thing, the State Department still offers its blessing — and all-important visas — to children from countries that do not participate in the convention. And the United States lobbied hard to keep the convention from banning private and for-profit adoption agencies and advisors.

"When Europeans first sense that there's trafficking or baby buying, they'll close their programs (in affected countries) pretty quickly," says Groza. "The U.S. will try to help, but only eventually, when there's pressure from UNICEF or Save the Children, will they shut down or question the program."

Although the Hague Convention has improved bilateral communications between sending and receiving countries, it has no international enforcement mechanism if things start to go wrong. However, its major provisions are being enforced pretty well when it comes to international adoptions involving American families, says Johnson, of the National Council for Adoption.

Minnesota pediatrician Johnson says the convention "has improved the quality of agencies in this country and kind of weeded out the ones that weren't doing a good job or had more suspicious processes."

Under the convention, adoption agencies can charge only for expenses and a "reasonable fee." Because of tighter rules — and because of the onset of the recession — at least 15 percent of American agencies that handled intercountry adoptions closed within a few months after the convention took effect in the United States in 2008.[10]

But there are ways to skirt the convention. Not every country that allows large numbers of its children to be adopted, such as Ethiopia, has signed on. And not every country that has agreed to abide by the convention has devoted the resources needed to make it effective. The same poverty that leads many children to become candidates for international adoption also can cripple bureaucratic systems meant to ensure that every child has a proper birth record as well as the police agencies and others handling the transactions.

"Countries that are under development can't comply and need help complying," says Johnson, of the National Council for Adoption.

Some critics of the treaty complain that its main effect has been to slow down an already cumbersome and emotionally draining process. The convention requires verification that the children being adopted were put up for adoption in the country where they were born. For American families, the U.S. consulate in the child's country of origin must approve additional paperwork.

"Whenever you regulate something that's been unregulated before, of course we're going to see challenges," says Susan Bissell, chief of child protection for UNICEF. "The Hague and other standards are forcing discussions that will put in place a system that gives children the protections they are entitled to, including a laminated proof that they exist."

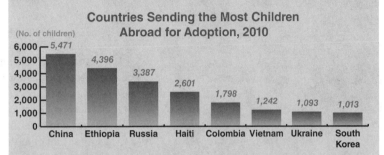

## Most Adoptees Come From Developing World

Nearly 5,500 Chinese children were adopted by foreign parents in 2010, more than from any other country. Ethiopia, Russia and Haiti had the second-, third- and fourth-largest number of adoptees, respectively. Adoptions in Haiti surged after a devastating earthquake in January 2010.

**Countries Sending the Most Children Abroad for Adoption, 2010**

(No. of children)

| Country | No. of children |
|---------|-----------------|
| China | 5,471 |
| Ethiopia | 4,396 |
| Russia | 3,387 |
| Haiti | 2,601 |
| Colombia | 1,798 |
| Vietnam | 1,242 |
| Ukraine | 1,093 |
| South Korea | 1,013 |

*Source:* Peter Selman, *The Rise and Fall of Intercountry Adoption in the 21st Century: Global Trends From 2001 to 2010,* Ashgate, 2011-2012 (forthcoming)

But centralizing oversight of the process has not necessarily weeded out all the problems, suggests E. J. Graff, a senior researcher at the Schuster Institute for Investigative Journalism at Brandeis University in Waltham, Mass.

"India is the prime example," Graff wrote in the liberal journal *Democracy* last year. "Ongoing scandals suggest the central authority may be either inept or perhaps corrupt."[11]

## Can the decline in international adoptions be reversed?

Some people blame plummeting international adoptions on the strictures imposed by the Hague Convention, but multiple factors appear to be at work.

The number of intercountry adoptions already had climbed significantly over roughly 25 years before reaching a peak in 2004. "Everybody expected the numbers to go up and up and up," says Selman at Newcastle University.

The decline has been dramatic. The United States received 22,884 foreign adoptees in 2004, but only 9,320 in fiscal 2011.[12]

Back in 2004, Russia, China and Guatemala accounted for two-thirds of the intercountry adoptions in the United States. But each of those countries is sending far fewer children now. The number of adopted Russian children fell from 5,865 in 2004 to 970 in 2011.

Brad Pitt and Angelina Jolie arrive at Haneda International Airport in Tokyo, Japan, with their family in tow on Nov. 8. The couple leads the celebrity world in adopting children from abroad. In addition to their own three children — Shiloh, 5, (fourth from right) and 3-year-old twins Knox (second from left) and Vivienne (right) — the couple has adopted three from overseas: Maddox, 10, from Cambodia (third from right); Pax, 8, from Vietnam (center) and Zahara, 6, from Ethiopia (left).

In China, the drop was from 7,044 to 2,589. In Guatemala adoptions essentially stopped, falling from 3,264 in 2004 to just 32 in 2011.[13]

Other receiving countries have seen similar declines. "For Holland, intercountry adoptions have dropped more than 50 percent in four or five years, and it will go on," says Hoksbergen, the Utrecht University professor. "You see the same processes in Sweden and Denmark and Norway and Belgium."

Developing countries have slowly built up their child-protective services programs, says UNICEF official Bissell — including a new emphasis on promoting domestic adoptions in countries such as South Korea, Russia and China.

"More and more Third World countries have changed their politics regarding the surrender of children," Hoksbergen says. "They adopt more and more of the children themselves."

"I have been going to India for the past 20 years, and when I first went there no one was talking about national adoption," says Hofstetter of Terres des Hommes. "Now, 75 to 80 percent of those adopted are adopted in India,

which means these children are not available for international adoption."

It's clear that many countries will not be giving up as many children to outsiders. Brazil, for instance, which two decades ago sent many children abroad, now bans international adoption of children under 5.

But Samford University's Smolin argues that other factors are at work as well. He blames what he calls the "slash and burn" adoption practices of supporters of intercountry adoption. Many African and Latin American countries have put their children off-limits, he says, because of concerns about abuses they have seen perpetrated elsewhere.

"You go into countries, you bring in a lot of agencies and a lot of money," Smolin says. "You're happy for a few years, and inevitably corruption and abuses follow, and then the numbers come down. It has not been developed in a sustainable way."

Having seen the abuses elsewhere, he says, developing countries will not open themselves up to outside adoption, thereby filling the gap left by countries that are closing their programs, as has happened repeatedly over the years.

But others see things differently. Hague rules may be slowing things down now, they say, but as countries are able to clean up their processes, they'll likely open again to intercountry adoptions. "Maybe Vietnam and Cambodia will start again after ratifying Hague and when they have clean adoptions," Hofstetter says.

However, countries that had been doing "thousands and thousands of adoptions a year" will not contribute such numbers again as they put stricter procedures in place, he predicts.

That may be why prospective parents and the adoption agencies seem constantly on the lookout for new countries willing to part with more of their neediest children. For instance, after Romania banned intercountry adoption a decade ago, agencies turned to countries with less regulation — first Moldova, then Ukraine. Last month, the Congressional Coalition on Adoption Institute in Washington announced projects to promote international adoptions in six African nations: Ethiopia, Ghana, Kenya, Malawi, Rwanda and Uganda.[14]

While the number of international adoptions has declined markedly, the need has not, say adoption proponents. "Particularly in Sub-Saharan Africa, with children orphaned by the AIDS epidemic, you can't find any care at all for those children," says Whitehead, the OASIS official. "It would seem appropriate for people who are seeking to find families for children to be looking for families outside of those countries, due to the lack of families within them." Some 16.4 million children in developing countries have lost one or both parents to HIV-AIDS, 15 million of them in Africa.[15]

Neither has the demand for children — on the part of both parents and adoption agencies — diminished. While many African nations have outlawed adoption of their children by foreigners, some that weren't major players in the international adoption arena before — such as the Democratic Republic of Congo and Ethiopia, neither of which have signed the Hague Convention — suddenly are seeing more of their children adopted abroad.

At the peak of international adoption in 2004, only 284 Ethiopians were among the nearly 23,000 foreign children adopted by Americans. In 2010, that number had increased nearly tenfold — to 2,513.[16]

"To some extent, it's a movable feast," says Groza, the Case Western Reserve professor. Now, "everyone who doesn't want to deal with the Hague goes to Ethiopia." But, due to concerns about corruption, Ethiopia now is putting on the brakes. In 2011, the number of Ethiopian children adopted by Americans dropped by 30 percent from the previous year.[17]

# BACKGROUND

## New Phenomenon

Famine, war and disease have left children as orphans since time immemorial, but wide-scale adoption is a relatively new phenomenon. And international adoptions had barely been heard of before the mid-20th century.

In ancient Rome, adoptions were usually used to promote ties between powerful families. "Several Roman emperors, including Augustus Caesar Octavius, Constantius I and Marcus Aurelius, were adopted sons," writes NPR host Scott Simon in his 2010 book about adopting two children from China.[18] But in many cultures throughout human history, orphans were typically taken in as slaves or future concubines and were not considered equal members of the family.

A teenage girl in Bucharest, Romania, peeps out of a manhole leading to an underground steam heating system, where she and other teenagers live. After former communist dictator Nicolae Ceausescu outlawed abortion and birth control, Romania's state orphanages were flooded with abandoned children. When his regime fell and nightmarish conditions in the orphanages were exposed, foreigners adopted thousands of Romanian orphans. Unadopted older children often ended up living on the streets, where many sniff glue, steal and prostitute themselves. But because of fraud and child trafficking allegations involved in international adoptions, Romania banned most foreign adoptions in 2001.

Muslim societies, for example, rarely allow adoption in the Western sense. In pre-Islamic Arab societies, adoption was akin to slavery, with boys taken in to be used eventually as warriors. To prevent such abuses, Islamic law is so restrictive that adoption rarely occurs. For instance, Islamic law bars Muslims from treating adopted children as equal to biological children in terms of naming and inheritance, unless the adopted child was breast fed by the adoptive mother. It also prohibits boys from being alone with girls they could potentially marry.[19]

Adoption also was unknown in American common law. Massachusetts became the first state to pass an adoption law, in 1851.[20] In 1909, President Theodore Roosevelt hosted a White House conference on the care of dependent children, which called for children in orphanages to be placed in families.[21] By 1931, every state had passed laws governing adoption.[22]

Children became tragic pawns during World War II. Nazi Germany kidnapped tens of thousands of children from countries it invaded, including Ukraine, Czechoslovakia and, especially, Poland, seeking those whose racial appearance indicated "Nordic blood" and thus were

# CHRONOLOGY

**1950s-1970s** *Families begin adopting large numbers of children from foreign war zones.*

**1953** Americans have adopted nearly 6,000 European children since 1947 — mostly from Germany and Greece — and 2,400 Asians, two-thirds of them from Japan.

**1955** Harry Holt, a wealthy Oregon businessman, persuades Congress to allow him to adopt Korean orphans, setting up formal procedures for international adoption and kicking off a decades-long wave of American adoptions from Korea.

**1973** Abortion is legalized in the United States, leading to fewer births of unwanted children.

**1978** China limits most families to one child; tens of thousands of baby girls are abandoned in orphanages in the coming decades.

**1980s-1990s** *International adoptions spike dramatically as more countries permit foreign adoptions.*

**1988** Adoptions from South Korea begin to fall after media reports during Seoul Olympics depict Korea as a "baby exporting nation."

**1990** Horrific conditions in Romania's orphanages are exposed after fall of Ceau?escu regime; European and American families adopt thousands of Romanian orphans.

**1993** Russia emerges as a leading source of adoptive babies. . . . Hague Convention established by 55 countries to regulate international adoption.

**1998** China sends 4,206 children to the United States, becoming America's leading supplier of Asian orphans.

**2000s-Present** *Corruption and child trafficking lead many countries to slow or stop international adoptions.*

**2001** Romania bans all international adoptions, save those involving biological grandparents.

**2004** International adoptions by Americans peak at 22,884.

**2005** Chinese police arrest 27 members of a ring that reportedly abducted or bought up to 1,000 children in Guangdong province and sold them to orphanages in Hunan; at least 100 children were put up for foreign adoption.

**2007** China bars adoption applicants who are older than 50, morbidly obese, unmarried or taking antidepressants. . . . Six workers from Zoé's Ark, a French charity, are sentenced to eight years in prison at hard labor on charges of kidnapping 103 children in Chad for adoption in France; most of the children were not orphans, nor from Sudan's Darfur region, as claimed.

**2008** Guatemala becomes source of most U.S. foreign adoptions but suspends the process in order to establish better regulations. . . . Kyrgyzstan suspends adoptions because of suspected corruption, leaving more than 60 U.S. families with pending adoptions in limbo. . . . Vietnam stops accepting adoption applications after a U.S. embassy investigation finds many cases in which poor birth parents had been paid or deceived into placing their children in an orphanage.

**2009** Malawi judge rejects Madonna's request to waive an 18-month residency requirement to adopt a Malawian child, saying it would set a dangerous precedent. The pop singer had been granted such an exemption in 2006 when she adopted another Malawian boy.

**2010** Foreign families adopt more than 1,000 Haitian children after earthquake devastates Haiti's capital. . . . Tennessee woman puts her 7-year-old adopted Russian boy alone on a plane to Moscow with a note saying she no longer wished to be his parent. . . . U.S. follows other Western countries in suspending adoptions of Nepalese children due to concerns about fabricated birth certificates.

**2011** U.S. and Russian foreign ministers agree to regulate adoptions of Russian children by American families (July 13). . . . Guatemalan court sentences a lawyer and an adoption-agency representative to 21 and 16 years in prison, respectively, for trafficking a stolen baby for adoption to a U.S. family (Oct. 24). . . . State Department reports that international adoptions in the United States have dropped below 10,000 — a fall of nearly 60 percent from the peak in 2004 (Nov. 16).

considered "Germanizable." Nazi policy called "for Polish children who appeared to be 'racially valuable' to have their ties severed with their parents and to be transferred into German care with new names," writes historian Mark Mazower.[23]

Greek communists pursued a similar policy during the Greek civil war of 1946 to 1949. An estimated 30,000 children were sent off to other Eastern-bloc countries to be brought up as communists.[24]

## Humanitarian Impulses

But World War II also led to international adoptions based on humanitarian needs. Having seen the ravages of war, Americans between 1948 and 1953 adopted 5,814 European children — primarily from Germany and Greece — and 2,418 children from Asia, two-thirds from Japan.[25]

As the economies of Europe and Asia recovered, the door to intercountry adoptions soon shut tight. Novelist Pearl S. Buck, who grew up in China as the daughter of American missionaries and won a Nobel Prize in Literature in 1938, became an advocate for transracial, special-needs and international adoptions. She adopted seven children, including several of mixed race. In 1949, after being unable to find an adoption agency that would place a mixed-race child, she founded Welcome House in Bucks County, Pa., the first international, interracial adoption agency.[26]

Harry Holt, a wealthy Oregon farmer and businessman, was another important early advocate for international adoption. In 1955 he was moved by a newsreel showing the wretched lives of Korean War orphans, nearly all of them biracial offspring of American soldiers. Adoption was practically unknown at the time in Korea, a Confucian society in which family heritage is central to establishing an individual's identity. Mixed-race children were especially spurned.

Holt and his wife, Bertha, adopted eight homeless Amerasian children from South Korea and founded an orphanage there. They also began Holt International, which remains one of the largest adoption agencies in the world. The Holts' own adoptions required an act of Congress, which spelled out for the first time "uniform procedures for adopting from other countries," Pertman, of the Donaldson Institute, writes in his 2011 book *Adoption Nation.*[27]

Over the next four decades, South Korea would remain the largest supplier of adopted children to the United States and other Western nations, with more than 100,000 children leaving Korea between the 1950s and mid-1980s. From 1965 to 1976, Asia supplied about two-thirds of the children adopted from abroad in the United States, most coming from South Korea.[28]

## One-Child Policy

The Korean War, of course, was not the last conflict that would lead to an increase in international adoptions. After the Vietnam War, Americans began to adopt Vietnamese children — including many babies fathered by U.S. soldiers. Vietnam's communist rulers blocked adoptions at first, but their numbers began to jump during the 1990s. Since then, however, foreign adoptions have been halted due to concerns about corruption, kidnapping and trafficking.

While natural disasters and crises such as the AIDS epidemic in Africa have triggered increased interest in adoption, the dramatic spike in adoptions of children from China — mostly girls — has been attributed to that country's one-child policy. "The overwhelming majority [of international adoptees] are the victims of much larger domestic tragedies, from civil strife and disease in Africa to the devaluation of girls in China," writes Pertman.[29]

Because most Chinese families are allowed to have only one biological child, baby girls — viewed as less desirable than boys in Chinese culture — have been abandoned by the tens of thousands each year. China has been the leading supplier of children for international adoptions over the last two decades.

Only 33 Chinese children were adopted by Americans in 1989, but by 1998 China was the top supplier of Asian orphans, sending some 4,200 children to the United States that year.[30] The numbers kept rising until they peaked in 2005 at 7,903.[31]

Compared with other countries, China's international adoption process has long been considered quick and efficient. But there have been ongoing accusations about the process for international adoptions, including kidnapping and the selling of babies for body parts or household labor.

In 2005, Chinese police arrested 27 members of a trafficking ring that allegedly had abducted or bought up

# Interracial Adoptions Raise Prickly Issues

*White parents today rarely adopt black children.*

After World War II, changing adoption policies and social mores eventually led to greater demand for international adoptions.

Influenced by social science research suggesting that strong ties with a parent or caregiver are crucial for the mental health of a developing child, Congress in 1961 created a federally funded foster-care system designed to move children out of orphanages and into family homes. By 1965, only 4 percent of American orphans remained in institutions, and today orphanages seem to be a thing of the past.[1] Children without parents almost universally live with foster parents, although some teens do live in "group homes" or shelters.

In the 1960s and early '70s, racial issues became central to adoption discussions, in part because black children made up nearly half of the foster-care population but only about 12 percent of the nation's population. To address that imbalance, some child-welfare groups sought to promote transracial adoptions.

But in 1972 the National Association of Black Social Workers (NABSW) passed a resolution calling the adoption of African-Americans by whites a "particular form of genocide."[2] Despite studies showing that transracial adoptions worked as well for the children as white-only adoptions, William T. Merritt, president of the NABSW, said, "Black children in white homes are cut off from the healthy development of themselves as black people."[3]

Transracial adoptions promptly plummeted. In 1971, 2,574 white families had adopted African-American children. By 1973, the number had dropped to less than 1,000.[4]

Two decades later, in 1994, Congress passed a law prohibiting the use of race or national origin as a factor in placing children in adoptive or foster-care homes, wiping out state laws that required children to be placed within their own racial group. But by then the pattern of whites rarely adopting African-Americans had been set.

Howard Altstein, a University of Maryland professor of social work, suggests that transracial adoption is no longer as controversial as in the past, but it's still relatively rare for black children to be adopted by white parents, who do most of the adopting in the United States. About two-thirds of the children in foster care today are black.

Alstein estimates that about 70,000 children in foster care are adoptable —"a whole lot of kids," he says. Others say the number could be even higher. "Many are not infants, many are not white, but if you want a kid, there they are."

Similarly, during the 1970s American Indians expressed concern that Native American children being raised by

to 1,000 children in Guandong Province over the previous three years and then sold them to orphanages in Hunan, presumably for trafficking or adoption by Westerners. A 2005 report from a U.S. congressional commission found that "trafficking of women and children in China remains pervasive."[32]

The government has tried to crack down on corruption and limit international demand for its children. In 2007, it imposed new restrictions, blocking adoptions by applicants older than 50 (except for those willing to adopt children with special needs) or who are morbidly obese, unmarried or taking antidepressants.

"It used to be, in the heyday of things, if you wanted to adopt from China you submitted your paperwork and you'd get a referral within months," says Minnesota pediatrician Johnson. "Now, it takes years before you get a referral."

## After the Fall

In the late 1980s and early '90s the collapse of communist regimes in Eastern Europe opened up another part of the world to international adoptions.

"At the time of the fall of the Berlin Wall, we did not think of it as an adoption event," the Donaldson Institute's Pertman says. "But we discovered orphanages teeming with children."

Under the heavy-handed rule of Romania's Nicolae Ceau?escu, abortions were illegal, and women were given incentives to have children, facing possible financial penalties if they didn't. As a result, thousands of babies were

whites would lose touch with their culture. In 1978, Congress passed the Indian Child Welfare Act, which virtually prohibits the adoption of Indian children by non-Indians. "In the case of Native American adoptions, there is truly the issue of the survival of a people," says Vincent Cheng, an English professor at the University of Utah and author of the 2004 book *Inauthentic: The Anxiety Over Culture and Identity.* "Native American groups are very sensitive about losing any children to adoptions to non-Native Americans."

Even as white families were becoming less likely to adopt American children of other races, the number of white American children available for adoption was falling for several reasons. The 1973 *Roe v. Wade* Supreme Court decision legalizing abortion led to abortions becoming widely available in the United States and fewer births of unwanted children. In addition, single parenthood was becoming more socially acceptable in American and other Western societies.

"Today, less than 2 percent of unwed mothers relinquish babies for adoption," compared to 20 to 30 percent in the past, says David Smolin, a professor at the Cumberland School of Law in Birmingham, Ala.

That means only about 30,000 babies are available for adoption in a given year, Smolin estimates. "There's a tremendous demand for babies," he says. "The demand side has probably been bigger for quite some time than the supply available, if you're talking about healthy babies."

And many Americans looking abroad are in the market for healthy babies. But not all children available for adoption in the United States are babies, and some prospective parents fear that American children who are put up for adoption may be the children of drug or alcohol addicts.

Another reason: the growing popularity of so-called open-records adoption laws. Such state laws allow the birth parents to share in the child's upbringing, which means the child can find out who his or her birth parents were.

"As adoptions become increasingly open here, there [still] are a small number [of birth parents] who want to maintain their privacy and confidentiality," says Charles Johnson, president of the National Council for Adoption.

For people who don't want to worry about the complications of their children interacting with their birth parents at some point down the road, international adoption provides some peace of mind.

"If you go abroad and you get a kid from country X, Y or Z, the likelihood of a birth father or grandmother or family member getting involved in your adoption and your raising the kid is minimal, maybe zero," Alstein says.

— *Alan Greenblatt*

---

[1]Darshak Sanghavi, "The Lonely Lives of Russian Orphans," *The Washington Post*, April 25, 2010, p. B2, www.washingtonpost.com/wp-dyn/content/article/2010/04/23/AR2010042302223.html.

[2]In an editorial about the condemnation of transracial adoption by the National Association of Black Social Workers, *The New Republic* called the organization a "little-known black nationalist group," "All in the Family," *The New Republic*, Jan. 24, 1994, pp. 6-7.

[3]Rita J. Simon and Howard Altstein, *Adoption Across Borders: Serving the Children in Transracial and Intercountry Adoptions* (2000), p. 52.

[4]*Ibid.*, p. 15.

abandoned, often ending up being raised in nightmarish conditions in institutions where they were neglected, malnourished and often left untreated for illness.

"They had thousands and thousands of children in orphanages that Ceau?escu just locked up," says Howard Altstein, an expert on adoption at the University of Maryland.

After the horrific conditions in the orphanages were exposed, thousands of European and American families began adopting Romanian children in the early 1990s. But complaints about bribery led the government to shut down the process. In 2001, Romania banned all intercountry adoptions, save those involving biological grandparents.

"There's definitely more capacity, and certainly more kids are assigned to adoptive parents in Romania now," says Wolfe Murray, who served as a consultant to the Romanian government on children's issues. "The system is by no means ideal. It's slow and bureaucratic, but adoption is always difficult."

But the Ceau?escu-era orphans who were not adopted by foreign parents had a bleak future. Once they became old enough to be released from the institutions, many of them — some who had AIDS or had been chained to iron beds for long periods — began living on the streets of Romania's cities. Many turned to prostitution or became addicted to drugs and sniffing glue. One former "street kid" named Cola, who had lived in a sewer and survived years of addiction, found work at a Bucharest fairground, organized with the help of Save the Children.

## Chile Has Longest Adoption Waiting Time

Americans adopting children from Chile, Armenia and India had to wait the longest — up to nearly two years — for the adoption process to be completed in fiscal 2011. Adoptions were quickest in Madagascar, Estonia and Panama.

### Average Time for an International Adoption
### (Number of days, by country, fiscal 2011)

| Longest Wait Times | No. of Days | Shortest Wait Times | No. of Days |
| --- | --- | --- | --- |
| Chile | 694 | Madagascar | 79 |
| Armenia | 620 | Estonia | 154 |
| India | 553 | Panama | 166 |
| Lithuania | 524 | Canada | 207 |
| Mexico | 519 | China | 254 |

*Source:* "FY 2011 Annual Report on Intercountry Adoptions," U.S. State Department, November 2011, http://adoption.state.gov/content/pdf/fy 2011_annual_report.pdf

"You have to pass through all that hell to get to this stage," he told a reporter. "You have to know what hell is like to get out of it. That's what we tell them if they come to live in the hole: that we went through the same, that you cannot live by buying crack or heroin, doing your shot. . . . We urge them to come and clean at the fairground instead. No one can save us, . . . only we can save ourselves," Cola said in 2009. "That's the law of the street in Romania these days."[33]

AP Photo/Richard Vogel

Vietnamese orphans with AIDS are cared for at a facility in Ha Tay province, 40 miles from Hanoi. UNICEF estimates that 16.4 million children in developing countries have lost one or both parents to HIV-AIDS, most of them in Africa and Asia.

### Looking East

Adoption agencies and their clients soon looked eastward to countries such as Russia, Ukraine and Georgia. There, too, international adoptions soon ran into resistance.

In Georgia, first lady Nanuli Shevardnadze successfully pushed for a moratorium on international adoptions in 1997, claiming that the process was riddled with bribery and deceit, with agencies exaggerating the medical needs of healthy, adoptable children to get them out of the country. "Our nation's gene pool is being depleted," she told *The New York Times.* "No more children should leave Georgia."[34]

Shevardnadze dismissed arguments that Georgia's conditions were miserable for children who might prosper elsewhere. "All the Georgian people are suffering hardships," she said. "Let our children suffer, too."

Since then, a handful of Georgian children have been adopted by foreigners, but none in 2009 or 2011 and only two in 2010.

"The pattern for intercountry adoption seems to be that as one source of adoptable children diminishes, other countries increase the number of children they allow to be adopted abroad, or else new sources appear," write Alstein and Rita Simon, an adoption expert at American University.[35]

For example, until 1993, Russia did not allow Americans to adopt any of its children. That year, 695 Russian children were adopted by Americans, and nearly twice as many the following year. Russia has also been one of the leading sources of children for European adopters over the past 20 years, along with Vietnam and China. Russian children, for instance, made up 30 percent of the foreign children adopted by Irish families from 1993 to 2010.[36]

But Russia generally has had an ambiguous attitude toward foreign adoptions. In 1994, the country mandated thorough searches for prospective adoptive families within Russia before orphans could be considered for international adoptions. The following year, President Boris Yeltsin signed a law making all children eligible for international

# Should international adoption be promoted?

## YES
**Stevan Whitehead**
*Vice President, Overseas Adoption Support and Information Service, United Kingdom*

Written for *CQ Global Researcher*, December 2011

Without a doubt, children need early, permanent, stable, nurturing parenting in order to flourish. This right to a family is enshrined in the United Nations Convention on the Rights of the Child. Yet, millions of children worldwide are denied this fundamental right: 2.2 million children worldwide are in orphanages, and more than 150 million are living on the street, according to UNICEF.

Equally without question, adoption provides the best form of substitute parenting. That's why in Western countries we do not shut down entire adoption programs just because there may be occasional instances of scandal and abuse. The benefits of adoption far outweigh the risks. Only in international adoption do breaches of the law by fraudsters, profiteers or traffickers result in the wholesale closure of adoption programs and the condemnation of children to institutional care or life on the streets. Often this results from critics sensationalizing or using false or exaggerated charges to characterize international adoption — with equally inflated claims about the benefits of their own solutions.

British and U.S. laws already exist to penalize those who commit serious adoption abuses. Where laws don't exist, they should be created, but they should be used wisely. Equal care should be given to the efficacious regulation of all adoptions in order to address real problems and avoid counterproductive moratoria and over-regulation.

Closing international adoption without having a viable alternative in place punishes unparented children — whether they are orphans or victims of abuse or neglect.

Adoption comes from harm and loss, but it is intended to prevent greater continuing harm by providing a nurturing, therapeutic family environment. When one considers the lack of success in finding social interventions that significantly improve children's lives, the proven positive impact of adoption should be applauded and promoted.

Adoption, whether domestic or international, is inherently sound. For all the risks it might pose in any individual case, it remains the best way to achieve a stable nurturing family life for thousands of children who don't have one. Thus, to ensure that children retain their right to a family and protection from the detrimental effects of multiple placements, institutionalization or worse, foreign adoption should be part of a spectrum of services to children, including family support and preservation, reunification with relatives and domestic adoption.

## NO
**Rupert Wolfe Murray**
*Former European Union Adviser on Children's Welfare, Romania*

Written for *CQ Global Researcher*, December 2011

I live in Romania, which was once one of the big "sending" countries in the international adoptions business: More than 30,000 Romanian children were sent abroad for adoption between 1990 and 2001. In Romania, and I suspect in all the "sending" countries, the lobby for international adoptions is highly effective in persuading the government and media that this is a solution to their child-welfare problems. The adoption lobby doesn't advertise, but it does offer generous "commissions" to politicians, journalists, lawyers, judges, social workers, medics and others who facilitate this secretive and highly profitable business.

In the chaos following Romania's violent revolution in 1989, adoption agencies were able to facilitate deals with directors of children's homes, medics in maternity hospitals and poor families in villages. The minimum price for a child was about $30,000. I recently asked the Romanian government for information about these cases, and they said there are no records for those who were sold between 1990 and 1997.

The international adoptions business is built on a false promise. Decent families in the United States are told they are giving a home to orphans and abandoned children. In reality, the demand for children far outstrips the supply of orphans, and the result is kidnapping and fraud — in countries with weak legal systems that can be easily corrupted.

A series of court cases in China revealed how the business operates there: Babies are snatched from the arms of mothers in one province and "abandoned" at an orphanage in another. The charity Against Child Trafficking, based in the Netherlands, is helping to pay the court costs for poor families in Ethiopia and India who were tricked into declaring that they had "abandoned" their children, who were then sold into the international adoption system.

When Romania's government discovered how unaccountable the business was (each child disappeared without trace), it banned international adoptions in 2001. Romania then reformed its child-welfare system, closed down the orphanages, developed a network of foster families and encouraged local adoptions. There is now a waiting list of Romanian families who want to adopt. All this will be undermined if international adoptions are reintroduced in Romania — and there is constant pressure to do so. Romania's social services will be unable to resist the cash that the foreign adoption agencies can offer.

International adoption should not be promoted. It should be banned.

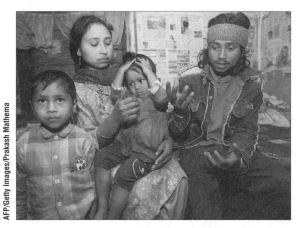

Illiterate Nepalese parents Rajan Kumar Nepali (right) and his wife Maya nearly lost their children after a nearby orphanage promised to care for them while the 28-year-old Nepali tried to kick his drug addiction. Instead, Nepali learned that the children had been declared orphans and put up for foreign adoption. Eventually, a local charity rescued both children. Child-protection groups say the family's ordeal is typical in Nepal, where unscrupulous agents traffic children to foreign couples for large profits.

adoption, not just the children of the mentally ill or alcoholics.

Nevertheless, the number of Russians adopted abroad continued to spike. In 1998, Russia was the leading supplier of foreign-born orphans to the United States, at 4,491.

## CURRENT SITUATION

### Abused Russians

Today Russia, like other "sending countries," is having second thoughts about its foreign adoption program. Problems and circumstances vary, but seemingly every country that experiences rapid growth in the number of its children adopted abroad comes to worry about what effects a large international adoption industry is having. They begin to worry about whether the process leads to corruption or abuse and what it says about their standing as a nation to have thousands of their children sent abroad to find homes.

And there have been some well-publicized problems. Last year, a Tennessee woman, Torry Ann Hansen, put her 7-year-old adopted Russian son alone on a plane to Moscow with a note saying, "I no longer wish to parent

this child." She said the child was difficult and sometimes violent.

The incident drew international attention, with Russian President Dmitry Medvedev calling it "a monstrous deed." But it wasn't the first time an adoptive parent had mistreated a Russian orphan.

In 1997, an American couple returning with two adopted Russian girls was arrested after slapping and verbally abusing the girls in flight, which led the Russian Duma to threaten to block all U.S. adoptions. The following year, Pittsburgh businessman Matthew Mancuso adopted a 5-year-old Russian girl, whom he immediately began to abuse sexually. She was freed three years later when the FBI raided Mancuso's home in a child pornography sting.[37]

"We've had 14 Russian adoptees killed by parents," says Smolin, the Samford University law professor. "Even though the whole world has been concerned about the kid sent back, there has been less concern about the kids who've been killed."

In response, Russia slowed down the adoption process. From a peak of 5,862 in 2004, Russian adoptions by Americans fell to 970 in 2011. Adoption of Russian children in countries such as Sweden, France and Germany have been falling in recent years as well, although the numbers continue to climb in Italy — from 380 in 2003 to 704 in 2009.[38]

In July, Russian Foreign Minister Sergei V. Lavrov and U.S. Secretary of State Hillary Rodham Clinton signed an accord designed to curb the worst abuses. The agreement allows the Russian government to decide which foreign adoption agencies can operate in their country and calls for improved screening of families prior to adoption and more careful post-adoption monitoring.

"This will help us remove the irritants that have been emerging quite rightfully in the realm of public opinion concerning the destiny of Russian children who were adopted by Americans," Lavrov said.[39]

Hansen, the Tennessee woman, was not alone in her complaint that a Russian adoptee was violent or abusive. Due to the lack of nurturing in orphanages in countries such as Russia and Bulgaria, many adopted children have emotional problems, often referred to as reactive attachment disorder (RAD).

But adoption proponents point out that the vast majority of the 50,000 Russians adopted by Americans are living healthy, successful lives, while more than 100,000 Russian children still languish in orphanages.[40]

Although the Russian institutions have been much improved, they remain less than ideal places for children to thrive, according to Boris L. Altshuler, a Russian who directs an advocacy group in Moscow called Children's Rights. He called international adoption a "giant rescue operation" for Russian orphans.

"For children who remain in Russian orphanages because of the difficulties of international adoption, this has been a calamity," he said. "It is a crime committed by us all."[41]

### Domestic Adoptions

Nascent domestic adoption programs in countries such as South Korea and China are having difficulty making much headway.

"They've been trying to foster a native adoption culture," says Pertman of the Donaldson Institute. "They want to keep more people at home. "But most countries don't have a native adoption culture," he continues. "You don't take in people who are not your blood in most countries."

Many developing countries are improving their systems to care for children, but resources are often lacking, says UNICEF's Bissell. "What we're seeing in countries where UNICEF has a presence in the global south is an increasing awareness of the state of child protection services," she says. "I don't want to say there's a groundswell, but there is definitely a lot more going on to build up child protective systems than we've ever seen before — an increased ability of countries to take care of their children and a desire to do so."

Pro-adoption groups say they support countries that want to keep more of their children at home. The best option for a child, all seem to agree, is to remain within its family or extended family and, if that's not possible, within its home country.

But international adoption must remain an option, its advocates argue, when it's not possible to find a good home for a child within its own country. "Anybody who looks at the situation of what I categorize as unparented children growing up in institutions or on the streets, you would say, 'Let's find them what they most need.' And what young children most need is a parent to nurture them," says Bartholet, the Harvard law professor.

But groups such as UNICEF say that if parents can't support their children, then they should be given help.

"UNICEF is very much a proponent of supporting the vulnerable mother who wants to keep her kid," says Bissell. "No one wants children in institutions. The phrase I often use is 'having the right children adopted at the right time.'"

Some adoption advocates accuse UNICEF of slowing down processes in certain places for altruistic but possibly misguided reasons, leaving millions of children desperately in need of a good home. Denying them the love and care they could receive from parents who happen to live in Europe or the United States out of either national pride or a well-intentioned desire to build up support systems in developing countries — which could take years — is a mistake, they say.

Brian Franklin, chairman of the board of the Joint Council on International Children's Services, a pro-adoption group based in Washington, says a two-pronged approach is needed: a long-term strategy to deal with the problems of corruption and inadequate support for families and children and a short-term commitment to placing young, institutionalized children in the best possible environment.

"There is enough evidence now that early placement in a permanent family environment for a child that can't go back to their birth family is truly in their best interest," says pediatrician Johnson.

## OUTLOOK

### Market Effects

Over the last 20 years, one country after another has gone through a roller-coaster ride of adoption cycles, experiencing the unintended consequences of upwards of $100 million a year being spent by agencies and prospective families to adopt children from another country.

Countries have tried to clean up the corruption that almost inevitably results when that amount of money is being spent. Then, when cleanup fails, governments shut down entire programs or watch foreign adoption agencies and governments cease doing business with them.

Some predict that the structures being put in place as a result of the Hague Convention will lead to a more sustainable system of international adoptions.

"There has been a slightly false picture of intercountry adoptions generally, a lot of it by the media," says Whitehead of OASIS. "It doesn't help that we have the media portraits of people swooping in and grabbing kids and swooping back out again."

Because of that image, countries that traditionally have furnished thousands of children to the West will send far fewer children in the future, some experts say, and adoptions will be limited to special needs or handicapped children.

"There are countries, such as Brazil, that moved to only send older children many years ago," says Newcastle University fellow Selman. "From the point of view of the Americans or Spanish, the hope for a healthy white baby girl is no longer there." Today, even agencies specializing in placing disabled children often have waiting lists of hopeful parents.

Under the Hague Convention, "Each country has a database, so they are able to match the child and the parent," says the State Department's Jacobs. "If a family that wants to adopt says they can take a child with special needs, then their central authority will find a child that wants a loving home."

Many people concerned about child welfare want to give homes to children who face emotional or physical difficulties. "My son would have been a beggar in Guatemala," said Michele Greene, an American television actress who was initially drawn to him by a photo showing his severe cleft palate. "He was a throwaway child."[42]

But not everyone will have the desire — or the skills — necessary to adopt a child with special needs. Part of what has made international adoption attractive for many prospective parents was the hope of adopting a healthy baby. "Obviously, the average infertile or gay couple is not going to be interested and cannot handle special-needs children," says Smolin, the Samford law professor.

It's always possible that new countries will open up to international adoption due to war or disease. But Smolin and others believe the global shifting of wealth toward emerging economies such as Brazil, Russia, India and China, will continue to put downward pressure on international adoptions as the countries become wealthier. Already, India and South Korea, which have enjoyed improved economic fortunes, are keeping more of their children home.

"Intercountry adoption was about the relationships of the U.S., Canada, Italy and Spain with either poor, developing or transitioning-from-communism countries," Smolin says. "The gap [in wealth] between those countries and the U.S. is going to decline."

Pertman, the Donaldson Institute director, says international adoptions could spike again in the face of future crises, which can create vast numbers of new orphans. Barring that, the number of international adoptions is likely to continue to fall, he agrees.

"If nothing institutional changes, if we keep on the path that we're on, then I think international adoption is going to keep falling," Pertman says.

In terms of U.S. adoptions, he says, it will continue to drop from its 2004 high of nearly 23,000. "I don't know where the basement is, but if I had to guess it's somewhere in the four- to seven-thousand range."

## NOTES

1. Sheila Wayman, "Why Adopting Abroad Is Appealing," *The Irish Times*, March 25, 2008, p. 11.

2. Beth Nonte Russell, "For Mercy's Sake, It's Madonna," *Los Angeles Times*, April 6, 2009, p. A21, http://articles.latimes.com/2009/apr/06/opinion/oe-russell6.

3. From an e-mail exchange with Rebecca Fordham, communication specialist with UNICEF. The 17.8 million figure comes from "Orphan Estimates," UNICEF, www.childinfo.org/hiv_aids_orphanestimates.php.

4. For background, see Robert Kiener, "Gendercide Crisis," *CQ Global Researcher*, Oct. 4, 2011, pp. 473-498.

5. "Saviours or Kidnappers?" *The Economist*, Feb. 4, 2010, www.economist.com/node/15469423.

6. Ginger Thompson, "Case Stokes Haiti's Fear for Children, and Itself," *The New York Times*, Feb. 2, 2010, p. A1, www.nytimes.com/2010/02/02/world/americas/02orphans.html?pagewanted=all.

7. Deborah Sontag, "A Year Later, Haunted But Hopeful, Haiti Struggles Back," *The New York Times*, Jan. 4, 2011, p. A1, www.nytimes.com/2011/01/04/world/americas/04haiti.html.

8. "Haiti Leader Vows to Tighten Adoption Rules," Agence France-Presse, June 23, 2011, www2.canada.com/edmontonjournal/news/story.html?id=41099646-fcc4-49f7-9ab5-167ab0cad540.

9. N. C. Aizenman, "Guatemalan Children in Limbo of Orphanages," *The Washington Post*, June 18, 2009, p. B1, www.washingtonpost.com/wp-dyn/content/article/2009/06/17/AR2009061703641.html.

10. Dan Frosch, "New Rules and Economy Strain Adoption Agencies," *The New York Times*, May 11, 2008, p. A16, www.nytimes.com/2008/05/11/us/11adopt.html.

11. E. J. Graff, "The Baby Business," *Democracy*, summer 2010, www.democracyjournal.org/17/6757.php?page=all.

12. "FY 2011 Annual Report on Intercountry Adoptions," U.S. State Department, November 2011, p. 3, http://adoption.state.gov/content/pdf/fy2011_annual_report.pdf. (The State Department keeps track of foreign adoptions by fiscal years that run from Oct. 1 to Sept. 30.)

13. Figures for 2004 were supplied by Pamela A. Quiroz of the University of Illinois-Chicago.

14. "The Way Forward Project Report," Congressional Coalition on Adoption Institute, November 2011, http://img-assets.s3.amazonaws.com/thewayforwardproject/files/The%20Way%20Forward%20Project%20Report.pdf.

15. "Orphan Estimates," ChildInfo, UNICEF, January 2011.

16. David Crary, "Adoptions From Ethiopia Rise, Bucking Global Trend," The Associated Press, Oct. 12, 2010, www.boston.com/news/nation/articles/2010/10/12/adoptions_from_ethiopia_rise_bucking_global_trend/.

17. "FY 2011 Annual Report on Intercountry Adoption," Bureau of Consular Affairs, U.S. Department of State, November 2011, http://adoption.state.gov/content/pdf/fy2011_annual_report.pdf.

18. Scott Simon, *Baby, We Were Meant for Each Other* (2010), p. 14.

19. Rachel Zoll, "Muslim Orphans Caught Between Islam and the West," The Associated Press, Nov. 29, 2010, www.usatoday.com/news/religion/2010-11-29-orphans29_ST_N.htm.

20. Rita J. Simon and Howard Alstein, *Adoption Across Borders* (2000), p. 37.

21. Simon, *op. cit.*, p. 17.

22. Simon and Alstein, *op. cit.*, p. 37.

23. Mark Mazower, *Hitler's Empire: How the Nazis Ruled Europe* (2008), p. 190.

24. C. M. Woodhouse, *Modern Greece* (1992), p. 259.

25. Adam Pertman, *Adoption Nation* (2011), p. 69. (Revised edition of his 2001 book by the same name.)

26. Hilary Spurling, *Pearl Buck in China* (2010), p. 245. Also see "About Welcome House," Pearl S. Buck International, www.psbi.org/page.aspx?pid=384.

27. Pertman, *op. cit.*, p. 69.

28. Simon and Altstein, *op. cit.*, p. 21.

29. Pertman, *op. cit.*, p. 69.

30. Simon and Alstein, *op. cit.*, p. 23.

31. Pertman, *op. cit.*, p. 72.

32. Martha Groves, "Painful Questions for Adoptive Parents," *Los Angeles Times*, Nov. 11, 2009, p. A6, http://articles.latimes.com/2009/nov/11/local/me-china-adopt11.

33. Ed Vulliamy, "Notes From the Underground," *The Observer*, Aug. 9, 2009, p. 32, www.guardian.co.uk/world/2009/aug/09/romania-street-children-revisited.

34. Alessandra Stanley, "Hands Off Our Children, A Georgian Tells America," *The New York Times*, June 29, 1997, p. 1, www.nytimes.com/1997/06/29/world/hands-off-our-babies-a-georgian-tells-america.html.

35. Simon and Altstein, *op. cit.*, p. 33.

36. Julia Werdigier and Judy Dempsey, "Europe Fears Fallout From U.S.-Russia Adoption Tiff," *The New York Times*, April 13, 2010, www.nytimes.com/2010/04/14/world/europe/14iht-parents.html.

37. The girl, Masha Allen, submitted testimony to the House Energy and Commerce Committee, May 3, 2006, http://energycommerce.house.gov/108/Hearings/05032006hearing1852/Allen.pdf.

38. "International Adoption Statistics," Australian Intercountry Adoption Network, www.aican.org/statistics.php?region=0&type=birth.

39. Robert Bridge, "Lavrov and Clinton Iron Out Differences in Washington," RT.com, July 14, 2011, http://rt.com/politics/lavrov-clinton-washington-reset/.

40. Boris Altshuler, "The Orphan Factory," *Russia Beyond the Headlines*, Nov. 21, 2011, www.rbth.ru/articles/2011/11/21/the_orphan_factory_13777.html.

41. Michael Schwirtz, "Pact on Adoptions Ends a U.S.-Russian Dispute," *The New York Times*, July 14, 2011, p. A12, www.nytimes.com/2011/07/14/world/europe/14moscow.html.

42. Pertman, *op. cit.*, p. 74.

## BIBLIOGRAPHY

### Selected Sources

### Books

Pertman, Adam, *Adoption Nation: How the Adoption Revolution Is Transforming Our Families — And America*, Harvard Common Press, 2011.
In this updated edition of his 2001 book, the executive director of the Evan B. Donaldson Adoption Institute in New York describes the changing landscape of adoption law.

Simon, Rita J., and Howard Altstein, *Adoption Across Borders: Serving the Children in Transracial and Intercountry Adoptions*, Rowman & Littlefield, 2000.
Two social scientists sketch the history of international adoptions and present research on how well children adopted from abroad acclimate in comparison with transracial domestic adoptions.

Simon, Scott, *Baby, We Were Meant for Each Other: In Praise of Adoption*, Random House, 2010.
The NPR host tells the story of his experience adopting two daughters from China and interviews other families who have adopted children from abroad.

### Articles

Cornell, Drucilla, "The 'Enabling Violation' of International Adoption," "Opinionator" blog, *NYTimes.com*, Oct. 23, 2011, http://opinionator.blogs.nytimes.com/2011/10/23/the-dilemmas-of-international-adoption/.
A Cornell University literature professor who adopted her daughter from Paraguay wonders about the moral repercussions of children being kidnapped in the international adoption process.

Crary, David, "Despite Hurdles, Families Pursue Nepal Adoptions," The Associated Press, Jan. 22, 2011, www.huffingtonpost.com/2011/01/22/despite-hurdles-families-_n_812618.html.
After the United States suspended its visa program for Nepalese adoptees, some American families waited there for months in hopes of being able to bring children home.

Ellingwood, Ken, "On the Trail of a War's Lost Kids," *Los Angeles Times*, July 13, 2011, http://articles.latimes.com/2011/jul/13/world/la-fg-salvador-dis appeared-20110713.
A group searching for hundreds of children who went missing during the 1980s civil war in El Salvador — seized from their parents by Salvadoran soldiers and funneled by unscrupulous lawyers into the lucrative international adoption market — finds that many ended up in the United States, Belgium, Italy, Mexico and Germany.

Graff, E.J., "The Baby Business," *Democracy*, summer 2010, www.democracyjournal.org/17/6757.php.
Foreign adoption programs in most countries are "relatively clean," but several — including Guatemala, Cambodia and Ethiopia — have had problems with corruption and kidnapping.

Leland, John, "For Adoptive Parents, Questions Without Answers," *The New York Times*, Sept. 16, 2011, www.nytimes.com/2011/09/18/nyregion/chinas-adoption-scandal-sends-chills-through-families-in-united-states.html.
After reports that thousands of adopted children may have been stolen from their birth parents, many American parents worry that their adopted children may have been kidnapped.

"Saviors or Kidnappers?" *The Economist*, Feb. 4, 2010, www.economist.com/node/15469423.
Problems arise when adoptions after natural disasters are rushed.

Seabrook, John, "The Last Babylift," *The New Yorker*, May 10, 2010, www.newyorker.com/reporting/2010/05/10/100510fa_fact_seabrook.
A journalist describes his family's experience adopting a Haitian child after the 2010 earthquake.

Thompson, Ginger, "After Haiti Quake, the Chaos of U.S. Adoptions," *The New York Times*, Aug. 3, 2010, www.nytimes.com/2010/08/04/world/americas/04adoption.html.

More than three times as many Haitian children were adopted by Americans immediately after the 2010 earthquake than over the previous three years.

## Studies and Reports

"FY 2011 Annual Report on Intercountry Adoptions," U.S. State Department, November 2011, http://adoption.state.gov/content/pdf/fy2011_annual_report.pdf.

The number of international adoptions completed in the United States in fiscal 2011 was down nearly 60 percent from its high in 2004 and fell 15 percent from the previous year.

Lammerant, Isabelle, and Marlène Hofstetter, "Adoption: At What Cost?" Terre des Hommes International Federation, 2007, www.terredeshommes.org/pdf/publication/adoption_embargo.pdf.

Receiving countries too often bow to pressure from prospective parents who want more countries to allow foreign adoptions. Instead, the authors argue, receiving countries should be more concerned with protecting adopted children.

Selman, Peter, "The Rise and Fall of Intercountry Adoption in the 21st Century," International Social Work, 2009, p. 52, http://isw.sagepub.com/content/52/5/575.abstract.

Demographic surveys of 22 receiving countries show a marked decline in international adoptions after decades of rapid growth.

# For More Information

**Against Child Trafficking**; +32 474974740; www.against childtrafficking.org/. A nonprofit, registered in the Netherlands, which fights child trafficking, particularly in the international adoption business.

**Australian Intercountry Adoption Network**, P.O. Box 7420, Bondi Beach 2026, New South Wales, Australia; www.aican.org. A national network of nonprofit groups involved in international adoptions; collects statistics on sending and receiving countries around the world.

**Both Ends Burning**, 16009 N. 81st St., Suite 130, Scottsdale, AZ 85260 USA; 480-699-5161; www.bothends burning.org. International organization founded by an American who has adopted three children from Haiti; promotes international adoption.

**Congressional Coalition on Adoption Institute**, 311 Massachusetts Ave., N.E., Washington, DC 20002 USA; 202-544-8500; www.ccainstitute.org. A nonprofit group that seeks to educate policymakers on the need for children to have safe, permanent homes.

**Evan B. Donaldson Adoption Institute**, 120 E. 38th St., New York, NY 10016 USA; 212-925-4089; www.adoption institute.org. Conducts research on adoption to help improve adoption laws, policies and practice.

**Hague Conference on International Private Law**, Scheveningseweg 6, 2517 KT The Hague, The Netherlands; fax +31 70 360 4867; www.hcch.net. The consortium of more than 70 member states that oversees the primary accord governing international adoptions.

**Joint Council on International Children's Services**, 117 S. Saint Asaph St., Alexandria, VA 22314 USA; 703-535-8045; www.jointcouncil.org. A coalition of more than 200 child welfare organizations, including adoption agencies.

**National Council for Adoption**, 225 N. Washington St., Alexandria, VA 22314 USA; 703-299-6633; www.adoption council.org. A nonprofit group that advocates for policies that promote adoption.

**Terre des Hommes International Federation**, 31 Chemin Franck Thomas, CH-1223 Cologny, Geneva, Switzerland; +41 22 736 33 72; www.terredeshommes.org. A coalition of organizations that provide support for children and children's rights; consults with the United Nations, the Council of Europe and other international organizations.

**United Nations Children's Fund**, 3 United Nations Plaza, New York, NY 10017 USA; 212-326-7000; www.unicef.org. Known today simply as UNICEF; provides long-term humanitarian assistance to mothers and children in developing countries.

# Voices From Abroad:

## JEAN-CHARLES BERTHONNET

**French Ambassador to Kazakhstan**

*Ties that bind*

"Kazakhstan's ratification of the Hague Convention is a positive step towards the protection of childhood in the country. International relationships should not be limited only to economic, political and cultural ties. Humane aspects should be an integral part of international ties."

*Times of Central Asia (Kyrgyzstan), May 2011*

## PAVEL ASTAKHOV

**Children's rights ombudsman, Russia**

*Agreements necessary*

"International adoptions between Russia and the United States have been in place for 16 years, but there has been no official bilateral agreement yet. It has been quite a revelation to me that children are being shipped out of Russia in their dozens, without any agreements. . . . Such agreements should be signed not only with the United States, but also with the U.K., France, Germany and other countries."

*Thai Press Reports, January 2011*

## FRANCES FITZGERALD

**Minister for Children Ireland**

*Trying our best*

"As a Hague member, we join a group of countries which aim to promote high standards and good practice in adoptions of children between countries. There will always be risks associated with adoption. However, we are doing our best to improve the protections surrounding Hague adoptions and reduce that risk."

*Irish Times, May 2011*

Bulgaria/Christo Komarnitski

## JASMINE WHITBREAD

**CEO, Save the Children England**

*Adoption's drawback*

"Taking children out of the country would permanently separate thousands of children from their families — a separation that would compound the acute trauma they are already suffering."

*Daily Telegraph (England) January 2010*

## JEAN LUC LEGRAND

**Adviser, UNICEF, Haiti**

*Links to trafficking*

"UNICEF has been working in Haiti for many years, and we knew the problem with the trade of children in Haiti that existed before. . . . Unfortunately many of these trade networks have links with the international adoption 'market.'"

*Guardian Unlimited (England) January 2010*

## CARLO GIOVANARDI

**Undersecretary for the Family, Italy**

*Italian laws are effective*

"Italy is a world leader in these matters and has no need to modify its laws. The criteria we use to allow couples to adopt abroad has earned us international credibility, and each year some 4,000 children are adopted from 62 countries."

*ANSA News Service (Italy) January 2010*

## PHILIP HOLMES

**Country Director Esther Benjamins Trust\* Nepal**

*Keeping options open*

"Domestic options, including adoption, should take precedence over intercountry adoption in line with the Hague Convention's 'Subsidiarity Principle.' [But] suspending intercountry adoption means denying a child the prospects that droves of their fellow Nepalis are leaving Nepal to access."

*Nepali Times, February 2010*
*\*An anti-child trafficking charity*

## VERONIQUE TAVEAU

**Spokeswoman, UNICEF Switzerland**

*Reunification first*

"UNICEF's position has always been that whatever the humanitarian situation, family reunification must be favored. The last resort is intercountry adoption."

*EFE News Service (Spain) January 2010*

# 3

# Child Poverty

Peter Katel

Impoverished Los Angeles residents queue up for free food, household items and toys at the Miracle in South Central event on Dec. 13, 2008. The national poverty rate is 15.1 percent — the highest in 28 years. More than a third of the 46.2 million people living below the poverty line are children.

From *CQ Researcher*, October 28, 2011.

Jason Barnett and his two brothers have better reason than many kids to welcome Friday afternoons. That's when they open a special backpack full of donated food that Jason brings home from his elementary school in Belen, N.M.

Inside are plastic-wrapped single servings of peanut butter and jelly, crackers, raisins, milk, juice and other healthy items. "You should see their eyes," says the boys' mother, Shannon Barnett. "There's usually cereal in it, which helps with breakfast over the weekend. If they're still hungry, I'm able to give them another bowl."

The Roadrunner Food Bank, New Mexico's major food charity, started the program 11 years ago after school officials in Albuquerque said some students went hungry on weekends. Now, demand is booming throughout the state, where 40 percent of New Mexicans — 806,000 out of a total population of 2 million — missed meals last year, according to a Roadrunner study.[1]

How many children went hungry isn't known. But children make up one-fourth of the population of New Mexico, which has a child-poverty rate of 30 percent, second only to Mississippi's (33 percent).[2]

Jason, 7, and his brothers — Andrew, 5, and Elias, 11 — weren't in danger of missing meals until about three years ago, their mother says. The family lives on about $15,000 a year that Paul Barnett earns at a building-supply company. That's well below the government's poverty threshold of $26,023 for a family of five with three children.[3]

The Barnetts had managed to scrape by with the help of food stamps, a federal housing subsidy and a federal income-tax credit for low-income families. But about three years ago, when gas and food

## Parental Unemployment Fuels Child Poverty

More than 12 percent of children in 14 states — including two of the biggest, California and Florida — have at least one unemployed parent, a factor that experts say contributes significantly to child poverty. In another dozen states, including New York and Texas, between 8 and 9 percent of children have at least one jobless parent. The national poverty rate has risen to 15.1 percent as unemployment hovers above 9 percent because of the recent recession.

### Percentage of Children With At Least One Unemployed Parent, 2010

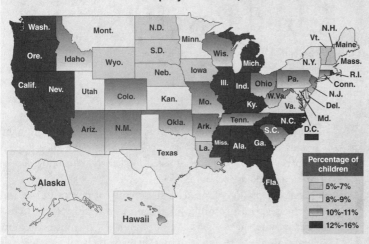

Percentage of children
- 5%-7%
- 8%-9%
- 10%-11%
- 12%-16%

*Source:* "America's Children, America's Challenge," Annie E. Casey Foundation, 2011, www.aecf.org/~/media/Pubs/Initiatives/KIDS COUNT/123/2011KIDSCOUNT DataBook/2011KCDB_FINAL_essay.pdf

1959, the rate hit 22.4 percent, concentrated among whites in isolated Appalachian mountain hollows and blacks in squalid urban ghettos and the rural South. The era spawned a spate of reform efforts, culminating in President Lyndon B. Johnson's War on Poverty program, which centered on providing welfare benefits to low-income families with children.

But by the mid-1990s, conservatives and some liberals alike were arguing that many of the Johnson-era reforms had created a culture of dependency on government aid. In 1996 Congress overhauled the welfare system, imposing work requirements and putting time limits on cash payments to the needy.

Welfare rolls plunged in the aftermath of the reforms. But the economic crisis, which began in 2007 and has pushed the national unemployment rate above 9 percent, has forced millions of families to seek government or private aid, or both. In response, Congress has expanded the welfare caseload, but only by 13 percent — not enough, advocates argue, to keep millions of children out of poverty. They are urging renewal of an emergency fund that Congress created in 2009 through the so-called economic stimulus bill — with an expiration date of Sept. 30, 2010.[7]

Child poverty arouses special concern because its effects can last a lifetime. "Children who are reared in poor families are more likely to fail in school, drop out of school, get arrested," says Ron Haskins, co-director of the Center on Children and Families at the Brookings Institution, a centrist think tank in Washington. "And the earlier the poverty starts, and the more years that a kid is reared in a household in poverty, the more likely those bad things are to happen."

Experts on both sides of the liberal-conservative divide agree that child poverty is causing the gap between rich and poor to widen. But they disagree on why more

prices rose sharply, the family sought help: monthly baskets from the food bank, and the backpack for the boys.[4]

"I just kind of suck in my pride and just get help," Paul Barnett says. "I was kind of embarrassed at first. But a lot of my friends are in a lot worse shape."

Indeed, millions of Americans are in dire financial straits. The national poverty rate, 15.1 percent, is the highest in 28 years. In 1983 it hit 15.2 percent.[5]

The picture is even bleaker for children, who make up a fourth of the U.S. population and more than a third of the 46.2 million people living below the poverty threshold. Over all, one in five U.S. children lives below the poverty line, a far higher rate than adults (13.7 percent) and the elderly (9 percent).[6]

It has been 52 years since the United States suffered a sustained bout of poverty as bad as the current one. In

than 16 million Americans under age 18 live below the poverty line — and on how to improve the situation.

For conservatives skeptical of government anti-poverty projects, child poverty above all is a behavioral issue — a reflection of the growing tendency to have children out of wedlock. A report last year by the National Center for Health Statistics shows that unwed mothers — a growing number of them in their 20s — accounted for 40 percent of U.S. births in 2008, the most recent year for which data are available. That rate has risen steadily over two decades. It was 26 percent in 1988 and 33 percent in 1998.[8]

And last year, children below the poverty line in single-mother households outnumbered poor children in married-couple families, by 8.6 million to 5.8 million.[9]

"Our society is bifurcating into one of upper-middle-class children raised by college-educated couples who are married and children born out of marriage to . . . women who have an overwhelming probability of being poor and remaining poor," says Robert Rector, a senior research fellow at the Heritage Foundation, a conservative think tank in Washington.

But liberal poverty experts, while acknowledging a link between single motherhood and poverty, reject the notion that out-of-wedlock child-bearing is either the main cause of child poverty or the key to its solution. "People are poor because they don't have enough income," says LaDonna Pavetti, vice president for family-income support policy at the liberal Center on Budget and Policy Priorities. "There is also a problem of people not having the skills to qualify for jobs that will move them out of poverty."

That problem is especially acute among Hispanics, who account for the single biggest number of children in poverty of any ethnic or racial group — 6.1 million.

## Poverty Most Prevalent in Single-Parent Families

More than half of poor children in the U.S. come from households with single mothers — whether divorced, separated, widowed or never having married — compared with one-fourth for all children. Two-thirds of all children live in families headed by married couples. Only about one-third of children in poverty come from such families.

### Family Living Arrangements for All Children and Poor Children, 2009

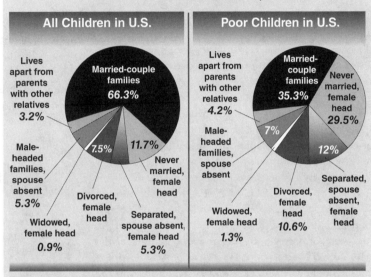

*\* Poverty measures are based on families' annual pre-tax income. In 2009, the threshold for a family consisting of a single mother with one child was $14,787; with two children it was $17,285. The poverty line for a married couple with one child was $17,268; with two children it was $21,756.*

*\*\* Percentages do not total 100 because of rounding.*

*Source:* Thomas Gabe, "Welfare, Work, and Poverty Status of Female-Headed Families With Children: 1987-2009," Congressional Research Service, July 2011, digitalcommons.ilr.cornell.edu/cgi/viewcontent.cgi?article=1852&context= key_workplace

Non-Hispanic whites account for 5 million poor children and African-Americans for 4.4 million.[10]

Educational achievement — closely tied to employment skills — traditionally has lagged among Hispanics. And that deficiency is greatest among immigrants, many without legal status. About 68 percent of poor Hispanic children have at least one immigrant parent. And though a relatively small proportion of poor Latino children have unemployed parents — about 19 percent — that proportion has risen significantly, from about 12 percent, in 2007.[11]

Anti-poverty activists want the federal government to boost spending on programs aimed at helping millions of people climb the socioeconomic ladder. Conservatives, on the other hand, contend that Washington already spends billions on such programs.

"I have no doubt that we have more people in poverty," says Michael Tanner, a senior fellow at the Cato Institute, a libertarian think tank in Washington. "But we're spending more money fighting poverty than ever before."

Conservatives also complain that in calculating the poverty rate, the government doesn't count food stamps, medical care, housing subsidies and other benefits for the poor. (The Census Bureau is studying how to devise a new poverty-calculation method that would include the value of benefits.)[12]

But anti-poverty advocates argue that including the benefits would simply show that while the government safety net is keeping some people from the severest levels of need, many more Americans are sliding beneath the poverty threshold.

"If you try various ways of correcting the data, you find fewer people in the most extreme forms of poverty," says Arloc Sherman, a senior researcher at the Center on Budget and Policy Priorities. "That has a bigger effect on counts of deeply poor people than on counts of the poor overall."

Such policy debates can seem far removed from the everyday lives of children living in poverty, but they ultimately shape the economic trajectory of families struggling to make ends meet.

Jane Trujillo and her husband, both deaf, have been unable to find jobs in Belen and can't afford to commute 60 miles roundtrip to Albuquerque.

Speaking by phone through a sign-language interpreter, Mrs. Trujillo says the backpack-food program has become essential to ensuring that her 6-year-old son and 9-year-old daughter don't go to bed hungry on weekends. "I have had to restrict the amount of milk," she says. "The backpack really helps, particularly toward the end of the month. We get $300 a month in food stamps, but $300 is not enough. Toward the end of the month, when food is tight, the kids eat first. They're more important than we are."

As policy advocates, lawmakers and anti-poverty groups seek solutions to the nation's child-poverty problem, here are some of the issues they are discussing:

## Should Congress expand welfare funding?

When Congress overhauled the welfare system in 1996, it made a major change in the way Washington disburses welfare funds to the states. Under the old system, the government made annual appropriations that Congress adjusted according to need, as reflected in the number of eligible applicants in each state. Under the new system, states receive fixed amounts in the form of "block grants" that they then use to make monthly payments to the poor.[13]

Conservatives hail block-grant funding because it limits the expansion of a program that many of them distrust. But liberals complain that it leaves states with little or no flexibility to expand welfare rolls when economic disaster hits and poverty rises.

Total outlays to the states under the block-grant program — called Temporary Assistance to Needy Families (TANF) — have remained unchanged since 1996, at $16.5 billion per year. In addition, states contribute a total of $10.4 billion to TANF and related programs for the needy. That amount also has remained the same since 1996.[14]

But inflation eroded the value of the federal block grants by 28 percent from 1997 through last January, the nonpartisan Congressional Research Service calculated.[15]

A safety mechanism created by Congress when it switched to the block-grant approach provided $63 million, divided among 16 of the hardest-hit states, in fiscal 2010.[16] A separate "emergency contingency fund" created by the American Recovery and Reinvestment Act of 2009 — the "stimulus" law — gave states another $5 billion for TANF programs, including job-subsidy payments to employers, in fiscal 2009 and 2010.[17]

But critics say those measures haven't done nearly enough to keep millions of Americans from falling out of the middle class or sliding deeper into poverty.

"It used to be the case that TANF and its predecessor" — Aid to Families with Dependent Children (AFDC), the old welfare program Congress eliminated in 1996 —"kept millions of people above the poverty line and responded during recessions," says Sherman of the Center on Budget and Policy Priorities. "Now, having dwindled to a fraction of the previous real [inflation-adjusted] funding level, it is protecting many fewer people from recession and bouts of joblessness."

Indeed, argue Sherman and other critics, the TANF caseload has grown only modestly compared with the scale of the recession and what they see as the true level of need. In September 2010, the caseload stood at 1.9 million families — representing 4.4 million people, three-fourths of them children. That was only 200,000 more families than in July 2008, when the worst of the economic crisis began to grip the nation.[18] Yet, between 2009 and 2010, the number of people below the poverty line rose by 2.6 million — including 900,000 more children.[19]

Critics such as Sherman look to another program for needy families — food stamps — as a better approach than TANF for adjusting benefits during hard times. Unlike TANF, food-stamp allocations rise and fall according to need. "When the unemployment rate soared, the food stamp program responded," Sherman says.

The number of food-stamp recipients increased by nearly 82 percent, from 24.9 million to 45.3 million people, from July 2006 to July of this year, according to the nonprofit Food Research and Action Center, an advocacy organization. During that period, the nation's unemployment rate rose from 4.7 percent to 9.1 percent.[20]

But conservative policy analysts cite the food-stamp increase for a different reason than proof of flexibility. They point to it as evidence that the welfare system as a whole has been steadily expanding, not contracting. Along with TANF cash payments and food stamps, they also cite continuing funding increases in medical assistance for the poor, child development programs such as Head Start, subsidized housing and other programs.[21] In this context, says the Heritage Foundation's Rector, TANF "only supplies 10 percent of assistance given to families with children."

As for expanding TANF funding, Rector argues, "I can't think of anything more foolish to do, and I can't think of anything more unpopular with the public than resurrecting an entitlement program for single parents. It would put a Band-Aid on the problem of single parenthood while ignoring the causes of poverty and the ever-increasing problem of dependency and poverty."

Some liberal poverty experts acknowledge that TANF is no panacea. "No one gets out of poverty by receiving cash assistance," says Elizabeth Lower-Basch, senior policy analyst for the Center for Law and Social Policy (CLASP), an advocacy organization in Washington. But, she says, welfare payments have been effective at lifting or keeping people out of extreme poverty. "One of the

AFP/Getty Images/Mark Ralston

Children of homeowners facing eviction in Long Beach, Calif., eat Thanksgiving dinner on Nov. 24, 2010, during a protest outside a bank. The economic crisis has forced millions of families to seek government or private aid, or both. Congress has expanded welfare benefits, but not enough, advocates argue, to keep millions of children out of poverty.

places where you see the weakness of TANF showing up is the growth of extreme child poverty."

Lower-Basch argues that the TANF emergency fund of 2009 provides a worthy model of how to extend the program's reach. But she acknowledges that the outlook for increasing anti-poverty funding in general is poor. "Not having things become worse feels like an accomplishment," she says.

The views expressed in September by Rep. Geoff Davis, R-Ky., chairman of the House Ways and Means Committee's Subcommittee on Human Resources, suggest that the priority of the House Republican majority, at least, is to tighten work requirements and curb reported abuses by recipients rather than expand funding.

"Not enough adults on welfare are working or preparing for work today," Davis said at a hearing he called on welfare-to-work rules and enforcement. He cited a July report by the Department of Health and Human Services that said only about one-fourth of "work-eligible adults" were meeting work requirements under TANF.[22]

Davis did say that "TANF can and should be strengthened to help more low-income families support themselves." But his remarks focused on what he said are abuses by state administrators. "Instead of the state helping more adults prepare for and begin work," he said, "they scour their books to uncover more spending they can credit to the TANF program and thereby reduce the number of people they have to engage in work activities."[23]

### Are poor children now in elementary school a lost generation?

Experts of all political orientations agree that the longer children spend in poverty, the less their chances for bettering themselves as they grow up.

Researchers for Child Trends, a nonpartisan Washington think tank, wrote in 2009 that 10 studies found strong links between child poverty and poor academic performance, especially during early childhood. A host of social, emotional and behavioral problems are associated with child poverty as well, the researchers noted. One possible cause, they said, is that poor families are more likely to live in single-parent households, often under less supervision and amid more turmoil.[24]

"Studies find that those who experienced persistent poverty as children are much more likely to be poor as adults than those who were not poor during childhood," the researchers wrote. That trend runs more strongly in the black than the white population, they added, with 33 percent of African-Americans who were poor as children remaining in poverty as young adults. Among their white counterparts, only 7 percent were poor in their mid-20s.[25]

Haskins, the Brookings Institution scholar, disputes the notion that a generation of young people living through today's economic woes has, on the whole, lost its chance at advancement. But he says their circumstances are cause for "great concern."

## Poverty Highest Among Minorities

Some 46 million Americans — 15.1 percent of the U.S. population — lived below the poverty line in 2010, including more than one-fourth of blacks and Hispanics. About one-fifth of those younger than 18 and a third of families headed by a single mother lived below the poverty threshold.

### Percentage of People and Families in Poverty, 2010

| Race | |
|---|---|
| White | 22.9% |
| Black | 27.4% |
| Asian | 12.1% |
| Hispanic (any race) | 26.6% |
| **Age** | |
| Under 18 | 22.0% |
| 18 to 64 | 13.7% |
| 65 and older | 9.0% |
| **Family type** | |
| Married couple | 6.2% |
| Female head, no husband present | 31.6% |
| Male head, no wife present | 15.8% |
| **Total** | **15.1%** |

*Source:* "People and Families in Poverty By Selected Characteristics: 2009 and 2010," U.S. Census Bureau, March 2011, www.census.gov/hhes/www/poverty/data/incpovhlth/2010/table4.pdf

"We want people to have an equal chance," he said. "That's been the whole idea of the country — and they don't."

Nevertheless, the possibility of upward mobility still exists, Haskins says. "If kids from the bottom get to college, they increase their odds of making it to the top by a factor of four."

Yet, college is not a sure ticket to stability or upward mobility. Linda Gonzales, 63, of Corrales, N.M., who helps take care of her 4- and 12-year-old grandchildren, is questioning her son's decision to pursue a college degree in civil engineering. "A lot of people are wanting to go back to school because they'll get better jobs, but I don't think the jobs are there," says Gonzales, who lost her nursing-care business last year. Gonzales says her son's part-time job selling hot tubs may not have much of a future either.

Joseph T. Jones, president and CEO of the Center for Urban Families, a Baltimore nonprofit that runs job-training and "responsible fatherhood" projects, argues that very young poor children may have better prospects than present conditions indicate. "Elementary-school students have a better shot at the economy turning around" by the time they are in their teens, he says.

But teenagers in poverty are in danger, Jones says. Speaking after meeting with African-American high-school students in Louisville, Ky., he says, "We are really at risk of saying to them, 'We don't care how much effort you put into education, once you graduate we don't have a darn thing for you.'"

Sherman of the Center on Budget and Policy Priorities argues strongly against the idea that poverty is an immovable obstacle to poor children's futures.

Early-childhood education programs alone, he says, "deliver huge impacts on academic achievement and behavior even decades later."

In general, Sherman says, disadvantages that come with poverty are not immutable. "Successful interventions enable children to get the stimulation they need to grow," he says. At the same time, policies such as the Earned Income Tax Credit for poor families, or employment opportunities for struggling parents, can go a long way toward "removing the strains of poverty on the rest of the family, which might otherwise interfere with a child having a nurturing home environment," he says.

But analysts who contend that poverty is a cultural phenomenon more than an economic one offer a grimmer prognosis for today's poor young people. "Certainly a generation of kids who are going to struggle through a host of social problems — very poor school performance, marginal work ethic when they get out of school, drugs, a lot of criminal behavior — they're likely to repeat those problems when they become adults," says Rector of the Heritage Foundation.

He argues that government programs, especially those that involve boosting income, miss the point. "We clearly are not going to make any progress until we deal with the real causes of why families are poor," he says. Chief among them, he says, is the growing number of single-mother families.

### Is single motherhood a bigger cause of child poverty than the low-wage economy?

A striking increase in out-of-wedlock births is adding fuel to a debate that's been running for decades — or, by some lights, for more than a century: To what extent does single motherhood lead to child poverty?

The two trends clearly are connected. The latest U.S. Census report on poverty notes that the poverty rate for children in single-mother households was 47 percent, but 11.6 percent in married-couple households. Overall, 31.6 percent of single-mother households were below the

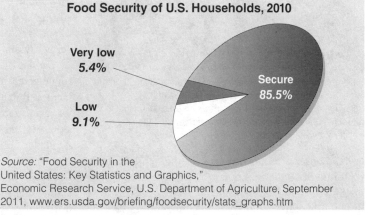

**One in Seven Households Is Short of Food**

Nearly 15 percent of U.S. households lack enough food to meet their needs. Those with low food security have enough to avoid disrupting eating patterns if they turn to such strategies as dieting, using food stamps or visiting food pantries. Households with very low food security lack adequate income or other resources to obtain food and must periodically reduce their food intake.

**Food Security of U.S. Households, 2010**

Very low
5.4%

Secure
85.5%

Low
9.1%

*Source:* "Food Security in the United States: Key Statistics and Graphics," Economic Research Service, U.S. Department of Agriculture, September 2011, www.ers.usda.gov/briefing/foodsecurity/stats_graphs.htm

poverty line, compared with only 6.2 percent of married-couple families.[26]

In Mississippi, 48 percent of children lived in single-parent families.[27]

Academics and advocates have been studying links between single motherhood and child poverty for decades. James Heckman, a Nobel laureate economist at the University of Chicago who specializes in social inequality, has written that the consequences of growing up in poverty can be deep and far-reaching. "There are large gaps in cognitive stimulation and emotional support at early ages," between children in two-parent and those in single-parent households, he wrote this year. But he went on to argue that early-childhood programs can compensate for some of the disadvantages.[28]

As Heckman noted, the issue has taken on greater urgency because childbirth by married women is on the decline. Among African-Americans, 72 percent of births are to single women. The statistic stands out given the disproportionate extent of poverty in the black population: 27.4 percent of African-Americans live below the poverty line. In the white, non-Hispanic population, the rate is about 10 percent.[29]

Reuters/Lucy Nicholson

Children from homeless shelters walk to an after-school program at the South Los Angeles Learning Center on March 16, 2011. School on Wheels runs the program, which uses volunteers to tutor children in shelters, parks and motels around the city, as well as at two centers.

For conservative poverty experts, the trends indicate that unmarried motherhood is by far the greatest cause of child poverty. "Those women have an overwhelming probability of being poor and remaining poor," says the Heritage Foundation's Rector. "In general, being married reduces the probability of poverty by about 80 percent."

Rector acknowledges that joblessness caused by the recession has put more families below the poverty line. "But when the recession goes away," he says, "we'll have the same child poverty we had before it began. The reality of this debate is that it is politically incorrect to ever discuss why people are actually poor. This factor — marriage — is more important than dropping out of high school, but we never tell anyone."

Nevertheless, few dispute that households headed by married couples are less vulnerable to poverty. Jones, of the Center for Urban Families, says, "We shouldn't be shy about talking about the institution of marriage. It's pretty clear that children who are raised in two-parent households, particularly if they are married households, fare better than their counterparts in single-parent families."

But Jones — who fathered a son out of wedlock before settling down to married life, and another son, with another woman — warns that single-minded focus on marriage as the cure for poverty is potentially danger-ous. Single parenthood should not be a reason for excluding people from benefits, he argues. "We should not be so rigid as to say you are not worthy of support if you are not on a path to marriage," Jones says.

Yet no other way to significantly reduce single parent-hood may exist other than curtailing benefits, says Tanner of the Cato Institute. "You can't go on just giving people money for having kids," he says. Such a move undoubtedly would cause personal crises for any number of women — and their children — he acknowledges, adding that private charities could soften some of the blows. But, he says, "Without crises you're not going to get behavioral changes."

Unlike Rector, Tanner says he doesn't believe that single parenthood outranks all other poverty-generating factors. But, he says, it's important enough for policy-makers to zero in on. "Having a child out of wedlock is a pretty good guarantee of being in poverty," he says.

Haskins of Brookings argues that unemployment out-ranks unmarried motherhood on the list of poverty's causes. In a recent paper, he cited a 30 percent decrease in poverty among single mothers and their children, from 47 percent in 1991 to 33 percent in 2000.[30] During that period — just before and after the 1996 welfare overhaul —"we saw a 40 percent increase in work rates of never-married mothers," he says. "Poverty fell like a rock for single-parent families to its lowest level ever."

Nevertheless, Haskins says, marriage — along with education — is almost as important as work in reduc-ing child poverty. "If we don't do something about reducing the proportion of kids in female-headed fami-lies and don't do something about getting kids through at least two years of post-secondary school or vocational training," he says, "we are not going to have an impact on poverty."

## BACKGROUND

### Focus on Children

Children have been the main concern of U.S. anti-poverty efforts since such endeavors began in systematic fashion in the early 1900s. Until the last years of the 20th century, government's emphasis was on ensuring that mothers raising children on their own wouldn't have to enter the workplace.[31]

Likewise, officials wanted to ensure that orphans and poverty-stricken children could be raised in families rather than institutions. In 1909, the White House Conference on the Care of Dependent Children, presided over by President Theodore Roosevelt, led to establishment of a federal Children's Bureau and a foster-care system designed to place children in homes rather than orphanages.[32]

State governments, meanwhile, were making their own efforts to keep needy children at home. At a time when nearly all families depended on a father's paycheck, a movement to establish widows' pensions scored its first victory when Missouri enacted a pension law in 1911.

In reality, the promise of subsidized child care was not always kept, historians write. Payments were small enough that widows and divorced or abandoned women had to supplement them with paid work. In Philadelphia, 84 percent of pension recipients held jobs. In Chicago the rate was 66 percent and in Los Angeles 57 percent. County pension administrators worried that more substantial payments would encourage wives to walk out on their husbands, or husbands to desert their families.[33]

An even greater weakness of the state pension laws was that counties didn't have to participate. In 1931, the Children's Bureau reported that half of the nation's counties had not established pension systems.

At that point, the widespread misery of the Great Depression had created enormous demand for a comprehensive nationwide system of providing for children whose families had fallen on hard times. Part of the New Deal package of social legislation pushed through Congress by President Franklin D. Roosevelt's administration was the Aid to Dependent Children (ADC) program, created by the Social Security Act of 1935.

Under ADC, the federal government contributed to states' pension programs. Payments to families, which by the law's language were intended to help provide a "reasonable subsistence compatible with decency and health," were capped at $18 a month for the first child and $12 monthly for subsequent children.[34]

Nearly all the child beneficiaries lived with widowed mothers. Women who had been abandoned, or were divorced, accounted for most of the remaining pensioners.

President Lyndon B. Johnson greets a resident during a tour of the impoverished Appalachia region in June 1964. Widespread poverty in Appalachian mountain hollows, urban ghettos and the rural South spawned a spate of reform efforts, culminating in Johnson's War on Poverty program, which targeted low-income families with children.

*Lyndon Baines Johnson Library & Museum*

Only 2 percent of the children in the program lived with mothers who had given birth out of wedlock.

The overall population of households headed by unwed mothers was greater than the number who received government assistance. State ADC administrators tended to bar support to families of unmarried women, who were considered far outside the bounds of respectability and traditional morality. During the 1950s, at least 19 states adopted policies that prohibited aid to children who were born to unwed mothers after they had begun receiving welfare.[35]

ADC gave state officials considerable power in setting eligibility standards. Under rules that were struck down by courts in 1960, states could require that aid go only to children living in so-called "suitable homes." In practice, that provision was used to block aid to unmarried mothers as well as many black mothers.[36]

Distinctions between categories of single mothers were reinforced by a change to the Social Security law in 1939. A separate Social Security benefit was created for widows and their surviving children. The effect was to divide beneficiaries of government support between the children of women whose husbands had died and the offspring of mothers who had divorced, been abandoned or had never married.

## CHRONOLOGY

**1909-1935** *Early welfare goals include keeping widowed mothers from having to join the workforce.*

**1909** President Theodore Roosevelt calls first White House Conference on Care of Dependent Children.

**1911** Missouri passes nation's first pension for widows, to free them from working.

**1931** Nearly all states have widows' pensions, but half the counties don't participate.

**1935** New Deal's Social Security Act includes first federal welfare system, Aid to Dependent Children.

**1960s** *Democratic president launches biggest package of domestic social programs since New Deal.*

**1962** President John F. Kennedy praises new book, *The Other America*, documenting widespread poverty. . . . Aid to Dependent Children is renamed Aid to Families with Dependent Children (AFDC).

**1964** Democratic President Lyndon B. Johnson declares War on Poverty, which sparks a number of federal initiatives, including Head Start.

**1965** *The Negro Family: A Case for National Action*, by Labor Department staffer Daniel Patrick Moynihan, argues for jobs for men over welfare, expresses concern at the growth in single-mother black households.

**1967** In an early effort to link welfare to work, Congress establishes voluntary Work Incentive (WIN) program to encourage AFDC recipients to obtain job training and jobs.

**1971-1987** *Welfare opponents argue AFDC fosters dependency.*

**1971** Congress makes WIN mandatory but doesn't fully fund revamped program.

**1972** Children in single-mother families account for 50 percent of all children below poverty line.

**1981** Congress lets states use welfare funds to subsidize job training.

**1986** President Ronald Reagan decries "welfare culture" marked by family breakdown.

**1988** Family Support Act requires AFDC recipients to log 20 hours a week of job training or employment.

**1992-2010** *Democratic president oversees major transformation of welfare system.*

**1992** Vowing to "end welfare as we know it," Democratic presidential candidate Bill Clinton promises to revamp the system into a "second chance, not a way of life."

**1995** New Republican House majority introduces welfare-revamping Work Opportunity Act, which passes both houses.

**1996** President Clinton vetoes the bill. . . . White House negotiations with both parties produce Personal Responsibility and Work Opportunity Reconciliation Act, with stiff work requirements for welfare recipients.

**1999** Work rate of never-married mothers on welfare rises to 66 percent, up from 46.5 percent in 1995.

**2000** Poverty among single mothers and their children falls to all-time low of 33 percent of population.

**2008** Forty percent of U.S. births are to unmarried mothers.

**2009** "Stimulus" law creates $5 billion emergency fund for national welfare system.

**2010** Poverty rate grows to 15.1 percent, with population below poverty line growing by 2.6 million to 46.2 million in one year.

**2011** Agriculture Department reports nearly 15 percent of population, including 16.2 million children, lives in "food-insecure" households. . . . Florida and three other states require drug tests for welfare applicants.

By 1961 nearly all families headed by widowed mothers were receiving Society Security benefits, while only 7.7 percent of families receiving ADC funds were headed by widows.

## War on Poverty

President John F. Kennedy's inauguration in 1961 followed a campaign in which poverty surfaced as a national issue for the first time since the 1930s.

Kennedy's campaign visit to impoverished Appalachian communities in West Virginia made an obvious impression on the candidate and received wide media coverage. One year after becoming president, Kennedy praised a new book, *The Other America*, by writer and political activist Michael Harrington, who reported on and denounced the extent of poverty in a rich nation.[37]

Harrington's book also influenced Kennedy's successor, Lyndon Johnson.

Providing children the opportunity to rise from poverty was one of the threads running through Johnson entire War on Poverty — the name he gave to a collection of social programs passed during his administration — and the main idea animating Head Start, an early-childhood education program still operating today.

Specifically, Head Start owed its existence to data presented to Johnson's poverty czar, Sargent Shriver. Shriver's researchers told him that half of the nation's 30 million poor were children, most of them under age 12. "It was clear that it was foolish to talk about a 'total war against poverty,' the phraseology the president was using, if you were doing nothing about children," Shriver told associates.[38]

The "war," in combination with the social and political changes that rocked the country during the 1960s, helped shape welfare policy and law during the decades that followed.

## Child Poverty Most Prevalent in South

Mississippi has the nation's highest child-poverty rate, with one in three residents under age 18 below the poverty threshold. Three other Southern states — Alabama, Arkansas and Louisiana — are in the top five. New Mexico ranks second, with 30 percent of children in poverty. California far outpaces other states in the total number of children in poverty, at slightly more than 2 million.

### Percentage and Number of Children Under 18 in Poverty
(by state, 2010)

| State | Percent | Number | State | Percent | Number |
|-------|---------|--------|-------|---------|--------|
| United States | 22% | 15,749,000 | Illinois | 19% | 600,000 |
| Mississippi | 33% | 242,000 | Pennsylvania | 19% | 522,000 |
| New Mexico | 30% | 154,000 | Rhode Island | 19% | 42,000 |
| Alabama | 28% | 311,000 | Wisconsin | 19% | 250,000 |
| Arkansas | 28% | 193,000 | Delaware | 18% | 37,000 |
| Louisiana | 27% | 300,000 | Kansas | 18% | 131,000 |
| Kentucky | 26% | 263,000 | Maine | 18% | 48,000 |
| South Carolina | 26% | 278,000 | Nebraska | 18% | 82,000 |
| Tennessee | 26% | 377,000 | South Dakota | 18% | 36,000 |
| Texas | 26% | 1,751,000 | Washington | 18% | 284,000 |
| Georgia | 25% | 611,000 | Colorado | 17% | 211,000 |
| North Carolina | 25% | 560,000 | Vermont | 17% | 21,000 |
| Oklahoma | 25% | 227,000 | Iowa | 16% | 115,000 |
| West Virginia | 25% | 96,000 | North Dakota | 16% | 24,000 |
| Arizona | 24% | 392,000 | Utah | 16% | 136,000 |
| Florida | 23% | 924,000 | Minnesota | 15% | 192,000 |
| Michigan | 23% | 539,000 | Hawaii | 14% | 41,000 |
| Ohio | 23% | 624,000 | Massachusetts | 14% | 201,000 |
| California | 22% | 2,013,000 | New Jersey | 14% | 295,000 |
| Indiana | 22% | 342,000 | Virginia | 14% | 265,000 |
| Nevada | 22% | 144,000 | Wyoming | 14% | 19,000 |
| Oregon | 22% | 184,000 | Alaska | 13% | 24,000 |
| Missouri | 21% | 291,000 | Connecticut | 13% | 103,000 |
| New York | 21% | 901,000 | Maryland | 13% | 173,000 |
| Montana | 20% | 44,000 | New Hampshire | 10% | 28,000 |
| Idaho | 19% | 80,000 | | | |

*Source:* "Data Across States," Annie E. Casey Foundation, 2011, datacenter.kids count.org/data/acrossstates/Default.aspx

One way it did so was by spurring a notable expansion in welfare rolls. The federal family-support program — renamed Aid to Families with Dependent Children (AFDC) in 1962 — saw beneficiaries more than double, from 3.5 million in 1962 to 7.4 million in 1970.[39]

Poverty itself didn't double in that period. But, encouraged by a welfare-recipients movement that

# States to Welfare Seekers: Drug Test Comes First

*"Taxpayers deserve to know money is being used for its intended purpose."*

As the bad economy drives up demand for welfare and employment aid, some state governments are imposing a controversial new condition for assistance: drug screening.

This year alone:

- Florida required welfare applicants to pay for — and pass — a drug test. They are reimbursed the $25 to $35 fee unless they fail. However, a federal judge in late October temporarily blocked enforcement of the new law on constitutional grounds.
- Missouri authorized drug testing of welfare recipients suspected of drug use — a step Arizona took two years ago. Those who test positive lose benefits unless they sign up for treatment.
- Indiana required aid recipients applying for job training to be tested for drugs. A positive result for drug use bars an applicant from training for 90 days, or for one year after a second positive result.

And legislators in some 35 other states have introduced similar drug-testing measures.[1]

"The taxpayers deserve to know that the money they are spending is being used for its intended purpose," said Joe Follick, a spokesman for the Florida Department of Children and Families. "If a family receiving [cash assistance] includes someone who has a substance-abuse problem, the odds of that money being used for purposes other than helping that family increases."[2]

But the American Civil Liberties Union (ACLU) won the first round in a legal challenge to the lawsuit when U.S. District Judge Mary Scriven of Orlando ruled that the new law was unlikely to survive a lawsuit that claims the law violates the Fourth Amendment's protection against unreasonable search and seizure. Scriven was appointed by President George W. Bush.

The judge said the state had failed to show a "special need" warranting exemption from the requirement to show probable cause or reasonable suspicion. "If invoking an interest in preventing public funds from potentially being used to fund drug use were the only requirement to establish a special need," she wrote, "the state could impose drug testing as an eligibility requirement for every beneficiary of every government program." The injunction she granted suspending the law remains in effect pending a full hearing, not yet scheduled.[3]

The ACLU sued on behalf of Luis Lebron, a 35-year-old Navy veteran who is caring for his 4-year-old son and disabled mother while studying accounting at the University of Central Florida. Responding to Scriven's order, he said he was "happy that the judge stood up for me and my rights and said the state can't act without a reason or suspicion."[4]

The lawsuit's Fourth Amendment argument echoed a federal court decision in 2000 that threw out a similar drug-test law in Michigan.

Drug testing of individuals not suspected of a crime is constitutionally permissible only where public safety is concerned, the court said, citing testing of people whose work requires them to carry a gun. "In this instance, there is no indication of a concrete danger to public safety which demands departure from the Fourth Amendment's main rule and normal requirement of individualized suspicion," the ruling said.[5]

Despite the resistance from civil-liberties advocates, however, conservative politicians and lawmakers see drug testing as a way to avoid channeling welfare money to people they view as undeserving of it.

In advocating for Florida's law, Republican Gov. Rick Scott asserted that drug abuse is more common among welfare recipients. "Studies show that people that are on welfare are higher users of drugs than people not on welfare," Scott said in a CNN interview in June. "Our taxpayers don't want to subsidize somebody else's drug addiction."[6]

The results from the first batch of about 1,000 tests didn't bear out Scott's impression, however. About 2 percent of applicants tested positive for drug use, the state's Department of Children and Families announced. Another 2 percent did not complete the application process, including the drug test for unspecified reasons. Test supporters said the abstainers knew they would fail the drug exam. Opponents said the walkaways couldn't afford to advance the drug test fee or couldn't reach a testing facility.[7]

By comparison, in 2010 just under 9 percent of the population age 12 and above reported using illicit drugs in the preceding month, according to the Department of Health and Human Services.[8]

Like Florida's governor, Rep. Geoff Davis, R-Ky., chairman of the House Ways and Means Human Resources Subcommittee, has spoken approvingly of drug tests for welfare applicants.

"In a world where many employers require drug testing to ensure workers are clean and sober, neither taxpayers nor welfare recipients are helped if we have a lower standard for those collecting welfare benefits designed to help them enter work," Davis said.

He spoke at a recent hearing on the federal welfare law, Temporary Assistance for Needy Families (TANF). Passed in 1996 with bipartisan support, the law imposed work requirements, put time limits on cash payments to the needy and authorized drug tests as a condition of aid.

But others in Congress are questioning whether money spent on drug testing might divert funds from the poor.

"Do you think it's a better investment, given the limited nature of the resources that we have, to drug test everyone?" Rep. Joseph Crowley, D-N.Y., asked Scott Wetzler, chief of psychology at New York's Montefiore Hospital, who runs a treatment program for welfare recipients with histories of drug abuse.[9]

"It would be a huge, huge, practical problem to actually drug test everybody," said Wetzler, whose program tests only people in drug treatment. "And it's not clear that you actually would be able to have the treatment capacity to receive all those people into treatment. So it's not clear what you even do with that information if you had it."[10]

*— Peter Katel*

Republican Gov. Rick Scott of Florida contends that drug abuse is more common among welfare recipients and that "our taxpayers don't want to subsidize somebody else's addiction."

[1] A.G. Sulzberger, "States Adding Drug Test as Hurdle for Welfare," *The New York Times*, Oct. 11, 2011, www. nytimes.com/2011/10/11/us/states-add ing-drug-test-as-hurdle-for-welfare.html? ref=us; Mike Schneider and Kelli Kennedy, "Florida Welfare Drug Testing Law Blocked by Federal Judge," The Associated Press, Oct. 24, 2011, www .huffingtonpost.com/2011/10/24/ rick-scott-drug-testing-welfare-florida_ n_1029332.html; Tom Coyne, "Indiana the first state to require drug tests for job training," The Associated Press, *Chesterton Tribune* (Indiana), July 11, 2011, http://chestertontribune.com/ Business/indiana_the_first_state_to_requi. htm; Rebecca Berg, "Missouri Legislature approves drug tests for welfare recipients," *St. Louis Post-Dispatch*, May 11, 2011, www.stltoday.com/news/local/ govt-and-politics/article_953196cf-8104-5758-8198-60e151debe90.html; Amy B. Wang, "Welfare recipients face drug tests," *Arizona Republic*, Nov. 25, 2009, www.azcentral.com/arizonarepublic/local/articles/2009/11/25/20091125urinetesting1125.html.

[2] Quoted in Catherine Whittenburg, "Welfare drug-testing yields 2% positive results," *Tampa Bay Online*, Aug. 24, 2011, www.tbo.com/news/politics/2011/aug/ 24/3/welfare-drug-testing-yields-2-percent-positive-res-ar-252458/.

[3] Quoted in Rebecca Catalenello, "Florida's welfare drug testing halted by federal judge," *The Miami Herald*, Oct. 25, 2011, www.miamiherald.com/2011/ 10/24/2470519/florida-welfare-drug-testing-halted .html.

[4] Quoted in Schneider and Kennedy, *op. cit.*

[5] *Marchwinski v. Howard*, 113 F.Supp.2d 1134, www.aclufl.org/pdfs/ March winski.pdf.

[6] Aaron Sharockman, "Rick Scott Says Welfare Recipients Are More Likely to Use Illicit Drugs," *St. Petersburg Times*, June 9, 2011.

[7] Whittenburg, *op. cit.*; Kelli Kennedy, "Nearly 1,600 welfare applicants decline drug test," The Associated Press, Oct. 11, 2011.

[8] "Results from the 2010 National Survey on Drug Use and Health: Summary of National Findings," Health and Human Services Department, September 2011, http://oas.samhsa.gov/NSDUH/2k10NSDUH/2k10Results .htm#Fig7-1.

[9] "Hearing of the House Ways and Means Committee, 'Improving Work and Other Welfare Reform Goals, Focusing on Reauthorization of the Temporary Assistance for Needy Families Program,'" Federal News Service, Sept. 8, 2011.

[10] *Ibid.*

considered benefits a right, not a privilege, low-income citizens became more likely to apply for welfare. During the 1960s, an estimated 33 percent of eligible families received assistance. By 1971, more than 90 percent of eligible households were on the welfare rolls.

Also promoting welfare expansion were U.S. Supreme Court decisions that overturned state welfare rules limiting eligibility. They included so-called "man in the house" policies that barred or stopped payments when adult males were found in recipients' or applicants' homes. Another court decision eliminated long-term residency requirements for recipients.

By 1971, a backlash was already under way. *U.S. News & World Report*, the most conservative of the three national newsweeklies, published a piece reporting that welfare spending threatened to "bankrupt the States and cities, and to drain the U.S. Treasury with chronic federal deficits."[40]

The magazine pointed to one development in particular: the growth in mother-headed households. AFDC child recipients whose fathers had deserted or whose mothers had never wed accounted for 80 percent of young beneficiaries, up from 60 percent a few years earlier, the magazine reported (without specifying the number of years).[41]

While some may have viewed *U.S. News*'s take on the issue as political spin, there was no question that female-headed households were becoming more common, especially in the poor population. In 1960, children in such households accounted for 9.2 percent of all children and 23.7 percent of all poor children. By 1972, children in single-mother families represented 14.2 percent of all children and more than 50 percent of poor children.[42]

## Families in Crisis

Single motherhood was especially prevalent among African-Americans, who were also disproportionately represented on welfare rolls. As early as 1965, Daniel Patrick Moynihan, a liberal New Deal-style Democrat who was then a staff member of the Labor Department's Office of Policy Planning and Research, zeroed in on that trend. In a report titled, "The Negro Family: The Case for National Action," he argued that employment of fathers was far more valuable than welfare payments in lifting families out of poverty.[43]

"In the beginning, the number of AFDC families in which the father was absent because of desertion was less than a third of the total," Moynihan wrote. "Today it is two-thirds." He linked paternal abandonment to persistent joblessness for black men. "Negro unemployment, with the exception of a few years during World War II and the Korean War, has continued at disaster levels for 35 years."[44]

Initially, Moynihan's report was greeted positively by African-American leaders, including the Rev. Martin Luther King Jr., many of whom had also expressed alarm at a growing number of black households headed by single mothers. They were echoing concerns of earlier generations of black leaders. W. E. B. DuBois, the most prominent African-American scholar and intellectual activist of the 20th century, had condemned the single-motherhood trend as far back as 1899.[45]

Nevertheless, applause for Moynihan's report faded quickly. Reactions among black leaders and white liberals turned hostile, guided by the view that Moynihan was holding African-Americans entirely responsible for black poverty.

To some extent, that response may have been inspired less by Moynihan's paper than by the favorable reception that the report got from conservatives. They took it, wrote John McWhorter, a present-day analyst of race-related issues, "as a statement rather than as a 'case for action.'"

Nonetheless, McWhorter argued that the decades that followed provided evidence that Moynihan had focused accurately on one element of the poverty equation in the country's most disproportionately poverty-stricken population: "Multigenerational welfare dependency and all-but-fatherless neighborhoods became a norm in poor black communities," McWhorter wrote. "Surely the burden of proof is upon those who would argue that this was unconnected with the relaxation of eligibility rules for AFDC benefits in the 1960s."[46]

Other scholars argue from a more liberal perspective that Moynihan's emphasis on male employment discouraged efforts to raise AFDC payments or provide well-paying jobs for welfare mothers. At the same time, liberals contend, the report strengthened efforts to require AFDC mothers to get jobs. "Requiring welfare recipients to work, the argument went, might put pressure on mothers and fathers to stay together or not have children in the first place," three historians wrote in a history of welfare.[47] As debate swirled over the Moynihan report, its examination of the links between family structure, economics and poverty may have influenced the first War on Poverty-era congressional efforts to promote employment for welfare recipients.

In 1967, Congress established the Work Incentive (WIN) program, which required states to provide training and employment programs for "appropriate" AFDC beneficiaries. And to encourage recipients to work, some of what they earned — the first $30, plus one-third of the remaining amount — wouldn't be counted against their welfare payments. (A similar, smaller program set up in 1961 had stricter incentives for recipients to find employment.)[48]

Overall, the welfare-law amendment that created WIN marked a shift in attitude, notes Thomas Gabe, a social policy analyst for the Congressional Research Service. The law replaced requirements that services to recipients be "rehabilitative" and "competence-enhancing." Instead, the law now emphasized practical, job-finding assistance, such as job and training referral.[49]

## Requiring Work

The WIN program only hinted at the transformation ahead. Discontent with the idea of paying people who didn't work, even if they were single mothers, was increasing both in Washington policy circles and in the states.[50]

In 1971, Congress changed WIN from a voluntary program to one in which welfare recipients were required to participate if they had no preschool-age children at home or other special circumstances. However, the practical effects of the new requirement were limited because the program wasn't fully funded.

Similarly, in 1971, California's Republican governor, Ronald W. Reagan, promoted a new approach to welfare that he dubbed "workfare." The legislature authorized a pilot program that required welfare recipients to get jobs. The program never got fully off the ground, however. A 1976 study by the state Employment Development Department concluded that it was badly designed, but a legislative sponsor said that counties ignored the project.[51]

Still, the appeal of requiring welfare recipients to work continued to grow. In 1981, during the first year of Reagan's presidency, Congress granted states the power

Seven-year-old Jayla gets ready for her weekly tutoring session last March 16 at the shelter in Los Angles where she lives with her mother. One in five U.S. children lives below the poverty line, a far higher rate than adults (13.7 percent) and the elderly (9 percent).

Reuters/Lucy Nicholson

to tailor WIN programs as they saw fit. States also gained authority to use federal welfare funds to subsidize on-the-job training.

States got further encouragement to step up work requirements from a 1986 report by the private, non-profit Manpower Demonstration Research Corp. (MDRC), a think tank on poverty-related issues. After studying reorganized welfare-to-work programs in eight states, Manpower concluded that they could increase employment and be cost-effective — though not to an extraordinary extent.

In his 1986 State of the Union address, Reagan called for changing the welfare system, arguing that it should be judged by how many recipients left the program because they no longer needed support. "In the welfare culture, the breakdown of the family, the most basic support system, has reached crisis proportions — in female and child poverty, child abandonment, horrible crimes and deteriorating schools," Reagan declared. He announced that his domestic-policy council would develop a new approach to aiding the poor.[52]

By the following year, Congress took another step toward making work a condition of welfare. The Family Support Act of 1988 obliged AFDC recipients, unless specifically exempted, to enroll in job training or find employment. That goal was reflected in the name given

# Food Banks Support Many in New Mexico

*"We always ate, but sometimes just a little."*

On a sunny morning in late September, 75 mothers and children, mostly Spanish-speaking Mexican immigrants, lined up in the parking lot of a mobile home community in the dusty South Valley of Albuquerque, N.M.

The crowd waited in line to fill baskets with cucumbers, onions, jalapeño chilies, cartons of long-life milk, dry pasta and other supplies from the Roadrunner Food Bank.

In the days before the monthly food deliveries started, "We always ate," says Laura Sánchez, the mother of a 4-month-old girl and two older children, "but sometimes just a little." Her husband works construction, earning about $350 a week when there's work, but often there is none.

"We started to see this two years ago," says Guillermo Yelo, pastor of Camino de Vida (Pathway of Life) church, who organized the food distribution. "A lot of people here don't have jobs. It made me realize the need for help."

A few hours later and about 10 miles north, another group gathered in a school gym in Corrales, a village that began as an 18th-century land grant by the Spanish crown.[1]

Among them was Lynette Bratvold, a homeowner who works two clerical jobs to support her husband and 3-year-old son. "My husband stays home with our child so that we don't have to pay outrageous child-care costs," she says. "So we need assistance with food."

Her husband, a high-school graduate, worked as a security guard when he was employed — earning at most $10 an hour. "I'm working 50-60 hours a week, and it's still not enough," she says.

As more people, even those working full time, needed assistance, the food bank, the state's main food charity, saw its distribution rise to about 24 million pounds in fiscal 2010-11 — a 10 percent increase over the previous year, says spokeswoman Sonya Warwick.

Nationally, food banks served 5.7 million a week in 2009 (the latest numbers available), a 27 percent increase since 2005, according to Feed America, a national alliance of food charities.[2]

Now, Feed America is warning Roadrunner and other food operations in New Mexico of a looming cutback in the free food it receives from the U.S. Department of Agriculture, which contributes about 20 percent of Roadrunner's stock. "We've been told to expect a reduction of 40 percent to 50 percent of that food," Warwick says. "We are trying to make sure we have various food sources so that when the cuts hit we don't have a crisis."

In fact, New Mexico is a state with two distinct populations, and one already is in crisis. Affluent New Mexicans, those who support the state's international reputation as an artists' haven, skiing destination and nuclear research center, are doing just fine, on the whole.

But the other New Mexico has been suffering a slow-motion crisis for several years. The state's 30 percent child-poverty rate is exceeded only by Mississippi's 33 percent.[3] And while the unemployment rate of 6.6 percent is lower than the national average of 9.1 percent, the state's 18.2 percent poverty rate in 2009 is significantly higher than the latest national rate of 15.1 percent. A longtime prevalence of low-wage work, compounded by the scarcity of regular employment in parts of the state, including the New

to related state programs, Job Opportunities and Basic Skills Training (JOBS). Because recipients who could not obtain child care were exempt from the new standard, Congress stepped up funding for that service. JOBS participants were required to work or train for 20 hours a week.

But by the standards of those who hoped that the 1988 law would transform the welfare system, actual changes were modest. The General Accounting Office (now the Government Accountability Office) reported in 1995 that about 20 percent of eligible AFDC recipients participated in some JOBS activity each month, though not all of them for the mandated 20 hours a week.

But the law set a new tone concerning welfare recipients and what was expected of them. Politicians took

Mexico portion of the Navajo Nation (most of which is in Arizona), explain the disparity between relatively low joblessness and high poverty.

"We have chunks of counties where people just aren't in the formal economy," says Gerry Bradley, research director at New Mexico Voices for Children, a nonprofit advocacy group.

"We're sort of bouncing along the bottom," Bradley says. He adds, citing 0.9 percent employment growth during the 12 months ending last August, "Maybe we're starting to turn around."[4]

New Mexico is a so-called "majority minority" state, with a population that's 46 percent Hispanic (both citizens and immigrants) and 9 percent Native American, a white, non-Hispanic population of 40 percent, plus small percentages of black, Asian and multi-racial people. The state ranks fourth from the bottom nationwide in a composite score of child-development indicators assembled by Voices for Children that includes the percentages of low-birth-weight babies and households with no stable employment.[5]

Hispanic New Mexicans tend to be concentrated in occupations that require less education — construction, above all. And construction, Bradley says, was "hammered by the recession."

Echoing Bradley's conclusion are the mothers gathered for food in South Valley.

"My husband works sometimes for two days, sometimes for a couple of weeks," says Soledad Murillo, a 47-year-old grandmother of six and mother of three daughters, none married. A 15-year New Mexico resident who comes from Durango, Mexico, Murillo says that jobs used to be far easier to find.

Linda Aguayo, who fled the ultraviolent Mexican border town of Ciudad Juárez three years ago, then returned, then fled again five months ago, says her husband fixes refrigerator cases and other store appliances.

*Roadrunner Food Bank*

The Roadrunner Food Bank's Mobile Food Pantry helps struggling families throughout New Mexico. The program served 85,000 children and 127,500 adults last year.

"But it's not stable work," she says. "Whatever he makes just pays the rent."

Without the donated food, she says, "We'd be eating less."

*— Peter Katel*

[1]"Brief History of Corrales," Corrales Historical Society, 2004, www.corrales history.com/html/morehistory.html.

[2]"Hunger in America: Key Findings," 2010, http://feedingamerica.org/hunger-in-america/hunger-studies/hunger-study-2010/key-findings.aspx.

[3]"Children in Poverty (Percent) — 2010," Kids Count Data Center, Annie E. Casey Foundation, undated, http://datacenter.kidscount.org/data/acrossstates/ Rankings.aspx?ind=43.

[4]*Ibid.*

[5]"Early Childhood Supports in New Mexico," New Mexico Voices for Children, updated 2010, www.nmvoices.org/attachments/ece-supports-2010-update.pdf.

note that those expectations reflected attitudes among a broad swath of voters in both parties.

Accordingly, Democratic presidential candidate Bill Clinton vowed during his 1992 campaign to "end welfare as we know it." Elaborating, Clinton said in a campaign commercial: "Those who are able must go to work. . . . It's time to make welfare what it should be — a second chance, not a way of life."[53]

Slightly more than two years later, newly triumphant Republicans who had overturned longtime Democratic control of the House introduced the Work Opportunity Act of 1995. The bill reflected Republicans' campaign pledge, laid out in their "Contract With America" political platform, to "achieve what some 30 years of massive welfare spending has not been able to accomplish: reduce illegitimacy, require work and save taxpayers money."[54]

As debate over welfare intensified, Clinton vetoed two Republican-crafted bills that he said were too harsh in their treatment of welfare mothers. He pointed to their failure to provide adequately for child care and medical care for AFDC recipients entering the job market.[55]

For a Democratic president, welfare was politically tricky. Clinton's party was divided between so-called "neo-liberals" (like himself), who strongly supported replacing the old welfare system, and traditional Democrats, who found more to support than to oppose in AFDC.[56]

In 1996, intense negotiations between Clinton and Republican leaders, and between Clinton and his fellow Democrats, produced the Personal Responsibility and Work Opportunity Reconciliation Act of 1996.

Hailed as the most significant piece of social legislation since the War on Poverty, the law required that recipients of what had become TANF go to work within two years of receiving aid and that aid be limited to five years. Moreover, the welfare-funding system was changed to fixed "block grants," replacing need-gauged appropriations.[57]

In the context of the economic boom of the late 1990s, the new law showed some remarkable results. The work rate of never-married mothers shot up from 46.5 percent of their total population in 1995 to 66 percent in 1999, an increase of about 40 percent in four years.[58]

As a result, Haskins of Brookings reported in a study last summer that poverty among single mothers and their children decreased from a 1991 peak of 47.1 percent to 33 percent in 2000 — the lowest level ever for that group.[59]

When the full force of the recession hit in 2009, however, another feature of the new welfare system became apparent. The block-grant funding scheme had the effect of limiting expansion of welfare rolls, the Congressional Research Service reported. "The fixed nature of TANF funding imposes some financial risk on states," it said. "Generally states bear the risk of increased costs from a cash welfare-caseload rise."[60]

## CURRENT SITUATION

### Budget Worries

Poverty experts worry that deficit-reduction efforts could shortchange funding for medical care for poor children and their families. Up to now, they say, the medical system for the poor has been responding effectively to the nation's worsening economic conditions.

While the number of poor children has grown in recent years, the population of those not covered by medical insurance declined — from 7.9 million in 2007 to 7.3 million in 2010, the Census Bureau reported. During that period, the number of children covered by Medicaid — the state- and federally funded medical-care system for the poor — grew from 20.9 million to 26 million.[61]

Medicaid and the Children's Health Insurance Program (CHIP) "stepped into the void," says Bruce Lesley, president of First Focus, a child-policy advocacy organization in Washington. CHIP provides low-cost medical care to children whose family incomes are low but above the poverty line.

But advocates have grounds for concern. Decisions by the Joint Committee on Deficit Reduction — the so-called congressional "super committee" charged this fall with proposing measures to reduce federal deficits by $1.5 trillion over 10 years — could lead to an erosion of medical care for the poor.[62]

And the Obama administration, as part of its own deficit-reduction proposal, has recommended cutting $72 million from Medicaid. "The Medicaid cuts in the president's proposal shift the burden to states and ultimately onto the shoulders of seniors, people with disabilities and low-income families who depend on the program as their lifeline," Ronald F. Pollack, executive director of Families USA, an organization that advocates for expanded health-care coverage, told *The New York Times*.[63]

As evidence of subsidized health care's vulnerability, Lower-Basch of the Center for Law and Social Policy (CLASP) cites lawmakers' reluctance to make sharp cuts in Social Security and Medicare, plus Obama's aim of raising $1.5 trillion over 10 years largely by raising taxes on high earners and cutting subsidized health programs.

"The president commented that 'it's not class warfare, it's math," Lower-Basch says. "At some point there are, mathematically, only a certain number of things to cut. Particularly if you take Social Security and Medicare off the table, that doesn't leave a lot of targets" besides food stamps and Medicaid, she says.

The political mechanics of deficit reduction also work in favor of cutting Medicaid funding because most Americans don't understand the technical language surrounding entitlements, Lower-Basch says.

# Should mothers who have children out of wedlock be denied welfare?

## YES  Michael D. Tanner
*Senior Fellow, Cato Institute*

Written for *CQ Researcher*, October 2011

Since Lyndon Johnson declared a War on Poverty in 1965, the federal government has spent roughly $18 trillion fighting poverty, almost $700 billion this year alone, on some 107 separate programs. Yet, the poverty rate stands at 15.1 percent. While this number may be partially inflated because of the poor economy, it is important to realize that, despite trillions in spending, we have never gotten the poverty rate below 11 percent. Clearly we are doing some things wrong.

One is perpetuating government programs that create an incentive for behavior that is likely to lead to poverty. In particular, our welfare programs continue to provide benefits to women who give birth out of wedlock.

The concern over this trend is not about personal morality. Having a child out of wedlock often means a lifetime of poverty. Children living with single mothers are almost six times more likely to be poor than those living with two parents. More than 20 percent of welfare recipients start on welfare because they have an out-of-wedlock birth. They also tend to stay on welfare longer than other recipients.

The trend is even worse among unwed teenage mothers. Half go on welfare within one year of the birth of their first child; 75 percent are on welfare within five years of the child's birth. Women who started on welfare because of an out-of-wedlock birth average more than nine years on welfare and make up roughly 40 percent of all recipients who are on welfare for 10 years or longer.

While there are many factors behind the rise in out-of-wedlock births, the availability of welfare is one. Of the more than 20 major studies of the issue, more than three-quarters show a significant link between benefit levels and out-of-wedlock childbearing.

Obviously no one gets pregnant to get welfare. But by softening the immediate as opposed to the long-term economic consequences of out-of-wedlock births, welfare has removed a major incentive to avoid them. As Charles Murray, a political scientist at the American Enterprise Institute, put it, "The evil of the modern welfare state is not that it bribes women to have babies — wanting to have babies is natural — but that it enables women to bear children without the natural social restraints."

A good start to a welfare policy that might actually reduce poverty would be to set a date — say nine months from today — after which an out-of-wedlock birth would no longer make one eligible for welfare.

## NO  LaDonna A. Pavetti
*Vice President for Family Income-Support Policy, Center on Budget and Policy Priorities*

Written for *CQ Researcher*, October 2011

The case for rejecting a policy that would deny cash assistance to mothers who have children out of wedlock was compelling in 1996, when Congress created Temporary Assistance for Needy Families (TANF) — the current welfare law — and it's even more compelling now.

For starters, such a policy would deny support to children who bear no responsibility for their parents' actions. With growing evidence that poverty among young children reduces their chances of success throughout their lives, we should do everything we can to make sure that all children have the support they need to become productive adults.

A recent article by University of California, Irvine, education professor Greg J. Duncan and University of Wisconsin, Madison, professor of social work Katherine Magnuson provides all the evidence we need. Duncan is one of the most respected academic researchers on the consequences of childhood poverty, and he has always been particularly cautious in drawing policy conclusions from academic research. Two key points from the article stand out:

- Income matters for young, low-income children's learning;
- Poverty in early childhood may reduce earnings much later in life.

The authors recommend that states avoid TANF policy changes that threaten the well-being of young children. Indeed, we should be seeking more ways to remediate deep and persistent poverty in early childhood — not fewer.

Besides, although TANF provides an important safety net for single-parent families, it is not the main source of support for families with out-of-wedlock children. So, denying them these benefits will play no role in changing societal behavior. In the late 1990s, when the economy was strong, record numbers of single parents entered the labor force, reaching a high of 83 percent by 2000. Even in the current economy, 74 percent of them still work. In contrast, only 27 families for every 100 in poverty receive TANF benefits. And, TANF benefits are meager: In the median state in 2011, a family of three received $429 per month; in 14 states, such a family received less than $300.

In 1968, the Supreme Court ruled that children born to unmarried parents could not be punished for their parents' actions. The question we should be answering is: How can we make investments in our children that guarantee bright and productive futures for all of them? The answers matter not only for our children, but for all of us.

Eight-year-old Briana, left, and her sister, Daneen, 9, watch as their mother asks for a Thanksgiving turkey at the "banquet in a box" food-distribution event held by the Denver Rescue Mission in Colorado on Nov. 23, 2010. In 2009 food banks served 5.7 million people a week in the United States (the latest figure available), according to Feed America, a national alliance of food charities.

"Part of what we worry about is the process of getting to these very high-level procedural issues that are abstract," she says. "People don't know what they mean, and what they mean is cuts in critical programs for low-income families."

Alarm among liberal advocates has stepped down a notch since earlier in the year, when Rep. Paul Ryan, R-Wis., a top Republican deficit hawk, proposed a federal budget in which Medicaid would be funded by fixed block grants to the states. The Center on Budget and Policy Priorities calculated that the proposal would have reduced Medicaid funding by at least 25 percent, based on 2009 budget figures.[64]

Obama and congressional Democrats would firmly oppose any such move, advocates say. But Haskins of the Brookings Institution suggests that the logic behind the block-grant idea remains plausible. He says, in fact, that he would support a Medicaid block grant if it came with annual funding increases.

Citing the growing costs of Medicaid and Medicare, Haskins says, "We've got to get hold of that or it's going to bankrupt us."

But Haskins adds, "If you gave a block grant with no mechanism for increasing funding, or just an increase

with the rate of inflation, states would either have to cut services or spend more, and they can't spend more."

## Child Support

For some poverty experts, enforcement of child-support payments is an anti-poverty tool that gets too little attention.

"We've actually reduced our investment in child-support enforcement," says Lesley of First Focus. "If we think that fathers should have responsibility for their kids, one way to address that is enforcement."

Federal "incentive" grants had been awarded to states that showed enforcement results, but those grants were eliminated by deficit-reduction legislation in 2005. The grants, which supplied from 6 percent to 39 percent of state enforcement budgets, were restored for 2009 and 2010 by the "stimulus" bill at the beginning of the Obama administration.[65]

"In 2008, 625,000 children would have been poor if they had not received child support, increasing child poverty by 4.4 percent," Elaine Sorensen of the Urban Institute, a centrist think tank in Washington, wrote last year in laying out the case for strengthening enforcement efforts. In that year, by her calculation, child-support payments aided 17 million children, ranking second to Medicaid, whose child caseload was 22.8 million — in the number of young people who received support.[66]

Sorensen also noted that among poor families with children, child support represents an average of 10 percent of family income — marginally more than the 9 percent that welfare payments represented.[67]

Nevertheless, the high and persistent joblessness that dominates the economy is having an effect on child support. The Government Accountability Office (GAO), Congress's nonpartisan investigative arm, reported in a study early this year that child-support collections had decreased for the first time in 2009, by $641 million.[68]

"Obtaining collections from a noncustodial parent with a limited ability to pay, such as those whose employment or earnings have been affected by the economic recession, is more difficult," the GAO noted.[69]

Some anti-poverty advocates point to a finding in the GAO study that they believe supports their view that enforcement is useful to only a minority of poor families, at least in present economic circumstances. The GAO found that only a third of families eligible for child-support and welfare payments actually received child-support money.[70]

Child-support payments "make a huge difference to families that receive it," says Lower-Basch of CLASP. But, she adds, most fathers of children who live under the poverty line with their mothers aren't in any position to provide significant support. "People talk about deadbeat dads, then figured out that many of them are dead broke, not deadbeat. They have minimal incomes themselves."

Jones of the Center for Urban Families warns that child-support enforcement laws, if not written with an eye to the realities that dominate families who live in poverty, can end up making matters worse. Maryland law authorizes the state to claim 65 percent of a worker's take-home pay for child support, he notes.[71]

"You take 65 percent from somebody who makes less than $10,000 a year," Jones says, and "you're setting someone up to live in the underground economy: 'I'm not going to take a legal job because I can't afford to have my money taken.' And when I become a senior citizen, I have no Social Security to draw on."

## Cartoon Debate

The increase in child poverty may not have gotten much notice from politicians. Over on "Sesame Street," though, the development has prompted a new Muppet to join the cast for a special program. Lily, a purple-faced girl in a denim jumper, was created to represent the 16.2 million children who live in what the U.S. Agriculture Department calls "food-insecure" households.[72]

These are families who don't have guaranteed access at all times to nutritious food — a condition affecting nearly 15 percent of the U.S. population, according to the Agriculture Department.[73]

Lily appeared on a one-hour Public Broadcasting System special in early October, "Growing Hope Against Hunger." "While collecting foods at a food drive and from a community garden, the Sesame friends meet Lily, a new character whose family has an ongoing struggle with hunger," the show's production company, "Sesame Workshop," said in a press release. "The Sesame characters learn how their simple actions, such as planting a seed, can make a world of difference to others. . . . The special reassures children that they are not alone: There are people who care and can help."[74]

At a time when poverty and related issues have generated little political debate, the addition of Lily to the "Sesame Street" cast prompted sniping in some conservative media.

"I just don't understand why this Muppet is hungry," Andrea Tantaros, co-host of a Fox News talk show, "The Five," said on her Oct. 7 show. "Obama has expanded Medicaid by $60 billion, he's expanded food stamps, he's expanded WIC — Women's, Infants and Children (nutrition). . . . Why is Lily hungry? Bob, should Lily be taken away from her parents? . . . There's so much money out there to feed these kids."[75]

Tantaros was echoing a theme sounded by conservative analysts, who point to the expanded food-stamp program and other anti-poverty programs as evidence of liberal mischaracterization of U.S. poverty as severe deprivation.

Nevertheless, another school of conservative commentary takes poverty indicators at face value to criticize Obama's presidency. "With a record number of Americans on food stamps, increased debt and record poverty, Sesame Street will introduce a poor, starving muppet to educate on the growing number of starving children in Obama's America," Jim Hoft, a conservative blogger, wrote at his site, "Gateway Pundit."[76]

Hoft's comment was circulated on the left side of the blogosphere by "Media Matters for America," which monitors conservative media for a liberal audience. In the same way, another liberal site, *Crooks and Liars*, posted a clip of the Fox News discussion.[77]

Liberals, for their part, have been applauding "Sesame Street" for tackling the hunger issue. "Good they're doing it, sad it's necessary," wrote Laura Clawson, a contributor to the *Daily Kos*.[78]

# OUTLOOK

## Needed: Poverty Target

If the poor and the well-off occupy different spheres of reality, so do poverty policy experts of opposing political views. Their differences run far deeper than disagreements over specific policies.

Lesley of First Focus, for instance, insists that the political establishment — Democrats and Republicans alike — is neglecting the issue of poverty. "What we really need in this country is something like a poverty-reduction target," he says. "Every year you would have the target, and the administration would be required to come up with its agenda on how to address the problem. If we had a conversation among Republicans and Democrats about who is not doing enough about child poverty, I would retire."

For now, despite the Census Bureau poverty statistics that got policy experts talking, politicians have taken a pass, Lesley says. "The conversations are among advocates and think tanks. There's 22 percent of children in poverty — where's Barack Obama? [House Speaker John] Boehner, where's his agenda?"

Rector of the Heritage Foundation dismisses the idea that poverty is being ignored. "That's just a ploy," he says. "Programs are growing like crazy. The sky is always falling from their perspective. There's been a gargantuan expansion of welfare spending that's not going to go down when the recession ends," he says.

Rector and two colleagues wrote in 2009 that welfare spending aimed at poor and low-income people had grown thirteen-fold, after adjusting for inflation, to more than $700 billion, since President Johnson launched the War on Poverty in 1964.[79]

At the same time, Rector sees no end to the growth in out-of-wedlock births — the major source, in his view, of poverty. "We're on a trajectory where the working-class white family is slowly disintegrating. That creates an automatic poverty population."

Liberal analysts raise their own fear about changes in the social structure. "It's widely thought in the United States that we're the land of opportunity," says Gerry Bradley, research director at New Mexico Voices for Children, an Albuquerque-based advocacy group. "But we're getting to the point where it's more difficult for people to move out of their income group than it is in European countries that are thought to be more stratified."

The likelihood of Congress cutting benefit programs that help lower-income people afford higher education will worsen the picture, Bradley argues. "Cutting these programs is going to ensure that we have a more rigid class structure than we already do."[80]

Jones of the Center for Urban Families sounds a guardedly optimistic note. "I have to believe that in 10 years the economy will be better," he says. But he's less certain about the level of national leadership.

"Our democracy depends on our political system to make the necessary recalibration to respond to circumstances," he says. "Unless the people in control change, or our system changes, we will be worse off than we are now. I think the American people are going to have rise up and say to policy makers, 'You've got to stop the ideological warfare.'"

On another note of tempered optimism, Jane Trujillo and Shannon Barnett of Belen, N.M., are both counting the value of education. Trujillo is studying for an associate's degree in nursing. Barnett vows to do likewise.

"I didn't finish school, so I've now started classes for my GED," Barnett says. "As soon as I'm done with that I'm going to try to get into nursing school. I'm hoping that once that happens we won't be struggling so much. I am just focusing on my education."

## NOTES

1. "Missing Meals in New Mexico," Roadrunner Food Bank, December 2010, www.rrfb.org/wp-content/uploads/2011/02/Executive-Summary-Version-2.pdf; "New Mexico QuickFacts," U.S. Census Bureau, updated June 3, 2011, http://quickfacts.census.gov/qfd/states/35000.html.

2. "Children in Poverty (Percent) — 2010," Kids Count Data Center, Annie E. Casey Foundation, undated, http://datacenter.kidscount.org/ data/acrossstates/Rankings.aspx?ind=43.

3. "Poverty thresholds," U.S. Census Bureau, updated Sept. 13, 2011, www.census.gov/hhes/ www/poverty/data/threshld/index.html.

4. Increases in food and gasoline prices in 2009-2011 are major reasons that U.S. incomes have fallen in value, a study by two former Census Bureau professionals concluded. See Robert Pear, "Recession Officially Over, U.S. Incomes Kept Falling," *The New York Times*, Oct. 10, 2011, www.nytimes.com/2011/10/10/us/recession-officially-over-us-incomes-kept-falling.html?_r=1&hp.

5. Carmen DeNavas-Walt, *et al.*, "Poverty Status of People by Family Relationship, Race, and Hispanic Origin: 1959 to 2010," U.S. Census Bureau, updated Sept. 13, 2011, p. 62, www.census.gov/

hhes/www/poverty/data/historical/ people.html. For background, see Thomas J. Billitteri, "Domestic Poverty," *CQ Researcher*, Sept. 7, 2007, pp. 721-744, updated April 27, 2011.

6. "Income, Poverty, and Health Insurance Coverage in the United States: 2010," U.S. Census Bureau, September 2011, p. 17, www.census.gov/ prod/2011pubs/p60-239.pdf.

7. Gene Falk, "The TANF Emergency Contingency Fund," Congressional Research Service, Dec. 22, 2010, Summary page, www.fas.org/sgp/crs/misc/ R41078.pdf.

8. Joyce A. Martin, *et al.*, "Births: Final Data for 2008," National Vital Statistics Reports, National Center for Health Statistics, Dec. 8, 2010, p. 44, www.cdc .gov/nchs/data/nvsr/nvsr59/nv sr59_01.pdf; "U.S. Births Rise for First Time in Eight Years," Family Planning Perspectives, Guttmacher Institute, September-October 2000, www.guttmacher.org/ pubs/journals/3226300. html; Current Trends in Fertility and Infant and Maternal Health — United States, 1980-1988," Centers for Disease Control, June 14, 1991, www.cdc.gov/mmwr/preview/ mmwrhtml/00014440.htm; Stephanie J. Ventura, "Changing Patterns of Nonmarital Childbearing in the United States," National Center for Health Statistics, May 2009, www.cdc.gov/nchs/data/data-briefs/ db18.pdf.

9. "Related Children Under 18 by Householder's Work Experience and Family Structure: 2010," Current Population Survey, U.S. Census Bureau, Labor Department, updated Sept. 13, 2011, www.census .gov/hhes/www/cpstables/032011/pov/new21_ 100_01.htm.

10. Mark Hugo Lopez and Gabriel Velasco, "Childhood Poverty Among Hispanics Sets Record, Leads Nation," Pew Hispanic Center, Sept. 28, 2011, p. 4, http://pewhispanic.org/files/reports/147.pdf.

11. *Ibid.*, pp. 11-14; "Educational Attainment: Better Than Meets the Eye, But Large Challenges Remain," Pew Hispanic Center, January 2002, http://pew hispanic.org/files/factsheets/3.pdf.

12. See Kathleen S. Short, "The Supplemental Poverty Measure: Examining the Incidence and Depth of

Poverty in the U.S. Taking Account of Taxes and Transfers," U.S. Census Bureau, June 30, 2011, www.census.gov/hhes/pov meas/methodology/ supplemental/research.html.

13. "A Brief History of the AFDC Program," Health and Human Services Department, June 1998, http:// aspe.hhs.gov/hsp/afdc/afdc base98.htm.

14. Gene Falk, The Temporary Assistance for Needy Families (TANF) Block Grant: Responses to Frequently Asked Questions," Congressional Research Service, May 4, 2011, www.work forceatm .org/assets/utilities/serve.cfm?path=/sections/pdf/ 2011/TheTemporaryAssistancefor NeedyFamilies TANFBlockGrantResponsesto FrequentlyAsked Questions3.pdf.

15. *Ibid.*, p. 6.

16. *Ibid.*, pp. 1, 3, 7.

17. *Ibid.*, p. 2.

18. *Ibid.*, p. 9; "Caseload Data 2011," Administration for Children and Families, Health and Human Services Department, updated July 25, 2011, www .acf.hhs.gov/programs/ofa/ data-reports/caseload/ caseload_current.htm# 2011.

19. Sabrina Tavernise, "Soaring Poverty Casts Spotlight on 'Lost Decade,' " *The New York Times*, Sept. 13, 2011, www.nytimes.com/ 2011/09/14/us/14census .html?pagewanted=1&_r=1&sq=census%20 2010%20poverty&st=cse&scp=2; DeNavas-Walt, *op. cit.*, pp. 14, 17.

20. "Supplemental Nutrition Assistance Program: Number of Persons Participating," Food Research and Action Center, updated monthly, http://frac .org/wp-content/uploads/2011/03/ snapdata2011_ july.pdf; "Labor Force Statistics from the Current Population Survey," U.S. Bureau of Labor Statistics, updated regularly, http://data.bls.gov/timeseries/ LNS14000000.

21. Robert Rector, *et al.*, "Obama to Spend $10.3 Trillion on Welfare," Heritage Foundation, Sept. 16, 2009, www.heritage.org/Research/Reports/2009/09/ Obama-to-Spend-103-Trillion-on-Welfare-Uncovering-the-Full-Cost-of-Means-Tested-Welfare-or-Aid-to-the-Poor.

22. "Hearing of the House Ways and Means Committee, 'Improving Work and Other Welfare Reform Goals, Focusing on Reauthorization of the Temporary Assistance for Needy Families Program," Federal News Service, Sept. 8, 2011; "Engagement in Additional Work Activities and Expenditures for Other Benefits and Services, a TANF Report to Congress," March 2011, (no page numbers), www.acf.hhs.gov/programs/ofa/data-reports/cra-report-to-congress/cra_report-to-congress.html#_Toc29 8161525.

23. Hearing, *ibid.*

24. Kristin Anderson Moore, *et al.*, "Children in Poverty: Trends, Consequences, and Policy Options," Child Trends, April 2009, www.child trends.org/files/child_trends-2009_04_07_rb_ childreninpoverty.pdf.

25. *Ibid.*

26. DeNavas-Walt, *et al.*, *op. cit.*, pp. 17-18, 74.

27. "2011 Kids Count Data Book," Annie E. Casey Foundation, 2011, p. 62, http://datacenter.kids count.org/databook/2011/OnlineBooks/2011 KCDB_FINAL.pdf; Vanessa R. Wight, *et al.*, "Who are America's Poor Children?," National Center for Children in Poverty, Columbia University, March 2011, www.nccp.org/publications/pub_1001.html.

28. James J. Heckman, "The Economics of Inequality," *American Educator*, Spring 2011, p. 33, www.aft.org/pdfs/americaneducator/spring2011/Heckman.pdf.

29. "Income, Poverty, and Health Insurance Coverage," *op. cit.*, p. 15.

30. Ron Haskins, "Fighting Poverty the American Way," Brookings Institution, June 20, 2011, p. 32, www.brookings.edu/~/media/Files/rc/ papers/2011/0620_fighting_poverty_haskins/ 0620_fighting_poverty_haskins.pdf.

31. Except where otherwise indicated, this subsection is drawn from Premilla Nadasen, *et al.*, *Welfare in the United States: A History With Documents 1935-1996* (2009); Thomas Gabe, "Welfare, Work and Poverty Status of Female-Headed Families With Children: 1987-2009, Congressional Research Service, July 15, 2011, http://digitalcommons.ilr.cornell.edu/cgi/viewcontent.cgi?article=1852&context=key_work place; for background, see Kathy Koch, "Child Poverty," *CQ Researcher*, April 7, 2000, pp. 281-304.

32. Jennifer Michael and Madeleine Goldstein, "Reviving the White House Conference on Children," Children's Voice, Child Welfare League of America, January-February 2008, www.cwla.org/voice/0801whconf .htm.

33. Nadasen, *et al.*, *op. cit.*, pp. 15-16.

34. Quoted in Susan W. Blank and Barbara B. Blum, "A Brief History of Work Expectations for Welfare Mothers," *Future of Children* (Journal), Spring 1997, p. 30, www.princeton.edu/futureofchildren/publi cations/docs/07_01_02.pdf.

35. *Ibid.*, p. 30.

36. Blank and Blum, *op. cit.*, p. 30.

37. Richard B. Drake, *A History of Appalachia* (2001), p. 173; Maurice Isserman, "Michael Harrington: Warrior on Poverty," *The New York Times*, June 19, 2009, www.nytimes.com/2009/ 06/21/books/review/ Isserman-t.html. Except where otherwise indicated, this subsection is drawn from Gabe, *op. cit.*

38. Quoted in Edward Zigler and Susan Muenchow, *Head Start: The Inside Story of America's Most Successful Educational Experiment* (1992), p. 3.

39. "Trends in the AFDC Caseload since 1962," U.S. Health and Human Services Department, undated, p. 15, http://aspe.hhs.gov/hsp/afdc/baseline/2case load.pdf.

40. Report included in Nadasen, *et al.*, p. 169.

41. *Ibid.*

42. Gabe, *op. cit.*, p. 69.

43. Daniel Patrick Moynihan, "The Negro Family: The Case for National Action," U.S. Department of Labor, March 1965, www.dol.gov/oasam/programs/history/webid-meynihan.htm.

44. *Ibid.*

45. Nadasen, *et al.*, *op. cit.*, pp. 45-46; John McWhorter, "Legitimacy at Last," *The New Republic*, April 16, 2010, www.tnr.com/book/review/legitimacy-last.

46. *Ibid.*

47. Nadasen, *et al.*, *op. cit.*, p. 47.

48. Gabe, *op. cit.*, pp. 59-60.

49. *Ibid.*, p. 60.

50. For background, see Peter Katel, "Straining the Safety Net," *CQ Researcher*, July 31, 2009, pp. 645-668. Except where otherwise stated, this subsection draws on Blank and Blum, *op. cit.*

51. Katel, *ibid.*

52. "Address Before a Joint Session of the Congress Reporting on the State of the Union," Feb. 4, 1986, http://reagan2020.us/speeches/state_of_the_union_1986.asp.

53. Quoted in Richard L. Berke, "Clinton: Getting People Off Welfare," *The New York Times*, Sept. 10, 1992, www.nytimes.com/1992/09/10/us/the-1992-campaign-the-ad-campaign-clinton-getting-people-off-welfare.html.

54. Quoted in Gabe, *op. cit.*, p. 8.

55. "Fact Sheet, The Personal Responsibility and Work Opportunity Reconciliation Act of 1996," Health and Human Services Dept., September 1996, http://aspe.hhs.gov/hsp/abbrev/prwora96.htm; "Interview: Welfare reform, 10 years later (with Ron Haskins)," Brookings Institution, Aug. 24, 2006, www.brookings.edu/interviews/2006/0824welfare_haskins.aspx.

56. *Ibid.*, Haskins; Ronald Brownstein, "A Stormy Debate Is Brewing Within GOP Over Clinton's Big Lead in Polls," *Los Angeles Times*, Sept. 9, 1996, p. A5.

57. *Ibid.*

58. Ron Haskins, "Fighting Poverty the American Way," Brookings Institution, June 20, 2011, pp. 4, 32, www.brookings.edu/~/media/Files/rc/papers/2011/0620_fighting_poverty_haskins/0620_fighting_poverty_haskins.pdf.

59. *Ibid.*

60. Gene Falk, "The Temporary Assistance for Needy Families (TANF) Block Grant: Responses to Frequently Asked Questions," Congressional Research Service, Jan. 21, 2009, p. 1, http://stuff.mit.edu/afs/sipb/contrib/wikileaks-crs/wikileaks-crs-reports/RL32760.pdf.

61. "Income, Poverty, and Health Insurance . . .," *op. cit.*, p. 82.

62. "Joint Select Committee on Deficit Reduction," undated, www.deficitreduction.gov/public.

63. Quoted in Robert Pear, "In Cuts to Health Programs, Experts See Difficult Task in Protecting Patients," *The New York Times*, Sept. 20, 2011, www.nytimes.com/2011/09/21/us/politics/wielding-the-ax-on-medicaid-and-medicare-without-wounding-the-patient.html.

64. Edwin Park and Matt Broaddus, "What if Ryan's Medicaid Block Grant Had Taken Effect in 2000," Center on Budget and Policy Priorities, April 12, 2011, www.cbpp.org/cms/index.cfm?fa=view&id=3466.

65. "Child Support Enforcement," Government Accountability Office, January, www.gao.gov/new.items/d11196.pdf.

66. Elaine Sorensen, "Child Support Plays an Increasingly Important Role for Poor Custodial Families," Urban Institute, December 2010, p. 1, www.urban.org/publications/412272.html.

67. *Ibid.*, p. 3.

68. "Child Support Enforcement," *op. cit.*, p. 11.

69. *Ibid.*, p. 14.

70. *Ibid.*, p. 14.

71. "Department of Human Resources, Child Support," Maryland state government, undated, www.dhr.state.md.us/csea/download/EMPLOY ERJOBAID.doc.

72. Dave Itzkoff, " 'Sesame Street' Special on Hunger Introduces New Muppet Character," *The New York Times*, ArtsBeat blog, Oct. 3, 2011, http://artsbeat.blogs.nytimes.com/2011/10/03/sesame-street-special-on-hunger-introduces-new-muppet-character; "Food Security in the United States," U.S. Agriculture Department, updated Sept. 7, 2011, www.ers.usda.gov/Brief ing/FoodSecurity/stats_graphs.htm.

73. *Ibid.*

74. "Project Overview, growing hope against hunger," Sesame Workshop, Oct. 4, 2011, www.s2.cinemagnetics.com/press-release/english.html.

75. "Sign of the Times: Poverty-Stricken Muppet," "The Five" transcript, Oct. 7, 2011, www.fox news.com/on-air/the-five/transcript/sign-times-poverty-stricken-muppet.

76. Melody Johnson, "Strings Attached: Right-Wing Media Take Shots At New Poverty-Stricken Sesame

Street Character," *Media Matters for America*, Oct. 6, 2011, http://mediamatters.org/blog/ 201110060010.

77. "Fox Panel Attacks Sesame Street for Wanting to Educate Children About Poverty," *Crooks and Liars*, Oct. 8, 2011, http://videocafe.crooks andliars.com/heather/fox-panel-attacks-sesame-street-wanting-ed.

78. Laura Clawson, "This week in the War on Workers: The hungry Muppet," *Daily Kos*, Oct. 8, 2011, http://labor.dailykos.com.

79. Robert Rector, Katherine Bradley, Rachel Sheffield, "Obama to Spend $10 trillion on Welfare," Heritage Foundation, Sept. 16, 2009, p. 1, www.heritage.org/research/reports/2009/09/obama-to-spend-103-trillion-on-welfare-un covering-the-full-cost-of-means-tested-welfare-or-aid-to-the-poor.

80. For background, see Marcia Clemmitt, "Student Debt," *CQ Researcher*, Oct. 21, 2011, pp. 877-900.

# BIBLIOGRAPHY

## Selected Sources

### Books

**Mead, Lawrence M., *Expanding Work Programs for Poor Men*, AEI Press, 2011.**
A leading conservative poverty-policy expert lays out a case for requiring low-income men to work, following the example of the 1996 welfare law and its demands on largely female welfare recipients. Poor children would benefit, he writes, as child-support payments increased.

**Nadasen, Premilla, Jennifer Mittelstadt and Marisa Chappell, *Welfare in the United States: A History With Documents, 1935-1996*, Routledge, 2009.**
Three historians chronicle and analyze welfare history from a pro-welfare recipients' perspective.

### Articles

**Alderman, Lesley, "Government Helps to Insure Children, Even Above the Poverty Line," *The New York Times*, Oct. 9, 2010, p. B6, www.nytimes.com/2010/10/09/health/ 09patient.html.**
Successful results are reported for the federal-state health coverage program for low-income children.

**Crary, David, *et al.*, "Behind the poverty numbers: real lives, real pain," *The Associated Press*, Sept. 19, 2011.**
In a series of profiles from across the country, AP correspondents report on the hardships faced by growing numbers of families.

**D'Innocenzio, Anne, and Dena Potter, "Food-stamp shoppers buy at midnight across the country," *The Washington Post*, Oct. 24, 2010, p. A8, www.washington post.com/wp-dyn/content/article/2010/10/23/AR2010 102300179.html.**
*The Post* uncovers a nationwide trend of families racing to stock up on food as soon as their electronic food-stamp cards are recharged once a month at midnight.

**Davey, Monica, "Families Feel Sharp Edge of State Budget Cuts," *The New York Times*, Sept. 7, 2011, p. A22, www.ny times.com/2011/09/07/us/07states .html?pagewanted=all.**
Hard-pressed states are reducing aid to poor families, a correspondent reports from the Midwest.

**Egger, Robert, "5 Myths about hunger in America," *The Washington Post*, Nov. 21, 2010, p. B2, www .washington post.com/wp-dyn/content/article/2010/ 11/19/AR2010111 906872.html.**
The founder of a Washington food-preparation business argues that hunger and poor nutrition are far bigger problems than generally recognized.

**Gordey, Cynthia, "Welfare, Fathers and Those Persistent Myths," *The Root*, June 17, 2011, www.theroot.com/views/welfare-fathers-and-those-persistent-myths.**
A writer for an online magazine on African-American issues reports on the growing recognition of fathers' importance for children growing up in mother-headed households.

### Reports and Studies

**Falk, Gene, "The Temporary Assistance for Needy Families (TANF) Block Grant: Responses to Frequently Asked Questions," Congressional Research Service, Feb. 16, 2011, www.naswa.org/assets/utilities/serve.cfm? gid=231C9E08-41AA-4283-9E35-7625F0575B4E.**
A social-policy expert for Congress' nonpartisan research arm provides a wealth of basic information on the welfare system.

**Gabe, Thomas, "Welfare, Work, and Poverty Status of Female-Headed Families with Children: 1987-2009," Congressional Research Service, July 15, 2011, http://digitalcommons.ilr. cornell.edu/cgi/viewcontent .cgi?article=1852&context=key_workplace.**
Another CRS specialist provides a detailed, data-rich analysis of one of the most long-running issues in anti-poverty policy.

**Haskins, Ron, "Fighting Poverty the American Way," Brookings Institution, June 2011, www.brookings.edu/ papers/2011/0620_fighting_poverty_haskins.aspx.**
A key figure in the 1996 welfare overhaul examines welfare policy against the backdrop of American political culture.

**DeNavas-Walt, Carmen, *et al.*, "Income, Poverty, and Health Insurance Coverage in the United States: 2010," U.S. Census Bureau, September 2011, www .census.gov/ prod/2011pubs/p60-239.pdf.**
Census Bureau experts marshal enormous quantities of data to illustrate ongoing trends in income and well-being.

**Rector, Robert, *et al.*, "Obama to Spend $10.3 Trillion on Welfare," Heritage Foundation, Sept. 16, 2009, www.heritage.org/research/reports/2009/09/ obama-to-spend-103-trillion-on-welfare-uncovering-the-full-cost-of-means-tested-welfare-or-aid-to-the-poor.**
Analysts for a leading conservative think tank present a case for extreme skepticism about government anti-poverty programs.

**Seith, David, and Courtney Kalof, "Who Are America's Poor Children?" National Center for Children in Poverty, Columbia University, July 2011, www.nccp.org/publications/ pdf/text_1032.pdf.**
Researchers for a leading child-poverty think tank analyze the defining characteristics of children in poverty.

# For More Information

**Center for Urban Families**, 2201 North Monroe St., Baltimore, MD 21217; 410-367-5691; http://cfuf.org/ index. Develops and runs training programs in job skills and fatherhood.

**Center on Budget and Policy Priorities**, 820 First St., N.E., Suite 510, Washington, DC 20002; 202-408-1080; www .cbpp.org. Research and advocacy organization specializing in legislative and policy analysis.

**CLASP**, 1200 18th St., N.W., Washington, DC 20036; 202-906-8000; www.clasp.org. Advocacy organization focusing on children and family law and policy.

**Feeding America**, 35 East Wacker Drive, Chicago, IL 60601; 800-771-2303; http:// feedingamerica.org. National alliance of food banks that provides information on hunger, nutrition conditions and relevant laws and policies.

**Heritage Foundation**, 214 Massachusetts Ave., N.E., Washington, DC 20002-4999; 202-546-4400; www.heritage. org/Issues/Poverty-and-Inequality. Conservative think tank that conducts research on poverty and related issues.

**National Center for Children in Poverty**, 215 W. 125th St., 3rd Floor, New York, NY 10027; 646-284-9600; www .nccp.org. Columbia University think tank providing data-analysis tools on poverty and health.

**U.S. Census Bureau**, 4600 Silver Hill Road, S.E., Washington, DC 20233; 301-763-4636; www.census.gov/ hhes/www/poverty/poverty.html. Federal agency providing a vast amount of current and historical information on poverty.

# 4

# Home Schooling

Marcia Clemmitt

Josh Powell, a senior at Georgetown University, said his parents' efforts to home school him were less successful as material got more advanced. Some educators argue the public interest warrants more oversight of the quality of home schooling, but most states allow home-schoolers to operate with little or no government regulation.

From *CQ Researcher*, March 7, 2014.

"My early education was great," said Josh Powell, a home-schooled Virginian and a senior at Georgetown University, in Washington, D.C. "I learned to read when I was 4."

But as his curriculum grew more advanced, Powell said, his parents were not equipped to teach it. For instance, when he asked his mother for help on a pre-algebra problem, she said, "'Pray. Ask God. He'll help you,'" he recalled, "and that wasn't working for me."[1]

Powell asked his parents' permission to enroll in public school. But the Powells educate their children at home under a Virginia law that frees those who home-school for religious reasons from government oversight. A lawyer advised the family that allowing one child to attend public school might jeopardize that legal status. Eventually Powell enrolled in a public library's GED classes, which can lead to a high school equivalency diploma.

Still, Powell worried that some of his younger siblings might not be learning well. One who is middle-school-age cannot read, he said. And some play video games most of the day, said one of Powell's brothers.

Powell reasoned that children's views should be considered alongside those of their parents when decisions about schooling are made. He wanted his hometown school board to ask his brothers and sisters whether they shared their parents' religious beliefs and conviction that the family should receive Virginia's religious exemption to home school without any oversight. But the board rejected Powell's request.[2]

*Getty Images/The Washington Post/Bill O'Leary*

## Parents Cite Safety, Drugs as Key Reasons for Home Schooling

One in four parents surveyed about why they home schooled their children in 2011-12 cited concerns about safety, drugs, negative peer pressure or other problems in traditional schools as the most important reason. A desire to provide religious instruction was cited by about one in six parents as their primary reason.

**Most Important Reasons for Home Schooling, 2011-12 (% of parents surveyed)**

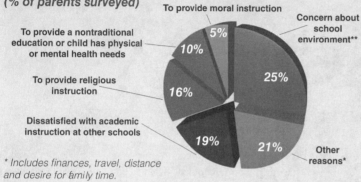

To provide moral instruction — 5%

Concern about school environment** — 25%

To provide a nontraditional education or child has physical or mental health needs — 10%

To provide religious instruction — 16%

Dissatisfied with academic instruction at other schools — 19%

Other reasons* — 21%

*\* Includes finances, travel, distance and desire for family time.*

*\*\* Such as safety, drugs and negative peer pressure.*

*Note: Percentages do not add to 100 due to margin of error*

*Source: Amber Noel, et al., "Parent and Family Involvement in Education, from the National Household Education Surveys Program of 2012," National Center for Education Statistics, August 2013, Table 8, p. 18, http://nces ed.gov/pubs2013/2013028.pdf*

Beginning as a tiny, distrusted minority in the 1960s and '70s, the number of home-schooling families has burgeoned since the 1980s. Today, education experts estimate that about 2 million American children ages 5-17 — out of a total of 52 million — are being home schooled, up from about 850,000 in 1999.[3] Official government studies put the figure at 1.8 million, but a group of leading scholars in the field notes that, "given the reluctance of home-schoolers to identify themselves or respond to surveys (especially from government agencies)," the 2-million-plus figure is likely more accurate.[4]

Thirty-one percent of home-schooled students live in rural areas, compared to only 20.7 percent of all U.S. students; 28 percent of home-schooled students live in cities, compared to 31.3 percent of students overall. Among home-schooling parents, 16.6 percent have a graduate or professional degree, 33.3 percent a bachelor's

degree, 36.4 percent some college or postsecondary training, and 13.7 percent a high school diploma or less.[5]

The fast-growing but poorly documented and loosely regulated phenomenon has led some lawmakers, educators and academics to question whether the public interest requires at least minimal government oversight of home education. Such concerns pit parents' right to direct the upbringing of their children against the public's responsibility to ensure an educated populace and the well-being of children.

The oversight debate is periodically thrust into the limelight, particularly when a home-schooled child like Powell says his education was inadequate or, in some extreme cases, when child abuse in the home goes unnoticed because the usual linkage between home and school life is missing.[6]

Home-schooling proponents say, however, that oversight is unnecessary because most home-schooled students are well-educated, and child safety can be ensured by improving the efficiency of existing social service agencies.

The majority of home-schooling families are white, politically conservative evangelical Christians, according to experts who study the field. However, in a 2012 government survey of why parents choose to home school their children, concerns about safety and drugs in the public schools were among the top reasons given, while the desire to provide a religious education ranked fourth in priority.[7]

In the past decade families representing many ethnic groups and a wide range of religious, political and philosophical beliefs have joined the home-schooling ranks. That includes a small minority of so-called unschooling families, in which children pursue only studies and activities they choose for themselves.[8] A number of high-profile entertainers and celebrities also are home-schoolers, from NASCAR star Darrell Waltrip and Wikipedia founder

Jimmy Wales and his wife Christine to superstars Brad Pitt and Angelina Jolie.

After decades of advocacy by the home-schooling community on behalf of parents who insist on their right to educate their children in their own way, most states now allow home-schoolers to operate with little or no government regulation.[9]

"As with most U.S. education policy, requirements [for home-schooling parents] vary from state to state" and have generally become looser as the years have gone by, said the International Center for Home Education Research (ICHER), a group of international scholars formed in 2012 to produce independent research on home schooling around the world. "A few states have no home-school regulations," the group added, while others require standardized testing, curriculum approval, portfolio review, teacher qualifications or some combination of those. However, "home-school advocacy groups, on the whole, have been quite effective in reducing regulations in several states in recent years."[10]

The National Education Association (NEA), a labor union and professional organization representing more than 3 million teachers, has repeatedly argued that public interest warrants more oversight of the quality of home-school education. Students educated at home should fulfill the same general curriculum requirements as public-school students and be tested "to ensure adequate academic progress," and states should require home-schooling parents to obtain licenses as instructors, the NEA argues.[11]

However, the country's main home-school advocacy and legal-support group, the Purcellville, Va.-based Home School Legal Defense Association (HSLDA), strongly contends that virtually any government regulation of home schooling violates parents' right to raise their children according to their own principles. Virginia's exemption of religious home-schooling families from all

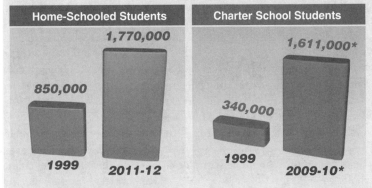

## Home-Schooling Population Doubled

The number of home schooled American children ages 5-17 doubled — from 850,000 to 1.8 million — between 1999 and the 2011-2012 academic year (graph at left). But the total represents only about 3.5 percent of the public school population of 52 million. As the home-school population was doubling, the charter school population rose more than fourfold (graph at right).

### Number of Home-Schooled and Charter School Students

**Home-Schooled Students**

1,770,000

850,000

1999    2011-12

**Charter School Students**

1,611,000*

340,000

1999    2009-10*

*Most recent data available*

Sources: *Digest of Education Statistics*, National Center for Education Statistics (NCES), http://1.usa.gov/N4inBO; Noel, *et al.*, "Parent and Family Involvement in Education, from the National Household Education Surveys Program of 2012," NCES, August 2013, Table 7, p. 17, http://1.usa.gov/NxEcK2; Figure 4-1, Section 1, "Participation in Education," in *The Condition of Education*, 2012, http://1.usa.gov/1gCRj5c

oversight, for example, is a "bedrock component of religious freedom in the state," wrote HSLDA Senior Counsel Scott Woodruff.[12]

As for the quality of home education, HSLDA says two large surveys it helped sponsor in 1998 and 2009 show that home-schooled students score better than public school students on standardized tests. But independent academic researchers say that because participation in both surveys was voluntary, they reveal nothing about the achievement of the average home-schooled student compared to the average public school student as measured by random-sample surveys.[13]

Woodruff also dismisses Josh Powell's contention that children should have a say in whether they are educated at home. Parental rights supersede those of minor children, he contends. "Children have many rights. Many of them are the same as adult rights," Woodruff wrote. But "while a child is a minor, his or her parent makes the final decision about how the child's right is to be exercised, if at all."[14]

The growth of the current home-schooling population also raises questions about whether and how home-schooling may change the American education system as a whole. Some scholars, for example, hope that home-schooling will have a positive influence on public education. "If we can get public schools and policymakers to look at the motivations people have for pulling kids out," it could ultimately lead to improvements in the public-school system, says Cheryl Fields-Smith, an associate professor of elementary education at the University of Georgia.

Frequently debated is whether home-schooled students should be allowed to participate in certain classes and extracurricular activities at their local public schools. About half the states and some individual school districts have laws or athletic-association rules that allow at least some home-schooled students to use certain public school facilities or attend activities or classes. On the whole, though, little interaction takes place between home-schooling families and the public schools.

Allowing more home-educated students to use public school facilities and encouraging home-schooling parents to talk more with public school officials could benefit both sides, Fields-Smith argues.

For example, if more schools offered science-lab or art-studio time to home-schooling families, the home-schooled students' education would be richer, and the schools would receive extra state funding to pay for the children's part-time attendance, she says.

Some parents who home-school their children do so not out of religious or moral conviction but because they believe the practice offers superior educational opportunities to their children. Many current school practices, such as "10-minute, fragmented spots of learning," conflict with "the way our kids learn naturally," says Beatrice Ekoko, who trained as a school teacher before unschooling her three daughters in Ontario, Canada. When children follow their own interests in learning and play, "they get into things for hours and hours, relax into them. That's how the mind focuses."

A weekly radio show that Ekoko and her husband ran for unschoolers often followed their daughters' intellectual interests, she says. "We did a show on poo, and went to see an organic farmer" and an academic researcher who studied "DNA in two-million year-old [animal] poo in China." she says. As teens, Ekoko's daughters chose to attend school but continued to cherish intense interests they'd developed as children, she says. "My oldest always made time for her music and writing and started university with a huge scholarship."

Some critics of home schooling argue that it can isolate children within like-minded communities, undercutting what the critics see as a key purpose of public education in a diverse democracy: encouraging students to work alongside others with different points of view.

"There are legitimate reasons why some individual families want to home school," says Christopher Lubienski, an associate professor of educational organization and leadership at the University of Illinois College of Education, in Champaign. However, some conservative Christian groups home school mainly to shield children from encountering other beliefs, he says, which he argues "drives polarization" of society by teaching children to avoid anyone who does not think as their parents do.

But such criticism is deeply alarming, according to HSLDA Chairman Michael Farris. For such commentators, Farris said, "the purpose of schooling includes mandatory instruction in tolerance. . . . And they conclude that Christian home-schoolers deny the value of tolerance — as they define tolerance. Because we teach our children that Jesus is the only way to God, we necessarily deny the validity of other religions." Contrary to Lubienski and others, home schooling children to ensure that they are not taught otherwise in the public schools is a proper decision for parents to make, he argued.[15]

As public officials, the home-schooling community and the public mull how to balance children's and parents' interests in home education, here are some of the questions being debated:

## Should governments oversee home schooling more strictly?

Some educational theorists, policy-makers and child-welfare advocates are calling for stricter oversight of home schooling. A key issue is whether children who are home schooled receive an adequate education.

Some experts argue that the public interest in ensuring that all children have the opportunity to obtain basic literacy warrants at least minimal academic oversight of home-schoolers.

The states' best course might be to set relatively minimal but firmly enforced rules aimed at "helping young people and balancing their rights and their parents' rights," says Robert Kunzman, a professor at the Indiana University School of Education, in Bloomington, and author of the 2009 book *Write These Laws on Your Children: Inside the World of Conservative Christian Homeschooling.*

For example, he says, because "students need basic skills to be self-sufficient down the road," states might require home-schooling families to register with the state and periodically conduct "basic skills testing" to ensure that reasonable education goals are being met.

Even if parents purchase off-the-shelf workbooks that walk students through the curriculum, they "must still have the ability to explore curricular options, oversee lessons, and help a child who is having trouble," wrote Laura Brodie, an author, college English instructor and former home-schooler. For that reason, some requirements probably should be imposed, although whether rules should require achievement tests or for parents to attend classes on teaching and curriculum is an open question, she said.[16]

Rob Reich, an associate professor of both political science and ethics at Stanford University, argued that regulation of home schooling is necessary to ensure that children are exposed to other perspectives. "Unregulated home schooling opens up the possibility that children will never learn about or be exposed to competing or alternative ways of life," a necessity if they are to grow into autonomous adults capable of functioning in a diverse, modern democracy, he argued. "[T]he education of children ought to be regulated in such a way that they learn about and engage with the diversity of ways of life in a democracy."[17]

But some home-schooling advocates resist any form of government regulation, arguing that it would trample parental rights.

Will Estrada, HSLDA director of federal relations, says interest in greater oversight or regulation of home schooling "is slim among Americans," except among "those who philosophically oppose home schooling." He points to his organization's repeated success at persuading states to reduce regulation of parents over the decades.

When it comes to maintaining educational standards, Estrada argues that the government is simply unfit to determine whether home-schoolers are doing a good job or not. "We live in a day and age when the public schools are doing horribly," he says. Furthermore, he says, many home-schoolers "tailor instructional models to their child's individual style" and view the increasing standardization of tests and curricula promoted by the government as an inferior approach. It would be a mistake to "take any more of the decision-making away from people who know the kids" and put it into the hands of education officials, he contends.

HSLDA opposes virtually all proposals for increased oversight or rule-setting on parental behaviors and in some cases also actively opposes increased regulation of the public schools. Any such regulation of how individual parents and teachers behave, the group says, opens the door to government micromanagement of child rearing and home teaching.

In 2013, for example, HSLDA backed state bills to stop states from implementing the Common Core academic standards in public schools. Requiring public schools to adopt the nationwide standards would likely be only a first step toward incorporating them into all education that receives government funds — including the online courses and virtual schools used by some home-schooled students — ultimately constraining home-schooling parents' right to fully determine what learning their children pursue, HSLDA said.[18]

Beyond concerns about education quality, some child advocates worry that home-schooled children could fall victim to abuse or physical or educational neglect that goes undiscovered because the youngsters are not interacting regularly with school nurses, guidance counselors or nonfamily teachers.

Cases of physical abuse in home-school settings appear to be extremely rare, but more than a few have occurred nationwide.[19] And some home-schooling parents have either inadvertently or deliberately neglected their children's education, such as by refusing to educate daughters beyond a certain age or entrusting a child's learning to a parent who is unfit for the responsibility because of mental illness or some other problem.[20]

To some observers, the fact that even a handful of home-schooled children face such risks warrants increased oversight.

Rachel Coleman, a home-schooled Ph.D. candidate in history at Indiana University and a founder of the Coalition for Responsible Home Education, says that in the 1980s, when the number of home-schoolers was tiny but rising, there may well have been legitimate reasons for home-schoolers to fear a ban on their activities by a government leery of having families opt out of the public education system.

"But we don't live in the 1980s anymore," and "home schooling is not in danger of being banned," says Coleman, whose group advocates for home-school reform through joint efforts of the public, governments and the home-schooling community.

The near-total lack of oversight of home schooling in most places today allows some educationally incompetent, neglectful and abusive parents to escape scrutiny, Coleman contends. For example, she says, in most states "convicted sex offenders and child abusers can home school" as long as they have custody of their children, on the argument that "if it's safe for the children to stay at home, then it's also safe to school them there." But school attendance might "provide an extra pair of eyes" to watch for signs of abuse in such cases, Coleman says. "We just want to make sure that children are being taught basic subjects and are safe."

Four high-profile cases of extreme child abuse among home-schooling families brought the oversight question to the forefront in North Carolina in 2010. The North Carolina Pediatric Society's Committee on Child Abuse and Neglect analyzed the state's medical, child-protection and educational systems for clues about how to prevent such incidents and recommended increased oversight by the state agency that oversees home-schoolers — the North Carolina Division of Nonpublic Education (DNPE).

Charged with monitoring that state's private schools and 45,000 home schools serving an estimated 80,000 students, the agency manages to meet with only about 300 home-schooling families per year, said the pediatricians' group. But no DNPE staffer had conducted a home-monitoring visit for a decade, the doctors pointed out, before calling for a dramatic increase in funding to allow DNPE to exercise more oversight.[21]

Home-school advocates such as the Home School Legal Defense Association (HSLDA), however, argue that increased government regulation of parental behavior with regard to educational neglect, abuse or any other aspect of family life is a slippery slope. Tighter oversight would eventually rob Americans of their legally protected right to raise their children as they wish, they contend.

Estrada says that "even one incident" of abuse "is too many." However, he says, in "almost every instance" of a brutal or life-threatening case involving home-schoolers, social service agencies "were already involved" in the case by the time extreme abuse occurred. This means that it was either the child-protection system or an individual social worker who failed to prevent the abuse from escalating, not the lack of home-schooling oversight, Estrada says.

Rather than doing more checking up on home-schooling families, governments should end the requirement that child protection agencies follow up all anonymous tips alleging child abuse, Estrada argues. Social workers would no longer waste time chasing down false allegations and be able to keep a closer watch on families — home schooling or not — already known to be at risk, he says.

## Is home schooling academically superior to public schooling?

Despite representing only a tiny percentage of all students, home-schooling has produced many children who have shone on the academic stage. In 1997, Rebecca Sealfon of Brooklyn, N.Y., became the first home-schooled student to win the Scripps Howard National Spelling Bee, and numerous children educated at home followed in her footsteps. In 2000, the first-, second- and third-place finishers were home-schooled.[22]

Home-school advocates also cite the results of 1998 and 2009 surveys, in which home-educated students "typically score 15 to 30 percentile points above public-school students on standardized achievement tests," said Brian D. Ray, president of the National Home Education Research Institute (NHERI), a Salem, Ore., think tank that produces and disseminates information mainly about Christian home schooling.[23]

However, top academic education researchers note that none of the studies conducted so far of home-schooled students' provides a statistically valid picture of the average academic achievement of a home-schooled student compared to that of an average student in a traditional public school. That's because the surveys of home-schooled children's achievement — except for state studies in Alaska and Arkansas — have involved only home-schooled students who volunteered to be surveyed. Results from such self-selected groups produce no information about actual statistical averages and therefore cannot be validly compared with the existing research on public school students, which is based on a random sampling and does provide information about the average student's achievement.

The 1998 study of home-schooled students, for example, included 20,760 students who volunteered to be surveyed. It showed that such students "scored significantly higher" on widely used student-achievement tests than the average of either public- or private-school students "in every subject and at every grade level," says HSLDA, which commissioned the survey. The study found that home-schooled students in grades 1 through 4 performed one grade level higher than the average traditionally schooled student. At grade 5 the score gap began widening, until it was four grade levels above the national average by grade 8. The research was conducted by Lawrence Rudner, vice president for research at the Reston, Va.-based Graduate Management Admission Council, which sponsors the Graduate Management Admission Test (GMAT).[24]

In a 2009 study by NHERI's Ray, the average scores of a volunteer group of 11,739 home-schooled students ranged between the 84th and 89th percentile on a set of subject-matter achievement tests.[25] And that survey too is "frequently cited as definitive evidence" that home-schooled students do better academically than traditionally schooled students, says Milton Gaither, an associate professor of education at Messiah College, a nondenominational Protestant institution with roots in the Anabaptist and Mennonite traditions, in Mechanicsburg, Pa.

But because all respondents in both surveys were volunteers, their performance reveals nothing about the average performance of the entire home-schooling population, says Gaither, a home-schooling father and author of the 2008 book *Homeschool: An American History*. Statistically, the main finding of the studies is the same that virtually all studies of academic achievement now confirm: that socioeconomic status (SES) plays a determining role in student achievement, Gaither says. "It's all SES. If you're a rich kid, you're going to do well," regardless of educational venue.

The International Center for Home Education Research, of which Gaither is a founding member, concurs. The families of the students surveyed in the cited studies have been "far whiter, more religious, more married, better educated and wealthier than national averages" for home-schooling families, the group says. "We simply can't draw any conclusions about the academic performance of the 'average home-schooler,' because none of the studies so often cited employ random samples representing the full range" of students educated at home, according to the scholars' group.

When the academic achievement of small but random samples of home-schooled students has been evaluated, the scholars say, analyses do not generally back up the claim that home-schooled youngsters far outperform traditionally schooled students.

In fact, a large study of Canadians, ages 24-39, educated in public, private and home schools, found that children educated at home "reported far lower rates of preparedness for college than all private school graduates," said Gaither. The Cardus Education Survey also found that home-schooled students "were more likely to attend 'open admission' universities (the least selective kind of higher education), less likely to attend prestigious universities, and in general less likely to attend college and especially graduate school," he continued. Their SAT scores were also lower than the other private-schoolers in the sample.[26]

Among the states, Alaska and Arkansas gather and publish some of the most extensive, randomly sampled data on home-schooled students' achievement, says Coleman, the Indiana University doctoral student. Arkansas found third- through ninth-grade home-schooled students scored above the 60th percentile, on average — far higher than their public school counterparts. In math, however, home-schooled students lagged slightly behind public school students, scoring, on average, at or below the 50th percentile in third through ninth grade.[27]

Alaska's data — which cover only part of the state's home-schooling population — show that "when we corrected for economic situation, home-school students' reading scores are about the same as the public school students' scores," Coleman says.

As for the approximately 10 percent of children learning at home who are "unschoolers" — students who decide

## Half of States Lightly Regulate Home Schooling

Twenty-six states require minimal or no regulation of home schooling, with 11 of those states requiring no contact at all between a home-schooling parent and state education authorities. Two dozen states and the District of Columbia require a moderate to high degree of regulation of home schooling. The five states with the greatest amount of regulation are in the Northeast.

### Levels of State Regulation of Home Schooling

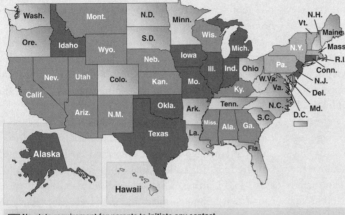

■ No state requirement for parents to initiate any contact.
■ Low regulation: State requires parental notification only.
■ Moderate regulation: Parents must notify the state and send test scores and/or professional evaluation of student progress.
■ High regulation: Parents must notify the state and send achievement test scores and/or professional evaluation, plus other requirements (such as state approval of curriculum or parents must be qualified as teachers).

*Source:* Home School Legal Defense Association, https://www.hslda.org/laws/

Some argue that home schooling is a valuable alternative for students who struggle in ordinary classrooms and a potentially good source of insights for improving traditional schools. Others, however, argue that any such help home schooling might offer is trivial compared to the serious threat it could pose to public education in a diverse democracy: depriving large numbers of students the experience of working and learning together with people different from themselves.

As public schools struggle with the 21st-century need to educate all students to a level that was unheard of half a century ago, home schooling could provide both temporary and long-term assistance, some commentators say.

Large public school classrooms that impose standardized expectations on all students simply don't work well for some children, home-schooling advocates contend. That's especially the case, they say, with students who have learning disabilities or who are unusually gifted.

The University of Georgia's Fields-Smith says home schooling can benefit both children who don't learn well in conventional classrooms and those in the schools they leave behind. "If Johnny is misbehaving in class, isn't it perfectly possible that Johnny is above what they're trying to teach?" she asks. "Why are smart children sitting in the principal's office? But often the teachers won't even entertain this idea."

At least one Baltimore teacher did entertain the idea of home schooling for one of her gifted students. "Our son had been reading, already in kindergarten, and [the teacher] had 30 people in her class and no TA," or teaching assistant, said Shawn Spence, the student's mother. "She said, 'I can't help him. He is bored. He is spending his entire day with his head down. . . . We can tell that he's just going to be lost here.'" Spence counts her son's home-schooling experience as a great success.[28]

In the long run, says Gary Houchens, an associate professor of educational administration, leadership and

entirely for themselves what interests to pursue — many skeptics question whether they can fare well in college.

But in a study of a volunteer group of unschooled young adults, "absolutely none of them seem to have suffered in any way in terms of learning or higher education," says Peter Gray, a research professor of psychology at Boston College. "Even one who complained that she didn't learn anything because her mother didn't teach her anything, is in an anthropology Ph.D. program at UCLA."

Gray acknowledges that his volunteer survey does not provide solid information about the average unschooler because it was not a random sample.

### Can home schooling help the public school system?

As home schooling grows, analysts debate whether the phenomenon could help or harm public education.

research at Western Kentucky University, the public schools badly need fresh ideas about how to tackle today's tough education demands, and the experiences of home-schoolers might provide some insights.

"The current structures of education have outlived their usefulness," Houchens says. That's largely because, for the first time in history, "we have to figure out how to do something that schools were never designed to do — educate all students to proficiency," he says. It's clear by now that this unprecedented task cannot be achieved using many standard school practices, such as "age-level groupings, a fragmented curriculum, days broken up into 60-minute periods by traditional subject matter such as reading or math, and letter grades," he says.

But what new practices and structures might effectively replace those models remains a mystery, Houchens says. He argues that the embrace of home schooling by more and more parents might provide some answers, if educators study them. "What does it mean that kids can be educated in their own homes at least to a comparable level that they are in schools" and that some people find home-schooling "a personalized model that schools don't provide and that seems to work better for their child?" he asks.

Other analysts, however, argue that no matter what good ideas home-schoolers may have about learning, some varieties of home schooling pose such a serious threat to one of the key purposes of the public schools that the danger may override other considerations. In a diverse democracy, they maintain, public schools are one of the few institutions that routinely encourage children to learn and work with people whose beliefs and backgrounds differ from their own.

If very large numbers of home-schoolers pull their children out of the schools in order to shield them from encountering such differences, this vital function will be undercut, some argue. Even as America becomes more diverse, home-schoolers form ever-larger enclaves of very similar families, such as upper-middle-class professional families in cities such as New York, where home schooling is increasingly common, according to Amy Stuart Wells, a professor of sociology and education at Columbia University Teachers College, in New York City. Wells argues that it's important for learning to "be challenged and confronted with other points of view." To the extent that home schooling doesn't provide such experiences "we have to question [it]," she said.[29]

The strongest statements about the dangers homogeneous home schooling might pose to a society that seeks to be both diverse and harmonious come from abroad, especially from Germany, where home schooling is generally banned in order to discourage religious and ideological isolation.

Some children likely would benefit from the personal attention home schooling provides, wrote Von Henrik Schmitz, a journalist for *Evangelische*, the website of the Evangelical Church in Germany, a federation of several Protestant denominations. Encompassing about 30 percent of the German population, the federation works together on some issues despite theological differences. Nevertheless, Germany's insistence on compulsory attendance at common schools is "an achievement" that "should not be abandoned," he wrote. "Were it not for compulsory education, our society would drift apart," and ideological conflicts would be exacerbated.[30]

On March 3, the Supreme Court refused to hear the appeal of a German evangelical Christian couple, Uwe and Hannelore Romeike, who sought U.S. asylum, arguing that Germany's home schooling ban constitutes religious persecution. In 2013, a federal appeals court denied their request on the grounds that Germany bans all home schooling, not just home schooling for religious reasons.[31]

## BACKGROUND
### Religious Differences

Home schooling did not become a growing trend until the late 20th century, but the religious disputes and dissatisfaction with standardized public education that led some families to home school have a long history in the United States.[32]

America's founders pondered how best to create an educated population to sustain the democratic republic. "I have indeed two great measures at heart, without which no republic can maintain itself in strength," wrote third President Thomas Jefferson. The first is "general education, to enable every man to judge for himself what will secure or endanger his freedom," he wrote. And second, "to divide every county" into subdivisions "of such size that all the children of each will be within reach of a central school in it."[33]

## CHRONOLOGY

**1840s-1910s** *Compulsory schooling spreads. Public schools limit religious activities.*

**1842** New York legislature bans religious instruction in public schools and state funding for religious schools.

**1844** Rumors among Protestants that Catholics want all religious materials removed from public schools spark riots in Philadelphia.

**1852** Massachusetts enacts first compulsory-education law, requiring children ages 8-14 to attend school for 12 weeks annually.

**1896** Education philosopher John Dewey creates the Laboratory Schools of the University of Chicago to demonstrate child-centered learning.

**1920s-1970s** *States struggle to enforce compulsory-attendance laws. Supreme Court limits states' right to regulate nonpublic education. Conservative Protestants grow more distrustful of public schools, and the so-called hippie movement refuels interest in child-centered learning.*

**1925** In *Pierce v. Society of Sisters*, a unanimous Supreme Court strikes down an Oregon ban on private schooling.

**1963** In a case stemming from a Pennsylvania law, the Supreme Court bans daily Bible readings in public schools.

**1972** In *Better Late than Early*, educators Raymond and Dorothy Moore recommend home schooling children up to at least ages 8 or 12.

**1977** Education theorist John Holt founds *Growing Without Schooling*, a magazine promoting the child-centered "unschooling" movement.

**1980s-1990s** *Interest in home schooling grows.*

**1982** After influential evangelical psychologist James Dobson hosts Raymond Moore on his radio program, more families pull their children from public schools.

**1983** The home-schooling legal and legislative support and advocacy group Home School Legal Defense Association (HSLDA) is founded.

**1988** The nation's largest teachers' union, the National Education Association, passes the first of many annual resolutions calling for increased regulation of home-schoolers.

**1992** Between 1985 and 1992, a total of 25 states pass laws explicitly exempting home-schooled children from compulsory school attendance.

**1999** Students being home-schooled total 850,000.

**2000s-Present** *Two decades of advocacy and the rise of the Internet help spur continuing increase in home schooling.*

**2000** The first, second and third place finishers in the Scripps Howard National Spelling Bee are home schooled.

**2011** Federal government finds that 1.8 million Americans ages 5 to 17 are home schooled; scholars say likely undercounting puts the total at more than 2 million, more than attend charter schools.

**2013** HSLDA mobilizes home-schooling families to pressure an Ohio lawmaker to withdraw a bill that would have required school and child-protection officials to check a database of child-abuse allegations before granting requests to home school; the association also mobilizes pressure to get New Mexico to withdraw a regulation requiring parents seeking a faith-based waiver of immunization requirements to state specific reasons. . . . A group of young adults home schooled in conservative Christian families forms the Coalition for Responsible Home Education to urge home-schoolers to develop an accountability system to prevent abuse or neglect of home-schooled children.

**2014** HSLDA persuades Virginia lawmakers to reject a study of the consequences of a state law exempting religiously motivated home-schoolers from oversight.

But in a nation founded on the principle of preserving religious liberty, the question of how public schools would accommodate a range of theological opinion quickly spurred controversy. Many parents preferred that their children not encounter differing theological ideas in school. America's Protestant religious majority mistrusted Catholics, and vice versa, while different Protestant denominations disagreed on theology.

For a time, such disagreements were held in check because taxpayer funds assisted a variety of separate schools "that we would now consider 'private' and religious," wrote Charles L. Glenn, a professor of educational administration and policy at Boston University. While most of them were Protestant, some were Catholic, he noted.[34]

By the mid-19th century, however, a growing influx of Catholic immigrants alarmed many Protestants and spurred them to push for ending tax support for Catholic schooling and for including Protestant studies and activities in the public schools while rigorously excluding Catholic texts or practices.

Some school leaders tried to maintain what they saw as the American principle of religious pluralism. In the 1840s, for example, Philadelphia school officials allowed Catholic children to use the Catholic-approved Douay-Rheims Bible during morning Scripture readings, rather than the Protestant King James translation, and decreed that no child would be forced to participate in religious activities. But the move spurred rumors among Protestants that Catholics were trying to rid the schools of religious material entirely, leading in 1844 to a series of lethal riots in the city.

Weary of the constant, apparently unsolvable, disputes, from the 1840s to the 1870s many public schools phased out religious activities such as Bible reading, most states banned taxpayer funding of religious schools and some banned religious instruction in public schools.

## Compulsory Schooling

The 19th century also saw states enact and expand compulsory-schooling laws, in part to advance Jefferson's aim of producing educated citizens and in part to improve children's lives by banning their use as fulltime workers.

In 1852, Massachusetts was first to require school attendance. With few exceptions, the state required children ages 8 through 14 to attend school for at least three months each year and spend at least six consecutive weeks in class. Other states followed, and over the years the age range was broadened and the number of compulsory days increased. Most Southern states did not compel attendance until the 20th century, but by 1918 compulsory-schooling laws were in place nationwide.[35]

Even as all children were moving into classrooms, however, a renowned American psychologist and philosopher, John Dewey, developed an alternative vision of learning that would play a key role in creating the home-schooling movement.

For the most part, American classrooms have used standardized curricula, to be mastered according to fairly strict timetables, and consisting mainly of facts and skill instruction poured from teachers' minds into students' minds, which have been envisioned as empty vessels.

By contrast, Dewey, who in 1896 founded the Laboratory Schools of the University of Chicago to try out his ideas, sharply criticized the "passive, receptive or absorbing attitude" that traditional classrooms require. Often dubbed "progressive" or "child-centered" education, Dewey's learning philosophy rejects standardized curricula and timetables in favor of personalized learning that follows each student's interests and rate of development.[36]

Many scholars and teachers praised Dewey's ideas as an accurate description of how effective learning occurs. As enrollments swelled and the nation continued to industrialize, however, public schools opted instead for standardization and vocationally oriented curricula.[37]

Meanwhile, in a series of landmark cases challenging the constitutionality of compulsory-school laws, the Supreme Court limited the degree to which states could curtail freedom of choice in education, providing wiggle room for families who sought alternatives to public school.

In 1922 in Oregon, for example, anti-immigrant and anti-Catholic sentiment had spurred passage of a particularly strict law that banned private schooling altogether. In 1925, in *Pierce v. Society of Sisters*, a unanimous court struck down the ban. While states have authority to require students to attend "some school" and to ensure that "certain studies plainly essential to citizenship" be part of each child's education, "the fundamental theory of liberty upon which all governments in this Union repose excludes any general power of the State to standardize its children by forcing them to accept instruction from public teachers

# 'Child-Centered Learning' Finds a Home(school)

*"I was amazed at my own kids."*

Beginning with University of Chicago philosopher John Dewey in the late 19th century, a persistent strain of educational thought has urged educators to stop force-feeding students an adult-created curriculum in favor of tailoring learning experiences to children's individual interests and pace of development. From the beginning, many teachers praised Dewey's ideas — a later version of which eventually became known colloquially as "unschooling" — as an accurate description of how effective learning happens. But schools never really embraced them.

A revival of Dewey's ideas in the 1960s and '70s by critics of traditional classrooms formed the underpinning of the home-schooling movement. And now, as home schooling burgeons, even some conservative Christian homeschooling families with generally authoritarian views have adopted versions of the unschooling approach.

Tailoring learning to the interests and abilities of individual children simply makes sense, many advocates of progressive education say.

For example, the rate at which children learn to read varies enormously, according to Carolyn McKeon, an adjunct and online faculty member in early childhood education at colleges including Northampton Community College, in Williamsport, Pa. For her doctoral dissertation, McKeon, who describes herself as a "radical unschooler" of four sons, interviewed many home-schooling families on the subject of reading. Among her interviewees, she said, were children who learned to read effortlessly, on their own, at age 4 as well as others in the same family who didn't learn until age 10 or 11.

"The middle son didn't really start reading until sixth grade, but as an eighth-grader he read parts of Plato's *Republic* and understood it," one mother said. She told

McKeon that she began early to instruct her children in phonics — reading instruction based on recognizing the sound of letter combinations. She also consistently read good books with them. But when she realized that the children picked up reading at different ages, she "quit worrying and hurrying them," the mother told McKeon. She was rewarded when, as she told McKeon, the children "blossomed before my eyes."[1]

Not just timetables but modes of learning vary widely, unschoolers say. "I was amazed at my own kids," says Beatrice Ekoko, a mother in Hamilton, Ontario, Canada, and co-editor of an independently published 2014 book, *Natural Born Learners*. "They had such unique ways of learning," with one figuring out at age 3 how gears worked and another loving Shakespeare before she could read it herself.

"Being slow to pick up on a major skill" doesn't mean failure at that skill, Ekoko says. "One of my kids learned to read at 4, but the oldest hadn't learned to read well by 8," yet ultimately entered a university on a scholarship. "My youngest learned to read by writing" — wanting to express things on paper and learning words by "asking how you spell this or that," Ekoko says.

Families who choose home schooling for practical reasons — such as to address problems a child is having in school — are most likely to employ progressive approaches. Charles Howell, a home-schooling father and former second-grade teacher who is dean of Beeghly College of Education at Youngstown State University in Ohio, says his son was taken out of school when he didn't respond well "to being forced to do things he wasn't interested in." Meanwhile, his daughter began to be home schooled because of some learning difficulties, he says.

only. The child is not the mere creature of the State," wrote Associate Justice James McReynolds.[38]

## Rise of Home-Schooling

Beginning in the 1960s, two divergent sets of beliefs came together to create the home-schooling movement:

conservative Protestants' objection to lack of religious instruction in public schools and some education reformers' belief that traditional classrooms hinder learning.

Over the years, many evangelical Christians had come to view public schools as "unaccepting of — and perhaps

Schools can be judged based on how child-centered they are as well, Howell maintains. "How responsive the school is to the kids' needs determines how willing the kid is to go there," he says.

Initially, many home-schoolers "try to replicate a school," since that's the educational model most are familiar with, "but over time they begin to mellow out," says Milton Gaither, an associate professor of education at Messiah College, in Mechanicsburg, Pa. "Even a very conservative Christian mother tends to become more progressive." Overall, the pedagogy of much home schooling "is essentially Deweyan," Gaither says, referring to education pioneer John Dewey.

Nevertheless, child-centered education isn't easy. McKeon says that when her children want to do something, "we make it happen."

"Each of my kids is delight-driven, every day," says McKeon. Each year around July, "we talk about, 'What are your goals for the year?' " she says.

At 14, McKeon's third son attended community college for the first time. "He's not going to go right back, though," she says. Music is his passion, she says, and "college classes took away from the five to six hours a day he used to spend on it." He plays bagpipes, after the family conducted an all-out search for a teacher. It's difficult to switch "this model in our head" from adult-centric priorities to child-centric ones, says Pat Farenga, an author and advocate who was a close associate of teacher and educational theorist John Holt, a pioneer of unschooling in the 1970s. "Just the idea of trusting children is hard because we were never trusted."

"When you start this journey, you discover that you have to unschool yourself," says Ekoko. "You have to train yourself to not be so hands-on. You're exposing them to things, but you're not to try to impose things on them. Benign neglect is very important."

Unschooling can sometimes lead to charges of educational neglect, because of traditional schooling's strong presumption "that you have to learn things by a particular time," says Farenga.

Critics also take aim at some subjects that may simply be skipped when children decide what to learn. For example,

Movie stars Angelina Jolie and Brad Pitt are among a number of celebrities and entertainers who home school their children.

"I don't teach my kids math," says McKeon. Nevertheless, when her oldest son decided to go to community college, he entered at the lowest level of math remediation and worked his way to algebra in a year. "He could do it well because he knew how to learn, and it was important to him" to master the prerequisites for future study, she says.

Some believe that student-centered learning is the wave of the future.

"Once there is a tipping point, when everybody knows someone who is doing this, and they're doing OK — getting jobs, going to college — people may start to ask, 'Why do I have to fight my kid over school?' " says Peter Gray, a research professor of psychology at Boston College. "Whenever people see that there is a real choice, they choose freedom."

— *Marcia Clemmitt*

[1] Quoted in Carolyn C. McKeon, "A Mixed Methods Nested Analysis of Homeschooling Styles, Instructional Practices, and Reading Methodologies," dissertation, Capella University, 2007, http://tinyurl.com/pqhyvau.

even hostile toward — their moral instruction," and some mid-20th-century modernizing trends increased that mistrust, says Indiana University's Kunzman. For example, he says, by teaching sex education and evolution, public schools incorporated teachings that conservative Protestants viewed as directly contradictory to their faith.

Then, in 1962 the Supreme Court prohibited oral readings in New York state public schools of a prayer especially composed for the purpose by the state's Board of Regents. And in a 1963 landmark Pennsylvania case, the court banned daily devotional Bible readings in any public school.[39]

# Home-Schooling Is Mostly Moms' Job

*Strong religious beliefs can shape how women see the work.*

In home-schooling families of all kinds, mothers do most of the teaching. How women envision and cope with home schooling's rigors varies significantly, though, depending on philosophical and religious beliefs, scholars say.

Home schooling "takes an incredible amount of work for the person doing it, and most of that falls on mothers," says Jennifer Lois, a sociology professor at the University of Western Washington, in Bellingham, and author of the 2012 book *Home Is Where the School Is.* Between 2002 and 2009 Lois conducted in-depth interviews for the book with 24 home-schooling mothers. Twenty-one were Christian, 14 politically and religiously conservative; and 21 were white. Most of the mothers were college graduates.

In the home-schooling boom of the 21st century, highly paid working women who are not evangelical Christians have grown somewhat more likely to home school than in the past, leaving their jobs to do it, says Lois. The non-evangelical mothers in Lois' sample chose home schooling because of problems, such as bullying, that their children experienced in conventional classrooms, not because they philosophically oppose public schools or traditional classroom teaching.

The entrance of such women into the home-schooling ranks "dovetails with a trend of the past half century" in society's view of mothering, Lois says. As women have entered the workforce in great numbers, there has been "a progressive ratcheting up of what it means to be a good mother," she says. As reflected in headlines in parenting magazines and in advertising imagery, it is sometimes called the trend of the supermom.

"We increasingly ask mothers to have a very close relationship with all of their children, to know all their friends,"

Lois says. That leaves many women feeling pressured both to work and to be highly involved superparents, and home schooling provides the opportunity for both — a job and 24/7 parenting rolled into one. "I do think there's an element of this" in the recent boom, Lois says.

Home-schooling parents of all sorts generally acknowledge that "there's potential for a lot of conflict and emotional button-pushing" between home-schooling parents and their children, says Lois. But conservative Christian and other home-schooling mothers generally describe such problems quite differently, Lois says.

Non-evangelical moms are more likely to remark that "we're not meant to be together all the time; we're not well matched for that," Lois says. In her study, Lois found these mothers also were more likely to home school for only a few years and to say that they wished their children's fathers would contribute more to home schooling, she says.

By contrast, most evangelical Christian women whom Lois studied made very long-term home-schooling commitments, often lasting from preschool through high school, most likely because they view home schooling as part of their commitment to their religious faith, she and other scholars say.

The fact that many home-schooling evangelical mothers view home schooling as an integral part of their faith — and virtually a requirement for some evangelical Christians — also changes how many evangelical mothers view its stresses. Evangelical mothers tended to describe conflicts less as problems and more as opportunities "to figure out ways to make their relationships with their children grow," Lois says.

Basing one's home-schooling philosophy on strong religious faith may lead to greater commitment even among

In response, some conservative Christian families quietly began teaching their children at home.

Meanwhile, some education analysts were reviving Dewey's criticisms of traditional schooling. John Holt was a fifth-grade teacher whose first critique of schools, *How Children Fail*, was published in 1964. Learning is hard — sometimes impossible — when children must follow adults' predetermined plans but flourishes when

children's own interests lead the way, Holt declared.[40] By the mid-1970s, he had shifted his attention from urging classroom teachers to use child-centered approaches to exploring possibilities for learning outside of the schools and providing information to a small group of mostly liberal families who practiced what came to be called unschooling — home schooling in which children's own desires entirely determine what they do and learn.

women who hold some feminist views. "Much as I loved what [feminist] women did for us in the '80s, I thought it was a false idea that I could be both a professional and a great mom," says Carolyn McKeon, a Pennsylvania-based Christian home-schooling mom who works as a facilitator for home-schooling families and as a college instructor in early-childhood education.

Feminism stresses the importance of empowering women, "but I am empowering my kids," says McKeon, who is home schooling her four sons fulltime from pre-school through high school by the "unschooling" method, in which children's individual interests set the entire curriculum.

Many religiously conservative home-schoolers are not motivated by feminist ideals, however.

"The wife's job is to stay home and home school the husband's children," says Rachel Coleman, who was home schooled in an evangelical Christian family. "That goes back to the 19th century, when men and women had separate spheres. The man does the public things. The woman is in the home." Coleman, a Ph.D. candidate in U.S. history at Indiana University, is a home schooling researcher and author of a master's thesis on the subject. In addition, she started *Homeschooling's Invisible Children*, a website that tracks home schooling-related child abuse.

Coleman says the division of labor between males and females is evident at the many Christian home-schooling conferences held around the country each year. Male headliners typically dominate the speaker lists, Coleman says. "The women are home schooling, the guys are keynoting," she says.

Among at least a small group of conservative Christian home-schoolers, the embrace of a patriarchal system — in which males have the authority — can lead to educational neglect of girls, say Coleman and others. "More of these stories are coming to light as more home-schooled young adults come of age," Coleman says.[1]

Erika Diegel Martin was pulled out of public school to be home schooled at age 14, but when she was ready to try for a GED that would provide potential employers or post-secondary educational institutions with proof of her high-school education, "the girls weren't allowed [by their parents] to get [one] because we were told we wouldn't need it," she said. "It would open up opportunities that were forbidden to us. . . . When I talked about wanting to go to college, my parents said, 'Well, you're a girl. You don't go to college.'"[2]

Debate over home schooling sometimes touches on its costs, and in such discussions an often hidden factor in society's view of female roles comes to light, said Milton Gaither, an associate professor of education at Messiah College, a nondenominational Protestant liberal arts school in Mechanicsburg, Pa., with roots in the Anabaptist and Mennonite traditions. "Home schooling is perhaps the purest expression of the failure of modern economics to account for the economic and social contributions of mothers," he said.

Even many home-schooling advocates "claim, insultingly, that home schooling only costs a family a few hundred dollars a year," said Gaither. "Tell that to the women who do it. Home-schooling costs them a lot more than that."[3]

— *Marcia Clemmitt*

---

[1] For background, see Homeschoolers Anonymous, http://homeschoolersanonymous.wordpress.com, a website where young adults home schooled in some fringe groups tell their stories, and Kathryn Joyce, *Quiverfull: Inside the Christian Patriarchy Movement* (2010).

[2] Quoted in Kristin Rawls, "Barely Literate? How Christian Fundamentalist Homeschooling Hurts Kids," Alternet, March 14, 2012, www.alternet.org/story/154541/barely_literate_how_christian_fundamentalist_homeschooling_hurts_kids?page=0%2C1&paging=off&current_page=1#bookmark.

[3] Milton Gaither, "Does Homeschooling 'Work': A Critique of Advocacy Research," International Center for Home Education Research Reviews, Sept. 2, 2013, http://icher.org/blog/?p=827.

By 1980, the two trends — one conservative and one countercultural — together had led to no more than a few tens of thousands of children being home schooled. Numbers would soon soar, however, as some influential evangelical Christian leaders embraced home schooling.

In 1972, Raymond Moore — a California teacher, public school administrator and college president — and his wife, Dorothy, a remedial-reading specialist, published a critique of traditional schooling with similarities to Holt's. *Better Late than Early* recommended home schooling children up to at least age 8 and perhaps age 12, to allow them to develop interests at their own pace and to provide time for strengthening families' emotional bonds.

The Moores' prioritizing of family life resonated with conservative Protestants, but their recommendations failed to take hold, at least partly because the couple were

Seventh-day Adventists. Founded in the 1840s in the United States, the Adventist church celebrates the Sabbath on Saturday, and for this and other reasons some Protestants do not regard its members as true Christians.

In 1982, however, Raymond Moore appeared on a weekly radio show hosted by evangelical Christian psychologist James Dobson, founder of the social-conservative advocacy group Focus on the Family. When Dobson gave Moore a national platform to promote home schooling, "it was huge for evangelicals" and encouraged many families to take the leap, says Coalition for Responsible Home Education founder Coleman.

"The Dobson interviews were the instrument that God used to introduce" home schooling to two couples who would become some of its strongest advocates, Michael and Vickie Farris, then of Washington state, and J. Michael and Elizabeth Smith, then of California, who in 1983 founded the Home School Legal Defense Association (HSLDA), according to a 2007 obituary tribute to Moore in the HSLDA's *The Home School Court Report*.[41] In 2000, Farris went on to found Patrick Henry College, a conservative, evangelical Protestant institution in Purcellville, Va., that is especially welcoming to home-schooled students.[42]

During the second half of the 1980s, the home-schooling population increased as much as sixfold to around 300,000, mostly among conservative Protestants.[43]

## Home-School Boom

Home schooling's initial boom saw Christian conservative home-schoolers and liberal unschooling families sharing support, scholars say.[44] After a few years, however, many groups split along religious lines. Unschoolers' belief in the "inherent goodness of children did not sit well with conservative Protestants, who tended to balance their high regard for children's potential with a strong conviction about the inherent sinfulness of humankind," wrote Mitchell Stevens, an associate professor of sociology at the Stanford University School of Education.[45]

Views also diverged about how best to protect families' rights to home school.

In the early 1980s, laws in most states neither permitted nor banned teaching children at home. Numerous court rulings had declared that states must allow parents to choose alternatives to public school education. Nevertheless, states and localities also had leeway to regulate education, including penalizing families when school officials deemed children truant from school and imposing some academic standards on private schools and home schools. Six states required home-schooling parents to hold teaching licenses, for example.[46]

Home-schoolers realized they would need to defend their right to home school, by opposing restrictive rules such as the teaching-license requirement. Nevertheless, many believed that the legal foundations for home schooling were strong and that many public officials could be persuaded to respect the Supreme Court's declarations that parents had a right to school choice. Moore claimed that in at least 80 percent of disputes over home schooling, "local public school administrators and primary teachers . . . are understanding," according to Indiana University's Coleman.[47]

The Supreme Court had repeatedly upheld parents' constitutional right to educate their children according to their own principles, including in cases such as *Pierce v. Society of Sisters*. With a general constitutional right to educational freedom well established, enacting multiple state laws specifically permitting home schooling might actually make the legal right to home-school appear weaker, some argued.[48]

To many in the conservative Christian home-schooling movement, though, the 1980s legal landscape seemed fraught with danger. "Home education was treated as a crime in almost every state" as school officials accused home-schooling families of truancy, wrote HSLDA attorney Scott Somerville in 2001. Accused parents "had no legal excuses, no useful precedents" to back up the "unwritten freedom" to home school, he wrote.[49]

Taking this view, HSLDA waged many legal and legislative battles, on several fronts. They sought enactment of state laws that explicitly declared home schooling legal, defended families accused of breaking compulsory-attendance laws and sought the rollback of home-schooling requirements such as submitting test scores or academic reports to schools.

HSLDA's approach got strong backing from some influential conservative Christians. Calvinist theologian Rousas John Rushdoony testified in courts around the country on behalf of Christian home-schoolers battling school rules. Rushdoony's advocacy sprang from his belief that Christ will return only after believers have transformed Earth into God's kingdom.[50] Key to the transformation will be "control of education and of the child," he said. "Hence, for Christians to tolerate statist education, or to allow their children to be trained thereby, means to renounce power in society . . . and to deny Christ's lordship over all of life."[51]

Between 1985 and 1992, a total of 25 states passed laws explicitly exempting home-schooled children from compulsory attendance.[52] By the mid-1990s, regulation had eased everywhere, and home-schooling numbers were rising steadily, a trend that continues today.

Home schooling had become a far easier choice than in the past, scholars say. And the rising numbers made it more familiar and thus a more comfortable choice for parents. Media portrayals, too, were becoming less negative than in earlier decades, says Joseph Murphy, a professor of education at Vanderbilt University's Peabody School of Education, in Nashville, Tenn.

The rise of the Internet also played a huge role, says Messiah College's Gaither. Families could easily find learning materials of innumerable kinds. No state requires the use of any specific curricular materials, and home-school students use everything from extremely structured arithmetic workbooks to materials produced by small companies specifically for Christian conservative home schoolers, such as biology textbooks that teach so-called young Earth creationism. There are also video games and museum and government websites.

The Internet has allowed parents to share materials with one another online, effectively breaking a monopoly that HSLDA had held on information and support, Gaither says. Now home-schooling families could seek help and information from like-minded parents near and far.

## CURRENT SITUATION

### Coming of Age

Home schooling's steadily increasing numbers have established it firmly in the educational mainstream. Home-schooled students comprise about 3 to 4 percent of the country's student population, and home-schooled children outnumber students enrolled in charter schools, which are increasingly popular among public school parents.[53]

"The market has responded" to parental demands for help, adding to the increased home-school numbers, says unschooling expert Pat Farenga, an author and advocate who was a close associate of teacher and educational theorist John Holt, an unschooling pioneer in the 1970s. For example, to keep antsy teenagers from demanding to enroll in or return to school, businesses, nonprofits and home-schooling families have created tutoring programs, online courses, field trips, resource centers and co-ops that sponsor social events and provide pricey art and science equipment, he says.

Businesses providing curriculum materials and services such as online courses to home schoolers today constitute "a billion-dollar industry," says HSLDA's Estrada.

And while the numbers are impossible to pin down precisely, home-schooling demographics are gradually broadening. More families today home school for what Indiana University's Coleman calls "pragmatic" reasons, such as to remove a child from a bullying situation or meet special learning needs that are hard for large classrooms to accommodate. Researchers point out that pragmatic home-schooling parents tend to home school for fewer years than those who home school for religious reasons.

Another growing phenomenon is the popularity of home schooling among urban professionals, says Gina Riley, a New York-based educational psychology researcher who has studied home-school and unschool parents. Often such parents "are seeing this as a way to set their kids apart" when college-application time rolls around, says Riley. "I've gotten a lot of calls from people talking about getting their kids into the Ivies."

Finding like-minded people with whom to share information and support online may help drive demographic diversification. Online support groups exist for many faiths and ethnicities. Home schooling is on the rise, at least to some degree, among Native Americans, Hawaiian natives, Catholics, Jews, Muslims and other groups.[54] In the most recent federal data, 8 percent of home-schooled students were identified as non-Hispanic blacks, 15 percent as Hispanics, and 4 percent as non-Hispanic Asians or Pacific Islanders — all slightly lower percentages than in the general population.[55]

Furthermore, "I was amazed by the diversity of income, family structure and education level I found" among home-schooling African-American families, says Fields-Smith of the University of Georgia.

However, an "unhappy paradox" exists when black people home school, she says. "We've always looked to

AT ISSUE

# Should states let home-schoolers play on public school teams?

## YES   Isaac Sommers
*Policy Analyst,*
*Texas Home School Coalition*

Written for *CQ Researcher*, March 2014

Twenty-eight states already permit home-schooled students to participate in athletic teams and other competitive extracurricular activities, such as debate, governed by state school associations like Texas' University Interscholastic League (UIL). They do so for good reason: By home-schooling, parents save states billions of dollars. Home-schooling in Texas saves almost $3.5 billion annually, and the parents of home-schoolers pay property taxes that fund public schools. Unfortunately, current policy in Texas and some other states bars home-schooled families from participating in extracurricular activities that their taxes help to fund.

In Texas, this legislative oversight has its roots in discriminatory policy. In 1913, Texas law established UIL activities for all Texas students. Two years later, however, eligibility was restricted to white, public school students. (Ironically, the majority of Texas students were home schooled at the time.) Finally, in 1967, the right of minority groups to participate was recognized and restored, but home-schooled students continue to be deprived of this simple yet important opportunity.

To counter this discrimination, several Texas legislators, as well as home-school advocacy groups like the Texas Home School Coalition, have worked tirelessly to promote legislation fondly referred to as the Tim Tebow bill, named for the home-schooled Heisman Trophy winner who played football thanks to Florida's equal-participation law. The bill would allow home-school students who live in and pay for a given public school district, and who meet the eligibility specifications required of public school students, to try out for that school's UIL activities. Simple provisions in the bill would prevent failing public school students from attempting to game the system by claiming they are "home schooled."

Determinations that students meet grade-average requirements are easily made by requiring written verification of passing grades from parents, who are home-schooled students' legally recognized teachers. Considering that home school students who participated in a number of large studies have scored an average of 30 points higher on national standardized achievement tests than their public school peers, we can easily create a trustworthy system that provides equal opportunity to each student. This allows students to excel both academically and athletically, regardless of the method of their education.

The Tim Tebow bill would ultimately benefit families — especially those in rural areas — by restoring equality to the UIL system.

## NO   William C. Bosher Jr.
*Distinguished Professor of Public Policy,*
*Virginia Commonwealth University*

Written for *CQ Researcher*, March 2014

For public school administrators who have historically supported school choice and competition, so-called Tebow bills allowing home-schooled students to participate in public school extracurricular activities offer a conundrum. It would seem that true advocates of choice should oppose any limitation to it; however, equality must be balanced with equity. What may seem like an effort to treat all students the same could actually treat some students unfairly. Students who must comply with attendance requirements, maintain grade-point averages and meet behavior expectations would compete for team slots with students who cannot be held to the same rules. Unfairness could also result if public school teams began recruiting home-schooled athletes.

Many home-schooling parents approach the issue as taxpayers. It is certainly true that home-schoolers as well as the 70 percent of homes with no school-age children heavily support the school system. However, it is also true that most citizens opt out of particular public services without being entitled to any benefit or compensation for taxes paid. If I choose never to use a public library, the purchases for my Nook are not paid by the public sector. If I never use a public recreation facility, my private gym fees will not be subsidized.

When I served as a local school superintendent and as state superintendent for Virginia, prorated funding was awarded to public schools when home-schooled and private school students participated in their programs. The focus of that policy was on academics, however, which have been and should remain the focus of school-choice movements. Nonpublic school students were guaranteed access to classes, but if they wanted to participate in extra activities such as athletics, they needed to enroll. Tim Tebow is admirable for his faith, athletic ability and role-model status, but what if the next "Tebow" movement presses for allowing home-schooled students to stand for election as student government president or homecoming queen?

Tebow bills proposed in many states have become a marketing tool for home-schoolers to advance an emotional rather than a rational appeal for fairness. But why were home-schooling policies first created? To solidify the right of each family to teach its children at home in its own way. That being the case, the push for Tebow laws violates home-schoolers' core mission, since at the same time as home-schooling families are seeking even greater separation from state requirements for academic testing, they are requesting much closer integration with public schools through athletics.

public school for racial uplift," so families who decide to remove their children often are criticized for disloyalty to that concept, she says. Much African-American home schooling is pragmatic, she says. "It's often just one kid who's home-schooled, and it's often a boy. Parents will say, 'Well, the kid is a nonconformist, and the school doesn't know what to do with him.'"

Even as diversity rises, though, white, conservative Protestant home-schoolers may be growing more homogeneous, at least in some ways, say Gaither at Messiah College and others.

In interviews with Indiana home-schoolers, Coleman found that some who began for pragmatic reasons gradually adopted strict conservative Christian views after joining support groups led by veteran home-schoolers. And, according to Coleman's research, as home-schoolers who aren't conservative Christians migrate to their own support groups, some older Christian home-schooling groups focus even more on adopting strict Christian worldviews and parenting approaches.[56]

Several scholars of conservative Christian home schooling have found that "the longer you [home school], the more hardcore you become," says Gaither. For many, home schooling "gradually becomes not just something you've done for your kid, but part of a general opting out of mainstream America. The women start wearing long dresses" to demonstrate modesty, for example, he says.

## Home Schools and Government

As more parents tackle home education, and some public schools see pupils and dollars slip away to home schooling, more schools and families are considering working together.

Since public schools are allotted government dollars based on the number of pupils they enroll, districts where home schooling's growth is greatest inevitably lose cash. Arizona's Maricopa County school district, for example, had lost $34 million by the year 2000 because 7,526 students were being home-schooled.[57] In response, the district offered popular courses in subjects such as sign language and karate to home schooled students and reaped funds for each home-schooling pupil who enrolled.

Such arrangements are not the norm, but some states, as well as some individual districts and schools, allow home-schooled students to enroll part time. Laws in states including Hawaii, Iowa, New York and Utah provide for

some such arrangements.[58] Also on the books — in states such as Arizona, Minnesota and Ohio and under debate in others — are laws or state athletic association rules permitting home-schooled kids to participate in extracurricular activities such as sports teams.[59] Known as Tim Tebow laws, some of this legislation was inspired by the story of Heisman Trophy winner and former NFL quarterback Tebow, a home-schooled student who played football at a public high school after Florida passed legislation allowing it.[60]

The Home School Legal Defense Association (HSLDA), meanwhile, continues to oppose regulatory requirements for parents. For instance, HSLDA was instrumental in killing an Ohio bill that would have required school superintendents and child-protection workers to consult child-abuse databases for prior abuse allegations before signing off on requests to home school.[61] Also in 2013, HSLDA persuaded New Mexico officials to scrap a requirement that home-schooling parents who opt out of state immunization requirements explain their specific reasons for doing so.[62]

In 2014, HSLDA members persuaded Virginia lawmakers to kill a bill calling for a study of whether a state law exempting from oversight families who home school for religious reasons might allow some parents to neglect their children's education.[63]

"Right now the HSLDA continues to run the policy world," says Indiana University's Kunzman. But with home-schooled students now numbering in the millions, it's not clear whether continued rollback of regulation will prevail.

"There are times when the state abuses its privilege by getting involved in people's lives, but that doesn't mean the state never has a role to play," such as by setting basic academic requirements to help "balance the rights of young people with those of their parents," Kunzman says.

## OUTLOOK

### Part of the System?

Few question that home schooling has become a mainstream phenomenon. Whether home schools have lessons to teach traditional schools — and whether traditional schools would learn them — remains in doubt, however. There is also the question of whether and how the home-schooling community will respond to public concerns about abuse or educational neglect.

Many home-schooling parents take highly individualized approaches to teaching their children, a fact that argues powerfully against the increasing standardization of public education, says HSLDA's Estrada. The lesson for public schools is, "Let's just, for crying out loud, let teachers teach," he says, and "get state and federal departments of education out of it." But whether public schools and home-schoolers can cooperate "is up to the teachers' unions," which he says looks doubtful since unions continue to recommend greater regulation of home schooling.

Meanwhile, however, while many early home-school proponents embraced the principles that home schooling should recognize the individual needs and interests of a child, many conservative Christian home-schoolers took an opposite tack, said Heather Doney, a writer and blogger who was home schooled in what she says was an abusive and socially isolated evangelical Christian household until age 13.[64]

The home-schooling situation in which she and her nine siblings grew up before her grandparents intervened and sent them to public school "is a framework where parents have all the power" and in some cases make "extreme" choices about what is good for their children, such as hitting them "with objects," placing them in arranged marriages and, in the case of girls, discouraging them from attending college or, in some cases, even completing high school, said Doney.

She urges home-schoolers who don't condone such practices to speak up in support of greater oversight. "Vulnerable populations [such as children] do best when there are multiple checks and balances tasked with ensuring that they are well treated by the dominant group (in this case, adults)," she argues. "Stop being so scared of government that you don't allow it" to do its job, "which is to keep citizens (including children) safe."[65]

Home-schoolers' black-and-white view of both public schools and home schools blocks progress toward cooperation, says Indiana University's Coleman. "From the inside, the rhetoric about public schools is so negative," she says. "I'd been taught that no one who went to public schools ever learned to think for themselves. When I got to college, I was shocked at how many creative people I met who'd been to public schools."

By the same token, idealizing home schooling, as many of its advocates do, is also off the mark, Coleman says. A healthier and more accurate view would be to deem it "a neutral tool that can be used for great good or great evil, depending on the parents."

## NOTES

1. Quoted in Michel Martin, "Brother Wants Parents to Stop Siblings' Homeschooling," *Tell Me More*, NPR, Aug. 6, 2013, www.npr.org/templates/story/story.php?storyId=209512311; and "Josh Powell, Class of 2014," Department of Sociology, Georgetown University, Aug. 6, 2013, http://sociology.georgetown.edu/page/1242728833848.html.

2. Martin, *op. cit.*, and Susan Svrluga, "Student's Homeschooling Highlights Debate Over Va. Religious Exemption Law," *The Washington Post*, July 28, 2013, p. A1, www.washingtonpost.com/local/students-home-schooling-highlights-debate-over-va-religious-exemption-law/2013/07/28/ee2dbb1a-efbc-11e2-bed3-b9b6fe264871_story.html.

3. "How Many Homeschoolers Are There in the United States?" U.S.-Focused FAQs, International Center for Home Education Researcher, http://icher.org/faq.html; and Amber Noel, *et al.*, "Parent and Family Involvement in Education, from the National Household Surveys Education Program of 2012: First Look," National Center for Education Statistics, August 2013, http://nces.ed.gov/pubs2013/2013028.pdf.

4. "How Many homeschoolers Are There in the United States?" *ibid.*

5. "Table 40. Number and percentage of homeschooled students ages 5 through 17 with a grade equivalent of kindergarten through 12th grade, by selected child, parent, and household characteristics: 1999, 2003, and 2007," *Digest of Education Statistics*, National Center for Education Statistics, https://nces.ed.gov/programs/digest/d11/tables/dt11_040.asp.

6. For background, see "Homeschooling's Invisible Children," http://hsinvisiblechildren.org; and

"Children killed or abused within their homeschooling adoptive family," Pound Pup Legacy, http://poundpuplegacy.org/node/20821.

7. "U.S.-focused FAQs," International Center for Home Education Research, http://icher.org/faq.html; and Milton Gaither, "Homeschooling Goes Mainstream," *EducationNext*, Winter 2009, http://educationnext.org/home-schooling-goes-mainstream. Also see Noel, *et al.*, *op. cit.*

8. *Ibid.*

9. For background, see Rachel S. Cox, "Home Schooling Debates," *CQ Researcher*, Jan. 17, 2003, pp. 25-48; and Thomas J. Billitteri, "Parental Rights," *CQ Researcher*, Oct. 25, 1996, pp. 937-960.

10. "U.S.-focused FAQs," *op. cit.*

11. "B-82 — Homeschooling," 2012-2013 NEA Resolutions, p. 249, www.nea.org/assets/docs/2013-NEA-Handbook-Resolutions.pdf.

12. Scott A. Woodruff, "Why the Religious Exemption From School Attendance Belongs and the Study Proposed in HJ 92 Is Unnecessary," Home School Legal Defense Association, www.hslda.org.

13. Milton Gaither, "Brian D. Ray and NHERI, Part I," *Homeschooling Research* Notes, Sept. 30, 2008, http://gaither.wordpress.com/2008/09/30/brian-d-ray-and-nheri-part-1.

14. *Ibid.*

15. "Attorney Michael P. Farris, Esq.: Homeschool Conference Speaker and Workshop Leader Details," Balancing the Sword, www.balancingthesword.com/homeschool/speakers/speaker_detail.asp?ID=2406.

16. Laura Brodie, "Should Homeschooling Parents Have College Degrees: Round Two," *Love in a Time of Homeschooling* blog, *Psychology Today*, July 28, 2010, www.psychologytoday.com/blog/love-in-time-homeschooling/201007/should-homeschooling-parents-have-college-degrees-round-two.

17. Rob Reich, "Why Homeschooling Should Be Regulated," 2005, www.stanford.edu/group/reichresearch/cgi-bin/site/wp-content/uploads/2011/01/Reich-WhyHomeSchoolsShouldBe Regulated.pdf.

18. "House Bill 1427: Removing Common Core Standards in Indiana," Home School Legal Defense Association, www.hslda.org/cms/?q=bill/house-bill-1427-removing-common-core-standards-indiana, and 7. "Will the Common Core Impact Home Schools and Private Schools?" HSLDA: Common Core Issues, www.hslda.org/commoncore/topic7.aspx.

19. For background, see "Themes in Abuse: An Introduction," Homeschooling's Invisible Children, http://hsinvisiblechildren.org/themes-in-abuse, and Mary McCarty and Margo Rutledge Kissell, "Home School Oversight Lacking, Investigation Finds," *Dayton Daily News*, March 17, 2012, www.daytondailynews.com/news/news/home-school-oversight-lacking-investigation-finds/nMzRG.

20. For background, see "Child Neglect," American Humane Association, www.americanhumane.org/children/stop-child-abuse/fact-sheets/child-neglect.html; and "Would you report a homeschooling family for educational neglect if . . ." The Well Trained Mind Community, Dec. 2, 2011, http://forums.welltrainedmind.com/topic/328906-would-you-report-a-homeschooling-family-for-educational-neglect-if.

21. Meggan Goodpasture, V. Denise Everett, Martha Gagliano, Aditee P. Narayan and Sara Sinal, "Invisible Children," *North Carolina Medical Journal*, January/February 2013, www.ncmedicaljournal.com/wp-content/uploads/2013/01/74124-goodpasture-posting.pdf.

22. "Homeschoolers Making Headlines," *The Home School Court Report*, Home School Legal Defense Association, July/August 2000, www.hslda.org/courtreport/V16N4/V16N402.asp.

23. Brian D. Ray, "Research Facts on Homeschooling," National Home Education Researcher Institute, Jan. 1, 2014, www.nheri.org/research/research-facts-on-homeschooling.html, and *Homeschool Progress Report: 2009*, www.hslda.org/docs/study/ray2009/2009_ray_studyfinal.pdf.

24. "Home Schooling Works: Pass It On," Home School Legal Defense Association, www.hslda.org/docs/study/rudner1999/Rudner0.asp.

25. *Homeschool Progress Report 2009, op. cit.*

26. Milton Gaither, "The Cardus Education Survey and Homeschooling," *Homeschooling Research Notes* blog, Sept. 23, 2011, http://gaither.wordpress.com/2011/09/23/the-cardus-education-survey-and-homeschooling.

27. Rachel Coleman, "Homeschoolers and Academics: The Alaska Data," *The Politics of Childhood* blog, Nov. 19, 2013, http://politicsofchildhood.org.

28. Quoted in Michel Martin, "Parents on the Pros and Cons of Homeschooling," *Tell Me More*, NPR, Aug. 6, 2013.

29. Quoted in Lisa Miller, "Homeschooling, City-Style," *New York Magazine*, Oct. 22, 2012, http://nymag.com/guides/everything/urban-homeschooling-2012-10/index2.html.

30. Von Henrik Schmitz, "Die allgemeine Schulpflicht muss erhalten bleiben," "Compulsory Education Must Be Maintained," *Evangelisch.de*, Jan. 27, 2010, www2.evangelisch.de/themen/gesellschaft/die-allge meine-schulpflicht-muss-erhalten-bleiben10753.

31. Sarah Pulliam Bailey, "Supreme Court Rejects Asylum Bid for German Homeschooling Family," *The Washington Post*, March 3, 2014, www.washingtonpost.com/national/religion/supreme-court-rejects-asylum-bid-for-german-home-schooling-fam ily/2014/03/03/06a987e8-a31b-11e3-b865-38b254d92063_story.html.

32. For background, see Milton Gaither, *Homeschool: An American History* (2008); Joseph F. Murphy, *Homeschooling in America: Capturing and Assessing the Movement* (2012); and *School: The Story of American Public Education* (2001), PBS, www.pbs.org/kcet/publicschool/about_the_series/program.html.

33. Thomas Jefferson, letter to John Tyler, May 26, 1810, "American History from Revolution to Reconstruction and Beyond," University of Groningen [Netherlands], Faculty of Arts, www.let.rug.nl/usa/presidents/thomas-jefferson/letters-of-thomas-jefferson/jefl205.php.

34. Charles L. Glenn, "Disestablishing Our Secular Schools," *First Things*, Jan. 1, 2012, www.firstthings.com/article/2011/12/disestablishing-our-secular-schools.

35. "State Compulsory Attendance Laws," *Infoplease*, www.infoplease.com/ipa/A0112617.html.

36. John Dewey, "My Pedagogic Creed," *The School Journal*, Jan. 16, 1897, pp. 77-80, http://playpen.meraka.csir.co.za/~acdc/education/Dr_Anvind_Gupa/Learners_Library_7_March_2007/Resources/books/readings/17.pdf.

37. David F. Labaree, "Progressivism, Schools and Schools of Education: An American Romance," *Paedagogica Historica*, February 2005, pp. 275-288, www.stanford.edu/~dlabaree/publications/Progres sivism_Schools_and_Schools_of_Ed.pdf.

38. *Pierce v. Society of Sisters*, 268 U.S. 510 (1925), www.oyez.org/cases/1901-1939/1924/1924_583; for background, see Paula Abrams, *Cross Purposes: Pierce v. Society of Sisters and the Struggle Over Compulsory Public Education* (2009), http://muse.jhu.edu/books/9780472021390?auth=0.

39. The cases are *Engel v. Vitale*, 370 U.S. 421 (1962) and *Abington School District v. Schempp*, 374 U.S. 203 (1963).

40. Marlene Bumgarner, "A Conversation with John Holt," The Natural Child Project, www.natural child.org/guest/marlene_bumgarner.html.

41. "The Passing of a Pioneer," *The Home School Court Report*, Home School Legal Defense Association, September/October 2007, www.hslda.org/courtre port/V23N5/V23N503.asp.

42. "The Man Behind the Parental Rights Amendment," Patrick Henry College, www.phc.edu/20090429_parental.php.

43. Robert Kunzman, *Write These Laws on Your Children: Inside the World of Conservative Christian Home-schooling* (2009), p. 4.

44. Mitchell Stevens, *Kingdom of Children: Culture and Controversy in the Homeschooling Movement* (2001), p. 6.

45. *Ibid.*, p. 25.

46. Rachel Coleman, "A Brief History of Homeschooling," Politics of Childhood, May 16, 2013, http://politic sofchildhood.org/2013/05/16/a-brief-history-of-homeschooling.

47. Quoted in *ibid.*

48. Larry and Susan Kaseman, "HSLDA's 'History' Erodes the Foundations of Our Freedom," *Home Education Magazine*, September-October 2001, homeedmag.com/HEM/185/sotch.php.

49. Scott W. Somerville, "The Politics of Survival: Home Schoolers and the Law," Home School Legal Defense Association, www.hslda.org/docs/nche/000010/politicsofsurvival.asp.

50. Chris Smith, "His Truth Is Marching On," *California Magazine*, Cal Alumni Association/UC Berkeley, Fall 2012, http://alumni.berkeley.edu/california-maga zine/fall-2012-politics-issue/his-truth-marching.

51. Quoted in Cheryl Seelhoff, "A Homeschooler's History, Part I," *Gentle Spirit Magazine*, Vol. 6, No. 9, P. 37, http://a2zhomeschooling.com/documents/hsh1.pdf; original quotation in J. Rousas Rushdoony, "The Philosophy of the Christian Curriculum," in Samuel Blumenfeld, "The Reconstructionist View of Education," *Chalcedon Report*, February 1996, p. 12.

52. Stevens, *op. cit.*, p. 14.

53. Noel, *et al.*, *op. cit.*

54. Gaither, "Homeschooling Goes Mainstream," *op. cit.*

55. "Table 7: Number and percentage of all children ages 5-17 who were homeschooled and homeschooling rate, by selected characteristics 2011-2012," *op. cit.*; and "People Quick Facts: USA," United States Census Bureau, http://quickfacts.census.gov/qfd/states/00000.html.

56. Milton Gaither, "Coleman on Homeschoolers in Middletown," *Homeschooling Research* Notes, May 24, 2010, http://gaither.wordpress.com/2010/05/24/coleman-on-homeschoolers-in-middletown.

57. Gaither "Home Schooling Goes Mainstream," *op. cit.*

58. "State Laws Concerning Participation of Home-school Students in Public School Activities," Home School Legal Defense Association, September 2013, www.hslda.org/docs/nche/issues/e/equal_access.pdf.

59. For background, see Joey Johnston, "A Cut Above," *Tampa Tribune/Tampa Bay Online*, Dec. 25, 2005, web.archive.org/web/20070109042139/http://gators.tbo.com/gators/MGBQVFCAMHE.html; and Mike Schwartz, "'Tim Tebow' Law for Students Signed in South Carolina," NFL.com, Aug. 21, 2012, web.archive.org/web/20070109042139/http://gators.tbo.com/gators/MGBQVFCAMHE.html; and "State Laws Concerning Participation of Homeschool Students in Public School Activities," *op. cit.*

60. Johnston, *ibid.*

61. For background, see Raymond L. Smith, "Teddy's Law Would Battle Child Abuse," *Tribune Chronicle* [Warren, Ohio], Dec. 17, 2012, www.tribtoday.com/page/content.detail/id/597010.html, and "Senate Bill 248: Require Children's Services Review for Homeschooling," Home School Legal Defense Association, Dec. 19, 2013, www.hslda.org/cms/?q=bill/senate-bill-248-require-childrens-ser vices-review-homeschooling, and "Victory! SB 248 Suspended No More Calls Needed at This Time," Home School Legal Defense Association, Dec. 19, 2013, www.hslda.org/elert/archive/elertarchive.aspx?6879.

62. For background, see "Positive Change to Immunization Waiver Form," Home School Legal Defense Association, Dec. 6, 2013, www.hslda.org/hs/state/nm/201312060.asp.

63. Susan Svrluga, "Virginia Lawmaker Seeks to Clarify Education Law on Religious Exemptions," *The Washington Post*, Jan. 14, 2014, www.washington post.com/local/education/virginia-lawmaker-seeks-to-clarify-education-law-on-religious-exemptions/2014/01/14/71a686dc-7c8c-11e3-9556-4a4bf7b cbd84_story.html, and "Call Committee to Protect the Religious Exemption," Home School Legal Defense Association, Jan. 17, 2014, www.hslda.org/elert/archive/elertarchive.aspx?6901.

64. Heather Doney, "About Me," *Becoming Worldly* blog, http://becomingworldly.wordpress.com/about-me.

65. Heather Doney, "To Homeschooling's 'Old Guard': 20 Truths You Need to Hear," *No Longer Quivering*, Patheos, May 13, 2013, www.patheos.com/blogs/nolongerquivering/2013/05/to-homeschoolings-old-guard-20-truths-you-need-to-hear/.

# BIBLIOGRAPHY

## Selected Sources

## Books

Gaither, Milton, *Homeschool: An American History*, Palgrave Macmillan, 2008.
An associate professor of education at Messiah College, in Mechanicsburg, Pa., describes the roots of American home schooling in the Colonial era and the historical forces that created the home-schooling boom over the past several decades.

Kunzman, Robert, *Write These Laws on Your Children: Inside the World of Conservative Christian Homeschooling*, Beacon Press, 2009.
An associate dean for teacher education at the Indiana University School of Education, in Bloomington, profiles several home-schooling families, analyzing ways in which conservative Christian home schooling may or may not contribute positively to children's education, with a special emphasis on citizenship education and the families' political participation.

Lois, Jennifer, *Home Is Where the School Is: The Logic of Homeschooling and the Emotional Labor of Mothering*, New York University Press, 2012.
Through in-depth interviews conducted in 2002 and again in 2008-2009, a professor of sociology at the University of Western Washington, in Bellingham, explores how the philosophical and religious beliefs of 24 home-schooling mothers help shape their and their children's experiences.

Murphy, Joseph F., *Homeschooling in America: Capturing and Assessing the Movement*, Corwin, 2012.
The chair of Vanderbilt University's Peabody College of Education, in Nashville, describes the forces behind the current boom in home schooling and discusses home-schooling's place in the educational landscape, with its focus on privatization and choice.

## Articles

"The Everything Guide to Homeschooling," *New York*, Oct. 4, 2012, http://tinyurl.com/o9lsyst.
A series of *New York* magazine stories introduces the people and activities of a relatively small but possibly growing home-schooling trend: home schooling by urban professional families who are not conservative Christians but who hope to use cities' multiple resources to enrich their children's education with an eye to college admission and other achievements.

Anne, Libby, "HSLDA: Man Who Kept Children in Cages 'A Hero,'" *Love, Joy, Feminism blog, Patheos*, May 6, 2013, http://tinyurl.com/ofhwy3g.
A home-schooled woman who left her church and blogs at Patheos under a pseudonym argues that mainstream home-school advocates don't do enough to distinguish between responsible and reckless home schooling, allowing some abusers to hide their crimes.

Johnson, Hannah, "Learning at Home," *Bakken Breakout* [North Dakota], Feb. 9, 2014, http://tinyurl.com/ohdj2ej.
A North Dakota home-education support group is rapidly gaining members, partly because the state's oil boom is drawing many workers to the area whose transient employment makes it more convenient to teach their own children rather than repeatedly pulling them out of school.

Marshall, Konrad, "Home-schooling on the Rise," *The Age* [Melbourne, Australia], Jan. 30, 2014, http://tinyurl.com/kgpy2hr.
Home-schooling numbers are growing outside the United States, doubling in the Australian state of Victoria over the last six years, for example.

Milweard, Christy, "Public School Online," *KFVS* [Cape Girardeaux, Mo.), Jan. 31, 2014, http://tinyurl.com/khftt9l.
More families may consider keeping their children out of public school if states make free online public schooling available as an alternative to other forms of home education, a Missouri survey suggests.

Woodruff, Betsy, "With Iowa Trip, Cruz Courts Homeschoolers," *The Corner, National Review Online*, Feb. 11, 2014, http://tinyurl.com/me8en2p.
This spring, Sen. Ted Cruz, R-Texas, long a favorite of home-schoolers in his state, could become the first 2016 presidential contender to reach out to home-schooling families in Iowa, a key state for those seeking their party's presidential nomination.

## Reports and Studies

**"Parent and Family Involvement in Education,"** National Center for Education Statistics, August 2013, http://tinyurl.com/n5wz5yo.
The latest edition of this recurring government survey describes families' reasons for home schooling and includes demographic data.

**Goodpasture, Meggan, V. Denise Everett, Martha Gagliano, Aditee P. Narayan and Sara Sinal, "Invisible** Children," NCMJ, January/February 2013, http://tinyurl.com/ox2xmws.
The North Carolina Pediatric Society Committee on Child Abuse and Neglect has asked the state to beef up oversight capabilities of North Carolina's Division of Nonpublic Education after studying cases in which children were murdered by parents who were — or who claimed to be — home schooling.

# For More Information

**A2Z Home's Cool**, http://a2zhomeschooling.com. Online publication and resource website on all aspects of home-schooling, founded by a longtime home-schooling mother.

**Coalition for Responsible Home Education**, www.responsiblehomeschooling.org. Advocates for greater protection against abuse and educational neglect.

**Homeschool Alumni Reaching Out**, http://homeschoolersanonymous.wordpress.com/haro. Largely founded by young people home-schooled in conservative Christian traditions to shed light on abuse of some home-schooled children.

**Homeschool Legal Defense Association**, P.O. Box 3000, Purcellville, VA 20134-9000; 540-338-5600; www.hslda.org. The main legal defense and legislative advocacy group for home-schoolers, chiefly oriented toward conservative Christians.

**Homeschool World, Home Life Inc.**, P.O. Box 1190, Fenton, MO 63026-1190; 636-343-6786; www.home-school.com. Website of conservative Christian home-schooling pioneer Mary Pride; has home-schooling information and commentary.

**International Center for Home Education Research**, 812-856-3382; http://icher.org. Scholars committed to non-advocacy home-schooling research.

**John Holt GWS**, www.johnholtgws.com. Provides information and commentary on home-schooling; "unschooling," and the work of John Holt.

**National Home Education Research Institute**, P.O. Box 13939, Salem, OR 97309; 503-364-1490; www.nheri.org. Conducts surveys of home-schoolers and disseminates commentary and information to the public and lawmakers.

# 5

# Tea Party Movement

Peter Katel

Republican Scott Brown celebrates in Boston on Jan. 19, 2010, after winning a special election to fill the seat of the late U.S. Sen. Edward M. Kennedy. Tea Party activity typically occurs in Republican territory — "red states" — in the South, West and Midwest. But Tea Party activists also cite Brown's upset election in Massachusetts, considered among the bluest of blue states, as indicative of their broad appeal.

From *CQ Researcher*, May 23, 2011.

I t's lock and load time, a pumped up Dana Loesch told several thousand attendees at the Conservative Political Action Conference (CPAC) in Washington last month. "We're in the middle of a war. We're fighting for the hearts, minds and souls of the American people."

Forget politeness, the St. Louis-based radio host and Tea Party activist told the equally energized crowd. "It's all about amplifying your voice." Conservatives, she said, should declare often and loudly, "'I don't like Barack Obama.'"

And as for the president's supporters, said the 31-year-old home-schooling mother, "Make them uncomfortable. . . . Attack, attack, attack. Never defend."

Many tea partiers may favor a softer approach, but Loesch's take-no-prisoners intensity reflects the dynamic and triumphant spirit emanating from the country's newest political trend, which arose in early 2009 in reaction to economic stimulus legislation, corporate bailouts and the Democrats' health insurance reform effort.

Indeed, as CPAC's enthusiastic embrace of Loesch and other tea partiers makes clear, the Tea Party movement is on the cutting edge of a conservative surge that aims to undercut, or even defeat, the Obama administration and what foes call its big-government, socialist agenda. Tea partiers are also trying to push the national Republican Party to the right, with Tea Party-affiliated candidates this year running in GOP primaries for at least 58 congressional and state offices, including three governorships.

A major wing of the movement, Tea Party Patriots, has helped set up a fundraising arm, Liberty Central, in the Washington suburb of Burke, Va. Its president and CEO is Virginia Thomas, wife of

## Tea Partiers Running in 25 States

At least 58 candidates — mostly Republican — in 25 states in the upcoming election say their beliefs align with those of the Tea Party movement. Most are running for House seats, but three candidates are in contention for governorships.

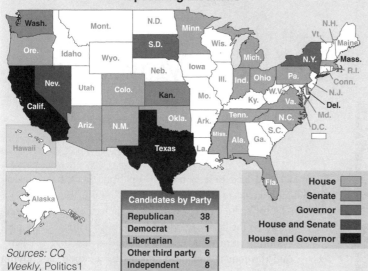

**States with Tea Party-aligned Candidates in Upcoming Elections**

| Candidates by Party | |
|---|---|
| Republican | 38 |
| Democrat | 1 |
| Libertarian | 5 |
| Other third party | 6 |
| Independent | 8 |

House
Senate
Governor
House and Senate
House and Governor

*Sources: CQ Weekly*, Politics1

"At a time of heavy recession and joblessness, giving banks a bailout rankles people across the spectrum," says Joseph Lowndes, a University of Oregon political scientist. "A lot of Brown supporters might have been in that camp."

But a vote for Brown doesn't equate to Tea Party membership, he adds, because the movement's sharply defined conservative political perspective doesn't travel well across the left-right divide. "A lot of people who are independents and disenchanted with Obama aren't going to be tea partiers," he says.

The decentralized and loosely defined Tea Party movement takes its name from the Boston Tea Party — the 1773 protest against British taxation. Tea Party Patriots is a national grassroots organization that claims to support more than 1,000 community-based Tea Party groups around the country. The Patriots-organized Tax Day protests last year drew 1.2 million people, says Tea Party activist Jenny Beth Martin of Woodstock, Ga., a founder of the group. She and her husband lost their home and filed for bankruptcy in August 2008 after their business failed. They owed $510,000 to the Internal Revenue Service (IRS). "We've been hit by the financial crisis and the recession," Martin told Fox News, just like other "everyday Americans."[3]

Martin was especially angered by the federal bailouts of ailing banks and financial institutions by the outgoing Bush administration just before the 2008 presidential election and then of the auto companies in 2009 by the incoming Obama administration. After her husband's temp firm failed, "We started cleaning houses and repairing computers to make ends meet," she told Fox News, while big corporations that were struggling got billions in aid from the federal government. "We were saying, these businesses they were bailing out, there's already a [bankruptcy] process in place," she said. "We've gone through it. It sucks and it's not fun, but its part of how the system works."

Supreme Court Justice Clarence Thomas. She appeared on the same CPAC platform with Loesch and two other movement members. Obama's "hope and change agenda certainly became a leftist agenda pretty fast," she said. "We saw what they were doing, and it was just a big ol' power grab."[1]

The movement proved itself a political force to be reckoned with in the special Senate election in January of Republican Scott Brown for the Massachusetts Senate seat held by the late liberal Democratic lion, Edward M. Kennedy.[2]

"The Tea Party movement had a lot to do with that election," says John Hawkins, publisher of the online *Right Wing News.* "[Brown] had millions and millions of dollars flooding in from the Internet, which showed people getting energized and excited." And some on the left acknowledge that the Tea Party campaign for Brown could have stirred support among Republican and GOP-leaning independents.

Grassroots anger at political and business elites has fueled political movements on both the right and left throughout history. A prolific right-leaning blogger, University of Tennessee law professor Glenn Harlan Reynolds, even views the Tea Party as continuing another tradition — the Great Awakening evangelical religious movements that have emerged periodically throughout American history. "It's a symptom of dissatisfaction with politics as usual," he says.

But Republican Indiana Gov. Mitch Daniels is more cautious. "I wouldn't overestimate the number of people involved," he told *The New York Times*, also offering faint praise to tea partiers' "net positive" effects on the party.[4]

Indeed, doctrines supported by some Tea Party followers would give pause to many politicians. Featured speakers at a Nashville Tea Party convention in February included, aside from former Alaska Gov. Sarah Palin, Web news entrepreneur Joseph Farah, who said Obama may not qualify for the presidency because of his possible foreign birth. Another speaker, ex-Republican Rep. Tom Tancredo of Colorado — known for his anti-immigrant stance — urged voter literacy tests, a discriminatory practice rooted in the Jim Crow South. "Because we don't have a civics literacy test to vote," Tancredo said, "people who couldn't even spell 'vote' — or say it in English — put a committed socialist ideologue in the White House named Barack Hussein Obama."[5]

For some on the left, the Tancredo and Farah appearances — along with xenophobic and racist signs and

## Tea Partiers Have 'Unfavorable' View of Obama

More than three-quarters of Tea Party supporters have unfavorable views of President Obama, compared with a third of all Americans. Forty-four percent of tea partiers think erroneously that the administration has raised taxes, compared with 24 percent of all Americans.

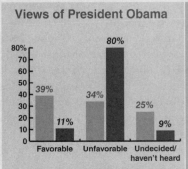
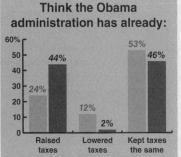
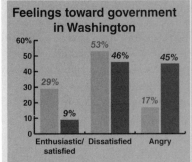

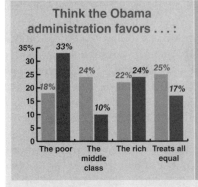

*\* Percentages may not add up to 100 due to rounding or respondents who didn't answer*

Source: CBS News/NY Times Poll, Feb. 11, 2010

slogans that have popped up at other Tea Party events — represent the core identity of the movement. "Tea Partiers have unjustly and unfairly targeted the Latino community to further their political agenda," say the organizers of a new Facebook community called *Cuéntame* ("tell me about it").[6]

Others insist that anti-immigrant xenophobia represents only a fringe. "I was concerned that the anti-immigrant people would try to hijack the Tea Party movement, and they have tried," said Grover Norquist, president of Americans for Tax Reform and a longtime Washington-based conservative who favors liberalized immigration policies. "Not succeeded to date."[7]

In any event, most Tea Party activists stayed away from the $549-per-person Nashville event, organized by the group Tea Party Nation, a social-networking site focusing on social issues that some other Tea Party activists discourage; among Tea Party Nation's "strategic partners" is Farah's *WorldNetDaily*. "It wasn't the kind of grassroots organization that we are, so we declined to participate," said Mark Meckler, a cofounder of Tea Party Patriots (TPP).[8]

The TPP network, which represents the movement's mainstream, steers away from social issues and instead has forged a consensus largely on economic matters: Government spending should be cut, government should be limited and the free-market system should prevail. Specifically, members argue, the federal government shouldn't expand its role in a health-care system that they say already provides adequate care to the poor and the elderly.

"Even if this bill were to have me insured tomorrow, it's still not the right thing to do for America," says Georgia TPP activist Martin. Although she and her husband lost their health coverage when his business failed, they oppose pending health-care legislation on the grounds it would add to the federal budget. "There are a lot of people in this movement who are unemployed. They don't want to burden future generations."

Martin shares a background in Republican politics with many other Tea Party activists — and a critical attitude toward the party. "There's no question the GOP has lost the mantle of fiscal responsibility and small government," writes John M. O'Hara, a former Labor Department staffer in the George W. Bush administration. But, he adds, "The GOP is the most likely breeding ground for the fiscally responsible constitutionalists the Tea Party movement — and America — craves."[9]

A rally O'Hara helped to organize last year in Washington was part of a series of protests that launched the movement. A cable TV moment provided the mobilizing spark: On Feb. 19, 2009, CNBC business reporter Rick Santelli launched a tirade against a plan by the new Obama administration to help homeowners facing foreclosure.

"How about this, President and new administration?" Santelli yelled from the floor of the Chicago Board of Trade. "Why don't you put up a Web site to have people vote on the Internet as a referendum to see if we really want to subsidize the losers' mortgages."[10]

Santelli went on: "We're thinking of having a Chicago Tea Party in July. All you capitalists that want to show up to Lake Michigan, I'm gonna start organizing." Within four days, Santelli's rant had been viewed 1.7 million times on the CNBC Web site.[11]

O'Hara and others used Twitter and other social-network links to find compatriots and launched their rallies on Feb. 27. Protesters showed up in more than a dozen cities — including Atlanta, Fort Worth, Nashville, New York, St. Louis, San Diego Omaha and Tampa.[12] Later events included a Sept. 12 march on Washington promoted by conservative Fox News commentator Glenn Beck.

But fledgling activist Keli Carender — who blogs as "Liberty Belle" — beat them all to the punch. The 30-year-old Republican convert organized a Feb. 16 rally in her hometown, liberal Seattle, against the Obama administration's economic stimulus bill, which she dubbed "porkulus."[13]

Carender's playful approach — she distributed pulled pork at the event — seems distant from Loesch's militancy at the CPAC convention. So distant, in fact, that the conservative *Washington Examiner* issued a warning that echoed the remarks of some in the Republican establishment. "The approach [Loesch] suggests . . . could easily be mistaken for a rallying cry for angry yelling," the paper said. "She must realize that when it comes to making change, it's not about who yells loudest but who actually makes people want to listen. Claiming that the tea parties and conservative activists have declared war on the left only serves to marginalize the right."

As the tea partiers gear up to challenge politics as usual in the 2010 congressional elections later this year, here are some of the questions being raised about the movement:

## Does the Tea Party represent only a narrow segment of the population?

Some Tea Party activists are quite candid about what they see as the movement's base. "They've been listening to Rush Limbaugh for years, they've been railing against the mainstream media for years, they've been voting Republican for years," J. P. Freire, a *Washington Examiner* editor and Tea Party activist, said at a Washington panel discussion in February organized by the America's Future Foundation, which trains young conservatives in economics. "I'm talking about mom-and-pop suburban dwellers."

Indeed, some key Tea Party issues do coincide with key Republican positions: The federal budget deficit is out of control; the administration's health-care proposal is unnecessary and fiscally risky; the $787 billion stimulus represented a grave threat to the nation's economic health.

Only three Republican senators voted for the stimulus. And party leaders have been arguing ever since that the stimulus didn't fulfill Obama's promise to jumpstart the economy and create and save jobs. Celebrating Republican gubernatorial victories in New Jersey and Virginia last November, GOP Chairman Michael Steele condemned "an incredibly arrogant government in Washington that has put our country, our freedoms and our economy at risk with unprecedented spending."[14]

Tea partiers insist they don't just blame Obama and the Democrats for excessive spending. "There was a loss of enthusiasm for Republicans" triggered by deficit spending, says blogger and law professor Reynolds, who co-founded Porkbusters, a political initiative that attacked Republicans as well as Democrats for allegedly wasteful spending. "It was one of the things that cost them Congress, and cost them the whole 2008 election."

Tea Party activity typically occurs in Republican territory —"red states" — in the South and Midwest. Like the GOP itself, Tea Party event attendees are overwhelmingly white. But Tea Party activists also cite Brown's upset election in Massachusetts, considered among the bluest of blue states, as indicative of their broad appeal.

"A lot of Democrats voted for Scott Brown," says Reynolds. "And he had massive Tea Party support. That is at least an indicator we're moving beyond the red state-blue state thing."

While labeling the Tea Party a red-state trend "isn't entirely false," he says, the number of "disaffected Democrats" is growing. "I actually think you'll see this spread to an insurgency in the Democratic Party." The theory is that the Tea Party appeals to a bipartisan sense that Congress and the White House are listening only to powerful lobbyists and not looking out for the interests of the average American.

But non-tea partiers view the movement as fitting comfortably within the Republican fold. "Given the pretty fervent conservatism that exists in this group, it is unlikely that there are a significant number of Democrats in it," says John Sides, a political scientist at George Washington University who studies political polarization. "You may be able to find people who say they voted for Obama, but I don't think that is the central tendency of the movement."

In fact, he argues, the concentration of conservatism in suburbs and smaller cities will make it difficult for the Tea Party to build strength in big urban centers. But the movement could play a big role in areas that are up for grabs. "You can imagine that activism by the Tea Party could have a measurable impact on 'blue dog' [conservative, usually Southern] Democrats in close races," he says.

Indeed, a cofounder of the TPP points to the movement's popularity outside of red-state America. "Three of the five coordinators in New York City are Democrats," says Georgia activist Martin. And she says she's ready for the emergence of a New York politician of either party who supports Tea Party principles but who is too socially liberal to win an election in her state.

Martin spent years as a Republican Party volunteer, heading Sen. Saxbe Chambliss' reelection campaign in her county. But she deplored his vote for the TARP (Troubled Asset Relief Program) bill — the emergency "bank bailout" legislation enacted in October 2008, signed into law by George W. Bush a month before Obama was elected. She has renounced completely partisan activity and doesn't exempt the GOP from criticism on big spending. But she acknowledges, "I think the Republican Party is probably the one most Tea Party people more closely align with."

Georgetown University historian Michael Kazin says the movement's espousal of strict market principles determines the Tea Party's political makeup. "It's hard to think of too many people who voted for Barack Obama who really care about the budget deficit."

Kazin, who specializes in populism and other social movements, draws a distinction between the Tea Party and other grassroots upsurges. "Social movements aren't as connected to one of the main parties as this one seems to be. I know that leaders of the Republican Party are trying to appear more moderate, but clearly if you have tens or hundreds of thousands of people whose views you would like to use, you don't push them out."

## Will the Tea Party movement reshape the Republican Party?

It remains to be seen whether the Tea Party can foment national political change. But some political observers think the movement is well-placed to drive the GOP rightward, especially on economic policy issues. Others say it's a fringe faction that ultimately will lose steam.

One outcome is fairly certain: The Tea Party movement would be seriously undercut if it evolved into a third political party — historically the route taken by new movements that want to broaden the national debate. Most Tea Party activists argue against such a move. "If you create a third party you guarantee that it's going to split Republican votes and guarantee socialist Democrat victories," says *Right Wing News* publisher Hawkins. He predicts that the Tea Party instead will effectively take over the GOP.

To be sure, the prevailing view in liberal circles is that the Republican Party has already moved far to the right. Even some senior Republicans are delivering much the same message.

"To those people who are pursuing purity, you'll become a club not a party," Republican Sen. Lindsey Graham of South Carolina told *Politico*, a Washington-based online newspaper, last November. He spoke following the failed attempt by Conservative Party candidate Doug Hoffman to win a congressional seat in upstate New York, replacing the Republican incumbent, who was judged by the party establishment as too liberal. (Democrat Bill Owens won the seat.)

"Those people who are trying to embrace conservatism in a thoughtful way that fits the region and the state

and the district are going to do well," Graham said. "Conservatism is an asset. Blind ideology is not."[15]

Some Washington-based conservatives question the possibility that any movement based on political principles can exert deep and lasting influence on the political process, where fulltime participants tend to act as much — or more — from self-interest as from ideology.

A movement that channels itself into a party inevitably suffers the dilution of its ideas, a conservative writer argued during the February panel discussion in Washington organized by the America's Future Foundation. "Politics is a profession, and the temptation, once we're in charge, is to say, 'We're going to fix everything, we're going to solve everything,' not realizing that people involved in these parties are human beings and susceptible to compromise," said Kelly Jane Torrance, literary editor of the Washington-based *American Conservative* magazine.

The absence of a Tea Party institutional presence makes its absorption by professional politicians inevitable, she added. "People seem to need a charismatic leader or organizer or an institution, which is why I think the movement is basically being eaten up by the Republican Party," she said.

But some Tea Party activists argue that promoting their ideas within the GOP is essential if the movement is to avoid being marginalized. "There's got to be communication with the political party establishment," says Karin Hoffman, a veteran Republican activist from Lighthouse Point, Fla. "The Democratic Party has done everything to ridicule the movement," she says, while the GOP platform "matches what the grassroots movement feels."

Hoffman orchestrated a Washington meeting this February between 50 Tea Party-affiliated activists and Republican Chairman Steele. Hoffman says she's on guard against the danger of Tea Party activists becoming nothing more than Republican auxiliaries.

"I've not been happy with how Republicans have behaved," she says, citing the reduced-price system for prescription drugs under Medicare that President Bush pushed through in 2003. "We don't need an increase in government."

Disillusionment with Bush is commonplace among tea partiers, who tend to have been Bush voters in 2000 and 2004. The shift in their support — or, alternatively, their view that he abandoned principles they thought he shared with them — underscores the potential obstacles to reshaping national parties. "Even with a relatively diffuse organization, they can have influence just because of visibility, and can pull conventions and rallies," says Sides of George Washington University. "But that's not a recipe for transformational change."

Sides cites the history of the Club for Growth, an organization of economic conservatives that rates lawmakers on their votes on taxes, spending and related issues. "No one would say that the Club for Growth has been able to remake the Republican Party," Sides says, "but it has exerted influence in certain races."

Republican consultant and blogger Soren Dayton disputes that view. "If you look at the electoral and policy successes of the conservative movement — look at the Republican Party," Dayton said at the America's Future Foundation event. "Abortion, guns and taxes are settled issues. If you're an activist on these issues, the point is actually changing the minds of Democrats."

The reason for that ideological victory is easy to identify, Soren said. "We're winning these [electoral] fights on the ground because the Republican Party is solid — because it's been taken over in certain significant ways by conservatives."

### Does the Tea Party attract conspiracy theorists?

Advocates of ideas and policies from far outside the mainstream are the bane of grassroots movements of any stripe. A classic case is the takeover in the 1960s of the New Left by self-styled revolutionaries, who cited Communist Vietnam and China as economic and political models.

Conservative movements, for their part, have always faced the danger of identification with far-right defenders of segregation and, more recently, with those who question President Obama's legitimacy on the grounds of his supposed foreign birth — a notion that has been laid to rest.

Tensions over ideas tinged with discredited notions about race and conspiracies surfaced publicly at the controversial Tea Party convention in Nashville. Speechmakers included Tancredo, the former Republican House member from Colorado. He advocated voter-literacy tests — a now-illegal procedure that was part of segregation law in the Deep South designed to deny

black citizens the right to vote. And *WorldNetDaily's* Farah insisted that Obama's birthplace remains an unsettled issue. "The president refuses to produce documents proving he meets the Constitution's natural-born citizen requirement," *WorldNetDaily* said in paraphrasing his argument.[16]

The publication reported that "the crowd cheered wildly, whistled and applauded" when Farah made his claim. But observers from both right and left reported a different impression.

Jonathan Raban, writing in the left-leaning *New York Review of Books*, said the favorable response was not universal: "I saw as many glum and unresponsive faces in the crowd as people standing up to cheer."[17] And conservative blogger, columnist and professor Reynolds says, "I did not hear a single person say a good thing about Farah or the 'birther' issue."

In fact, the dispute went public. After his speech, Farah engaged in a heated argument outside the convention hall with Andrew Breitbart, publisher of the conservative *Breitbart.com* news and commentary sites.[18] Breitbart called Farah's focus on Obama's citizenship "a fundamentally controversial issue that forces a unified group of people to have to break into different parts."[19]

The surfacing of the tensions among the tea partiers did lend substance to press reports of fringe constituencies attaching themselves to the movement, whose primary concerns publicly center on economic policy.

Les Phillip, a Tea Party candidate for the Republican nomination for a House seat in Alabama, blames the mainstream media for characterizing the Tea Party constituency as "white, racist old men." To be sure, he says, "You do have some folks on the far right." But, he adds, "Most are in the center."

Himself a black immigrant from Barbados, Phillip calls Farah's insistence on the Obama birth issue a diversion. But he voices sympathy for Tancredo's call for voter-literacy tests, despite their unsavory history. "I know more about the country than many people who were born here," he says. "If you're going to be a voter, you need to understand the history and governing documents and how the government should work."

Nevertheless, Lowndes of the University of Oregon argues that racial fears and xenophobia do play a role in some Tea Party movements, whose agendas may vary widely from place to place. "Certainly one does get the

## Tenets of the Tea Party

*The Tea Party Patriots organization says its impetus comes from "excessive government spending and taxation," according to the TPP's Web site. Here are the group's three core values:*

**"Fiscal Responsibility —** *Fiscal Responsibility by government honors and respects the freedom of the individual to spend the money that is the fruit of their own labor. . . . Such runaway deficit spending as we now see in Washington, D.C., compels us to take action as the increasing national debt is a grave threat to our national sovereignty and the personal and economic liberty of future generations.*

**Constitutionally Limited Government:** *We, the members of the Tea Party Patriots, are inspired by our founding documents and regard the Constitution of the United States to be the supreme law of the land. . . . Like the founders, we support states' rights for those powers not expressly stated in the Constitution. As the government is of the people, by the people and for the people, in all other matters we support the personal liberty of the individual, within the rule of law.*

**Free Markets:** *A free market is the economic consequence of personal liberty. The founders believed that personal and economic freedom were indivisible, as do we. Our current government's interference distorts the free market and inhibits the pursuit of individual and economic liberty. Therefore, we support a return to the free-market principles on which this nation was founded and oppose government intervention into the operations of private business."*

*Source:* Tea Party Patriots, www.teapartypatriots.org

sense that the movement is made up mostly of older folks, 50 and older," he says. "I think these are people who are most likely to be uncomfortable with cultural differences and certainly with racial differences."

Racial and cultural concerns may outweigh suspicion of the business establishment, which used to predominate among many of today's Tea Party supporters. They also denounce excessive government intrusion in citizens' lives, though typically with little reference to the Patriot Act, the Bush-era law that expanded government's surveillance and monitoring authority over e-mail and other communications. "If these folks are concerned about overweening executive power, then why did the movement not arise during the Bush years?" Lowndes asks.

Hawkins of *Right Wing News* counters that the same kind of inconsistency shadows the liberal activist world. Antiwar marches and protests of all kinds marked the Bush presidency, he observes. Yet, with tens of thousands of U.S. troops fighting hard in Afghanistan and still present in Iraq, "Where's the antiwar movement?" he asks.

Similarly, he argues, the presence of fringe activists who attach themselves to a broader cause is no less a problem on the left than on the right. "There's a very tiny percentage of people who generally are not welcome at tea parties," Hawkins says, adding that he distinguishes members or sympathizers of the militia movement from those who question Obama's presidential eligibility. "I guarantee you that, percentage-wise, there are as many Democrats who think Bush stole the election in 2004 as people who think Barack Obama is not a citizen. I would put those as complete equivalents."

Sides, of George Washington University argues, however, that the Tea Partys' big tent may limit the movement's effectiveness for reasons that go beyond issues of political respectability. The presence of the "birthers" and some militia members, along with people concerned about taxes and spending, likely will add to what he sees as a fundamental weakness. "There is an extraordinarily diffuse organizational structure with a lot of internecine conflict," he says. "That makes coalescing extremely difficult."

## BACKGROUND

### People's Party

Historians trace the origins of populism to the early years of the new republic. President Andrew Jackson, who served two terms (1829-1837), helped formulate the fear that a financial elite threatened popular control of national institutions.[20]

Jackson's distrust of "money power" led him to veto a bill to extend the charter of a privately owned national bank that served the federal government as well as private interests. "It is to be regretted that the rich and powerful too often bend the acts of government to their selfish purposes," his veto message said.[21]

Jackson's admonition resounded for generations. But it wasn't until the late 19th century that a national political movement was organized to wrest control of the country from intertwined political and business classes. The People's Party of America, formed in 1892 in St. Louis, united an array of activists that included small farmers from the South and Great Plains who were overwhelmed by debt; the Woman's Christian Temperance Union, which advocated alcohol prohibition; two early union organizations, the Knights of Labor and the American Federation of Labor; and evangelical Christians with socialist politics.

All saw themselves as oppressed by big business and its political allies. The prohibitionists viewed big business as profiting from the vice of alcoholism. But the Populists — as they were dubbed — dodged the issue of race because they counted on Southern supporters of segregation.

Still, the Populist alliance generated enough enthusiasm to drive a presidential campaign in the 1892 election. The Populist candidate, former Union Army officer James B. Weaver, garnered 8.5 percent of the national vote, an impressive showing for a third-party candidate.

Realizing that their party stood no chance of winning the presidency on its own, the Populists forged an electoral alliance in 1896 with the Democratic Party (founded by Jackson). The Democrats' nominee was William Jennings Bryan, who had worked closely with the Populists as a House member from Nebraska.

Known for his spellbinding oratory, Bryan wanted the U.S. currency based on both gold and silver, not just gold. That would lower the value of debt-ridden farmers' obligations by lowering the value of the dollar.

"Having behind us the commercial interests and the laboring interests and all the toiling masses," Bryan said in his electrifying speech to the Democratic Convention that nominated him, "we shall answer their demands for a gold standard by saying to them, you shall not press down upon the brow of labor this crown of thorns. You shall not crucify mankind upon a cross of gold."[22]

However, the Democrat-Populist alliance proved no match for the Republicans. Populists' weaknesses included their strong ties to the Farm Belt and support of strict Protestant moral codes — turn-offs to big-city voters, many of them Catholic immigrants.

Republican William McKinley won the election, which marked the high point of the People's Party's fortunes. By 1908 it had dissolved.

## Right Turn

Populist leaders spoke eloquently of corporate oppression, a classic issue of the left. But their handling of race would seem to place them on the political right. While Tom Watson, a Georgia Populist leader, made joint speaking appearances with black populists (who had their own organization), he defended Jim Crow laws, as did party rank and file. (After the party ceased to exist, Watson incited and then defended the lynching of Jewish factory manager Leo Frank of Atlanta, wrongly accused of the rape and murder of a 13-year-old girl.)[23]

In other respects, the Populists' attacks on big business, as well as ties to the early labor movement, marked them as left-liberal. President Franklin D. Roosevelt's New Deal policies of 1933-1940 drew on the Populists' doctrines. They influenced his campaigns to impose regulatory controls — such as creation of the Securities and Exchange Commission — on the "economic royalists" of Wall Street. And his administration's agricultural policies, which sought to stabilize prices by subsidizing farmers for not overproducing, also grew out of the Populists' search for solutions to farmers' financial woes.[24]

Nevertheless, Watson's career had shown that populism can whip up hatred as well as inspire ordinary citizens to demand that government serve their interests, as was exemplified during the Roosevelt era by the career of the Rev. Charles E. Coughlin, a figure of far greater influence than Watson. The Catholic priest from Royal Oak, Mich., went from being a New Deal supporter to a furious critic, whose weekly radio speeches became wildly popular. He then took a sharp right turn into anti-Semitism in 1938, attempting to link Jews to communism — a longtime target of his wrath — and financial manipulation.[25]

Dislike of Jews was commonplace in pre-World War II America, but Coughlin's calls for action against

## CHRONOLOGY

### 1830s-1900s *Movements expressing citizen outrage at government and business elites begin.*

**1832** President Andrew Jackson vetoes a bill to expand the national bank, calling it a tool of the "rich and powerful."

**1892** People's Party of America (populists) formed in St. Louis by small farmers, evangelical Christians, labor unions and alcohol prohibition advocates.

**1896** Populists unite with Democratic Party behind presidential candidate William Jennings Bryan, who is defeated.

**1908** People's Party dissolves, unable to develop an urban base to match its rural constituency.

### 1930s-1950s *Populist politicians begin directing anger toward government, and sometimes ethnic minorities, and away from big business.*

**1938** The Rev. Charles E. Coughlin, a Catholic priest with a large radio following, switches from support of President Franklin D. Roosevelt's New Deal to virulent opposition.

**1954** After leaping to prominence by accusing the State Department and other agencies of harboring Soviet loyalists, Sen. Joseph R. McCarthy wrecks his career by charging the U.S. Army is also protecting communists.

**1955** Liberal academics alarmed by McCarthyism argue that far-right tendencies lurk within all populist-oriented movements.

### 1960s-1970s *Civil rights and antiwar movements prompt middle-class whites to become Republicans.*

**1966** Activists in Oakland, Calif., form Black Panther Party, embodying the worst fears of many middle-class whites about surging left-wing radicalism and "black power."

**1968** Violence at Democratic National Convention in Chicago deepens divide between pro- and anti-Vietnam War Democrats and further alienates middle-class whites from protest movements. . . . Alabama Gov. George C. Wallace wins 13 percent of ballots for his third-party candidacy, built on anti-Washington message.

**1969** Referring to Americans turned off by protesters, President Richard M. Nixon calls on "great silent majority" to support his plan to end the war.

**1972** Sen. George S. McGovern, D-S.D., the Democratic presidential candidate, wins only one state as incumbent Nixon successfully ties Democrats to privileged, unpatriotic elites who look down on "good, decent people."

**1979** Former Gov. Ronald Reagan, R-Calif., wins the presidency, largely by appealing to the "silent majority" constituency identified by Nixon.

### 1990s-2000s *Populism returns as a third-party movement, and then as a group with strong political party ties.*

**1992** Texas billionaire H. Ross Perot launches himself as a third-party presidential candidate, attacking deficit spending and outsourcing of jobs abroad. . . . Perot wins 19 percent of the vote, drawing votes from both winning candidate Bill Clinton and the defeated George H. W. Bush.

**2008** Congressionally approved financial bailout creates discontent among grassroots Republicans and Democrats.

**2009** Seattle woman outraged by Obama administration-proposed economic stimulus holds protest against "porkulus." . . . CNBC reporter Rick Santelli calls for a "tea party" while denouncing administration's rescue plan for homeowners facing foreclosure. . . . Dozens of activists network to plan "tea party" demonstrations on Feb. 27. . . . Tea Party activists take part in town hall meetings with lawmakers, denouncing administration's health-care proposal. . . . Fox News commentator Glenn Beck promotes a "9/12" rally in Washington, which draws heavy crowd of Tea Party supporters.

**2010** Tea Party activists contribute to surprise election victory of Republican Sen. Scott Brown in Massachusetts. . . . "Tea Party Nation" convention in Nashville sparks dissension in movement due to high ticket price and presence of anti-immigration and "birther" speakers. . . . Tea Party opponents begin organizing Coffee Party alternative.

**November** — Tea Party protests and marches provide momentum to Republican candidates who win a decisive House majority, though Senate remains majority-Democrat.

## 2011

**Jan. 5** — Congress convenes with more than 50 House members in Tea Party Caucus; only four senators join Senate counterpart.

**Jan. 25** — House Tea Party Caucus Chair Michele Bachmann, R-Minn., delivers response to president's State of the Union speech that is separate from official Republican response.

**Feb. 22** — Newly elected Sen. Scott Brown, R-Mass., declines to join Tea Party Caucus in Senate.

**March 31** — Tea Party Republican Mike Pence of Indiana urges House leaders negotiating with the Senate and White House to maintain demands for major spending cuts even at cost of shutting down government.

**April 28** — Arizona Legislature authorizes Tea Party license plates, but some movement members oppose the move as government intrusion.

**May 9** — Group of Tea Party leaders attacks House Republican leaders for willingness to accept raising the national debt limit.

Jews found little support outside the ranks of his hardcore supporters. He raised enough concern in the Catholic hierarchy, however, to lead the archbishop of Detroit to order Coughlin to end his radio broadcasts in 1941. And in 1942, at the U.S. Justice Department's request, the church ordered him to stop publishing his weekly newspaper.

Although the infamous "radio priest" never returned to the public arena, he left his mark. In depicting communism as a menace to ordinary Americans, Coughlin anticipated the early-1950s career of Sen. Joseph R. McCarthy, R-Wis., and his supporters. To be sure, some of McCarthy's followers abhorred anti-Semitism; *National Review* founder William F. Buckley Jr., a leading defender of McCarthy, was credited with purging that prejudice from mainstream conservatism.[26] Ethnic hatred aside, McCarthy owed an intellectual debt to Coughlin with his portrayal of working people preyed upon by communist-inspired elites or outright communist agents.

McCarthy himself saw his career go down in flames in 1954 after a conflict with the U.S. Army in which the senator accused the military of harboring communists. But McCarthyism left a foundation upon which later conservative politicians built, writes Georgetown historian Kazin.

By stirring up distrust of the highly educated graduates of elite schools who predominated in the top reaches of public life — especially the foreign policy establishment — McCarthy and his allies caused serious

alarm among liberal academics. McCarthyism "succeeded in frightening many liberals into mistrusting the very kinds of white Americans — Catholic workers, military veterans, discontented families in the middle of the social structure — who had once been foot soldiers of causes such as industrial unionism, Social Security and the GI Bill."[27]

## The 'Silent Majority'

The tensions fanned by McCarthy burst into flame in the mid-1960s. Some of the most active and visible leaders of the civil rights movement — such as Stokely Carmichael of the Student Non-Violent Coordinating Committee — adopted the "black power" slogan. The term was elastic — covering everything from affirmative action to armed self-defense — but many whites heard a threat.

Adding to the tension, the Black Panther Party, formed in 1966 in Oakland, Calif., paraded with firearms to illustrate its goal of "self-defense" against police officers and soon embraced the Cuban and North Korean versions of communist doctrines.[28]

The anti-Vietnam War movement also was gathering strength on college campuses, where potential male foot soldiers benefited from draft deferments, unlike working-class high school graduates who weren't going on to college. Antiwar activists also began openly advocating draft-dodging and draft resistance, some even burning their draft cards in protest — stirring outrage among many among the World War II-Korean War generations.

# Tea Partiers Take Aim at Health Reform

*Movement plans a replay of last summer's town hall meetings.*

Joblessness hovers near 10 percent. Yet in a country where most Americans get health insurance through their employers, opposing health insurance reforms proposed by congressional Democrats at the urging of President Barack Obama has been a driving force in the Tea Party movement.

"The Tea Party . . . did help destroy health reform," Kelly Jane Torrance, literary editor of the *American Conservative*, claimed at a Washington panel discussion in February. "I think that's an amazing accomplishment."

Torrance's remarks at the America's Future Foundation event may have been premature. Since the event, prospects for passage of the legislation seem to have improved.

With a congressional recess starting on March 29, tea partiers are aiming for a replay of last summer's fractious "town hall" meetings with legislators, when the movement's opposition to health reform — especially its added cost to the deficit — first erupted. "We're gonna hit 'em when we know they're back in [the] district, and we're gonna hit 'em hard," Tom Gaitens, a Tampa Tea Party organizer, told Fox News.

Final passage of the legislation before the recess would short-circuit that plan. But the prospects are uncertain.

In any event, plans to destroy the health-care plan, a longtime centerpiece of the Democratic agenda, might seem counter-intuitive, given that the Tea Party hopes to grow — in a country with up to 45 million uninsured residents.[1]

Among them is Tea Party organizer Jenny Beth Martin of Woodstock, Ga. Martin's family lost health coverage when her husband's business failed more than two years ago. When one of the Martins' children gets sick, "We tell the doctor we don't have insurance, and make arrangements to pay cash," Martin says.

The hardships brought on by the Great Recession hit even deeper for Martin's family. She and her husband lost their home, and for a while the couple was cleaning houses to make ends meet.

Nevertheless, she opposes the Obama plan. "I think that we do need health insurance reform," she says. "I just don't think this bill is a good idea."

Her political response, even in the face of personal hardship, illustrates a major facet of the movement, and of American conservatism in general. "People don't connect the economic crisis to the need for any kind of government intervention," says Joseph Lowndes, a political scientist at George Washington University. "People come to this movement with a pretty strong level of conservatism in place already. So there is that irony: to some extent these movements are facilitated by a poor economy, but their reaction . . . does not embrace the government's effort to fix things."

Political and social tensions exploded in 1968. First, the April 4 assassination of civil rights leader the Rev. Dr. Martin Luther King Jr. led to rioting in black communities across the country, notably in Washington, D.C., where the National Guard was called out to quell the violence. Also that spring, tensions over the Vietnam War within the Democratic Party — and within the country as a whole — came to a head during the Democratic Convention in Chicago, marked by large antiwar demonstrations and violent police repression. Although Vice President Hubert H. Humphrey won the nomination, his campaign against Republican Richard M. Nixon was hobbled by the escalation of the war under outgoing President Lyndon B. Johnson.

Nixon's victory enabled him to indulge a deep grudge against the East Coast-based Democratic political elite. In 1969, soon after taking office, he used a term that echoed old-school populist rhetoric, urging the "great silent majority" to support his peace plan.[29] In effect, Nixon was effectively telling ordinary Americans repelled by the civil disorder and protests that they were the backbone of the nation, despite all the noise generated by the demonstrators.

But another high-profile politician tapped even deeper into the vein of outrage that ran through blue-collar America. Gov. George C. Wallace of Alabama had propelled himself into the national spotlight by dint of his fervent resistance to the civil rights movement. As the presidential

John Hawkins, publisher of the *Right Wing News* Web site, suggests another reason for conservative distrust of the health-reform plan. "I think people fear there is going to be a massive decrease in the quality of care," he said. "The idea that you'll cover more people, but the quality won't drop and it won't cost more — people don't believe that."

And, Hawkins says, conservatives understand another deep-seated element of American political culture. "People don't, with good reason, trust the competence of government."

Martin opposes health reformers' plans to penalize businesses that don't provide health insurance for employees and to raise taxes to help subsidize mandatory coverage for those who couldn't afford it. Although the legislation hasn't been finalized, proposals so far would pay for the expanded insurance coverage by raising taxes on high-end health insurance plans or on wealthy Americans (those earning more than $250,000 a year). Martin also does not like the proposal to delay implementation of benefits until 2014, after some higher taxes take effect (though a prohibition would be immediate on insurance companies refusing clients with pre-existing conditions).[2]

A tea partier protests President Obama's health-care reform plans before his arrival at Arcadia University in Glenside, Pa., on March 8, 2010.

*AP Photo/Mark Stehle*

Martin does favor making coverage "portable," not dependent on employment — which would be compatible with the Obama plan, in principle. And she agrees that individuals who can't qualify for insurance could benefit from high-risk insurance pools, which some states have set up. Tea Party organizer John M. O'Hara laid out these and other proposals in a book on the movement.[3]

The book doesn't propose dismantling Medicare, the massive health-care subsidy program for the elderly, and neither does Martin. "It's there now, and we need to deal with it as it is."

And, she adds, "I don't think there is anything wrong with government providing safety nets. I understand that sometimes things happen to people."

— *Peter Katel*

[1] Carl Bialik, "The Unhealthy Accounting of Uninsured Americans," *The Wall Street Journal*, June 24, 2009, http://online.wsj.com/article/SB124579852347944191.html#articleTabs%3Darticle. Some question that U.S. Census Bureau estimate, in part because it includes illegal aliens who wouldn't be covered under a new law.

[2] Alec MacGillis and Amy Goldstein, "Obama offers a new proposal on health care," *The Washington Post*, Feb. 23, 2010, p. A1.

[3] John M. O'Hara, *A New American Tea Party: The Counterrevolution Against Bailouts, Handouts, Reckless Spending, and More Taxes* (2010), pp. 175-201.

candidate of the American Independent Party, he tried to expand his segregationist appeal (he later repudiated Jim Crow) to cast himself as the voice of the common American. He demonstrated his familiarity with his constituency by ticking off its members' occupations: "The bus driver, the truck driver, the beautician, the fireman, the policeman and the steelworker, the plumber and the communications worker and the oil worker and the little businessman." They knew more about the nation's problems, he said, than snobbish politicians, academics and journalists.[30]

As a third-party candidate, Wallace had no chance of winning, but he garnered nearly 10 million votes — 13 percent of ballots — showing that his appeal ran strong.[31] Many of those Wallace votes would have gone to Nixon

if the Alabama governor hadn't launched his third-party bid, and Nixon concluded that he didn't want to face that challenge again.[32]

## Enduring Appeal

In 1972 Wallace had plans for another presidential run. But the outsider candidate apparently wasn't above making insider deals. In a book on Nixon's presidential campaigns, author Rick Perlstein reports that Nixon made moves to benefit Wallace in exchange for the Alabaman dropping his third-party strategy and running instead in the Democratic presidential primary. As a Democratic candidate, Wallace wouldn't siphon off Republican votes in the general election, as he had in 1968.[33]

# Sarah Palin Shines at Tea Party Convention

*Some see her as a potential party leader.*

Tea partiers pride themselves on their lack of formal leadership, but that hasn't stopped speculation about who will emerge to lead the movement. So far, the speculation largely has zeroed in on Sarah Palin. And the former vice-presidential candidate's insistence that she isn't seeking a leadership role hasn't squelched the topic.

In fact, Palin has actually fueled the speculation, possibly inadvertently. After her surprise resignation last year as Alaska's governor and the publication of *Going Rogue*, her best-selling book, she addressed the Tea Party's February convention in Nashville — the only speech she's given this year at an overtly political event. Her political ideas, to the extent she has spelled them out, seem consistent with the tea partiers' call for lower taxes and smaller government.

In the eyes of Tea Party activists who skipped Nashville — in part because they objected to its $500-plus ticket price — Palin made a mistake in going. That view was even more prevalent after the influential online political newspaper *Politico* reported she had received $100,000 for the speech. "This has nothing to do with the grassroots movement — nothing," said Robin Stublen, who helped organize a Tea Party group in Punta Gorda, Fla.[1]

Palin didn't deny that account, but she wrote in *USA Today* that "any compensation for my appearance will go right back to the cause."[2] She didn't specify the precise destination for the money.

Some tea partiers saluted her presence in Nashville and its effects on the movement. "I think the Tea Party is gaining respect when we're able to attract some of the quality representation . . . a caliber of person such as this," said Bob Porto, an attendee from Little Rock.[3]

Palin's star power certainly generated media attention for the convention, even though a relatively modest 600 people attended, and the convention was controversial within the movement. Her speech, in fact, was carried live on C-SPAN, CNN and Fox News.

Palin made a point of waving off the idea that she wants to take the helm. "I caution against allowing this movement to be defined by any one leader or politician," she said. "The Tea Party movement is not a top-down operation. It's a ground-up call to action that is forcing both parties to change the way they're doing business, and that's beautiful."[4]

For all of her attention-getting capabilities, Palin comes with baggage. A new book by Steve Schmidt, top strategist for the McCain-Palin campaign, described her as dishonest. And another book, by journalists Mark Halperin and John Heilemann reported that she was ignorant of even basic national and international matters. "[S]he still didn't really understand why there was a North Korea and a South Korea," Heilemann said on CNN.[5]

Even a friendlier figure, Stephen F. Hayward of the conservative American Enterprise Institute, warned Palin that she's nowhere near as ready for a national position as Ronald Reagan was. "Palin has as much as admitted that she needs to acquire more depth, especially on foreign policy," he wrote in *The Washington Post.* "One thing above all is required: Do your homework. Reagan did his."[6]

But in Nashville, the crowd loved her, wrote Jonathan Raban in the liberal *New York Review of Books.* Many

---

In the summer of 1971, Wallace met with Nixon during a flight to Alabama from the president's vacation home in Key Biscayne, Fla. Three months later, a federal grand jury investigating alleged tax fraud by Wallace's brother dissolved without issuing indictments. Shortly thereafter, the Justice Department announced — "suddenly and improbably," in Perlstein's words — that Alabama's civil rights enforcement plan was superior to other states' plans.

In January 1972 Wallace announced he would run for the Democratic presidential nomination. In Florida, the first primary, he won first place in a five-man race, with 42 percent of the vote.

In the end, Wallace (who was shot and paralyzed midway through the campaign) won only two primaries outside the Old Confederacy, in Michigan and Maryland. The Democratic nomination went to Sen. George S. McGovern of South Dakota, an anti-Vietnam War candidate.

Unfortunately for McGovern, he came to symbolize a social gap between hard-working, ordinary Americans,

had been cool not only to the anti-immigrant talk of Tom Tancredo, the former Colorado congressman and 2008 GOP presidential candidate, but also the Obama-birthplace suspicions of Web news entrepreneur Joseph Farah, Raban reported.

But the crowd embraced Palin. "A great wave of adoration met the small black-suited woman. . . . The entire ballroom was willing Sarah to transport us to a state of delirium with whatever she chose to say."[7]

The speech was something of a letdown, Raban added, because Palin's delivery was better suited to the TV cameras than to the live audience. Still, she got a big sendoff. "The huge standing ovation ('Run, Sarah, Run!') was more for the concept of Palin . . . than it was for the lackluster speech," Raban wrote.[8]

Sarah Palin answered questions from attendees at the National Tea Party Convention in Nashville on Feb. 6, 2010.

Getty Images for NASCAR/Jerry Markland

Palin hasn't revealed whether she'll run for president in 2012, but she pointedly avoids denying it. "I won't close the door that perhaps could be open for me in the future," she told Fox News.[9]

However, University of Tennessee law professor Glenn Harlan Reynolds, who covered the Nashville convention for the Web-based *Pajamas TV*, warned that Palin's popularity could exact the same price that he argues President Obama has made his political allies pay for hero-worshipping him.

"The biggest risk that the Tea Party movement faces is that it will create its own Obama in the person of Sarah Palin and get a similar result," he says. "She made a point of saying she didn't want to be their leader, and most people agreed. But the tendency of people to run after a charismatic leader is probably genetically hardwired."

— *Peter Katel*

[1]Quoted in Chris Good, "Is Palin's Tea Party Speech a Mistake?" *The Atlantic*, Feb. 4, 2010, www.theatlantic.com/politics/archive/2010/02/is-palins-tea-party-speech-a-mistake-tea-partiers-have-mixed-opinions/35360/.

[2]Ben Smith and Andy Barr, "Tea partiers shell out big bucks for Sarah Palin," *Politico*, Jan. 12, 2010, www.politico.com/news/stories/0110/31409.html; Sarah Palin, "Why I'm Speaking at Tea Party Convention," *USA Today*, Feb. 3, 2010, http://blogs.usatoday.com/oped/2010/02/column-why-im-speaking-at-tea-party-convention-.html.

[3]*Ibid.*

[4]"Sarah Palin Speaks at Tea Party Convention," CNN, Feb. 6, 2010, http://transcripts.cnn.com/TRANSCRIPTS/1002/06/cnr.09.html.

[5]Jonathan Martin, "Steve Schmidt: Sarah Palin has trouble with truth," *Politico*, Jan. 11, 2010, www.politico.com/news/stories/0110/31335.html.

[6]Steven F. Hayward, "Would Reagan Vote for Sarah Palin?" *The Washington Post*, March 7, 2010, p. B1.

[7]Jonathan Raban, "At the Tea Party," *New York Review of Books*, March 25, 2010, www.nybooks.com/articles/23723.

[8]*Ibid.*

[9]Quoted in "Palin says 2012 presidential bid a possibility," CNN, Feb. 8, 2010, www.cnn.com/2010/POLITICS/02/07/palin.presidential.run.tea.party/index.html.

and pampered liberals and radicals. In fact, he had earned a Distinguished Flying Cross as a bomber pilot in World War II and hardly fit the stereotype.[34]

But McGovern's supporters did include the liberal wing of the Democratic Party, Hollywood stars among them. So the "McGovern Democrats" neatly symbolized one side of the social gap that right-wing populists had identified, and that Nixon had done his best to widen. "It is time that good, decent people stop letting themselves be bulldozed by anybody who presumes to be the self-righteous moral judge of our society," Nixon said in a radio address shortly before Election Day.[35]

His strategy proved spectacularly successful. McGovern won only one state, Massachusetts, and Washington, D.C. But Nixon's even more spectacular political downfall during the Watergate scandal prevented him from taking advantage of his victory. He was forced to resign in 1974.

Though President Ronald Reagan, another Republican, adopted Nixon's "silent majority" paradigm, Reagan's overall optimism effectively sanded off the doctrine's sharp

# New Coffee Party Drawing Supporters

*"People are tired of the anger."*

An alternative to the Tea Party is taking shape, as citizens who oppose its message and tactics are forming their own grassroots network — the Coffee Party.

The Tea Party's nascent rival takes a deliberately toned-down approach to political conflict. "We've got to send a message to people in Washington that you have to learn how to work together, you have to learn how to talk about these issues without acting like you're in an ultimate fighting session," founder Annabel Park, who launched the movement from a Coffee Party Facebook page, told *The New York Times* recently.[1]

Tea partiers put themselves on the map with rallies, pointed questions to politicians at town hall meetings and election campaign organizing. How the coffee partiers plan to project themselves into the national debate isn't clear yet. But there's no question that the effort grows out of the liberal, Democratic Party-oriented part of the political spectrum — a counterpart to the veteran Republicans who launched the Tea Party. Park, a documentary filmmaker in the Washington suburb of Silver Spring, Md., had worked on the Obama campaign.

By mid-March, when enthusiasts nationwide held a coordinated series of get-togethers in — of course — coffee shops across the country, the Coffee Party page had collected more than 100,000 fans. "Coffee partiers seem to be more in favor of government involvement — as in envisioning a greater role for government in the future of health care — but denounce the 'corporatocracy' that holds sway in Washington," *The Christian Science Monitor* reported from a Coffee Party meeting in Decatur, Ga.[2]

Whether the Coffee Party grows into a full-fledged movement, there's no denying the initial appeal. The organizer of a Dallas-area gathering in March had expected 15 people at most. She got 40. "This is snowballing," Raini Lane said. "People are tired of the anger, tired of the hate."[3]

*— Peter Katel*

---

[1]Quoted in Kate Zernike, "Coffee Party, With a Taste for Civic Participation, Is Added to the Menu," *The New York Times*, March 2, 2010, p. A12.

[2]Patrik Jonsson, "'Coffee party' movement: Not far from the 'tea party' message?" *The Christian Science Monitor*, March 13, 2010, www.csmonitor.com/USA/Politics/2010/0313/Coffee-party-movement-Not-far-from-the-tea-party-message.

[3]Quoted in Cassie Clark, "Coffee Party energizes fans," *Dallas Morning News*, March 14, 2010, p. B2.

---

edges. And Reagan didn't have to contend with directing an unpopular war.

During the 1992 reelection campaign of Reagan's successor (and former vice president), President George H. W. Bush, another populist figure emerged, Texas billionaire H. Ross Perot. In his brief but influential third-party campaign for president, Perot declared, "America today is a nation in crisis with a government in gridlock. We are deeply in debt and spending beyond our means."[36]

A pro-choice, law-and-order conservative, Perot paid little attention to social issues. Instead, he emphasized the need to cut government spending and strongly opposed the proposed North American Free Trade Agreement (NAFTA) with Mexico and Canada. Business' "job is to create and protect jobs in America — not Mexico," he said shortly before formally announcing.[37]

And he decried what he saw as the lavish perks of government service. "We have government turned upside down, where the people running it act and live at your expense like royalty, and many of you are working two jobs just to stay even."[38]

Perot's intolerance for criticism and a strong authoritarian streak (he praised Singapore, notorious for its rigid enforcement of laws on personal behavior) limited his appeal. Still, he wound up with 19 percent of the vote, including 29 percent of all votes by independents. "He showed the nation's ruling elites," wrote *The Washington Post*'s John Mintz, "that millions of Americans are deeply disturbed by what they believe is a breakdown in American society."[39]

Political professionals had assumed Perot would draw far more Republican votes away from Bush than

Democratic ones from Bill Clinton. But post-election surveys showed that Perot voters — often casting what amounted to protest votes — came from both Republican- and Democratic-oriented voters.

"Those who said they voted for Perot," *The Washington Post* reported, "split almost evenly between Bush and Clinton when asked their second choice."[40]

## CURRENT SITUATION

### The Election Test

Across the country, Tea Party-affiliated candidates — or those who claim the movement's mantle — are running for a range of Republican nominations, in races that will test both the movement's strength and its potential to influence GOP politics. The races will also set the stage for the 2012 Republican presidential nomination.

So far, at least one potential Republican candidate seems to think the Tea Party will have run its course by then. Former Massachusetts Gov. Mitt Romney is criticizing populism among both Republicans and Democrats. "Populism sometimes takes the form of being anti-immigrant . . . and that likewise is destructive to a nation which has built its economy through the innovation and hard work and creativity of people who have come here from foreign shores," Romney told *The Boston Globe*.[41]

Some candidates seeking Tea Party votes do take an anti-immigrant line. In Arizona, former Rep. J.D. Hayworth is challenging veteran Sen. John McCain, the GOP candidate for president in 2008. "In Arizona, you can't ignore the Republican animus against Sen. McCain on immigration," Jason Rose, a spokesman for Hayworth, told *Roll Call*, a Washington political newspaper.[42]

Meanwhile, another Tea Party-backed candidate, Mike Lee, is challenging Republican Sen. Bob Bennett of Utah, whose backers include the state's senior senator, Republican Orrin Hatch. And in Kentucky, Tea Party enthusiast Rand Paul (son of libertarian Rep. Ron Paul, R-Texas) is competing against a Republican officeholder, Secretary of State Trey Grayson, for the GOP nomination to a Senate seat left open by a Republican retirement. Florida's GOP Gov. Charlie Crist, whom tea partiers consider insufficiently conservative, is fighting hard for the Senate nomination against Marco Rubio, a lobbyist and former state legislator who has become a national star among conservative Republicans. "America already has a Democrat Party, it doesn't need two Democrat parties," Rubio told CPAC in February.[43]

And Sen. Jim DeMint, the South Carolina Republican who has become a Senate liaison for the Tea Party, made clear to the CPAC crowd where his sympathies lie, tacitly drawing a parallel between Crist and Sen. Arlen Specter of Pennsylvania. who defected from the GOP last year to save his seat. "I would rather have 30 Marco Rubios in the Senate than 60 Arlen Specters."[44]

In the Deep South, where the Tea Party runs along the same conservative Republican tracks, two Tea Party-friendly candidates for Congress are opposing each other in north Alabama. "A lot of Tea Party activists are split between Les Phillip and Mo Brooks," says Christie Carden, who organized a Tea Party group in Huntsville. So far, at least, she and her fellow members have not endorsed either candidate.

Complicating matters, a third Republican is running as well. Incumbent Parker Griffith was welcomed into the GOP fold after he switched from Democrat to Republican last December. Party-establishment backing for Griffith makes sense, given the GOP's interest in providing a defector with a favorable reception, says blogger and Tennessee law professor Reynolds. But, he adds, "One of the Tea Party complaints is that there is too much *realpolitik*" — or compromising — in the GOP establishment.

Elsewhere, even where Tea Party candidates might have traction, Republican organizations won't necessarily welcome them with open arms. "The Republican Party in Pennsylvania is pretty good at controlling its side of the ballot," says Dan Hirschorn, editor and publisher of the Philadelphia-based political news site *pa2010*. "When . . . Tea Party candidates are in a race where there already are establishment Republicans, the political landscape the Tea Party candidates face is really formidable."

Democrats view the tension between party professionals and conservative insurgents as a potential advantage. "You've got these very divisive primaries," Rep. Chris Van Hollen, D-Md., chairman of the House Democratic campaign organization, told *CQ Weekly.* "In many instances it's driving the primary way to the right."[45]

In some districts, Van Hollen suggested, primary victories by Tea Party-style Republicans could spell victory for centrist Democrats.

# Does the Tea Party movement represent another Great Awakening?

## YES

**Glenn Harlan Reynolds**
*Professor of Law, University of Tennessee*

Written for *CQ Researcher*, March 2010

In the 18th and 19th centuries, America experienced two Great Awakenings, in which mainstream religious institutions — grown too stodgy, inbred and self-serving for many — faced a sudden flowering of new, broad-based religious fervor. Now we're experiencing a third Great Awakening, but this time it's political, not religious, in nature.

Nonetheless, the problem is the same: The existing institutions no longer serve the needs of broad swaths of the public. The choice between the two parties is increasingly seen as a choice between two gangs of thieves and charlatans. While Americans always joked about corruption and venality in politics, now those jokes don't seem as funny.

The Tea Party movement is one symptom of this phenomenon: Millions of Americans are aligning themselves with a bottom-up insurgency angered by bailouts, growing deficits and the treatment of taxpayers as cash cows. Though often treated as a red-state phenomenon, the Tea Party movement is strong even in deep-blue states like Massachusetts, where Scott Brown was elected to the Senate, or California, where one out of three voters told a recent poll that they identified with the Tea Party.

But the Tea Party movement is a symptom of a much broader phenomenon, exemplified by earlier explosions of support for Howard Dean via Meetup and Barack Obama and Sarah Palin via Facebook. They were triggered by the growing sense that politics has become a cozy game for insiders, and that the interests of most Americans are ignored.

Thus, Americans are becoming harder to ignore. Over the past year they've expressed their dissatisfaction at Tea Party rallies and town hall meetings, and at marches on Washington and state capitals. And they're planning what to do next, using the Internet and talk radio.

Traditional politics is still wedded to 20th-century top-down models, where mailing lists, organizations and message control are key. But in the 21st century, the real energy is at the grassroots, where organization can take place on the fly. When Tea Party activists decided to support Brown, they sent him money through his Web site, and put together an online "Moneybomb" campaign to bypass the Republican Party, which got behind Brown's seemingly quixotic campaign only after the momentum was established by the grassroots.

Coupled with widespread dissatisfaction at things as they are, expect a lot more of this grassroots activism, in both parties, over the coming years.

## NO

**Joseph Lowndes**
*Professor of Political Science, University of Oregon*

Written for *CQ Researcher*, March 2010

The Tea Party movement is indeed revivalist, but it revives not the egalitarian impulses of the 1740s or 1830s that fed the zeal of the Revolution and abolition. Rather it rehashes a tradition of racial, antigovernment populism that stretches from George Wallace's American Independent Party through Reagan Democrats to Sarah Palin Republicans.

In this tradition's origins mythology, a virtuous white citizenry became squeezed between liberal elites above and black dependents below as a result of civil rights and Johnson's Great Society. Since then, these Americans have resented taxation and social welfare, linking it to those whom they believe are recipients of special rights and government coddling. Thus, for the tea partiers and their immediate forebears the state is what monopoly capital was for 19th-century populists: a parasitic entity controlling their lives through opaque and malevolent machinations. It is worth noting that a significant percentage of tea partiers appear to be in their 60s or older — placing them in the generation that expressed the most negative reaction to the advances of the civil rights movement.

Why are we seeing this wave of protest now? The Tea Party movement has emerged out of the confluence of two momentous events: an enormous economic crisis and the election of a black president. The dislocations produced by the former have stoked the latent racial nationalism ignited by the latter. Obama represents both aspects of modern populist resentment — blackness and the state, and his perceived coziness with Wall Street taps into outrage felt toward banks right now. Add to this Glenn Beck's continual attacks on Obama and progressivism more generally, and you get a demonology that allows tea partiers to see tyranny wherever they look. (If "demonology" seems too strong a word here, look no further than the grotesque Joker-ized image of Obama over the word "Socialism" that has been omnipresent at Tea Party rallies.)

Will this movement transform the landscape? Third-party movements have impact when they can drive a wedge into the two-party system, creating a crisis that reframes the major political questions of the day. But the stated principles of the various Tea Party groups show them to be entirely consistent with the social conservative wing of the GOP. And there is a great overlap in leadership ties and funding sources as well, making it likely that the movement will find itself reabsorbed by the party with little independent impact.

## Political Realities

Fresh from his victory in Massachusetts, Sen. Brown is now a certified hero to Republicans, especially the Tea Party movement, which worked its heart out for him. Brown's victory was made all the sweeter by its location in the heart of blue-state America. But his first vote on Capitol Hill has conservatives talking about political realities.

Less than three weeks after he formally took office on Feb. 4, Brown joined four other Republicans in voting for a $15-billion jobs bill pushed by the Obama administration and Democratic Senate leader Harry Reid of Nevada. "I came to Washington to be an independent voice, to put politics aside and to do everything in my power to help create jobs for Massachusetts families," Brown said after the vote. "This Senate jobs bill is not perfect. I wish the tax cuts were deeper and broader, but I voted for it because it contains measures that will help put people back to work."[46]

His words did nothing to stem the tide of rage that poured onto his Facebook page — 4,200 comments in less than 24 hours after his Feb. 22 vote, the vast majority of them furious. As gleefully documented by the liberal *Huffington Post* news site, the comments included "LYING LOW LIFE SCUM HYPOCRITE!" and "YOU FAILED AT THE FIRST CHANCE" and "You sir, are a sellout."

But Michael Graham, a radio talk-show host and *Boston Herald* columnist in the Tea Party fold, mocked the outrage. "This is still Massachusetts," Graham wrote. "Brown will have to win a general election to keep this seat. . . . This one, relatively insignificant vote sent a powerful message to casual, Democrat-leaning voters that Brown isn't in the GOP bag. . . . It's brilliant politics."[47]

Graham is a political veteran, unlike many tea partiers. The movement, in fact, prides itself on its many political neophytes. "These are not people," Tea Party activist Freire, the *Washington Examiner* editor, said at the Washington panel discussion in February, "who are used to getting engaged in the process."

Although the panel discussion preceded Brown's vote by about a week, it delved into the tension between principles and pragmatism that surfaced after Brown's move. Other conservative lawmakers also have disappointed conservative backers, Freire noted. Rep. Paul Ryan, R-Wis.,

Chris Van Hollen, D-Md., chairman of the influential House Democratic Congressional Campaign Committee, helps guide House Democrats' fundraising and strategizing. He thinks the Tea Party activists may be driving the Republicans to the right and that primary victories by Tea Party-style Republicans could spell victory for centrist Democrats in November.

Freire said, "is a pretty reliable guy when it comes to his fiscal conservatism; he still voted for the bailout."

## Third-Party Option

Democrats are nourishing the fond if unlikely hope that the Tea Party will turn into a full-fledged political party. "[That] would have a negative effect on Republicans, as would threatening to do that and influencing Republican candidates to move further to the right," says Neil Oxman of Philadelphia, cofounder of The Campaign Group political consulting firm.

For that reason, the third-party idea has not caught fire among tea partiers. "We don't need another party," says Carden, the Huntsville organizer. "We just need to use the vehicles for political change that are already there."

History points to that course as the most promising. Socialists, conservatives, libertarians and other political movements have long used third-party campaigns to build national support or at least publicize their ideas. Winning the White House isn't the goal.

In state races, candidates outside the two major parties have won, though such cases at the moment can be counted on one hand. Sen. Bernard Sanders of Vermont, a socialist who ran as an independent, is serving his first

Senate term after 16 years in the House. Another senator, lifelong Connecticut Democrat Joseph I. Lieberman, is technically an independent, but he dropped that affiliation after losing a primary race to an Iraq War opponent.

The outcome of a bitter political fight in upstate New York last November would seem to confirm the two-party strategy as best for Republicans. In a special election to fill a newly vacated "safe" GOP House seat, the choice of a Republican legislator raised the hackles of conservatives nationwide, who viewed her as too liberal on abortion and gay rights. Instead, they backed a Conservative Party candidate — who eventually lost to Democrat Owens. His backers included the onetime Republican candidate Dede Scozzafava, who denounced what she viewed as betrayal by the GOP.[48]

"This election represents a double blow for national Republicans and their hopes of translating this summer's Tea Party energy into victories at the ballot box," Van Hollen, the Democratic Congressional Campaign Committee chairman, said.[49]

In New York state, Conservative Party candidate Hoffman's backers included Sarah Palin and former Rep. Dick Armey of Texas, a Tea Party booster and former House Republican leader who is president of Freedom-Works, a Washington-based activist-training organization whose politics run along Tea Party lines.

The New York debacle was followed by Brown's triumph in Massachusetts. That Brown ran as a Republican seemed to confirm the wisdom of channeling Tea Party activism into GOP campaigns.

Republican strategy guru Karl Rove, the top campaign and White House adviser to former President George W. Bush, is warning Tea Party groups to stay in the Republican fold. "There's a danger from them," he told *USA Today* recently, "particularly if they're used by political operators . . . to try and hijack" elections.[50]

Rove could have had Nevada in mind. There, a candidate from the "Tea Party of Nevada" has filed to oppose Senate Majority Leader Reid in the GOP primary.

Leaders of Nevada's Tea Party movement told the conservative *Washington Times* that they don't recognize the names on the Tea Party of Nevada filing documents. They claimed the third party was created on Reid's behalf to siphon Republican votes. But the candidate said by mail, "I am not for Harry Reid. . . .

My candidacy is real." The Reid campaign didn't return a call to the *Times'* reporter.[51] Whatever the

sincerity of the Nevada Tea Party, grassroots conservatives elsewhere who are disenchanted with the GOP argue that the best course is to fight within the party. "Use the Republican Party to your advantage," Chicago tea partier Eric Odom wrote on his blog. "Move in and take it over."[52]

## OUTLOOK

### Short Life?

In the hyperspeed political environment, evaluating the 10-year prospects for a newly emerged movement is an iffy proposition. Still, a consensus is emerging that the Tea Party's ideas will last longer than the movement itself.

"These ideas are endemic in American political culture," says Sides of George Washington University. "Whether we will be able to attach them to a movement or an organization we call the Tea Party is an open question."

Georgia Tea Party activist Martin acknowledges the movement may dissolve over the next decade. "If there isn't a movement 10 years from now, I hope it's faded away because people understand what the country's core values are and don't need to be reminded."

Whatever the state of national consciousness in the near future, the life cycle of social movements in their most influential phase arguably has never been very long, even before the pace of modern life quickened to its present pace. "In their dynamic, growing, inspirational, 'we-can-change-the-world' stage, they last five to seven years," says Kazin of Georgetown University.

The labor union movement's high point ran from 1933 to 1938, Kazin says. And the civil rights movement in its nationwide, unified phase ran from just 1960 to 1965. "And those were movements that were more independent of a political party structure," he adds.

As a movement closely linked to the Republican Party, the Tea Party's future will depend greatly on the course of the 2010 elections, Kazin argues. And which GOP candidates are nominated for president in 2012 will offer an even clearer gauge of the movement's influence.

Hawkins of *Right Wing News* thinks he knows where the Tea Party will be in 10 years. "I tend to doubt it will exist," he says. "It will have been absorbed into the Republican Party."

But the University of Oregon's Lowndes argues that beyond the country's Republican strongholds, the Tea

Party won't acquire enough influence to reconfigure the entire party. "It will shape politics in certain places, and shape the Republican Party, but it won't take it over."

For now, however, Lowndes credits the Tea Party with effectively pulling together strands of discontent. "With enormous power concentrated in the executive branch and in corporations, there is a sense of powerlessness at work that can be picked up and interpreted different ways by different folks," he says. "These people have found a language for it that the left has not."

Jonah Goldberg, high-profile editor of *National Review Online*, urged conservatives during the America's Future Foundation panel discussion in February to come to terms with the nature of the political system. "The American people aren't as conservative as we would like them to be, and they never will be," he said, despite what seem to be favorable conditions for the right that largely grow out of the Tea Party's success.

"Things are so much better than they seemed to be a little while ago," he continued. "Will Republicans blow it? They have a great history of that. One of the things that movements do is try to keep politicians honest. That's going to be hard work because politicians are politicians."

Reynolds of the University of Tennessee Law School acknowledges that the Tea Party's promise may go unfulfilled. Conservative hopes ran high after the 1994 Republican takeover of Congress midway through the first Clinton administration, he notes. "But that didn't have long-lasting legs."

On the other hand, Reynolds says, the Reagan legacy has been long-lasting. "And this is probably bigger," he says of the Tea Party.

But there are no guarantees, he cautions. "A lot of people are involved in politics who never were before. In 10 years, some will have gone back to their lives. Of the people who stay in, the odds are that many will become politicians as usual. The question is how much this will happen."

# UPDATE

A political activist dressed as a hero of the American Revolution joined with a small group of fellow conservatives in early May to denounce Washington politicians in the name of the Tea Party. Nothing surprising in that — except that the politicians under attack are Republicans.

"Yes, we've been deeply disappointed," said William Temple of Brunswick, Ga., at a Washington news conference. He named House Speaker John Boehner, R-Ohio, as the main source of disenchantment. "Mr. Boehner has been a 'surrenderist' who waves the white flag before the first shots are fired." Temple, wearing a tricorner hat, boots and other 18th-century garb, leaned his musket against a wall when he took to the lectern at the National Press Club in Washington.[53]

The episode was one of many marking the complicated follow-up to Tea Party-driven Republican election successes in 2010. Temple and his half-dozen companions vowed that Boehner, House Budget Committee Chairman Paul Ryan, R-Wis., and other House Republicans would pay a political price if they defied demands of the loose-knit Tea Party movement. At the top of their wish list: massive government spending cuts.

Instead, House leaders have signaled they're willing to go along with raising the "debt ceiling," the limit on how much government can borrow. "This debt limit . . . provides the perfect opportunity to substantially reduce the size and scope of the federal government," said Bob Vander Plaats, vice chair of a Tea Party convention scheduled for Kansas City in October. A loser in last year's Republican gubernatorial primary in Iowa, Vander Plaats remains a top political player in a state whose early primaries are a critical early test for presidential candidates.[54]

## Testing Time

The Tea Party's ability to sustain the support it gathered last November will be tested as well. Tea Party members and sympathizers played a major part in helping shift control of the House to a 242-193 Republican majority — about 30 of whom had been endorsed by Tea Party groups. That victory, which followed months of demonstrations, marches and frenetic organizing activity by Tea Party members, was limited to the House. The Senate remains in the hands of a Democratic majority though Republicans gained six seats.[55]

Speaker Boehner, who presides over the House GOP majority, seemed to confirm the Tea Party activists' increasingly dire view of him in a speech he gave on the evening following their press conference. As they expected, he signaled willingness to approve a debt-ceiling increase. But in a nod to the Tea Party, he conditioned approval on trillions of dollars of cuts in federal spending.[56]

Sporting patriotic red, white and blue, a Tea Party supporter attends a Tax Day rally in Chicago on April 18, 2011, calling for massive government spending cuts and tax reform. Tea Party members have been angry at House Republican leaders for signaling they may support raising the nation's debt ceiling.

Whether that would satisfy the activists remains to be seen. Joining with their staunchest congressional allies, they had previously failed in an effort to convince Boehner and other leaders to refuse to reach a temporary budget compromise with the Senate and White House. The move averted a government shutdown. But Rep. Mike Pence, R-Ind. had urged holding fast. "It's time to pick a fight!" he had told a small rally outside the Capitol. "If liberals in the Senate want to play political games . . ., I say shut it down."[57]

### 'Unrealistic Expectations'

In another show of Tea Party independence from the Republicans, Rep. Michele Bachmann, R-Minn., chair of the Tea Party Caucus in the House, delivered a response to President Obama's State of the Union address separate from the official Republican response.[58]

Political observers have been arguing that politicians who identify with the Tea Party may have overestimated their power. "The standards they set for themselves in terms of budget cutting and deficit reduction were very high, and the expectations were unrealistic," said Robert Bixby, executive director of the Concord Coalition, a nonpartisan organization directed by members of the political establishment that advocates spending cuts. "Some of the leaders in the House, Boehner and Ryan,

do have a bit of a problem in trying to write a tough and realistic budget that can get done, and tamping down some of the unrealistic expectations," Bixby told the *Los Angeles Times*.[59]

And Tea Party strategists may have overestimated the movement's appeal outside its red-state, suburban base. Sen. Scott Brown, R-Mass., who scored a stunning victory last year in a special election for the seat of the late Sen. Edward M. "Ted" Kennedy, a Democratic icon, has taken pains to distance himself from the movement. Along with others more closely identified with the movement, Brown didn't join the Senate Tea Party Caucus. And, asked if he was a Tea Party member, he told *USA Today*, "No, I'm a Republican from Massachusetts."[60]

### Pressure to Deliver

For their part, Tea Party-backed lawmakers have expressed frustration at being hemmed in on one side by Democratic opposition in the Senate, and on the other by political commitments to constituents.

"If we don't do a real serious job with spending these next two years, then I think that voters in my district will feel that I didn't deliver," Rep. Joe Walsh, R-Ill., a freshman who was part of the Tea Party wave of House members in last year's election, said in January.[61]

By early May, Walsh was echoing activists' criticisms of Republican House leaders. In his case, he took issue with their abandonment of a proposal to transform Medicare, the program of government subsidies of health-care costs for the elderly. Under a plan that the House passed in March, senior citizens (starting in 2022) would get vouchers to buy private insurance.[62]

"I would be very disappointed if we didn't follow through," Walsh said, after top Republicans indicated they wouldn't try to push the Medicare plan any further. A fellow Illinois Tea Party Republican, Rep. Bobby Schilling, went further. Giving up on the proposal, he said, would amount to surrendering "to lies and deceit told by the other side."[63]

But the Medicare proposal was turning into a rallying cry for Democrats, as well as for some Medicare beneficiaries who had voted for Republicans in 2010. Republican lawmakers came face-to-face with that reality at town hall meetings they held in their districts during the spring recess. Some of those meetings turned into role-reversed versions of constituent meetings in 2009, at which Tea Party opposition to the administration's health-care legislation seized the headlines and spurred the movement's rapid growth.

## Signs of Discord

At this year's meetings, however, crowds turned out to grill and heckle Republicans who had voted for the Medicare plan. A woman in Racine, Wis., attending a meeting held by Rep. Ryan, the author of the plan, held up a sign that read, "We use up the voucher, and then what?" In Orlando, shouts and arguments over Tea Party Republican Rep. Daniel Webster's support for the plan grew so loud that Webster at one point quit talking.[64]

Not all town meetings turned raucous. But the Medicare plan seemed to be turning into a liability. Even after top Republicans backed away from the proposal, Democrats vowed to keep exploiting the issue. "The Republicans are slowly realizing their plan to privatize Medicare is a political disaster," said Sen. Charles E. Schumer, D-N.Y., a spokesman for Senate Democrats. "But until they renounce their vote for it, they are still going to own it."[65]

Yet, as they continue marking a distance between themselves and the Republican establishment, Tea Party members are showing signs of discord within their movement.

In Arizona, some Tea Party members have rallied against the creation of automobile license plates emblazoned with a Revolutionary War slogan they've adopted —"Don't Tread on Me." Tea Party groups can sell the tags to raise money. But, Tea Party member Jim Wise of Surprise, Ariz., isn't buying one. "I realize the people behind this had the best of intentions," he said, "but it goes against what we stand for, which is limited government."[66]

Despite such rifts, there's little doubt that Tea Party movement supporters do agree on the issue of federal spending. The anti-Boehner press conference was only one sign of Tea Party members' determination on that score, expressed as resistance to a debt-ceiling increase. The Tea Party Express, one of the movement's national organizations, was planning a national TV ad campaign on that theme.

"The GOP is on probation," the organization's chair, Amy Kremer, told *The Atlantic*, "because under President Bush they spent a lot of money, and added $3 trillion to the national debt." She added, "You will see that the Tea Party will have no problem whatsoever challenging the very freshmen they put in."[67]

## NOTES

1. Kathleen Hennessey, "Justice's wife launches 'tea party' group," *Los Angeles Times*, March 14, 2010, www.latimes.com/news/nation-and-world/la-na-thomas142010mar14,0,3190750,full.story.

2. Mark Leibovich, "Discipline Helped Carve Path to Senate," *The New York Times*, Jan. 21, 2010, www.nytimes.com/2010/01/21/us/politics/21brown.html.

3. Zachary Ross, "Top Tea Partier, Husband, Owed IRS Half a Million Dollars," *Talking Points Memo*, Oct. 8, 2009, http://tpmmuckraker.talkingpointsmemo.com/2009/10/top_tea_partier_husband_owed_irs_half_a_million_do.php.

4. Jeff Zeleny, "Daniels Offers Advice to Republicans," *The New York Times*, The Caucus (blog), March 9, 2010, http://thecaucus.blogs.nytimes.com/2010/03/09/daniels-offers-advice-to-republicans/.

5. "Tom Tancredo's Feb. 4 Tea party speech in Nashville," *Free Republic*, Feb. 5, 2010, http://freerepublic.com/focus/f-news/2445943/posts.

6. Cuéntame, www.facebook.com/cuentame?v=app_11007063052.

7. John Maggs, "Norquist on Tea and Taxes," *National Journal*, Feb. 4, 2010, http://insiderinterviews.nationaljournal.com/2010/02/-nj-were-you-surprised.php.

8. *Ibid.* Also see Tea Party Nation, teapartynation.com; and Kate Zernike, "Seeking a Big Tent, Tea Party Avoids Divisive Social Issues," *The New York Times*, March 13, 2010, p. A1.

9. John M. O'Hara, *A New American Tea Party: The Counterrevolution Against Bailouts, Handouts, Reckless Spending, and More Taxes* (2010), pp. 256-257.

10. "Rick Santelli Rant Transcript," www.reteaparty.com/2009/02/19/rick-santelli-rant-transcript/.

11. *Ibid.*; Brian Stelter, "CNBC Replays Its Reporter's Tirade," *The New York Times*, Feb.23, 2009, p. B7.

12. Mary Lou Pickel, "Tea Party at the Capitol," *Atlanta Journal-Constitution,* Feb. 28, 2009; Aman Batheja, "Several hundred protest Obama stimulus program in Fort Worth," *Fort Worth Star-Telegram*, Feb. 28, 2009; "Tea Party Time," *New York Post*, Feb. 28, 2009, p. 16; Tim O'Neil, "Riverfront tea party protest blasts Obama's stimulus plan," *St. Louis Post-Dispatch*, Feb. 28, 2009, p. A7; Christian M. Wade, "Tax Protesters Converge on Federal Courthouse," *Tampa Tribune*, Feb. 28, 2009, p. A4; "Protesters bemoan stimulus funds at Tenn. Capitol," The Associated Press, Feb. 28, 2009.

13. Kate Zernike, "Unlikely Activist Who Got to the Tea Party Early," *The New York Times*, Feb. 27, 2010, www.nytimes.com/2010/02/28/us/politics/28keli.html.

14. Quoted in David M. Halbfinger and Ian Urbina, "Republicans Bask in Glow of Victories in N.J. and Va.," *The New York Times*, Nov. 5, 2009; Janet Hook, "Stimulus bill battle is only the beginning," *Los Angeles Times*, Feb. 15, 2009, p. A1.

15. Quoted in Manu Raju, "Lindsey Graham warns GOP against going too far right," *Politico*, Nov. 4, 2009, www.politico.com/news/stories/1109/29131.html.

16. Chelsea Schilling, "'Government wants to be your one and only god,'" *WorldNetDaily*, Feb. 6, 2010, www.wnd.com/index.php?pageId=124326.

17. Jonathan Raban, "At the Tea Party," *New York Review of Books*, March 25, 2010, www.nybooks.com/articles/23723.

18. For background, see Peter Katel, "Press Freedom," *CQ Researcher*, Feb. 5, 2010, pp. 97-120.

19. Quoted in David Weigel, "Birther Speaker Takes Heat at Tea Party Convention," *Washington Independent*, Feb. 6, 2010 (includes audio clip of argument), http://washingtonindependent.com/75949/birther-speaker-takes-heat-at-tea-party-convention.

20. Except where otherwise indicated, this subsection is drawn from Michael Kazin, *The Populist Persuasion: An American History* (1998).

21. Quoted in Daniel Feller, "King Andrew and the Bank," *Humanities*, National Endowment for the Humanities, January-February, 2008, www.neh.gov/news/humanities/2008-01/KingAndrewandtheBank.html.

22. "Bryan's 'Cross of Gold' Speech: Mesmerizing the Masses," *History Matters*, undated, http://historymatters.gmu.edu/d/5354/.

23. Steve Oney, "The Leo Frank case isn't dead," *Los Angeles Times*, Oct. 30, 2009, http://articles.latimes.com/2009/oct/30/opinion/oe-oney30. Except where otherwise indicated, this subsection is drawn from Kazin, *op. cit.*

24. William E. Leuchtenburg, *Franklin D. Roosevelt and the New Deal* (1963), pp. 33, 255, 335-336.

25. For background, see Peter Katel, "Hate Groups," *CQ Researcher*, May 8, 2009, pp. 421-448.

26. Douglas Martin, "William F. Buckley Jr., 82, Dies," *The New York Times*, Feb. 28, 2008, p. A1.

27. Kazin, *op. cit.*, p. 193. For background on the G.I. Bill, see "Record of 78th Congress (Second Session)," *Editorial Research Reports*, Dec. 20, 1944, available at *CQ Researcher Plus Archive*; K. Lee, "War Veterans in Civil Life," *Editorial Research Reports*, Vol. II, 1946; and William Triplett, "Treatment of Veterans," *CQ Researcher*, Nov. 19, 2004, pp. 973-996.

28. Todd Gitlin, *The Sixties: Years of Hope, Days of Rage* (1993), pp. 348-351.

29. Quoted in Kazin, *op. cit.*, p. 252.

30. *Ibid.*, pp. 234-235.

31. Richard Pearson, "Former Ala. Gov. George C. Wallace Dies," *The Washington Post*, Sept. 14, 1998, p. A1, www.washingtonpost.com/wp-srv/politics/daily/sept98/wallace.htm.

32. Rick Perlstein, *Nixonland: The Rise of a President and the Fracturing of America* (2008), pp. 631-632.

33. Except where otherwise indicated, this subsection draws from *ibid.*

34. "George McGovern Interview," The National World War II Museum, undated, www.nationalww2museum.org/wwii-community/mcgovern.html.

35. Quoted in Perlstein, *op. cit.*, pp. 732-733.

36. H. Ross Perot, "What Americans Must Demand," *The Washington Post*, March 29, 1992, p. C2.

37. Quoted in John Dillin, "Possible Presidential Bid by Perot Is Seen Posing a Threat to Bush," *The Christian Science Monitor*, March 24, 1992, p. 1.

38. Quoted in *ibid.*

39. John Mintz, "Perot Embodied Dismay of Millions," *The Washington Post*, Nov. 4, 1992, p. A26; Jeffrey Schmalz, "Clinton Carves a Wide Path Deep Into Clinton Country," *The New York Times*, Nov. 4, 1992, p. B1.

40. Thomas B. Edsall and E. J. Dionne, "White, Younger, Lower-Income Voters Turn Against G.O.P.," *The Washington Post*, Nov. 4, 1992, p. A21.

41. Quoted in Sasha Issenberg, "In book, Romney styles himself wonk, not warrior," *Boston Globe*, March, 2, 2010, www.boston.com/news/nation/washington/articles/2010/03/02/mitt_romneys_no_apology_is_not_light_reading?mode=PF.

42. Emily Cadei, "Sands of GOP Discord in Arizona," *Roll Call*, Jan. 28, 2010.

43. Quoted in Liz Sidoti, "Excited GOP: Energy on the right, divisions within," The Associated Press, Feb. 19, 2010. Adam Nagourney and Carl Hulse, "Re-energized, G.O.P. Widens Midterm Effort," *The New York Times*, Jan. 25, 2010, p. A1; Thomas Burr, "GOP's Armey backs Lee, scolds Bennett," *Salt Lake Tribune*, Feb. 18, 2010.

44. Quoted in *ibid.*

45. Quoted in Joseph J. Schatz, "Reading the Leaves," *CQ Weekly*, March 1, 2010, pp. 480-489.

46. Quoted in James Oliphant, "Scott Brown's 'tea party' fans feel burned by jobs vote," *Los Angeles Times*, Feb. 23, 2010, http://articles.latimes.com/2010/feb/23/nation/la-na-scott-brown24-2010feb24.

47. Michael Graham, "Still right cup of tea," *Boston Herald*, Feb. 25, 2010, www.bostonherald.com/news/opinion/op_ed/view.bg?articleid=1235356.

48. Jeremy W. Peters, "Conservative Loses Upstate House Race in Blow to Right," *The New York Times*, Nov. 3, 2009, www.nytimes.com/2009/11/04/nyregion/04district.html?_r=1&scp=9&sq=HoffmanScozzafava&st=cse.

49. Quoted in *ibid.*

50. Judy Keen, "Rove: 'Tea Party' may be risk to GOP," *USA Today*, March 10, 2010, p. A1.

51. Quoted in Valerie Richardson, "New party brings its own 'tea' to election," *The Washington Times*, Feb. 22, 2010, p. A1.

52. Quoted in Kate Zernike, "In Power Push, Movement Sees Base in G.O.P.," *The New York Times*, Jan. 15, 2010, p. A1.

53. For a video of the press conference, see "Federal Debt Ceiling and Debt," C-Span, May 9, 2011, www.c-span.org/Events/Tea-Party-Activists-Take-on-GOP-on-Deficit/10737421394-1/.

54. *Ibid.*; Kerry Howley, "The Road to Iowa is Paved With Pizza," *The New York Times*, March 11, 2011, www.nytimes.com/2011/03/13/magazine/mag-13YouRHere-t.html?scp=1&sq=%22Bob%20vander%20Plaats%22&st=cse; Joshua Green, "The Iowa Caucus Kingmaker," *The Atlantic*, May 2011, www.theatlantic.com/magazine/archive/2011/05/the-iowa-caucus-kingmaker/8446/.

55. Rick Rojas, "Last midterm House, governor races end," Los Angeles Times, Dec. 9, 2010, p. A24.

56. Carl Hulse, "Boehner Outlines Demands on Debt Limit Fight," *The New York Times*, May 9, 2011, www.nytimes.com/2011/05/10/us/politics/10boehner.html?_r=1&ref=politics.

57. Quoted in Doyle McManus, "No party for John Boehner," *Los Angeles Times*, April 3, 2011, p. A28.

58. David A. Farenthold, "Republicans decry debt, offer few detailed fixes," *The Washington Post*, Jan. 26, 2011, p. A9.

59. Quoted in Lisa Mascaro, "Cracks show as GOP tackles budget," *Los Angeles Times*, Jan. 25, 2011, p. A1.

60. Quoted in Susan Page, "Sen. Brown keeps 'an open mind,'" *USA Today*, Feb. 21, 2011, p. A4.

61. Quoted in ibid.

62. Noam N. Levey, "Rep. Paul Ryan's Medicare privatization plan increases costs, budget office says," *Los Angeles Times*, April 7, 2011, http://articles.latimes.com/2011/apr/07/nation/la-na-gop-budget-20110408.

63. Quoted in Carl Hulse and Jackie Calmes, "G.O.P. Rethinking Bid to Overhaul Medicare Rules," *The New York Times*, May 5, 2011, www.nytimes .com/2011/05/06/us/politics/06fiscal.html? ref=politics.

64. Mike Schneider and Dinesh Ramde, "Congressional Republicans go home to mixed reviews," The Associated Press, April 26, 2011.

65. Quoted in Hulse and Calmes, op. cit.

66. Quoted in Marc Lacey, "In Arizona, Tea Party License Plate Draws Opposition From its Honorees," *The New York Times*, May 4, 2011, www.nytimes .com/2011/05/05/us/05plates.html.

67. Eliza Newlin Carney, "Tea Party Puts the Screws to House Republicans Over Debt Ceiling," The Atlantic.com, May 9, 2011, www.theatlantic.com/ politics/archive/2011/05/tea-party-puts-the-screws-to-house-republicans-over-debt-ceiling/238640/.

## BIBLIOGRAPHY

### Selected Sources

### Books

**Continetti, Matthew, *The Persecution of Sarah Palin: How the Elite Media Tried to Bring Down a Rising Star*, Sentinel, 2009.**
An editor of the conservative *Weekly Standard* chronicles the rise of Tea Party-friendly Palin from a sympathetic perspective.

**Kazin, Michael, *The Populist Persuasion:* An American History, Cornell University Press, 1998.**
A Georgetown University historian traces the forms that an enduring American distrust of elites has taken.

**O'Hara, John M., *A New American Tea Party: The Counterrevolution Against Bailouts, Handouts, Reckless Spending, and More Taxes*, John Wiley & Sons, 2010.**
A manifesto in book form by one of the first Tea Party activists tells of the movement's formation and ideas.

**Perlstein, Rick, *Nixonland: The Rise of a President and the Fracturing of America*, Scribner, 2008.**
A non-academic historian adds to the Tea Party story with this account of Nixon and his appeal to the "silent majority."

### Articles

**Barstow, David, "Tea Party Lights Fuse for Rebellion on Right," *The New York Times*, Feb. 15, 2010, www .nytimes.com/2010/02/16/us/politics/16teaparty .html.**
A lengthy, detailed report traces the formation of a Tea Party undercurrent of conspiracists and militia members.

**Continetti, Matthew, "Sarah Palin and the Tea Party, Cont.," *Weekly Standard*, Feb. 8, 2010, www.week lystandard.com/print/blogs/sarah-palin-and-tea-party-cont.**
The author of a sympathetic book on Palin argues she made a powerful case for herself as a 2012 presidential candidate.

**Good, Chris, "Some Tea Partiers Question Meeting With Steele," *The Atlantic*, Politics site, Feb. 16, 2010, www.theatlantic.com/politics/archive/ 2010/02/some-tea-partiers-question-meeting-with-steele/36027/.**
Some Florida tea partiers questioned the movement credentials of a political activist who organized a meeting with Michael Steele, the controversial Republican national chairman.

**Hennessey, Kathleen, "Justice's wife launches 'tea party' group," *Los Angeles Times*, March 14, 2010, www.latimes.com/news/nation-and-world/la-na-thomas14-2010mar14,0,3190750,full.story.**
This is the first report of the Tea Party activism of Virginia Thomas, wife of Supreme Court Justice Clarence Thomas.

**Markon, Jerry, "'Wired' conservatives get the message out," *The Washington Post*, Feb. 1, 2010, p. A1.**
Tea Party organizers made extensive use of social networking tools and Republican connections in getting the movement up and running, a political correspondent reports.

**Naymik, Mark, "GOP stumbles with Tea Party as movement gains foothold," *Cleveland Plain Dealer*, Feb. 21, 2010, p. A1.**
A leading newspaper in a key political state reports on ambivalent relations between tea partiers and the Republican Party.

**Parker, Kathleen, "The GOP's misguided hunt for heretics," *The Washington Post*, Feb. 24, 2010,**

www.washingtonpost.com/wp-dyn/content/article/
2010/02/23/AR2010022303783.html.
A conservative columnist warns of a tendency to zealotry
and intolerance among tea partiers.

Rucker, Philip, "GOP woos wary 'tea party' activ-
ists," *The Washington Post*, Jan. 20, 2010, p. A4.
Republican officials are courting Tea Party members,
Washington's leading newspaper reports.

Sidoti, Liz, "Primary time: Let the political family
feuds begin," The Associated Press, Jan. 30, 2010.
The Tea Party movement's political strength will be
tested in some key primary elections, a political correspondent reports.

Tanenhaus, Sam, "The Crescendo of the Rally Cry," *The
New York Times*, Jan. 24, 2010, Week in Review, p. 1.
A *Times* editor who writes on the history of conservatism
examines the Tea Party movement in light of past populist surges.

Wilkinson, Howard, "Tea Partiers aim to remake
local GOP," *Cincinnati Enquirer*, Jan. 30, 2010.
Tea partiers in southwest Ohio are making a concerted
effort to take over Republican precinct organizations.

Zernike, Kate, "Seeking a Big Tent, Tea Party Avoids
Divisive Social Issues," *The New York Times*, March
13, 2010, p. A1.
Some Tea Party activists deliberately bypass controversial
social issues, a correspondent specializing in the Tea
Party reports.

### Reports

"AEI Political Report," *American Enterprise Institute
for Public Policy Research*, February 2010, www.aei
.org/docLib/Political-Report-Feb-2010.pdf.
A compilation of survey results from a variety of
sources includes data on public knowledge of the Tea
Party.

# For More Information

**Coffee Party**, www.coffeepartyusa.com. A new network of
Tea Party opponents.

**FreedomWorks**, 601 Pennsylvania Ave., N.W., North Building, Washington, DC 20004; (202) 783-3870; www.freedom
works.org. Created by former House Republican Leader Dick
Armey, the conservative organization trains local activists.

**Politics1**, 409 N.E. 17th Ave., Fort Lauderdale, FL 33301;
www.politics1.com/index.htm. Comprehensive political site
offering a guide to races involving Tea Party candidates.

**Right Wing News**, rightwingnews.com. Independent Web
site covers Tea Party movement, often critically.

**Talkingpointsmemo**, www.talkingpointsmemo.com.
Democratic-oriented news site provides critical but fact-based
coverage of Tea Party.

**Tea Party Patriots**, www.teapartypatriots.org. An extensive
network of Tea Party groups around the country offering
movement news and views from its Web site.

# 6

# Climate Change

Jennifer Weeks

A villager rafts through flood waters in northeastern India on Sept. 25, 2012. Scientists say the negative effects of climate change, including flooding caused by sea-level rise, as well as heat waves and storms, will affect developing countries most severely because they are less prepared for disaster and have limited funds for disaster relief.

From *CQ Researcher*, June 14, 2013.

N ews reports last month marked a scientific milestone: Earth's atmosphere now contains more carbon dioxide ($CO_2$) than at any time in up to 3 million years.[1] And the average annual rate of increase for the past decade was more than twice as steep as during the 1960s.[2]

With carbon dioxide levels climbing at such a rapid pace, scientists said, it is clear that humans already have set dramatic climate change in motion. "Even if we all decided to stop emitting $CO_2$ immediately, it would take at least 20 years to start putting new [low-carbon or carbon-free] systems in place, and another 50 years for the climate to adjust," says Kevin Trenberth, a senior scientist at the National Center for Atmospheric Research in Boulder, Colo.

Carbon dioxide is a "greenhouse gas" (GHG) that traps heat in the atmosphere, warming Earth's surface. It is generated by natural sources such as wildfires and volcanic eruptions, and by human activities — primarily burning fossil fuels such as coal, oil and natural gas. Before the Industrial Revolution, Earth's atmosphere contained about 280 parts per million of $CO_2$. Now, numerous scientific studies warn, GHG concentrations have reached levels that will cause drastic warming with widespread consequences.[3]

"We cause global warming by increasing the greenhouse effect, and our greenhouse gas emissions just keep accelerating," climate scientist Dana Nuccitelli wrote in May. In a review of more than 4,000 peer-reviewed studies, Nuccitelli and others found that 97.1 percent endorsed the idea that human activities were contributing to climate change.[4]

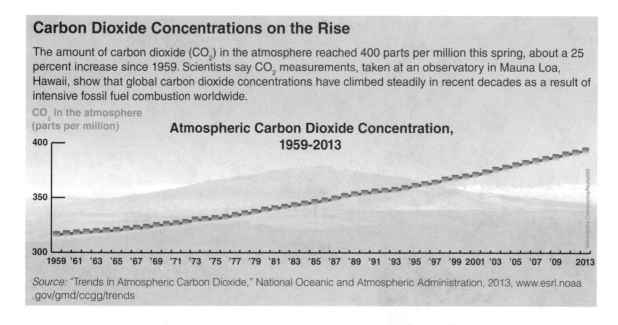

**Carbon Dioxide Concentrations on the Rise**

The amount of carbon dioxide ($CO_2$) in the atmosphere reached 400 parts per million this spring, about a 25 percent increase since 1959. Scientists say $CO_2$ measurements, taken at an observatory in Mauna Loa, Hawaii, show that global carbon dioxide concentrations have climbed steadily in recent decades as a result of intensive fossil fuel combustion worldwide.

$CO_2$ in the atmosphere (parts per million)

**Atmospheric Carbon Dioxide Concentration, 1959-2013**

*Source:* "Trends in Atmospheric Carbon Dioxide," National Oceanic and Atmospheric Administration, 2013, www.esrl.noaa .gov/gmd/ccgg/trends

Other researchers say that while human activities may be warming the Earth, climate scientists are drawing conclusions that go beyond the evidence. "[T]here is no *prima facie* reason to think that global warming will make most extreme weather events more frequent or more severe. . . . Extreme events are by definition rare, and the rarer the event the more difficult it is to identify long-term changes from relatively short data records," said Judith Curry, chair of the School of Earth and Atmospheric Sciences at Georgia Tech, testifying to Congress in April.[5]

But many experts are deeply concerned. "The clock is ticking," said Jerry Melillo, a scientist at the Marine Biological Laboratory in Woods Hole, Mass., and chairman of a committee that published a national assessment earlier this year of the science and impacts of climate change.[6] According to the assessment, average U.S. temperatures have risen about 1.5° Fahrenheit since 1895, most of it in the past 20 years.

That change may not seem large, but small shifts can have big impacts. During the so-called Little Ice Age (1300s-1800s), when average temperatures fell by just under 1°C (1.8°F), widespread crop failures in Europe caused millions of deaths.[7] At the end of the last full-scale ice age about 10,000 years ago, average temperatures were only 5 to 9 degrees Fahrenheit cooler than

modern levels, and much of North America and Europe was covered by glaciers.[8]

Recent warming already has caused significant changes. "Certain types of weather events have become more frequent and/or intense, including heat waves, heavy downpours, and, in some regions, floods and droughts," authors of the assessment report wrote. "Sea level is rising, oceans are becoming more acidic and glaciers and arctic sea ice are melting."[9]

During his 2008 presidential campaign, President Obama called for action to slow climate change, but prospects faded in 2010 after a Democratic controlled Congress failed to enact legislation and control of the House shifted to the GOP. Most congressional Republicans and some conservative Democrats oppose legislation to limit climate change.[10]

Campaigning for reelection in 2012, Obama supported developing all types of energy sources, including fossil fuels. In his second inaugural address in January he issued a strong call for action. Ignoring climate change, he said, "would betray our children and future generations."[11] In his State of the Union address in February he asked Congress to pass a "bipartisan, market-based solution to climate change." If not, Obama said, he would direct federal agencies to propose steps that could be taken through regulations.[12]

But the politics of climate change remain highly polarized. Some Republican politicians question the overwhelming scientific consensus that human actions are altering Earth's climate.[13] "All the things they're [the Obama administration] saying happened, they're all part of [former Vice President] Al Gore's science fiction movie, and they've all been discredited," said Oklahoma Sen. James Inhofe, former chairman of the Senate Environment and Public Works Committee.[14]

Others say the case is not proven, focusing on issues that researchers are still analyzing. "There is a great amount of uncertainty associated with climate science," wrote Rep. Lamar Smith of Texas, chairman of the House Science Committee.[15] And many legislators oppose measures that would raise fossil fuel prices. More than a dozen moderate and conservative Democrats joined Republicans in symbolic votes earlier this year against a carbon tax — which would raise the price of fossil fuels based on their carbon content — and for construction of the Keystone XL pipeline. The pipeline would facilitate development of Canadian "tar sand" oil and is opposed by many environmentalists who say it will enable greater use of fossil fuels.[16]

At the same time, polls show a growing share of Americans — including Republicans — believe climate change is occurring and support some kind of action. And some observers say Republican legislators' opposition is eroding.[17]

"There is a divide within the party," said Samuel Thernstrom, a scholar at the conservative American Enterprise Institute who served on the White House Council on Environmental Quality under President George W. Bush and has written that humans are changing Earth's climate, with potentially severe effects. "The position that climate change is a hoax is untenable," he says.[18]

Other conservatives view climate change as a serious problem but question whether government actions — particularly through regulation — can slow it. "The real

## Partisan Divide Is Wide on Climate Change

About 70 percent of Americans say there is solid evidence the Earth is warming, and about 40 percent say the planet is warming mainly because of human activity. The percentage of those with either view declined between 2006 and 2009-2010 but has risen since, including among Republicans. Nevertheless, the partisan divide over climate change remains wide: Fewer than 20 percent of Republicans believe human activity causes it. And although 42 percent of Republicans favor stricter environmental limits on power plants, significantly more Democrats and Independents want such restrictions.

(percentage)

● Is there solid evidence the Earth is warming?
■ Is the Earth warming mostly because of human activity?

### Percent Who Think the Earth Is Warming, by Party, 2013

**Yes**

| | |
|---|---|
| Republicans | 44% |
| Democrats | 87% |
| Independents | 68% |

**Yes, and mostly due to human activity**

| | |
|---|---|
| Republicans | 19% |
| Democrats | 57% |
| Independents | 43% |

### Percent Who Think Scientists Agree Human Activity Is Causing Climate Change, by Party, 2012

| | |
|---|---|
| Republicans | 30% |
| Democrats | 58% |
| Independents | 45% |

### Percent Who Favor Setting Stricter Limits on Power Plants to Address Climate Change, by Party, 2013

| | |
|---|---|
| Republicans | 42% |
| Democrats | 72% |
| Independents | 64% |

*Source:* "Climate Change: Key Data Points From Pew Research," Pew Research Center, April 2013, www.pewresearch.org/2013/04/02/climate-change-key-data-points-from-pew-research

## China, U.S. Emit the Most Carbon Dioxide

China emitted more carbon dioxide ($CO_2$) in 2011 than any other country. Its nearly 9 billion metric tons of carbon dioxide emissions were about 60 percent greater than the 5.5 billion metric tons emitted in the United States, which ranked second. Worldwide, $CO_2$ emissions from energy use totaled nearly 33 billion metric tons in 2011. Most carbon dioxide, a major source of heat-trapping greenhouse gases, comes from energy consumption. Emissions of other types of greenhouse gases — such as methane and nitrous oxide — are not included in these totals.

(millions of metric tons of carbon dioxide)

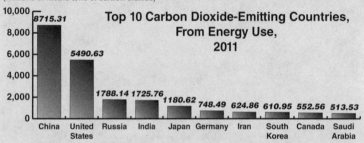

**Top 10 Carbon Dioxide-Emitting Countries, From Energy Use, 2011**

*Source:* "International Energy Statistics," Energy Information Administration, 2013, www.eia.gov/cfapps/ipdbproject/iedindex3.cfm?tid=90&pid=44&aid=8

motion. However, scientists and policymakers are debating how much climate change is inevitable.

During negotiations over the past decade, some officials — particularly from Europe — have called for limiting carbon emissions enough so global temperatures do not rise more than 2°C (3.6°F) above pre-industrial levels. That target recognizes that some climate change is unavoidable but strives to prevent more disastrous effects, such as large-scale melting of polar ice caps. The goal was noted at a 2009 climate conference in Copenhagen, although nations did not formally commit to reductions large enough to achieve it.[19]

Limiting warming to 2°C would require capping $CO_2$ concentrations at about 450 parts per million, a level the planet could hit by mid-century if emissions keep rising at current rates, scientists say. Warming could be limited to that level if governments make polluters pay for their carbon emissions, eliminate subsidies for fossil fuels and increase investments in energy efficiency and renewable energy, according to Maria van der Hoeven, executive director of the International Energy Agency, which works to help nations secure reliable, affordable and clean energy. "While ambitious, a clean energy transition is still possible," van der Hoeven said. "But action in all sectors is necessary to reach our climate targets."[20]

Other experts are more pessimistic. Sir Robert Watson, a British scientist and former chair of the Intergovernmental Panel on Climate Change (IPCC), an international organization established to advise governments on climate change science and impacts, argues that nations have 50-50 odds of limiting warming to 3°C (5.4°F), but should prepare for an increase of up to 5°C (9°F). At that level, scientists say the effects will be severe, especially for developing countries.

"When I was chairing the IPCC . . . we were hopeful that emissions would not go up at the tremendous rate they are rising now," Watson said in February.

obstacle to making meaningful emissions reductions is that it's unbelievably difficult to do," says Jonathan Adler, a professor of law and director of the Center for Business Law and Regulation at Case Western Reserve University. Adler describes himself as a conservative who believes that climate change is a serious problem, but is skeptical that government can mandate solutions. "We don't know how to do it at anything remotely approaching a cost that countries are willing to bear," he says. Instead, Adler favors policies that encourage energy innovation without prescribing specific technical solutions.

As Congress, the Obama administration and advocacy groups debate how to address climate change, here are some issues they are considering:

### Are catastrophic climate change impacts inevitable?

Scientists say human activities have increased the amount of $CO_2$ in the atmosphere by more than 40 percent from pre-industrial levels. $CO_2$ remains in the atmosphere for years, so some climate change has already been set in

While cost-effective and equitable solutions exist, he added, "political will and moral leadership is needed" to address climate change. And the substantial changes in policies, practices and technologies are "not currently under way."[21]

Climate scientist Trenberth of the National Center for Atmospheric Research (NCAR) also doubts that it will be possible to limit warming to 2°C. "But it matters enormously how rapidly we get to that number," he says. "The rate of change matters as much as the change itself. Getting to 2°C in 50 years is quite different than if it takes 200 years or longer."

Yet he believes it is still possible to limit the rate of warming to a pace that will allow societies to adapt. "We can slow things down enough to make a big difference and push the 2°C mark well into the 22nd century," Trenberth says.

To meet that target, nations would have to sharply cut fossil fuel use. "To stay at 2°C we can't emit more than 565 gigatons of carbon dioxide into the atmosphere by mid-century," he explains. "World $CO_2$ emissions in 2011 were 31.6 gigatons, which was a 3.2 percent increase from the year before. At current rates, we'll go through our limit in 16 years."*

Scientists say many of the effects of climate change will occur even if the planet warms by 2°C or less. "There's an impression that if we hold warming below two degrees we're safe, which is demonstrably false," says Christopher Field, a professor of global ecology at Stanford University and lead author of IPCC climate change assessment reports. "Climate change in the next 20 to 40 years will be the result of actions that are already baked into the system."

In the United States average temperatures are rising; frost-free seasons are lasting longer; precipitation is up in the Midwest, southern Plains and Northeast and down in parts of the Southeast, Southwest and Rocky Mountain states; and extreme weather events, such as heat waves and flooding, are becoming more frequent and intense.[22]

Some experts, such as James Hansen, who retired early this year as director of NASA's Goddard Institute for Space Studies, calls the 2-degree target "a prescription

---

*A gigaton is one billion tons.

Getty Images/Sean Gallup

A coal-fired power plant spews smoke over Mehrum, Germany, on March 4, 2013. Burning fossil fuels — such as coal, natural gas and oil — creates carbon dioxide ($CO_2$), a greenhouse gas that traps heat in the atmosphere, warming the Earth's surface. $CO_2$ is also generated by natural sources, such as volcanoes and wildfires.

for disaster." Hansen says nations should cut $CO_2$ emissions back sharply enough to reduce atmospheric concentrations to 350 parts per million — a level last seen in 1987 — to avoid effects such as melting most of the world's glaciers and ice caps.[23]

Other scientists share his perspective. "Two degrees is actually too much for ecosystems," Thomas E. Lovejoy, a professor of environmental science and policy at George Mason University, wrote in January. "A 2-degree world will be one without coral reefs (on which millions of human beings depend for their well-being)." At current warming levels, he noted, U.S. and Amazonian forests already have been heavily damaged. "The current mode of nibbling around the edges is pretty much pointless," he concluded.[24]

## Is climate engineering a good idea?

As atmospheric concentrations of greenhouse gases climb and international negotiations fail to make progress, some say it is time to begin researching ways to alter Earth's climate system on a large scale to slow the rise of global temperatures, at least until nations make serious commitments to cut emissions.

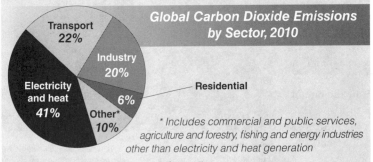

## Electricity, Heat Generation Biggest CO₂ Sources

More than 40 percent of global carbon dioxide ($CO_2$) emissions in 2010 came from electricity and heat generation. The transportation and industrial sectors each accounted for about one-fifth of $CO_2$ emissions, the main component of human-generated greenhouse gases.

**Global Carbon Dioxide Emissions by Sector, 2010**

Transport 22%
Industry 20%
Electricity and heat 41%
Other* 10%
Residential 6%

\* Includes commercial and public services, agriculture and forestry, fishing and energy industries other than electricity and heat generation

*Figures do not total 100 because of rounding.*

*Source:* "$CO_2$ Emissions From Fuel Combustion," International Energy Agency, 2012, p. 9, www.iea.org/co2highlights/co2highlights.pdf

Various climate engineering schemes (also called geoengineering) have been proposed, such as injecting particles into the atmosphere to reflect sunlight back into space or removing tons of carbon from the atmosphere and injecting it deep underground. But these concepts raise difficult technical, political and ethical questions, and some say they are unworkable or unnecessary.

The National Research Council concluded in 2010 that more research was needed on ways to reduce carbon emissions, such as improving energy efficiency, capturing and storing power plant emissions and developing more low-carbon energy sources. Geoengineering strategies "may also warrant attention, provided that they do not replace other research efforts," the authors wrote.[25]

Similarly, the Royal Society, Britain's national science academy, said in 2009 that "properly researched geoengineering methods . . . could eventually be useful to augment conventional mitigation [emission-reducing] activities, even in the absence of an imminent emergency."[26] Both academies emphasized that little was known about how well various geoengineering methods work or how easy they would be to deploy.

But some advocates are undeterred. Many cite the 1991 eruption of Mt. Pinatubo in the Philippines, which injected millions of tons of sulfur dioxide into the atmosphere. There the gas formed sulfate particles, which reflected some of the sun's radiation back into space, lowering average global temperatures the following year by just under 1°C.

David Keith, a professor of physics and public policy at Harvard University, calls strategies to reduce incoming sunlight an imperfect but fast and cheap way to partly offset climate risk. "You can stop the warming or even do cooling if that's what you wanted to do," Keith said in January. "All the really hard problems [with geoengineering] are public policy problems."[27] For example, there are no broad international rules for governing geoengineering research or policies for assigning liability if an experiment harms natural resources or alters weather patterns.

Other scientists say geoengineering cannot be evaluated without better understanding of Earth's complex climate systems. For example, researchers at California's Scripps Institution of Oceanography have used shipboard generators to produce smoke (the same type used in skywriting) to see how it affects clouds on a small scale. They found that smoke particles brightened the clouds, making them more reflective, but that low clouds and multiple cloud layers made the process less effective.[28]

Clouds are still poorly understood, according to Scripps atmospheric chemistry professor Lynn Russell, lead author of the cloud brightening study. "Cloud droplets are measured in micrometers, but the heating and cooling that makes clouds appear occurs over areas of many kilometers. And droplets form in microseconds, but clouds form and dissipate in hours or days," she says. Computer models have trouble combining such large- and small-scale measurements, so they usually represent some variables well and approximate others, Russell notes.

Moreover, she says, scientists do not have good ways to measure some conditions that affect cloud formation, such as extremely high humidity or three-dimensional turbulence in the atmosphere. Nonetheless, Russell believes more small-scale experiments would be useful. "Before you think about investing money in long-term geoengineering studies, you need to know what's possible," she says.

Trenberth, of the National Center for Atmospheric Research, worries that adding particles to the atmosphere could harm Earth's weather and climate cycles. For example, an NCAR study of the impacts of the Mt. Pinatubo eruption found that besides temporarily lowering global temperatures, the event caused large declines in rainfall over land and extensive droughts worldwide.[29] "It was an extreme event," Trenberth says. "Geoengineering might cool off temperatures, but if it also shuts down parts of the weather and hydrological cycles, the cure could be worse than the disease."

In a recent article in the journal *Science*, Keith and UCLA law professor Edward Parson suggested governments start organizing modest field experiments in geoengineering to see how various techniques affect the atmosphere — on a scale small enough that it won't alter the climate — and start developing cooperative rules and limits.

"If research is blocked, then in some stark future situation where geoengineering is needed, only unrefined, untested and excessively risky approaches will be available," they contended.[30]

## Should the United States adopt a carbon tax?

Although there is little prospect that Congress will adopt broad climate change legislation in the next several years, many liberal and conservative experts advocate taxing carbon — more specifically, the carbon content of fossil fuels. That would promote low-carbon and carbon-free fuels and technologies without having government agencies pick specific solutions, they argue.

"A carbon tax would encourage producers and consumers to shift toward energy sources that emit less carbon — such as toward gas-fired power plants and away from coal-fired plants — and generate greater demand for electric and flex-fuel cars and lesser demand for conventional gasoline-powered cars," wrote George P. Shultz, a former budget director, Treasury secretary and secretary of State during Republican presidential administrations, and Gary S. Becker, a Nobel laureate in economics and professor at the University of Chicago.[31]

AFP/Getty Images/Romeo Gacad

A snorkeler views a coral reef near Mansuar Island, in eastern Indonesia's Papua region. The surrounding Raja Ampat archipelago, considered one of the most important biodiversity environments in the world, was nominated as a UNESCO World Heritage Site. A 2°C temperature rise would kill the world's remaining coral reefs, according to scientist Thomas Lovejoy of George Mason University.

Nearly a dozen nations or regions have adopted some version of carbon taxes, including the Canadian province of British Columbia, Australia, Japan, South Africa, Switzerland, Norway, Sweden, Finland and Denmark.[32] In 2009-2010 Congress debated another way of pricing carbon: emissions trading through a so-called cap-and-trade system, which also has been adopted or is being considered by countries and regions in Europe, North America, Latin America and Asia.[33] The Waxman-Markey bill, which passed the House, would have created a U.S. emissions trading system, but it was never brought up in the Senate.*

Waxman-Markey illustrated the complexities of cap-and-trade systems, in which government agencies set a ceiling, or a cap, on total emissions of a pollutant, then issue emissions allowances to businesses that generate that pollutant. Companies must obtain allowances to cover all of their emissions or pay fines. Sources that reduce their emissions can sell their extra allowances, so they have a financial incentive to clean up their operations.

---

* The measure was named after its sponsors, Democratic Reps. Henry A. Waxman of California and Edward J. Markey of Massachusetts.

The Amazon rain forest — already being devastated by global warming — faces further damage from climate change. Scientists say a 2°C temperature rise would decrease water flow in the Amazon basin by 20-40 percent, causing widespread drought and other environmental problems.

Conservatives lobbied hard against Waxman-Markey, which they labeled "cap-and-tax" because government would keep the revenues from selling allowances. But many liberal activists also disliked the bill. They said it gave businesses permission to pollute. And most Americans had trouble understanding how the complex program would work or how it would benefit them.[34] Many observers say carbon taxes can be simpler and more understandable.

In addition, a carbon tax can be revenue-neutral, many supporters argue. Government could collect taxes on high-carbon fuels, either by taxing fuel producers (the simplest approach) or energy purchasers, then rebate the money to consumers when they file their annual income tax returns.

This approach "would make energy more expensive, but would greatly offset the regressive impact of increasing the cost of energy," says Adler of Case Western Reserve University. "It's also transparent. The more clearly we tax one thing and then send money directly back to people, the less ominous a carbon tax appears to be. Waxman-Markey was littered with special-interest giveaways, which magnified the suspicions that people have about this kind of legislation."

But many business interests strongly oppose a carbon tax, which they say would increase production costs, making their companies less competitive, especially if they compete with manufacturers in other countries where carbon isn't taxed. A study released earlier this year by the National Association of Manufacturers (NAM) contended that a carbon tax would reduce total U.S. manufacturing output by up to 15 percent in energy-intensive sectors. Higher production costs would put millions of jobs at risk and impel companies to reduce wages, which in turn would reduce workers' income. Eventually, workers would reduce their spending, which would dampen economic growth, the study said.[35]

"Manufacturers use one-third of all energy consumed in the U.S. and depend on reliable, low-cost energy sources to compete in a global marketplace," a coalition of manufacturing trade associations wrote to members of Congress in May, citing the NAM study.[36]

Industry representatives also say a carbon tax would hurt their ability to compete against fast-growing developing countries like China, which overtook the United States in 2006 as the world's largest GHG emitter. Earlier this year, however, China pledged to adopt its own carbon tax, although it has not yet offered details.[37]

Carbon tax advocates respond that emitting greenhouse gases imposes costs on society, in the form of climate change and all of its negative environmental effects. In their view, taxing carbon corrects an unfair advantage that fossil fuel producers reap when they are not required to pay the costs of carbon pollution.

"Oil and coal companies have been sending carbon pollution into the atmosphere since the Industrial Revolution. When these industries started, the risks were poorly understood. Today they know better," argued Sen. Sheldon Whitehouse, D-R.I., who has cosponsored legislation to impose a carbon tax. "On average, [economists'] estimates of the social cost of carbon are about $48 per ton of carbon dioxide — $48 per ton that these big businesses dodge and that we all pay for."

## BACKGROUND

### Measuring GHGs

Anthropogenic (human-driven) climate change is a relatively new scientific field, but it has deep roots. Scientists have understood for well over a century that Earth's climate has fluctuated between warm and cold phases

## CHRONOLOGY

**1890s-1950s** *Scientists study weather and the role of heat-trapping greenhouse gases (GHGs).*

**1896** Swedish chemist Svante Arrhenius develops first theory of human-caused climate change.

**1945** U.S. military agencies start funding basic weather and climate research.

**1950** The World Meteorological Organization is founded; it becomes a U.N. agency the next year.

**1957** American geochemist Charles David Keeling begins measuring atmospheric carbon dioxide ($CO_2$) levels at Mauna Loa, Hawaii.

**1980s** *Environmentalists push for pollution limits in developed countries. Scientists warn that human activities are warming the planet.*

**1988** Testifying before Congress, NASA scientist James Hansen warns that Earth's climate is warming with potentially disastrous impacts.

**1987** Nations adopt the Montreal Protocol, setting international limits on gases that destroy Earth's ozone layer.

**1988** U.N. creates Intergovernmental Panel on Climate Change (IPCC) to provide governments with expert views on climate change science.

**1990s** *Governments pledge to tackle climate change, but worry about costs.*

**1990** First IPCC assessment report says global temperatures have risen and are likely to continue warming.

**1992** At the Earth Summit in Rio de Janeiro, the United States and more than 150 other nations sign the Framework Convention on Climate Change (FCCC), pledging to cut all GHG emissions to 1990 levels by 2000.

**1995** Second IPCC report finds scientific evidence of human-driven warming.

**1997** FCCC member nations adopt the Kyoto Protocol, which requires developed countries to cut GHG emissions 5.2 percent, on average, by 2012. The Senate votes 95-0 not to adopt binding U.S. targets until developing nations also have to make cuts.

**2000s-Present** *Evidence mounts that human activities are warming the planet. Scientists find increasing evidence that climate change is altering weather patterns, ocean chemistry and other Earth systems.*

**2001** Third IPCC report says major global warming is "very likely."

**2005** The Kyoto Protocol enters into force after Russia ratifies it, leaving the United States and Australia as the only nonparticipating industrialized nations.

**2006** Dutch Nobel laureate Paul Crutzen calls for active research into geoengineering.

**2007** Fourth IPCC assessment finds with more than 90 percent certainty that human activities are warming the climate. . . . Australia ratifies Kyoto Protocol. . . . U.S. Supreme Court rules that the Environmental Protection Agency can regulate $CO_2$ as a pollutant.

**2008** Newly elected President Barack Obama pledges quick action on climate change

**2009-2010** Legislation creating a system of marketable permits to emit GHGs narrowly passes House (2009), fails to reach Senate floor. . . . Republicans win control of House in midterm elections.

**2011** A conservative government announces that Canada will withdraw from the Kyoto Protocol because Canadian companies would have to buy too many carbon emission credits in order to meet the country's emission-control target.

**2012** Kyoto Protocol member countries extend the agreement at the last minute and commit to developing a follow-on treaty requiring cuts from more countries by 2015.

**2013** President Obama calls for action to slow climate change, pledging to use regulations if Congress will not pass legislation.

# Global Warming Will Hit Poor the Hardest

*"The heat must be turned down."*

Will the planet warm by 2°C in coming decades, or 4 degrees — or even more? The question may seem trivial, but the difference could mean life or death for millions of people worldwide, especially in poor nations.

A 2012 report commissioned by the World Bank warned that while all countries will be affected by climate change, "the poor will suffer most, and the global community could become more fractured and unequal than today." That scenario is especially likely if the world warms by 4°C (7.2° F) above pre-industrial levels — the likely outcome if nations don't start cutting emissions sharply.[1]

"The projected 4°C warming simply must not be allowed to occur — the heat must be turned down," the report asserted.[2]

Scientists are still quantifying all of the potential impacts from a 4°C jump in temperature, but the report warns that risks from heat waves, altered rainfall patterns and drought will increase — even with a 2°C (3.6°F) temperature rise — and will be much more severe with 4°C of warming. For example:

- With a 2-degree rise in temperature, the average amount of water flowing yearly through the Danube, Mississippi and Amazon river basins would fall 20 to 40 percent, while flow in the Nile and Ganges river basins would rise by about 20 percent. With 4°C of warming, those changes would roughly double, increasing the likelihood and severity of droughts and flooding.

- If temperatures rise 1.5 to 2 degrees Celsius by 2050, the number of forest fires in the Amazon rain forest could double. With 4°C of warming, the number of fires would increase even more.[3]

Geophysical factors are part of why climate change will affect poor countries more than rich countries. Sea-level rise is likely to be 15 to 20 percent higher in the tropics than the average increase around the globe because of warming-related changes in ocean circulation patterns. And warming is expected to make tropical cyclones (hurricanes) more intense, while dry areas in many tropical and subtropical regions are likely to become drier as the climate warms.[4]

In addition, developing countries typically are less prepared for disasters and may not be able to provide adequate disaster relief to those whose lives will be uprooted by storms, floods or heat waves. According to the Intergovernmental Panel on Climate Change (IPCC), a scientific organization that advises national governments, more than 95 percent of deaths from natural disasters between 1970 and 2008 occurred in developing countries. However, economic losses were higher in wealthy countries, where more buildings and infrastructure were at risk.[5]

throughout history, and have studied factors that contribute to such changes.

For example, in 1864 Scottish physicist James Croll theorized that regular variations in Earth's orbit could trigger ice ages by changing how and where the sun's energy fell on the planet. Eighty years later Milutin Milankovic, a Serbian geophysicist, calculated these shifts more precisely and developed a theory of glacial periods, now known as Milankovic cycles.

Swedish chemist Svante Arrhenius was the first scientist to suggest that human activities could affect planetary climate cycles. In 1896 Arrhenius published the first explanation of how two greenhouse gases — $CO_2$ and water

vapor — trapped heat in the atmosphere. He also recognized that humans were increasing $CO_2$ concentrations by burning fossil fuels, but assumed that it would take thousands of years for those activities to have a measurable impact.

In 1938 Guy Callendar, an English inventor, estimated that humans had added about 150 billion tons of $CO_2$ to the atmosphere since the 1880s. He collected temperature records from around the world and concluded that rising GHG concentrations were raising the planet's temperature. Like Arrhenius, he thought warming would benefit humans by extending growing seasons. "In any case, the return of the deadly glaciers should be delayed indefinitely," he wrote.[38]

The IPCC's definition of disaster risk is based on three factors:

- Weather and climate events, such as hurricanes or heat waves;
- Exposure — people living in areas where those events occur; and
- Vulnerability — whether victims have well-built homes or shelters, access to medical care, insurance and other resources to help them through the disasters.

"For the poor and vulnerable, a non-huge disaster can have huge consequences," says Christopher Field, a professor of global ecology at Stanford University and co-chair of the IPCC's working group on impacts, adaptation and vulnerability. For example, during urban heat waves the poor, elderly and infirm are much more likely to die than their more affluent neighbors.[6]

"Societies can moderate impacts of high heat by setting up cooling centers and increasing access to electricity for air conditioning, but if they're unprepared there can be very heavy loss of life," says Field.

Climate change threatens basic needs for the poor, such as access to clean drinking water and adequate food supplies. According to the World Bank report, 2°C to 2.5°C of warming would increase the rate of childhood stunting (failure to grow at normal rates because of undernourishment), especially in sub-Saharan Africa and South Asia, a problem likely to be more severe as warming increases. Higher temperatures also will expand the geographic ranges of many infectious diseases such as malaria, with higher risks for those without access to vaccinations and medical care.[7]

Climate change is a "clear and present danger . . . to our development plans and objectives and the health of economies large and small in all regions," United Nations Secretary-General Ban Ki-moon said in April. "The poor and vulnerable are the ones most hit and targeted, but no nation will be immune."[8]

— *Jennifer Weeks*

[1]"Turn Down the Heat: Why a 4°C Warmer World Must Be Avoided," Potsdam Institute for Climate Impact Research and Climate Analytics, (prepared for the World Bank), November 2012, p. xviii, http://climate change.worldbank.org/sites/default/files/Turn_Down_the_heat_ Why_a_4_degree_centrigrade_warmer_world_must_be_avoided.pdf.

[2]*Ibid.*

[3]*Ibid.*, p. xvi.

[4]*Ibid.*, p. xiii.

[5]"Managing the Risks of Extreme Events and Disasters to Advance Climate Change Adaptation," Intergovernmental Panel on Climate Change, 2012, p. 7, http://ipcc-wg2.gov/SREX/images/uploads/SREX-SPMbrochure_FINAL.pdf.

[6]For example, see Micah Maidenburg, "The 1995 Heat Wave Reflected Chicago's 'Geography of Vulnerabilty,' " *ChicagoNow.com*, July 20, 2011, www.chicagonow.com/chicago-muckrakers/2011/07/the-1995-heat-wave-reflected-chicagos-geography-of-vulnerability/.

[7]"Turn Down the Heat," *op. cit.*, p. xvii.

[8]"Climate change is a 'clear and present danger,' says UN Chief," United Nations, April 19, 2013, www.unmultimedia.org/radio/eng lish/2013/04/climate-change-is-a-clear-and-present-danger-to-human kind-says-un-chief/.

But after further study, scientists began to worry about where all of the excess $CO_2$ would go. In 1957 Roger Revelle and Hans Suess of California's Scripps Institution of Oceanography published a study showing that most human-generated $CO_2$ emissions up to that time had been absorbed by the world's oceans. But the oceans were nearing their capacity for absorbing $CO_2$, so the gas was accumulating in the atmosphere, they contended, with unknown results.

"[H]uman beings are now carrying out a large-scale geophysical experiment," Revelle and Suess warned. "Within a few centuries we are returning to the atmosphere and oceans the concentrated organic carbon [that was] stored in sedimentary rocks over hundreds of millions of years."[39]

Climate science expanded rapidly in the 1950s and 1960s. International research groups in the United States, England, Mexico and elsewhere began designing general models to simulate the many complex processes that created Earth's climate, such as ocean currents and wind patterns. Scientists used these models to test theories about how the system might change in response to natural or manmade events.

French, Danish, Swiss, Russian and U.S. scientists drilled into ice sheets in Greenland and Antarctica and analyzed air bubbles from thousands of years earlier to

President Obama has called for cutting emissions of heat-trapping gases from power plants and other sources and pledged to use regulations if Congress fails to act. Environmental advocates say the president could take other steps as well, including rejecting the proposed Keystone XL crude oil pipeline from Alberta, Canada, and tightening restrictions on hydraulic fracturing, or fracking.

determine how the atmosphere's composition had changed over time. A growing body of research showed that many processes shaped global climate patterns, and that human actions could disrupt the system.

## Calls for Action

In the late 1960s public concerns about pollution and over-development in industrialized countries triggered a global environmental movement. Governments began setting standards for air and water quality, waste management and land conservation.

Congress established the Environmental Protection Agency (EPA) in 1970 and a wave of major environmental laws followed, including the Clean Air and Clean Water acts, the Endangered Species Act and the National Environmental Policy Act, which required federal agencies to consider the environmental impacts of major government projects. A 1972 international conference on the environment in Stockholm set lofty goals for international cooperation and led to creation of the United Nations Environment Programme.

Global climate change had not yet become a policy issue, but scientists were drawing more connections between

atmospheric GHG concentrations, rising temperatures and alarming potential consequences, such as a melting and breaking apart of Antarctic ice sheets. By the early 1980s, many prominent scientists were warning that heavy fossil fuel use was warming the planet, with possible widespread effects.[40]

By the late 1980s, environmental groups were calling for reductions in fossil fuel use. But critics argued that scientific evidence for climate change was uncertain and that reducing emissions would seriously harm economic growth by forcing businesses and households to use more expensive low-carbon energy sources.

Western Europe, with its strong Green parties, pressed for an international agreement to limit GHGs. In 1992 nations signed the Framework Convention on Climate Change (FCCC) at the Earth Summit in Rio de Janeiro, Brazil. The treaty called for voluntarily reducing GHGs to 1990 levels, but did not set binding national limits or timetables.

## Climate Wars

As it became clear that nonbinding pledges would not slow rising GHG concentrations, the focus shifted to numerical limits. In 1997 nations adopted the Kyoto Protocol, which required developed countries to reduce their GHG emissions, on average, by 5.2 percent below 1990 levels by 2012. It also created programs to slow emission growth in developing countries, including international trading of emission allowances and credits for wealthy countries that paid for emission reduction projects in developing countries.[41]

The framework recognized that developed countries were responsible for virtually all warming above pre-industrial levels that had already occurred, but fast-growing developing nations such as China, India and Brazil also were becoming major emitters. But the U.S. Senate made clear that it would not ratify the pact unless developing countries also were required to make binding reduction pledges. Accordingly, President Bill Clinton, who had signed the Kyoto Protocol in 1997, never submitted it to the Senate for ratification, although both he and Vice President Al Gore supported action to address climate change.

The prospect of national legislation to cut GHG emissions energized fossil-fuel interests, which were funding work by some conservative think tanks and media outlets to discredit scientific evidence of a human role in climate change. As long as the scientific evidence was uncertain, these advocates argued, it did not make sense to limit GHG emissions. Over time, the Republican Party came to strongly oppose government efforts to address climate change.[42]

Shortly after he was sworn into office, Republican President George W. Bush (2001-2009) renounced Clinton's decision to sign the Kyoto agreement and said cutting GHG emissions would harm the U.S. economy. Bush's presidency was also marked by what many observers came to refer to as "climate wars" — harsh debates over the accuracy of climate science. "There is still a window of opportunity to challenge the science," Republican political consultant Frank Luntz wrote in a 2002 strategy memo. To prevent voters from supporting action to slow climate change, he argued, politicians should "continue to make the lack of certainty a primary issue in the debate."[43]

Despite these arguments, some national leaders — including Republicans — pressed for the United States to take action. In 2003, 2005 and 2007, Sens. John McCain, R-Ariz., and Joseph Lieberman, D-Conn., introduced bills to create a cap-and-trade system for reducing U.S. carbon emissions. And some major corporations began endorsing carbon controls. "We know enough to act on climate change," the U.S. Climate Action Partnership (an alliance of major corporations including Alcoa, DuPont and General Electric) said in January 2007.[44]

Also in 2007 the IPCC and former Vice President Gore — who had argued strongly for action on climate change in the Academy Award-winning documentary *An Inconvenient Truth* — were awarded the Nobel Peace Prize, a sign of strong international concern about climate change.[45]

## Obama's Record

Many observers expected progress on climate change after Obama was elected in 2008. As a candidate, he had pledged to support clean-energy options and work for passage of a national cap-and-trade system to limit GHG emissions.

Initially, however, Obama's attention was consumed by the worldwide recession that had begun in 2007. Obama's major legislative successes in 2009 were economic rescue measures, including a $787 billion economic stimulus package and a bailout plan for U.S. automakers.

In such economic circumstances, proposing policies that would raise the price of fossil fuels was much more challenging than it would have been in a strong economy.

In June 2009 the House passed the Waxman-Markey cap-and-trade bill by a narrow 219-212 margin.[46] Many environmental advocates hailed it as a first step, but others complained it set what they saw as weak emissions limits and allowed polluters to "offset" some of their emissions by paying for cleanup projects elsewhere.[47]

Without strong support from the public or liberal environmentalists, and with conservatives labeling it an "energy tax," Senate Democratic leaders opted not to bring the bill up for consideration.[48] Then in the 2010 midterm elections Republicans won control of the House, making it effectively impossible to enact climate change legislation. Conservative legislators, particularly those affiliated with or seeking support from the conservative anti-tax Tea Party movement, challenged numerous laws and regulations as government intrusions into private decisions — including previously uncontroversial policies such as efficiency standards for light bulbs.[49]

Obama's main climate-related success was negotiating tighter fuel efficiency and greenhouse gas pollution standards for new cars and trucks. These changes, announced in 2011, were projected to cut U.S. oil use by 12 billion barrels and avoid 6 billion metric tons of $CO_2$ emissions — equivalent to all of U.S. emissions in 2010.[50]

During the 2012 presidential race, Obama and his GOP opponent, former Massachusetts Gov. Mitt Romney, largely avoided the topic of climate change. (Romney had supported state GHG limits as governor, then reversed his position shortly before leaving office.) Instead, they both emphasized producing energy from as many sources as possible, including coal, oil and natural gas. Obama also advocated more government support for solar, wind and other renewable energy sources, while Romney called for leaving energy choices up to the market.[51]

Just before the election, New York City Mayor Michael Bloomberg, an independent who had been courted by both campaigns, endorsed Obama, partly because he believed Obama was more likely to act to slow climate change. Bloomberg made his announcement just after Superstorm Sandy, an immense hurricane, flooded parts of Manhattan and devastated coastal New Jersey.

# Geoengineering Proposals Would Alter Earth's Climate

*Scientists say the controversial techniques demand more study.*

Shooting small particles into Earth's upper atmosphere to reflect incoming sunlight back into space. Dumping large quantities of iron into the oceans to stimulate the growth of pollution-eating plankton. Those are just two of the futuristic methods engineers have considered as ways to keep the planet from overheating.

So-called geoengineering techniques involve large-scale efforts to alter Earth's climate system in order to reduce the impact of climate change. They fall into two broad categories: Managing the amount of energy from the sun that falls on Earth's surface, and scrubbing millions of tons of heat-trapping carbon dioxide ($CO_2$) from the atmosphere.

Strategies designed to control the amount of heat from the sun striking the Earth include:

- Injecting small reflective particles, such as sulfates, into the upper atmosphere to reflect some sunlight back to space.
- Spraying salt water into the lower atmosphere, which makes clouds brighter and more reflective (water vapor in the atmosphere condenses around salt particles, increasing the number of droplets in clouds).
- Installing reflective objects in space between the Earth and sun; and
- Increasing the percentage of Earth's surface covered with light-colored, reflective surfaces, through such techniques as painting millions of roofs white.

Engineers believe shooting reflective particles into the atmosphere would be the most cost-effective and feasible approach, but some scientists worry that it could change rain and snowfall patterns, damage the Earth's ozone layer or increase air pollution.[1]

Strategies for removing carbon dioxide from the atmosphere include planting more forests, which consume and store carbon as trees grow; "fertilizing" the oceans by dumping large quantities of iron to stimulate the growth of plankton, which absorbs $CO_2$ as it multiplies; and capturing $CO_2$ by passing air through "scrubbers" that remove carbon dioxide. The $CO_2$ would then be injected into deep underground reservoirs.

No international treaty or agency governs geoengineering, and many critics say efforts to manipulate weather and climate on such massive scales could threaten human health, forests or fisheries.

One widely publicized geoengineering experiment was conducted by Russ George, an American businessman who has tried several ocean-fertilization experiments, seeking to demonstrate that by locking $CO_2$ up in the deep ocean a company can generate marketable "carbon credits." But studies have not yet shown that ocean fertilization actually removes significant amounts of carbon from the atmosphere, so he doesn't have any buyers yet.

Spain and Ecuador barred George from their ports after he sought to carry out ocean fertilization experiments near the Galápagos and Canary islands, which officials contended would pollute the seas and threaten biodiversity.[2] Controversy over his proposals spurred the United Nations to adopt a moratorium on ocean fertilization experiments. Nonetheless, George dumped 100 metric tons of iron sulphate off Canada's west coast last fall, generating a large plankton bloom. He said international treaties barring ocean dumping and actions that might threaten biodiversity were "mythology" and did not apply to his activities.[3]

"Our climate is changing. And while the increase in extreme weather we have experienced in New York City and around the world may or may not be the result of it, the risk that it might be — given this week's devastation — should compel all elected leaders to take immediate action," Bloomberg said.[52]

## CURRENT SITUATION

### Bypassing Congress

With Congress sharply divided along party lines, observers see little prospect for legislation to address climate change during Obama's second term. But environmental

The Canadian government belatedly launched an investigation into George's experiment, which was partly funded by a native Haida community on the coast in hopes that a plankton bloom would help restore traditional salmon runs.[4] But the president of the Haida Nation, Guujaw, denounced the village's action. "Our people, along with the rest of humanity, depend on the oceans and cannot leave the fate of the oceans to the whim of the few," he said.[5]

In its last major climate change assessment report, the Intergovernmental Panel on Climate Change (IPCC) called geoengineering techniques such as ocean fertilization "speculative" and noted that many of the potential environmental side effects had yet to be studied, no detailed cost estimates existed and there was no legal or political framework for implementing such projects.[6] The IPCC held an expert workshop on geoengineering in 2011, and its next assessment, scheduled to be published in late 2014, will consider the science, potential impacts and uncertainties of geoengineering in more detail.

Meanwhile, many nations are concerned about how geoengineering strategies could affect climate cycles and natural resources. A 2012 report for the U.N. Convention on Biological Diversity (an international treaty signed by 193 countries that aims to protect Earth's natural resources) concluded that few proposed geoengineering strategies had been well researched and no good systems had been designed for regulating them. In short, the report concluded, much more study was needed.[7]

Large-scale application of geoengineering techniques "is near-certain to involve unintended side effects and increase sociopolitical tensions," the report observed. "While technological innovation has helped to transform societies and improve the quality of life in many ways, it has not always done so in a sustainable manner."[8]

*— Jennifer Weeks*

AFP/Getty images/Arlan Naeg

The 1991 eruption of Mt. Pinatubo in the Philippines caused global temperatures to drop temporarily by nearly 1°C by sending millions of tons of sulfur dioxide into the atmosphere. The gas formed sulfate particles, which reflected some of the sun's radiation back into space.

[2]Kalee Thompson, "Carbon Discredit," *Popular Science*, July 1, 2008, www.popsci.com/environment/article/2008-07/carbon-discredit?single-page-view=true.

[3]Martin Lukacs, "World's Biggest Geoengineering Experiment 'Violates' UN Rules," *The Guardian*, Oct. 15, 2012, www.guardian.co.uk/environment/2012/oct/15/pacific-iron-fertilisation-geoengineering.

[4]"B.C. Village's Ocean Fertilization Experiment Probed," CBC News, March 28, 2013, www.cbc.ca/news/canada/british-columbia/story/2013/03/27/bc-iron-restoration-fifth-estate.html.

[5]"West Coast Ocean Fertilization Project Defended," CBC News, Oct. 22, 2012, www.cbc.ca/news/canada/british-columbia/story/2012/10/19/bc-ocean-fertilization-haida.html.

[6]"Climate Change 2007: Mitigation of Climate Change," Intergovernmental Panel on Climate Change, section 11.2.2, 2007, www.ipcc.ch/publications_and_data/ar4/wg3/en/ch11s11-2-2.html.

[7]"Impacts of Climate-Related Geoengineering on Biological Diversity," Convention on Biodiversity, April 5, 2013, pp. 3, 9, www.cbd.int/doc/meetings/sbstta/sbstta-16/information/sbstta-16-inf-28-en.pdf.

[8]*Ibid.*, p. 8.

[1]"IPCC Expert Meeting on Geoengineering," Intergovernmental Panel on Climate Change, June 20-22, 2011, pp. 19-20, www.ipcc.ch/pdf/supporting-material/EM_GeoE_Meeting_Report_final.pdf.

advocates say he can make significant progress through executive actions and regulations.

"By far the most important step the president can take is using his authority under the Clean Air Act to finalize carbon pollution limits for new power plants [i.e., plants not yet constructed] and develop limits for existing power plants," says David Goldston, government affairs director for the Natural Resources Defense Council (NRDC), a national environmental advocacy group. "That could reduce $CO_2$ output from power plants by 25 percent."

The EPA proposed a carbon pollution standard for new power plants in 2012 after the Supreme Court ruled

The glaciers at Glacier National Park in Montana (above) are melting, along with many of the world's other glaciers and Arctic ice. Some officials have called for limiting temperature increases to 2°C, but some climate experts say even that could cause most of the world's glaciers and ice caps to melt.

in 2007 that the agency had authority to regulate carbon dioxide as a pollutant under the Clean Air Act.[53] The proposed standard would limit carbon emissions from fossil-fuel-burning power plants to 1,000 pounds of $CO_2$ per megawatt-hour of electricity generated.[54]

According to the agency, new natural gas plants should be able to meet the standard without additional controls. But coal-fired plants emit carbon dioxide at about twice that rate, so new coal plants would need extra pollution controls. Because the price of natural gas has dropped sharply in recent years, the EPA and Department of Energy (DOE) expect that new power plants likely will burn gas, so they don't expect the coal plant rule to affect energy prices or reliability.[55]

But in April the EPA put the new rule on hold indefinitely after energy companies said it would effectively kill any new coal-fired power plants. Agency officials said the rule would be rewritten to provide more flexibility.[56] And during her confirmation hearings this spring to be administrator of EPA, Gina McCarthy said the agency was not developing GHG regulations for existing power plants.[57]

Environmentalists also suggest other steps Obama could take to limit GHG emissions, including:

- Rejecting the proposed Keystone XL pipeline, which would carry crude oil from tar sand deposits in Alberta, Canada, to refineries on the U.S. Gulf Coast. "Tar sand oil is far more polluting than traditional fossil fuels," says Goldston.
- Further tightening energy efficiency standards for appliances, electronics and other equipment.
- Maintaining robust funding for renewable energy research and development; and
- Regulating the environmental impacts of hydraulic fracturing, or "fracking," for natural gas, including limits on methane emissions.[58] Methane, the main component of natural gas, is a greenhouse gas, and critics contend that methane leaks from fracking operations contribute significantly to climate change, although energy companies say the problem can be managed.[59]

Any new regulations could face legal challenges, especially if industry says they would cost too much to implement. But Goldston believes courts will uphold reasonable climate protection rules. "Everyone knows there will be challenges, but there's no reason that well-written standards shouldn't survive in court," he says.

Republican opposition to greenhouse gas regulations figured prominently in debate over Obama's choice of McCarthy as EPA administrator. McCarthy currently heads the agency's Air and Radiation program (a position for which the Senate confirmed her by voice vote in 2009) and has also worked for Republican governors in Massachusetts and Connecticut. Her nomination was praised by business leaders: Gloria Bergquist, vice president of the Alliance of Automobile Manufacturers, called her a "pragmatic policymaker" who "accepts real-world economics."[60]

But Republicans on the Senate Environment and Public Works Committee asked McCarthy more than

AT ISSUE

# Should the United States adopt a carbon tax?

## YES
**William G. Gale**
*Co-Director,*
*Urban-Brookings Tax Policy Center*

From "The Tax Favored by Most Economists," Brookings Institution, March 12, 2013, www.brookings.edu/research/opinions/2013/03/12-taxing-carbon-gale

Looking for a public policy that would improve the . . . economy, lower our dependence on foreign oil, reduce pollution, slow global warming, allow cuts in government spending and decrease the long-term deficit? Then a carbon tax is what you want. . . .

Energy consumption [involves] substantial societal costs — including air and water pollution, road congestion and climate change. Since many of these costs are not directly borne by those who use fossil fuels, they are ignored when energy production and consumption choices are made, resulting in too much consumption and production of fossil fuels. Economists have long recommended a tax on fossil-fuel energy sources as an efficient way to address this problem. . . .

Most analyses find that a carbon tax could significantly reduce emissions. Tufts University economist Gilbert Metcalf estimated that a $15 per ton tax on $CO_2$ emissions that rises over time would reduce greenhouse gas emissions by 14 percent. . . .

A carbon tax . . . has been implemented in several other countries, including the Scandinavian nations, the Netherlands, Germany, the United Kingdom and Australia. . . . Estimates suggest that a well-designed tax in the United States could raise . . . up to 1 percent of GDP, [which] could . . . address the country's . . . medium- and long-term budget deficits.

A carbon tax could [also reduce U.S.] dependence on foreign sources of energy and [create] better market incentives for energy conservation, the use of renewable energy sources and the production of energy-efficient goods. . . .

Two problems are sometimes raised in response to a federal carbon tax proposal. The first is its impact on low-income households, who use most of their income for consumption. However, this . . . could be offset [through] refundable income tax credits or payroll tax credits.

The second concern is whether the U.S. should act unilaterally. Without cooperation from the rest of the world, critics fear that a U.S. carbon tax would reduce economic activity here and make little difference to overall carbon emissions or levels. This view . . . discounts the experience of other countries that unilaterally created carbon taxes; there is no evidence that they paid a significant price, or any price at all, in terms of economic activity levels.

No one is claiming the carbon tax is a perfect outcome. But relative to the alternatives, it has an enormous amount to offer.

## NO
**Kenneth P. Green***
*Senior Director, Energy and Natural Resources*
*Studies, Fraser Institute, Calgary, Canada*

From "Why a Carbon Tax is Still a Bad Idea," American Enterprise Institute, Aug. 28, 2012

Taxes on carbon are not simply taxes on consumption, they're a tax on production as well, since energy is a primary input to production. Taxing both production and consumption seems like a poor way to stimulate your economy, reduce your costs of production or make your exports more competitive.

Carbon taxes are regressive. Poorer people spend a higher portion of their household budget on energy than do the better off. [Unless] you were to posit redistributing the tax to the poor, higher energy costs [will] slap the lower-end of the income spectrum hard.

Taxing carbon gets you virtually no climate or health benefit unless it exists within some binding, international carbon control regime, which is unlikely. China and India will dominate global carbon emissions for the next century, while emissions in the developed world are already level or in decline. And, global negotiations over carbon controls have become a farce in which developing countries fish for wealth and intellectual property transfers, while developed countries make promises they have little intention of keeping.

Carbon taxes would put a share (potentially a large share) of the U.S. tax system under the influence of bureaucrat-scientists at the U.N. You can guarantee that there would be steady pressure to tax carbon at ever-higher rates (and transfer some of that booty to developing countries!). Do we really want "the science" of climate change as developed by the U.N. setting our tax rates?

We already have a vast array of regulations aimed at reducing carbon emissions, [so] new carbon taxes would represent double-taxation. You're already paying carbon taxes in the additional costs of new vehicles with higher fuel emission standards, more expensive appliances that aim to conserve energy, renewable energy standards that raise your cost of electricity, etc.

For the record, I'm a "lukewarmer" [on global warming] and I've written (since 1998) that some resilience-building actions would be wise in the face of climate risk, but a carbon tax? In the real world, like other eco-taxes, carbon taxes would quickly morph into just another form of taxation that feeds the ever-hungry maw of big government.

*Green was a policy analyst at the American Enterprise Institute when he wrote this commentary.

1,100 questions for the record during her confirmation process — seven times as many as McCarthy's predecessor, Lisa Jackson, faced. The Republican Policy Committee contended that McCarthy had "played a central role in authoring environmental regulations that could effectively ban the use of coal as an energy source," alluding to the carbon standards for new power plants. The committee also charged that EPA was working to undercut approval of the Keystone XL pipeline by criticizing the State Department's environmental review of the project.[61]

All eight committee Republicans voted against McCarthy's nomination, which was supported by all 10 Democrats. The nomination could face a Republican filibuster on the Senate floor. A *Boston Globe* editorial said the GOP was trying to "bully the EPA into lowering pollution standards." If McCarthy is eventually confirmed, *The Globe* observed, she will face looming challenges — in particular, rising GHG emissions.[62]

## Public Concern

Recent polls show that while climate change remains a divisive issue, the public is much less polarized than Congress, with a majority of respondents believing global warming is occurring. And while Democrats are more likely than Republicans to believe in global warming, some polls show that Republicans increasingly agree. For instance:

• A March Gallup poll found that 66 percent of Americans believe global warming has already begun or will begin soon or within their lifetimes. And the share of those who believe human activity causes climate change has jumped from 50 percent in 2010 to 57 percent today.[63]

• An April Pew Research Center poll found that 69 percent of Americans believe there is solid evidence Earth is warming (including 44 percent of Republicans), and 42 percent believe it is caused mostly by human activity. Both beliefs have been increasing since about 2010.[64]

• A University of Michigan study conducted last fall found that the percentage of Republicans who believe in global warming rose from 33 percent in 2010 to 51 percent in 2012.[65]

• Similarly, a George Mason University survey in January found that 52 percent of Republicans and Republican-leaning independents believe climate change is occurring.[66]

However, Stephen Ansolabehere, a professor of government at Harvard University who has conducted numerous surveys of public views about energy and climate change, says "the public is of two minds about climate change. People generally accept that it's happening, but they don't see it as an urgent issue." The Gallup survey, for instance, found that 64 percent of respondents did not see climate change as a threat to them or their lifestyles, while the Pew poll found that only 33 percent of respondents called global warming a "very serious" problem.

Since climate change is not considered an impending crisis, surveys indicate Americans are only willing to make minor sacrifices to deal with it. Ansolabehere has found that respondents, on average, would spend only $10 per month to shift to low-carbon energy sources. "That's an important first step, but it's only a modest one," he says.

Polls also suggest that many Americans do not support broad national, taxpayer-supported solutions. In a March survey commissioned by Stanford University, respondents were asked who should pay for projects to protect coastal communities from flooding, such as building sea walls and manmade dunes. More than 80 percent said such projects should be funded by raising local property taxes for those who live near shorelines.[67]

More extreme weather events could convince Americans that climate change is an imminent threat. "Big galvanizing examples can change public opinion across generations in a lasting way," says Ansolabehere. "The cleanest examples are the accident at Three Mile Island, which completely reset the nuclear power industry in the United States, and Chernobyl, which did the same in Europe. But Hurricane Sandy plus droughts in Texas and the Midwest are starting to make people realize they need to be concerned about weather."

Indeed, wrote Trenberth, at the National Center for Atmospheric Research, and Princeton's Michael Oppenheimer, "There is conclusive evidence that climate change worsened the damage caused by Superstorm Sandy. Sea levels in New York City harbors have risen by more than a foot since the beginning of the 20th century. Had the storm surge not been riding on higher seas, there would have been less flooding and less damage.

Warmer air also allows storms such as Sandy to hold more moisture and dump more rainfall, exacerbating flooding."[68]

## OUTLOOK

### Adapting and Leading

As the impacts of climate change become increasingly clear, scientists say the United States must spend more money and resources to help the nation adapt to extreme weather and other climate-related events.

"Water will be one of the biggest pressure points on society," says NCAR's Trenberth. "The intensity and frequency of rain and storms will increase, with longer dry spells. Even if we get the same average amount of precipitation yearly, the way it's distributed over time will become harder to manage, and shortages will be more likely."[69]

Rising sea levels are also highly likely. "Storm surges, high tides and flood events all are amplified by rising seas. A few inches of sea level rise can make a big difference in the amount of damage," says Stanford's Field.

Other effects could be devastating for many regions. "Droughts are becoming longer or more severe in some parts of world, but shortening in others," says Field. Hurricane frequency "probably won't change, but more storms will grow to the most damaging levels. Tornadoes are a very active area of research, and we may see some new results over the next decade."

As the science of climate change improves, prospects for leadership from the United States or other major greenhouse gas emitters remain murky. Environmental advocates hope for strong action from the Obama administration, especially on power plant emissions. "President Obama took very important actions in his first term, especially raising mileage standards for passenger cars," says the NRDC's Goldston. "That policy will save money, reduce fuel consumption, and cut a large chunk of carbon pollution. Power plant standards are the next logical step."

Others see promoting innovative low-carbon energy sources and technologies as a better long-term strategy. "We need ways to drive down the cost of decarbonization, and regulatory mandates aren't likely to do that," says Adler of Case Western Reserve University. "Encouraging more innovation is the way to get large developing countries onto a low-carbon development path. Going after energy subsidies, especially for high-carbon fuels, would also help. So would reducing regulatory barriers that impede nontraditional energy sources like offshore wind energy, tidal power, solar generation on federal lands and next-generation nuclear reactors."

Meanwhile, environmentalists and policymakers are closely watching China, the world's largest GHG source. "If China puts a price on carbon, that could really change the international dynamic," says Arvind Subramanian, a senior fellow at the Center for Global Development, a research center in Washington, D.C. "And if China becomes a leader in green technologies, that would have an even bigger impact. It could make developed countries fear that they were losing leadership and rouse the United States into stronger action."

Field would like to see more emphasis on potential profits from building low-carbon economies. "There are rich and exciting prospects for developing new technologies that will help us solve the climate problem," Field says. "I'd like to shift away from viewing climate policies as scary economic choices and frame them as exciting business opportunities. One person's risk is another person's opportunity to capture markets."

## NOTES

1. Justin Gillis, "Carbon Dioxide Level Passes Long-Feared Milestone," *The New York Times*, May 10, 2013, www.nytimes.com/2013/05/11/science/earth/carbon-dioxide-level-passes-long-feared-milestone.html?hp.

2. John Vidal, "Large Rise in $CO_2$ Emissions Sounds Climate Change Alarm," *The Guardian*, March 8, 2013, www.guardian.co.uk/environment/2013/mar/08/hawaii-climate-change-second-greatest-annual-rise-emissions.

3. For recent overviews see "Climate Change Science Overview," U.S. Environmental Protection Agency, April 22, 2013, www.epa.gov/climatechange/science/overview.html; and "Climate Change: Evidence, Impacts, and Choices," National Research Council, 2012, http://nas-sites.org/americasclimatechoices/files/2012/06/19014_cvtx_R1.pdf.

4. John Cook, *et al.*, "Quantifying the Consensus on Anthropogenic Global Warming in the Scientific Literature," *Environmental Research Letters*, vol. 8, 2013, http://iopscience.iop.org/1748-9326/8/2/024024.

5. Testimony before the Subcommittee on Environment, House Committee on Science, Space and Technology, April 25, 2013, p. 8, http://science.house.gov/sites/republicans.science.house.gov/files/documents/HHRG-113-SY18-WState-JCurry-20130425.pdf.

6. Melillo's comments are from the American Association for the Advancement of Science annual conference, Feb. 18, 2013. The draft report is online at "Draft Climate Assessment Report," National Climate Assessment and Development Advisory Committee, January 2013, http://ncadac.globalchange.gov, and is scheduled to be finalized later in 2013.

7. "Research Highlight: The Little Ice Age Was Global, Scripps Researchers Say," *Explorations Now*, June 7, 2012, http://explorations.ucsd.edu/research-highlights/2012/research-highlight-the-little-ice-age-was-global-scripps-researchers-say/; Edna Sun, "Little Ice Age," *Scientific American Frontiers*, Feb. 15, 2005, www.pbs.org/saf/1505/features/lia.htm.

8. "The Current and Future Consequences of Global Change," National Aeronautics and Space Administration, http://climate.nasa.gov/effects.

9. "Draft Climate Change Assessment Report," *op. cit.*, p. 3, http://ncadac.globalchange.gov/download/NCAJan11-2013-publicreviewdraft-chap1-execsum.pdf.

10. For background see Marcia Clemmitt, "Energy and Climate," *CQ Researcher*, July 24, 2009, pp. 621-644.

11. "Inaugural Address by President Barack Obama," Jan. 21, 2013, www.whitehouse.gov/the-press-office/2013/01/21/inaugural-address-president-barack-obama.

12. "Remarks by the President in the State of the Union Address," Feb. 12, 2013, www.whitehouse.gov/the-press-office/2013/02/12/remarks-president-state-union-address.

13. John Cook, *et al.*, *op. cit.* See also "Consensus: 97% of Climate Scientists Agree," National Aeronautics and Space Administration, http://climate.nasa.gov/scientific-consensus.

14. Roger Aronoff, "The Greatest Hoax? Global Warming, Says Sen. James Inhofe," *AIM Report*, May 30, 2012, www.aim.org/aim-report/the-greatest-hoax-global-warming-says-sen-james-inhofe/.

15. Lamar Smith, "Overheated Rhetoric on Climate Change Doesn't Make for Good Policies," *The Washington Post*, May 19, 2013, http://articles.washingtonpost.com/2013-05-19/opinions/39376700_1_emissions-carbon-dioxide-climate-change.

16. Andrew Restuccia and Darren Goode, "Obama's Achilles' Heel on Climate: Senate Democrats," *Politico*, March 25, 2013, www.politico.com/story/2013/03/obamas-achilles-heel-on-climate-senate-democrats-89295.html.

17. See "Continuing Partisan Divide in Views of Global Warming," Pew Research Center, April 2, 2013, p. 4, www.people-press.org/files/legacy-pdf/4-2-13%20Keystone%20Pipeline%20and%20Global%20Warming%20Release.pdf; and Lydia Saad, "Americans' Concerns About Global Warming on the Rise," *Gallup Politics*, April 8, 2013, www.gallup.com/poll/161645/americans-concerns-global-warming-rise.aspx. For details, see "Gallup Poll Social Series: Environment," March 7-10, 2013, question 25, www.usclimatenetwork.org/resource-database/poll-global-warming-fears-rising.

18. Coral Davenport, "The Coming GOP Civil War Over Climate Change," *National Journal*, May 9, 2013, www.nationaljournal.com/magazine/the-coming-gop-civil-war-over-climate-change-20130509. For a sample of Thernstrom's position see "Resetting Earth's Thermostat," American Enterprise Institute, June 2008, www.aei.org/files/2008/06/27/20080627_OTIThernstrom.pdf, p. 2.

19. William R. Moomaw, "Can the International Treaty System Address Climate Change?" Fletcher Forum of World Affairs, vol. 37, no. 1, winter 2013, p. 109, www.fletcherforum.org/wp-content/uploads/2013/02/Moomaw_37-1.pdf. For more background on limiting warming to 2ºC see Samuel Randalls, "History of the 2ºC Climate Target," *WIREs Climate Change*, vol. 1, July/August 2010, http://wires.wiley.com/WileyCDA/WiresArticle/wisId-WCC62.html.

20. "Limiting the Long-Term Increase of Global Temperature to 2º Celsius is Still Possible," International Energy Agency, Aug. 17, 2012, www.iea.org/newsroomandevents/news/2012/august/name,30638,en.html.

21. Alex Kirby, "Ex-IPCC Head: Prepare for 5°C Warmer World," *Climate Central*, Feb. 17, 2013, www.climatecentral.org/news/ex-ipcc-head-prepare-for-5c-warmer-world-15610.

22. "Draft Climate Assessment Report," *op. cit.*, pp. 25-26.

23. Mark Fischetti, "2-Degree Global Warming Limit is Called a 'Prescription for Disaster,'" *Scientific American.com*, Dec. 6, 2011, http://blogs.scientificamerican.com/observations/2011/12/06/two-degree-global-warming-limit-is-called-a-prescription-for-disaster/. For more on the 350 target, see http://350.org/en.

24. Thomas E. Lovejoy, "The Climate Change Endgame," *The New York Times*, Jan. 21, 2013, www.nytimes.com/2013/01/22/opinion/global/the-climate-change-endgame.html.

25. "Advancing the Science of Climate Change," National Research Council, 2010, p. 174, www.nap.edu/catalog.php?record_id=12782.

26. *Geoengineering the Climate: Science, Governance and Uncertainty* (2009), p. 56, http://royalsociety.org/uploadedFiles/Royal_Society_Content/policy/publications/2009/8693.pdf.

27. "David Keith on Climate Change and Geo-Engineering as a Solution," *Harvard PolicyCast*, Jan. 23, 2013, https://soundcloud.com/harvard/david-keith-on-climate-change.

28. Lynn M. Russell, "Offsetting Climate Change by Engineering Air Pollution to Brighten Clouds," *The Bridge*, Winter 2012, www.nae.edu/File.aspx?id=67680.

29. Kevin E. Trenberth and Aiguo Dai, "Effects of Mount Pinatubo Volcanic Eruption on the Hydrological Cycle as an Analog of Geoengineering," *Geophysical Research Letters*, vol. 34, Aug. 1, 2007, www.cgd.ucar.edu/cas/adai/papers/TrenberthDai_GRL07.pdf.

30. Edward A. Parson and David W. Keith, "End the Deadlock on Governance of Geoengineering Research," *Science*, vol. 339, March 15, 2013, www.keith.seas.harvard.edu/preprints/163.Parson.Keith.DeadlockOnGonvernance.p.pdf.

31. George P. Shultz and Gary S. Becker, "Why We Support a Revenue-Neutral Carbon Tax," *The Wall Street Journal*, April 7, 2013, http://online.wsj.com/article/SB10001424127887323611604578396401965799658.html.

32. "Mapping Carbon Pricing Initiatives: Development and Prospects," The World Bank, May 2013, http://www-wds.worldbank.org/external/default/WDSContentServer/WDSP/IB/2013/05/23/000350881_20130523172114/Rendered/PDF/779550WP0Mappi0til050290130morning0.pdf, pp. 57-58.

33. *Ibid.*, p. 43.

34. Theda Skocpol, "Naming the Problem: What It Will Take to Counter Extremism and Engage Americans in the Fight Against Global Warming," Harvard University, January 2013, http://www-wds.worldbank.org/external/default/WDSContentServer/WDSP/IB/2013/05/23/000350881_20130523172114/Rendered/PDF/779550WP0Mappi0til050290130morning0.pdf, pp. 45-55.

35. "Economic Outcomes of a U.S. Carbon Tax: Executive Summary," National Association of Manufacturers, March 2013, www.nam.org/~/media/ECF11DF347094E0DA8AF7BD9A696ABDB.ashx, p. 1.

36. National Association of Manufacturers, www.nam.org/~/media/9C72C0E7823B4E558DF3D49B65114615.ashx.

37. "China to Introduce Carbon Tax: Official," Xinhua, Feb. 19, 2013, http://news.xinhuanet.com/english/china/2013-02/19/c_132178898.htm; Adele C. Morris, *et al.*, "China's Carbon Tax Highlights the Need for a New Track of Carbon Talks," East Asia Forum, March 19, 2013, www.eastasiaforum.org/2013/03/19/chinas-carbon-tax-highlights-the-need-for-a-new-track-of-climate-talks/.

38. G. S. Callendar, "The Artificial Production of Carbon Dioxide and its Influence on Temperature," in Bill McKibben, ed., *The Global Warming Reader* (2011), p. 37.

39. Roger Revells and Hans E. Suess, "Carbon Dioxide Exchange between Atmosphere and Ocean and the Question of an Increase of Atmospheric $CO_2$ During the Past Decades," in McKibben, *ibid.*, pp. 41-42.

40. For a chronology of climate change research see "The Discovery of Global Warming: Timeline," American Institute of Physics, www.aip.org/history/climate/timeline.htm.

41. For background, see Jennifer Weeks, "Carbon Trading," *CQ Global Researcher*, Nov. 1, 2008, pp. 295-320.

42. Carolyn Lochhead, "How GOP Became Party of Denial on Global Warming," *The San Francisco Chronicle*, April 28, 2013, www.sfchronicle.com/politics/article/How-GOP-became-party-of-denial-on-warming-4469641.php; and Riley E. Dunlap and Aaron M. McRight, "Organized Climate Change Denial," *The Oxford Handbook of Climate Change and Society* (2011).

43. Oliver Burkeman, "Memo Exposes Bush's New Green Strategy," *The Guardian*, March 3, 2003, www.guardian.co.uk/environment/2003/mar/04/usnews.climatechange.

44. "A Call for Action," U.S. Climate Action Partnership, Jan. 22, 2007, p. 2, www.us-cap.org/ClimateReport.pdf.

45. "Nobel Peace Prize Citation," *The Guardian*, Oct. 12, 2007, www.guardian.co.uk/environment/2007/oct/12/gorecitation.

46. A cap-and-trade system sets a ceiling on emissions and requires large GHG sources to buy marketable allowances to cover their emissions.

47. For a survey of views see "The Waxman-Markey Bill: A Good Start or a Non-Starter?" *Yale Environment 360*, June 18, 2009, http://e360.yale.edu/feature/the_waxman-markey_bill_a_good_start_or_a_non-starter/2163/.

48. Bryan Walsh, "Why the Climate Bill Died," *Time*, July 26, 2010, http://science.time.com/2010/07/26/why-the-climate-bill-died/.

49. Mark Clayton, "House Republicans fail to save 30-cent light bulbs from extinction," *The Christian Science Monitor*, July 12, 2011, www.csmonitor.com/USA/Politics/2011/0712/House-Republicans-fail-to-save-30-cent-light-bulbs-from-extinction. For background, see Peter Katel, "Tea Party Movement," *CQ Researcher*, March 19, 2010, pp. 241-264, updated May 23, 2011.

50. The White House, July 29, 2011, www.whitehouse.gov/blog/2011/07/29/president-obama-announces-new-fuel-economy-standards.

51. John M. Broder, "Both Romney and Obama Avoid Talk of Climate Change," *The New York Times*, Oct. 25, 2012, www.nytimes.com/2012/10/26/us/politics/climate-change-nearly-absent-in-the-campaign.html?pagewanted=all.

52. Michael R. Bloomberg, "A Vote for a President to Lead on Climate Change," Bloomberg News, Nov. 1, 2012, www.bloomberg.com/news/2012-11-01/a-vote-for-a-president-to-lead-on-climate-change.html.

53. *Massachusetts v. Environmental Protection Agency*, 549 U.S. 497, 2007, www.supremecourt.gov/opinions/06pdf/05-1120.pdf. In 2009 EPA issued a formal determination that carbon pollution threatened American's health and welfare by contributing to climate change, laying the ground for issuing regulations to limit carbon emissions.

54. "Proposed Carbon Pollution Standards for New Power Plants," U.S. Environmental Protection Agency, March 27, 2012, http://epa.gov/carbonpollutionstandard/pdfs/20120327factsheet.pdf, p. 2.

55. *Ibid.*, p. 3.

56. John M. Broder, "E.P.A. Will Delay Rule Limiting Carbon Emissions at New Power Plants," *The New York Times*, April 12, 2013, www.nytimes.com/2013/04/13/science/earth/epa-to-delay-emissions-rule-at-new-power-plants.html.

57. Erica Martinson and Jennifer Epstein, "Where's President Obama's Climate Agenda?" *Politico*, May 25, 2013, www.politico.com/story/2013/05/obama-climate-change-agenda-91877.html.

58. For background see Daniel McGlynn, "Fracking Controversy," *CQ Researcher*, Dec. 16, 2011, pp. 1049-1072.

59. Kevin Begos, "EPA Methane Report Could Reshape Fracking Debate," *The Boston Globe*, April 29, 2013, www.bostonglobe.com/business/2013/04/28/

epa-methane-report-further-divides-fracking-camps/Ft7DVUvAHE6zctsgbcGuZN/story.html.

60. Daniel J. Weiss, *et al.*, "EPA Nominee Gina McCarthy Has Strong History of Bipartisan leadership," *Climate Progress*, April 10, 2013, http://thinkprogress.org/climate/2013/04/10/1846181/epa-nominee-gina-mccarthy-has-strong-history-of-bipartisan-leadership/.

61. "Questions for EPA Nominee Gina McCarthy," Republican Policy Committee, April 11, 2013, www.rpc.senate.gov/policy-papers/questions-for-epa-nominee-gina-mccarthy.

62. "Under Fire, EPA Nominee Can't Give Ground on Climate Change," *The Boston Globe*, May 17, 2013, www.bostonglobe.com/editorials/2013/05/16/epa-nominee-can-give-ground-climate-change/4fTQci7wlXK1mJw0qYH6kO/story.html.

63. See Lydia Saad, "Americans' Concerns About Global Warming on the Rise," *Gallup Politics*, April 8, 2013, www.gallup.com/poll/161645/americans-concerns-global-warming-rise.aspx. For details, see "Gallup Poll Social Series: Environment," March 7-10, 2013, question 25, www.usclimatenetwork.org/resource-database/poll-global-warming-fears-rising.

64. See "Continuing Partisan Divide in Views of Global Warming," Pew Research Center, April 2, 2013, p. 4, www.people-press.org/files/legacy-pdf/4-2-13%20Keystone%20Pipeline%20and%20Global%20Warming%20Release.pdf.

65. Christopher Borick and Barry G. Rabe, "The Fall 2012 National Surveys on Energy and the Environment: Findings Report for Belief-Related Questions," The Center for Local, State, and Urban Policy, Gerald R. Ford School of Public Policy, University of Michigan, March 2013, http://closup.umich.edu/files/nsee-climate-belief-fall-2012.pdf.

66. "A National Survey of Republicans and Republican-leaning Independents on Energy and Climate Change," George Mason University Center for Climate Change Communication, April 2, 2013, http://climatechangecommunication.org/sites/default/files/reports/Republicans%27_Views_on_Climate_Change_2013.pdf.

67. "2013 Stanford Poll on Climate Adaptation," Stanford Woods Institute for the Environment, March 2013, pp. 10-12, http://woods.stanford.edu/research/public-opinion-research/2013-Stanford-Poll-Climate-Adaptation.

68. Michael Oppenheimer and Kevin Trenberth, "Will we hear Earth's alarm bells?" *The Washington Post*, June 9, 2013, p. A19. Oppenheimer is a professor of geosciences and international affairs at Princeton University. Trenberth is a distinguished senior scientist at the National Center for Atmospheric Research.

69. For background, see Peter Katel, "Water Crisis in the West," *CQ Researcher*, Dec. 9, 2011, pp. 1025-1048.

# BIBLIOGRAPHY
## Selected Sources
### Books

**Guzman, Andrew T., *Overheated: The Human Cost of Climate Change*, Oxford University Press, 2013.**
A University of California, Berkeley, law professor explores the consequences of climate change, including deaths from flooding, water shortages, strains on global food supplies and growing competition for resources.

**Hamilton, Clive, *Earthmasters: The Dawn of the Age of Climate Engineering*, Yale University Press, 2013.**
An ethics professor at Australia's Charles Sturt University describes geoengineering proposals and considers how these concepts could alter humans' relationship with Earth.

**Mann, Michael E., *The Hockey Stick and the Climate Wars: Dispatches from the Front Lines*, Columbia University Press, 2012.**
A prominent climate scientist at Penn State University describes well-funded efforts to discredit climate science.

**Mattoo, Aaditya, and Arvind Subramanian, *Greenprint: A New Approach to Cooperation on Climate Change*, Center for Global Development, 2013.**
A World Bank research manager (Mattoo) and a global development scholar propose new strategies for achieving global cooperation on climate change.

McKibben, Bill, ed., *The Global Warming Reader*, Penguin, 2011.

A prominent journalist and climate activist provides a collection of articles and documents about climate change, from its 19th-century discovery to the present day.

## Articles

Ansolabehere, Stephen, and David M. Konisky, "The American Public's Energy Choice," *Daedalus*, vol. 141, no. 2, Spring 2012.

Political scientists at Harvard and Georgetown universities, respectively, contend that American attitudes about energy are largely unrelated to views about climate change, so the most politically efficient way to reduce greenhouse gas emissions may be to regulate the burning of fossil fuels.

Drajem, Mark, "Obama Will Use Nixon-Era Law to Fight Climate Change," Bloomberg News, March 15, 2013, www.bloomberg.com/news/2013-03-15/obama-will-use-nixon-era-law-to-fight-climate-change.html.

The Obama administration is reportedly preparing to direct federal agencies to consider global warming impacts when they review major projects under the National Environmental Policy Act, which industry leaders say could delay infrastructure projects.

Gillis, Justin, "Carbon Dioxide Level Passes Long-Feared Milestone," *The New York Times*, May 10, 2013, www.nytimes.com/2013/05/11/science/earth/carbon-dioxide-level-passes-long-feared-milestone.html?hp.

In the spring of 2013 atmospheric concentrations of carbon dioxide reached 400 parts per million, the highest level in perhaps 3 million years.

Moomaw, William R., "Can the International Treaty System Address Climate Change?" Fletcher Forum of World Affairs, vol. 37, no. 1, Winter 2013, www.fletcherforum.org/wp-content/uploads/2013/02/Moomaw_37-1.pdf.

A professor of international environmental policy and contributor to past global climate assessments argues that a new approach is needed for international progress, led by the United States and China.

Parson, Edward A., and David W. Keith, "End the Deadlock on Governance of Geoengineering Research," *Science*, vol. 339, March 15, 2013, pp. 1278-1279, www.sciencemag.org/content/339/6125/1278.

A professor of law at UCLA (Parson) and a professor of applied physics at Harvard (Keith) call for creating rules and procedures to allow geoengineering research to proceed.

## Reports and Studies

"Draft Climate Assessment Report," National Climate Assessment and Development Advisory Committee, January 2013, http://ncadac.globalchange.gov/.

A draft of a report mandated under the Global Change Research Act of 1990, finds that climate change already affects the United States in several ways, causing — among other things — more frequent extreme weather events and damage to ocean life.

"The Global Climate Change Regime," Council on Foreign Relations, updated March 22, 2013, www.cfr.org/climate-change/global-climate-change-regime/p21831.

A broad overview of the international framework for addressing climate change finds that the system is underdeveloped and offers options to strengthen it, according to a prominent think tank.

Hansen, J., M. Sato, and R. Ruedy, "Global Temperature Update Through 2012," *NASA* Goddard Institute for Space Studies, Jan. 15, 2013, www.nasa.gov/pdf/719139main_2012_GISTEMP_summary.pdf.

NASA scientists report that global surface temperature in 2012 was 1° Fahrenheit warmer than the 1951-1980 average, continuing a long-term warming trend since the mid-1970s.

# For More Information

**Center for Global Development**, 1800 Massachusetts Ave., N.W., 3rd floor, Washington, DC 20036; 202-416-4000; www.cgdev.org. An independent think tank that works to reduce global poverty and inequality through research and outreach to policymakers.

**National Association of Manufacturers**, 733 10th St., N.W., Suite 700, Washington, DC 20001; 800-814-8468; www.nam.org. An industrial trade association representing small and large American manufacturers.

**National Center for Atmospheric Research**, P.O. Box 3000, Boulder, CO 80307; 303-497-1000; www.ncar.ucar.edu. A federally funded research and development center devoted to service, research and education in the atmospheric sciences, including weather, climate and atmospheric pollution.

**Natural Resources Defense Council**, 40 West 20th St., New York, NY 10011; 212-727-2700; www.nrdc.org.

A national environmental advocacy group that lobbies and conducts public education on issues including ways to combat global climate change.

**Scripps Institution of Oceanography**, University of California at San Diego, 9500 Gilman Dr., La Jolla, CA 92023; 858-534-3624; www.sio.ucsd.edu. Center for ocean and Earth science research, including atmosphere and climate.

**U.S. Global Change Research Program**, 1717 Pennsylvania Ave., N.W., Suite 250, Washington, DC 20006; 202-223-6262; www.globalchange.gov. A congressionally mandated program that coordinates and integrates climate change research across 13 government agencies and publishes scientific assessments of potential impacts in the United States from global warming.

# 7

# Gay Rights

Reed Karaim

Moses, a gay Ugandan seeking asylum in the United States, hides his identity out of fear for his safety as he tells a press conference in Washington, D.C., on Feb. 2, 2010, about being terrorized in his home country for being homosexual. The conference was held to kick off the American Prayer Hour, a multi-city event organized to "affirm inclusive values and call on all nations, including Uganda, to decriminalize the lives of gay, lesbian, bisexual and transgender people."

From *CQ Researcher*, March 1, 2011.

The movie poster shows two shirtless young men in a passionate embrace. But the film is not "Brokeback Mountain," the acclaimed Hollywood story featuring Jake Gyllenhaal and Heath Ledger as closeted, gay cowhands.

This film was produced, surprisingly, in Mumbai, India, home of the Bollywood extravaganza. Until last year, Bollywood films were long on exuberant singing and dancing, and virtually devoid of sex scenes. Even heterosexual kissing was primly avoided.

But after Delhi's high court in 2009 overturned a 148-year-old colonial law criminalizing homosexual acts between consenting adults, Bollywood moved quickly to keep up with the times. Soon afterwards, "Dunno y — Na Jaane Kyun" changed all that with the first gay kiss in an Indian movie. Indeed, the film by director Sanjay Sharma was billed as India's "Brokeback Mountain." And as Indian bloggers made clear, it had its share of both defenders and critics.

"Dunno y" reflects what could, by one measure, be considered the culmination of the "Gay Rights" decade. In a relatively short time, countries around the world have addressed concerns of homosexual or bisexual individuals.

Beginning with the Netherlands in 2001, gay marriage morphed almost overnight from a largely ridiculed notion to a legal reality in at least 10 countries. Sixteen other nations recognized same-sex civil unions. And anti-sodomy laws were struck down in nations as disparate as the United States and India. On every continent, lesbian, gay, bisexual and transgender (LGBT) people stepped out in "pride marches." The trend continued, or even accelerated, in 2010. Argentina became the first Latin American country to legalize

# Muslim and African Nations Have Toughest Anti-Gay Laws

Africa and the Middle East have the strictest laws governing homosexual behavior. At least five countries in those regions allow the death penalty for homosexual acts, and gays can be jailed in at least 75 countries, some for life. Australia, Canada, Europe and South Africa have the most liberal laws.

## Status of Lesbian and Gay Rights Around the World

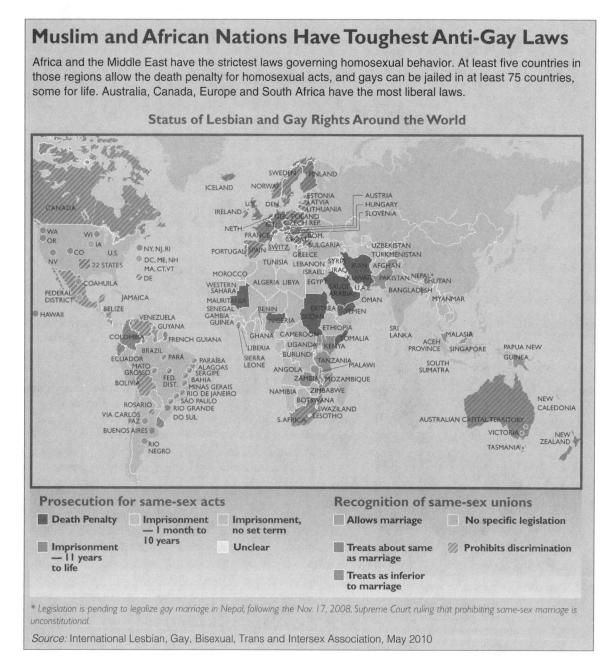

### Prosecution for same-sex acts

- Death Penalty
- Imprisonment — 1 month to 10 years
- Imprisonment, no set term
- Imprisonment — 11 years to life
- Unclear

### Recognition of same-sex unions

- Allows marriage
- No specific legislation
- Treats about same as marriage
- Prohibits discrimination
- Treats as inferior to marriage

*\* Legislation is pending to legalize gay marriage in Nepal, following the Nov. 17, 2008, Supreme Court ruling that prohibiting same-sex marriage is unconstitutional.*

*Source:* International Lesbian, Gay, Bisexual, Trans and Intersex Association, May 2010

same-sex marriage. The United States is in the process of ending its "don't ask, don't tell" policy requiring gay military personnel to hide their sexual orientation, joining at least 36 countries that allow gays and lesbians to serve openly in the armed services.[1]

Polls show growing U.S. support for same-sex marriage, and in a major policy shift on Feb. 23, the Obama administration decided it could no longer defend the Defense of Marriage Act, the 1996 law that bars federal recognition of same-sex marriages.

President Barack Obama says the law is unconstitutional.[2]

But a happy Bollywood movie tells only part of the global story of gay rights. While it seems the best of times for the LGBT community in an increasing number of countries, large parts of the world continue to view same-sex relationships as unnatural, a sin and a threat to the traditional family.

Homosexual acts remain illegal and severely punished in most of Africa and the Muslim world. Uganda made international headlines last year when *Rolling Stone*, a local newspaper not connected to the U.S. publication, publicly identified 100 gays and called on the public to "hang them."[3] A member of the Ugandan parliament introduced a bill that would impose the death penalty on anyone engaging in repeated homosexual activity.[4] If approved, Uganda would join the five other countries and parts of Somalia and Nigeria where homosexual activity is punishable by death.

In the formerly communist states of Eastern Europe, gay-pride marches were met with outrage and violence, sometimes organized by far-right political groups.[5] China, where homosexuality is not illegal, still stifles public gatherings or rallies for gays.[6] And in the United States, a spate of gay teen suicides in 2010 at year's end provided evidence that, even in countries with "hate crime" laws and other legal protections for LGBT people, "coming out" remains an agonizing experience for many, often greeted with disapproval or cruelty.[7]

Within the scientific community the question of whether sexual orientation is inherent or learned — a debate often referred to as "nature vs. nurture" — is largely over. "The consistency of the genetic, prenatal and brain findings has swung the pendulum toward a biological explanation," writes David Myers, a psychology professor at Michigan's Hope College, in his textbook *Exploring Psychology*. "Nature more than nurture, most psychiatrists now believe, predisposes sexual orientation."[8]

## Gays Face Harsh Penalties in 75 Nations

Individuals engaging in homosexual behavior can face the death penalty in five countries and can be imprisoned in 75 others. However, more than 50 countries and 57 states, districts or other governmental entities have enacted anti-discrimination laws protecting gays. Three dozen countries allow gays to serve openly in the military, and 26 nations recognize same-sex unions.

*Number of countries that:*

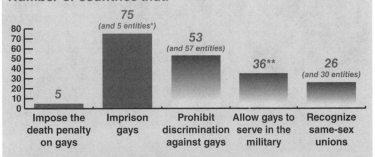

*\* Includes part of a federation state, a district or any other administrative or territorial unit.*

*\*\* Includes Israel but does not include the United States, which is repealing its ban on gays in the military.*

*Sources:* International Lesbian, Gay, Bisexual, Trans and Intersex Association, May 2010; "Report of the Comprehensive Review of the Issues Associated with a Repeal of Don't Ask Don't Tell," Pentagon Working Group Study, Nov. 30, 2010

The evidence, however, has failed to convince the most fervent opponents of treating homosexual relationships as equal to heterosexual ones. In fact, the rhetoric seemed to grow even more heated on the most strident anti-gay edge of the debate as public animosity faded and legal rights were extended to gay couples. Gay-rights supporters speak of their battle as part of the broader movement to assure equal rights for all.

"I don't like the phrase 'LGBT rights' because what we're really talking about are fundamental human rights, like the right to privacy. When you talk about LGBT rights or gay rights, people immediately think you want something special. We don't want anything special. We want to be treated like everyone else," says Boris Dittrich, a former member of parliament in the Netherlands who initiated that country's same-sex marriage and adoption bills. He now serves as advocacy director for the LGBT program at Human Rights Watch, an international organization dedicated to defending and protecting human rights.

AFP/Getty Images/Ilmars Znotins

Waving banners and bibles, anti-gay activists hold a counter-protest during a 2009 Baltic Gay Pride rally in Riga, Latvia. The backlash against gay and lesbian rights in several former Soviet satellite states has been led by far-right parties that also have campaigned against other minorities. Government officials often cite the threat of violence from such groups to justify outlawing gay-pride parades and other events.

This perspective has gained strength in the American debate about same-sex marriage, even among conservatives. Theodore B. Olson, who served as solicitor general under President George W. Bush, argued in *Newsweek* last year that legalizing same-sex marriage would "be a recognition of basic American principles." Marriage is an "expression of our desire to create a social partnership, to live and share life's joys and burdens with the person we love," and honoring these desires in all people strengthens society's bonds, he concluded.[9]

Opponents of gay rights, not surprisingly, do not speak in unison. Some support civil unions and legal safeguards against discrimination for gays and lesbians but oppose same-sex marriage, believing it should be reserved for heterosexual couples to promote the traditional family. Others do not accept the idea of natural differences in sexual orientation or gender identity.

Religious communities around the world take a range of positions on homosexuality, from acceptance to prohibition. Many Christians and Muslims believe gay sexual relations are proscribed by God but emphasize charity and forgiveness. The Catholic Church says homosexual acts are a sin but recognizes that homosexual orientation is strongly felt and may be innate in some people.

But the Catholic Church, with 1.2 billion faithful worldwide, adamantly opposes extending certain legal rights to same-sex couples, particularly the right to marry. Pope Benedict XVI has called same-sex marriage one of the "most insidious and dangerous challenges that today confront the common good."[10]

Some American evangelical Christians take a harsher view of both homosexuality and the idea of gay rights. In a still widely disseminated 2002 essay against granting "rights" to gays, Scott Lively, president of the Springfield, Mass.-based group Abiding Truth Ministries, says the idea that homosexuals can be the subject of "discrimination" and that those who support their cause are "tolerant" distorts both words. He discounts the possibility that homosexual preference could be innate and says that, even if it is, acting on that impulse is a choice equivalent to "pedophilia, sado-masochism, bestiality and many other forms of deviant behavior."[11]

The Southern Poverty Law Center, the Montgomery, Ala.,-based anti-bigotry advocacy group, calls Lively's organization a hate group.[12] But the message of Lively and others who consider homosexuality deviant and dangerous continues to find a receptive audience overseas, particularly in Africa, where he met with Ugandan political leaders shortly before they introduced their punitive legislation.[13]

But support for allowing gay marriage or equal partnerships can be found among Christian leaders and scholars, including in the Catholic Church. More than 140 German, Austrian and Swiss Catholic theologians signed a petition earlier this year calling for reforms in the church, including acceptance of homosexual partners.[14]

Daniel Maguire, a professor of moral theology at Catholic Marquette University in Milwaukee, has argued that the love of some people for members of the same sex is a fact of God's creation and should be accepted. "Homosexuality is not a sin. Heterosexism (prejudice against people who are homosexual) is a sin," Maguire writes. "It is a serious sin because it violates justice, truth and love."[15]

Tolerance is also gaining support in some developing nations. Nepal's highest court has said gays should have the right to marry, and the Philippine Supreme Court recently ruled that an LGBT political party could field candidates for office. And there was the overturning by India's high court of a British-era anti-sodomy law, declaring it a vestige of colonialism that did not square with the country's constitution.

"People feel much freer in their minds. Their hands are untied," says Arvind Narrain, one of the lawyers who brought the case. "I never thought I'd see this in my lifetime, but we've seen how quickly things can change."

But in parts of socially conservative Eastern Europe, changes have gone in the other direction. Romania and other countries in the region have legally defined marriage as a union between a man and woman. Romania also prohibits recognition of same-sex marriages or civil unions that were entered into legally abroad.

"In the last couple of years, Romanians realized what was happening in Holland, Sweden and Spain [countries where gay marriage is legal], and they became very concerned" about the trend spreading to Romania, says Peter Costea, a lawyer and president of the Alliance of Romania's Families, which worked for adoption of the new definition. "They decided that right now, they did not wish such an institution to be legalized in Romania."

Costea believes a backlash is growing against what many conservative Europeans see as a gay-rights "agenda" that discounts the importance of the traditional family. But while resistance to same-sex marriage or civil unions remains strong in many parts of the world, far fewer countries are now willing to accept discrimination based on sexual orientation. For instance, Costea notes, it is illegal under Romanian law to discriminate against gays seeking housing or jobs.

As gay rights evolve across the globe, here are some of the questions being debated:

## Five U.S. States Allow Same-Sex Marriage

Five states and the District of Columbia issue marriage licenses to same-sex couples. Twelve other states give some spousal rights to same-sex couples or recognize marriages initiated in other jurisdictions.

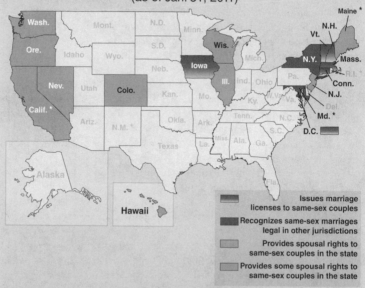

**States That Recognize Same-sex Marriage**
**(as of Jan. 31, 2011)**

Issues marriage licenses to same-sex couples

Recognizes same-sex marriages legal in other jurisdictions

Provides spousal rights to same-sex couples in the state

Provides some spousal rights to same-sex couples in the state

**\* California:** *Marriages that took place between June 16 and Nov. 4, 2008, continue to be defined as marriages. An Oct. 12, 2009, law recognizes out-of-jurisdiction same-sex marriages that occurred in the June-November 2008 time frame as marriages in California, and all other out-of-jurisdiction same-sex marriages as domestic partnerships.*

**\* Maine:** *Marriage equality legislation enacted May 6, 2009; repealed by a ballot measure in November 2009.*

**\* Maryland:** *Provides certain benefits to statutorily defined domestic partners. In 2010, attorney general said the state can recognize out-of-jurisdiction marriages.*

**\* New Mexico:** *In January 2011, attorney general issued an advisory opinion saying the state can recognize out-of-jurisdiction same-sex marriages.*

**\* Rhode Island:** *Provides certain benefits to statutorily defined domestic partners. In February 2007 attorney general issued an opinion saying the state can recognize out-of-jurisdiction marriages. However, in December 2007 state Supreme Court refused to grant a divorce to a same-sex couple legally married in Massachusetts.*

*Source:* "Marriage Equality & Other Relationship Recognition Laws," Human Rights Campaign, Jan. 31, 2011

# Sexual Orientation: Is It Due to Nature or Nurture?

*For scientists, the debate is largely over.*

Is human sexual orientation predetermined at birth or something that is learned? That question is not only part of the scientific inquiry into the nature of human sexual relationships but, to many, central to the political debate over gay rights.

If it's an innate characteristic like left-handedness or red hair, then arguments that homosexuality is "unnatural" or against God's plan become much harder to justify, as does treating sexual relationships — and the idea of love — between adults of the same gender differently than heterosexual relationships.

Since the "nature vs. nurture" question concerning sexual orientation is so fraught, some people will never accept the answer unless it coincides with their political or religious beliefs. But within the scientific community, a consensus has emerged.

"Most of today's psychologists view sexual orientation as neither willfully chosen nor willfully changed," writes David Myers, a psychology professor at Hope College in Michigan in his textbook *Psychology*. "Sexual orientation is in some ways like handedness. Most people are one way, some the other. A very few are truly ambidextrous. Regardless, the way one is endures."[1]

A wide range of research has found biological connections to sexual orientation. Identical twins are more likely to share a homosexual orientation than fraternal twins. Another study found that a certain cell cluster in the hypothalamus of the brain is reliably larger in heterosexual men than in women or homosexual men. Hormonal activity in the womb also seems to have an effect on sexual orientation.[2]

Several organizations, mostly religion-based, claim "corrective therapy" can reorient gays and lesbians toward heterosexuality. But studies by researchers have found that same-sex attractions typically persist, as do those of heterosexuals, who are no more capable of changing their sexual orientation.[3]

Since the days of the ancient Greeks, whenever philosophers have argued against homosexual love, some have argued that it is against the natural order, in part because it was found nowhere else in the animal kingdom.

Scientists now know this is incorrect. Some birds, sheep, monkeys and more than 450 other species of animals have at least occasional same-gender sex.[4] In some cases, animals form long-lasting same-sex relationships, even raising young together. Studies have found that roughly 8 percent of male sheep are sexually attracted only to other males — an example of an animal subpopulation that seems exclusively homosexual.[5]

In his book *The Science of Sexual Attraction*, noted neurobiologist Simon LeVay examines same-sex animal behavior. "The bonobo monkeys are interesting, because they're fairly close to us (genetically)," he says, "and they're polymorphously perverse — they use sex for many interactions that aren't tied to procreation. As far as we know, you don't really have gay or straight . . . bonobos."

LeVay discovered the difference in the hypothalamus between gay and straight men and published his results in *Science* in 1991. He initially found the results — some of the earliest evidence indicating biological differences between gay and straight men — startling.

The research briefly made him a scientific celebrity. "I was really shocked when I came in the day after it was published," he says, "and saw satellite trucks waiting outside the office."

Twenty years later, in the middle of a tour promoting *The Science of Sexual Attraction* — LeVay says the reaction has been far more muted. "There was no sense of shock with my book coming out as there was when my research came out," he says. "I think a lot of people have come to accept that biology is relevant to sexual orientation."

— *Reed Karaim*

---

[1]David Myers, *Psychology* (2010), p. 472.

[2]*Ibid.*

[3]*Ibid.*

[4]Jon Mooallem, "Can animals be gay?" *The New York Times Magazine*, March 31, 2010, www.nytimes.com/2010/04/04/magazine/04animals-t.html.

[5]John Cloud, "Yep, they're gay," *Time*, Jan. 26, 2007, www.time.com/time/magazine/article/0,9171,1582336,00.html.

## Are governments and society more receptive to gay rights?

LGBT activists seem generally optimistic that they are succeeding, albeit only incrementally in some places. "We are on a very positive trajectory," says Mark Bromley, chairman of the Washington, D.C.-based Council for Global Equality, founded to encourage a stronger American voice on LGBT human rights concerns. "There will be some plateaus and some inevitable backlash, and there is a gap between parts of the globe, but I think we've seen tremendous progress over all."

But opponents of gay-friendly initiatives see exactly the opposite. "We work with groups in more than 70 countries. We've been holding our world congresses since 1997, and in that time we've seen participants realize they represent a much larger voice in the world," says Larry Jacobs, managing director of the Illinois-based World Congress of Families, which insists heterosexual marriage is fundamental to society and is threatened by same-sex marriage and other social changes.

Government policies in most of the world's industrialized democracies have become far more supportive of equal treatment of gays and lesbians than would have been imaginable only a generation ago. More than 50 countries and 57 states, districts or other governmental entities have enacted anti-discrimination laws protecting gays, and 26 countries and 30 government entities recognize same-sex unions. Meanwhile, 36 countries now allow homosexuals to openly serve in the military, and the United States is in the process of repealing its ban on gays in the services.[16] Same-sex consensual sexual acts also have been decriminalized throughout these countries.

In some Western European nations the question of equal treatment under the law for same-sex couples seems largely settled. In the Netherlands, for instance, Jan Willem Duyvendak, a sociologist at the University of Amsterdam who studies the gay-rights movement, says, "The opening up of marriage to gay people will never be reversed. Even the political parties that were originally against it now support it."

Indeed, in countries where homosexuality still faces disapproval, governments have decriminalized sex between same-sex partners. In Russia, for example, authorities have refused to allow gay-pride marches and other gatherings, and public antipathy toward homosexuals remains strong, but homosexual acts have been legal since 1993.

Still, in many countries — especially in Eastern Europe — majority sentiment appears to be against taking further steps, particularly when it comes to legalizing same-sex marriage. In addition to Romania, three other countries — Bulgaria, Estonia and Lithuania — have taken legal steps to reserve marriage for heterosexuals.[17]

Reflecting much of the opinion across Eastern Europe, Costea of the Alliance of Romania's Families says, "Romania is a deeply religious country, mainly an orthodox one with a fairly substantial evangelical minority. The church has retained a fairly firm position with respect to marriage, and it's a position shared by the overwhelming majority of the Romanian people."

At least one LGBT rights activist, however, believes anti-gay opinion is tempering in parts of Eastern Europe. Greg Czarnecki — a board member for the Brussels-based International Lesbian, Gay, Bisexual, Trans and Intersex Association (ILGA) in Europe — lives in socially conservative, predominantly Catholic Poland. In recent years, Polish governments have drafted a bill to punish teachers who "promoted" homosexuality. European officials criticized the measures as homophobic, and recently Czarnecki sees the tone changing.[18] "The Democratic-left alliance now supports a form of civil partnership for gays," he says, "and the conservatives have tempered some of their rhetoric, too."

But social attitudes rarely change as fast as government policy. "Most people aren't actively, violently against gay people. They just kind of say, 'Okay, if you're gay, just don't talk about it,'" he says. "That's a very Polish way to look at an issue. If there's an uncomfortable situation, we try to find a way around it. With the younger people, I see a real hunger to join the West, and I think there's definitely a more cosmopolitan, tolerant attitude."

Focusing on Europe, however, can create a false impression. In other parts of the world — especially in Africa and the Middle East — signs that policies or attitudes are becoming more supportive of the LGBT community are difficult to find. The proposed death-penalty legislation in Uganda has gotten the most attention, but several other African nations are considering or have adopted similar measures. LGBT activists also worry about violent public sentiment worked up by politicians and the media elsewhere in Africa.

AFP/Getty Images/Esdras Ndikumana

Up to 20,000 people took to the streets in Burundi's capital city of Bujumbura on March 6, 2009, to protest the failure of the Senate to outlaw homosexuality. Anti-gay sentiment is on the rise in many African countries, where Christian and Muslim fundamentalism is growing, and homosexuality is seen as foreign to many African cultures.

"Genocide is brewing in Uganda, and the influence of this bill is spilling over to other countries like Zambia, Democratic Republic of Congo, and Malawi, where similar bills are being proposed," says Valentine Kalende, a Ugandan LGBT activist who was identified in the *Rolling Stone* article. "It seems like the whole world is focusing on Uganda, and ignoring what's happening to LGBT people in other African countries."

On the other side, Theresa Okafor, the CEO of Life League, a Nigerian organization that believes homosexuality is unnatural, does not think gays and lesbians should be executed; she believes counseling or therapy is in order. But she rejects the notion they are victims of prejudice in Africa. "I have heard accusations that they are being discriminated against," she says, "but this is completely false because if you think deeply about it, it is not the person that is being despised, it is the conduct."

But why does Africa seem to be growing more intolerant toward gays? That topic is hotly debated. Some blame it on the recent rise in Christian and Muslim fundamentalism in the region, while some say it is a reaction against Western influence and an expression of traditional attitudes, although others say that misrepresents the diversity of views in the African past. Some political observers say authoritarian regimes are scapegoating gays in order to redirect public ire.

"By and large, these are countries with very difficult economic and political problems, with political leaders who are not popular who can score easy victories by targeting the gays," says the Council for Global Equality's Bromley.

Meanwhile, in the Middle East there are few signs of a thaw in government policies. Homosexual acts remain illegal in most of the region and are often punished severely. Iran presents a particularly harsh case study. Human Rights Watch has documented a series of allegations of rape, torture and executions of sexual minorities by Iran's police and paramilitary forces.[19]

"Executions take place in Iran," says Human Rights Watch's Dittrich. "It's one of very few places where that happens." Four other countries and two regions — all Muslim countries — allow executions for consensual same-sex acts, according to the organization: Saudi Arabia, Yemen, Sudan, Mauritania and the ultra-conservative parts of Somalia and Nigeria.

But elsewhere in the developing world, change is happening with surprising swiftness. Marcelo Ferreyra, Buenos Aires-based program coordinator for Latin America and the Caribbean with the International Gay and Lesbian Human Rights Commission (IGLHRC), which works for LGBT rights worldwide, notes that Argentina's legalization of same-sex marriage is part of a broader trend in the region.

"Two or three years ago, Uruguay was the first country in Latin America to recognize civil unions. Mexico City allows same-sex marriages. Colombia is going through a recognition process for same-sex couples. There's a lot happening in Brazil," says Ferreyra. "This is not just coming from Argentina."

In Asia, the picture is as complex as it is in Europe. Gay-rights advocates have won important victories in Nepal, India and, to a lesser degree, the predominantly Catholic Philippines. In China, however, which has one-fifth of the world's population, the situation seems largely static. Laws criminalizing homosexuality were taken off the books in the 1997, but no law bars discrimination on the basis of sexual preference, and the government continues to block gay public gatherings and websites.[20]

In Indonesia, observers see an example of another phenomenon: a backlash against the increasing visibility of the LGBT community.

## Does a backlash threaten advances made by gays?

During a regional gay-rights conference in Surabaya, Indonesia, last year, Grace Poore, IGLHRC coordinator for Asia and the Pacific Islands, got a first-hand look at how some political and religious groups are responding to the gay-rights movement.

As the conference was about to begin, protesters from hardline Islamic groups arrived at the hotel, demanding that the conference be shut down and the attendees leave the country. Conference members were told to stay in their rooms as the protesters moved through the halls. Eventually, after hearing that a larger group of protesters was on the way and that the police could not guarantee members' safety, organizers decided to cancel the conference.

"We were basically under siege in the hotel," Poore says. "We were forced to leave. We were threatened with violence. I think it's the only time I have been afraid. It was such a situation of anarchy, and the police were saying they would not protect us."

Indonesia has the world's largest Muslim population, but it is a secular state, and homosexual acts are not illegal. But conservative Muslim groups have been increasingly strident in their opposition to equal treatment of LGBT relationships. To Poore it's an example of a counteroffensive being mounted in many countries.

"We're seeing religious backlash," particularly by hardliners, whether it's Islamic hardliners or Christian fundamentalists," she says. "Even in India, where Hindu has been considered very open, the Hindu right wing has suddenly claimed that homosexuality is anathema to Indian culture and Hindu beliefs. It's all part of this trend where religious conservatives and extremists, on their own or with the support of governments, are really pushing back in severe ways."[21]

The backlash has made it harder for LGBT people to publicly make their case and complicates the political landscape. For instance, in some Eastern European countries the reaction against gay and lesbian rights has been led by the rise of far-right parties that also have

---

## 19 Nations Allow Both Same-Sex Unions and Gays in Military

In 36 countries the military either allows gays to serve openly or does not ban homosexual conduct, and at least 26 countries recognize same-sex unions. Nineteen nations do both.

### Gay Rights in Selected Countries

| Country | Allows gays to serve in the military* | Recognizes same-sex unions | Country | Allows gays to serve in the military* | Recognizes same-sex unions |
|---|---|---|---|---|---|
| Albania | X | | Iceland | X | X |
| Andorra | | X | Ireland | X | |
| Argentina | | X | Israel ** | X | |
| Australia | X | | Italy | X | |
| Austria | X | X | Latvia | X | |
| Azerbaijan | X | | Lithuania | X | |
| Belgium | X | X | Luxembourg | X | X |
| Bosnia and Herzegovina | X | | Netherlands | X | X |
| Canada | X | X | New Zealand | X | X |
| Colombia | | X | Norway | X | X |
| Croatia | X | | Portugal | X | X |
| Czech Republic | X | X | Romania | X | |
| Denmark | X | X | Slovakia | X | |
| Ecuador | | X | Slovenia | X | X |
| Estonia | X | | South Africa | X | X |
| Finland | X | X | South Korea | X | |
| France | X | X | Spain | X | X |
| Georgia | X | | Sweden | X | X |
| Germany | X | X | Switzerland | | X |
| Greece | X | | Ukraine | X | |
| Hungary | X | X | United Kingdom | X | X |
| | | | Uruguay | | X |

*Among NATO and ISAF (International Security Assistance Force in Afghanistan) partner nations, and in Israel, which is not a member of either organization. Does not include the United States, which is in the process of repealing its ban on gays serving openly in the military.*

** *Israel allows a limited common-law marriage for same-sex couples.*

*Sources: "Report of the Comprehensive Review of the Issues Associated with a Repeal of Don't Ask Don't Tell," Pentagon Working Group Study, Nov. 30, 2010; International Lesbian, Gay, Bisexual, Trans and Intersex Association*

campaigned against other minorities, including Roma (Gypsies) and Jews. The threat of violence from such groups has been cited by government officials to justify outlawing gay-pride parades and other events.

In some countries the backlash has resulted in hate crimes — even in countries without a hostile government and where the dominant religion, such as Catholicism, opposes homosexuality but does not condone violence against the LGBT community.

"We're facing some backlash in different ways," Ferreyra, of the International Gay and Lesbian Human Rights Commission, says about Latin America. "We are experiencing a high rate of hate crimes — in Honduras, where five LGBT activists were just murdered but also in Mexico and other places. You see it happen especially where LGBT people have become more visible."[22]

But even in the most dangerous countries the backlash is not suppressing the LGBT movement, say some observers. "In virtually every country, there are brave individuals who are standing up and saying I'm gay or I'm lesbian, and I have rights, too. We're seeing this activism in virtually every corner of the world," says Bromley, of the Council for Global Equality.

Activist Kalende says this is true even in Uganda. "The LGBT movement in Uganda is more organized than before," she says. Kalende believes the movement's work with other concerned groups in Uganda and abroad has helped to prevent passage of the bill so far.

Despite violent incidents, the backlash against gay rights is not just about intimidation, hatred or prejudice. "We're not anti-homosexual; they're not the 'evil people' that need to be destroyed," says Jacobs, of the World Congress of Families. "What we're saying is that what's best for society is the natural family."

In some cases the backlash is coming from people who feel their own rights are being trampled by the movement to recognize gay rights. In Great Britain, Andrea Minichiello Williams is a lawyer and the founder of Christian Concern, which represents people who feel they've been treated unjustly because of their Christian beliefs. Her organization represents British citizens who've been reprimanded or fired because they refused to take certain actions regarding the treatment of gays and lesbians, such as presiding over a civil union ceremony or teaching about homosexuality, required under Britain's Equality Act of 2010.

Williams says many rank-and-file Britons who feel their beliefs aren't being respected could become more extreme if they're not listened to. "My sense is that the British people are longing to get their country back, their country founded on great Christian principles," she says.

In the United States, a backlash against court rulings in favor of same-sex marriage has been evident in several states. Voters in California overturned — through referendum — a state Supreme Court ruling in favor of same-sex marriage.[23] In Iowa, voters removed three state Supreme Court judges who voted to allow same-sex marriage.[24] "We've won every time it's been put before the people of any state, including liberal states like California and Maine," says Maggie Gallagher, chairman of the board of the U.S. National Organization for Marriage, which opposes same-sex marriages.

Todd Shepard, a historian at The Johns Hopkins University in Baltimore who studies the history of sexuality, believes it's a mistake to assume the increasing freedom many LGBT people are experiencing represents an unstoppable historical current. "One of the things we want to do in America is make every story a progress story, where things are getting better and better," he says. "But there have been plenty of other times where there were all sorts of freedoms, and then — there weren't."

However, sociologist Duyvendak of the Netherlands believes history has turned a corner. "There will be local fights and backlash in some areas, but I think the trends will continue. Even in the United States we still see progress, step-by-step. Now the army is open, and marriage will be the next thing. Things may go slow, but I'm really quite optimistic. I don't think the gains that have been made will be reversed."

### Should the United Nations and other international bodies be promoting gay rights?

The United Nations does not mention same-sex relations in its main human rights treaties, although the documents do include declarations of the right of all people to be treated with dignity and respect regardless of circumstances. U.N. agencies also disseminate information on a variety of topics, including basic human rights and educational materials on sexual behavior, which includes information about homosexuality.

The European Union (EU), however, does prohibit discrimination based on sexual orientation, and the EU's

Fundamental Rights Agency monitors and recommends policies to end discrimination within member countries.

Not surprisingly, gay-rights supporters and opponents view the activities of these international organizations very differently.

Human Rights Watch's Dittrich helped develop the Yogyakarta Principles, which were drawn up in 2006 by a group of international experts to apply human rights to sexual orientation and gender identity.[25] The principles are not a legally binding treaty but represent a template for treatment of the LGBT community. While acknowledging legitimate differences in cultures, Dittrich believes the responsibility of the U.N. and EU in this regard is clear.

"In many countries, they say the words 'gay' or 'homosexual' are from the West. They have this vision of the gay parades in New York or Amsterdam, and they say, 'We don't want that,' and that stops the discussion," Dittrich says. "But we're not talking about people dancing in the streets, we're talking about people being evicted or thrown into prison and being raped in prison without having access to lawyers. We are talking about fundamental human rights."

But few critics of the U.N. and EU activity on behalf of LGBT rights advocate throwing people into prison on the basis of sexual orientation or denying them lawyers. However, they do object to what they say are the bureaucracies of these international bodies adopting "agendas" that promote homosexual relationships as equivalent to heterosexual relationships, a position that enforces an ideology deeply at odds with the religious and cultural convictions of many people.

For instance, says Brussels lawyer Jakob Cornides, the European Union's Fundamental Rights Agency has pushed a "radical" gay-rights agenda that includes the false proposition that European nations must enact same-sex marriage laws to correspond to international law. "They're not reacting to the number of cases or complaints," he says. "They have their own agenda, and part of it is promotion of LGBT rights."

But the Council for Global Equality's Bromley says the agency's work has been within the legal and human rights mainstream and does not require nations to adopt same-sex marriage. "They have an agenda that is far broader than LGBT concerns. It includes programs to respond to religious discrimination, racism and other forms of discrimination that are of equal concern across the EU region," he says. "While they do not have a radical LGBT agenda, they do have an important tolerance agenda that focuses on equality for all."

Austin Ruse, president of the Catholic Family and Human Rights Institute, based in New York and founded to affect debate at the U.N., says his organization is fairly satisfied with the U.N. position "because all these agendas have been stopped. Sexual orientation and gender identity are not part of the human rights treaties, and they're not going to be anytime soon."

In December, 2008, Ruse's group joined the Vatican in opposing a nonbinding U.N. "declaration" — sponsored by France with broad support in Europe and Latin America — recommending that countries decriminalize homosexuality. It was the first time a measure specifically dealing with gay rights was discussed by the U.N. General Assembly. Proponents, who included representatives of 66 countries, said laws making it a crime to be gay conflicted with the Universal Declaration of Human Rights. But representatives from the Vatican and 60 nations opposed the declaration, saying it could lead to legalizing same-sex marriage.[26]

Some critics say the U.N. still promotes policies at odds with the Universal Declaration of Human Rights, passed by the General Assembly in 1948. It proclaims that "Men and women of full age, without any limitation due to race, nationality or religion, have the right to marry and found a family," and, "The family is the natural and fundamental group unit of society and is entitled to protection by society and the State."[27]

To some social conservatives, the two provisions were intended to establish the primacy of the heterosexual marriage and traditional family. "Many of the foundational human rights documents being used today to undermine the family actually provide a remarkable defense of the natural family, marriage between a man and a woman," William Saunders Jr., senior vice president for legal affairs of Americans United for Life, wrote in *The Family in America, A Journal of Public Policy.*[28]

U.N. officials have ignored the vision of human rights expressed in these documents because "they've been taken over by activists who focus 24/7 on issues that really only affect a small minority," says Jacobs, of the World Congress of Families. "They've taken over the human rights committees in the U.N. — the Committee on the

## CHRONOLOGY

### 1st-15thCenturies *Judeo-Christian tradition against homosexuality takes hold.*

**50-58** Apostle Paul denounces homosexuality, forming foundation for subsequent religious and legal rulings.

**313-380** Roman Empire converts to Christianity; adopts its views on homosexuality.

**1480s** Homosexuals are persecuted during Spanish Inquisition.

### 19th Century *Homosexuality is defined, defended and viewed as scandalous.*

**1867** German intellectual Karl Heinrich Ulrichs becomes first modern openly gay activist.

### 1900s-1950s *Homosexuality remains largely hidden, but research illuminates its prevalence.*

**1924** First U.S. gay-rights organization, Society for Human Rights, is founded in Chicago, but soon disbands.

**1930s-40s** Nazis imprison, murder gays.

**1948-52** Pioneering sex researcher Alfred Kinsey reveals unexpectedly high prevalence of male homosexuality.

### 1960s-1970s *Gay-rights movement emerges.*

**1967** England and Wales decriminalize sex between male adults, except in armed forces and merchant marines.

**1969** Police raid Stonewall Inn, a gay bar in New York City, triggering riots and launching modern gay-rights movement.

**1974** Netherlands allows gays to serve openly in the military.

### 1980s-1990s *Rising gay activism results in policy changes but prompts conservative backlash.*

**1983** U.S. Rep. Gerry Studds, D-Mass., becomes the first openly gay member of Congress. . . . The Rev. Jerry Falwell describes AIDS, a new disease that has appeared among homosexual men, as a "gay plague."

**1989** Denmark is first to grant same-sex couples rights similar to marriage.

**1993** "Don't ask, don't tell" law allows gays and lesbians to serve in the U.S. military, but only if they hide their sexual orientation.

**1996** U.S. adopts Defense of Marriage Act (DOMA), which allows states and the federal government not to recognize same-sex marriages legal in another state.

**1997** World Congress of Families holds its first international gathering devoted to defending the heterosexual, or as the Congress terms it, "natural" family.

### 2000s *Worldwide gay-rights movement builds despite growing resistance.*

**2001** Denmark becomes first to allow same-sex marriage.

**2008** Nepal legalizes same-sex marriage. For the first time, U.N. General Assembly discusses gay rights, debating a nonbinding resolution to recommend that countries decriminalize homosexuality.

**2009** India's high court overturns British-era anti-sodomy law.

**2010** U.S. Congress votes to allow gays to serve openly in the military, but it does not take effect immediately. . . . Romania, Estonia and Bulgaria take legal steps to define marriage as between a man and a woman. . . . Uganda and other African nations consider stronger sanctions — including the death penalty — for homosexual acts.

**2011** Ugandan gay activist David Kato is murdered in January, after he is identified by a newspaper that urged Ugandans to kill gays. . . . British government lifts ban on same-sex civil union ceremonies in churches. . . . Obama administration stops defending DOMA in court.

Rights of the Child, the Commission on the Status of Women — all these things have been taken over by NGOs [nongovernmental organizations] that don't really represent the values of the people of the world."

Proponents of LGBT rights say their concerns warrant inclusion based on a basic concept of human rights. They note that the Universal Declaration of Human Rights says that "everyone is entitled to all the rights in this declaration without distinction of any kind," including "race, colour, sex, language, religion . . . birth or other status." The declaration also proclaims "no one shall be subjected to arbitrary interference with his privacy, family, (or) home."[29]

Gay-rights supporters say the U.N. and other international organizations must ensure that the rights expressed in these documents are applied to the LGBT community, which has suffered from discrimination and violent oppression throughout history. Current events provide regular evidence that the battle against both is far from over, they say.

For example, IGLHRC director of programs Jessica Stern points to what happened when a General Assembly committee recently was renewing a declaration condemning "extrajudicial, summary or arbitrary executions." Benin, on behalf of several African nations, tried to strike "sexual orientation" from the list of discriminatory grounds on which these killings often take place — a list that has been in the declaration for the past 10 years.

But the amendment to eliminate the reference passed, with 79 votes in favor, 70 against, 17 nations abstaining and 26 not present.[30] Only after lobbying by the United States and other nations did sexual orientation go back into the resolution.

"We were forced to mobilize the vote, and in the end we picked up three African votes." Stern says. "But the fact is, it's still the only explicit LGBT resolution passed at the U.N., and what is it about? It's about killing, and we had to fight for it. It really underscores the fragility of the whole human rights framework."

## BACKGROUND

### Ancient Practice

Those who oppose granting same-sex relationships equal legal and social footing with heterosexual relationships often refer to being gay or lesbian as a "lifestyle choice." If so, it's a lifestyle that has survived since the beginnings of recorded civilization, often in the face of sanctions that included torture and death.

"If you just take a look at homoerotic love, it crosses all cultures, it goes through all time. You can always find people who are having sex with members of their own sex and falling in love with them," says John G. Younger, a gay-studies scholar and professor of the classics at the University of Kansas. "What society does with it is the question."

Some cultures viewed same-sex behavior benignly, as just another aspect of human sexuality. Some have accepted it under certain conditions, for example, as part of rites of passage or initiation rituals. Others have viewed it as contrary to God's natural order but have largely tried to ignore it. Some have punished it severely.

Most of the attitudes that existed in the past can still be found today.

From ancient Greece to the early dynasties in China, historical documents make clear that homosexual behavior has been around since humanity began recording its own existence. Some of the most esteemed literature from the pre-Christian era in Greece celebrates same-sex love. Sappho's poems to young women on the island of Lesbos spawned the words "lesbian" and "Sapphic."

Some Greek philosophers considered sex between adolescent boys and older men, who also served as their intellectual and societal mentors, as the highest form of love. But other Greeks believed it represented a distortion of the natural business of sex, which was procreation.

In China, court historians recorded the homosexual affairs and infatuations of many Han Dynasty emperors, who ruled for roughly 400 years from the 2nd century B.C.[31] In the 18th century several Manchu emperors openly engaged in sex with both men and women.[32] Although these choices were often considered unwise, they weren't considered unnatural. The Arab world in the first millennium also took a more benign view of homosexual relations than many later cultures.

Men and women engaging in homosexual behavior in ancient times did not necessarily think of themselves as gay or lesbian in the modern sense, say scholars. Most historians of human sexuality believe the idea of sexual preference as a defining part of one's identity did not become a popular concept until much later. This was

# Gays in the Military Create Few Problems Abroad

*Transition has been much less wrenching than the debate.*

A t least 36 nations already allowed gays and lesbians to serve openly in their armed forces before the U.S. Congress in December voted to have the United States join them. Those nations included most of America's NATO allies, plus Israel and South Korea, countries where hostile neighbors make maintaining military capability a priority.[1]

During America's heated debate over whether to end "don't ask, don't tell" — the controversial U.S. policy that required gays to keep their sexual orientation hidden — opponents claimed that allowing gays to serve openly would undermine American military readiness and lead to dissent in the ranks. Congress was being "asked to impose a risky military social experiment that has not been duplicated anywhere else in the world," said Elaine Donnelly, president of the Center for Military Readiness, which opposed ending the policy.[2]

The record, however, indicates little risk. Several key U.S. allies now have more than a decade of experience with openly homosexual sailors and soldiers in uniform. Despite dire predictions by some foreign officers that would be echoed years later in the United States, the transition seems to be much less wrenching than the debate.

"It was a nonevent," retired Maj. Gen Simon Willis, the former head of personnel for the Australian Defense Force,

told the Brookings Institution, "and it continues to be a nonevent."[3]

In Great Britain, a review after the policy was instituted found that only three service members, out of more than 250,000, had resigned because of the change. In addition, discussions with foreign military personnel in several nations conducted by a special Pentagon Working Group and the Rand Corporation think tank found no evidence that the shift had undermined training or morale.[4]

The study said none of the nations directly assessed the effects of the policy on combat effectiveness. "However, most of these nations have been engaged in combat operations in the years since changing their policy. Uniformly, these nations reported that they were aware of no units that had a degradation of cohesion or combat effectiveness, and that the presence of gay men and lesbians in combat units had not been raised as an issue by any of their units deployed in Iraq or Afghanistan."[5]

In Canada, the United Kingdom and Australia, the military expected "noticeable numbers" of gays and lesbians to come out following the change, "but in fact very few did so." Officials in Canada and the U.K. also said recruitment did not suffer, nor did retention of personnel.[6]

Most nations instituted the policy relatively quickly, usually after amending their training methods in order to emphasize respect for people of different sexual orientation.

---

true, they say, even after Christian disapproval of homosexuality took hold in Western culture.

"People thought of sex acts primarily as sinful acts available to everyone, rather than identity," says Shepard, the Johns Hopkins University historian.

The triumph of Judeo-Christian beliefs, particularly the adoption of Christianity by the Roman Empire in the 4th century, ushered in a long period in which homosexuality was considered a sin, generally outlawed and sometimes punished by torture or death. The roots of the Judeo-Christian attitude toward gays can be found in

Chapters 18 and 20 of the Old Testament book of "Leviticus," which prohibit same-sex relations. Chapter 18, verse 22, is the most succinct: "You shall not lie with a male as with a woman. It is an abomination." Chapter 20, verse 13, adds that the two men "shall surely be put to death."[33]

But Leviticus spends more time condemning incest, adultery and consorting with evil spirits than it does on male homosexuality (female homosexuality isn't mentioned). It also establishes dietary and hygiene rules to which Christianity does not generally adhere. Nonetheless,

A survey of American military personnel conducted by the Pentagon Working Group as part of its study found that 70-78 percent expected the change to either improve or make little difference in the ability of their unit to work together or get along socially.[7]

Aubrey Sarvis, executive director of the Servicemember's Legal Defense Network, which is dedicated to allowing gays to serve in the military, says he suspects most Americans believe that gays could serve openly as soon as President Barack Obama signed the law repealing "don't ask, don't tell." But the law requires the president, the Defense secretary and the joint chiefs of staff to certify that the military is ready for the change and then includes a 60-day transition period before open service becomes the rule.

The administration has not yet issued the certification, and groups that fought for the repeal are watching the process closely. "I don't see any foot-dragging at the Pentagon, but I think it's clear they want to have a sizeable number of the force receiving training around open service before certification can take place," says Sarvis.

Still, Sarvis expects the process to proceed quickly from here. "Moving to open service really isn't that complicated, for two reasons," he says. "One, gays and lesbians are already serving side by side with their straight counterparts, and many of them know who the gays and lesbians are, even if they haven't come out. We're talking about a lot of young people, and they have pretty good radars. Second, the education and training around open service isn't that complicated either. How many different ways do you have to say: 'Treat your fellow soldier with the respect and dignity you expect to receive?'"

— *Reed Karaim*

Members of the British Royal Navy march during the Euro Pride parade in London, England, on July 1, 2006. The U.K. is one of 36 nations — including most of America's NATO allies — that allow gays and lesbians to serve openly in their armed forces.

[1]"Report of the Comprehensive Review of the Issues Associated with the Repeal of 'Don't Ask, Don't Tell,'" Pentagon Working Group Study, Nov. 30, 2010, p. 89, www.defense.gov/home/features/2010/0610_gatesdadt/DADTReport_FINAL_20101130(secure-hires).pdf.

[2]Elaine Donnelly, "At Issue: Should the U.S. follow the example of nations that allow gays to serve openly in the military?" *CQ Researcher*, Sept. 18, 2009, p. 781.

[3]Charles McLean and Peter Singer, "What Our Allies Can Tell Us About the End of Don't Ask, Don't Tell," The Brookings Institution, June 7, 2010, www.brookings.edu/opinions/2010/0607_dont_ask_dont_tell_singer.aspx.

[4]"Report of the Comprehensive Review of the Issues Associated with the Repeal of 'Don't Ask, Don't Tell,'" *op. cit.*

[5]*Ibid.*, p. 92.

[6]*Ibid.*, p. 91.

[7]*Ibid.*, p. 64.

it's hard to overstate the impact Leviticus has had on the Christian world's view of homosexuality. "The authors of Leviticus wrote two dozen words which sealed the fate of men who loved men for more than 14 centuries," wrote pioneering gay studies scholar Louis Crompton in his sweeping *Homosexuality and Civilization*.[34]

The Apostle Paul harshly condemned homosexuality in his epistles to the Romans and Corinthians. It was also defined as unnatural and morally wrong by Saint Thomas Aquinas, a 13th-century Italian priest and philosopher whose writings still form the underpinnings of Catholic

philosophy.[35] In the Middle Ages and through the Renaissance, the Catholic Church and civil governments generally proscribed homosexual acts, whether by gays or heterosexuals.

The penalties were often severe, including branding, castration and death, but punishments varied from one city or country to another and from one generation to the next. The situation was far more complex than a simple reading of the laws would indicate, say historians.

"Michelangelo had male lovers; Leonardo da Vinci had lovers. Nobody cared, mostly because the people they were having sex with were young men from the lower classes," says Younger, who edited the encyclopedia *Sex in the Ancient World*. "If they had been doing it with the sons of nobles, it would have been different. The act might be illegal, but the law is applied in different ways."

For instance, during a 100-year period in Florence, a principal Renaissance city, the uncertainty surrounding how seriously to punish homosexuals is recorded in Crompton's history. The laws were changed, on the average, "more than once a decade and contain such elaborately gradated punishments that they resemble a kind of commercial tariff," Crompton wrote.[36] Records indicate 4,062 accusations of sodomy were lodged in just 24 years, at a time when the city had less than 50,000 occupants.[37]

On the other hand, officers of the Spanish Inquisition — which executed about 100 men for sexual relations with other males — were far less troubled by ambiguity, according to Crompton. Harsh punishments, primarily torture, were also common.[38]

In the ensuing centuries punishments for homosexual behavior became less severe across most of Europe, and some authorities showed far less zeal in pursuing men suspected of same-sex relations. Female homosexual behavior was of even less concern.

In Asia, Africa and elsewhere the view of same-sex behavior and of minorities that crossed traditional gender identities — such as the Hijras, men who have dressed like women for centuries in India — varied widely during this period. Heterosexual relationships, whether polygamous or monogamous, remained the dominant form of sexual pairing everywhere, however.

In the West, the most significant change in ideas about same-sex behavior since Christianity began occurred in 19th-century Germany, where the modern notion of a "homosexual" was born.

## Modern Movement

Karl Heinrich Ulrichs, a 19th-century German intellectual, is considered by many historians and LGBT activists as the father of the modern homosexual-rights movement. But his journey was an intensely personal one that began as an examination of his own sexual attraction to men. Eventually he concluded that "sexual orientation was a stable, inherent human characteristic and homosexuality a valid and natural form of sexual expression," wrote Francis Mark Mondimore, author of

*A Natural History of Homosexuality.* Mondimore is an associate professor at The Johns Hopkins University medical school in Baltimore, Md.[39]

Ulrichs was considered a pioneer because he publicly acknowledged his sexual orientation and began crusading for his ideas, even arguing against anti-sodomy laws before a congress of German jurists. Although he had barely begun to speak before he was shouted down, today the International Lesbian and Gay Law Association presents an annual award in his memory.[40]

The word "homosexual" first appeared in an 1869 political pamphlet by Karl Maria Kertbeny, a German journalist and crusader who also opposed having anti-sodomy statutes included in the unified German state's proposed constitution. The word "heterosexuality" came to be used in its modern sense slightly later. Taken together, these words would eventually help to create an idea of human sexuality built around two opposite poles of attraction, with humans' sexual compass needle more or less pointing one way or the other. They would also help to tie sexuality more closely to a person's sense of identity.

The notion of sexuality as identity would flower in the 20th century. "There's this idea that there's something in you that's really you, and that sexuality is one of the key aspects of who you are as an individual," says Shepard of The Johns Hopkins University. "Sexuality, or sex, goes from being something you do to this key measure by which people can know something about you. It becomes revelatory."

The idea that sexual orientation is largely innate is widely accepted within the scientific community now but continues to be debated by the public. It was viewed even more skeptically through most of the 20th century. The American Psychiatric Association classified homosexuality as a mental disorder until 1973, and pop culture often referred to it as a disease, or an aberrant, repulsive act.

A sense of shared identity began to strengthen in homosexual subcultures, which flourished at various times and places in several countries. For instance, in Berlin in the 1920s and in Paris in the '20s and '30s attitudes toward homosexuality were relaxed, and gays and lesbians lived fairly openly.

"We're always trying to build this story where things are headed in one direction, but even if you just look at the 20th century and the West, we've really gone back and forth," Shepard says. "The fact is, there were lots of moments and places in time when people had good things happening to them and were living their lives without too much trouble."

But those periods also can end abruptly, Shepard adds, such as during the Nazi persecution of homosexuals in the 1930s. And in the United States and many European nations "the 1950s and '60s were a pretty dramatic period of repression," Shepard says. France, for example, passed its first anti-homosexual laws during that period.

Still, homosexual organizations were slowly raising their profile, both in the United States and in Europe. In 1965, a group picketed in front of the White House against U.S. policies concerning homosexuality.

But in 1969 the modern gay-rights movement was suddenly and violently born. On June 28, police raided the Stonewall Inn, a gay bar in the Greenwich Village section of Manhattan. Police raids on gay bars were hardly rare at the time and had generally been greeted with submission. But this time the patrons, who were not charged, did not disperse. A crowd quickly gathered outside the bar, and a riot eventually broke out. It raged, off and on, for several days, gathering world attention. By the time it ended, gays and lesbians were demanding fair treatment and establishing a defiantly public gay culture that included annual parades and other events.

"Stonewall was enormously influential, basically all across Europe, from Argentina to Japan," says Shepard. "You had all these people making connections. The world is much more mobile, and you're getting this massive transfer of information."

The gay-liberation movement would intersect with other social currents, such as the international youth movement seeking to overturn existing social norms and a burgeoning feminist movement. It would include an ethos of sexual freedom and experimentation that in the 1980s ran smack up against the AIDS epidemic and a growing emphasis on safe sexual practices.

AIDS (Acquired Immune Deficiency Syndrome) was originally viewed as a disease afflicting only gay men until researchers began finding cases among heterosexual women and realized it could be transmitted through blood, semen, vaginal fluid and breast milk. Gay activists played a leading role in pressuring governments for more money for research and treatment.[41]

Political organizing eventually won greater legal and cultural recognition for LGBT relationships. The cause

Thousands of gays, lesbians, bisexuals and supporters of equal rights for sexual minorities march in a gay-pride parade in Warsaw, Poland, on July 17, 2010, urging the government to legalize same-sex partnerships. The socially conservative, predominantly Catholic country has not legalized gay marriage and recently tried to punish teachers who "promote" homosexuality. But the measure was condemned as homophobic by European Union officials.

AFP/Getty Images/Janek Skarzynski

also expanded to embrace bisexuals and transgender people. Although the LGBT movement has had little or limited impact on policies or social attitudes in some countries, it has encouraged LGBT people around the globe to speak up, often at personal risk. In the West, it has led to dramatic changes in laws and attitudes. Homosexuality has been generally decriminalized in most places except Africa and the Middle East, more and more nations accept civil unions or gay marriage, and gays have won elective office and serve openly in the military in three dozen countries.[42] More significant, perhaps, are polls showing that the young are particularly unconcerned about sexual orientation.

All this has happened in about four decades. "In today's world we get so caught up in what's happening right now," says Younger at the University of Kansas, "it's easy to forget how much has changed in recent years."

# CURRENT SITUATION

## Same-Sex Marriage

Amid the remnants of a worldwide recession, unprecedented immigration levels and a continuing conflict between Islamic fundamentalism and secular Western democracies, the debate over sexual rights often gets caught in the political and social crosswinds. And frequently, same-sex marriage seems to be at the center of the storm.

In Europe, for instance, Hungary has shown how shifts in larger political sentiments can affect the gay-rights debate. Since the 1990s, gay-rights activists have considered Hungary one of Eastern Europe's more progressive countries. In 2010, it passed a law recognizing "registered partnerships," which give gay couples most of the benefits of marriage.

But Hungary also was hit hard by the economic downturn, fueling frustration with failed economic policies seen as imported or imposed by the West as Hungary was integrated into the EU. That anger helped the far-right Jobbik Party, known for anti-gay rhetoric, win 16.7 percent of the vote in the last general election.[43]

"I think it's sort of a Euro-fatigue," says Czarnecki, the LGBT activist in Poland. "I think overall people are a little disenchanted with the [economic and cultural] integration process."

Particularly in rejecting the idea of same-sex marriage, Eastern Europeans seem to be staking out their national identity. "To Romanians, the only thing that saved them as a nation [during communism] was the family, marriage and their faith in God," says Costea, whose Alliance of Romania's Families worked to get the law to define marriage as between a man and a woman.

On the other side of Europe's political spectrum, support for gay and lesbian rights has become a litmus test for cultural assimilation in some countries where LGBT rights have progressed the farthest, such as the Netherlands and Scandinavia. Norway, for example, now requires asylum seekers to watch a movie on gays and lesbians. "We want to show that homosexuality is normal and accepted," said the movie's director, Mari Finnestad. "If you want to live in Norway and be part of the Norwegian society, you have to accept that."[44]

Some observers believe that in such situations LGBT rights are being used as a way to define Muslim immigrants as outsiders — not really part of the nations they have joined. Randi Gressgård, a researcher at the Centre for Women's and Gender Research at the University of Bergen, Norway, recently coauthored a paper examining the phenomenon: "Intolerable Citizens: Tolerance, Islam and Homosexuality."[45] Ironically, she says, the concept of tolerance is being used to exclude people —"as a political strategy to create a division between what are considered proper citizens, liberal and tolerant citizens, and improper or intolerant citizens."

Gressgård points out that as anti-Muslim sentiment has grown in Europe, the cause of "homo-tolerance" has been embraced even by conservative parties that originally opposed same-sex marriage and a previously indifferent general public.[46] "People don't care about gender and sexuality issues," she says, "but when it comes to Muslims it's suddenly really important. It's not enough that they follow the laws, they have to embrace the social norm."

Yet, a recent survey in the Netherlands found that most of the country's minorities, including Muslims, feel that "gay people should be free to live their lives as they wished."[47]

Still, the perceived cultural split has led even some gays to join far-right political parties and anti-Muslim groups, says Gressgård, who believes the actions reflect a shift in strategies by far-right parties across much of Europe. France's National Front Party, for example, has gained public support by changing its tune and supporting gay rights while focusing on Muslim immigration as a threat to national identity.[48]

## The Americas

Gay rights have been at the center of America's culture war for at least two decades. Legislative proposals limiting gay rights, often used to whip up turnout among culturally conservative voters, have been a political staple during election years. They've also been convenient political sledgehammers to batter an opponent — such as the initial uproar over allowing gays to serve openly in the military that forced President Bill Clinton to accept the controversial "don't ask, don't tell" approach.[49]

Thus, the most surprising thing about the December votes by the U.S. Congress to repeal the "don't ask, don't tell" measure may be how little heat it generated. Although Sen. John McCain, R-Ariz., brandished a petition from 1,000 retired officers opposing the idea, polls showed strong public support for repeal, and a Pentagon study

# Should same-sex couples be allowed to marry?

## YES
### Rosa M. Posa Guinea
*Coordinator, Latin American Human Rights Advocacy Institute, International Gay and Lesbian Human Rights Commission, Paraguay*

Written for *CQ Global Researcher*, March 2011

"We do not want to marry! And we want that that be our own choice! We do not want the State to regulate our relations in any way, even forbidding marriage!" That statement — which is how the Colombian women's community organization Mujeres al Borde qualifies its endorsement of same-sex marriage — summarizes my thoughts on equal marriage. We celebrate the progress toward equal rights that same-sex marriage indicates. But, we recognize that equal marriage is not the pinnacle of the fight for the rights of lesbian, gay and bisexual people, nor does it end discrimination on the basis of sexual orientation and gender identity.

In January a lesbian and bisexual organization in Argentina — where same-sex marriage was legalized in July 2010 — faced an unusual discrimination case. Members of the group were forbidden from entering a swimming pool because the women were wearing "non-feminine" swimwear (shorts and shirts). They were told they must "respect the family environment" and that the recent victory for the rights of same-sex couples to marry was merely "a left-wing issue!" Clearly, the legalization of same-sex marriage in Argentina had not really changed people's prejudices.

Limiting marriage to heterosexual couples encourages homophobia, discrimination and exclusion. The specter of same-sex marriage is used by opponents of lesbian, gay, bisexual and transgender (LGBT) rights to further persecute us. It is invoked in countries that criminalize homosexuality to arrest people exercising their freedom of association rights or by legislatures seeking to blame systemic problems on vulnerable minorities. In countries where same-sex marriage is a viable goal or already a reality, leaders who still oppose allowing same-sex couples to marry play on this prejudice, painting same-sex couples as less important to society.

Consider South Africa, a country that legalized same-sex marriage in 2006. There lesbian activists fight to end "corrective rape" (when a man rapes a lesbian in order to "turn" her heterosexual) and have it recognized as a hate crime. Dozens of lesbians are raped and murdered there every week, even though the South African Constitution prohibits discrimination on the basis of sexual orientation.

The right to marry a person of the same sex is not the only right LGBT people still seek. In all countries, even those where marriage equality exists, we still have a long way to go to reach real equality as citizens.

## NO
### Margaret Somerville
*Professor, Centre for Medicine, Ethics and Law, McGill University, Montreal, Quebec, Canada*

Written for *CQ Global Researcher*, March 2011

I oppose same-sex marriage but approve of "civil unions." Civil unions can provide the protections and benefits same-sex couples seek and send the message that discrimination on the basis of sexual orientation is wrong, while leaving children's rights unaffected.

Same-sex marriage presents a conflict between the claims of children and homosexual adults. Children's claims relate to their biological origins, family structure and societal norms. Homosexual adults' claims are to not be discriminated against in public recognition of their committed, intimate relationships and the benefits of such recognition. In that conflict I give children priority, since they are the most vulnerable.

In law, marriage confers two rights: to marry and create a family. Giving same-sex couples the latter right changes our societal norms regarding children's human rights. It divests all children of the right to be reared in a natural family structure, with a mother and a father, who optimally should be the child's biological parents. It also gives married, gay adults the right to use reproductive technologies to create families. Thus, a same-sex couple could potentially create a shared genetic child, contravening the child's right to have natural, biological origins — unmanipulated by science.

Rather than being defined primarily by biological ties, all parenthood would be defined primarily by legal ties, as Canada's same-sex marriage law shows. Civil unions do not establish the right to create a family, so they do not affect children's rights. Thus, they are the ethical way to deal with this conflict.

Same-sex marriage was always possible, but it's been an anomaly. Over millennia, the core of marriage across all kinds of societies, cultures and religions has been its biological, procreative reality. Same-sex marriage negates this core. Marriage is built around procreation because it is primarily intended to benefit children and only secondarily, adults. Today, marriage as a cultural construct built around a biological reality is more important than ever, due to the advent of assisted human reproductive technologies and how those can affect the rights of children resulting from their use.

Proponents of same-sex marriage correctly point out that children's rights often are not respected in opposite-sex marriages and not all opposite-sex couples procreate. But those cases do not erase existing societal norms, basic values or symbolism regarding children's rights with respect to their biological origins and family structure. Same-sex marriage does exactly that, which is why we should not introduce it.

**Tying the Same-Sex Knot**

South Africa and Nepal are among the countries where gay marriage is legal. Sonia Souls (left) and Charmaine Weber (center) embrace after their wedding in Capetown, South Africa, on Feb. 14, 2010 (top), and Diya Mahaju and Anil Mahaju prepare to wed in Kathmandu on Aug. 26, 2006, in Nepal's first public gay marriage (bottom). Sixteen other countries recognize same-sex civil unions.

concluded it would cause little disruption in the ranks. In a year of bitter partisan division, eight Republicans joined with the Democratic majority to pass the Senate measure.[50]

The vote left same-sex marriage as the last flashpoint in what had once been a fiery battle over LGBT rights in the United States. Younger, director of the Women, Gender and Sexuality Studies Program at the University of Kansas, believes that's because marriage is considered more than a civil contract. "Most people think of marriage

as a religious ceremony," he says. "We all know that what makes it legal is when you go in the back room and sign the papers, but it's a religious sacrament, and I think that's one reason you see people drawing the line."

Some opponents, however, stress the benefit they believe comes with having children raised by parents of both sexes, and what they consider the right of children to know their biological parents. "A child's got a right to a mother and a father, and preferably its own biological parents," says Margaret Somerville, a law and ethics professor at Canada's McGill University in Montreal, Quebec, who supports civil unions, but not same-sex marriage.

In the United States, five states and the District of Columbia currently allow same-sex marriage, and six others allow some legal spousal rights to gay couples.[51] Although some polls showed Americans inching toward a roughly even split on the issue, the fight over same-sex marriage seemed likely to continue in courts and statehouses across the nation in 2011.

LGBT activists believe they have a good chance to see gay marriage legalized in several other states, including Maryland, New York and Delaware within the next year. But opponents, pointing to their success with voter referendums, believe they will be able to prevail at the ballot box.

Surprisingly, same-sex marriage may have a better chance in some predominantly Catholic Latin American countries. The movement exists, says Ferreyra, IGLHRC's representative in Argentina, because past authoritarian regimes have left the public sensitive to the need to protect human rights. "It's also related to the overall political climate," he says. "There are many left-wing governments that have taken power, in countries such as Argentina, Brazil, Venezuela, Ecuador, and they are supporting LGBT rights."[52]

## Western Influence?

David Kato — a gay activist in Uganda who had been publicly identified by the local newspaper *Rolling Stone*, which urged Ugandans to kill local gays — was murdered in January.

Claims and counterclaims about his death were still being made in mid-February, the motive uncertain. But to many gay activists, Kato's death represents the dangerous situation that exists in the homophobic climate of Uganda and several other African nations, including Cameroon, Senegal and Nigeria.[53]

Many gay activists blame a 2009 visit by American evangelist Lively, of Abiding Truth Ministries, and two other U.S. anti-gay crusaders for inflaming existing homophobic sentiment in Uganda and spurring a local lawmaker to introduce the bill imposing the death penalty for repeated homosexual offenses.

"Lively is said to have spent four hours with Ugandan parliamentarians talking to them about homosexuality," says Kalende, the Ugandan gay activist. "In April 2009, the first version of the bill was written, and the language of this first version reiterated Lively's comments." Ugandan lawmaker David Bahati, however, said on MSNBC's "Rachel Maddow Show" that he alone authored the legislation. In the same interview, Bahati claimed foreigners are coming into Uganda and spending millions of dollars to recruit children into homosexuality, but, despite repeated requests, he has provided no evidence to support the assertion.

The Rev. Kapya Kaoma, a Zambian Episcopal priest, says the foreigners spending money to spread their views about homosexuality are on the other side of the issue. "It's a political agenda being driven by so-called evangelism in the U.S. and being pushed on to Africa," Kaoma concluded after spending 16 months interviewing people in Uganda, Kenya and Nigeria. His report, "Globalising the Culture Wars; U.S. Conservatives, African Churches and Homophobia," warned that preaching intolerance could lead to mob violence against African gays.[54]

Likewise, some leaders in the Middle East see tolerance for homosexuality — and even homosexuality itself — as something imposed on them by the West. Iranian President Mahmoud Ahmadinejad notably expressed that idea at Columbia University in New York City in 2007, when responding to a question about the recent execution in Iran of two gay men. "In Iran we don't have homosexuals like in your country," he said. "In Iran we do not have this phenomenon. I do not know who has told you we have it."[55] African leaders have made similar claims.

As some Ugandans have begun speaking out in opposition to the bill, and international criticism has grown,

the Ugandan anti-gay bill appears to have stalled.[56] But with homosexuality already illegal in almost all the countries of the region, and more punitive legislation pending in several, the situation for LGBT people in Africa seems unlikely to improve in the immediate future.

Meanwhile, a continent away in the world's second-largest nation, the 2009 decision of the Indian Supreme Court to strike down a colonial-era law and decriminalize homosexuality may have had as much of an effect on the lives of LGBT people as any other action in the world. The case attracted support from a broad array of public organizations, but it also was opposed by some religious groups that have continued legal efforts to restore bans on homosexual behavior.

"There's a continuing legal battle, but as far as the public is concerned, the fight is over," says Indian lawyer Narrain. "To change the law you need a public movement, and that's what we have had in India."

## OUTLOOK
### Sweeping Transformation?

Both proponents and opponents of gay rights seem to share the sense that things have been moving quickly. Those who feel that the changes threaten the traditional heterosexual family have developed a fierce determination to halt the process. Among those who believe they stand at the cusp of an era when gays and lesbians will see their relationships treated just like everyone else's, there is an equal determination to complete the transformation.

American psychiatrist and author Mondimore believes the arguments for discrimination are "just falling away" and that attitudes about same-sex relationships could get to the point "where it's like it is with interracial marriage. Once people got all worked up about it, and now that reaction just seems strange."

But Ruse, head of the Catholic Family and Human Rights Institute, believes the "status quo" will prevail and that gay-rights activists overestimate how much opinion is shifting. "We are told incessantly that homosexual marriage is just on the cusp of widespread acceptance," he says, "but I don't see that happening."

The University of Amsterdam's Duyvendak, however, believes a fundamental shift in attitudes has taken place in much of Europe, at least, that will help to make same-sex couples unexceptional in the near future. "Sexuality and procreation have been totally decoupled," he says. "This very idea that love and sexuality is only reserved for straight people, I cannot imagine that coming back."

In Latin America, Ferreyra of the International Gay and Lesbian Human Rights Commission sees the next 10 to 15 years of gay-rights advocacy as part of a larger regional effort to build institutions that support stable democracies and "increase the internal bonds within the countries, support civil society and human rights." And the current LGBT movement in Latin American is limited largely to urban elites, he says. The next step is to reach out to "the whole population."

The World Congress of Families' Jacobs believes LGBT activists who are optimistic about the future overlook a key factor: global demographic trends. Declining birth rates and aging populations among the largely secular Western nations contrast with higher birth rates in regions that are hostile to gay rights. Even within the developed world, he says, portions of the population that oppose equal treatment for homosexual couples are growing. "The arrow points to the natural family," he says, "because it's only the religious who are having children."

But reflecting the general sense of optimism within the LGBT community, activist Kalende looks past today's troubles in her native Uganda and sees a brighter future there, too. "Things will get better," she says, "because whenever there is a noble cause for justice, freedom finds a way."

# NOTES

1. "Report of the Comprehensive Review of the Issues Associated with a Repeal of Don't Ask Don't Tell," Pentagon Working Group Study, Nov. 30, 2010, p. 89, www.defense.gov/home/features/2010/0610_gatesdadt/DADTReport_FINAL_20101130(secure-hires).pdf.

2. "Americans split evenly on gay marriage," CNN Politics, Aug. 11, 2010, http://politicalticker.blogs.cnn.com/2010/08/11/americans-split-evenly-on-gay-marriage/. Also see Charlie Savage and Sheryl Gay Stolberg, "U.S., in Shift, Sees Marriage Act as Violation of Gay Rights," The New York Times,

Feb. 23, 2011, www.nytimes.com/2011/02/24/us/24marriage.html.

3. Sudarsan Raghavan, "Gays in Africa face growing persecution, activists say," The Washington Post, Dec.12, 2010, www.washingtonpost.com/wp-dyn/content/article/2010/12/11/AR2010121103045.html.

4. Ibid.

5. Mark Lowen, "Scores arrested in Belgrade after anti-gay riot," BBC News, Oct. 10, 2010, www.bbc.co.uk/news/world-europe-11507253.

6. "Sexual Orientation/Gender Identity References, Human Rights Report for 2009," U.S. Department of State, March 10, 2010, http://paei.state.gov/g/drl/rls/hrrpt/2009/.

7. Jeremy Hubbard, "Fifth Gay Teen Suicide Sparks Debate," ABC News, Oct. 3, 2010, http://abcnews.go.com/US/gay-teen-suicide-sparks-debate/story?id=11788128.

8. David Myers, Exploring Psychology (2007), p. 368.

9. Theodore Olson, "The Conservative Case for Gay Marriage," Newsweek, July 10, 2010, www.newsweek.com/2010/01/08/the-conservative-case-for-gay-marriage.html.

10. Nick Squires, "Pope says gay marriage is 'insidious and dangerous,'" The Telegraph, May 13, 2010, www.telegraph.co.uk/news/newstopics/religion/7719789/Pope-says-gay-marriage-is-insidious-and-dangerous.html.

11. Scott Lively, "Deciphering 'Gay' word-speak and language of confusion," newswithviews.com, May 25, 2002, www.newswithviews.com/conspiracy/conspiracy6.htm.

12. Evelyn Schlatter, "18 Anti-Gay Groups and their Propaganda," Southern Poverty Law Center, winter 2010, www.splcenter.org/get-informed/intelligence-report/browse-all-issues/2010/winter/the-hard-liners.

13. Zoe Alsop, "Uganda's Anti-Gay Bill: Inspired by the U.S.," Time, Dec. 10, 2009, www.time.com/time/world/article/0,8599,1946645,00.html.

14. Thomas Fox, "140 theologians call for women's ordination, end of mandatory celibacy," The National Catholic Reporter, Feb. 4, 2011, www.ncronline.org/

blogs/ncr-today/143-theologians-call-womens-ordination-end-mandatory-celibacy.

15. Daniel Maguire, "A Catholic Defense of Same-Sex Marriage," *The Religious Consultation*, April 20, 2006, www.religiousconsultation.org/Catholic_ defense_of_same_sex_marriage.htm.

16. "Lesbian and Gay Rights in the World," International Lesbian, Gay, Bisexual, Trans and Intersex Association, May 2010, http://ilga.org/ilga/en/arti cle/1161.

17. "Homophobia, Transphobia and Discrimination on Grounds of Sexual Orientation and Gender, 2010 Update," European Union Agency for Fundamental Rights, 2010, p. 7.

18. "Poland urged to halt 'homophobia,'" BBC News, April 27, 2007, http://news.bbc.co.uk/2/hi/ europe/6596829.stm.

19. "We Are a Buried Generation: Discrimination and Violence Against Sexual Minorities in Iran," Human Rights Watch, Dec. 15, 2010, www.hrw.org/en/ reports/2010/12/15/we-are-buried-generation.

20. Kathy Chu and Calum MacLeod, "Gay life in China is legal but remains hidden," *USA Today*, Feb. 22, 2010, www.usatoday.com/news/world/2010-02-21-gays-China-closeted_N.htm.

21. For background, see Brian Beary, "Religious Fundamentalism," *CQ Global Researcher*, Feb. 1, 2009, pp. 27-58.

22. Rafael Romo, "Hate crimes, killings rising, say Honduras activists," CNN, Feb. 1, 2011, www.cnn .com/2011/WORLD/americas/01/31/honduras .hate.crimes/index.html.

23. Tamara Audi, Justin Scheck and Christopher Lawton, "California Votes for Prop 8," *The Wall Street Journal*, Nov. 5, 2008, http://online.wsj.com/ article/SB122586056759900673.html.

24. A. G. Sulzberger, "Ouster of Iowa Judges Sends Signal to Bench," *The New York Times*, Nov. 3, 2010, www .nytimes.com/2010/11/04/us/politics/04judges.html.

25. "The Yogyakarta Principles," www.yogyakartaprin ciples.org/.

26. Neil MacFarquhar, "In a First, Gay Rights Are Pressed at the U.N.," *The New York Times*, Dec. 19, 2008, p. 22.

27. Article 16, "The Universal Declaration of Human Rights," United Nations, www.un.org/en/docu ments/udhr/index.shtml.

28. William J. Saunders, "Committees Gone Wild: How U.N. Bureaucrats Are Turning 'Human Rights' Against the Family," *The Family in America, A Journal of Public Policy*, winter 2010, www.familyinamerica .org/index.php?doc_id=15&cat_id=6.

29. Articles 2 and 12, "The Universal Declaration of Human Rights," *op. cit.*

30. "Governments Remove Sexual Orientation from UN Resolution Condemning Extrajudicial, Summary or Arbitrary Executions," IGLHRC press release, Nov. 17, 2010, www.iglhrc.org/cgi-bin/ iowa/article/pressroom/pressrelease/1257.html.

31. Louis Crompton, *Homosexuality and Civilization* (2003), location 4751 in the Kindle edition.

32. *Ibid.*, location 5161 in the Kindle edition.

33. The Holy Bible, New King James version.

34. Crompton, *op. cit.*, location 888 in the Kindle edition.

35. A concise summary of Aquinas's philosophical argu-ment and objections to it can be found at Stephen Law's blog, under "Aquinas on Homosexuality," March 14, 2007, http://stephenlaw.blogspot .com/2007/03/aquinas-on-homosexuality.html.

36. Crompton, *op. cit.*, location 5397 in the Kindle edition.

37. *Ibid.*

38. *Ibid.*, location 6208.

39. Francis Mark Mondimore, *A Natural History of Homosexuality* (1996), p. 28.

40. "The Karl Heinrich Ulrichs Award," International Lesbian and Gay Law Association, www.ilglaw.org/ cnfaward.htm.

41. For background, see Nellie Bristol, "Battling HIV/ AIDS," *CQ Researcher*, Oct. 26, 2007, pp. 889-912.

42. Gay and Lesbian Leadership Institute, www.glli.org/ home.

43. Dan Bilefsky, "World Briefing/Europe; Hungary: New Leader Assails Far-Right Party's Rise," *The New York Times*, April 13, 2010, www.nytimes.com/2010/04/13/ world/europe/13briefs-Hungary.html.

44. "Asylum seekers have to watch gay movie," DR Forside (Danish Public Broadcasting), Feb. 10, 2010, www.dr.dk/Nyheder/Andre_sprog/English/2011/02/10/151816.htm.

45. Randi Gressgård and Christine Jacobsen, "Intolerable citizens: Tolerance, Islam and Homosexuality," presented at the conference on Sexual Nationalisms: Gender, Sexuality and the Politics of Belonging in the New Europe, in Amsterdam, Jan. 27-28, 2011.

46. For background, see Sarah Glazer, "Europe's Immigration Turmoil," *CQ Global Researcher*, Dec. 1, 2010, pp. 289-320.

47. "Just Different, That's All, Acceptance of Homosexuality in the Netherlands," The Netherlands Institute for Social Research, August 2010, p. 17, www.scp.nl/english/Publications/Publications_by_year/Publications_2010/Just_different_that_s_all.

48. Sarah Wildman, "Neo-Nazis No Longer? Marine le Pen Tones Down France's Far Right," *Politics Daily*, August 2010, www.politicsdaily.com/2010/05/31/neo-nazis-no-longer-marine-le-pen-tones-down-frances-far-right/.

49. For background, see Kenneth Jost, "Gays in the Military: Update," *CQ Researcher*, Oct. 15, 2010.

50. Ed O'Keefe, "'Don't ask, don't tell,' is repealed by Senate; bill awaits Obama's signing," *The Washington Post*, Dec. 19, 2010, www.washingtonpost.com/wp-dyn/content/article/2010/12/18/AR2010121801729.html.

51. "Marriage and Relationships Recognition" webpage, Human Rights Campaign, www.hrc.org/issues/marriage.asp.

52. For background, see Roland Flamini, "The New Latin America," *CQ Global Researcher*, March 1, 2008, pp. 57-84.

53. Jeffrey Gettleman, "Ugandan who spoke up for gays is beaten to death," *The New York Times*, Jan. 27, 2011, www.nytimes.com/2011/01/28/world/africa/28uganda.html.

54. Jacqui Goddard and Jonathan Clayton, "Anti-gay laws in Africa are product of American religious exports, say activists," *The Times*, May 22, 2010.

55. "'We don't have any gays in Iran,' Iranian president tells Ivy League audience," *The Daily Mail*, Sept. 25, 2007, www.dailymail.co.uk/news/article-483746/We-dont-gays-Iran-Iranian-president-tells-Ivy-League-audience.html.

56. "Uganda gay bill critics deliver online petition," BBC News, March 1, 2010, http://news.bbc.co.uk/2/hi/8542341.stm.

# BIBLIOGRAPHY

## Selected Sources

## Books

**Carlson, Allan, and Paul Mero, *The Natural Family: A Manifesto*, Spence Publishing Co., 2007.**
Two leaders of a movement to protect the heterosexual, or what they call the "natural," family outline their view of its societal role and threats it faces from same-sex marriage.

**Crompton, Louis, *Homosexuality and Civilization*, Belknap Press, 2003.**
A comprehensive history of homosexuality and how different societies have responded to it, written by a professor who founded one of the first interdisciplinary gay studies programs, at the University of Nebraska, in 1970.

**LeVay, Simon, *Gay, Straight and the Reason Why: The Science of Sexual Orientation*, Oxford University Press, 2010.**
A neuroscientist looks at the research on the development of sexual orientation.

**Mondimore, Francis Mark, *A Natural History of Homosexuality*, The Johns Hopkins University Press, 1996.**
A psychologist at The Johns Hopkins University provides an accessible survey of homosexual history, along with research into sexual biology and sexual identity.

## Articles

**"Gay Rights in Eastern Europe: The long march," *The Economist*, Oct. 26, 2010, www.economist.com/blogs/easternapproaches/2010/10/gay_rights_eastern_europe.**
A blogger reviews the tension between European Union calls for equitable treatment of gays and antipathy toward gay rights felt in many Eastern European countries.

Kaphle, Anup, and Habiba Nosheem, "After string of gay-friendly measures, Nepal aims to tap valuable tourist market," *The Washington Post*, Jan. 9, 2011, www.washingtonpost.com/wp-dyn/content/article/2011/01/07/AR2011010702762.html.
Reporters examine how Nepal became the first South Asian country to decriminalize homosexuality and allow same-sex marriage.

Kurczy, Stephen, "Don't ask, don't tell: How do other countries treat gay soldiers?" *The Christian Science Monitor*, May 26, 2010, www.csmonitor.com/World/Global-News/2010/0526/Don-t-ask-don-t-tell-How-do-other-countries-treat-gay-soldiers.
The reporter examines which countries allow gays and lesbians to serve openly in the military and how the transformation has gone.

Mooallem, Jon, "Can animals be gay?" *The New York Times Magazine*, March 31, 2010, www.nytimes.com/2010/04/04/magazine/04animals-t.html.
Research shows that same-gender relationships are common among many animals.

O'Flaherty, Michael, and John Fisher, "Sexual Orientation, Gender, Identity and International Rights Law: Contextualizing the Yogyakarta Principles," *Human Rights Law Review*, 2008.
Two scholars look at the significance and impact of the Yogyakarta Principles, a set of human rights standards relating to sexual orientation and gender identity.

Raghaven, Sudarson, "Gays in Africa Face Growing Persecution, activists say," *The Washington Post*, Dec. 12, 2010, www.washingtonpost.com/wp-dyn/content/article/2010/12/11/AR2010121103045.html.
Persecution of gays is intensifying across Africa, the author says, spurred by evangelical preachers, local politicians and a virulently anti-gay local media.

## Studies and Reports

"2009 Country Reports on Human Rights Practices," U.S. Department of State, March 2010, www.state.gov/g/drl/rls/hrrpt/2009/index.htm.
The annual report examines human rights issues around the world, including discrimination against LBGT people.

"Homophobia, Transphobia and Discrimination on grounds of Sexual Orientation and Gender Identity, 2010 Update," European Union Agency for Fundamental Rights, www.fra.europa.eu/fraWebsite/attachments/FRA-LGBT-report-update2010.pdf.
The agency that monitors human rights across Europe reviews how the LGBT population is being treated.

"Religious Groups' Official Positions on Same-Sex Marriage," Pew Forum on Religion and Public Life, July 2010, http://pewforum.org/Gay-Marriage-and-Homosexuality/Religious-Groups-Official-Positions-on-Same-Sex-Marriage.aspx.
The nonprofit Pew center looks at every major religion's position on same-sex marriage.

Tozzi, Piero, "Six Problems with the 'Yogyakarta Principles,'" Catholic Family and Human Rights Institute, April 2007, www.c-fam.org/publications/id.439/pub_detail.asp.
A conservative reviews the Yogyakarta Principles, intended to provide a human rights framework for the LGBT community.

# For More Information

**Catholic Family and Human Rights Institute**, 211 East 43rd St., Suite 1306, New York, NY 10017; (212) 754-5948; www.c-fam.org. A research and lobbying group that works "to defend life and family at international institutions" and otherwise support the values of the Catholic Church.

**Council for Global Equality**, 1220 L St., N.W., Suite 100-450, Washington, DC 20005; (202) 719-0511; www.globalequality.org. Brings together experts and organizations to encourage a U.S. foreign policy supportive of LGBT people around the world.

**European Union Fundamental Rights Agency**, Schwarzenbergplatz 11, 1040 Vienna, Austria; (+43 (1) 580 30 - 60; www.fra.europa.eu. An advisory body of the European Union that monitors human rights.

**International Gay and Lesbian Human Rights Commission**, 80 Maiden Lane, Suite 1505, New York, NY 10038; (212) 430-6054; www.iglhrc.org. Opposes discrimination or abuse based on a person's actual or perceived sexual orientation, gender identity or expression.

**International Lesbian, Gay, Bisexual, Trans and Intersex Association (ILGA)**, http://ilga.org. A network of groups that have been working for LGBT rights since 1978, with regional offices throughout the world.

**World Congress of Families**, Howard Center for Family, Religion and Society, 934 N. Main St., Rockford, IL 61103; (815) 964-5819; www.worldcongress.org. Seeks to unite groups from around the world who believe the "natural" family is threatened by societal changes.

**The Yogyakarta Principles**, www.yogyakartaprinciples.org. An effort by an international group of experts to outline a broad range of human rights standards relating to sexual orientation and gender identity.

# Voices From Abroad:

## MORGAN TSVANGIRAI

### Prime Minister, Zimbabwe

*Ruling party practices homosexuality*

"Nowhere in our (Movement for Democratic Change political party) principles document is there any reference to gays and lesbians. For the record, it is well-known that homosexuality is practised in Zanu PF (political party) where senior officials from that party have been jailed while others are under police probe on allegations of sodomy. It is in Zanu PF where homosexuality is a religion."

*Guardian Unlimited (England) March 2010*

The Rome News-Tribune/Mike Lester

## PETER TATCHELL

### Coordinator, Equal Love Campaign, England

*Double standards*

"If the government banned black people from getting married and offered them civil partnerships instead, it would provoke public outrage. It is equally outrageous for the government to deny gay couples the right to marry."

*Yorkshire (England) Evening Post, November 2010*

## PAUL SEMUGOMA

### Physician, Uganda

*A deadly policy*

"In Uganda, our once-lauded AIDS programmes are failing. They refuse to serve major vulnerable populations like gay men. Puritanism may make attractive politics, but it's a deadly policy."

*The Independent (Sierra Leone) February 2010*

## DAVID WATKINS

### Teacher, Schools Out (LGBT organization) England

*Other types of people exist*

"When you have a math problem, why does it have to involve a straight family or a boyfriend and girlfriend?

Why not two boys or two girls? It's not about teaching about gay sex, it is about exposing children to the idea that there are other types of people out there."

*Sunday Telegraph (England) January 2011*

## MAHMOUD AHMADINEJAD

### President, Iran

*No gays in Iran*

"In Iran we don't have homosexuals like in your country (United States). In Iran we do not have this phenomenon. I don't know who has told you that we have it."

*Agence France-Presse September 2007*

## JUNG YEON-JU

### Law professor Sungshin Women's University, South Korea

*Consider the majority*

"Yes, there are some countries making efforts to accept gay [service] members, but at the same time, many others oppose them. Especially given that Korea maintains a mandatory [military] draft system, we should think about the majority in the big picture."

*Korea Times (South Korea) June 2010*

# NICHOLAS OKOH

### Archbishop, Uganda

*A threat to the church*

"Homosexuality is not a new phenomenon in the society but the only trouble is that the issues dividing us (church) now are very difficult to handle. They are threatening the unity of the church because they disobey the authority of the scriptures."

*The Monitor (Uganda) August 2010*

# ZHANG BEICHUAN

### Gay-rights advocate, China

*An added benefit*

"To legalize same-sex marriage could help stabilize and sustain gay relationships, thereby lowering the risk of contracting HIV/AIDS."

*Chinadaily.com.cn November 2010*

# VITIT MUNTARBHORN

### Law professor Chulalongkorn University Thailand

*Thailand welcomes gays*

"Thailand is in a good position to promote LGBT rights internationally. We have an environment conducive to LGBT rights. Our constitution also contains a nondiscrimination clause for their protection."

*The Nation (Thailand) December 2010*

# KELVIN HOLDSWORTH

### Provost, St. Mary's Episcopal Cathedral, Scotland

*'The time has come'*

"I am aware of couples in Glasgow who are prevented by law from celebrating their relationship in the form of marriage. The time has come for a marriage law that does not discriminate, and I look forward to the day when I can marry gay members of my congregation in church."

*The Herald (Scotland) November 2010*

# 8

# Homeless Students

Marcia Clemmitt

Zach Montgomery and his niece Alexys watch TV in the Clermont, Fla., motel their homeless family was staying in on Feb. 9, 2012. Efforts to identify homeless students and get them into the classroom are beginning to pay off. In the 2010-2011 school year, public schools enrolled a record number of homeless students — more than a million.

From *CQ Researcher*,
April 5, 2013.

"I struggled in school . . . because of having to sleep in different places . . . and not being able to rest," 11-year-old Rumi Khan of Carlisle, Pa., told a congressional committee investigating student homelessness in 2011.

Rumi said he and his mother became homeless after his father committed several acts of domestic violence. But his mother was so worried about the effects on Rumi of not having a stable home that she "was thinking that we should maybe go back to my dad," the sixth-grader said.[1]

Homelessness is "especially hard for my 2-year-old brother," seventh-grader Brooklyn Pastor, 12, from Shirley, N.Y., told the panel. Pastor said that instead of doing her homework, she often played with her baby brother to keep him from crying.[2]

"When you are sitting in class you are . . . worried about where are you going to go after, where are you going to eat, how are you going to get your homework done," said Army Pvt. Brittany Koon, of Fort Hood, Texas, who lost her access to permanent shelter when she "aged out" of the foster-care system at 18. "I had a scholarship to college, but I lived in my car and on [relatives' and friends'] couches," said Koon.[3]

In the 2010-2011 school year, for the first time, America's public schools enrolled more than a million pre-K-12 students who had been homeless at some time during the previous school year.[4] That statistic, together with worry about the lingering effects of the 2007-2008 recession and the home-foreclosure crisis, has increased public concern about student homelessness. Media coverage of

## Vermont Leads in Curbing Child Homelessness

Led by Vermont, states in New England and the Midwest ranked highest in efforts to reduce child homelessness, while those in the South and West ranked lowest. Low rankings were due to such factors as weak state policies, the poor overall well-being of children and, in the South, the lasting effects of hurricanes Katrina and Rita.

### State Rankings on Addressing Child Homelessness, 2010*

Top 10
11 to 20
21 to 30
31 to 40
Bottom 10

*The study considers the extent of homelessness relative to population size, the overall well-being of children, the risk of homelessness and state policy and planning efforts.*

Source: "America's Youngest Outcasts 2010: State Report Card on Child Homelessness," National Center on Family Homelessness, December 2011, p. 13, www.homeless childrenamerica.org/media/NCFH_ AmericaOutcast 2010_web.pdf

struggling students and cash-strapped schools attempting to help them has heightened the concern.[5]

The problem is not new, however. Beginning around 1980, local housing agencies and homelessness advocates began noticing more families with children appearing in shelters alongside the adult men who formerly had made up most of the homeless population. Furthermore, they discovered, many children and teens in this new population were not enrolled in school.

In response, a 1987 federal law — known as the McKinney-Vento Act* — charged the nation's public schools with seeking out homeless students in their communities, enrolling them and reporting their numbers

---

*The law was named after two of its chief sponsors, Rep. Stewart B. McKinney, R-Conn., and Rep. Bruce Vento, D-Minn.

annually to the U.S. Department of Education (DoE). The aim: to help the government craft policies to decrease student homelessness and ensure that homeless children get equal access to schooling.

A quarter-century into the effort, however, advocates warn that poverty, a lack of affordable housing and family problems such as domestic violence continue to fuel student homelessness. A broader societal effort is needed to tackle the problem, they contend.

"Today the number of homeless kids is at a historic high," says Carmela DeCandia, director of the National Center on Family Homelessness, a research and advocacy group based in Needham, Mass.

But understanding the numbers is difficult. More than 1 million children and teens were homeless at some time during the 2010-2011 school year, and the number has been rising for years, according to a June 2012 DoE report. The department bases its tally on reports from schools around the country and counts as homeless anyone living in a homeless shelter, on the streets, in a cheap hotel or involuntarily with friends and relatives.

Furthermore, "kids under 6 — the most likely to be homeless — aren't in those numbers," says DeCandia. When those younger children are included, she says, the center estimates that 1.6 million youngsters experienced homelessness in 2010.

However, the Department of Housing and Urban Development (HUD) has a more conservative estimate — about 634,000 "literally" homeless Americans in 2012. HUD also finds that the number of homeless has been dropping slightly, probably because of increased efforts by the Obama administration to help homeless people find permanent housing.[6]

The differences stem from the departments' differing missions, how they define homelessness and how they conduct their counts. HUD counts only those who on any given night are sleeping in homeless shelters, on the streets or in places not intended for human habitation, such as cars. The HUD total therefore does not include many of the children and teens that DoE counts, since a majority of them are living in cheap motels or involuntarily "doubled up" in homes or apartments with friends and relatives.

It's unclear why DoE's numbers are rising and the HUD numbers falling. Dennis Culhane, a professor of social policy at the University of Pennsylvania in Philadelphia, says the decreasing trend HUD reports is probably more credible. HUD counts homeless people in a national census conducted by trained observers, he says, while DoE relies on self-reporting by homeless families and reports from school homeless liaisons (employees responsible for seeking out homeless students in their communities and helping them get enrolled). Improved detection by educators — 25 years after they began reporting the numbers — probably accounts for at least part of the recent DoE increases, Culhane says.

Nevertheless, researchers and advocates agree about most of the demographic facts on student homelessness. "The typical family experiencing homelessness is a young, single mother with a couple of kids, and about 42 percent of children who are homeless are under the age of 6," says Christina Murphy, director of policy and communications at the National Center for Family Homelessness.

"Homelessness drops sharply when children turn 5 or 6 because they can go into the subsidized child care called 'public schools,'" says Marybeth Shinn, a professor of human and organizational development at Vanderbilt University's Peabody School. Homelessness is higher among very young families, she says, because "the youngest children take a toll on a parent's ability to work."

Most people experience only one spate of homelessness — using the HUD definition of living in a shelter or a place not meant for human habitation — and half

## Homeless Students "Double Up" for Shelter

Most of the more than 1 million students who were homeless at some point during the 2010-2011 school year found nighttime shelter by "doubling up," or living with extended family, friends or adult guardians. Nearly one-fifth slept in homeless shelters, while 5 percent lived in motels or hotels. Five percent had no shelter at all.

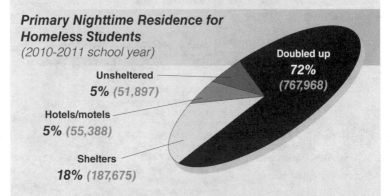

*Primary Nighttime Residence for Homeless Students*
*(2010-2011 school year)*

Unsheltered **5%** *(51,897)*

Hotels/motels **5%** *(55,388)*

Shelters **18%** *(187,675)*

Doubled up **72%** *(767,968)*

*Source:* "Education for Homeless Children and Youth Programs: Data Collection Summary," National Center for Homeless Education, June 2012, p. 17, center.serve. org/nche/downloads/data_comp_0909-1011.pdf

of all homeless stints last fewer than 30 days, says Culhane. Nevertheless, a single bout of homelessness often signals that the family has had an unstable housing situation for some time, he says. "Many have multiple moves before they come in" to a shelter.

"I worked for a dozen years with a family shelter, and we'd hear stories about moving around, getting separated," says DeCandia. "There is a period of instability before the shelters, and those kids may or may not be in school."

In the 2010-2011 school year, for example, the Education Department reported that of the nation's more than 1 million homeless students, 72 percent were living doubled up, 18 percent were in homeless shelters, 5 percent were unsheltered and 5 percent lived in hotels or motels.[7]

Researchers cite two primary reasons for youth and family homelessness.

For the most part, "it's a manifestation of poverty" coupled with the lack of affordable permanent housing, says Shinn. In addition, especially for teenagers living on their own, "family dysfunction" such as domestic violence, substance abuse or conflict with parents over sexual preference are key drivers, she says.

## Affordable Housing Is Biggest Challenge

More than 40 percent of the nation's school districts say their biggest challenges in dealing with student homelessness are the lack of affordable housing and difficulty in identifying homeless students. Other big challenges include providing transportation and health care.

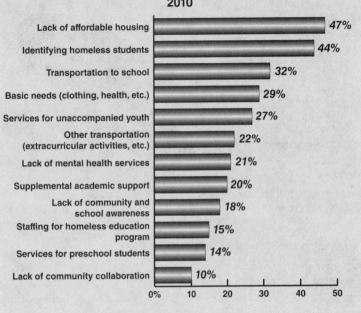

**School Districts' Greatest Student-Homelessness Challenges, 2010**

| Challenge | Percent |
|---|---|
| Lack of affordable housing | 47% |
| Identifying homeless students | 44% |
| Transportation to school | 32% |
| Basic needs (clothing, health, etc.) | 29% |
| Services for unaccompanied youth | 27% |
| Other transportation (extracurricular activities, etc.) | 22% |
| Lack of mental health services | 21% |
| Supplemental academic support | 20% |
| Lack of community and school awareness | 18% |
| Staffing for homeless education program | 15% |
| Services for preschool students | 14% |
| Lack of community collaboration | 10% |

*Source:* "A Critical Moment: Child & Youth Homelessness in Our Nation's Schools," First Focus, July 2010, www.firstfocus.net/sites/default/files/HomelessEd_0.pdf

Young people living on their own are almost certainly the most undercounted homeless group, analysts agree. Often, they aren't in school, and many who do attend school "probably aren't telling the schools that they aren't with their families," says DeCandia. They also are less likely than single adults or families to be in homeless shelters, she says.

Based on reports that HUD undercounts teens living on their own, the agency this year stepped up efforts to find and count homeless young people and to study the best ways to reach them with services such as temporary or permanent housing assistance and counseling.[8]

In the early 1980s, as student homelessness began to rise, researchers began to study how schools might better serve that population, focusing on questions such as how homelessness affects young people's learning and whether homelessness puts students more at risk than poverty alone. Because of the difficulty of locating large study populations and defining "homelessness," however, findings have largely remained "inconclusive," says Kerri Tobin, an assistant professor of education at Marywood University in Scranton, Pa., and co-author of the 2011 book *Homelessness Comes to School.*

Nevertheless, many scholars continue to believe that homelessness adds academic risk to low-income students' lives. "The more risk factors you add on," the worse students' outcomes are likely to be, says Joseph Murphy, a professor at Vanderbilt University's Peabody College of Education in Nashville and Tobin's co-author. Homeless students also experience a lot of school "churn," Murphy says, which means they are "late, then out a day, then late," which often leads to poor academic performance.

Many also question how effectively federal law addresses the problems of homeless students and how much more school districts can do to help.

A 2010 study of 1,668 school districts indicated that the McKinney-Vento law's education-related provisions — grants and rules collectively dubbed the Education for Homeless Children and Youth (EHCY) program — help foster "more productive education opportunities" for homeless students, wrote Peter M. Miller, an assistant professor of educational leadership and policy analysis at the University of Wisconsin, Madison. For example, in the 2008-09 school year, more than 70 percent of districts that received federal funding for homelessness assistance had given their staffs professional training on homelessness issues, provided extra resources to transport homeless students to appropriate schools, helped families get non-school-related services and provided school supplies for students.[9]

Nevertheless, most of the federal law's requirements constitute "unfunded mandates" for states and localities, making them difficult to fulfill, says Marywood's Tobin. Each year a small proportion of school districts receive competitively awarded federal grants to assist homeless students, but the law's requirements "are generally underfunded," she says.

On the plus side, many districts' homeless liaisons "are doing better" at informing homeless people about what assistance is available, says Ronald Hallett, an assistant professor of education at the University of the Pacific, in Stockton, Calif.

Some school leaders don't do more about student homelessness because of anxiety over whether resources will hold out as more students in need are identified, says Tobin. "Even some principals who know what to do are hesitant to speak out and tell parents to fight for resources [outlined in federal law] because the principals often know that they can't fund those things," she says.

As schools, housing agencies and advocates for the homeless consider how best to help homeless children and youth, here are some of the questions being asked:

## Are federal programs to assist homeless students working?

When Congress passed the McKinney-Vento Act in 1987 to help homeless families with children, many homeless students were not enrolled in school. The law requires school districts to locate homeless students in their communities and help them enroll. But while the act clearly has spurred improvements, gaps in federal policy and inadequate funding make McKinney-Vento less effective than it should be, many analysts say.

"Federal law did exactly what you hoped a federal law would do," says Vanderbilt's Murphy. "It alerted people to the problem and stated that we need to take care of these children."

Under the program, each school district employs a homeless liaison. Thus, Wisconsin's Miller says, the law has created a highly important "critical mass" of school staff nationwide who are aware of the scope of homelessness and what kind of help students need. Still, he says, some liaisons could be better informed about how to help.[10]

Indeed, the program's influence on school-district practices hasn't always been — and likely still isn't — adequate, says Miller. In 1995, for example, eight years

A teenager living in a shelter in New York City earned money by collecting cans. Numerous studies have found that homeless students and low-income students with stable housing have similar academic performance.

Getty Images/Spencer Platt

after the law's enactment, 48 percent of 102 school districts in the nation's 50-largest cities still "had no specific plans for the education of homeless students," and 54 percent hadn't named a homeless liaison. Many district leaders continued to say that student homelessness was "nonexistent or very minor in scope" in their communities, Miller wrote.[11]

"Homelessness plus mobility" — the movement of students from school to school as their housing situations change — poses "tremendous problems" both for the students and for the schools they attend, says John Fantuzzo, a professor of human relations at the University of Pennsylvania's Graduate School of Education in Philadelphia. But while numerous specific and practical national policies for how to serve such students are badly needed, they have not yet been developed, he says.

For example, thoughtfully developed national standards are needed to guide schools' practices, such as those specifying how quickly a child's information must be transferred to his new school, Fantuzzo says. A delay in teachers' learning about a new child in class harms the child and can disrupt the classroom, he notes.

Researchers say vaguely framed federal requirements allow halfhearted implementation and time-consuming

## Family Rejection Causes Most LGBT Homelessness

Nearly half of the lesbian, gay, bisexual or transgender (LGBT) youths who are homeless or at risk of homelessness left home because of family rejection; a comparable number were forced out for similar reasons. Others left because of physical or emotional abuse at home.

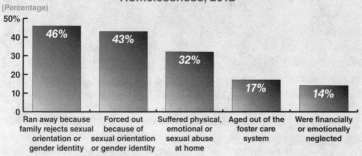

### Reasons LGBT Youths Are Homeless or at Risk of Homelessness, 2012*

* Percentages exceed 100 percent because LGBT homelessness may be caused by multiple factors.

Source: "Serving Our Youth," Williams Institute, UCLA School of Law, July 2012, williamsinstitute.law.ucla.edu/wp-content/uploads/Durso-Gates-LGBT-Homeless-Youth-Survey-July-2012.pdf

disputes that harm students. For instance, homeless liaisons in many districts have a host of other duties, such as coordinating the federal government's assistance program for low-income students, making it difficult to focus on homelessness, says Marywood University's Tobin.

The law requires school districts to enroll homeless students in the most appropriate school — often the same one they attended before they lost their homes, even if it is in a different district from the one where the student is temporarily living. However, the law doesn't specify which locality is responsible for how much of the transportation costs (which are paid with a combination of district, state and federal funds). The result is sometimes long-term wrangling and miscommunication between districts, with the students caught in the middle and "forced to spend extended periods away from school," wrote Miller.[12]

Moreover, the McKinney-Vento transportation requirement is much more difficult to meet in some locations than others, Miller said. In rural New Hampshire,

for example, public transportation is "nearly nonexistent." Such differences have led to spotty implementation of this key provision, he wrote.[13]

While federal law has helped more homeless students enroll in school, federal policies do too little to ensure that students have permanent — or even suitable temporary — roofs over their heads, many homelessness experts say.

"On the education side we've made wonderful progress," says Patricia Popp, state coordinator of Project HOPE-VA, the Virginia Education Program for Homeless Children and Youth, referring to the extra training and resources districts now receive to address homelessness. "But on the housing side we're struggling."

HUD and local housing agencies traditionally focus on the chronically homeless, most of whom are adults, and on people who literally lack a roof over their heads. But most homeless students live "doubled up" with friends or relatives and experience only short stretches of "literal" homelessness.

As a result, "hundreds of millions a year are spent on men's shelters," while few resources help children and youth, said Diane Nilan, president of Naperville, Ill.-based Hear Us, an advocacy group for homeless children.

"Displaced families desperately turn to any possible place to sleep because many cities and towns have no shelters" for them, or the shelters that exist have non-family-friendly rules such as "age limits on boys . . . and curfews that prevent the parent from working third-shift jobs," said Nilan.[14]

### Are school systems doing enough to help homeless students?

Since 1987, federal law has laid out steps that state and local school systems must take to ensure that homeless students receive the same quality of education as others. Researchers say local schools have taken significant actions to meet those standards. But the picture is uneven.

The McKinney-Vento Act "began with very general kinds of statements," says Popp, Virginia's state coordinator for homeless education, and school districts have added meat to the bones. When she started working on homeless-student issues in 1995, she says, the response from schools was, "We don't have any" homeless students. "Now it's, 'How do we implement this?'"

Shame and anxiety make many families reluctant to identify themselves as homeless, even when doing so could qualify them for vital services, says Hallett of the University of the Pacific. But liaisons are learning better ways to make families more comfortable with identifying as homeless. As a result, "we're getting a better idea of the number" of homeless students, he says. For instance, he says, by replacing the term "homeless families" on questionnaires with the term "families in transition," one district has encouraged more families to acknowledge housing problems.

Many school districts now make school showers, meals, closets, lockers, nurses' services and laundry facilities available to teens living on their own.[15]

"I'm amazed," says Popp, "because some schools are doing so much more" than the law requires.

One dedicated liaison found a family living in a motel in a dangerous neighborhood, located an apartment for them, talked the landlord into renting to them despite their recent difficulties, found them a security deposit and helped the family plan a long-term budget, Popp says. "That was about four years ago, and the family is still doing well."

In addition, some "bus drivers go out of their way" to let school officials know when a family "isn't living where they say they're living" and may have lost their housing, she says.

Nevertheless, there's a long way to go, researchers say. "Even today some schools don't quite know who their homeless kids are," says Vanderbilt's Murphy.

Adds Popp, "Across the country there's still a lot of variability in implementation."

Seventy-five percent of districts still say providing transportation for homeless students is difficult, according to Hallett.

Too many teachers remain largely unaware of the problems that beset homeless families and the resources available to help them, says Tobin. As a result, many teachers have somewhat adversarial relationships with

In the wake of hurricanes Katrina and Rita in 2005, the Smith family of Port Sulphur, La., was forced to move to a trailer supplied by the federal government. The Smiths were among thousands of newly homeless families who moved to trailers or to other states, where schools struggled to accommodate the flood of new students. In 2007, Congress required Head Start, the preschool program for poor students, to identify homeless children and enroll them quickly.

homeless parents because they perceive them as being uncooperative rather than struggling to cope with extreme difficulties, she says. Many teachers remain "stuck in the paradigm of, 'I called them and nobody called back,'" so they don't reach out to help, she says.

It's not easy for schools to make homeless students a priority, says Hallett. The homeless population is less familiar than other student groups, such as those with disabilities, who have been incorporated into public schools over the years, he says. "How many of us have relationships with people who are admittedly homeless?" he asks. And it's difficult for teachers to make extraordinary efforts "to keep kids at your school who have big issues, who miss their homework, who don't come to school," Hallett says.

In addition, laws and policies — such as those that require school staff to contact law-enforcement or child-welfare authorities when they suspect neglect — likely drive some homeless teens from school, said the National Association for the Education of Homeless Children and Youth, an advocacy group with offices in Minneapolis and Washington, D.C.[16] Among other reasons, many teens living without parents already have been involved with the child-welfare system and feel betrayed by it, the group says.

"One option would be to revise reporting requirements to clarify that school personnel should not refer unaccompanied youths to police or child-welfare officials in the absence of an immediate danger to their health or safety," the association suggests.[17]

### Do homeless students have more academic troubles than other disadvantaged students?

Researchers have tried to determine whether homeless students have different types of problems in school from other poor children. "A lot of the research over the past 30 years has focused on trying to answer the question, 'Are they worse off?' " says Tobin of Marywood. The findings have been "inconclusive," she says.

For one thing, "homelessness" has no single standard definition, so it is difficult to locate enough subjects to ensure statistically valid results. Moreover, because homeless children's experiences vary tremendously depending on where they live, it is difficult to know whether findings are generally applicable, Tobin and others say.

For example, much of the existing homelessness research has been done in New York City, says Tobin. But the city's "family shelter system is so well developed it may actually be better" as a home environment for students than some permanent low-income housing, she says. So it's unclear whether findings about the difference between homeless and non-homeless New York students would apply to students elsewhere.

A substantial body of research has concluded that homeless students are very hard to distinguish from low-income students generally. For example, numerous studies have found that homeless students and poor students with stable housing have basically the same academic outcomes. That finding casts doubt on whether children's school struggles can be "attributable to homelessness per se or whether the broader confluence of negative events in their lives is to blame," wrote Wisconsin's Miller.[18]

Studies find that both homeless students and low-income students have worse school-attendance, achievement and graduation records than students who are neither poor nor homeless, Miller wrote.[19]

But other research finds school-related problems that beset homeless students in particular. After a stint of homelessness, "You can see the effect on the kid in the next school year," says Vanderbilt's Shinn. Essentially, a graph of the student's academic progress in the year following a homelessness episode shows a lower level of achievement than would be expected based on the student's pre-homelessness record, she explains.

Some studies find that students who change schools frequently are half as likely to graduate from high school, have lower attendance rates and are twice as likely as others to repeat a grade. Other research concludes that it takes four to six months for a student to recover academic ground lost by moving from one school to another — a potential long-term academic setback.[20]

Many experts say most homeless students already have poverty and other disadvantages such as domestic violence in their backgrounds, so homelessness can't help but increase their struggles beyond those of poor children living in stable homes.

"Homelessness is poverty and mobility in spades," says Shinn. For example, "poor kids have hardly any books," which makes it harder for them to succeed in school. "How many do you have when you're not only poor but moving in and out of shelters?"

In a first-of-its-kind study, published in 2012, the University of Pennsylvania's Fantuzzo and colleagues began with all of the third-graders in the Philadelphia school district in 2005-2006, a very large population compared to earlier studies.[21] The researchers then eliminated from the pool any students not born in the city, because their histories couldn't be tracked using Philadelphia's standardized records. Then the researchers followed the progress of homeless students (according to the strict HUD definition) and those who had changed schools an unusual number of times and compared it to that of students who had experienced neither problem.

The study found that homelessness alone — without an abnormal number of moves from school to school — made it harder for children to engage with teachers and other students. In addition, children who switched schools frequently — without actually ending up on the street or in a shelter — not only had significant trouble learning and engaging with others but also did more poorly in reading and math.

Problems with academic or social engagement "are very, very predictive of later academic problems," Fantuzzo says. However, it's the combination of "homelessness plus mobility" that turned out to be the clearest "indicator of tremendous problems" down the line.

Children with both experiences did substantially worse on all the measures, he says.

## BACKGROUND

### Family Affair

Children and teens with nowhere to call home are not new in America.

In the mid-19th century, private charities, religious institutions and state and local governments built many orphanages to house poor children. Generally, the institutions housed a mix of children. Some were orphans, but many — likely the larger share — had either been given up by their parents to the orphanage or been taken away by orphanage officials who deemed their poverty-stricken households unsuitable for child rearing.[22] In the poorest urban neighborhoods, so-called street children begged or did odd jobs to feed themselves or help their families. They sometimes shared makeshift shelters with other children.[23]

By the end of the 19th century, growing national prosperity made child homelessness less prevalent, and mistrust of many orphanages' harsh conditions and their practice of removing poor children from their parents led to the demise of those institutions.

Child and adolescent homelessness again became part of the national landscape during the Great Depression of the 1930s. However, this time many young people experienced homelessness alongside their parents, as rampant unemployment left hundreds of thousands of adults unable to pay their mortgages or rent.[24]

During the Depression the first federal programs emerged aimed at assisting homeless youths. In 1933, as many as 30 percent of the estimated 2 million to 5 million homeless Americans were boys. The federal Civilian Conservation Corps opened camps and shelters where more than a million older teens and young men in their 20s could live and receive small stipends for work, such as building parks and roads, cleaning up streams and planting trees.[25]

Homelessness declined after the Depression but picked up again in the 1980s, when public concern began to coalesce around the problem of keeping homeless students in school because a high school diploma had become a workforce prerequisite.

For decades most homeless Americans had suffered from mental illness or substance-abuse problems — most of them single men, but some single women. But after a 30-year decline, the period between 1978 and 1983 saw the number of families "doubling up" — involuntarily living in overcrowded multifamily dwellings — rise to about 2.6 million families nationwide, twice its previous level.[26] In 1981, New York City officials reported a sudden 25 percent increase in the number of families seeking emergency shelter.[27]

Analysts cite a variety of intertwined causes for the increases, including a decline in the availability of affordable housing, rising income inequality and stagnating wages, cuts in some federal safety-net programs, an increase in single-parent female-led households, the closing of many mental hospitals and a rise in recreational drug use.[28]

Soon, troubling facts emerged about the fate of children in homeless families.[29] Notably, in the early 1980s only about "one in four homeless kids were in school," says Vanderbilt's Murphy.

Despite the widespread belief that school attendance is mandatory in America, in reality schools have many barriers that make attendance difficult. For example, districts usually require students to show proof of residency to register, which is difficult or even impossible for families or teens living in cheap motels or cars or squatting with different friends on different nights. Registration rules usually also require a student to be in the care of a parent or legal guardian. But many homeless students bunk with relatives who fall into neither category or live on the streets unaccompanied by any adult caregiver.

Ultimately, "litigation was required to establish the legal right to public education for homeless children," according to the Children's Health Fund, a New York City-based child advocacy group. In 1987, when the McKinney-Vento law was passed, 43 percent of the estimated 500,000 homeless children nationwide did not attend school, mainly because of residency issues or inability to afford transportation from their temporary shelter to the district where they were registered before losing their homes.[30]

### Legislative Response

In the early 1980s, attempts to help homeless families occurred mainly at the local level. Eventually, however,

Homeless children board a school bus in Miami, Fla., on Oct. 1, 2008. Twins Kristian and Christian Ricardo, center, were living temporarily with their parents and four siblings at the Community Partnership for the Homeless assistance center while their father looked for construction work. The center, now called Chapman Partnership, helps homeless people get off the streets and find permanent housing.

advocates for the homeless demanded that the federal government treat homelessness "as a national problem requiring a national response," said the Washington, D.C.-based National Coalition for the Homeless. In response, Congress began considering a wide variety of measures — and enacting a few.

For example, in 1986 lawmakers removed permanent-address requirements that had barred the homeless from receiving federal assistance such as Aid to Families with Dependent Children, veterans' benefits and food stamps. Then, in 1987, large majorities of both parties approved the first comprehensive federal legislation to address homelessness, the Stewart B. McKinney Homeless Assistance Act, later renamed the McKinney-Vento Act. President Ronald Reagan signed the bill — the first to address barriers preventing homeless students from attending school — into law on July 22, 1987, and it has been amended frequently over the years.

While the original law addressed many issues that afflict homeless families generally, such as the need for temporary shelters and job training, it included a key provision designed to increase enrollment of homeless children and teens: the Education for Homeless Children and Youth (EHCY) program. It aimed to provide homeless students with the same easy access to free public education as other American students received. Among

other things, it required states to review and revise school-registration policies that could put homeless children and teens at a disadvantage, such as proof-of-residency requirements. It also authorized the Department of Education to provide state grants to carry out the work.[31]

By 1989, however, two years after enactment, DoE estimated that a third of school-age homeless children still did not attend school.[32] In response, 1990 amendments to the program ordered states to eliminate all enrollment barriers, increased the amount of money Congress could appropriate for the program and authorized use of McKinney-Vento grants to pay for direct educational services such as tutoring to help homeless students succeed.

Nevertheless, compliance remained spotty. Grants were inadequate, and the federal government did little to monitor progress. In 1990 half the homeless children in Washington, D.C., still did not attend school, mainly because of a lack of transportation.[33]

In 1994, the education portion of the McKinney-Vento Act was again amended and folded into the Elementary and Secondary Education Act, the massive law that spells out most federal requirements for the nation's schools. The amendments explicitly gave homeless children the same rights to free public preschool education, where available, as other children received; gave parents of homeless children and teens a say in which schools their children attend and stated that school districts should form partnerships with housing agencies to provide services to homeless families.

In 2001, Congress reauthorized the EHCY program as part of the No Child Left Behind Act, which President George W. Bush signed into law on Jan. 8, 2002. Under the law, each school district must appoint a liaison to locate and assist homeless students.[34] Congress also responded to qualms that temporary or permanent schools created by some districts to serve the homeless might stigmatize the students attending them. Congress called for a performance evaluation of existing schools established for that purpose and prohibited full segregation of homeless students into homeless-only institutions except as a temporary health or safety measure or to provide supplemental services.[35]

Preschool children are the most likely to be homeless, and in the 2007 reauthorization of Head Start, the federal preschool program for low-income families, local programs were required to identify homeless children and enroll

# CHRONOLOGY

**1970s-1980s** *Cities see rise in homeless families with children; concern grows that many of the children don't attend school.*

**1977** Runaway and Homeless Youth Act authorizes federal funds to provide temporary shelter, counseling and other supports to youths ages 16 to 21.

**1986** Congress ends requirement that food-stamp and welfare recipients have permanent addresses.

**1987** A large bipartisan majority in Congress passes the McKinney Homeless Assistance Act, which requires states to end school-registration policies that keep homeless students from enrolling; President Ronald Reagan signs the bill.

**1988** Education activist Jonathan Kozol's book-length *New Yorker* article, "Rachel and Her Children," increases public awareness of the problems of homeless families.

**1989** U.S. Department of Education estimates that a third of homeless children are not in school.

**1990s** *School districts struggle to adapt to federal requirements on homeless students.*

**1990** Congress authorizes use of McKinney funds to pay for direct services for homeless students, such as tutoring.

**1994** Congress says homeless preschoolers should get equal access to free public preschool, where available.

**2000s** *Homeless suburban student population rises as poverty in suburbs increases and families lose homes in the foreclosure crisis.*

**2001** Congress requires school districts to appoint liaisons to find homeless students in their districts and help them enroll.

**2005** Hurricanes Katrina and Rita devastate the Gulf Coast; thousands of temporarily homeless families relocate to other states, where local schools struggle to accommodate the students.

**2007** As hurricane-displaced families resettle, the number of homeless children drops by 25 percent. . . . Congress requires Head Start, the federal public preschool program for poor children, to identify homeless children and enroll them quickly. . . . Federal College Cost Reduction and Access Act encourages colleges to loosen financial-aid-application requirements to allow students living without their parents to apply; the law is unevenly enforced.

**2008** The housing crisis and recession begin driving up student homelessness.

**2009** President Obama's economic-stimulus law, the American Recovery and Reinvestment Act, provides a two-year, $70 million funding boost for programs that serve homeless students; it also provides $1.5 billion in time-limited grants for homelessness-prevention efforts. . . . Congress requires all shelters housing families to accept children of all ages, including teenage boys. . . . The share of people spending more than half their income on housing rises from 20.7 percent in 2001 to 26.1 percent.

**2010** The number of homeless students reported by public schools tops 1 million for the first time. . . . The Government Accountability Office, Congress' nonpartisan research arm, reports that students who frequently change schools have more absences, lower test scores and higher dropout rates than students with a stable homelife. . . . Obama administration pledges to end family and youth homelessness in a decade.

**2012** Federal law requires that homeless students be transported to their usual schools, if possible, but as gas prices rise, more school districts say it costs too much.

**2013** For the first time, the Department of Housing and Urban Development's "point-in-time" national homeless count includes special measures to ensure that young people ages 18 to 24 are counted. . . . Advocates press Congress to increase funding for education programs for homeless students. . . . Housing analysts estimate that at least 113,000 low-income families will lose rent aid in across-the-board "sequestration" spending cuts that began on March 1.

# Homeless Students Face Obstacles to College

*"The biggest barrier is the lack of a high school diploma."*

Teens who have lived in unstable housing and foster children who have "aged out" of government-subsidized foster care at age 18 face huge barriers to college admission or post-high school career training.

"Young people who have foster care or homelessness in their background often have no way of breaking free from the cycles of poverty except via success in postsecondary education or training," says a 2011 report for the California Community Colleges System and the National Association of Student Financial Aid Administrators. But, the report adds, "it is nearly impossible to secure that postsecondary education when life revolves around the struggle to survive."[1]

"The biggest barrier to postsecondary education for homeless youth is the lack of a high school diploma," says Ronald Hallett, an assistant professor of education at the University of the Pacific in Stockton, Calif.

While high school completion rates vary widely from place to place, the National Coalition for the Homeless estimates that 75 percent of young people who are homeless during their teen years drop out of school. The stress of trying to survive on their own, often on the streets, while attending school may be just too great for many.[2]

The graduation outlook for young people who have been homeless at some time in their lives is improving, however, at least in some places, says Patricia Popp, state coordinator of Project HOPE-VA, the Virginia Education Program for Homeless Children and Youth.

"We're doing so much better with the school-age population that there are more people graduating from high school," Popp says. "We're talking to colleges" about how to help students move on to the next phase of their education, she says.

It is unknown how many students who have experienced homelessness at some point in their lives graduate from high school. States aren't yet breaking down graduation rates in that way. But in Virginia, where data is disaggregated, or broken down, to reveal that information, a graduation rate that was once 25 percent has now risen to 70 percent, Popp says. "Many, many, many more [once-homeless students] ask questions about college now," she says.

Historically, the college-admissions process has put unintended barriers in the way of homeless students, the biggest being financial aid. Until a few years ago, the Free Application for Federal Student Aid (FAFSA) — the standardized form used by colleges and government-aid

programs to qualify students for financial assistance — required almost all students to provide financial information from their parents as well as a parental signature to qualify for aid. In 2007, however, Congress passed the College Cost Reduction and Access Act, which allowed homeless young people living on their own, without parents or guardian, as well as unaccompanied young people at risk of homelessness, to apply for aid on their own.[3]

Once accepted, though, students with no real homes can find some college policies daunting, says Hallett. For example, "residence halls that make students leave for Thanksgiving and Christmas" can make holidays a stressful, difficult time rather than a happy break from hard work.

Heightening the stress — as well as the difficulty for college administrators and others who might offer help — is the fact that many homeless college students hide their status. At the University of California-Los Angeles (UCLA), for example, "it's very affluent. . . . It's Westwood, Bel Air, Beverly Hills. Students . . . want to fit the norm here, so they're not going to tell you they're homeless," said Antonio Sandoval, director of community programs at UCLA.

Near Sandoval's office is an unmarked, unlocked utility closet stocked with food and toiletries donated by students. Abdallah Jadallah, now an engineer in Los Angeles, came up with the idea for the closet when, as a student, he realized that classmates he spotted sleeping overnight in the library or regularly crashing on friends' couches likely had little money and no permanent places to live.

"Thank you so much for the food and small items like soap and shampoo," one student wrote Jadallah. "It really does make a difference in my life. God bless you all."[4]

— *Marcia Clemmitt*

[1] Tracy L. Fried and Associates, "Providing Effective Financial Aid Assistance to Students from Foster Care and Unaccompanied Homeless Youth: A Key to Higher Education Access and Success," California Community Colleges/National Association of Student Financial Aid Administrators, September 2011, http://casey.org/Resources/Publications/pdf/ProvidingEffectiveFinancialAid.pdf.

[2] Danielle Ferrier, "Societal Failure in Each Dropout," *The Boston Herald*, June 2, 2012, p. 11.

[3] Tracy L. Fried and Associates, *op. cit.*

[4] Quoted in "College Students Hide Hunger, Homelessness," NPR, July 27, 2010, http://m.npr.org/news/front/128778321?textSize=medium.

them expeditiously. The change "was a federal recognition of the problem" and, as such, quite welcome, says Fantuzzo of the University of Pennsylvania.

But making the program work is easier legislated than done. For example, "in Philadelphia, Head Start is struggling" just to locate the eligible children, says Whitney LeBoeuf, a research analyst at the University of Pennsylvania's Graduate School of Education.

"We're having strong conversations with Head Start" about how to serve more homeless children, says Popp, Virginia's coordinator for homeless education. But Head Start regulations haven't yet been revised to incorporate the requirements, she says. Among other worries: Head Start agencies fear that "working with children who are going to miss days" could cause their programs to be evaluated harshly, Popp says. "That empty seat won't look good."

"If we want to help these vulnerable families, we need to be careful to create policies with an eye to how [the families] can really take advantage of them," says Fantuzzo.

Federal funding has always been tight. EHCY's annual funding for each state is based on the same formula that allocates money for services to disadvantaged students, and states award the funds to school districts on a competitive basis. In the 2008-2009 school year, for example, federal funds were sufficient to provide grants to only 11 percent of districts, generally those with the highest burden of homeless students. During the next two school years the percentage of districts receiving grants approximately doubled because President Obama's economic-stimulus package boosted EHCY funding by $70 million over two years.[36]

Apart from the temporary stimulus funds, total EHCY funding rose from $55 million in 2003 to $65 million in 2009 and has remained at that level since, despite a continued rise in the number of homeless students identified by school districts, as well as increases in the price of services such as transportation.[37]

## Homes for the Homeless

Many homelessness advocates and researchers say the key weakness in government efforts to help homeless

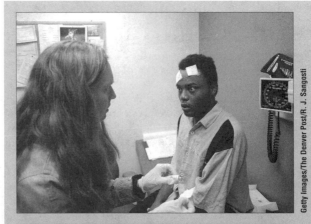

**Helping Hands**

Dominic McGee, 20 (top), receives treatment for a head injury at Urban Peak, a homeless shelter for youths in Denver, on Oct. 1, 2008. The shelter provides medical care for teens who live in the shelter or on the streets. High school senior Maricruz Rodriguez, 18 (bottom), tries on clothes at the Main Place clothing center in Irving, Texas, on Dec. 21, 2011. The store gives free, new clothing from corporate and private donors to homeless and other needy high school students.

students is the lack of attention paid to helping families find permanent homes.

"Rather than just making sure that kids are getting to school, we need to make them not homeless," says the University of Pennsylvania's Culhane. "In the social services arena there's a tendency to deal with related issues rather than solving the core problem, often under the misconception" that tackling the root-cause problem would cost

# LGBT Youths at High Risk of Homelessness

*Some wind up on the streets at age 13.*

Disowned by his parents after they learned he is gay, Mikael "Gatsby" Miller, now a law student at Columbia University in New York City, spent his senior year of high school without a place to call home. Instead, he "couch-surfed" among friends and teachers and worked full time to support himself.

Miller's experience is common among lesbian, gay, bisexual and transgender (LGBT) young people, researchers say. A significant percentage of LGBT young people face homelessness, as well as problems at school or in getting access to school.

Nevertheless, Miller was one of the lucky ones. He made it to college and found help paying for his education.

"The main factor that influenced my decision to attend" the University of California, Los Angeles (UCLA) was "their response to my family situation," Miller said. In letters, he described his situation to each school that accepted him, but only UCLA responded, he said.[1] There, he found a champion in the director of the university's LGBT center, who advised him on how best to navigate a financial-aid process that subjects applications lacking a parental signature to intense scrutiny.

A 2011 study found that about a quarter of Massachusetts high school students who identified themselves as gay or lesbian were homeless, as were 15 percent of students who said they were bisexual. Twenty percent of teens who said they were unsure about their sexual orientation also were homeless. Only 3 percent of students who described themselves as heterosexual were homeless.[2]

Furthermore, while many heterosexual teens were part of homeless families, the large majority of homeless LGBT teens lived on their own, unaccompanied by parents or guardians — a much more difficult and dangerous situation, the study's authors said.[3] Other analysts have found that between 25 and 40 percent of homeless LGBT young people report that they left home because of conflicts with their families over their sexual orientation or gender expression.[4]

Family conflicts are driving LGBT teens out of their homes at younger and younger ages, an ironic downside to society's increasing acceptance of LGBT people, says a report by the liberal Washington-based research and advocacy group Center for American Progress.

Two decades ago, most people "started coming out in their 20s, well after most left home and started working," so family rejection, while painful, at least wasn't life threatening. Today, by contrast, "the usual coming-out age is in the mid-teen years, when youth still depend on their families to meet their material needs," the report said. When unaccompanied teens become homeless, it said, they can find themselves "cascading through social safety nets that are not equipped to support them."[5]

An analysis of homeless teens in New York City found that the average age at which lesbian and gay teens had become homeless was about 14-and-a-half, while teens who identified themselves as transgender had wound up on the streets at an average age of 13-and-a-half.[6]

too much, he says. "Then, when you look back, you realize that you've actually spent that amount of money" on what's essentially a side issue. "Very-low-income families need permanent-housing vouchers," but existing programs are insufficient to meet the need.

Some promising federal efforts have emerged recently, many analysts say.

The 2009 economic-stimulus legislation launched a "very ambitious" program of homelessness prevention, called the Homelessness Prevention and Rapid Re-Housing Program, says Culhane. It provided $1.5 billion over a three-year period to cities, counties, states and territories to help low-income families at risk of becoming homeless but who had "the capacity to maintain stable housing" on their own. The grants could be used to pay for services such as legal counsel for landlord-tenant disputes, housing searches, credit repair and budget counseling.[38]

Also in 2009, Congress amended and reauthorized some McKinney-Vento housing programs. Among other things, the new law required all shelters or other housing that serve families to admit children of all ages rather than close their doors to older boys. More generally, it shifted the focus of federal policy from providing homeless people first with

Historically, providing shelter and other help for teens has been a low priority for homeless-assistance programs. Even private organizations that serve homeless teens have discriminated against LGBT teenagers, according to advocates for LGBT youths. For example, some shelters have reportedly denied entrance to male teens who dress as females and female teens who dress as males, and one facility in Michigan reportedly required gay and transgender teens to wear orange to set them apart from heterosexual residents.[7]

LGBT youths also face discrimination in school. One study found that 20 percent of LGBT youth said they skipped school at least monthly because they feared for their safety. Another study found that 28 percent of LGBT teens had dropped out of school because of harassment.[8]

Advocates are calling for a society-wide re-examination of the situations that leave LGBT teens vulnerable to becoming homeless, dropping out of school and being harassed.

LGBT teens' "homelessness isn't a failure of character but the result of a profound human tragedy," said Jean Ann Esselink, a writer for the online journal *The New Civil Rights Movement*.[9]

— *Marcia Clemmitt*

Gizmo Lopez, 19, who is bisexual and homeless, hangs out at a fast-food restaurant in New York City with her boyfriend on March 1, 2012. A significant number of LGBT youths face homelessness.

AP Photo/Bebeto Matthews

[1] Quoted in Joseph Gentile, "Disowned LGBT Students Need Financial Aid Help," *The Huffington Post*, Feb. 3, 2012, www.huffingtonpost.com/tngg/lgbt-students-financial-aid_b_1246762.html.

[2] Heather L. Corliss, *et al.*, "High Burden of Homelessness Among Sexual-Minority Adolescents: Findings from a Representative Massachusetts High School Sample," *American Journal of Public Health*, September 2011, pp. 1683-1689.

[3] *Ibid.*

[4] Shahera Hyatt, "Struggling to Survive: Lesbian, Gay, Bisexual, Transgender, and Queer/Questioning Homeless Youth on the Streets of California," California Homeless Youth Project, 2011, http://cahomelessyouth.library.ca.gov/docs/pdf/StrugglingToSurviveFinal.pdf.

[5] "On the Streets: The Federal Response to Gay and Transgender Homeless Youth," Center for American Progress, June 2010, www.americanprogress.org/wp-content/uploads/issues/2010/06/pdf/lgbtyouthhomelessness.pdf.

[6] "Gay and Transgender Youth Homelessness by the Numbers," Center for American Progress, June 21, 2010, www.americanprogress.org/issues/lgbt/news/2010/06/21/7980/gay-and-transgender-youth-homelessness-by-the-numbers.

[7] "On the Streets," *op. cit.*; for background, see Nicholas Ray, *et al.*, "Lesbian, Gay, Bisexual and Transgender Youth: An Epidemic of Homelessness," National Gay and Lesbian Task Force Policy Institute/National Coalition for the Homeless, 2006, www.thetaskforce.org/downloads/HomelessYouth.pdf.

[8] "LGBTQ Youth in the Foster Care System," National Center for Lesbian Rights, June 2006, www.nclrights.org/site/DocServer/LGBTQ_Youth_In_Foster_Care_System.pdf.

[9] Quoted in Gentile, *op. cit.*

temporary, transitional shelter — where services such as substance-abuse counseling are available on site — to moving them as quickly as possible into permanent housing.[39]

This approach is "what most people experiencing homelessness want," according to the National Alliance to End Homelessness, an advocacy group in Washington, D.C. Most people lose their homes after a temporary financial or personal crisis and, once set up in permanent housing, "need surprisingly little support . . . to achieve independence," said the group.[40]

Caution is needed, however, because the approach so far has been tested only on single people, says Wisconsin's

Miller. "We don't know what may be lost when families lose that attachment to institutions where support is easily available."

In 2010, the Obama administration pledged to end family and youth homelessness in a decade by having federal agencies partner with state and local governments and private groups. Among other things, the administration said it wanted to focus on finding housing for young people who age out of foster care at 18 and provide funds to support the creation of more affordable rental housing.[41]

Meanwhile, affordable housing has become harder to find. The share of people spending more than half of

> **"If a student has neither the place nor the tools with which to complete tasks sent home, they are often reprimanded or punished by missing recess. This makes our homeless population feel even more singled out and ostracized."**
>
> — *Mary J. Lechner,*
> *Lecturer on Education,*
> *University of Colorado-Denver*

their income for housing jumped from 20.7 percent to 26.1 percent between 2001 and 2009, noted Mary Cunningham, a senior research associate, and Graham MacDonald, a research assistant, at the nonpartisan Urban Institute in Washington. Furthermore, they cite estimates that the nation's stock of affordable low-income housing may be 6.4 million units lower than the demand because homes in low-income neighborhoods are being remodeled to attract high-income buyers, converted to nonresidential uses or demolished.[42]

## CURRENT SITUATION

### More Kids, Less Cash

As schools become more adept at identifying homeless students and economic times remain tough, schools continue to report higher numbers of homeless children and teens. Meanwhile, school funding is shrinking.

Housing vouchers are one of the first things to be eliminated in federal budget crunches such as this year's "sequestration" — across-the-board cuts that became effective in March as a temporary measure until Congress and the White House can agree on a plan to decrease the federal debt.[43]

Housing analysts estimate that between 113,000 and 125,000 low-income families will lose rental assistance due to sequestration, a blow to efforts to keep children stably housed.[44]

In Topeka, Kan., the number of students identified as homeless has climbed from 340 to 580 over the past decade, but this school year Topeka's federal aid for school supplies and city bus passes for homeless students has been cut to $50,000 — from $61,000 last year.[45] And like more than half of the states, Kansas also has cut its

state per-student school funding this school year — by $34 between fiscal years 2012 and 2013 — potentially making it even harder for schools to meet the needs of homeless or other disadvantaged populations.[46]

At the same time, fuel prices are rising, causing more local governments to chafe at the McKinney-Vento transportation requirement. A survey by the Massachusetts state auditor's office, for example, found that it would cost $11.3 million to bus the state's homeless students to school in 2012, up from $10.4 million in 2011. "We are 33 square miles, and we are obligated to get our kids to school. . . . There's got to be a short-term and long-term conversation about how to address this," said Domenic J. Sarno, mayor of Springfield, Mass.[47]

Meanwhile, debate continues among homelessness advocates and researchers on a proposal that a House committee discussed but did not vote on in 2012. It would require HUD to expand the pool of those eligible for its homelessness assistance to the larger group eligible under Education Department programs.

"In each state, between 41 percent and 91 percent of the homeless students identified by the U.S. Department of Education are not considered homeless" by HUD, said the Washington, D.C.-based advocacy group Alliance for Excellent Education, which favors the expansion. If these students and their families were eligible for HUD services, they would get more help finding temporary shelter and permanent housing as well as other assistance, the group said.[48]

But the University of Pennsylvania's Culhane says the proposal is inappropriate. "We have two definitions, and they exist for different purpose, based on the missions of the two departments," he says. "In HUD's case, they have to provide emergency housing," so they must look for people with no place to live. The Education Department's mission, on the other hand, is "to make sure that people are getting to school," which is imperiled by situations such as being forced to move in with relatives. "It wouldn't make sense for HUD to expand its definition because doing so wouldn't expand the amount of money available" for housing, he says. "We'd just be cutting the pie in smaller and smaller pieces. Living doubled up is a real problem, but it's not homelessness."

Meanwhile, homelessness and poverty, once largely rural and inner-city phenomena, are spreading to suburbia. A decade ago, the suburban Jefferson County, Colo., school district, west of Denver, identified 59 homeless students.

# Should federal agencies use the same definition of homelessness?

## YES
**Barbara Duffield**
*Policy Director, National Association for the Education of Homeless Children and Youth*

Written for *CQ Researcher*, April 2013

Most agree there are insufficient resources to meet the needs of all homeless people. How do we ensure that these few resources are used effectively for those in greatest need?

The Department of Housing and Urban Development (HUD) bases people's eligibility on where they happen to find refuge: with very few exceptions, HUD limits homeless assistance to people who are on the street or are fortunate enough to have found a shelter bed.

This approach excludes many of the most vulnerable people — specifically, families and youths staying in motels or with others temporarily. These situations are unstable and often unsafe, putting children at high risk of abuse, health problems and educational deficits.

Under federal law, public schools, Head Start programs and runaway-youth programs include families and youths in these living situations in their definition of homelessness.

Who are these families and youths? A parent struggling with mental illness, caring for three young children with significant developmental delays, moving between motels because there are no shelters in the community. A 17-year-old kicked out of his home, staying with friends of friends, raped by the apartment owner, not eating on weekends, whose high school found out only when he worked up the courage to ask for food. These are daily scenarios in schools across the country.

Homeless families and youth move from shelter to motel to car to couch, often at a moment's notice. Where they sleep on any given night is not the best measure of their vulnerability. There are more effective ways of determining who is in greatest need. HUD's definition of homelessness should be amended to include families and youths who are verified as homeless by public schools, Head Start programs and runaway-youth programs. Then, with these homeless people eligible for assistance, local communities can assess people's relative needs, considering factors such as income, employability, barriers to housing, illness, disability and children's developmental delays — all of which are more relevant than where they happened to sleep the previous night.

HUD's approach deprives communities of the flexibility to meet the needs of its most vulnerable children and youths. Research on brain development makes clear that adverse experiences in childhood can have lifelong impacts on physical and mental health. Ignoring the urgency of child and youth development threatens to create a new generation of homeless adults. We can and must do better.

## NO
**Dennis P. Culhane**
*Professor of Social Policy, University of Pennsylvania; Director of Research, National Center on Homelessness Among Veterans, Department of Veterans Affairs*

Written for *CQ Researcher*, April 2013

Proponents of expanding the definition of homelessness want HUD to include doubled-up households. Opponents want the definition more narrowly focused on those who are "literally homeless" — living in emergency and transitional shelters, on the streets or in places not meant for human habitation.

In 2009 the definition was expanded to include doubled-up families at risk of losing their housing within 14 days and families "unstably housed" for at least 60 days and likely to remain so. For now, the new definition will not greatly affect how funds are disbursed, because by statute and regulation most HUD funds must target the literally homeless. That's as it should be.

Proposals to further expand the definition — and hence eligibility — should be approached cautiously. Eligibility does not automatically entitle the homeless to housing, income or services, so expanding the definition without expanding the resources would effectively leave many more people with little or nothing. In simple terms, consider that HUD spends about $2 billion annually for a population of about 2 million "literally" homeless people — or $1,000 per person (though many receive nothing). The number of doubled-up poor is just under 4 million. So expanding the definition could triple the number of eligible persons, which — without new resources — would reduce average annual expenditures to $333 per eligible person. That would substantially lessen the aid's impact.

In contrast, 250,000 of the most vulnerable homeless on any given night in 2012 were living on the streets, in parks, transit stations and other places not meant for habitation and thus in imminent risk of injury, illness and death. With an expanded definition, these people would have to compete for scarce resources with those who at least have a roof over their heads.

Doubled-up, crowded or poorly housed people merit attention. But as one observer has noted, "a lousy home doesn't make you homeless any more than a lousy marriage makes you single." The Department of Education's definition of homelessness includes any temporarily displaced children living with others because the education mandate is to ensure that all children get to school, regardless of their housing status. HUD's mandate is to address the critical housing needs of the literally homeless, often with disabilities. Until there is substantial progress in reducing the number of unsheltered Americans — or new funds are appropriated to serve doubled-up households — that should remain HUD's focus.

The lingering effects of the recent recession and the home-foreclosure crisis, coupled with the precarious finances of cash-strapped schools and social service agencies, have heightened concern about student homelessness. Above, a foreclosed home in Richmond, Calif.

By 2012 there were nearly 3,000 in the 86,000-student district.[49]

Many suburban teachers are insensitive to the problems of homelessness, said Mary J. Lechner, a lecturer on education at the University of Colorado-Denver. As a result, "if a student has neither the place nor the tools with which to complete tasks sent home, they are often reprimanded or punished by missing recess," she said. "This makes our homeless population feel even more singled out and ostracized."[50]

### Seeking Improvements

A quarter-century since the first federal mandate that schools assist homeless students, progress is evident but slow, says Vanderbilt's Murphy.

Popp, Virginia's state coordinator for homeless education, says that in at least some places, "we've gotten so much better at working with school-age" homeless students "that our new challenges are working with college transition and preschoolers."

Historically, institutions have needed 20 to 30 years to figure out how to work with particular sets of clients with specific needs, such as homeless students, Murphy says. Today "we're just at the level of knowing that we need to make sure kids have meals, get to school, have a caring adult in the school," he says. Still lacking is "hard,

objective" information about the specific learning barriers homeless students face, how to overcome them and ways to measure how well schools achieve this goal, he says.

Some researchers are "trying . . . to create actionable intelligence" that schools can use to shape their practices, says the University of Pennsylvania's Fantuzzo. For example, improved data collection now makes it possible to rank the 175 elementary schools in Philadelphia by the number of homeless students enrolled in each — information the city might use to craft a "triage" system for directing limited resources to where needs are greatest.

Schools can't solve the problems that lead to homelessness — poverty, the shortage of affordable housing, family violence — says the University of the Pacific's Hallett. "But if we're not doing everything we can to remove any barriers" keeping homeless children and teens from succeeding in school, "we're doing a real disservice."

## OUTLOOK
### Collaborating

Student homelessness "is a complex problem, and it won't have a simple solution," says Murphy of Vanderbilt. "It's going to require an integrated set of players — social services, schools, food banks, charitable organizations" — to address and solve the problem. Collaborative efforts are on the horizon, however, some analysts say.

Some new homelessness-prevention initiatives and housing agencies are trying to look at a broader range of information about an individual's or family's situation when deciding who gets their assistance, rather than sticking firmly to the letter of current eligibility rolls, says Virginia homeless education coordinator Popp. Educators "need to be at the table," she says, because "we already know where [homeless] people are," and housing authorities do not.

Collaboration can provide integrated services in a "more thoughtful way," says Wisconsin's Miller. For example, many school districts send homeless children across town in taxis. But, he says, if districts worked together, they might find that homeless children are temporarily living near another school's bus route that could deliver them to their school with minor rerouting. Teachers, social workers and homeless-shelter workers who deal with the same homeless students should compare notes to avoid providing redundant services and base decisions on as much information as possible, he says.

In Pittsburgh, a local Homeless Education Network is fostering collaborations among housing agencies, public and parochial schools, libraries and other groups, Miller says. "People are sitting at the table from diverse sectors talking about housing and educational needs."

Meanwhile, some districts are helping to develop national standards for integrating data from schools and agencies providing services and housing, says the University of Pennsylvania's Culhane. Having nationally consistent data gathered from the full range of social service agencies will enable effective policy making. Officials in such places as Philadelphia, Michigan, South Carolina and Los Angeles County are already working toward that goal, he says.[51]

Nevertheless, the stigma and fear associated with youth and family homelessness will continue to make it difficult to identify what many experts call the "hidden homeless."

Homeless people fear that if they are discovered to be homeless, they will lose their children or their jobs, said Denise Giles, of the Cumberland Interfaith Hospitality Network in Fayetteville, N.C. "They become very cautious. . . . You borrow or you beg a couch for the night, stay in cars, use money for a hotel. They just live day by day and do all they can to not be found out."[52]

# NOTES

1. "The Homeless Children and Youth Act of 2011: Proposals to Promote Economic Independence for Homeless Children and Youth, Serial No. 112-93," U.S. Government Printing Office, 2012, www.gpo .gov/fdsys/pkg/CHRG-112hhrg72634/html/ CHRG-112hhrg72634.htm.

2. *Ibid.*

3. *Ibid.*

4. "One Million U.S. Students Homeless, New Data Show," press release, National Law Center on Homelessness and Poverty, June 2012, www.nlchp .org/view_release.cfm?PRID=148; "Education for Homeless Children and Youths Program: Data Collection Summary," National Center for Homeless

Education, June 2012, http://center.serve.org/nche/ downloads/data_comp_0909-1011.pdf.

5. For background, see Marcia Clemmitt, "Mortgage Crisis," *CQ Researcher*, Nov. 2, 2007, pp. 913-936 (updated Aug. 9, 2010).

6. "HUD Reports Slight Decline in Homelessness in 2012," press release, Department of Housing and Urban Development, Dec. 10, 2012, http://portal .hud.gov/hudportal/HUD?src=/press/press_releases _media_advisories/2012/HUDNo.12-191.

7. "Education Program for Homeless Children and Youths Program: Data Collection Summary," *op. cit.*, p. 17.

8. For background, see "2013 HIC and PIT of Homeless Persons Data Collection Guidance: Supplemental Guidance on Counting Homeless Youth," OneCPD Resource Exchange, December 2012, https://onecpd.info/resource/2796/2013-hic-and-pit-supplemental-guidance-counting-homeless-youth; and "The Youth Point-in-Time Count: Philanthropy Partnering with Government to End Youth Homelessness," *USICH Blog*, United States Interagency Council on Homelessness, Feb. 22, 2013, /www.usich.gov/media_center/blog/the_ youth_point_in_time_count_philanthropy_part nering_with_government_to_en.

9. Peter Miller, "A Critical Analysis of the Research on Student Homelessness," *Review of Educational Research*, July 2011, pp. 308-337.

10. *Ibid.*

11. *Ibid.*

12. Peter M. Miller, "Educating (More and More) Students Experiencing Homelessness: An Analysis of Recession-Era Policy and Practice," *Educational Policy* online, May 4, 2012, http://epx.sagepub.com/ content/early/2012/05/01/0895904812440500 .abstract.

13. Miller, "A Critical Analysis," *op. cit.*

14. Diane Nilan, " 'THE' Count — HUD Ignores Millions of Homeless Persons," *Alternet*, Jan. 17, 2013, www.alternet.org/speakeasy/diane-nilan/ count-hud-ignores-millions-homeless-persons.

15. Patricia Julianelle, "Using What We Know: Supporting the Education of Unaccompanied

Homeless Youth," National Association for the Education of Homeless Children and Youth, February 2008, www.naehcy.org/dl/uwwk_youth .pdf.

16. *Ibid.*

17. *Ibid.*

18. Miller, "A Critical Analysis," *op. cit.*

19. *Ibid.*

20. Patricia A. Popp, James H. Stronge and Jennifer L. Hindman, "Students on the Move; Reaching and Teaching Highly Mobile Children and Youth," National Center for Homeless Education at SERVE/ ERIC Clearinghouse on Urban Education, November 2003, http://center.serve.org/nche/ downloads/highly_mobile.pdf.

21. John W. Fantuzzo, *et al.*, "The Unique and Combined Effects of Homelessness and School Mobility on the Educational Outcomes of Young Children," *Educational Researcher*, December 2012, pp. 393-402, http://edr.sagepub.com/content/ 41/9/393.full.pdf+html.

22. Dale Keiger, "The Rise and Demise of the American Orphanage," *Johns Hopkins Magazine*, April 1996, www.jhu.edu/jhumag/496web/orphange.html.

23. Hannah Roberts, "The Slumdogs of New York: Remarkable Images Open a Window into the Squalor and Deprivation Endured by Immigrant Families in an Unrecognizable 19th Century America," *Mail Online* [U.K.], Jan. 20, 2012, www .dailymail.co.uk/news/article-2089243/Slum dogs-New-York-The-remarkable-images-capturing- immigrant-families-unrecognisable-19th-century- New-York.html; and Hugh Cunningham, "Work and Poverty," faqs.org, www.faqs.org/childhood/ Wh-Z-and-other-topics/Work-and-Poverty.html.

24. "Hoovervilles and Homelessness," The Great Depression in Washington State, http://depts.wash ington.edu/depress/hooverville.shtml.

25. Adrienne L. Fernandes, "Runaway and Homeless Youth: Demographics, Programs, and Emerging Issues," Congressional Research Service, Jan. 8, 2007, http:// assets.opencrs.com/rpts/RL33785_20070108.pdf.

26. "Still in Peril: The Continuing Impact of Poverty and Policy on America's Most Vulnerable Children,"

Children's Health Fund, September 2012, www .childrenshealthfund.org/sites/default/files/Still_in_ Peril_100212.pdf.

27. Kay Young McChesney, "Homeless Families Since 1980: Implications for Education," *Education and Urban Society*, August 1993, pp. 361-380.

28. For background, see Peter Katel, "Child Poverty," *CQ Researcher*, Oct. 28, 2011, and "Housing the Homeless," *CQ Researcher*, Dec. 18, 2009, pp. 1053-1076; Martha Burt, "Causes of the Growth of Homelessness During the 1980s," in *Understanding Homelessness: New Policy and Research Perspectives* (1997), http://content.knowl edgeplex.org/kp2/kp/report/report/relfiles/home less_1997_burt3.pdf; Paul Koegel, "Causes of Homelessness," in David Levinson and Marcy Ross, eds., *Homelessness Handbook* (2007), pp. 244-255.

29. For background, see Joseph Murphy and Kerry J. Tobin, *Homelessness Comes to School* (2011); "McKinney-Vento Act," National Coalition for the Homeless, *NCH Fact Sheet #18*, June 2006, www .nationalhomeless.org/publications/facts/McKinney .pdf; "H.R. 558, Bill Summary and Status," *CRS Summary*, The Library of Congress, http://thomas .loc.gov/cgi-bin/bdquery/z?d100:HR00558:@@ @D&summ2=m&.

30. "Still in Peril," *op. cit.*

31. "H.R. 558, Bill Summary and Status," *op. cit.*

32. "Still in Peril," *op. cit.*

33. *Ibid.*

34. "Education for Homeless Children and Youths Program," *op. cit.*

35. Lynnette Mawhinney-Rhoads and Gerald Stahler, "Educational Policy and Reform for Homeless Students: An Overview," *Education and Urban Society*, May 2006, pp. 288-306.

36. "America's Youngest Outcasts: State Report Card on Child Homelessness," The National Center on Family Homelessness, December 2011, www.home lesschildrenamerica.org/media/NCFH_America Outcast2010_web_032812.pdf.

37. "Education for Homeless Children and Youth Program," *op. cit.*

38. "Homelessness Prevention and Rapid Re-housing Program (HPRP) Fact Sheet," U.S. Department of

Housing and Urban Development, www.hudhre .info/index.cfm?do=viewHprpProgram.

39. Janel Winter, "The HEARTH Act: What Does It Mean for Your Community?" Corporation for Supportive Housing, June 2011, http://documents .csh.org/documents/nj/HEARTH-HUD%2711 .pdf.

40. "Housing First," National Alliance to End Homelessness, www.endhomelessness.org/pages/ housing_first.

41. Tony Pugh, "Obama Vows to End Homelessness in 10 Years," McClatchy, June 22, 2010, www .mcclatchydc.com/2010/06/22/96322/obama-administration-vows-to-end.html.

42. Mary Cunningham and Graham MacDonald, "Housing as a Platform for Improving Education Outcomes Among Low-income Children," Urban Institute, What Works Collaborative, May 2012, www.urban.org/UploadedPDF/412554-Housing-as-a-Platform-for-Improving-Education-Outcomes-among-Low-Income-Children.pdf.

43. For background, see Chelsea Kiene, "Sequestration Puts Rental Assistance Programs in Jeopardy," *The Huffington Post*, March 2, 2013, www.huffington post.com/2013/03/02/sequestration-rental-assis tance-federal-housing_n_2795038.html.

44. *Ibid.*

45. Celia Llopis-Jepsen, "Number of Homeless Students Rises, Funding Hits 10-Year Low," *The Topeka Capital-Journal* online, Jan. 23, 2013, http://cjon line.com/news/2013-01-20/number-homeless-stu dents-rises-funding-hits-10-year-low.

46. Phil Oliff, Chris Mai and Michael Leachman, "New School Year Brings More Cuts in State Funding for Schools," Center on Budget and Policy Priorities, Sept. 4, 2012, www.cbpp.org/cms/index.cfm? fa=view&id=3825.

47. Quoted in Stephanie Barry, "School Busing Costs Up $1 Million: Student Homelessness Rises," *The Republican* [Springfield, Mass.], Feb. 8, 2012, p. A1, www.masslive.com/news/index.ssf/2012/02/bus ing_costs_for_mass_homeless.html.

48. "Falling Through the Gaps: Homeless Children and Youth," Alliance for Excellent Education, April

2012, www.all4ed.org/files/HomelessFalling ThroughGaps.pdf.

49. David McKay Wilson, "Struggling in Suburbia," Teaching Tolerance, Southern Poverty Law Center, Fall 2012, www.tolerance.org/magazine/number- 42-fall-2012/feature/struggling-suburbia.

50. Quoted in *ibid.*

51. For background, see "About US," Actionable Intelligence for Social Policy website, University of Pennsylvania, www.gse.upenn.edu/child/about-u.s.

52. Quoted in Michael Futch, "The New Face of Homelessness," *The Fayetteville Observer* [N.C.], April 1, 2012.

# BIBLIOGRAPHY

## Selected Sources

## Books

**Kozol, Jonathan, *Rachel and Her Children*, Broadway, reprint, 2006.**
Originally published in *The New Yorker* in 1988 and based on interviews with homeless families in New York City, this book helped bring national attention to the issue of homeless children. Kozol is an educator and activist for educational equality for poor children.

**Murphy, Joseph, and Kerry J. Tobin, *Homelessness Comes to School*, Corwin, 2011.**
A professor at Vanderbilt University's Peabody College of Education (Murphy) and an assistant professor of educa- tion at Marywood University describe how homelessness or unstable living situations prevent children from obtaining an adequate education and explain how schools and policymakers can address those problems.

## Articles

**Knafo, Saki, "Homeless Children Living on the Highway to Disney World," *The Huffington Post*, April 19, 2012, www.huffingtonpost.com/2012/04/19/ homeless-children-disney-world_n_1420702.html.**
Many hotels and motels that serve Central Florida's tour- ist trade — which has dwindled since the recession — now house families who have lost their homes because of job layoffs or natural disasters and moved to Florida hoping for a new start.

**Llopis-Jepsen, Celia, "Number of Homeless Students Rises, Funding Hits 10-Year Low,"** *The Topeka Capital-Journal* **online, Jan. 23, 2013, http://cjon line.com/news/2013-01-20/number-homeless-stu dents-rises-funding-hits-10-year-low.**

The number of homeless students identified by the Topeka, Kansas, school system has risen over the past decade, but state and federal school funding are falling.

**Wilson, David McKay, "Struggling in Suburbia," Teaching Tolerance, Southern Poverty Law Center, Fall 2012, www.tolerance.org/magazine/number-42-fall-2012/feature/struggling-suburbia.**

As poverty and homelessness become more common in suburbia, teachers gain a whole new set of student problems and must develop new skills to deal with the homeless, according to an anti-discrimination advocacy group.

### Reports and Studies

**"America's Youngest Outcasts 2010: State Report Card on Child Homelessness," National Center on Family Homelessness, December 2011, www.home lesschildrenamerica.org/media/NCFH_America Outcast2010_web.pdf.**

A nonprofit group that conducts research and provides assistance to homeless families describes trends in family homelessness and in state programs designed to aid the population.

**Miller, Peter M., "Educating (More and More) Students Experiencing Homelessness: An Analysis of Recession-Era Policy and Practice,"** *Educational Policy***, May 4, 2012.**

An assistant professor of educational leadership and policy analysis at the University of Wisconsin, Madison, traces the long-term effects of a 1987 federal law that requires schools to identify and enroll homeless students in their districts.

**Perl, Libby,** *et al.***, "Homelessness: Targeted Federal Programs and Recent Legislation," Congressional Research Service, May 17, 2012, www.fas.org/sgp/ crs/misc/RL30442.pdf.**

Congress' nonpartisan research office describes the federal government's evolving definitions of homelessness and discusses existing or proposed federal policies to help the homeless.

**Popp, Patricia A., James H. Stronge and Jennifer L. Hindman, "Students on the Move; Reaching and Teaching Highly Mobile Children and Youth," National Center for Homeless Education at SERVE/ ERIC Clearinghouse on Urban Education, November 2003, http://center.serve.org/nche/downloads/ highly_mobile.pdf.**

Using case studies, members of the education department at Virginia's College of William and Mary present an overview of problems faced by homeless students and those who change schools frequently and suggest approaches schools can take to meet those students' needs.

**Quintana, Nico Sifra, Josh Rosenthal and Jeff Krehely, "On the Streets: The Federal Response to Gay and Transgender Homeless Youth," Center for American Progress, June 2010, www.americanprogress.org/wp-content/uploads/issues/2010/06/pdf/lgbtyouth homelessness.pdf.**

As gay and transgender youths declare their gender identities at earlier ages, more are ending up homeless after disputes with their families. But government assistance for the homeless is sparsest for teens living on their own, and some private service agencies for homeless people discriminate on the basis of sexual orientation.

**Tierney, William G., Jarrett T. Gupton and Ronald E. Hallett, "Transitions to Adulthood for Homeless Adolescents: Education and Public Policy," University of Southern California Center for Higher Education Policy Analysis, April 2008, www.uscrossier.org/ pullias/wp-content/uploads/2012/02/2008_CHEPA_ Transitions_to_Adulthood_for_Homeless_Adole scents.pdf.**

Based on interviews with homeless teens, researchers suggest how federal and California laws could better provide education assistance for homeless adolescents and propose additional steps that would be effective.

# For More Information

**Cato Institute**, 1000 Massachusetts Ave., N.W., Washington, DC 20001; 202-842-0200; www.cato.org. Think tank that analyzes housing policies and other public issues from a libertarian/conservative perspective.

**Homeless Children's Education Fund**, 2100 Smallman St., 2nd Floor, Pittsburgh, PA 15222; 412-562-0154; www.homelessfund.org. Advocacy group that supports stronger government efforts to help homeless children complete school and coordinates public and private assistance for homeless students.

**National Alliance to End Homelessness**, 1518 K St., N.W., Suite 410, Washington, DC 20005; 202-638-1526; www.endhomelessness.org. Nonpartisan group that conducts research and advocates for public policies aimed at ending homelessness.

**National Association for the Education of Homeless Children and Youth**, P.O. Box 26274, Minneapolis, MN 55426; 866-862-2562; www.naehcy.org. Membership group for professionals who work with homeless students; advocates for more federal support for such activities.

**National Association of Student Financial Aid Administrators**, 1101 Connecticut Ave., N.W., Suite 1100, Washington, DC 20036; 202-785-0453; www.nasfaa.org. Membership group for college financial-aid officers; provides information, training and advice on helping homeless youths obtain higher education.

**National Center for Homeless Education**, NCHE at SERVE, P.O. Box 5367, Greensboro, NC 27435; 800-755-3277; http://center.serve.org. Department of Education-funded information clearinghouse on homeless students, administered by the University of North Carolina, Greensboro.

**National Center on Family Homelessness**, 200 Reservoir St., Suite 200, Needham, MA 02494; 617-964-3834; www.familyhomelessness.org. Research group that disseminates information about causes and potential remedies and policy solutions for family homelessness.

**Urban Institute**, 2100 M St., N.W., Washington, DC 20037; 202-833-7200; www.urban.org. Nonpartisan research group that provides data and analysis on homeless youth.

# 9

# Caring for Veterans

Peter Katel

Eric Johnson, a scout from the 10th Mountain Division stationed at Fort Drum, near Watertown, N.Y., shares painful wartime experiences with friends at a coffeehouse catering to vets on April 16, 2008. Soldiers in Johnson's division have been deployed in Iraq and Afghanistan multiple times. Repeated deployments are creating an unprecedented number of cases of post-traumatic stress disorder, traumatic brain injury and associated mental-health conditions — overwhelming mental-health professionals in veterans' health care facilities.

From *CQ Researcher*, April 23, 2010.

Reuters/Mark Dye

T he car bomb exploded at dusk. Its target — a seven-ton U.S. Army personnel carrier — was blown about six feet by the force of the blast. Infantryman John Lamie came out alive, thanks to armor plating around his machine-gunner's cupola, but three of his buddies died in the Aug. 3, 2005, attack in Baghdad. Lamie went to Iraq a second time in 2007-2008, before the cumulative effects of combat eventually pushed him out of the Army.

Now he's fighting another kind of battle — with the Department of Veterans Affairs (VA). "I did two tours in Iraq and half my squad died," he says from his home in Cecil, Ga., only to "come home and get treated like a piece of crap in my own state."

Because of a series of complications over the validity of disability exams Lamie took for post-traumatic stress disorder (PTSD), traumatic brain injury (TBI) and other conditions, Lamie's most recent disability check amounted to $83.19. He and his wife have three children, and he's paying child support for a fourth child with his ex-wife.

Lamie says that when he tried to straighten out his case with staff of the VA's Veterans Benefits Administration (VBA), he ran into a wall of indifference. "The vet has no power, you are left to the wind," Lamie says. "You have to call and beg — I don't mean ask nicely, I mean beg — and I don't feel any vet should have to beg somebody to do their damn job."

However, by late April, Lamie had found a VA staffer who was trying to straighten out bureaucratic confusion involving multiple files shipped among multiple offices. "Fingers crossed," Lamie says.

213

## Brain Injuries Put Strain on VA Benefits

Nearly 91,000 U.S. soldiers have either died, been wounded or medically evacuated for noncombat-related reasons thus far in the Iraq and Afghanistan wars (top). The 760,000 veterans who suffer from either post-traumatic stress disorder (PTSD) or traumatic brain injury (TBI), or both, have put the Veterans Benefits Administration under increasing pressure to meet the needs of the country's injured veterans.

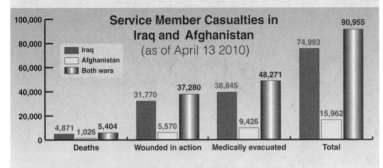

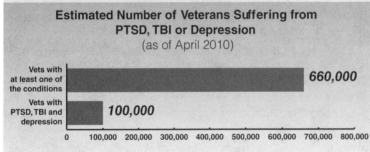

*Sources:* Veterans for Common Sense; RAND Center for Military Health Policy Research, 2008, www.rand.org/pubs/monographs/MG720

About 1 million claims of all kinds are backlogged at the VA, according to veterans' organizations, some of which help veterans on behalf of the VA, which says the backlog of initial claims alone totals 500,000, using a different calculation method.

While VA medical care, delivered through the Veterans Health Administration, tends to earn high marks from vets, the VBA presents a different picture. In 2007-2008, staff at VBA regional offices compiled an overall accuracy record on initial claims decisions of only 77 percent, Belinda J. Finn, VA deputy inspector general, told the House Veterans' Disability Assistance and Memorial Affairs Subcommittee in early March. "This equates to approximately . . . 203,000 total claims where veterans' monthly benefits may be incorrect," Finn told the subcommittee.[2]

The VA's scramble to meet mounting demand for its services is occurring amid continuing warfare on two fronts: Since U.S. forces entered Afghanistan in 2001, at least 5,190 service members have been wounded, 425 of them this year. Since the 2003 U.S. invasion of Iraq, 31,176 service members have been wounded there.[3]

Yet the VA's difficulties providing adequate care for veterans got only sporadic attention until 2007, when a prize-winning *Washington Post* series pushed them to the top of the national agenda. With the issue in the spotlight, Congress in 2008 authorized free medical care for all Iraq and Afghanistan veterans for five years after leaving the military. And GI Bill educational benefits were expanded for veterans who entered the service after the Sept. 11, 2001, terrorist attacks.

Vets welcomed the new benefits, but questioned the VBA's ability to process all the new claims. The VA's new boss, retired Gen. Eric K. Shinseki, is vowing to shake up the agency. "2010 is my year to focus on finding

"Within another two months something might work itself out." He emphasizes "might."

Veterans' advocates, the Government Accountability Office (GAO) and the VA's own inspector general have all reported similar communications breakdowns and wildly varying standards for evaluating disability claims among VBA regional offices, even as a steady stream of new claims pours into the VA.

Soldiers wounded while serving their country "are waiting — and waiting — for the help they have been promised," said Rep. Bob Filner, D-Calif., chairman of the House Veterans' Affairs Committee, after meeting with agency officials and veterans' organizations in March. "Frankly, it's an insult to our veterans and their service."[1]

and breaking the obstacles that deny us faster and better processing and higher quality outcomes," he told the Veterans of Foreign Wars in early March. To break the backlog while dealing with a rush of expected new claims, he proposes adding 4,000 claims examiners in the 2010-2011 fiscal year.[4]

His appointees aren't mincing words about what they found when they took over. "In my judgment, it cannot be fixed," Peter Levin, the VA's chief technology officer, said of the benefits claims system during a March meeting on Capitol Hill with veterans' organizations. "We need to build a new system, and that is exactly what we are going to do."[5]

Veterans' advocates cheered Levin's comments and praise Shinseki's vision, but some wonder if he can put his stamp on the VA. A West Point graduate who lost most of a foot in Vietnam combat, Shinseki has earned a reputation for speaking out regardless of consequences. As Army chief of staff, he told the Senate Armed Services Committee in 2003 that securing Iraq after invading it would require "something on the order of several hundred thousand soldiers." Shinseki's civilian boss, Defense Secretary Donald Rumsfeld, contemptuously brushed that assessment aside and marginalized its author. But time proved Shinseki more accurate than Rumsfeld, who endorsed a forecast of 30,000-50,000 troops in Iraq after the invasion. By fiscal year 2008, U.S. troop strength had reached nearly 160,000.[6]

Now, Shinseki's leading an agency trying to adjust to the special demands created by 21st-century warfare. Vast advances in battlefield care are enabling thousands of vets to survive injuries that would have been fatal in the past. But those injuries, often caused by homemade bombs, or so-called improvised explosive devices (IEDs), can be crippling.

"IED blasts alone often cause multiple wounds, usually with severe injuries to extremities, and traumatic brain and other blast injuries, and they leave many . . . with serious physical, psychological and cognitive injuries," the government-funded Institute of

## Appeals Take Longer Than Claims

The average processing time to complete a veteran's compensation claim in 2008 was nearly 200 days, more or less the same since 2003. Finalizing appeals, however, took nearly four times longer — a constant trend since 2000.

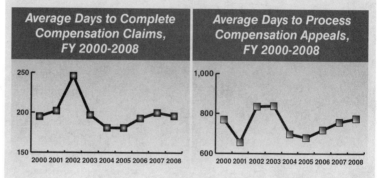

Source: "Veterans' Disability Benefits," Government Accountability Office, January 2010

Medicine (IOM) reported to Congress in a lengthy study published in March.[7]

Today's all-volunteer military is far smaller than past draftee-fed forces, requiring troops to be repeatedly recycled through combat zones. About a third of those who have been deployed to combat more than once have suffered from PTSD, TBI or major depression, and about 5 percent suffered from all three, according to the RAND Corp, a California think tank. Multiple deployments can double the risk of PTSD and other psychological problems, the Army surgeon general concluded in a 2008 report, which found mental health problems in 12 percent with one deployment and 27 percent with three or more deployments.[8]

Retired Army Capt. Anthony Kennedy, who attempted suicide after two tours in Iraq, described the nature of the fighting there and the psychological effects of the constant threat of being blown up by an IED. "One of my friends . . . had a friend whose arms and legs were blown off," Kennedy says. "All of us combat guys are thinking, 'Why do I want to go through life with no arms and no legs?' Our consensus: 'Can my battle buddy just put a bullet in me?' We talk about that."

Kennedy has had problems with the VA benefits system as well, but obtained a volunteer lawyer's help in pushing his PTSD rating from 30 percent to 70 percent

Double amputee Bradley Walker practices walking on his new prosthetic legs, using a moving sidewalk at Walter Reed Army Medical Center in Washington, D.C., on April 4, 2007. Wounded veterans' benefit claims are projected to rise 30 percent next fiscal year, to about 1.3 million, in part because additional illnesses are being classified as caused by military service, including ailments linked to the Agent Orange defoliant used during the Vietnam War.

disability. He says his 17 years in the service taught him how to deal with military-style bureaucracy. "I have the maturity and the knowledge to know that there's 100,000 applications out there, and I'm just one cog in the wheel," he says. "But I can imagine that if someone is completely disabled, and their father or mother comes in, the system can be a shock."

Even military reservists, accustomed to part-time service, can be taken aback by the VA system they encounter after active duty. Naval reservist Richard Sanchez of New York, a former paralegal for a Wall Street law firm, was discharged after his second deployment, which took

him to Kuwait, where he was injured when an ammunition and weapons container fell on him in 2005.

After discharge, Sanchez began to suffer intense back pain, failing memory and depression. In his confused state, the VA system overcame him, he says. Eventually, he encountered a VA counselor who helped him straighten out a long series of bureaucratic complications, and in March received a letter from the VA apologizing for erroneous ratings and promising to reevaluate claims for PTSD, TBI and depression.

"I don't hate the VA," says Sanchez, who is attending college thanks to VA education benefits. "There are some faults there, but you can't blame the whole system."

That system is about to be tested even more forcefully. The VA is predicting that its claims workload will rise 30 percent next fiscal year, to about 1.3 million, in part because the department added three new ailments to the list of illnesses presumed to result from exposure to the Vietnam-era defoliant known as Agent Orange. And more "presumptive" illnesses associated with exposure to other battleground chemicals in more recent wars may be added later this year.[9]

Still, it won't be easy to convince veterans that the VA has turned a new page. In Georgia, Iraq vet Lamie is trying to keep his family fed, his lights on and his car running on the small checks he receives now. "I've still got no faith in VA" — for now, he says.

As veterans' disablity claims mount, here are some of the questions being debated:

## Is the VA benefits system broken beyond repair?

Vietnam vet Elmer A. Hawkins filed a claim for disability benefits in 1990. Repeated errors by Regional Office (RO) staffers kept his case — based on exposure to Agent Orange decades earlier while serving in Vietnam — bouncing between them and VA appeals boards.

Last year Hawkins tried to inject some urgency into the proceedings. He asked the Court of Appeals for the Federal Circuit to order the VA to finally decide his case. But the court rejected the request. After all, wrote Judge Haldane Robert Mayer, a decorated Vietnam combat veteran, "The RO may yet grant Hawkins VA benefits."[10]

However, the fact that the case has been pending for 20 years shocked U.S. District Judge Claudia Wilken of Oakland, Calif. — a stranger to the VA benefits system and its slow-moving clock. Serving temporarily on the federal circuit, Judge Wilken wrote in a dissenting opinion that the VA had "made repeated errors which have prolonged the decision-making process." These errors "cannot be excused as products of a burdened system."[11]

Hawkins' wait was unusually long. But years-long battles over claims aren't at all unusual, say experts on the system. Barton Stichman, joint executive director of the nonprofit National Veterans Legal Services Program, testified last year that the first step alone in the appeal process took an average of 563 days in fiscal 2007-2008. "Frustrated veterans have to wait many years before receiving a final decision on their claims," Stichman told the House Veterans' Disability Assistance and Memorial Affairs Subcommittee.[12]

Meanwhile, claims pile up in the system. "This massive backlog has resulted in a six-month average wait for an initial rating decision, and a two-year average wait for an appeal decision," Thomas J. Tradwell, commander in chief of Veterans of Foreign Wars, testified in March to a joint hearing of the Senate and House Veterans' Affairs committees. "That is completely unacceptable."[13]

Finn of the VA inspector general's office cited the 22 percent error rate in regional office disability assessments when she testified that even VA staffers assigned to identify mistakes compiled an imperfect record. "They either did not thoroughly review available medical and non-medical evidence or identify the absence of necessary medical information," Finn told the Disability Assistance and Memorial Affairs Subcommittee. "Without an effective and reliable quality assurance program, VBA leadership cannot adequately monitor performance to make necessary program improvements and ensure veterans receive accurate and consistent ratings."[14]

Getting a disability rating is the key to the process. Veterans like Hawkins who claim their illnesses or conditions were "service-connected" must prove that connection. The VBA's staff then state their conclusions in the form of ratings — such as that a veteran is 50 percent disabled because of an event that occurred while in the military.

"A vet fills out a 23-page claim form, then VHA sends it to the VBA office and it takes six months to get an answer," says Paul Sullivan, executive director of Veterans for Common Sense, which has sued the VA over the workings of the benefit system. "And the appeals process takes four-five years. That's unconscionable. VBA leaders

failed, and they crashed the agency. It has suffered catastrophic meltdown."

A Gulf War veteran who worked at VBA in the 1990s, Sullivan praises the VA's new leaders but says even they cannot save the VBA without replacing it with an entirely new agency. With a war ongoing in Afghanistan, 98,000 troops still deployed in Iraq, the recent expansion of benefits for victims of Agent Orange and the proposed addition of other chemical exposures to the "presumptives" list, he says, "VBA is overwhelmed. It's broken beyond repair."[15]

Other veterans' advocates agree but not on Sullivan's proposed solution. "I got an e-mail yesterday from a vet who's been fighting with the VA for six years," says Tom Tarantino, legislative associate for Iraq and Afghanistan Veterans of America (IAVA). The organization is pressing for greater efficiency and accuracy in the benefits process.

But Tarantino says the current VA leadership is making great strides. "The VA has in the last year been incredibly aggressive in trying to address this issue" of claims processing, he says. "They have put in place a very solid, ambitious plan to upgrade the workflow, management, technology and customer service. Our challenge in the veterans' community is making sure that what we push and what Congress introduces do not interfere with actual progress at VA."

That big-picture perspective may not reassure veterans who are dealing with the current system. "When you contact people at these ROs [regional offices], they don't want to hear they did something wrong," says injured Iraq veteran Lamie, who has been disputing his 50 percent disability rating since shortly after retiring from the Army late last year. "Instead of coming together with the vet and going through it page by page and seeing what went wrong, they blow you off, because you did something wrong — not them. You are left to the wind."

David E. Autry, deputy national communications director of Disabled American Veterans (DAV), agrees that some veterans encounter a lack of cooperation from some VA staffers. "It's clearly in the law that the VA has a 'duty to assist' the veteran," he says. "But in many cases we find that the VA is throwing up unnecessary roadblocks: 'You need to provide me with a documentary statement,' and you turn it in, and the VA loses it."

The VA benefits system, Autry says, "has been approaching critical mass for some time." Still, he says,

## Backlog Claims Increase After Afghanistan, Iraq

After the war in Afghanistan began in 2001, compensation claims to the Veterans Administration nearly doubled. The pace picked up again after the start of the war in Iraq. Claims pending for more than six months have remained relatively constant.

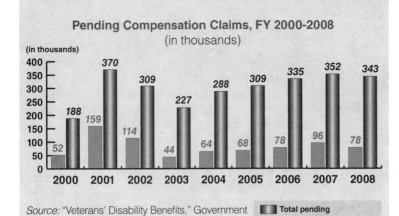

**Pending Compensation Claims, FY 2000-2008**
(in thousands)

*Source:* "Veterans' Disability Benefits," Government Accountability Office, January 2010

■ Total pending
■ Pending at least 6 months

"The good news is that the VA seems to be committed to making things work differently."

## Is the VA adjusting to the needs of 21st-century combat and technology?

The wars in Afghanistan ("Operation Enduring Freedom") and Iraq ("Operation Iraqi Freedom") have already lasted longer than World War II, which for the United States ran from 1941 to 1945. The wars also are presenting the VA with a new constellation of disabilities, along with heightened veteran expectations of government efficiency and attention.

Today's veterans grew up with the Web and with speedy online shopping. These experiences don't prepare them for dealing with the VA. "FedEx can track where your package is," Rep. Phil Roe, R-Tenn., ranking Republican on the House Veterans Affairs Oversight and Investigations Subcommittee, told VA technology officials last February. "You can order your coat from L.L. Bean and you know exactly where it is before it gets to you. Will it be possible when a veteran puts in for their benefits to track where their claim is with this current system that we're setting up?"[16]

"Absolutely," said Roger Baker, the VA's assistant secretary for information and technology, citing work on a system for tracking education benefits planned for release this fiscal year. The VA will eventually have "a Web site to which veterans can come and see the exact status of their claim from the point where it's received by the VA . . . to the point where the check is cut and sent to the veteran, and it will tell them everywhere along the process where they sit."[17]

But the technology gap is only part of the problem. The nature and severity of today's injuries also complicate the VA's job. Most casualties are caused by IEDs, the favorite enemy weapon in both conflicts. Victims of these powerful bombs may lose limbs, which typically aren't protected by torso-covering body armor. And even troops who avoid penetrating wounds may suffer harder-to-detect brain injuries.

Thanks to recent advances in battlefield care, "more service members survive to return home with severe combat-related injuries that require additional care," the Institute of Medicine concludes in a new research report.[18]

And repeated deployments are causing a growing incidence of PTSD and associated mental-health conditions, including depression. Veterans' demand for psychological services is outpacing the availability of mental-health professionals in areas with large vet populations, according to the IOM.[19]

Furthermore, family members increasingly must care full time for the growing number of vets who survive injuries that would have killed soldiers in earlier wars. The Wounded Warrior Project, a Jacksonville, Fla.-based nonprofit, estimates that the families of 2,000 severely disabled Iraq and Afghanistan veterans are now caring for them full time.[20]

"But the department has no systematic Family Caregiver Program," Anna Frese, sister of a severely brain-injured survivor of an IED attack in Iraq, told the House Veterans Affairs' Health Subcommittee last year. "It has mounted some pilot programs. But overall, our experience is that very little institutional attention is being paid to family caregivers even though they are a vital link in the veteran's lifelong rehabilitation process. Families are coping largely on their own."[21]

The VA doesn't support the comprehensive caregiver support program that Frese, the Wounded Warrior Project and other nonprofits advocate, which would provide financial support and health coverage for caregivers. One point of dispute is the agency's insistence that family care be overseen by a VA staff member or contractor, who, an official implied, would be more objective in dealing with the disabled patient. "Health-care providers maintain their relationships on a professional level," Dr. Madhulika Agarwal, chief of patient care services for the VA's Veterans Health Administration, told the Health subcommittee.[22]

More recently, the VA has said it needs more information before proposing any policies and programs. "VA does not have adequate information on the number of caregivers, the number of family caregivers and the number of veterans receiving . . . services from family caregivers," says the agency's budget proposal for fiscal 2010-2011.[23]

The effects of intense combat during repeated deployments are showing up in another disturbing pattern. According to the most recent statistics available, suicides among young Iraq and Afghanistan veterans jumped 26 percent from 2005 to 2007, the VA reported early this year.[24]

Though the VA has strengthened its suicide-prevention programs, the agency's image among veterans lessens its effectiveness, according to M. David Rudd, dean of the University of Utah's College of Social and Behavioral Science. "It is important for the VA to recognize that they fight a longstanding image as an inflexible and unresponsive bureaucracy," Rudd told the Senate Veterans Affairs Committee in March.[25]

Seventy percent of veterans shun VA help, said Rudd, a specialist in military suicide. He urged the agency to establish partnerships with other mental-health providers. "Expansion of the existing VA system may not be the most effective expenditure of available funds," he testified.[26]

But, a top VA official countered at the same hearing, "Young veterans receiving VA care are significantly less

**IED Aftermath**

Flames engulf a U.S. Army tank in Baghdad, Iraq, after it was struck by a homemade roadside bomb known as an improvised explosive device (IED) (top). Its crew escaped unharmed from the March 10, 2006, explosion, but Marine Sgt. Merlin German (bottom left), being promoted by Lt. Gen. James F. Amos (right) on May 21, 2007, suffered burns on 97 percent of his body after his vehicle struck an IED in Iraq. Blasts from IEDs — widely used by insurgents in both Iraq and Afghanistan — often cause multiple wounds, usually with severe injuries to extremities.

likely to commit suicide than those not receiving VA care." Gerald M. Cross, acting principal deputy undersecretary for health, cited U.S. Centers for Disease Control and Prevention statistics showing a drop from 39 suicides per 100,000 in 2001 to 35 per 100,000 in 2007 among patients of VA health services, a decline equivalent to about 250 lives saved.[27]

Nevertheless, another VA mental health specialist said the VA is open to joining forces with other organizations, by contract or other arrangements. "We need to have partnerships," said Antoinette Zeiss, associate chief consultant for mental health. "We can't do it alone. If there is a level of care that VA is not able to provide in rural or in urban or suburban settings we should look for . . . well-tested programs."[28]

Before declaring that policy, Zeiss conceded that suicide-prevention programs have only recently been strengthened. For vets in danger of suicide, "We have instituted throughout the system far more intensive outpatient programs, so that instead of one, one-hour-a-week session," Zeiss said, "there are at least three hours a day, three days a week with an interdisciplinary team trying to deliver very complex and intensive services."[29]

## Is the VA improving rapidly enough?

Debates about the quality of veterans' services are taking place amid a notable change in climate from the days of the Bush administration. Widespread agreement prevails that the VA's new leadership genuinely wants to make deep improvements and has the organizational competence to do so.

Under the Bush administration, even those who defended the VA against steadily increasing criticism from Iraq and Afghanistan vets didn't deliver more than pro-forma praise of top VA leaders. In October, 2007, under the pressure of months of revelations of substandard and inadequate care from the VA, VA Secretary James Nicholson, who had headed the agency since 2005, resigned.[30]

Shinseki's experience with the Bush-era Defense Department and his Vietnam service gave him considerable credibility in the veteran community. And he named as one of his assistant secretaries L. Tammy Duckworth, a former Illinois Veterans Affairs director and Illinois National Guard helicopter pilot who lost both legs in Iraq in 2004.

Measured by the size of his proposed new budget — an important gauge of intentions and administration support — Shinseki is planning to follow through on his modernization vows. He's asking for an increase of $9.4 billion in discretionary spending in fiscal 2011 — a 20 percent hike at a time of spending cutbacks and only modest increases elsewhere in government.[31]

Shinseki faced an early test in September, 2009, when the VA failed to send out scheduled checks to about 277,000 college-bound vets who had qualified for GI Bill education benefits. As the VA showed itself incapable of processing the payments on time, some vets were forced to borrow money or take other emergency measures.[32]

Shinseki ordered the agency to issue emergency checks of up to $3,000 and to distribute them to veterans at VA offices around the country. The fast action and acknowledgement of error struck many veterans' affairs specialists as a new approach. Shinseki explicitly endorsed that view. "We will change the [VA] culture," Shinseki told the House Veterans Affairs Committee three weeks later. "I assure you of that."[33]

Nevertheless, debate is still running strong on whether the agency's new leaders can transform the 300,000-employee department quickly enough to make a difference to the steadily growing ranks of veterans who depend on the VA.

Where benefits decision appeals are concerned, "The quality of decision-making hasn't improved," says Stichman of the National Veterans Legal Services Program. "It's in the same bad state."

Shinseki, he says, "does sound like he's intelligent and really wants to do something." But, the veterans-law expert says, "It's very difficult for a secretary to shake the bureaucracy. Can he get the lieutenants to follow orders?"

Autry of Disabled American Veterans acknowledges that giant institutions don't adapt to change easily or quickly. But the new leaders' determination is making a difference, he says. "The VA seems to be committed to making things work differently," he says.

To be sure, Autry, a Navy veteran of the Vietnam War, is also dissatisfied with the pace of transformation. "But this is an aircraft carrier," he says of the VA. "You don't just spin the wheel and turn it around."

But Sullivan of Veterans for Common Sense urges against accepting sluggishness as a given. "We're generally opposed to more layers of bureaucracy," he says. "But the agency has grown, and in order for Mr. Shinseki to leave his mark he is going to have to bring in new leaders."

Furthermore, growing pressures on the VA demand accelerated response, Sullivan says. The military is discharging a steady stream of combat veterans, at the same time as new data emerge that point to wartime conditions as causes of ailments suffered by Gulf War and

Vietnam vets. "Right now is the pivotal moment," he says. "Will we repeat the mistakes of how horribly mistreated Vietnam and Gulf War veterans were when they came home?"

At least some of those veterans are still inclined to trust that Shinseki is moving as fast as possible, based on improvements already in place. "From my experience with the VA, from 2005 to now, there has been great change," says retired Capt. Kennedy, who served two tours in Iraq.

Kennedy won his fight to increase his PTSD disability rating to 70 percent, though he is still dealing with what he calls a VA error that cost him $13,000 in retirement pay — which he expects to recoup. He attributes part of his success to the free legal representation he received though the National Veterans Legal Services program.

However, he adds, "By hiring Gen. Shinseki as secretary, the Obama administration made a statement that they are committed to disabled veterans. People like me can see light at the end of the tunnel, but I know I'll never be part of it."

## BACKGROUND

### The Big Change

Victory in World War II, the biggest armed conflict by far in U.S. history, brought a monumental shift in veterans' care and compensation. For the first time, they were given a major opportunity to improve their lives, not just tend to their injuries or subsist on tiny pensions.

The new doctrine may have been inevitable. To achieve victory, the United States had mobilized more than 16 million men (and accepted 210,000 female volunteers) for military service — many of them for the entire four-year span of the war. More than 405,000 were killed, and more than 671,000 wounded.[34]

To be sure, veterans hadn't been ignored before World War II. Long before, Congress and the executive branch had established a series of institutions and systems designed to provide care and compensation. These included the Asylum for Disabled Volunteer Soldiers, created (under another name) in 1865, at the end of the Civil War, and the Consolidation Act of 1873, which set up a pension

system based on the degree of disability, replacing a scale based on rank.

Of the 4.7 million men mobilized during World War I, 204,000 were wounded (and 116,000 were killed). But the veterans' system wasn't up to the challenge. In 1924, Congress made matters worse. Lawmakers created a bonus designed to make up the difference between military pay and the high wages earned by civilians who'd spent the war working in essential industries. But the money was granted in the form of a bond that would mature in 1945, and after the Great Depression began in 1929, vets needed their bonus immediately. Up to 40,000 veterans and their families — called the Bonus Marchers — set up an encampment in Washington in 1932, only to see it destroyed by Army troops, an event that shocked the nation.[35]

Fourteen years later, as World War II drew to a close, the Franklin D. Roosevelt administration and Congress were determined to prevent a repeat of the Bonus March disaster. Instead, the Servicemen's Readjustment Act of 1944 — known forever after as the "GI Bill of Rights" — created a broad range of opportunities for veterans.[36]

Under the bill, the Veterans Administration paid all or most of the costs of college or vocational training, provided guarantees for no-down-payment mortgages or business loans and granted unemployment compensation for up to a year. When the GI Bill expired in 1956, 7.8 million vets had received education or training, and the VA had guaranteed 5.9 million home mortgages worth a total of $50.1 billion.

The GI Bill, widely considered one of the most far-reaching pieces of social legislation ever enacted, "gave veterans from less-advantaged backgrounds chances they had never dreamed possible and a route toward the middle class," wrote Suzanne Metler, a political science professor at Syracuse University, author of a book about the law.[37]

In 1952, Congress passed a second version of the bill for veterans of the Korean War, which had begun in 1950. The new law was slightly less generous: For example, it covered only three years of college expenses instead of all four, and provided a smaller tuition subsidy.

Meanwhile, the magnitude of the veteran population created by World War II and the Korean conflict led to a vast expansion of the VA medical system, which by the early 1950s was caring for about 2.5 million vets.

## CHRONOLOGY

**1944-1950s** *GI Bill of Rights, enacted in final days of World War I, becomes the standard for all subsequent veteran care policy.*

**1944** As World War II nears an end, Congress passes GI Bill to provide for education, home mortgages and business loans; allows millions of vets to move into the middle class.

**1952** Korean War vets get their own, slightly downsized version of GI Bill.

**1958** Veterans' unemployment insurance extended to peacetime draftees.

**1967-1980s** *Vietnam War gives rise to complaints of shoddy VA medical care; scientists begin evaluating evidence of psychological trauma from combat and physical damage from radiation and chemical exposure.*

**1967** Six Vietnam veterans form Vietnam Veterans Against the War (VVAW), which grows into the thousands and directs much anger at VA.

**1970** *Life* magazine reports on rat-infested VA hospital in the Bronx, N.Y.

**1973** Paraplegic vet Ron Kovic leads takeover of Democratic Sen. Alan Cranston's office to call attention to deplorable conditions at VA hospitals.

**1979** Accumulating evidence of psychological troubles among Vietnam vets leads Congress to authorize opening of 92 "Vet Centers" for counseling and other assistance. . . . Years-long debate among psychiatrists leads to inclusion of newly named post-traumatic stress disorder (PTSD) in *Diagnostic and Statistical Manual of Mental Disorders.*

**1981** U.S. District Court in Washington throws out VA regulation that effectively excludes 400,000 radiation-exposed World War II and postwar vets from claiming benefits for cancer and other disabilities.

**1982** General Accounting Office reports that VA offices give short shrift to vets reporting physical symptoms from Agent Orange defoliant exposure.

**1988** President Ronald Reagan signs law granting disability benefits to "atomic veterans" suffering from 13 (later 16) specific cancers.

**1990s-2000s** *VA benefits system begins to buckle under strain of disability claims arising from wars in the Persian Gulf and Afghanistan, as well as recognition of disabilities arising from Vietnam War.*

**1991** VA recognizes two cancers are linked to Agent Orange.

**1992** Persian Gulf War ends; reports emerge of physical and psychological symptoms among up to 100,000 veterans of the conflict.

**1997** Medical researchers hypothesize that exposure to combinations of pesticide and nerve gas gave rise to "Gulf War syndrome." . . . VA begins providing benefits for Vietnam vets' children born with spina bifida.

**2002** U.S. troops in Afghanistan report first enemy use of improvised explosive devices (IEDs).

**2007** IEDs found to have caused two-thirds of 3,100 U.S. combat deaths in Iraq since U.S. invasion of 2003. . . . *Washington Post* publishes series on substandard conditions for outpatients at Walter Reed Army Medical Center in Washington.

**2008** Congress authorizes free medical care for Iraq/Afghanistan veterans for five years after leaving military. . . . RAND Corp. reports that about one-third of service members deployed to combat suffered from PTSD, traumatic brain injury or major depression. . . . Delay in considering appeals of VA ratings rises to 563 days.

**2009** VA issues emergency checks after agency fails to send education benefits to 277,000 college-bound vets. . . . IEDs reported to cause 55 percent of amputations among combat casualties.

**2010** VA technology chief calls claims-management system "broken beyond repair." . . . Compromise reached on legislation to aid families caring for severely disabled vets. . . . Institute of Medicine reports shortage of mental health services for vets and "evidence of association" between Persian Gulf War service and multisymptom illness.

## Vietnam's Neglected Vets

The Vietnam War influenced veteran law and policy every bit as deeply as World War II, even though the conflict was much smaller than World War II.[38]

By the time the fighting ended with victory for the communist government of North Vietnam in 1975, 3.4 million service members had been deployed to Southeast Asia.[39]

U.S. society divided sharply over the war; so did the veterans' community. In 1967, six returnees founded Vietnam Veterans Against the War, which grew over the years and held a series of high-profile demonstrations, including one in 1971 in which several thousand veterans threw their service decorations over a fence at the U.S. Capitol.[40]

Debate over the rights and wrongs of the Vietnam War faded somewhat with its end, but anger and bitterness among veterans over shoddy VA services and treatment grew steadily. The discontent eventually transcended political views on the war itself, but challenges to the VA came at first from antiwar vets.

In 1973, paraplegic vet Ron Kovic (later portrayed by Tom Cruise in the 1989 film, "Born on the Fourth of July")[41] led other severely disabled vets in a 17-day hunger strike and occupation of the Los Angeles office of Sen. Alan Cranston, D-Calif. They were publicizing appalling conditions at VA hospitals in Southern California. A Senate hearing produced testimony about neglect of patients, brutal retaliation against those who complained and violations of basic hygiene. The testimony mirrored a 1970 *Life* magazine exposé about a VA hospital in the Bronx, N.Y., which was plagued by rats, filth and deficient medical care.

Meanwhile, with far less public attention, a group of psychiatrists with ties to antiwar veterans had started trying to describe and define a condition that they'd noticed in many Vietnam returnees. Symptoms included sleep disturbance, anxiety and depression. Eventually, the psychiatrists proposed that the American Psychiatric Association add the condition — which colleagues were also seeing in disaster survivors — to a new edition of the *Diagnostic and Statistical Manual of Mental Disorders*, the bible of the mental-health profession.

The fight to include what eventually became known as post-traumatic stress disorder went on for more than four years. Like the military and the VA, much of the psychiatric establishment initially dismissed the idea that

intense combat or other wartime experiences could produce serious disturbances in a well-adjusted individual. Troubled veterans suffered from conditions that afflicted them before they joined the military, the skeptics argued.

But mounting evidence weakened their position. In 1979, PTSD was added to the manual. The move marked the beginning of a change in outlook, eventually of global dimensions, about the deep effects of war and disaster.

In a more immediate sense, the PTSD debate influenced Congress to pass in 1979 (shortly before the definition was formally added to the manual) a bill to create 92 Vet Centers, where Vietnam returnees could obtain psychological counseling. In 1991, the centers were opened to all combat veterans of any conflict.

## Chemicals and Radiation

Meanwhile, a major issue affecting Vietnam vets' physical health — and that of their children — was also emerging. In 1970, journalist Thomas Whiteside reported in *The New Yorker* that dioxin — the main ingredient of a defoliant nicknamed "Agent Orange" used in large quantities by U.S. forces to strip jungle cover in Vietnam — was a carcinogen.[42]

The article led the Pentagon to ban Agent Orange (the nickname came from the orange-banded barrels in which it was stored). But by then hundreds of thousands of vets already had been exposed. As the decade wore on, many developed diseases, including leukemia and other cancers, and were also reporting an unusual number of birth defects in their children.

Initially, the VA resisted vets' claims that Agent Orange was the cause of their symptoms. In 1982, a congressionally commissioned study by the General Accounting Office, now the Government Accountability Office (GAO), concluded that the VA had neglected the issue, for instance, taking medical histories from only 10 percent of the 90,000 vets who had filed Agent Orange-based claims.

Not until 1991 did the VA recognize links between two cancers — soft-tissue sarcoma and non-Hodgkin's lymphoma — and Agent Orange exposure. Several more were added in 1993, and still more in later years. And in 1997 — 22 years after the war ended — the VA began a program to provide medical benefits, vocational training and a monthly allowance for veterans' children born with spina bifida, one of the birth defects associated with exposure to the chemical.

# VA Benefits to Get High-Tech Overhaul

*Current system is 'hopelessly broken.'*

Members of today's tech-savvy military have grown up being able to buy virtually any product online and have it shipped overnight. Instantaneous communication by text, voice and video has been part of their everyday lives.

And it's now part of their military service as well. "I was battle captain for a unit that oversaw all the transportation into Iraq," says retired Army Capt. Anthony Kennedy about his second deployment there in 2007-2008. "Each night we had 3,000 trucks on the road. I needed to know where every truck was at every second."

Shortly thereafter, however, Kennedy retired from the military and encountered the VA benefits system. Suddenly, he was back in the mid-20th century, dealing with paper forms filled out by hand and sent by mail. His reaction: "Let's let Amazon run it," referring to the huge online retailer Amazon.com.

The VA recognizes the problem. "We have a manual, paper-bounded system; what we want is an automated electronic system," says Peter L. Levin, the VA's new chief technology officer. He has initiated several pilot projects designed to become the new system's backbone.

Levin became a "rock star" among veterans' organizations, says Tom Tarantino, legislative associate for Iraq and Afghanistan Veterans of America, by acknowledging at a March meeting organized by the House Veterans' Services Committee that the present system is hopelessly broken and must be replaced. "He said some of the gutsiest things I've ever heard a VA person say in front of Congress," Tarantino adds.[1]

But Levin makes clear that he isn't promising the new system will be up and running tomorrow, or even next year. The deadline, set by VA Secretary Eric K. Shinseki, is 2015 (though parts of the system are scheduled to be online before then). "I come from the private sector, and I think I got this job based on a good reputation for on-time, on-budget deliveries," he says. "That is a reputation I intend to keep. I don't want to give unrealistic dates. The instructions are clear that if it is going to move in any direction it is going to be earlier, not later."

Levin was hired last year away from DAFCA Inc., which he cofounded and where he was CEO. The Framingham, Mass.-based firm designs software to test the reliability of computer chips and block malicious circuitry. Levin, who has a doctorate in electrical and computer engineering from Carnegie Mellon University in Pittsburgh, served as a White House fellow and as expert consultant in the Office of Science and Technology Policy in the Clinton administration.[2]

Paper won't entirely disappear from the redesigned system. Some records, Levin says, are too important to exist in purely digital form — birth and marriage certificates in the civilian world, for example. But medical scans and lists of medications should be digitized, he says.

Still, the planned improvements won't make dealing with the benefits system like dealing with Amazon.

But the long-running Agent Orange dispute was only one of several controversies surrounding service members' exposure to dangerous substances and atomic radiation.

World War II veterans, including thousands who had been assigned to clear rubble in Hiroshima and Nagasaki, Japan, after atomic bombs were dropped there, had filed about 1,500 claims for benefits, claiming adverse health consequences from the intense radiation they'd absorbed. Some survivors of deceased veterans also filed for death benefits. But the federal government long resisted paying for the claims; in 1979 the VA adopted a rule effectively rejecting 98 percent of claims by "atomic veterans." The group was substantial — 200,000 personnel who had been exposed to radiation in postwar Japan, and another 200,000 who had participated in atmospheric testing of atomic weapons.[43]

In 1981, U.S. District Judge June L. Green of Washington threw out that rule. Eventually, President Ronald W. Reagan signed a bill in 1988 establishing that atomic veterans suffering from 13 (later 16) specific kinds of cancers were automatically entitled to benefits.[44]

The Persian Gulf War of 1990-1991 prompted another wave of veteran medical concerns. About 100,000 of the 694,000 Gulf War veterans reported symptoms including fatigue, skin rash, headache, muscle and joint pain,

Kennedy notes that Amazon's customers get invited to buy specific books, music and other merchandise based on their records of past purchases. A VA version, he says, could tell a user, "Your account shows you've been treated for this, this and this — you should apply for this disability."

But Levin, while acknowledging the appeal of the Amazon model, argues that it's not a precise fit. Amazon sells mass-produced goods, with one copy of a book or CD, for instance, indistinguishable from another. "It turns out that every vet is a little different," he says. Nevertheless, a VA variant could produce data that allow a records examiner to see how vets with similar characteristics were treated.

For a veteran with a given list of claims, "I want to know what guys who are about your age and who served about where you served, and did things like you did while serving — I want to know what they're talking about that maybe you forgot," Levin says. And at some point, an examiner might be able to instantly access information on specific health and environmental conditions in given areas of operation.

Meanwhile, even the basic system is complicated enough to design and install that Levin is trying to improve the present system pending its replacement. "We do not have the option of turning off the system for six months

*U.S. Department of Veterans Affairs*

Peter L. Levin, the Department of Veterans Affairs' new chief technology officer, became an instant "rock star" among some veterans' organizations when he told Congress the VA benefits system is hopelessly broken and must be replaced.

and building a new one really quickly."

For vets, the bottom line is that paper documents are still indispensable to dealing with the VA. Indeed, Richard Sanchez, a U.S. Navy veteran, says he's on his way to resolving four years of miscommunications with the VA, partly because he heeded an old sailor's advice.

"He said, 'Make copies of everything; doesn't matter if it's not important, it might be important later, it might have a date on it. And then make a copy, and then another copy.' I did that," says Sanchez, "and it was true. I have an archive at home, another with relatives and another one in a safe-deposit box."

— *Peter Katel*

[1] Rick Maze, "VA official: Disability claims system 'cannot be fixed,' " *Federal Times*, March 18, 2010, www.federaltimes.com/article/20100318/DEPARTMENTS04/3180302/1055/AGENCY.

[2] "Executive Biographies," U.S. Department of Veterans Affairs, undated, www1.va.gov/opa/bios; "Carnegie-Mellon Engineering Alumnus Peter L. Levin Named as Chief Technology Officer at U.S. Veterans Affairs," Carnegie Mellon University, press release, Aug. 3, 2009; John Markoff, "F.B.I. Says the Military Had Bogus Computer Gear," *The New York Times*, May 9, 2008, p. C4.

memory loss, difficulty concentrating, shortness of breath, sleep disturbance, gastrointestinal problems and chest pain. Over the years, the number of vets reporting symptoms rose to 250,000.

Scientists and others advanced various hypotheses, including exposure to destroyed Iraqi stocks of sarin nerve gas, smoke from oil well fires or pesticides. Government-sponsored and private medical and environmental studies offered contradictory conclusions on whether an identifiable "Gulf War Syndrome" existed.

Nevertheless, Gulf War veterans continued to report ailments, some of them serious. And after President George

W. Bush ordered troops into Afghanistan in 2001, and into Iraq, in 2003, veterans of both wars began reporting similar ailments, leading the VA and Defense Department to focus more closely on the possible effects of chemical exposure from "burn pits" on military bases, where plastics, electronics, lubricants and medical waste were incinerated, among other things.[45]

## 21st-Century Wounds

The nature of the wars in Afghanistan and Iraq, coupled with tremendous advances in battlefield medicine, produced significant increases in the numbers of severely disabled

# Full-time Caregiving Challenges Families

*Families make huge sacrifices to deal with soldiers' catastrophic injuries.*

For the Edmundsons of New Bern, N.C., veteran care is a family mission. On Oct. 2, 2005, Eric Edmundson, then a 25-year-old sergeant in the 172nd Stryker Brigade, took the impact of a roadside bomb, which sent shrapnel shooting into his brain and elsewhere in his body.

After emergency surgeries in Baghdad, the young soldier's heart stopped, depriving his brain of oxygen for a full 30 minutes. "Eric can't walk, talk; he has cognitive memory issues," says his father, Ed, from the family home, which used to house Eric, his wife Stephanie and their daughter, Gracie Rose, 5. Now Ed and his wife Beth live there as well.

"We downsized our lives to be here for Eric and Stephanie," says Ed, 52, who had worked as a warehouse supervisor at ConAgra Foods. "I took my retirement, burned down our debt load, basically got rid of all our possessions. We live in a bedroom in my son's house."

Eric returned to North Carolina after six months of intensive care and training at the Rehabilitation Institute of Chicago. His parents quickly realized that Eric would need full-time care, and that the load was too much for Stephanie to handle alone.[1] "There's a high rate of divorce among the injured," Eric's father says. "We don't want to allow that to happen. Eric has a beautiful family. What my wife and I do is take care of Eric, dealing with rehabilitation and his doctor visits. That allows Eric and Stephanie and Gracie to have as much of a life as possible."

Eric has been able to function more fully than initially expected. He is working as a greeter two days a week in a sporting-goods store. In January he attended the opening of a photo exhibit at the University of North Carolina, Wilmington, of images he took in Iraq before being wounded. He addressed the crowd using a computer voice-generating device.[2] The young family is expecting a second child.

As Eric napped on a recent afternoon, his father spoke by phone, recounting in a matter-of-fact tone the realities of life as a full-time caregiver. For one thing, Edmundson says, "We don't have any retirement or financial future."

Last year, after two bouts of pneumonia, he was able to see a doctor only because of financial help from Wounded Warriors Project, a Jacksonville, Fla.-based nonprofit. Another nonprofit, Homes For Our Troops, built a fully accessible house for the family.[3] "I can't imagine what we would be going through if we didn't have nonprofits," he says.

The Edmundsons' daughter, Anna Frese, has testified in support of legislation to provide financial support and health care to family caregivers, and Edmundson too would welcome some help. "Some small compensation would allow us to get a change of clothes or service our vehicle," he says, "and health care insurance would keep me moving forward." Under the pending legislation, health care would be available only for him or his wife, not both of them.

veterans. But some six years into the fighting, many began to question whether the military and VA were prepared for the consequences of the century's first two wars.

Initially, the focus was on the military. In 2007, *The Washington Post* published a devastating series of articles about conditions for injured service members recovering at Walter Reed Army Medical Center outpatient facilities in Washington, D.C. The exposé led to the firings of Army Secretary Francis Harvey and of the Walter Reed commander, Lt. Gen. George W. Weightman. Lt. Gen. Kevin Kiley, Army surgeon general and a former Walter

Reed commander who initially had minimized *The Post*'s accounts, was also forced to resign.[46]

The Walter Reed scandal focused media and political attention on the treatment of veterans in general. President George W. Bush appointed former Sen. Robert Dole, R-Kan., a disabled World War II vet, and former Health and Human Services Secretary Donna Shalala to co-chair a commission to examine the entire veterans' health care system. The commission recommended simplifying the ratings system and improving care for TBI and PTSD, among other steps.

Meanwhile, the Edmundsons are aware that they may represent only the first wave of families dealing with the after-effects of catastrophic wounds "The war wasn't supposed to last this long," he says. "The system hadn't been tested. But if they're going to take these young men and women and send them to war, they'd better be able to take care of them. They need to ramp up post-trauma care and rehabilitation."

Though the family is relying on Eric's VA benefit payments and on his VA-financed health care, the entire care mission otherwise has been independent of the VA. Edmundson says he's found the agency peopled with dedicated staff but somewhat snarled in its own procedures.

"For the first three years I spent almost 100 percent of my time dealing with VA red tape," Edmundson says. "We did a lot of self-education. We'd get up in the morning, take care of Eric and get on the computer and research and talk to people: Why were you able to do this or that? Why are we not able?"

Dealing with the VA isn't for the passive, Edmundson has concluded. "If you don't plead your case, you fall through the cracks." The Edmundsons located the Chicago Rehabilitation Institute on their own, for instance, and found it superior to the VA hospital where Edmundson had been previously. The VA did, however, finance the cost of the private rehab program.

The deeper issue, Edmundson says he's come to believe, is that the VA — and the government in general — are only now starting to adjust to advances in rehabilitative medicine. "For years, the answer was to institutionalize the soldier," he says. "But the soldiers of today don't want to be taken care of, they want to be rehabilitated, they want to go home."

*— Peter Katel*

U.S. Army Specialist Eric Edmondson (center), who suffered a severe traumatic brain injury in Iraq in 2005, and his father Ed (top) appear at a Nov. 10, 2009, news conference in Washington, D.C., to discuss legislation to provide financial support and health care for family members caring for wounded vets full time. The Edmondsons, who sold their house and moved in with their son and his family in order to care for him, may represent the first wave of families dealing with the after-effects of catastrophic wounds. Senate Majority Whip Dick Durbin (D-Ill.) (left) thanks Edmondson for his sacrifice.

[1] For a detailed account of Eric's stay at the Rehabilitation Institute, see "Eric Edmundson's Patient Story," Rehabilitation Institute of Chicago, undated, www.ric.org/aboutus/stories/EricEdmundson.aspx.

[2] Ashley White, "Photo collection at UNCW illustrates life as a soldier," News14 Carolina, Jan. 10, 2010, http://news14.com/triad-news-94-content/military/620344/photo-collection-at-uncw-illustrates-life-as-a-soldier.

[3] "Severely Wounded Army SGT Eric Edmundson Receives Specially Adapted Home from Homes for Our Troops," *Homes for Our Troops*, Nov. 5, 2007, www.homesforourtroops.org/site/News2?page=NewsArticle&id=5743.

The commission blamed much of the problem on the kind of war U.S. troops were fighting. Enemies in Iraq and Afghanistan were using IEDs as their major weapon. The bombs produce devastating effects without exposing the anti-American guerrillas to battlefield confrontations, in which U.S. forces held the advantage. Deployed as mines, packed into cars and trucks as well as bicycles and motorcycles, the bombs first appeared in Afghanistan in 2002 as radio-controlled roadside devices. But military officials planning the following year's invasion of Iraq didn't foresee the use of IEDs there, despite plentiful supplies of explosives.

By late 2007, IEDs were causing two-thirds of the 3,100 U.S. combat deaths registered through September of that year in Iraq. By then, IEDs had killed or wounded more than 21,000 Americans in Iraq. And by late 2009, the Pentagon calculated that the bombs accounted for up to 80 percent of U.S. and NATO casualties in Afghanistan.[47]

Aside from their appalling efficiency as killing machines, IEDs wrought damages on survivors that would have ended their lives in any previous war. Dramatic advancements in both the protective gear worn by soldiers and in military urgent care made the difference.

"This is the first war in which troops are very unlikely to die if they're still alive when a medic arrives," Dr. Ronald Glasser, who had treated troops wounded in Vietnam in 1968-1970, pointed out in *The Washington Post* in 2007.[48]

At that point, about 1,800 troops had survived brain injuries caused by penetrating wounds. But nearly a third of military personnel involved in heavy combat in Iraq or Afghanistan for at least four months were at risk of brain disorders from IED and mortar blasts. Symptoms of such shock-wave neurological disorders include memory loss, confusion, anxiety and depression, Glasser wrote.[49]

But the IEDs produced other types of injuries as well: As of mid-January, 2009, 1,184 U.S. personnel had suffered amputations, 55 percent of them the result of IED injuries.[50]

## CURRENT SITUATION

### 'Presumptive' Diseases

In veterans' jargon, they're "presumptives" — certain diseases or conditions presumed by the VA to arise from military service in a certain time or place. In addition to having recently added to the list of ailments associated with exposure to Agent Orange in Vietnam, the agency is proposing to add nine new conditions that have developed among veterans of the 1990-91 Gulf War and the Afghan and Iraq conflicts.

Vets suffering from the following diseases or their after-effects would be presumed to have contracted them while serving: brucellosis, campylobacter jejuni, coxiella burnetii (Q fever), malaria, mycobacterium, tuberculosis, nontyphoid salmonella, shigella, visceral leishmaniasis and West Nile virus.

"We recognize the frustrations that many Gulf War and Afghanistan veterans and their families experience on a daily basis as they look for answers to health questions and seek benefits from VA," Shinseki said in announcing the proposed rule.[51]

In addition, the VA is proposing to add a presumption of service connection for Gulf-Iraq-Afghanistan vets suffering from "medically unexplained chronic multisymptom illness." Characteristics include fatigue, pain and inconsistent laboratory reports. That definition would cover Gulf War Syndrome, noted Sullivan of Veterans for

Common Sense. "The proposed new VA rules may finally, after nearly two decades, open the door to a lifetime of free VA medical care for tens of thousands or more sick Gulf War veterans," he told *Military Times*.[52]

On the heels of the VA announcement, the Institute of Medicine issued the latest volume in its long study of Gulf War symptoms, finding that "sufficient evidence of association" exists between deployment to the Persian Gulf operations area and "multisymptom illness." That conclusion falls one step short of establishing a causal relationship between the illness and Gulf War service. "There is some doubt as to the influence of chance, bias and confounding," the report said, using a statistical term for an element of an issue that mistakenly leads to associating exposure with outcome.[53]

Still, given the long and contentious history of Gulf War veterans' attempts to obtain scientific confirmation that they were suffering from something other than random, imagined or exaggerated symptoms, the institute's report marked an important milestone.

"The multisymptom illness that affects so many Gulf War veterans is a terrible, distinct illness," James E. Finn, chairman of a VA-appointed advisory committee on Gulf War illnesses, told *The Washington Post*, "and . . . this nation can and should launch a Manhattan Project-style research program to identify treatments and prevent this from happening again."[54]

Meanwhile, the VA is trying to pinpoint specific causes of Gulf War illness, including exposure to substances including "smoke and particles from military installation burn-pit fires that incinerated a wide range of toxic-waste materials," Bradley Mayes, director of the VBA Compensation and Pension Service, wrote in a February letter to VA medical personnel and claims examiners. *The Military Times*, which has no ties to the Defense Department, had reported on growing suspicions of burn-pit exposure as a cause of disease.[55]

### Legal Benefits

The VA pipeline may be clogged for health and education claims, but vets facing criminal charges are getting a new form of assistance from federal and state court systems around the country.

At least 21 states, cities and counties have set up "veterans' courts." Modeled on "drug courts," which provide a chance at supervised addiction treatment — and

# Should the VA's Veterans Benefits Administration be scrapped and rebuilt?

## YES — Paul Sullivan
*Executive Director,*
*Veterans for Common Sense*

Written for *CQ Researcher*, April 2010

VA's top leaders and auditors have confirmed that benefit claim processing at the Veterans Benefits Administration (VBA) cannot be fixed, as it represents an obsolete and unsustainable model. VBA leaders have no permanent solution for the 60-year-old system, and VBA should eventually be replaced using a careful plan.

This year, VA Secretary Eric Shinseki has a rare window of opportunity to build a new, high-tech, veteran-friendly VBA when he names a new under secretary for benefits. Fixing VBA is vital because an approved disability claim usually opens the door for both disability payments and health care. VBA's current woes include:

- 500,000 veterans now waiting an average of six months for a disability claim decision, plus 200,000 more veterans waiting five more years for an appealed decision.
- 70,000 new pages of paper clog up VBA every day.
- VBA makes an error in nearly one-in-four decisions.
- VBA improperly shredded claims, lost claims and backdated records.
- VBA leaders paid themselves millions in cash bonuses while rank-and-file employees struggled.
- Distraught veterans call VA's suicide prevention hotline out of frustration with endless VBA delays.

We urge the VA to begin a series of public meetings with Congress, veteran advocates and academic experts to pass new laws to design, build and deploy a new VBA with the shortest path possible between the veteran and VA benefits, including health care. Here are practical solutions for a new, high-quality VBA:

- Use a one-page claim form, a single, automated computer system and decide each claim within 30 days.
- Use easy-to-understand rules that presume more medical conditions are linked to military service.
- Use the new, robust lifetime military medical record.
- Move claims staff, currently isolated in a single office in each state, into medical facilities to help veterans set up claim exams as well as quickly and accurately decide claims.
- Allow veterans to hire an attorney before they file a claim, especially veterans with brain injuries or mental health conditions.

When these common sense solutions are adopted, then more of our veterans are welcomed home with the VA benefits and health care they need and earned after defending our freedom. Learn more at: www.FixVA.org.

## NO — James B. King
*National Executive Director, AMVETS;*
*Marine Corps Veteran of Vietnam*

Written for *CQ Researcher*, April 2010

Since 2001, the Department of Veterans Affairs disability claims backlog has grown precipitously because of the ongoing conflicts in Iraq and Afghanistan and the establishment of new presumptive health conditions.

Thankfully, through constructive dialogue with the nation's top veterans' service organizations, the VA has implemented significant changes over the last few months that should help to alleviate strains on the system.

AMVETS is encouraged by the VA's recent steps to streamline the process, making a proposed scrapping of the current Veterans Benefits Administration (VBA) system duplicative and unnecessary. Today, VA has launched pilot programs at regional offices around the country, investigating ways to modernize the claims process, building on opinions and suggestions from leading veterans' groups. These pilot programs include the paperless claims process in Providence, the virtual regional office in Baltimore, team-based workload management in Little Rock and tiered case-management teams in Pittsburgh. AMVETS and other groups have had access to each of these programs, offering opinions and recommendations where necessary, based on decades of experience in the VA claims process. VA also recently implemented eight system-wide solutions to transform the mindset of all involved in the claims process — from the individual veteran to the VA adjudicator.

AMVETS will continue to monitor the progress of these initiatives to help find the best solutions to the daunting backlog. We encourage Congress to do the same before taking hasty legislative action. In AMVETS' opinion, plans to scrap the VBA would only exacerbate current benefits-delivery issues. Today, millions of veterans are entitled to care and compensation through their VBA ratings. By scrapping VBA, VA would need to develop a new corollary to deliver care and benefits to the millions of veterans already enrolled, dating back to World War II.

Plus, would veterans rated under the old system be entitled to reopen their claims? AMVETS believes that they must, which only creates more roadblocks to benefits. Forget the current 400,000-claim backlog — VA would be facing more than 3 million reopened claims and appeals.

AMVETS believes we are on the cusp of developing a modern VA claims process through constructive collaboration among VA and the veterans' groups that have helped our heroes navigate the system for decades. The proposed solutions could finally provide veterans with the timely and accurate claims processing they deserve. Thus, it's critical that the VBA be preserved.

in some cases a clean record — instead of jail time, the veterans' versions are designed to take into account the repercussions of military service, especially combat tours in Iraq and Afghanistan. PTSD, TBI and other after-effects have become widely acknowledged and, in the view of many in the criminal-justice system, deserve to be weighed when a vet is being prosecuted or sentenced.

In Buffalo, N.Y., where Judge Robert T. Russell Jr. pioneered the concept in 2008, the vets' court takes only those accused of nonviolent felonies and misdemeanors. But the Santa Ana, Calif., court is open to those charged with any offense. Judge Wendy Lindley, who established the program, told the *National Law Journal* that California criminal law specifically allows treatment instead of incarceration for a convicted veteran who has served in a combat zone and developed psychological or substance-abuse problems. Veterans' courts are also in session in Anchorage, Chicago, Pittsburgh and Tulsa.[56]

The VA started a program last year to work with veterans' courts, and VA Secretary Shinseki visited the Buffalo court in April to underline his support. "The secretary's purpose was to receive first-hand knowledge about how the program works in order to integrate and develop similar endeavors in other communities," the Erie County Veterans Service Agency said on its Web site.[57]

The VA formed its own Veterans' Justice Outreach Initiative last year. The program is designed in part to provide detailed reports to judges on a vet's medical history and on VA benefits and programs that might help him if he were sentenced to probation instead of jail. Staffers are also trained to work with vets serving jail time.[58]

As support grows, dissenters are making themselves heard. In Nevada, which along with Illinois and New York enacted statewide veterans' courts last year, the general counsel for the American Civil Liberties Union of Nevada argued that they represent a dangerous trend of creating different avenues of justice for certain kinds of people. Veterans' courts amount to establishing special courts for "police officers, teachers or politicians," Allen Lichtenstein told the Stateline.org news service.[59]

He also rejected the analogy to drug courts, which are open to defendants suffering from a condition. But all veterans are eligible for veterans' court, Lichtenstein pointed out.[60]

Nevertheless, federal judges are starting to take veterans' wartime experiences into account in sentencing. In Denver, Senior U.S. District Judge John Kane sentenced a federal prison guard to five years' probation, with mental-health treatment required, because of his Air Force service in Afghanistan and Iraq, where he dealt with seriously injured and dead service members and civilians. John Brownfield Jr. had pleaded guilty to accepting at least $3,000 in bribes for smuggling contraband to inmates.[61]

"It would be a grave injustice," Kane said in a written decision, "to turn a blind eye to the potential effects of multiple deployments to war zones on Brownfield's subsequent behavior."[62]

Sentencing guidelines aside, Kane's move seemed consistent with a U.S. Supreme Court decision in November, 2009, to throw out a death sentence for a Korean War veteran convicted of murdering his ex-girlfriend and her boyfriend. Ordering a new sentencing hearing, the justices cited "the intense stress and emotional toll that combat took" on George Porter Jr.[63]

## Aiding Caregivers

Legislation is pending in Congress to channel aid to families and others who have become full time caregivers for catastrophically disabled Iraq and Afghanistan veterans.

In a unanimous vote in November, the Senate passed the Caregivers and Veterans Omnibus Health Services Act, sponsored by Senate Veterans Chairman Daniel Akaka, D-Hawaii. House action was held up while Akaka's staff negotiated changes with his counterparts. The resulting compromise is ready for action, which is expected some time in April or May.

The legislation represents the first comprehensive attempt to assist those suddenly thrust into the 24-hour-a-day caregiver role. Approximately $3.7 billion would be spent on stipends — amount unspecified — for caregivers, on temporary alternative care ("respite care") arrangements to give caregivers a breather, on training caregivers and on other forms of support, including expense reimbursement to accompany disabled vets to distant hospitals.[64]

Only those caring for veterans from Operation Enduring Freedom (OEF) — the Afghanistan war — and Operation Iraqi Freedom (OIF) would be covered by the bill. Yet, as veterans of other wars age, issues of round-the-clock care for them are beginning to weigh on families. "Veterans' service organizations would like to see the legislation open to all," says Barbara Cohoon, deputy director of government relations for the National Military Families Association. "But we recognize that OIF and OEF caregivers are experiencing the biggest hardship right now and that resources are limited. But this needs to be done for all at some point."

## OUTLOOK

### National Priority?

Researchers have been trying for the past several years to forecast the medium-term effects of the Iraq and Afghanistan wars on veterans and, by extension, on the government agency that deals with them most closely.

Trend lines are exceptionally difficult to forecast, in part because fighting is still under way and may be for some time. Meanwhile, the VA "does not have the personnel, the funding, or the mandate from Congress to produce broad forecasts of service needs," the Institute of Medicine concluded in its recent report.[65]

The after-effects of past wars are of only limited usefulness, the institute noted, because so many more severely wounded service members are surviving combat now. The entire picture of the wounded veteran population has changed. "These survivors of very severe injuries need more intensive care than the most severely wounded service members from prior wars," the report said. "Extrapolating from past conflicts might result in an underestimation of the overall burden of need for persons impacted by OEF and OIF."[66]

What is clear, the institute reported, is that the needs of these veterans will be extensive. "The burden borne by wounded service members and their families, and thus the public responsibility to treat or compensate them, is large and probably will persist for the rest of their lives."[67]

Moreover, "peak demand for compensation" is likely to increase as veterans age, the institute said. "So the maximum stress on support systems for OEF and OIF veterans and their families might not be felt until 2040 or later."[68]

In the veterans' community, some express confidence in the VA's ability to keep up with an already growing demand for its services. "It has the potential to be as great as it needs to be," says Autry of Disabled American Veterans. "There are an awful lot of very dedicated people in the VA."

Their dedication is already being tested, and is certain to be tested even further, by the high incidence of PTSD,

TBI and depression among Afghanistan and Iraq vets. "The prevalence of those injuries is relatively high and may grow as the conflicts continue," RAND has reported. Yet, both the Defense Department and the VA "have had difficulty in recruiting and retaining appropriately trained mental health professionals to fill existing or new slots."[69]

The RAND report urges that dealing with the trio of conditions be elevated to a "national priority." But even some relatively optimistic veterans say raising public concern to that level requires some heavy lifting. "We're less than 1 percent of the population," says Kennedy, the retired Army captain.

For his own part, Kennedy is still "pretty sure" the VA will be "a lot better than it is" now, but he's not sure how it will have improved.

Sullivan of Veterans for Common Sense is a bit more skeptical. The VA is still trying to protect its reputation, he says, similar to shipping company officials who "were saying everything was fine while the *Titanic* was sinking."

But the potential exists to transform VA's benefits service into a smooth-running operation in which veterans have confidence. "A tremendous amount of effort must be invested in this moment of opportunity," Sullivan says. "We have a new administration, a Congress eager to help, veterans' groups who want to help and public understanding of an urgent need. We have a golden moment of opportunity now."

Sullivan's outlook is considerably sunnier than that of Lamie, the IED attack survivor. In 10 years, he says, "I think the situation will be worse. In 10 years, everybody is going to forget all about the Iraq war. If there's a war in 2020, those guys will probably be treated great. But if there's nobody dying on the TV screen nobody will care."

An outsider might say that Lamie's combat scars are still raw; his brother Gene, an Army sergeant, died in an IED attack in Iraq in 2007.[70] But dismissing his bleak outlook could be a mistake. The searing experiences that inform his forecast are shared by a growing number of young veterans.

## NOTES

1. "Radical Change Needed for Veterans Disability Claims Process," House Committee on Veterans Affairs, press statement, March 18, 2010, http://veterans.house.gov/news/PRArticle.aspx?NewsID=559.

2. "Statement of Belinda J. Finn, Assistant Inspector General for Audits and Evaluations, Office of Inspector General, Department of Veterans Affairs," VA Office of Inspector General, March 24, 2010, www4.va.gov/OIG/pubs/VAOIG-statement-2010 0324-Finn.pdf.

3. Icasualties.org, updated regularly, http://icasualties .org/OEF/Index.aspx.

4. "Remarks by Secretary Eric K. Shinseki," Veterans of Foreign Wars National Legislative Conference, March 8, 2010, www1.va.gov/opa/speeches/2010 /10_0308.asp; "Fiscal 2011 Budget: VA," Committee Testimony, Senate Veterans' Affairs Committee, Feb. 26, 2010; "FY 2011 Budget Submission," Department of Veterans Affairs, pp. 2B-4, 2C-2, www4.va.gov/budget/docs/sum mary/Fy2011_Volume_1-Summary_Volume.pdf.

5. Quoted in Rick Maze, "VA official: Disability claims system 'cannot be fixed,' " *Federal Times*, March 18, 2010, www.federaltimes.com/article/20100318/ DEPARTMENTS04/3180302/1055/AGENCY.

6. Quoted in Philip Rucker, "Obama Picks Shinseki to Lead Veterans Affairs," *The Washington Post*, Dec. 7, 2008, www.washingtonpost.com/wp-dyn/content/ article/2008/12/07/AR2008120701487.html; Bernard Weinraub and Thom Shanker, "Rumsfeld's Design for War Criticized on the Battlefield," *The New York Times*, April 1, 2003, p. A1; Amy Belaso, "Troop Levels in the Afghan and Iraq Wars," Congressional Research Service, July 2, 2009, Summary page, www.fas.org/sgp/crs/natsec/ R40682.pdf; "US Forces Order of Battle," Global Security.org, undated, www.globalsecurity.org/mili tary/ops/iraq_orbat.htm.

7. "Returning Home from Iraq and Afghanistan: Preliminary Assessment of Readjustment Needs of Veterans, Service Members, and Their Families," Institute of Medicine of the National Academies (2010), p. 52, http://books.nap.edu/openbook .php?record_id=12812&page=R1.

8. Terri Tanielian and Lisa H. Jaycox, eds., "Invisible Wounds of War: Psychological and Cognitive Injuries, Their Consequences, and Services to Assist Recovery," RAND Center for Military Health Policy Research, 2008, p. xxi, www.rand.org/pubs/mono

graphs/MG720; U.S. Army Surgeon General study cited in Kline, Anna, *et al.*, "Effects of Repeated Deployment to Iraq and Afghanistan on the Health of New Jersey Army National Guard Troops: Implications for Military Readiness," *American Journal of Public Health*, February 2010, http://ajph .aphapublications.org/cgi/content/abstract/100 /2/276.

9. The three are Parkinson's Disease, ischemic heart disease and B-cell leukemias. "FY 2011 Budget Submission," *op. cit.*, p. 1A-3; Gregg Zoroya, "VA to automate its Agent Orange claims process," *USA Today*, March 9, 2010, p. 4A.

10. *Hawkins v. Shinseki*, U.S. Court of Appeals for the Federal Circuit, 2009-7068, Dec. 7, 2009, www .cafc.uscourts.gov/opinions/09-7068.pdf.

11. *Ibid.*

12. "VA Appellate Processes," Committee Testimony, House Veterans' Affairs Committee, Subcommittee on Disability Assistance and Memorial Affairs, May 24, 2009.

13. "Legislative Presentations of Veterans' Organizations," House Veterans' Affairs Committee, Senate Veterans' Affairs Committee, March 9, 2010. For VA backlog figure, see "2010 Monday Morning Workload Reports," Department of Veterans Affairs, March 29, 2010, www.vba.va.gov/REPORTS/ mmwr/index.asp.

14. Finn, *op. cit.*

15. "Iraq Index: Tracking Variables of Reconstruction and Security in Post-Saddam Iraq," Brookings Institution, updated March 30, 2010, p. 19, www .brookings.edu/~/media/Files/Centers/Saban/Iraq Index/index.pdf.

16. "The House Veterans' Affairs Subcommittee on Oversight and Investigations," *op. cit.*

17. *Ibid.*

18. "Returning Home from Iraq and Afghanistan . . . ," *op. cit.*, pp. 29, 69.

19. *Ibid.*, p. 69.

20. *Ibid.*, p. 32.

21. "Needs of Family Caregivers," House Veterans' Affairs Committee, June 4, 2009.

22. *Ibid.*

23. "FY 2011 Budget Submission," Department of Veterans Affairs, p. 3A-7, www4.va.gov/budget/docs/summary/Fy2011_Volume_1-Summary_Volume.pdf.

24. Kimberly Hefling, "Increase in suicide rate of veterans noted," The Associated Press (*Army Times*), Jan. 12, 2010, www.armytimes.com/news/2010/01/ap_vet_suicide_011110.

25. "Veterans Suicide Prevention," Senate Veterans' Affairs Committee, March 3, 2010.

26. *Ibid.*

27. *Ibid.*

28. "Veterans Suicide Prevention," Senate Veterans' Affairs Committee, March 3, 2010, (Web video), http://veterans.senate.gov/hearings.cfm?action=release.display&release_id=d1a8548c-de2c-49a8-b7f9-d0855265d435.

29. *Ibid.*

30. Walter F. Roche Jr., and James Gerstenzang, "Doctor picked to head VA," *Los Angeles Times*, Oct. 31, 2007, p. A11.

31. "FY 2011 Budget Submission," *op. cit.*, p. 1A-1; Jackie Calmes, "In $3.8 Trillion Budget, Obama Pivots to Trim Future Deficits," *The New York Times*, Feb. 1, 2010, www.nytimes.com/2010/02/02/us/politics/02budget.html?pagewanted=all.

32. James Dao, "Late Benefit Checks Causing Problems for Veterans Attending College On New G.I. Bill," *The New York Times*, Sept. 25, 2009, p. A16.

33. "House Veterans' Affairs Committee Holds Hearing on the State of the Department of Veterans Affairs," CQ Congressional Transcripts, Oct. 14, 2009.

34. Except where otherwise indicated, this subsection is drawn from "VA History in Brief," Department of Veterans Affairs, undated, www1.va.gov/opa/publications/archives/docs/history_in_brief.pdf. For number serving in the World War II military, male and female, "Facts for Features," U.S. Census Bureau, April 29, 2004, www.census.gov/Press-Release/www/2004/cb04-ffse07.pdf.

35. For background, see P. Webbink, "Veteran-aid Policies of the United States," *Editorial Research Reports*, Vol. IV, Oct. 6, 1930; and B. W. Patch,

"The Bonus and Veterans' Pensions," *Editorial Research Reports*, Vol. I, Jan. 10, 1936, both available at *CQ Researcher Plus Archive*, www.library.cqpress.com.

36. For background, see R. McNickle, "Service Pensions for War Veterans," *Editorial Research Reports*, May 4, 1949, available at *CQ Researcher Plus Archive*, www.library.cqpress.com.

37. Suzanne Metler, "Why Skimp on GI Bill?" Military.com, Nov. 18, 2005, www.military.com/opinion/0,15202,80830,00.html. The book is Suzanne Metler, *Soldiers and Citizens: The GI Bill and the Making of the Greatest Generation* (2005).

38. Except where otherwise indicated, this subsection is drawn from Gerald Nicosia, *Home to War: A History of the Vietnam Veterans Movement* (2001), and "VA History in Brief," *op. cit.*

39. Neil Sheehan, *A Bright Shining Lie: John Paul Vann and America in Vietnam* (1988), p. 39; "Vietnam War," GlobalSecurity.org, undated, www.globalsecurity.org/military/ops/vietnam.htm; "America's Wars," Department of Veterans Affairs, updated November, 2009, www1.va.gov/opa/publications/factsheets/fs_americas_wars.pdf.

40. "VVAW: Where We Came From, Who We Are," Vietnam Veterans Against the War, undated, www.vvaw.org/about/; Jason Zengerle, "The Vet Wars," *The New York Times Magazine*, May 23, 2004, p. 30.

41. "Born on the Fourth of July," Internet Movie Database, www.imdb.com/title/tt0096969/.

42. Except as otherwise indicated, material in this section is drawn from "VA History in Brief," *op. cit.* For background, see Peter Katel, "Wounded Veterans," *CQ Researcher*, Aug. 31, 2007, pp. 697-720.

43. "Independent Review Could Improve Credibility of Radiation Exposure Estimates," GAO, January, 2000, p. 2, www.gao.gov/archive/2000/he00032.pdf; "Rules for Veterans' Radiation Benefits Voided," The Associated Press (*The New York Times*), Oct. 8, 1981, www.nytimes.com/1981/10/08/us/rules-for-veterans-radiation-benefits-voided.html.

44. "House Votes Bill Giving Benefits to Veterans Exposed to Radiation," The Associated Press (*The New York Times*), May 3, 1988, p. A26; "Independent

Review . . . ," *op. cit.*, p. 6; "Statement on Signing the Radiation-Exposed Veterans Compensation Act of 1988," Ronald Reagan, May 20, 1988 the American Presidency Project, www.presidency.ucsb.edu/ws/index.php?pid=35855.

45. David Zucchino, "Veterans speak out against burn pits," *Los Angeles Times*, Feb. 18, 2010, http://articles.latimes.com/2010/feb/18/nation/la-na-burn-pits18-2010feb18.

46. Thom Shanker and David Stout, "Chief Army Medical Officer Ousted in Walter Reed Furor," *The New York Times*, March 13, 2007, p. A5.

47. Rick Atkinson, " 'The single most effective weapon against our deployed forces,' " *The Washington Post*, Sept. 30, 2008, p. A1; Ann Scott Tyson, "U.S. combat injuries rise sharply," *The Washington Post*, Oct. 31, 2009, p. A1.

48. Ronald Glasser, "A Shock Wave of Brain Injuries," *The Washington Post*, April 8, 2007, Outlook, p. B1.

49. *Ibid.*

50. "Returning Home from Iraq and Afghanistan . . . ," *op. cit.*

51. Quoted in "VA recognizes 'presumptive' illnesses in Iraq, Afghanistan," Veterans Administration, March 24, 2010, www.army.mil/-news/2010/03/24/36272-va-recognizes-presumptive-illnesses-in-iraq-afghanistan.

52. Quoted in Kelly Kennedy, "VA may designate 9 infectious diseases as service-connected," *Military Times*, April 5, 2010, p. A12; "Proposed Rule," Department of Veterans Affairs, *Federal Register*, Vol. 75, No. 52, March 18, 2010, www1.va.gov/ORPM/docs/20100318_AN24_PresumptionsPersianGulf Service.pdf.

53. "Gulf War and Health, Vol. 8: Update of Health Effects of Serving in the Gulf War," Institute of Medicine, April 9, 2010, pp. 5-7, 25, www.iom.edu/Reports/2010/Gulf-War-and-Health-Volume-8-Health-Effects-of-Serving-in-the-Gulf-War.aspx.

54. David Brown, "Up to 250,000 Gulf War veterans have 'unexplained medical symptoms,' " *The Washington Post*, April 10, 2010, www.washington-post.com/wp-dyn/content/article/2010/04/09/AR2010040904712.html.

55. Quoted in Kennedy, *op. cit.*

56. Lynne Marek, "Courts for veterans spreading across U.S.," *National Law Journal*, Dec. 22, 2008, www.law.com/jsp/nlj/PubArticlePrinterFriendlyNLJ.jsp?id=1202426915992&hbxlogin=1; Carolyn Thompson, "Special court for veterans addresses more than crime," The Associated Press (*Boston Globe*), July 7, 2008, www.boston.com/news/nation/articles/2008/07/07/special_court_for_veterans_addresses_more_than_crime; John Gramlich, "New courts tailored to war veterans," Stateline.org, June, 18, 2009, www.stateline.org/live/details/story?contentId=407573.

57. Sergio R. Rodriguez, "VA Secretary Eric K. Shinseki visits the Buffalo Veterans Treatment Court," Veterans Service Agency, April 6, 2010, www.erie.gov/veterans/veterans_court.asp.

58. P. Solomon Banda, "Troubled Veterans Get a Hand," The Associated Press (*The Washington Post*), Aug. 7, 2009, p. A19.

59. Quoted in John Gramlich, *op. cit.*

60. *Ibid.*

61. Robert Boczkiewicz, "Veteran of Afghanistan, Iraq gets probation," *Pueblo Chieftain*, Dec. 19, 2009, www.chieftain.com/news/local/article_d2d823fb-19ee-5eb4-ac54-dca372dd75d4.html.

62. Quoted in *ibid.*

63. Quoted in John Schwartz, "Defendants Fresh From War Find Service Counts in Court," *The New York Times*, March 16, 2010, p. A14.

64. Leah Nylen and Jennifer Scholtes, "Senate Passes Vets' Package Despite Coburn's Concerns," *CQ Today*, Nov. 19, 2009; "S 1963 CRS Bill Digest Summary," March 10, 2010.

65. "Returning Home from Iraq and Afghanistan," *op. cit.*, p. 98.

66. *Ibid.*, p. 97.

67. *Ibid.*, p. 98.

68. *Ibid.*

69. "Invisible Wounds of War," *op. cit.*, pp. 452, 446.

70. "Sgt. Gene L. Lamie, United States Army, KIA 06 July 2007," www.ourfallensoldier.com/LamieGeneL_MemorialPage.html.

# BIBLIOGRAPHY

## Selected Sources

## Books

Glantz, Aaron, *The War Comes Home: Washington's Battle Against America's Veterans*, University of California Press, 2009.
A journalist who covered the Iraq war reports critically on the state of VA services.

Nicosia, Gerald, *Home to War: A History of the Vietnam Veterans' Movement*, Crown, 2001.
The influence of the groundbreaking movement still resonates today, having helped to get post-traumatic stress disorder classified as a disability caused by military service.

Schram, Martin, *Vets Under Siege*, St. Martin's Press, 2008.
A veteran Washington reporter examines the VA's efforts to meet the demands placed on it by the Iraq and Afghanistan wars.

## Articles

Cave, Damien, "A Combat Role, and Anguish, Too," *The New York Times*, Nov. 1, 2009, p. A1.
Women vets suffering from PTSD are more isolated than their male counterparts, because they are fewer in number and are expected to immediately jump back into household duties.

Chong, Jia-Rui, "Veterans' long-term ills linked to brain injuries," *Los Angeles Times*, Dec. 5, 2008, p. A25.
The first comprehensive report links TBI to long-term conditions including seizures and aggression.

Cullison, Alan, "On Battlefields, Survival Odds Rise," *The Wall Street Journal*, April 3, 2010, online.wsj.com/article/SB20001424052748704655004575114623837930294.html.
A journalist experienced in covering warfare in Afghanistan provides a close-in look at advances in battlefield medicine.

Dao, James, and Thom Shanker, "No Longer a Soldier, Shinseki Has a New Mission," *The New York Times*, Nov. 11, 2009, p. A21.
The VA's new boss as profiled by correspondents on the Pentagon and veterans' affairs beats.

Hefling, Kimberly, "The veterans hall is growing — online," *The Associated Press*, Dec. 7, 2008, p. A15.
The newest veterans are taking their postwar bonding to the Internet.

Kennedy, Kelly, "DoD concedes rise in burn-pit ailments," *Military Times*, Feb. 8, 2010, p. 10.
The Defense Department admits there are possible connections between waste-burning emissions and health problems.

Marcus, Mary Brophy, "Military families cry for help," *USA Today*, Jan. 27, 2010, p. 8B.
Families taking care of catastrophically wounded veterans struggle financially and emotionally, a medical correspondent reports.

Ungar, Laura, "Suicide takes growing toll among military, veterans," *The Courier-Journal* (Ky.), Sept. 13, 2009.
The health-affairs specialist for a newspaper situated near a big military base (Fort Knox) covers the rising tide of suicide.

Whitlock, Craig, "IED attacks soaring in Afghanistan," *The Washington Post*, March 18, 2010, p. A10.
A war correspondent for *The Post* charts the Taliban's growing use of the explosive devices.

Zoroya, Gregg, "Repeated deployments weigh heavily on troops," *USA Today*, Jan. 13, 2010, p. A1.
As repeat deployments continue, the newspaper's veterans-beat reporter covers the toll on service members.

## Reports and Studies

"Gulf War and Health: Vol. 8: Update of Health Effects of Serving in the Gulf War," *Institute of Medicine*, 2009, www.nap.edu/catalog/12835.html.
The federally funded institute is finding evidence of a link between service in the Gulf and multisymptom illness.

"Returning Home from Iraq and Afghanistan: Preliminary Assessment of Readjustment Needs of Veterans, Service Members, and Their Families,"

**Institute of Medicine, 2010, www.nap.edu/cata log/12812.html.**
A massive examination and analysis of research data that attempts to portray the effects of the present wars on service members and society at large.

**"Veterans' Disability Benefits: Further Evaluation of Ongoing Initiatives Could Help Identify Effective Approaches for Improving Claims Processing," Government Accountability Office, January 2010, www.gao.gov/new.items/d10213.pdf.**

In the most recent of its reports on the VA claims system, Congress' investigative arm concludes that the backlog problem remains serious.

**Mulhall, Erin, and Vanessa Williamson, "Red Tape: Veterans Fight New Battles for Care and Benefits," Iraq and Afghanistan Veterans of America, February 2010, media.iava.org/reports/redtape_2010.pdf.**
The advocacy organization reports on delays and complicated procedures that still characterize the VA's disability claims system.

# For More Information

**Amvets**, 4647 Forbes Blvd., Lanham, MD 20706; (301) 459-9600; www.amvets.org. Originally formed for World War II vets; specializes in public policy and legislative work and aids vets with claims to the U.S. Department of Veterans' Affairs (VA).

**Disabled American Veterans**, P.O. Box 14301, Cincinnati, OH 45250; (859) 441-7300; www.dav.org. Specializes in VA claims work and other services for severely wounded vets.

**Lawyers Serving Warriors**, P.O. Box 65762, Washington, DC 20035; (202) 265-8305; www.lawyersservingwarriors .com. Provides free lawyers to veterans in disability and other cases, but is not accepting new clients; Web site remains a valuable source of information.

**U.S. Department of Veterans Affairs**, 810 Vermont Ave., N.W., Washington, DC 20420; (800) 827-1000; www.va .gov. Maintains a Web site that is a rich source of information on benefits and policy.

**Veterans for Common Sense**, 900 2nd St., S.E., Suite 216, Washington, DC 20003; (202) 558-4553; www.veterans forcommonsense.org. Advocacy organization focuses on VA reform.

**Wounded Warriors Project**, 7020 AC Skinner Pkwy., Suite 100, Jacksonville, FL 32256; (877) 832-6997; www.wound edwarriorproject.org. Provides aid to severely disabled veterans and their families.

# 10

# Government Spending

Marcia Clemmitt

Construction crews demolish part of a bridge during a $1 billion freeway improvement project in Los Angeles on Sept. 29, 2012. Cuts in federal grants to the states affect numerous programs that are integral to citizens' everyday lives, including repairs and improvements to highways and other infrastructure.

From *CQ Researcher*,
July 12, 2013.

I f only federal budget-making were as straightforward as budgeting now is in Ward Five on Chicago's South Side. On May 4, in a middle school classroom, dozens of residents scrutinized descriptions and cost estimates for 13 proposed government spending projects for their neighborhood, ranging from a community vegetable garden to $400,000 for new street lights.

"I've been around here forever, and we've never been allowed to vote on how the money is spent," said Candace White, who had just voted for her six favorite projects, which included the community garden.[1]

The Fifth Ward's new "participatory budgeting" program is a utopian vision of democratic budgeting — citizen deliberations directly determining how tax dollars are spent. Nevertheless, the Chicago experiment, which now operates in four city wards, mimics how public budgets traditionally are created.[2]

Budgets "reflect the general public consensus about what kinds of services governments should provide," wrote Irene S. Rubin, a professor emeritus of public administration at Northern Illinois University, in DeKalb. Budgets also set priorities — choosing between police and flood control, day care and defense, by mediating among groups and individuals who want different things from government, she explained.[3]

But when it comes to the federal budget, the number of groups and individuals who want a say is seemingly endless. The government's priority-setting process consists of often lengthy annual negotiations led by the White House Office of Management and Budget, House and Senate appropriations committees and congressional

## Spending on Defense, Social Services Mushroomed

Federal spending on national defense has risen more than 700 percent from its World War II-era peak after adjusting for inflation, reaching an estimated $716 billion in 2012. Spending on Medicare, Social Security and other social services reached an estimated $2.5 trillion in 2012. It is projected to rise sharply as the baby boom generation ages, reaching a projected $3.1 trillion by 2017. Interest on federal loans to U.S. and foreign investors, such as the Chinese government, totaled about $225 billion in 2012. Total federal outlays — less than $10 billion in 1940 — amounted to an estimated $3.8 trillion in 2012.

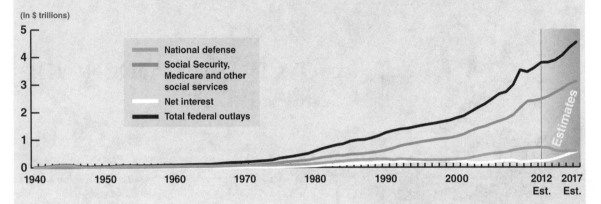

*Source:* "Outlays by Superfunction and Function: 1940-2017," Table 3.1, "Budget of the U.S. Government, Fiscal Year 2013," White House Office of Management and Budget, www.whitehouse.gov/sites/default/files/omb/budget/fy2013/assets/hist.pdf

panels that set spending rules for programs such as Social Security and Medicare. This year, however, annual deliberations have ground to a halt, stymied by the bitter, long-running division between Republicans and Democrats and the GOP insistence that spending cuts to decrease the national debt must be the government's top fiscal priority.

In hopes that a deadline would spur lawmakers to compromise on taxes and spending, Congress mandated in the 2011 Budget Control Act that dozens of federal agencies, including the Pentagon, be hit with across-the-board spending cuts this year if Congress had not reached agreement on a major tax and spending plan. When no such progress was made, the federal government in March was ordered to trim $85.4 billion from federal spending during fiscal year 2013. Similar cuts must be made each year through fiscal 2021, unless Congress decides to stop them.[4]

The hope was that across-the-board cuts — called "sequestration" and inevitably striking programs important to each party — would be so painful they would force Congress to work out a deal. But while lawmakers

did exempt the Federal Aviation Administration's air traffic control division and a few other programs from cuts, no substantive discussion of how federal dollars should be spent has occurred.

Worse, sequestration "didn't force action on the big stuff. It's just squeezing the part of the budget that's already small," says Alan Viard, a resident scholar at the free-market-oriented American Enterprise Institute (AEI), referring to the 30 percent of the budget called discretionary spending — the portion that Congress can change without amending major laws. Discretionary programs range from Head Start and hurricane forecasting to biomedical research, firefighting and foreign aid.[5]

Washington's inability to overcome its ideological divide to deliberate on national priorities shocks the international community, says Allen Schick, a distinguished university professor at the University of Maryland's School of Public Policy in College Park. "Countries used to say, 'What can we learn from the United States?' but now they say, 'Why can't the Americans get their act together?'"

Achieving budget compromise is daunting, but it can be done by those armed with good information and a willingness to consider different points of view, says Mattea Kramer, research director for the National Priorities Project (NPP), a Northampton, Mass., group that educates citizens about the impact of government programs and the tradeoffs public budgeting requires. "Once folks have good, solid information like lawmakers do, they can make very good decisions," she says.

Among Washington's most contentious spending programs are so-called entitlements — programs such as Medicaid and Social Security that promise a set level of benefits to anyone who meets enrollment criteria.

Open-ended benefit programs "funded by other people's money" foster a " 'something for nothing' mentality" that's weakening America,

## United States Leads in Military Spending

The United States accounted for nearly 40 percent of worldwide military spending in 2012, four times as much as China, the next biggest spender. However, Saudi Arabia spent a far greater percentage of its gross domestic product (GDP) on military needs than any other country, including the United States.

### Countries with the Highest Military Spending, 2012

| Country | % of total world military spending | % of national GDP | Military spending per capita |
|---|---|---|---|
| United States | 39.0% | 4.7% | $2,261 |
| China | 9.5% | 2.0% | $109 |
| Russia | 5.2% | 3.9% | $507 |
| United Kingdom | 3.5% | 2.6% | $1,013 |
| Japan | 3.4% | 1.0% | $459 |
| France | 3.4% | 2.2% | $932 |
| Saudi Arabia | 3.2% | 8.4% | $1,725 |
| India | 2.6% | 2.5% | $37 |
| Germany | 2.6% | 1.3% | $572 |

*Sources:* SIPRI (Stockholm International Peace Research Institute) www.sipri.org/research/armaments/milex/milex-graphs-for-data-launch-2013/States-with-the-highest-military-expenditure-in-2012.png; World Bank

contends Nicholas Eberstadt, lead scholar on political economy at AEI. For example, he says, entitlement programs for disabled people have precipitated a "flight from work" to government disability assistance. Disability payouts have swollen because "it is impossible for a health professional to ascertain conclusively whether . . . a patient is suffering from back pains or sad feelings" or is merely malingering, he says.[6]

But other analysts say unemployment and low wages in a tough economy are what cause most people to join the entitlement rolls.

"While corporate profits break records, the share of national income going to workers' wages has reached record lows," making more people income-eligible for assistance, argues a report by the Democratic staff of the House Committee on Education and the Workforce. Wisconsin Medicaid records, for example, show that just one 300-worker Walmart Supercenter may cost federal and state taxpayers more than $900,000 per year in Medicaid coverage of its low-income workers.[7]

Another hotly debated item is military spending, which eats up 60 percent of discretionary spending. "My greatest fear is that in economic tough times . . . people will see the defense budget as the place to solve the

nation's deficit problems, to find money for other parts of the government," said Robert Gates, former secretary of defense under Presidents Obama and George W. Bush. "As I look around . . . and see a more unstable world . . . my greatest worry is that we will . . . slash" the military budget.[8]

But other analysts say weapons systems' cost overruns, military health care spending that's risen faster than anywhere else in the economy, and an ever-lengthening list of U.S. foreign-policy and security projects indicate that some Pentagon spending is ripe for cutting. Indeed, they say, lawmakers are demanding that some weapons systems be included in the budget that the Pentagon says it doesn't need.[9]

"In 2010, the United States spent more on its armed forces than the next 14 nations combined," said Cindy Williams, a principal research scientist for security studies at the Massachusetts Institute of Technology (MIT). That being the case, "a more constrained [Pentagon] mission is arguably in order." For the past few decades, she noted, the United States has repeatedly expanded its slate of military goals to include "deposing dictators and building market economies," while giving "virtually no thought to cost."[10]

As policymakers and the public mull how government should spend taxpayers' dollars and how to improve the processes by which spending decisions are made, here are some questions that are being asked:

## Is too much being spent on mandatory programs?

Mandatory spending programs are some of the government's most hotly debated programs. They include some very large, well-known social insurance programs such as Social Security along with others such as farm subsidies and the Supplemental Nutrition Assistance Program (SNAP), formerly called food stamps.

Dubbed entitlements because anyone who applies and matches a legislated list of criteria may automatically receive benefits, mandatory spending programs currently amount to 64 percent of total government spending.[11]

Critics argue that all mandatory programs are potential budget busters. That's because, at least in the short run, the programs' costs can grow without limit, since qualified applicants must receive all benefits specified by law each year, regardless of how much those benefits cost. Unlike so-called discretionary spending programs — for which Congress specifies in law each year exactly how much each program may spend — Congress can limit costs for mandatory programs only for future years, by either enacting stricter eligibility criteria or trimming the benefits that future participants will receive.

Supporters of entitlements, though, argue that their hard-to-predict annual costs are necessary because the programs' aid is intended to be available to people in times of need.

This year, two high-profile battles over mandatory spending erupted as Congress struggled to write new legislation governing the Department of Agriculture, which administers both SNAP and farm subsidies.[12]

In May, the Republican-dominated House Committee on Agriculture approved eligibility limits and other cuts that would have removed 1.8 million people from SNAP and cut spending on the program by nearly $21 billion over a decade.[13] (Since the recession that began in 2007, about 15 percent of Americans — more than 45 million — have been receiving SNAP benefits.)[14] When the measure came before the full House on June 19, however, 62 Republicans joined most Democrats to reject it on a 234-195 vote.[15]

The "argument we're having today is, what's the duty of the federal government" when it comes to assisting the poor, said Rep. Stephen Fincher, R-Tenn., an agriculture panel member who voted for the measure. Offering assistance through programs such as SNAP means spending "other people's money," a responsibility Congress must take seriously, Fincher said. The Bible teaches that one should care for the poor but also that "if anyone is not willing to work, then he is not to eat, either," he observed.[16]

SNAP spending soared from $30 billion to $72 billion between 2007 and 2011, according to the nonpartisan Congressional Budget Office (CBO).[17] Eligible nonelderly, nondisabled SNAP recipients must have assets of $2,000 or less, not counting a home, and a gross monthly income equal to or lower than 130 percent of the federal poverty level, which is $2,069 for a family of three.[18] In fiscal 2010, the average SNAP household with children had a gross monthly income of $923 and received a monthly benefit of $419.[19]

The House panel bill would have ended the practice of granting SNAP benefits automatically to people enrolled in other means-tested programs, such as home-energy assistance, on the grounds that this makes it easy for otherwise unqualified applicants to enroll.[20] "If you qualify, we will help you, but no more automatic food stamps," said committee chairman Rep. Frank Lucas, R-Okla.[21]

But other analysts argue that low-income entitlements have grown mainly because of a poor economy, not because of cheating. Recession-triggered income loss pushed more people onto SNAP rolls beginning in 2007, accounting for 65 percent of the 2007 to 2011 spending growth, said the CBO.[22]

Food stamps played an "especially useful" role during the recession, argues Princeton University economics professor and *New York Times* columnist Paul Krugman. In the national economy, "your spending is my income, my spending is your income," he contends, so precipitous cuts to anyone's spending power lessen other peoples' incomes, further shrinking the economy. SNAP benefits helped families "spend more on other necessities," thus propping up the economy, argued Krugman, who won the Nobel Prize in economics in 2008.[23]

"While I think it's ridiculous to cut hundreds of billions of dollars, as some members have called for, it's also just not realistic to refuse to cut one penny" from nutrition-assistance programs, said Rep. Collin Peterson, D-Wis., ranking minority member of the agriculture panel. "I do believe that we can make some reasonable, responsible reforms and . . . find some middle ground."[24]

Mandatory spending on farm-subsidy programs, meanwhile, attracts criticism because much of the cash goes to very large farms.

Many farmers purchase so-called crop insurance to keep their incomes steady. It entitles them to be reimbursed if their crops produce smaller harvests or lower prices than projected, and the federal government subsidizes the cost of the premiums. However, a whopping portion of the subsidy helps industrial-size farms, according to an analysis by Congress' nonpartisan auditing arm, the Government Accountability Office (GAO). In 2011, capping the subsidy at $40,000 per owner would have saved taxpayers $1 billion yet affected only 3.9 percent of farmers in the program, such as one that received $1.3 million in subsidies to insure crops in eight counties, GAO said.[25]

"This level of corporate welfare should be unacceptable even if we had surpluses as far as the eye could see," said Ryan Alexander, president of the budget watchdog group Taxpayers for Common Sense.[26]

Some lawmakers who back SNAP cuts draw sharp criticism for supporting and receiving farm subsidies. Tennessee Rep. Fincher's arguments for SNAP cuts are "hypocritical with a capital H," said Donald Carr, senior policy and communications adviser to the advocacy organization Environmental Working Group, because Fincher has received nearly $3.5 million in farm subsidies since 1999, mostly for cotton.[27]

But there's nothing hypocritical about receiving the subsidies, said committee chairman Lucas. "Members of Congress are allowed to . . . have farming operations and participate in the programs," he said. "They're abiding by the law."[28]

## Is too much being spent on Social Security and Medicare?

The cost of mandatory spending programs is projected to consume 64 percent of the federal budget in fiscal 2014, compared to 30 percent for so-called discretionary programs — which include the Department of Defense — and 6 percent for interest on the federal

AFP/Getty Images/Mandel Ngan

Students await the arrival of President Obama to deliver the commencement address at Morehouse College in Atlanta on May 19, 2013. New college graduates' job prospects are suffering as federal agencies cut staff to meet sequestration spending caps. Hiring for the federal nonmilitary workforce already was sluggish during the post-recession period, and the number of 20- to 24-year-olds who landed federal jobs dropped 40 percent between 2008 and 2012.

debt.[29] Costs are driven mainly by the two biggest programs — Social Security and Medicare — which currently account for about 36 percent of federal spending, $812 billion for Social Security and $504 billion for Medicare.[30]

The two programs differ from other entitlements because they are types of social insurance — programs that derive all or much of their funds from taxes paid by workers, who eventually receive benefits.[31] Like other insurance, but unlike programs such as SNAP, "the only way [a person can] meet the criteria" for receiving Medicare and Social Security "is by paying past payroll taxes," making participation "to some extent an earned right," says John Palmer, a professor of public policy at Syracuse University.

In 1935, when Social Security was created by President Franklin D. Roosevelt in the midst of the worldwide Great Depression, Congress understood that the payroll tax wouldn't generate revenues that matched required payouts each year. To compensate, the law decreed that a so-called Social Security Trust Fund invest excess revenues in U.S. Treasury bonds, redeeming them later to pay benefits in years when payroll tax payments fell short. By law, Social Security may not pay out more

## Health, Social Security Take Most of Budget

Spending on Social Security and health care consumes nearly 60 percent of President Obama's proposed $3.8 trillion budget for fiscal 2014. Military spending represents nearly 60 percent of "discretionary" spending under the budget — spending not mandated by law that is requested by the president and allocated by Congress.

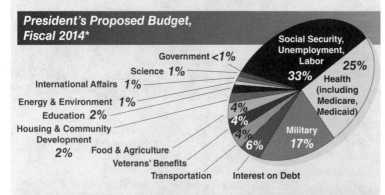

**President's Proposed Budget, Fiscal 2014***

- Social Security, Unemployment, Labor **33%**
- Health (including Medicare, Medicaid) **25%**
- Military **17%**
- Interest on Debt **6%**
- Transportation **4%**
- Veterans' Benefits **4%**
- Food & Agriculture **4%**
- Housing & Community Development **2%**
- Education **2%**
- Energy & Environment **1%**
- International Affairs **1%**
- Science **1%**
- Government **<1%**

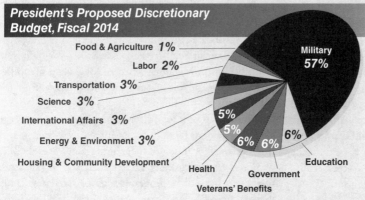

**President's Proposed Discretionary Budget, Fiscal 2014**

- Military **57%**
- Government **6%**
- Education **6%**
- Veterans' Benefits **6%**
- Health **5%**
- Housing & Community Development **5%**
- Energy & Environment **3%**
- International Affairs **3%**
- Science **3%**
- Transportation **3%**
- Labor **2%**
- Food & Agriculture **1%**

*\* Percentages may not total 100 because of rounding.*

*Sources: "Federal Budget 101: Where Does the Money Go?" National Priorities Project, http://nationalpriorities.org/budget-basics/federal-budget-101/spending/*

in annual benefits than it receives in tax revenues and trust fund investments.[32]

According to this year's Social Security actuarial report, the trust fund will have spent all its assets by 2033. From that point forward the program could pay only about 77 percent of benefits currently promised in law, unless some combination of benefit-formula cuts and payroll tax increases is enacted.[33]

Relative to the size of the economy, the cost of Social Security's old-age and survivors' benefits rose from about 4.5 percent of gross domestic product (GDP) in 1990 to 5.1 percent in 2013. The cost is projected to continue rising to about 6.2 percent of GDP by 2035 — at the height of the baby boomers' retirement — and then decline to about 6 percent by 2050, where it will remain for the foreseeable future.[34]

To some observers, those projections demonstrate that the program now costs more than the nation can afford. "Medicare and Social Security were not designed to cope with America's new demographic" of an older population with more retirees per worker, said Gary W. Loveman, CEO of casino operator Caesars Entertainment Corp. and chairman of the health and retirement committee at the Business Roundtable, a membership group for executives of large companies. The Roundtable recommends raising the eligibility age for full benefits from 67 (the eligibility age for people born after 1959) to 70, with some exceptions for people in physically demanding jobs.[35]

As lifespans increase, "Social Security has shifted from a program to protect the elderly from poverty to a potential decades-long income subsidy," wrote Romina Boccia, assistant director of economic policy studies, and Rachel Greszler, a senior policy analyst on economics and entitlements, at the Heritage Foundation, a conservative think tank. Among other changes, Congress should rein in Social Security's cost-of-living benefit increases, they contend.[36]

But others say focusing budget-trimming efforts on Social Security benefits is unfair and unnecessary.

According to the U.S. Census, 15 percent of seniors live in poverty, a percentage likely to tick upward as the age of eligibility for full benefits gradually rises to 67, said Richard Eskow, a senior fellow at the Campaign for America's Future, a liberal advocacy group. Furthermore, higher benefits help the economy by giving seniors more spending power, Eskow argues.[37]

In a 2012 survey of 2,000 people conducted by the nonpartisan analysis and public-education group National Academy of Social Insurance, 84 percent of respondents said Social Security currently doesn't provide enough benefits for retirees and that preserving benefits for future generations is important even if it means raising taxes on workers.[38]

Hiking both the employer and employee shares of the payroll tax from 6.2 percent of a worker's eligible wages to about 7.5 percent would allow the program to maintain full benefits for 75 years, said Alicia Munnell, director of the Center for Retirement Research at Boston College. Adding other changes, such as raising the cap on the amount of wages subject to the payroll tax, makes it even easier, she said.[39]

Whatever changes are made, they should be made sooner rather than later, says Syracuse's Palmer. Retirees depend on Social Security benefits, and workers and employers like predictability in their taxes, "so it makes sense to either phase things in or give people advance warning."

As for Medicare, the health insurance program for people over 65, virtually all observers agree that the program's rate of spending growth must be slowed to make it sustainable, but it's far from clear how to accomplish that.

Liberal and conservative analysts agree that many Medicare features are inefficient, says Michael Tanner, a senior fellow for domestic policy at the Cato Institute, a libertarian, free-market-oriented think tank. Tanner says policy analysts from many backgrounds generally agree that these things, among others, should be done to solve that problem:

- Shift Medicare's service-by-service payment structure to payment based on patient outcomes and on whole episodes of illness or injury;

- Devise a new system of copays and deductibles that makes enrollees conscious of the cost and benefits of services; and

- Provide more information about treatment costs and value.[40]

However, all these things are more easily said than done, Tanner concedes.

For one thing, Medicare's soaring costs result from a decades-long cost explosion throughout the "whole system [of U.S. health care, public and private], not from something about the structure of public programs," says Syracuse's Palmer.

Moreover, "every dollar of health care spending is someone's health care income, including fraud, waste and abuse," making simple changes, such as providing information about the quality of services, threatening to

---

## Individuals Benefit Most from Tax Breaks

Individual taxpayers receive far more in federal tax breaks than corporations. Many economists consider tax breaks a form of government spending, arguing that they deprive the government of money while providing benefits to individuals and corporations. Other economists contend that by allowing corporations and individuals to keep more cash, tax breaks stimulate spending and thus help the economy generate more tax revenue.

### Selected U.S. Tax Breaks and Cost to Federal Government (in $billions)

| Corporations:* | Individual:** |
|---|---|
| • Accelerated depreciation of machinery and equipment: **$76.1** <br> • Deferral of income earned offshore: **$41.4** <br> • Other: **$37.7** <br><br> Total: **$155.2 billion** | • Employer-sponsored health insurance: **$248** <br> • 401(k) and other pension contributions and earnings: **$137** <br> • State and local taxes: **$77** <br> • Mortgage interest deduction: **$70** <br> • Charitable contributions: **$39** <br> • Preferential tax rates on capital gains and dividends: **$161** <br> • Other: **$151** <br><br> Total: **$883 billion** |

\* *Fiscal 2011 figures*

\*\* *Fiscal 2013 figures*

*Source:* "Corporate Tax Expenditures," Government Accountability Office, March 2013, www.gao.gov/assets/660/653120.pdf; "The Distribution of Major Tax Expenditures in the Individual Income Tax System," Congressional Budget Office, May 2013, www.cbo.gov/sites/default/files/cbofiles/attachments/43768_DistributionTax Expenditures.pdf

many, wrote Uwe Reinhardt, a Princeton University economics professor.[41]

## Is too much being spent on discretionary programs?

Thirty percent of the federal budget is so-called discretionary spending — a grab bag of hundreds of programs for which Congress sets specific annual budgets. Fifty-seven percent of it goes to the Department of Defense, and the rest covers everything from foreign aid to national parks, biomedical research, community health centers that serve the poor, veterans' benefits, the Environmental Protection Agency and the Internal Revenue Service.

While non-military discretionary spending makes up only about 13 percent of the entire federal budget, it's often the focus of the fiercest budget-cutting efforts, largely because proposing cuts to the military — or to the middle-class assistance programs Social Security and Medicare — is a political minefield.

The bottom line: "As big as the budget is, there is never enough money to satisfy all demands. To budget is to fight over money and the things that money buys," wrote the University of Maryland's Schick.[42]

Many conservative arguments in favor of cutting discretionary programs hinge on the principle that better government nearly always means smaller, lower-spending government.

Sen. Tom Coburn, R-Okla., a committed foe of budget deficits, argued this year that, although the federal government often must help out in natural disasters, such spending should be offset by cuts elsewhere to keep total spending low. After his home state suffered devastating tornado damage in May, Coburn argued unsuccessfully for trimming other programs to offset what the federal government spent helping Oklahomans recover.[43]

Trimming the budgets of federal regulatory agencies also provides other benefits, say fiscal conservatives: It "prevents the [Environmental Protection Agency (EPA)] and other federal bureaucracies from stepping out of their lane and stifling our economic recovery," said Rep. Harold Rogers, R-Ky., chairman of the powerful House Appropriations Committee.[44]

Others, however, argue that adequate funding for assistance and regulatory agencies is vital.

With regard to paying for disaster relief by cutting other programs, House Minority Leader Nancy Pelosi, D-Calif., insists, "there has never been an offset for disaster assistance. When natural disaster strikes, the American people . . . don't need to fear that there's going to be a debate over how this is going to be paid for."[45]

Rep. Cedric Richmond, D-La., argues that agencies such as the EPA have a legal and "a moral duty to respond" when they find unsafe conditions. "There is a place for responsible environmental regulations, especially when we're talking about keeping our families . . . safe," he said. "Regulations aren't standing in the way of job creation."[46]

Robert Reich, a professor of public policy at the University of California-Berkeley and a former Labor secretary in the Clinton administration, notes that a West, Texas, fertilizer plant that exploded in April, killing 15, injuring hundreds and destroying homes and businesses, had not received a full federal or state safety inspection since 1985, because years of budget cutting have decimated staffs at the Occupational Safety and Health Administration and state offices that work with it. The trigger for the explosion remains undetermined, with investigators unable to rule out causes including an electrical fire or a criminal act.[47]

With more than half of discretionary spending earmarked for the military, the Defense Department's budget also has come in for intense debate. Military spending cuts that took effect this year will likely "seriously damage a fragile American economy," especially in communities that depend on military contractors for employment, and "degrade our ability to respond to crisis precisely at a time of rising instability," said then-Defense Secretary Leon Panetta in February.[48]

Some argue that since defense spending has doubled in the past 10 years, returning it to its level of a decade ago makes sense, but "that would mean returning to an era when general readiness was at a nadir and equipment was aging," said AEI fellow James Pethokoukis.[49]

However, defense spending is "high by historical standards," even without factoring in the costs of the Iraq and Afghanistan conflicts, wrote MIT's Williams. "Non-war budgets for national defense rose by about 50 percent in real terms between fiscal 1998 and fiscal 2010," then declined by 3.5 percent between fiscal 2010 and fiscal 2012.[50]

In the future, as nations such as China fund larger military forces, war will become riskier than in the recent past, making it crucial to favor diplomatic and economic initiatives over ever-higher military spending, according to the National Security Network, a progressive research and advocacy group for foreign policy analysts. The United States "should place a renewed emphasis on deterring conflict and coercion between [foreign] states," a task in which the Defense Department will play a "supporting" rather than a leading role, allowing a $500-billion drop in the defense budget over a decade, said the group.[51]

Military health care costs, which have doubled in a decade, are a major budget-buster, says MIT's Williams. Health-care spending for active and retired military makes up 10 percent of the Pentagon budget and may soon squeeze out other spending, she says. Spending has risen by an average 9 percent annually — faster than the 6 percent average annual increases seen in non-military health care, she says.

The rise in spending occurred partly for the same reasons that health costs have soared overall — rising prices and more diagnostic and treatment technology — but Congress has vastly expanded benefits for active and retired military. In 2000, the Defense Department began offering military retirees over age 65 supplemental insurance that picks up costs Medicare doesn't cover. The coverage "has absolutely no premium," and "any old year you can just jump on it" without a waiting period, Williams says.

Meanwhile, Defense Department coverage for working-age retirees is so cheap, most opt to use it, at taxpayer expense, rather than enrolling in their employers' health plans. Facing no out-of-pocket costs for care, enrollees use "significantly" more health services than the general population, says Williams. Hospitalization rates are 75 percent higher, for example.

# BACKGROUND

## Old Wars

"In a fundamental sense," government "is what it spends," observed the University of Maryland's Schick.[52] Leaders have struggled throughout history over who should hold the power of the purse — that is, the right to decide who is taxed, and how much, and who benefits from tax dollars.

By the time the United States declared nationhood in 1776, "the role of [elected representatives] in deciding revenues and spending was well established," after centuries of struggle between Parliament and the monarchy in England established the idea that elected legislators, not hereditary rulers, should have final authority to tax and spend, Schick wrote.[53]

As the United States and European countries shifted the power of the purse to the people's representatives, spending priorities also began to shift.

Historically, war has been the primary expense for most governments, observed Robert E. Wright, chairman of political economy at Augustana College in Sioux Falls, S.D. Ancient rulers also built infrastructure, such as dams and roadways, but kings, not commoners, saw most of the benefits. "Instead of building a canal that would have expanded trade . . . the pharaohs of ancient Egypt wasted untold hours and lives erecting elaborate pyramid tombs for themselves and a few loved ones," he noted.[54]

## Building an Economy

During the United States' first century, annual government spending began low but quadrupled during the War of 1812, doubled during the Mexican-American War (1846-1848) and increased twenty-fold during the Civil War (1861-1865). Between wars, spending did not drop to pre-war levels but remained relatively stable.[55]

Besides funding the military, U.S. spending in the 19th century included "extraordinary" efforts to spur economic development, says James Livingston, a history professor at Rutgers University in New Brunswick, N.J. Federal and state officials made public investments aimed at promoting industries that "would allow us to compete internationally, to become a manufacturing nation," such as by giving "enormous subsidies to railroads."

Limiting government power was among the founding ideas of the United States. However, except during the presidency of Andrew Jackson (1829-1837), a determined foe of government spending who even vetoed proposals to build national highways, the principle held little sway over the young country's leaders, who used the federal treasury to promote economic development, Livingston says. And as the young nation quickly gained economic prominence, the spending appeared beneficial, changing how many Americans thought about the role of government, he says. By the 1850s many citizens, at least in the

# CHRONOLOGY

**1780s-1880s** *Wartime and infrastructure spending make up most of federal budget.*

**1930s-1960s** *Social-welfare spending swells government budgets worldwide.*

**1935** Social Security is enacted as part of President Franklin D. Roosevelt's New Deal response to Great Depression.

**1937** Social Security begins dispersing funds. . . . Federal deficits prompt Roosevelt to cut federal spending; economic growth slows and still-high unemployment rises the following year.

**1940** Japan sets goal of extending health coverage to all citizens.

**1946** Britain's National Health Services Act promises tax-funded health care for all.

**1956** President Dwight D. Eisenhower commits $25 billion to create Interstate Highway System; federal government pays 90 percent of cost.

**1965** President Lyndon B. Johnson signs Medicare and Medicaid into law.

**1980s-1990s** *Anti-spending sentiment grows in Congress.*

**1988** Congressionally created National Council on Public Works Improvement recommends doubling infrastructure spending, but Congress balks.

**1993** Democratic President Bill Clinton proposes $30 billion economic-stimulus package for infrastructure and housing construction and energy efficiency retrofits, but withdraws the plan after criticism about high spending.

**1995** Two temporary shutdowns close federal agencies as Congress' Republican majority and the Democratic White House fail to agree on budget legislation; the next year, unhappy voters mostly blame anti-spending Republicans for the shutdowns and re-elect Clinton.

**1997** With bipartisan support, Congress passes and Clinton signs the Balanced Budget Act, cutting Medicare and Medicaid spending.

**2000s** *Wars and soaring health-care costs raise spending as recession and anti-tax sentiment depress government revenues.*

**2002** Congress mulls increased infrastructure spending to stimulate the economy but cuts taxes instead, despite vast defense expenditures from the war in Afghanistan. Within a year, the country will be involved in a second war, in Iraq.

**2005** Hurricanes Katrina and Rita hit the Gulf Coast, swelling spending as costly wars continue. . . . Signup begins for Medicare drug benefit to begin on Jan. 1, 2006, and expected to cost upwards of $60 billion per year.

**2008** First baby boomers begin collecting Social Security retirement benefits.

**2011** First baby boomers become eligible for Medicare. . . . Budget Control Act slates dozens of federal agencies for so-called sequestration, or required, across-the-board cuts from fiscal 2021 through fiscal 2023 if Congress can't agree on a budget deal. . . . Federal spending on low-income food assistance has swelled from $30 billion to $72 billion since a steep economic downturn began in 2007.

**2012** Federal government spends $100 billion on cleanup and disaster aid for weather events possibly worsened by climate change.

**2013** With no budget deal in place, automatic sequestration spending cuts take effect; Congress rescinds cuts for air traffic control and a few other programs. . . . United States accounts for 39 percent of world's military spending, more than the next 14 highest-spending countries combined. . . . After deadly tornados hit Oklahoma, some senators say disaster aid to the state should be paid for by cuts to other government programs. . . . House Agriculture panel approves cutting 1.8 million people from food-assistance rolls, but the full House rejects the measure. . . . Mandatory programs such as Medicare and Social Security account for 64 percent of federal budget.

Northern states, "complained about a do-nothing government" and pressed for more infrastructure spending.

U.S. lawmakers early on also saw the value to themselves of so-called pork-barrel spending — federally funded infrastructure projects such as lighthouses, roads, canals, dams and harbors slated for congressmen's home districts, relying on such grants to woo voters, wrote Diana Evans, a political science professor at Trinity College in Connecticut.[56]

As federal funding grew more important to voters and lawmakers alike, the budget process became more complicated and contentious, according to the University of Maryland's Schick. In pre-Civil War days, the same congressional committees that created government programs allocated the funds to carry them out. When the war and its aftermath increased Congress' workload, however, the House in 1865 created the Appropriations Committee to allocate funds annually.

Soon, though, the legislative committees became disgruntled with spending limits imposed by the appropriations panel and took back control over half the spending bills. The move decentralized deliberation of spending priorities and may have helped push federal spending higher, some scholars say. Only in the Budget and Accounting Act of 1921 did Congress finally give the president a formal role in budgeting, requiring him to submit an annual budget proposal to Congress. The budget was to include all spending proposals for federal agencies, which were thereafter barred from independently pitching budget plans to lawmakers.

## Social Spending

Beginning in the late 19th century, European governments began instituting a new spending category — assistance for needy individuals. Many programs amounted to social insurance — national funds built by pooling worker contributions, to be paid out later on health care for disabled workers or cash payments for retirees.

A conservative German government in 1883 was the first to enact social insurance, in hopes of fending off growing popular support for a more radical socialism, which would have had government take over private industries.[57] Social insurance programs soon became the European norm.

U.S. lawmakers resisted calls for government safety nets for decades, however. Conservatives successfully argued that social insurance unfairly required younger, healthier people to subsidize support for others and that private enterprise, not government, should provide services.

In 1935, however, in the depth of the Depression, with millions out of work, President Roosevelt signed into law the Social Security program that he had asked Congress to create. The new social insurance program provided cash assistance for retirees, severely disabled people, widows and under-age children without a working parent, funded by mandatory workplace contributions.

The advent of social-welfare programs greatly increased government spending. Spending on Social Security and other "human resource" budget items, such as worker training, biomedical research and veterans' benefits, accounted for $4.1 billion in 1940, just before the country entered World War II. By 2001, the most recent year when the U.S. budget contained no wartime spending, human resource spending totaled nearly $1.2 trillion — 287 times as much.[58]

In the latter half of the 20th century, it was health care that began to swell government budgets. Around 1900, medicine morphed from a relatively low-paid profession in which doctors could do little besides provide comfort into today's complex, high-tech medical system.[59] As the cost of care grew, many industrialized countries added health care to their social-insurance programs. By 1960, seven countries had passed legislation providing universal health care coverage.[60]

In the United States, however, most health insurance was provided by employers, who bought group coverage for employees. The country's largest physicians' group, the American Medical Association (AMA), strongly endorsed this system, fearing that government-provided insurance would limit their freedom to practice medicine. Worried by rising costs, in the 1940s and '50s, members of Congress from both parties repeatedly introduced legislation to provide "universal" care, but the bills were defeated.

Businesses' ability to provide health insurance was limited, however. Many retirees, disabled people and low-income families had no workplace-based insurance. And many — especially the elderly and disabled — couldn't afford individual policies, which usually charged higher premiums to older people because they already had chronic illnesses or were at higher risk for becoming ill.

Countries in which the government was the single or primary payer of medical bills were able to use their

# State Budget Battles Affect Everyday Lives

*Lawmakers scramble to preserve key services.*

**B**itter battles over government spending don't just take place in Washington. If anything, state spending conundrums may be more complex than at the federal level.

States support services that immediately affect people's everyday lives, from schools and universities to mental-health care, law enforcement and construction and maintenance of roads and transit systems.[1]

In recent months, as many state legislative sessions wound down, lawmakers scrambled to preserve government functions that matter most to voters.

In Washington state, for instance, legislators fought through a near-impasse over taxes to approve a last-minute budget in June adding about $1 billion to school funding and keeping state university tuitions at current levels. Most conversations between Democrats favoring some tax increases and Republicans staunchly against them dead-ended during the session. Highway improvements and expansion of public transit, for example, were put on hold when GOP lawmakers successfully defeated a Democratic plan to raise the gas tax.[2]

By session's end, however, an improving economy that promised higher tax receipts gave lawmakers leeway to transfer funds among accounts to pay for some school and university assistance. However, cost-of-living increases for

school employees that had already been approved by voters did not make it into the budget.

State budgeting is more difficult than federal budgeting because, unlike for Congress, every state except Vermont bans its legislature from borrowing money to carry out ongoing government activities. States may borrow for capital investments such as new infrastructure, however. The intricate interrelationship between federal budgets and state government activities also complicates the picture, especially when spending cuts to federal grant programs for states pinch citizens more quickly and keenly than cuts to federal programs, some analysts say.

State budgets took numerous hits during the 2007-'09 recession and its aftermath, and in the current congressional drive for spending austerity. Federal tax revenues funneled into state coffers through a variety of programs — including $414 billion for Medicaid in fiscal 2011 — make up 25 percent of all state revenues.[3]

And because states have "a variety of revenue streams that are very close to people" in their daily lives, cuts in federal grants to states may have quick, painful consequences for the public, says Linda Bilmes, a senior lecturer in public policy at Harvard's Kennedy School of Government. Jobs are cut, mental-health services eliminated, "the night nurse has to wait longer for the bus," she says.

bargaining clout to keep costs low, but American employers did not have such bargaining power. Partly for that reason, annual U.S. health-care spending by 1960 was 50 percent higher per capita than in any other industrialized nation.[61]

As a result, in the mid-20th century many Americans lacked access to health care, concludes a report by the *Tampa Bay Times* fact-checking website *PolitiFact*. In a 1963 survey of the general population, 25 percent said they had refrained from seeing a doctor after experiencing "pains in the heart," for example. In 1962, just over half of Americans over age 65 had insurance, and the uninsured —"who had to pay all or much of the costs [of a hospital stay] out of pocket" — found themselves "paying for [the] misfortune for years to come," wrote senior writer Louis Jacobson.[62]

With such problems in mind, in 1965 Congress enacted Medicare, a social insurance-entitlement program that provides health insurance for the elderly and some disabled people, partly funded by payroll taxes, and a new entitlement program — Medicaid — funded out of general tax revenues, to subsidize health care for poor families with children.

## Spending Backlash

Credited with helping keep generations of elderly, middle-class Americans from falling into poverty, Medicare quickly grew in popularity. Medicaid, which primarily benefited the poor who paid little or nothing in income taxes, was more controversial.

Beginning in the 1970s, a series of oil shocks, recessions and a globalizing economy shook Americans' confidence

Thus, federal lawmakers are ill-advised to cut spending without carefully examining how those cuts may also decrease revenues at other levels of government, Bilmes says. "When federal spending goes to states and localities it becomes revenue for them." Federal spending "that goes to infrastructure in states creates jobs, which in turn generate more revenues" — from income taxes paid —"for both the state and the federal government," she says.

The close relationship between federal spending and state economies and revenues is not lost on industries that thrive on government contracts, such as those that supply goods and services to the Pentagon, notes Cindy Williams, a principal research scientist for security studies at the Massachusetts Institute of Technology (MIT). Military contractors who manage the development of big weapons systems such as the F-35 fighter plane, which has been in the works for much of the past decade, "ensure that there is a subcontractor in every, or nearly every, congressional district," Williams says.

Then, when Washington policymakers threaten such a project with budget cuts, contractors "make sure that the fax machines are working, getting in touch with congressmen" in every one of the country's 435 congressional districts to convey the message, "Don't forget about the 200 jobs in your town."

— *Marcia Clemmitt*

The F-35 Joint Strike Fighter undergoes a test flight over the Chesapeake Bay on Feb. 11, 2011. Defense contractors who develop big weapons system such as the F-35 garner lawmakers' support for their projects by seeding congressional districts with subcontractors.

[2]Mike Baker, "Lawmakers Approve Budget to Avert Shutdown," The Associated Press/Komonews.com [Seattle], June 28, 2013, www.komonews.com/news/local/State-lawmakers-prepare-for-swift-budget-vote-213509661.html; and Jordan Shrader, "UPDATE: Senate Leaders Say No to Vote on Gas Tax Hike That Would Fund SR-167-to-Tacoma," *The News Tribune* [Tacoma, Wash.], June 29, 2013, http://blog.thenewstribune.com/politics/2013/06/29/senate-leaders-block-gas-tax-hike-that-would-fund-sr-167-to-tacoma.

[3]"The ABCs of State Budgets," *op. cit.*; and "Total Medicaid Spending," State Health Facts, Kaiser Family Foundation, http://kff.org/medicaid/state-indicator/total-medicaid-spending-fy2010.

[1]"Where Do Our State Tax Dollars Go?" Center on Budget and Policy Priorities, April 12, 2013, www.cbpp.org/cms/?fa=view&id=2783; and "The ABCs of State Budgets," Center on Budget and Policy Priorities, Feb. 7, 2013, www.cbpp.org/cms/?fa=view&id=3067.

in what had seemed to be an endlessly bright economic future. Soon, analysts saw rising government spending as a potential cause of the stalling economy.

By the 1980s, many Republicans — philosophically committed to keeping government's role in most people's lives small and taxes low — argued that most government spending was a drain on the economy that produced little of value. Most Democrats, on the other hand, supported government initiatives such as anti-poverty programs and environmental regulation of industry.

This divide has only deepened over the past 30 years but is more than a politicized slugfest, says the University of Maryland's Schick. The two sides "really do disagree about the role of government."

A key question underlying the debate is whether government spending boosts the economy by contributing things that are difficult for the private sector to provide, such as income support for the unemployed or infrastructure such as roads or schools, or whether it merely diverts cash from savvier private-sector investors who would use it more effectively.

On the anti-spending side, Dean Kalahar, a high-school economics and psychology teacher who writes for the free market-oriented blog and news aggregator RealClear Markets, says flatly: "As [influential conservative University of Chicago economist] Milton Friedman said, 'Nobody spends somebody else's money as carefully as he spends his own.. . . ' So any policy that reduces personal freedom in economic decision making" by allowing the government to spend tax dollars "inhibits economic growth."[63]

But history shows that government spending is fully capable of boosting the economy strongly, says Rutgers'

# Critics See Tax Breaks as Stealth Spending

*Supporters say breaks are needed for sound tax policy.*

Everybody loves a tax break. Homeowners happily lower their tax burdens each April 15 by claiming deductions for paying the interest on their mortgages. Businesses are excused from tax payments for, among other things, income they earn and keep offshore and investments in low-income housing.

Increasingly, though, many public-policy scholars and policymakers eye tax breaks as potentially budget-busting "tax expenditures" — no different in their effects on government budgets from spending programs. Tax-break advocates, however, argue that it's simply wrong to label as government spending any policy that allows people to keep money they earn rather than paying it in taxes.

Tax expenditures "represent dollars that the government is theoretically owed that it has decided not to collect," to encourage individuals or businesses to engage in certain activities or, in some cases, simply to help them financially, wrote Irene S. Rubin, a professor emeritus of public administration at Northern Illinois University, in DeKalb.[1]

For example, in response to fuel shortages in the late 1970s, the Carter administration and Congress approved tax breaks for adding energy-saving insulation to homes and other buildings, Rubin said.[2]

Tax expenditures fly under the normal budgeting radar, she points out. "Revenues are never collected or due," she said, "and hence they may never appear in the budget as an outlay, though the money is spent as surely as if the revenue were collected and then disbursed."[3]

This spring Congress' nonpartisan budget-analysis agency, the Congressional Budget Office (CBO), and its auditing arm, the Government Accountability Office (GAO), released reports tallying the amount of federal revenues lost due to tax breaks.

The GAO reported that in 2011 corporate tax breaks amounted to lost revenues of more than $181 billion — approximately the same amount it collected in corporate income taxes. Tax breaks incentivized such activities as producing products in the United States and doing more research and development.[4]

Ten of the biggest tax breaks aimed at individuals, on the other hand, will represent about $900 billion in so-called "forgone" federal income-tax revenues in fiscal 2013, or about 5.7 percent of gross domestic product (GDP), according to the CBO.[5]

Among the highest-dollar individual breaks are exemptions for employer-sponsored health insurance and for contributions to and investment earnings from pension-fund contributions.[6] (Individual income tax collected in 2013 totaled 7.6 percent of GDP, while corporate income taxes amounted to 1.8 percent of GDP.)[7]

Critics like Rubin say Congress often provides tax breaks in order to curry favor with a particular group, such as middle-class voters or energy companies, rather than to foster a public-policy goal such as encouraging home ownership or energy efficiency. That practice often leads to the tax break remaining in law long after it's no longer needed, she says. Worse, when one group gets a tax break, others can argue that it's only fair for them to get one, too, Rubin wrote.[8]

Moreover, while federal discretionary spending — such as for community health centers and small-business grants — is reviewed each year, tax expenditures get hardly any review once enacted, notes John Palmer, a professor of public policy at Syracuse University. "We've got to develop a way of having tax expenditures subject to more ongoing scrutiny," such as having some reviewed every several years or so "and some subjected to annual review. They should have to compete against spending" for a place in the budget, he says, so they can be required to prove that they do a job better than a direct spending program would.

The ineffectiveness of some tax breaks seems clear, says Palmer. For example, "$100 billion in tax expenditures"

Livingston. The years from 1933 to 1937, when America struggled to emerge from the Great Depression, saw some of the fastest economic growth rates of the 20th century, he says. "How did that happen? Private investment was nil. The banks did absolutely nothing" in the way of lending. "Consumer spending? Nobody had any income. The only possible explanation is the government's contribution" through infrastructure building and other activities, he says.

annually to encourage workers to save and invest in tax-deferred retirement accounts such as IRAs and 401(k)s "have not increased retirement preparedness" across society, he says. "And in the health care area, tax breaks that both employers and workers receive for the cost of employer-provided insurance had the perverse effect of driving up health-care costs," chiefly by subsidizing the generous insurance packages enjoyed by higher-income workers and shielding them from the true cost of care, thus encouraging them to be careless health care consumers, he says.

The century-old tradition of providing subsidies to encourage oil and gas production amounts to about $41 billion in forgone revenue over a decade — subsidies that are ripe for reconsideration, wrote Joseph Aldy, an assistant professor of public policy at Harvard University's Kennedy School of Government. Once, drilling was a risky business — likely justifying the subsidies — but that's no longer true, he said. Recent analyses suggest that tax breaks have little effect on fuel production, so eliminating them would not drive up prices, reduce employment or cause shortages.[9]

Other analysts argue strongly that calling tax breaks a stealth form of government spending is simply wrong.

"There is a huge moral and economic difference between government taxing income away from citizens and then spending it and allowing income earners to keep their money by reducing taxes through tax preferences," wrote Curtis Dubay, a senior policy analyst at the Heritage Foundation, a conservative think tank.

Many of the policies often called into question actually are "necessary for establishing a sound tax code," Dubay argues. For example, he contends that if home buyers paid taxes on the income that they spend on their mortgage interest, that money would unfairly and inefficiently be taxed twice — once as part of the householder's income and once as income for the bank that collects the interest.[10]

Not all conservative analysts agree, however.

Alan Viard, a resident scholar at the American Enterprise Institute (AEI), a free market-oriented think tank, recommends trimming the mortgage-interest deduction. Steeply cutting the size of eligible mortgages and changing the subsidy to a refundable tax credit would increase federal revenues by about $300 billion over a decade, he wrote.[11] "If you made it a credit, it would work better for the lower end of the income scale" — since poorer people get more money from tax credits than from deductions. "So there would arguably be a legitimate government interest" in maintaining the break but using it only to help poorer Americans buy homes, he says.

The middle class must take a hit if tax expenditures are phased out to increase revenues, Viard says. "People on both sides talk as if there are all these loopholes that can be eliminated without the average person even noticing it," he says. But with some of the biggest being the health-insurance exclusion and tax breaks for state and local taxes and mortgage interest, "that's not the case," he says.

— *Marcia Clemmitt*

[1] Irene S. Rubin, *The Politics of Public Budgeting* (2009), p. 49.

[2] *Ibid.*, p. 52.

[3] *Ibid.*, p. 151.

[4] "Corporate Tax Expenditures," Government Accountability Office, March 2013, p. 10, www.gao.gov/assets/660/653120.pdf.

[5] "The Distribution of Major Tax Expenditures in the Individual Income Tax System," Congressional Budget Office, May 2013, p. 1, www.cbo.gov/sites/default/files/cbofiles/attachments/43768_DistributionTaxExpenditures.pdf.

[6] *Ibid.*, p. 6.

[7] "Historical Source of Revenue as Share of GDP," Tax Policy Center, May 7, 2013, www.taxpolicycenter.org/taxfacts/displayafact.cfm?Docid=205.

[8] Rubin, *op. cit.*, p. 57.

[9] Joseph E. Aldy, "Proposal 5: Eliminating Fossil Fuel Subsidies," in "Innovative Approaches to Tax Reform," The Hamilton Project, February 2013, www.brookings.edu/~/media/research/files/papers/2013/02/thp%20budget%20papers/thp_15waysfedbudget_prop5.pdf.

[10] Curtis Dubay, "CBO Report on 'Tax Expenditures' Has It Wrong," Heritage Foundation, June 4, 2013, www.heritage.org/research/reports/2013/06/cbo-report-on-tax-expenditures-has-it-wrong.

[11] Alan Viard, "Proposal 8: Replacing the Home Mortgage Interest Deduction," in "Innovative Approaches to Tax Reform," Brookings Institution, February 2013.

Conservative opposition to government spending grew louder around 2008, when the crisis in financial markets plunged the world into deep recession.[64] As the U.S. economy sank, government debt burgeoned, due to increased spending to support the unemployed, and aid to businesses and state and local governments — all paid for out of a federal tax base shrunken by unemployment and the business slowdown.

Getty Images/Matt Cardy

A volunteer with The Fight Continues, an organization of disabled veterans, comforts a woman who lost her home in a devastating tornado in Moore, Okla., on May 20. While the federal government should help out in natural disasters, says Sen. Tom Coburn, R-Okla., a foe of budget deficits, he argues that such spending should be offset by cuts elsewhere. But House Minority Leader Nancy Pelosi, D-Calif., says that "when natural disaster strikes, the American people . . . don't need to fear that there's going to be a debate over how this is going to be paid for."

The nation's existing debt — and spending that can drive it further upwards — is the principal obstacle to economic recovery, said many conservatives. "A balanced budget is a reasonable goal, because it returns government to its proper limits," said House Budget Committee Chairman Paul Ryan, R-Wis., regarding his budget proposals that focus on large spending cuts.[65]

Liberals countered that when the economy is weak, precipitous cuts to government spending only weaken it further. "If I am out of work . . . almost any normal expenditure is beyond my means. If my lack of a job throws you out of work, . . . too, . . . the whole economy cascades downward," said Robert Kuttner, co-editor of the liberal journal *The American Prospect*. "If you put an entire nation under a rigid austerity regime, its capacity for economic growth is crippled."[66]

Exacerbated by a polarized political climate, this debate has effectively stalemated thoughtful discussion in Washington about government spending, many analysts say with regret.

"There's no imminent crisis" that will noticeably affect voters in the short run, says Palmer at Syracuse

University. "So lawmakers remain free to say, 'I can afford to hold onto my principles. I don't have to compromise.' "

## CURRENT SITUATION

### Sequester and Stalemate

This summer, across-the-board discretionary-spending cuts that took effect in March threaten some government workers' jobs as well as public services on which many people depend. Some Head Start programs have cut enrollments, Social Security offices are closing earlier in the day, and the Hanford nuclear-reactor site in Washington state — heavily contaminated with radioactivity — laid off 250 workers.[67]

The governmentwide sequester required federal agencies including the Pentagon to cut about $85.4 billion in spending during fiscal 2013 and make similar cuts through fiscal 2021, unless Congress agrees to a new taxation and spending plan.[68]

One group that may feel the pinch — new graduates applying for jobs at federal agencies. As agencies cut staff to meet spending caps and workers go on furlough, job offers are being withheld, reports *The Wall Street Journal*.[69] Hiring for the federal nonmilitary workforce already was sluggish during the post-recession period.[70] The number of 20-to-24-year-olds who landed federal jobs dropped 40 percent between 2008 and 2012. The sequester will likely worsen those numbers, at least temporarily, the paper reports.

### Better Budgeting

Sequestration originated in a deal congressional Democrats and the Obama White House struck in 2011 to get Republicans to agree to raise the so-called debt ceiling — a legislated limit on the level of debt the nation can carry. By law, Congress must raise the current limit if debt rises above it. Under the deal, a "super committee" of six congressional Democrats and six Republicans had three-and-a-half months to agree to $1.2 trillion in deficit reduction — from spending cuts, revenue increases or both. If they failed — which they did — automatic across-the-board cuts to Medicare and to military and nonmilitary discretionary spending would kick in on

# Should Social Security cost-of-living increases be trimmed?

## YES

**Marc Goldwein**
*Senior Policy Director, Committee for a
Responsible Federal Budget*

Written for *CQ Researcher*, July 2013

Should we measure inflation as accurately as possible? Of course we should, particularly when the fiscal implications of measuring inaccurately are so large. The so-called chained Consumer Price Index (CPI), a far more accurate inflation index than the one used now, would better reflect retirees' actual spending patterns and the cost increases they encounter. Economists from the left, right and center broadly agree on that, and their view is affirmed by the nonpartisan Congressional Budget Office (CBO) and the Bureau of Labor Statistics. Adopting this improved measure would also generate more tax revenue, slow government spending growth and strengthen the Social Security system.

So how can anyone oppose this change? Some special-interest groups do so for their own financial benefit, while others argue that seniors face faster price growth or the most vulnerable would be hurt by this change.

Yet alternative measures that purport to show seniors spending more are highly flawed — including in the ways they measure housing and health care — to the point that the CBO has concluded, "It is unclear . . . whether the cost of living actually grows at a faster rate for the elderly than for younger people."

Even if a better measure were produced for measuring cost increases affecting only retirees, adopting it would raise serious fairness concerns. Should the one-third of Social Security beneficiaries who are not retirees receive smaller cost-of-living adjustments so seniors can receive larger ones? Should New Yorkers, with their high cost of living, receive a higher percentage than Detroiters? Should each government program get its own index or only those backed by powerful interest groups?

As for the most vulnerable, it makes little sense to measure inflation incorrectly for everyone in order to retain a desired windfall for the neediest. Doing so would cut taxes for the top 1 percent by $1,000 each in order to keep an average $20 tax cut for the lowest fifth. Instead, desired tax relief and benefit enhancements for the most vulnerable should be achieved through targeted reforms designed specifically to strengthen those populations.

Ultimately, the best thing we can do for the most vulnerable in society — at least within Social Security — is to make the program sustainable and solvent and avoid the 23 percent across-the-board benefit cut currently scheduled for when the program's funds dry up. If we can't even measure inflation correctly, how can we hope to make the hard choices necessary to keep Social Security funded for future generations?

## NO

**Nancy Altman and Eric Kingson**
*Co-directors, Social Security Works*

Written for *CQ Researcher*, July 2013

Every January, Social Security benefits are automatically adjusted for inflation. Some refer to these cost-of-living adjustments (COLAs) as "increases," but they're not. They are designed to ensure that benefits do not erode over time.

That's important. Social Security benefits are modest, averaging just $15,000 a year for retirees. Even so, two out of three retirees rely on them for at least half their income; almost one out of two over age 79 for virtually all their income.

COLAs should allow beneficiaries to tread water, but they are sinking. The current index under-measures inflation experienced by seniors and people with disabilities, because, on average, they spend more than workers and the general population on health care and less on items for which prices rise more slowly, such as clothing.

Several members of Congress have introduced bills to use an index that better reflects elder spending patterns. But other leading policymakers have proposed a stingier index, called the "chained CPI," which purports to be more accurate by taking into account substitution of cheaper goods across categories when prices rise — for example, buying more blankets when the price of heating fuel rises. However, 300 economists and related experts have gone on record opposing the chained CPI for Social Security, emphasizing that "there is no empirical basis for reducing the Social Security COLA." Leading veterans' organizations, including the American Legion and Veterans of Foreign Wars, oppose the chained CPI for both veterans' benefits and Social Security.

Chained CPI proposals are not a "small tweak." They would cut benefits for all of today's 57 million Social Security beneficiaries. Over time, they would greatly diminish the value of disability benefits received by today's young, disabled veterans. And chained CPI cuts would increase every year, totaling an average $4,600 by age 75, $13,900 by age 85 and $28,000 by age 95 for a worker who begins receiving benefits at age 65.

No matter how politicians dress up the chained CPI, the proposal violates election promises not to cut benefits for today's beneficiaries. The most prominent advocates of this misguided plan also propose shielding some of the most vulnerable from the harshest aspects of the chained CPI, an implicit admission that it is a flawed, less accurate and harmful measure. Bottom line: Social Security beneficiaries need a more accurate measure of inflation, not one designed to inflict cuts by stealth.

Jan. 1, 2013, unless Congress canceled the cuts in the meantime.

The hope was that the across-the-board cuts would strike at programs important to both parties, spurring Congress to develop a compromise plan to stop them. In January, Congress approved delaying the cuts until March.[71]

Since sequestration went into effect, Congress has stepped in to exempt a few programs from cuts. After people complained about airline flight delays, Congress quickly exempted air traffic controllers from furloughs. Meat inspections at the Department of Agriculture, security funding for U.S. embassies and the Women, Infants and Children infant-nutrition program were among a handful of programs fully or partly exempted from this year's cuts.[72]

Supporters of other programs, many that serve the needy, aren't pleased. "It's perplexing that we're saving programs that are inconveniencing others, but we're not saving programs that are saving lives," said Ellie Hollander, president of the nutrition program for low-income seniors, Meals on Wheels.[73]

"The sequester is not just a bad idea for one program or group — it's a bad idea for everyone," said Rep. Mark Pocan, D-Wis. "Congress needs to come together [to eliminate the sequester] and support all of our hard-working families, not just those with influence."[74]

But more general outrage against the cuts has not materialized, dashing Democrats' hopes that voter pressure would force Congress back to the bargaining table. "Even federal employees just seem to be accepting their furloughs," says the University of Maryland's Schick.

Some members of Congress embrace the automatic cuts, observed ardent spending foe Sen. Jeff Flake, R-Ariz. "A lot of members . . . will publicly complain . . . about the sequester and privately say, 'Well, better somebody else makes a decision than us,' " Flake said.[75]

Meanwhile, many analysts say some procedural changes could lead to smarter spending.

Switching from the current one-year appropriations cycle to a two-year system could create a more deliberative process, many say. "Annual budgets are very inefficient, in terms of human resources," says Linda Bilmes, a senior lecturer in public policy at Harvard's John F. Kennedy School of Government. Federal workers are pulled from their primary duties every year to prepare lengthy budget documents. Furthermore, "many federal agencies have

long-term missions" — such as the National Park Service's charge to "protect the lands in perpetuity," but the yearly appropriations process encourages them to focus on short-term activities and goals.

Federal workers often have good ideas about how to save money "but they have no way to benefit from it," since money saved in one activity generally may not be switched to another that could use more resources, Bilmes says.

Giving the president a line-item veto of individual spending items "also might be a minor improvement," says Viard of AEI. The veto "wouldn't necessarily reduce spending, but the president, who represents the country as a whole, might be able to throw out some of the special-interest, localized spending" that Congress includes but that may not be the best use of federal dollars, he says.

Few analysts see much hope for quickly bridging the political and ideological divide that stymies Washington. "It'll only happen when one party wins all the marbles" — House, Senate and White House — in an election, Schick predicts.

## OUTLOOK

### Forever Sequester?

The essentially random nature of the sequester — which required dozens of federal programs to cut spending by the same percentage, no exceptions — was intended to force lawmakers to compromise. But it didn't work out that way. The question remains, however: Will constituent backlash develop as the cuts continue — potentially for almost a decade — or will reduced spending become the new normal?

"If a few months from now the economy is weakening," as many economists have predicted will happen, it "would reignite the warfare" over spending, says Maryland's Schick. It's likely, though, that Republicans and Democrats will simply return to their entrenched positions, he says. "The Pentagon may ultimately be the leading edge in saying that we can't make ends meet with the sequester."

On July 8, the White House announced that this year's federal budget deficit continues to shrink, projecting a $759 billion shortfall — $214 billion less than was expected in April. Congressional Republicans continue to fight for more cuts, however. "The president's plan is simply to tax more in order to spend more," said Alabama Sen. Jeff Sessions, the top-ranking Republican on the Senate Budget Committee.[76]

Furthermore, the GOP-led House of Representatives "is organized so that the majority party always wins without having to give any consideration whatever to the views of the minority party," Schick says. "That extraordinary fact means that the party that controls the House has no incentive to compromise."

Sequester pain will come, says Syracuse's Palmer. "Squeezing discretionary spending to the extent we're doing, that's going to turn out to be devastating."

Budgeting for an uncertain future requires tough deliberation today more than ever, analysts say.

When spending cuts hit the Pentagon in the past, each service branch — Army, Navy and Air Force — simply took the same cut. "But this time we're having a different conversation" — a complex, charged and nearly unprecedented examination of the actual structure of the military, says MIT's Williams.

Foreign policy analysts expect future military action to occur in Asia and the Pacific, requiring a larger Navy and Air Force and a smaller Army. Alarmed by this threat to their status, the Army opposes spending changes based on that idea, Williams says. The Army's argument: Asian nations now have the world's largest armies, with which the U.S. Army must pursue partnerships. Furthermore, Army analysts contend, it's not clear how soon, if ever, U.S. forces will actually leave the Middle East, where an Army presence is widely considered crucial.

In 2012, federal spending for droughts, storms, floods and forest fires that may have been worsened by the effects of climate change totaled nearly $100 billion, a whopping 16 percent of nonmilitary discretionary spending, wrote Daniel Lashof, director of the climate and clean air program at the Natural Resources Defense Council, an environmental-advocacy group.[77]

Lashof contends that the government must change its practice of spending heavily on post-event responses while spending skimpily on programs that might prevent or dampen the effects of climate change. Federal spending to respond to extreme weather in 2012 was eight times the EPA's total budget and eight times the total spending on development of new energy sources, energy cleanup technologies and so on, he said.

Meanwhile, "there's a long horizon" until sequestration's effects resonate with the public, says Kramer of the National Priorities Project. When that finally happens, "we could have a much more broad-based, popular movement" in favor of thoughtful budgeting, she says.

## NOTES

1. Joel Handley, "Whose Budget? Their Budget," *In These Times*, May 10, 2013, http://inthesetimes.com/article/14970/the_5th_ward_votes.

2. "Welcome to the Website of the First-ever Participatory Budgeting Process in the U.S.!" "Participatory Budgeting in the 49th Ward," March 29, 2012, http://participatorybudgeting49.word press.com.

3. Irene S. Rubin, *The Politics of Public Budgeting* (2009), p. 1.

4. Dylan Matthews, "The Sequester: Absolutely Everything You Could Possibly Need to Know, in One FAQ," *The Washington Post*, March 1, 2013, www.washingtonpost.com/blogs/wonkblog/wp/2013/02/20/the-sequester-absolutely-everything-you-could-possibly-need-to-know-in-one-faq.

5. "How Is the Sequester Affecting Federal Agencies," *Politics blog*, *The Washington Post*, www.washington post.com/wp-srv/special/politics/sequestration-fed eral-agency-impact.

6. Nicholas Eberstadt, "Yes, Mr. President, We Are a Nation of Takers," *The Wall Street Journal*, Jan. 24, 2013, http://online.wsj.com/article/SB1000142412 7887323539804578259940213918254.html.

7. "The Low-Wage Drag on Our Economy: Wal-Mart's Low Wages and Their Effect on Taxpayers and Economic Growth," Democratic Staff, House Education and the Workforce Committee, May 2013, http://democrats.edworkforce.house.gov/sites/democrats.edworkforce.house.gov/files/docu ments/WalMartReport-May2013.pdf.

8. News Transcript, Secretary of Defense Robert Gates, U.S. Department of Defense, Aug. 9, 2010, www .defense.gov/transcripts/transcript.aspx?transcrip tid=4669.

9. For background, see Josh Sweigart, "Congress Pushes for Weapons Pentagon Didn't Want," *Dayton* [Ohio] *Daily News*/Military.com, Aug. 20, 2012, www.daytondailynews.com/news/news/congress-pushes-for-weapons-pentagon-didnt-want/nRC7w/.

10. Cindy Williams, "Making Defense Affordable," The Hamilton Project, Brookings Institution, February 2013, www.hamiltonproject.org/files/downloads_and_links/THP_WilliamsDiscPaper.pdf.

11. "Federal Budget 101," National Priorities Project, http://nationalpriorities.org/budget-basics/federal-budget-101/spending. For background, see D. Andrew Austin and Mindy R. Levit, "Mandatory Spending Since 1962," Congressional Research Service, March 23, 2012, www.fas.org/sgp/crs/misc/RL33074.pdf.

12. For background, see Reed Karaim, "Farm Subsidies," *CQ Researcher*, May 1, 2012, pp. 205-228.

13. "Farm Bill 2013," Food Research and Action Council Action Center (FRAC), http://frac.org/leg-act-center/farm-bill-2012/#house; "HR 1947: Federal Agriculture Reform and Risk Management Act of 2013," govtrack.us, www.govtrack.us/congress/bills/113/hr1947; and "S. 954: Agriculture Reform, Food, and Jobs Act of 2013," govtrack.us, www.govtrack.us/congress/bills/113/s954.

14. Jeff Cox, "Record 46 million Americans Are on Food Stamps," CNBC, Sept. 4, 2012, www.cnbc.com/id/48898378.

15. Ron Nixon, "House Rejects Farm Bill as Food Stamp Cuts Prove Divisive," *The New York Times*, www.nytimes.com/2013/06/21/us/politics/house-defeats-a-farm-bill-with-big-food-stamp-cuts.html.

16. Arthur Delaney and Jaweed Kaleem, "Food Stamp Cuts Spark Bible Debate," *The Huffington Post*, May 17, 2013, www.huffingtonpost.com/2013/05/17/food-stamp-cuts-bible-debate_n_3293982.html.

17. "The Supplemental Nutrition Assistance Program," Congressional Budget Office, April 2012, www.cbo.gov/sites/default/files/cbofiles/attachments/04-19-SNAP.pdf.

18. "Supplemental Nutrition Assistance Program," Food and Nutrition Service, U.S. Department of Agriculture, www.fns.usda.gov/snap/applicant_recipients/eligibility.htm.

19. "The Supplemental Nutrition Assistance Program," Congressional Budget Office, *op. cit.*

20. "Glance: Senate, House Farm Bills to Be Considered by Committees this Week," Associated Press/*The Washington Post*, June 10, 2013, http://news.yahoo.com/glance-senate-house-farm-bills-075638678.htm.l.

21. Quoted in Chris Day, "Lucas: Farm Bill Approval Vital for State Farmers," CNHI News Service/*Edmond* [Okla.] *Sun*, June 17, 2013, www.edmondsun.com/local/x479813622/Lucas-Farm-Bill-approval-vital-for-state-farmers.

22. "The Supplemental Nutrition Assistance Program," Congressional Budget Office, *op. cit.*

23. Paul Krugman, "From the Mouths of Babes," *The New York Times*, May 30, 2013, www.nytimes.com/2013/05/31/opinion/from-the-mouths-of-babes.html?_r=0.

24. Collin Peterson, press release, House Committee on Agriculture-Democrats, June 18, 2013, http://democrats.agriculture.house.gov/press/PRArticle.aspx?NewsID=1178.

25. "Crop Insurance," Government Accountability Office, March 2012, www.gao.gov/assets/590/589305.pdf.

26. Ryan Alexander, "Farm Bill's Corporate Welfare Is Unacceptable," *U.S. News & World Report*, Jan. 29, 2013, www.usnews.com/opinion/blogs/economic-intelligence/2013/01/29/farm-bills-corporate-welfare-is-unacceptable.

27. Paul C. Barton, "Rep. Stephen Fincher Under Fire: 'Hypocritical with a Capital 'H,'" *The Tennessean*, June 5, 2013, www.tennessean.com/article/20130605/NEWS/306050181/Rep-Stephen-Fincher-under-fire-Hypocritical-capital-H-, and Bartholomew Sullivan, "Fincher Opponents Raise Issue of Crop Subsidies," *Memphis Commercial Appeal*, June 7, 2010, www.commercialappeal.com/news/2010/jun/07/fincher-faces-anger-over-farm-subsidies/?print=1.

28. Quoted in Erik Wasson, "Ag Chairman Defends Lawmakers Who Get Subsidies, Cut Food Stamps," *The Hill*, May 23, 2013, http://thehill.com/blogs/on-the-money/agriculture/301639-ag-chairman-defends-lawmakers-who-get-subsidies-cut-food-stamps.

29. "Federal Budget 101: Where Does the Money Go?" National Priorities Project, http://nationalpriorities.org/budget-basics/federal-budget-101/spending.

30. "The Budget for Fiscal Year 2014," Summary Tables, Table S-4, White House Office of Management and Budget, April 2013, www.whitehouse.gov/sites/default/files/omb/budget/fy2014/assets/tables.pdf.

31. For background, see Larry DeWitt, "The Development of Social Security in America," *Social Security Bulletin*, August 2010, www.ssa.gov/policy/docs/ssb/v70n3/v70n3p1.html.

32. For background, see Marcia Clemmitt, "National Debt," *CQ Researcher*, March 18, 2011, pp. 241-264.

33. "The 2013 Annual Report of Trustees of the Federal Old-age and Survivors Insurance and Federal Disability Insurance Trust Funds," Board of Trustees, Federal Old-age and Survivors Insurance and Federal Disability Insurance Trust Funds, May 31, 2013, www.socialsecurity.gov/oact/tr/2013/tr2013.pdf.

34. *Ibid.*

35. "Social Security Reform and Medicare Modernization Proposals," Business Roundtable, January 2013, www.scribd.com/fullscreen/120654297?access_key=key-ssy9spfp05slr2fw7zi.

36. Romina Boccia and Rachel Greszler, "Social Security Trust Fund Reports Massive Deficits, Benefit Cuts by 2033," Heritage Foundation, May 31, 2013, www.heritage.org/research/reports/2013/05/2013-social-security-trust-fund-reports-massive-deficits-benefit-cuts.

37. Richard Eskow, "A Vision for Social Security," *Campaign for America's Future blog*, May 28, 2013, http://blog.ourfuture.org/20130528/strengthening-social-securitys-bright-shining-web.

38. Jasmine V. Tucker, Virginia P. Reno, and Thomas N. Bethell, "Social Security: What Do Americans Want?" National Academy of Social Insurance, January 2013, www.nasi.org/sites/default/files/research/What_Do_Americans_Want.pdf.

39. Quoted in "How Underfunded Is Social Security and How Might It Be Fixed?" PBS NewsHour, May 6, 2013, www.pbs.org/newshour/business-desk/2013/05/how-underfunded-is-social-secu.html.

40. For background, see Marcia Clemmitt, "Rising Health Costs," *CQ Researcher*, April 7, 2006, pp. 289-312.

41. Uwe Reinhardt, "Divide et Impera: Protecting the Growth of Health Care Incomes (Cost)," *Health Economics*, January 2012, pp. 41-54, www.bettmartinezinsurancesolutions.com/uploads/MAYNARD_PAPER_25TH_JAN_2012.pdf.

42. Schick, *op. cit.*, p. 2.

43. Quoted in Christina Wilkie, "Oklahoma Senators Jim Inhofe, Tom Coburn, Face Difficult Options on Disaster Relief," *The Huffington Post*, May 20, 2013, www.huffingtonpost.com/2013/05/20/oklahoma-senators-disaster-relief_n_3309234.html.

44. Quoted in Mark Drajem, "House Republicans Propose Cutting EPA Budget, Preventing Rules," Bloomberg, June 19, 2012, www.bloomberg.com/news/2012-06-19/house-republicans-propose-cutting-epa-budget-preventing-rules.html.

45. Quoted in Felicia Sonmez, "Democrats Will Not Support Any Disaster Relief Offset," *2Chambers blog*, *The Washington Post*, Sept. 22, 2011, www.washingtonpost.com/blogs/2chambers/post/pelosi-democrats-will-not-support-any-disaster-relief-offset/2011/09/22/gIQA4bWOoK_blog.html.

46. Quoted in Bruce Alpert, [New Orleans] *Times-Picayune*, Oct. 18, 2011, www.nola.com/politics/index.ssf/2011/10/republican_congressmen_take_ai.html.

47. Robert Reich, "The Hollowing Out of Government," RobertReich.org, May 4, 2013, http://robertreich.org/post/49624800686; for background, see Matthew DeLuca, "FEMA Denies More Aid to Texas Town Devastated by Fertilizer Plant Explosion," NBC News, June 12, 2013, http://usnews.nbcnews.com/_news/2013/06/12/18921111-fema-denies-more-aid-to-texas-town-devastated-by-fertilizer-plant-explosion?lite. Lisa Marie Garza, "Arson Not Ruled Out in Fire That Caused West, Texas, Blast," Reuters/Yahoo!News, May 16, 2013, http://news.yahoo.com/arson-not-ruled-fire-caused-west-texas-blast-002635317.html.

48. Quoted in Tom Cohen, "Panetta Warns of Degraded Military Readiness from Spending Cuts," CNN Politics, Feb. 7, 2013, www.cnn.com/2013/02/06/politics/congress-spending-cuts.

49. James Pethokoukis, *AEI Ideas blog*, Nov. 16, 2012, www.aei-ideas.org/2012/11/5-myths-about-u-s-defense-spending.

50. Cindy Williams, "Making Defense Affordable," *Discussion Paper 2013-02*, The Hamilton Project, February 2013, www.hamiltonproject.org/files/downloads_and_links/THP_WilliamsDiscPaper.pdf.

51. Bill French, "Reshaping Pentagon Spending and Capabilities: Setting Priorities for the Future," National Security Network, March 2013, http://nsnetwork.org/wp-content/uploads/2013/03/Reshaping-Pentagon-Spending-and-Capabilities_Future-Priorities_FINAL-0313132.pdf.

52. For background, see Allen Schick, *The Federal Budget, Third Edition: Politics, Policy, Process* (2007), and Rubin, *op. cit.*

53. Schick, *op. cit.*, p. 10.

54. Robert E. Wright, *One Nation Under Debt* (2008), p. 9.

55. Schick, *op. cit.*, p. 12.

56. Diana Evans, *Greasing the Wheels: Using Pork Barrel Projects to Build Majority Coalitions in Congress* (2004), p. 5.

57. "Otto von Bismarck," *Social Security History*, www.ssa.gov/history/ottob.html.

58. "Table 3.1: Outlays by Superfunction and Function: 1940-2017," White House Budget, Fiscal Year 2014, Office of Management and Budget, April 2013, www.whitehouse.gov/omb/budget/historicals.

59. For background, see Henry J. Aaron, William B. Schwartz, and Melissa Cox, *Can We Say No: The Challenge of Rationing Health Care* (2005).

60. Gerard F. Anderson and Jean-Pierre Poullier, "Health Spending, Access, and Outcomes: Trends in Industrialized Countries," *Health Affairs*, May/June 1999, http://content.healthaffairs.org/content/18/3/178.full.pdf+html?sid=6eb9b3be-8aa1-460f-9687-5b2334fc0ebb. For background, see Marcia Clemmitt, "Universal Coverage," *CQ Researcher*, March 30, 2007, pp. 265-288.

61. *Ibid.*

62. Louis Jacobson, "Were the Early 1960s a Golden Age for Health Care?" PolitiFact.com, *Tampa Bay Times*, Jan, 20, 2012, www.politifact.com/truth-o-meter/article/2012/jan/20/was-early-1960s-golden-age-health-care.

63. Dean Kalahar, "Government Spending, and the 18 Percent of GDP Myth," *RealClearMarkets*, June 9, 2011, www.realclearmarkets.com/articles/2011/06/09/government_spending_and_the_18_of_gdp_myth_99063.html.

64. For background, see Marcia Clemmitt, "Mortgage Crisis," *CQ Researcher*, Nov. 2, 2007 (updated Aug. 9, 2010), pp. 913-936, and Kenneth Jost, "Financial Crisis," *CQ Researcher*, May 9, 2008, pp. 409-432.

65. Paul Ryan, "The GOP Plan to Balance the Budget by 2023," *The Wall Street Journal*, March 12, 2013, http://online.wsj.com/article/SB10001424127887323826704578353902612840488.html.

66. Robert Kuttner, "Austerity Never Works: Deficit Hawks Are Amoral — and Wrong," *Salon*, May 5, 2013, www.salon.com/2013/05/05/austerity_never_works_deficit_hawks_are_amoral_and_wrong.

67. "How Is the Sequester Affecting Federal Agencies," *op. cit.*

68. For background, see Matthews, *op. cit.*

69. Jonnelle Marte, "No College Grads Need Apply," MarketWatch, *The Wall Street Journal*, May 4, 2013, www.marketwatch.com/story/college-grads-uncle-sam-doesnt-want-you-2013-05-03.

70. For background, see "Total Government Employment Since 1962," Office of Personnel Management, www.opm.gov/policy-data-oversight/data-analysis-documentation/federal-employment-reports/historical-tables/total-government-employment-since-1962, and "Graph: Employment Level — Nonagriculture, Government Wage and Salary Workers," *Economic Research*, Federal Reserve Bank of St. Louis, http://research.stlouisfed.org/fred2/graph/?g=4LP.

71. For background, see "How Does the American Taxpayer Relief Act Affect You?" USA.gov, http://blog.usa.gov/post/40104053240/how-does-the-american-taxpayer-relief-act-affect-you.

72. Laurie True, "Sequester Reprieve but Danger Still Lurks," *WIC blog*, California WIC Association, April 12, 2013, www.calwic.org/news-a-publications/

wic-blog; and Nancy Cook, "Short-Term Flexibility Won't Help Long-Term Impact of Sequestration," *National Journal*, March 26, 2013, www.national journal.com/daily/short-term-flexibility-won-t-help-long-term-impact-of-sequestration-20130326.

73. Quoted in Sam Stein and Amanda Terkel, "Flight Delays Deal Has Other Sequestration Victims Asking, WTF?" *The Huffington Post*, April 27, 2013, www.huffingtonpost.com/2013/04/26/flight-delays-congress-sequester_n_3165593.html.

74. Quoted in Steve Frank, "Democrat Calls Out Washington's Hypocrisy on 'Sequester' Cuts," "The Ed Show," MSNBC, May 4, 2013, http://tv.msnbc .com/2013/05/04/democrat-calls-out-washingtons-hypocrisy-on-sequester-cuts.

75. Quoted in Elise Foley, "Jeff Flake on Sequestration: Some Lawmakers Relieved to Avoid Cut Decisions," *The Huffington Post*, June 12, 2013, www.huffing tonpost.com/2013/06/12/jeff-flake-sequestra tion_n_3429974.html.

76. Quoted in Zachary A. Goldfarb, "OMB Shrinks Its Budget Deficit Forecast," *The Washington Post*, July 8, 2013, www.washingtonpost.com/business/ economy/omb-shrinks-its-budget-deficit-forecast/2 013/07/08/0b2f9f4c-e812-11e2-a301-ea5a8116d 211_story.html.

77. Daniel Lashof, "Taxpayers Get Nearly $100 Billion Bill for 2012 Extreme Weather, Equivalent to One-Sixth of Non-defense, Discretionary Spending," *Dan Lashof's blog*, Natural Resources Defense Council, May 14, 2013, http://switchboard.nrdc .org/blogs/dlashof/post.html.

# BIBLIOGRAPHY

## Selected Sources

### Books

**Rubin, Irene S., *The Politics of Public Budgeting: Getting and Spending, Borrowing and Balancing*, CQ Press, 2009.**
A professor emeritus of political science at Northern Illinois University describes the politics and the administrative processes of public budgeting at the local, state and national levels.

**Shick, Allen, *The Federal Budget, 3rd ed., Politics, Policy, Process*, Brookings Institution Press, 2007.**
A professor of public policy at the University of Maryland, College Park, and longtime analyst of government budgeting explains the history of how budgets are made in Washington.

### Articles

**"With Austerity Under Fire, Countries Seek a More Balanced Solution," *Knowledge at Wharton*, May 22, 2013, http://knowledge.wharton.upenn.edu/article .cfm?articleid=3261.**
Many nations launched repeated rounds of government budget cutting — dubbed austerity programs — in response to the international economic downturn that began in 2007. Six years later, many economies remain mired in recession, sparking renewed debate among policymakers about whether austerity or increased government spending is the right medicine for slow economies.

**Cassata, Donna, "Senate Readiness Panel Says No to Defense Department's Request for Military Base Closings," The Associated Press/*Star Tribune* [Minneapolis], June 11, 2013, www.startribune.com/ politics/national/211028181.html.**
Worried about the economic health of their communities if military installations shrink or pull out, members of Congress have rejected a Defense Department proposal to close more bases.

**Cockburn, Andrew, "Flight of the Discords," *Harper's*, June 6, 2013, http://harpers.org/blog/2013/ 06/flight-of-the-discords.**
The F-35 fighter jet being developed has a long record of cost overruns, delays and technical problems. That's at least partly due to the collaboration by industry, the military and federal lawmakers, who use the Pentagon procurement process as a means of local economic development, journalist Cockburn argues.

**Frost, Peter, "Critics Say Medicare Competitive Bidding Program Not Ready to Fly," *Chicago Tribune*, June 21, 2013, http://articles.chicagotribune .com/2013-06-21/business/ct-biz-0621-medicare-billing-20130621_1_medicare-patients-bidding-pro gram-medicare-plans.**
Practically every dollar of government spending has advocates who argue that proposed cuts would be harmful.

Federal budget analysts estimate that instituting competitive bidding in Medicare for durable medical equipment would save taxpayers and enrollees nearly $43 billion by 2022. But as Medicare prepares to roll out a bidding program, equipment companies and some lawmakers say the program could put the companies out of business.

**Riccardi, Nicholas, and Mead Gruver, "As Fires Rage, Feds Cut Funding on Prevention," ABC News/The Associated Press, June 19, 2013, http://abcnews .go.com/US/wireStory/fires-rage-feds-cut-funding-prevention-19439477#.UdHRwtgmJ0Q.**

This summer's devastating wildfires throughout the West demonstrate the tough trade-offs involved in federal government spending cuts as agencies spend scarcer dollars to combat the blazes while stinting on the ongoing fire-prevention efforts needed to keep fires from occurring and spreading.

## Reports and Studies

**Aldy, Joseph E., "Proposal 5: Eliminating Fossil Fuel Subsidies,"** Innovative Approaches to Tax Reform, **The Hamilton Project, February 2013, www.brookings .edu/~/media/research/files/papers/2013/02/thp%20 budget%20papers/thp_15waysfedbudget_prop5.pdf.**

Tax breaks to companies that drill for oil and gas are no longer needed to encourage drilling, and eliminating many of the breaks would create a more level playing field between large and small operators, says an assistant professor of public policy at Harvard University's Kennedy School of Government.

**Kogan, Richard, "Sequestration by the Numbers," Center on Budget and Policy Priorities, March 22, 2013, www.cbpp.org/cms/?fa=view&id=3937.**

An analyst at a liberal think tank explains the percentage cuts in spending that federal agencies must make to meet sequestration requirements passed by Congress in 2011 and that took effect in March.

**Viard, Alan D., "Proposal 8: Replacing the Home Mortgage Interest Deduction,"** Innovative Approaches to Tax Reform, **The Hamilton Project, February 2013, www.brookings.edu/~/media/research/files/ papers/2013/02/thp%20budget%20papers/thp _15waysfedbudget_prop8.pdf.**

An analyst from the free-market-oriented American Enterprise Institute, a Washington think tank, argues that tax breaks connected to home-mortgage interest payments are budget busters and should be limited to lower-income home buyers.

# For More Information

**Cato Institute**, 1000 Massachusetts Ave., N.W., Washington, DC 20001; 202-842-0200; www.cato.org. Libertarian think tank that advocates limiting the scope of government.

**Center on Budget and Policy Priorities**, 820 1st St., N.W., Suite 510, Washington, DC 20001; 202-408-1080; www .cbpp.org. Think tank that analyzes federal and state government spending from a liberal viewpoint.

**Committee for a Responsible Federal Budget**, 1899 L St., N.W., Suite 400, Washington, DC 20036; 202-986-6599; http://crfb.org. Bipartisan group argues for lowering the national debt.

**The Hamilton Project**, The Brookings Institution, 1775 Massachusetts Ave., N.W., Washington, DC 20036; 202-797-6484; www.hamiltonproject.org. Researches how government spending and other public policies affect economic growth.

**Heritage Foundation**, 214 Massachusetts Ave., N.W., Washington, DC 20002; 202-546-4400; www.heritage.org. Think tank that provides budget analysis from conservative viewpoint.

**National Academy of Social Insurance**, 1776 Massachusetts Ave., N.W., Suite 400, Washington, DC 20036; 202-452-8097; www.nasi.org. Nonpartisan expert group provides analysis of Social Security and Medicare.

**National Priorities Project**, 243 King St., Suite 109, Northampton, MA, 01060; 413-584-9556; http://national priorities.org. Provides information about government budgets to encourage citizens to participate in national priority setting.

**Social Security Works**, www.strengthensocialsecurity.org. Coalition of groups that advocate improving and enhancing Social Security benefits.

# 11

# Minimum Wage

Barbara Mantel

President Obama, along with a majority of Americans, supports a hike in the federal minimum wage. "We know that there are airport workers, and fast-food workers, and nurse assistants and retail salespeople who work their tails off and are still living at or barely above poverty," he said recently.

From *CQ Researcher*,
January 24, 2014.

C rystal Dupont, 25, was trying to make ends meet on the federal minimum wage. Dupont worked 30 to 40 hours a week as a customer service representative and earned between $7.25 and $8 an hour.

"I try to live within my means, but sometimes you just can't," the Houston, Texas, resident told a reporter last March. Dupont said she had no health insurance, was behind on her car payments and had taken out pawn shop loans to cover expenses.

Dupont lived with her mother, whose disability benefits and food stamps helped. Enrolled in community college, Dupont studied as much as she could. "It tells me that there's more than what I'm doing now out there — there's more to life than this," she said.[1]

Pressure is building on Congress to raise the federal minimum wage, which has remained at $7.25 an hour since 2009. Polls show a majority of Americans support the idea, and last year low-wage workers captured national media attention with protests at retailers such as Macy's, Sears and Walmart and fast-food outlets such as Dunkin' Donuts, McDonald's and Subway.

More workers making the minimum wage are employed in the food-services industry than in any other, according to the U.S. Bureau of Labor Statistics (BLS). Workers in sales, office support, transportation and personal care follow.[2]

The protesters have helped to renew a perennial national debate about the minimum wage against a backdrop of growing income disparity, stagnant real wages and rising poverty. Advocates say increasing the federal minimum wage would help struggling

## Minimum Wage's Buying Power Peaked in 1968

The federal minimum wage rose after World War II as the U.S. economy expanded, but its purchasing power peaked in the mid-1960s and declined sharply in the 1980s and '90s. The minimum wage has risen from 25 cents an hour in 1938 — $4.08 in today's dollars — to $7.25 today. In 1968 it was $1.60 per hour — $10.77 in today's dollars after adjusting for inflation using the Consumer Price Index.

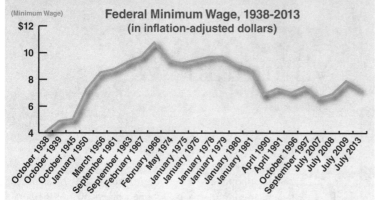

(Minimum Wage)

**Federal Minimum Wage, 1938-2013**
**(in inflation-adjusted dollars)**

Source: Craig K. Elwell, "Inflation and the Real Minimum Wage: A Fact Sheet," Congressional Research Service, Sept. 12, 2013, www.fas.org/sgp/crs/misc/R42973.pdf

low-income families, nudge down poverty and increase consumer demand, all with minimal loss of jobs. Opponents counter that it would lead employers to automate workplaces and reduce job opportunities for the lowest-skilled workers, while doing nothing to reduce poverty or help the economy.

Last year, congressional Democrats introduced legislation to raise the federal minimum wage, and five states raised their own wage floors. The bill before Congress, which President Obama supports, would raise the federal minimum in stages over a little more than two years — from $7.25 to $10.10 an hour — and then index it to inflation.

"Income inequality is one of the greatest threats to America's long-term economic vitality, yet we are widening that inequality with wages that subject people to live in poverty," the bill's co-sponsor, California Democratic Rep. George Miller, said last March.[3]

Congressional opponents insist the economy is too fragile for an increase in the minimum wage. "Listen, when people are asking the question, 'Where are the

jobs?' why would we want to make it harder for small employers to hire people?" said House Speaker John Boehner, R-Ohio, last February.[4]

Meanwhile, 21 states have minimum wages that exceed the federal minimum, with Washington state's, at $9.32 an hour, the highest.

It turns out relatively few people make the federal minimum of $7.25.

According to the Bureau of Labor Statistics, about 1.6 million Americans, or 2 percent of all hourly workers, earned the federal minimum wage in 2012. Mostly female, more than half were less than 25 years old and nearly a third were teenagers. The vast majority — 68 percent — worked part time.[5]

But if Congress raised the minimum wage to $10.10 an hour, many more than 1.6 million hourly workers would be affected. The nearly 17 million workers who earn between the current and proposed minimum wage would receive an automatic pay hike. And the wages of 11 million others who make just over $10.10 an hour would also rise, as employers adjust their pay scales upward, according to the Economic Policy Institute, a Washington-based think tank that favors a minimum wage hike and says raising the minimum would not cost jobs.[6]

This broader group of low-wage workers is older than those currently earning the $7.25 federal minimum wage. More than half are at least 30 years old; only 13 percent are teens. And, more than half are working full-time.[7]

Proponents of raising the minimum wage say it has not kept up with the rising productivity of low-wage workers and that its real value has eroded over time. Adjusted for inflation using the Consumer Price Index, the federal minimum has fallen from a high of $10.77 in 1968 to $7.25 in today's dollars.

But opponents of a higher minimum wage say the erosion has not been nearly that steep. James Sherk, a senior policy analyst in labor economics at the Heritage Foundation, a conservative think tank in Washington, uses an alternative government measure, the Personal Consumption Expenditure Price Index, to adjust the minimum wage. He says the real value of the minimum wage reached a high of only $8.28 in 1968. Thus, he says, "Raising the federal minimum wage to $10.10 an hour would be taking it well above anything we've seen before."

In any case, the main reason for raising the wage floor is "fairness," says Arindrajit Dube, an economics professor and minimum wage researcher at the University of Massachusetts, Amherst. The federal minimum wage represents about 37 percent of the median wage of all fulltime American workers, down from 55 percent in 1968, says Dube. "Raising it to $10.10 an hour would get us back to about 50 percent, which is more in line with the average for other OECD countries," he adds, referring to the Paris-based Organisation for Economic Co-operation and Development.*

According to a *Washington Post*-ABC News poll, about two-thirds of Americans say the minimum wage should be increased, although the average minimum suggested was $9.41 an hour. Breaking it down along party lines, 85 percent of Democrats support raising the minimum wage, while Republicans are split 50-45 on the issue.[8]

Meanwhile, it cost U.S. taxpayers about $243 billion per year between 2007 and 2011 to provide low-income working families with public aid through one or more of four programs — Medicaid, food stamps, the Earned Income Tax Credit and Temporary Assistance for Needy Families (TANF), according to a study by academic

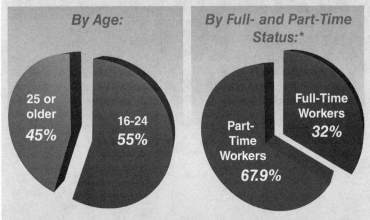

### Majority of Minimum-Wage Workers Are 16-24

More than half of minimum wage workers are between 16 and 24 years old, according to the U.S. Labor Department. More than two-thirds of workers earning the federal minimum wage are employed part time.

**Minimum Wage Workers by Age and Hours, 2012**

By Age:
- 25 or older 45%
- 16-24 55%

By Full- and Part-Time Status:*
- Part-Time Workers 67.9%
- Full-Time Workers 32%

*Figures do not add to 100 because of rounding.*

Source: "Characteristics of Minimum Wage Workers: 2012," Table 1, U.S. Bureau of Labor Statistics, www.bls.gov/cps/minwage2012tbls.htm#1

researchers. The study was funded by Fast Food Forward, a New York organizer of the fast-food strikes.[9]

"One answer to the feeling that public aid programs are too expensive is to raise the minimum wage so that more of workers' earnings come from employment," says Marc Doussard, a co-author of the study and professor of urban and regional planning at the University of Illinois at Urbana-Champaign.

According to the study, the restaurant and food services industries — at 44 percent — had the highest share of workers with a family member enrolled in one or more public-assistance programs. Thirty-five percent of agricultural, forestry or fisheries workers had a family member receiving some form of public assistance, and 30 percent of workers in the retail, leisure and hospitality industries lived in such families. In contrast, the share in manufacturing, where wages are higher, was just above 20 percent.[10]

But Thomas Fullerton, an economist at the University of Texas at El Paso, says that without low-wage jobs, "these workers would be much worse [off] because their income levels would be even lower and they would

---

*The OECD, made up of 34 market-oriented democracies, conducts economic research and provides a forum for governments to discuss solutions to common economic problems.

House Speaker John Boehner, R-Ohio, and other congressional opponents of increasing the minimum wage say the economy is too fragile to handle a hike now. "Listen, when people are asking the question 'Where are the jobs?,' why would we want to make it harder for small employers to hire people?" he said in February 2013.

require greater amounts of public assistance in order for their families to survive."[11]

Against this backdrop, these are some of the questions being debated:

## Would raising the federal minimum wage mean job losses?

Even the experts can't reach consensus on how raising the federal minimum wage would affect the number of low-skilled jobs. In a 2013 survey, about a quarter of 38 elite university economists from diverse backgrounds — including Nobel laureates, editors of leading scholarly journals and past Democratic and Republican presidential advisers — said they were uncertain whether "raising the federal minimum wage to $9 an hour would make it noticeably harder for low-skilled workers to find employment." The rest were almost evenly split between those who agreed and disagreed.[12]

"The empirical evidence now pretty decisively shows no employment effect," MIT economist Michael Greenstone wrote in his survey response, while Yale economist Joseph Altonji wrote, "The weight of the evidence is that a modest increase will have a small negative effect on employment of low-skill workers."[13]

Economists have been wrestling with this question for decades, with contradictory results. Many variables affect employment, such as oil shocks, recessions and population shifts, and economists must choose how to control for such variables to isolate the impact of the minimum wage.

"It really comes down to a judgment call," says John Schmitt, a senior economist at the Center for Economic and Policy Research, a liberal think tank in Washington.

Two different research approaches emerged in the early 1990s. One group of economists aggregated data from all 50 states, controlled for extraneous variables and concluded that minimum wage increases over the years had reduced employment.[14] At about the same time, Princeton economists David Card and Alan Krueger hit on the novel idea of conducting a "natural" experiment. It was 1992, and New Jersey had just raised its minimum wage, from $4.25 an hour to $5.05, while neighboring Pennsylvania had not. To test the notion that when the wage floor goes up employment goes down, the economists decided to use New Jersey as the experimental case and Pennsylvania as the control. The idea was that regional economic differences that might have skewed previous national research would disappear when comparing areas so close together and, presumably, economically alike.

For nearly a year, Card and Krueger surveyed employment levels at 410 fast-food outlets on either side of the state line. To the surprise of many, they found "no indication that the rise in the minimum wage reduced employment."[15]

"I think it was an exquisite piece of work," says Schmitt. "It definitely changed the way economists think about the minimum wage."

Critics complained, however, that the experiment focused on just one case at one point in time. So a new crop of economists expanded the research to include cross-border comparisons nationwide and over many years. They came to the same conclusion. "For the kinds of minimum wage increases that we have seen in the U.S. in the last 20 years, there isn't much evidence of any measurable job loss," says Dube of the University of Massachusetts, who is one of the economists.

Two explanations are possible, Dube says. Employees may stay on the job longer, reducing employers' turnover costs, such as recruitment and training expenses, and partially offsetting the cost of higher wages. Employers also could be passing on some of the increased labor costs to customers by raising prices. "And if customers continue to buy roughly, for example, the same number of burgers and fries that they were buying before, then there is less impetus to cut employee hours or the number of jobs," says Dube.

But William Dunkelberg, chief economist at the Nashville-based National Federation of Independent Business, an association of small-business owners, doesn't believe a higher wage lessens turnover or that small businesses can pass on much of the higher labor costs to consumers without affecting sales.

"Consumers buy less, and then maybe you fire a worker because you don't need 10 anymore, maybe you need 9," he says. "That's how the minimum wage gets paid for."

Researchers who say raising the minimum wage costs jobs have issued their own critique of Dube and his cross-border approach. "Maybe the counties that are separated by a state border are not so similar after all," which would make comparisons between them flawed, says J. M. Ian Salas, a fellow at the Harvard Center for Population and Development Studies.

In 2012, Salas co-wrote a paper with David Neumark, an economist at the University of California, Irvine, and William Wascher, a member of the board of governors of the Federal Reserve System, whose decades of research have found a negative impact on employment from raising the minimum wage. The three found what they considered a better comparison of counties for every state minimum wage increase between 1999 and 2011, and the counties weren't always adjacent.

"When we do our analysis, we found that for every 10 percent increase in the minimum wage, teen employment goes down by 1.5 percent" the following year, says Salas. Researchers often use teenagers as a proxy for low-wage earners.

Dube will be publishing a paper in response, as the debate continues, underscoring that what seems like a relatively simple question is anything but.

## Would raising the federal minimum wage reduce poverty?

In a speech last month, President Obama appealed to Congress to raise the minimum wage in order to help the poor. "We know that there are airport workers, and fast-food workers, and nurse assistants, and retail salespeople who work their tails off and are still living at or barely above poverty," he said.[16]

Nearly 47 million Americans, or 15 percent, live in poverty, according to the U.S. Census Bureau.[17] But economists continue to debate the merits of using the minimum wage as an antipoverty tool.

Opponents of raising the wage floor say it will help too many low-wage workers from middle-class households who are employed part time. Supporters say many of those households are struggling financially and some would be classified as poor if it weren't for the government's artificially low poverty thresholds.

But everyone agrees that raising the minimum wage won't help the non-working poor. "It's absolutely true that if you really want to address poverty, you have to help a lot of people who aren't working right now, and increasing the minimum wage is not going to do that," says David Cooper, an economic analyst at the Economic Policy Institute. The minimum wage was devised to bring fairness to the labor structure, not to fight poverty, he says. "But that doesn't mean it's not going to help a lot of people who are earning very low wages and who may be in or very close to being in poverty."

Others say increasing the base wage will do little to reduce poverty. Their argument partly harks back to the jobs debate. "There are winners, to be sure — those whose wages increase and who retain their jobs and don't have their hours reduced," said University of California, Irvine's Neumark. "But some low-skilled workers lose their jobs, and others fail to find work because of the higher wage floor."[18]

Cooper doesn't agree that jobs will be lost. Instead, he estimates that 28 million Americans would see their wages go up if the federal minimum wage were raised to $10.10 an hour, receiving "an additional $35 billion dollars in earnings over the phase-in period," which is a little over two years.

But conservative analysts say those in poverty won't be the biggest beneficiaries. First, nearly 40 percent of workers in poor families earn more than $10.10. "The reason they are poor is not the wage rate. They are poor because they don't have enough hours," says Richard Burkhauser, an economist at Cornell University in Ithaca, N.Y. The number of employees — at all income levels — working part-time because they can't find full-time work or their employers have cut their hours has nearly doubled since 2007.[19]

Second, many people earning less than the proposed new $10.10 wage floor are middle class, they say. "Mandated wage floors do a bad job of directing benefits to low-income families," said Neumark.[20]

"It's not perfectly targeted, true, but most of the water gets to the fire," counters economist Jared Bernstein, a senior fellow at the Center on Budget and Policy Priorities, a liberal think tank in Washington. In his analysis, 26 percent of the benefits of the proposed minimum wage increase would flow to the bottom 10 percent of the workforce with family incomes below $20,000 a year. "OK, some of those families will not be [officially designated as] poor because the poverty threshold for a parent with a kid, for example, is below that," he says. The threshold for a family of two is $14,937 a year.[21]

"But I don't care about that," Bernstein continues. "We must be careful not to be wedded to poverty thresholds that are inadequate measures of who needs the help." Half the benefits, he says, flow to the bottom quarter of the workforce with family incomes below $35,000. The official poverty threshold for a family of five is $27,827 a year.[22]

Still, that leaves the other half of the benefits flowing to those with family incomes above $35,000. "If it helps people further up the income ladder, great. But the point is having a floor under wages so people at the low end see improvement in their living standards," says Cooper.

Economists have tried to parse the impact of past minimum-wage increases on state poverty rates. Burkhauser, who wrote several of those studies, says, "We find none." After examining states that had raised their minimum wage, Burkhauser and his coauthors found "that a), there was no change in the overall poverty rate in the state, and b), there was no change in the poverty rate in households with workers," he says.

"What this evidence has more or less confirmed," he says, "is that if you are interested in helping the working poor, the minimum wage just doesn't do it."

But Dube says the previous studies didn't cover enough years. Using data from more than two decades, he concludes that "raising the minimum wage actually tends to have a moderate-sized reduction in the poverty rate."

Applying his results to the 39 percent increase in the wage floor proposed by congressional Democrats, he predicts 1.7 percentage points would be shaved from the 17.5 percent poverty rate among the non-elderly population. That would mean 4.6 million fewer non-elderly people living in poverty.[23]

Still, if the only goal was to fight poverty, other policies are better targeted than the minimum wage, says Dube. "You could significantly ramp up food stamps, for example."

Burkhauser suggests that the government raise the current Earned Income Tax Credit (EITC) and expand eligibility. The credit reduces the amount of tax owed or provides a tax refund for low- to moderate-income workers and shrinks as income rises. But while it provides a generous subsidy for low-income parents, it provides very little for childless adults and nothing for young adults with no children.

"I would much prefer to make all low-income kids between 18 and 25 eligible for the EITC," says Burkhauser, "rather than forcing employers to pay a wage to these kids higher than their skill level warrants."

But Cooper says if the government expanded the tax credit, it would also have to raise the minimum wage. The tax credit encourages more people to enter the workforce, putting downward pressure on wages as more people compete for jobs, research shows. "There have been some estimates that say for every dollar spent on the EITC, employers are essentially capturing about 27 cents" by being able to keep wages low, says Cooper.

## Would raising the federal minimum wage help the economy?

When Sen. Tom Harkin, D-Iowa, introduced his bill to raise the minimum wage last March, he said it would give hourly workers a fair wage and grow the economy. "With an increase in the minimum wage, workers will have more money to spend," Harkin said. "This is just basic economics: Increased demand means increased economic activity."[24]

"Wage stagnation is one of the key things holding back our economy from growing the way we need it to," says Paul Sonn, general counsel at the National Employment Law Project (NELP), a legal organization in New York that promotes worker rights. "We need to find ways to increase wages across the bottom of the economy to create consumer demand."

But Sherk of the Heritage Foundation says any economic boost triggered by a wage increase would be temporary and dissipate once economic growth resumes a more normal pace. "And then you must couple that with the straight-up losses in employment and that this money . . . is either coming from consumers in the form of higher prices or it's coming from reduced business earnings." The losses stemming from a minimum-wage increase would outweigh the benefits, says Sherk.

But analysts such as Cooper say transferring money from consumers and business owners to low-wage workers would help the economy. "You are going to be putting more money into the hands of people who are going to spend it right away because they have to," says Cooper. "And they are going to spend those dollars in their local economies instead of [having them] just sitting in banks."

But Dunkelberg of the National Federation of Independent Business says the spending habits of many consumers, small-business owners and low-wage workers aren't that different. "These aren't rich people coming into these restaurants. They're just kind of ordinary folk, like the minimum wage workers. And, again, many minimum wage workers are not poor people."

Sherk estimates that a minimum wage increase to $10.10 an hour would eliminate about 300,000 jobs and $40 billion a year from the nation's gross domestic product (GDP) by 2017.

Cooper, meanwhile, estimates that after accounting for some reduced corporate profits and higher consumer prices, GDP would increase by about $22 billion over the phase-in period — enough to create about 85,000 jobs.

The University of Massachusetts' Dube, who favors the congressional proposal, says he believes there would be some net increase in consumer spending. "But as I have tried to point out every chance I get, I think this is really small," he says, "and as a result, you just won't find anything on the aggregate economy."

## Food-Service Leads Minimum-Wage Ranks

More than 400,000 food-preparation and food-service workers earn the federal minimum wage of $7.25 an hour, the largest occupational category of minimum-wage workers. Retail and other sales-related occupations rank next, followed by office support, transportation and personal care jobs.

### Five largest occupational categories of minimum-wage workers, 2012

Food preparation and service-related jobs: **408,000**

Sales and related jobs: **400,000**

Office and administrative support: **150,000**

Transportation and material-moving jobs: **136,000**

Personal care and service jobs: **120,000**

*\* Data do not include self-employed persons.*

*Source:* "Characteristics of Minimum Wage Workers, 2012," Table 4, U.S. Bureau of Labor Statistics, www.bls.gov/cps/minwage2012tbls.htm#4

He supports raising the minimum wage because he believes it will reduce wage inequality. "This is why the vast majority of people in the U.S. support raising the minimum wage," he says.[25]

## BACKGROUND

### Early State Laws

The campaign for a minimum wage in the early 1900s was part of a broader program of social reform in response to urbanization and industrialization. Yet the first American minimum wage laws applied only to women, the result of two U.S. Supreme Court decisions.

In 1905, the Supreme Court (in *Lochner v. New York*) voided a New York law that established maximum working hours for bakers — all of whom were men at the time. The court said bakers, equal in intelligence and capacity to other working men, did not need state protection to assert their rights.[26] If a law regulating working hours for men was unconstitutional, it stood to reason that a "minimum wage law covering men was clearly doomed," wrote political scientist Jerold Waltman, of Baylor University in Waco, Texas, in *Minimum Wage Policy in Great Britain and the United States.* "However, since women, for any

Rep. George Miller, D-Calif., left, and Sen. Tom Harkin, D-Iowa, announce their sponsorship on March 5, 2013, of a bill that would raise the federal minimum wage to $10.10 an hour. "Income inequality is one of the greatest threats to America's long-term economic vitality, yet we are widening that inequality with wages that subject people to live in poverty," Miller said.

number of reasons, were not able to assert their rights in the workplace, and because their health affected children yet to be born, a case might be made that legislation applying to women could survive judicial scrutiny."[27]

That thesis was successfully tested in *Muller v. Oregon* (1908), when the Supreme Court upheld a new Oregon law regulating the working hours of women. The court cited women's smaller physical stature and lesser endurance compared to men and a lack of equal opportunities. "Education was long denied her, and while now the doors of the schoolroom are opened and her opportunities for acquiring knowledge are great, yet, even with that and the consequent increase of capacity for business affairs, it is still true that, in the struggle for subsistence, she is not an equal competitor with her brother," the court said.[28] The decision opened the way for female-specific minimum wage laws.

In 1912, Massachusetts became the first state to pass such a law, prodded by middle-class women reformers. Unions, for the most part, were less enthusiastic. Samuel Gompers, president of the American Federation of Labor, the largest labor federation at the time, opposed minimum wage laws, "fearing they would undermine collective bargaining," wrote Waltman.[29]

The Massachusetts measure established regulatory boards that set minimum wages for women equal to the

cost of living. Yet the law was, in essence, voluntary. The only penalty for employers who violated it was to have their names publicized in local newspapers. "However, the Massachusetts law had an important effect: It emboldened minimum wage advocates in other states," wrote Waltman.[30]

Within a decade, 14 other states and Puerto Rico had passed similar statutes, and Congress passed a minimal wage law for the District of Columbia.* Oregon, for example, set a minimum wage of $8.25 per week for women. Unlike the Massachusetts law, most other statutes imposed some kind of penalty on violators, although it was usually minimal.

Yet by the end of the 1920s, seven of the original minimum wage laws had been found unconstitutional; five were either never enforced or were repealed; and the remaining laws were enforced with "discretion," including targeting only small noncompliant firms that could not afford legal appeals, according to economist Clifford Thies in a review of the early laws.[31]

The cascade of reversals began in 1923 when the U.S. Supreme Court, in *Adkins v. Children's Hospital*, struck down the District of Columbia's minimum wage law as a violation of the Fifth Amendment's due process clause. In its 5-3 majority opinion, the court wrote that the inequality of the sexes cited in its *Muller v. Oregon* decision had been greatly diminished, especially in light of the 1920 ratification of the 19th Amendment giving women the right to vote. ". . . [I]t is not unreasonable to say that these differences have now come almost, if not quite, to the vanishing point," the court said.[32] Working women, in other words, no longer needed the protection of the state when entering into contracts with employers.

Chief Justice William Howard Taft issued a strong dissent, writing that minimum wage laws rightly assumed that the lowest paid employees are not on equal footing

---

*The states are Arizona, Arkansas, California, Colorado, Kansas, Minnesota, Nebraska, North Dakota, Oregon, South Dakota, Texas, Utah, Washington and Wisconsin.

with their employers and "are prone to accept pretty much anything that is offered."[33]

## Congress Acts

Amid the economic pressures of the Great Depression, the Supreme Court revisited state minimum wage laws and reversed course in March 1937. In *West Coast Hotel Co. v. Parrish*, the court upheld the constitutionality of Washington state's long-standing minimum wage law in a 5-4 vote. "The exploitation of a class of workers who are in an unequal position with respect to bargaining power, and are thus relatively defenceless against the denial of a living wage, is not only detrimental to their health and well-being but casts a direct burden for their support upon the community," wrote Chief Justice Charles Evans Hughes.[34]

Two months after the landmark decision, Democratic President Franklin D. Roosevelt called on Congress to pass a national minimum wage law. "All but the hopeless reactionary will agree that to conserve our primary resources of manpower, government must have some control over maximum hours, minimum wages, the evil of child labor and the exploitation of unorganized labor," Roosevelt said in proposing a minimum wage law.[35]

The initial draft of the bill set a 40-cent-per-hour minimum wage, a 40-hour maximum workweek and a minimum working age of 16. It applied to both sexes. The proposed legislation also would establish a five-member labor standards board that could authorize even higher pay and shorter hours after holding public hearings.

Opponents argued that a wage floor would cost jobs and impose anti-business government mandates. The National Association of Manufacturers called the president's bill "a step in the direction of communism, Bolshevism, and Nazism."[36]

Organized labor was split in its support. "Some leaders, such as Sidney Hillman of the Amalgamated Clothing Workers Union and David Dubinsky of the International Ladies' Garment Workers' Union, supported a strong bill," according to a Department of Labor history of the era. But both William Green of the American Federation of Labor and John L. Lewis of rival labor group Congress of Industrial Organizations "favored a bill which would limit labor standards to low-paid and essentially unorganized workers," the Labor Department history said. They feared that a minimum wage would become a maximum

wage and that a wage board would interfere with collective bargaining. As a result, Congress amended the bill to exclude work covered by collective bargaining.[37]

After bruising political battles and additional revisions that, among other things, lowered the minimum wage to 25 cents an hour in the first year and postponed its rise to 40 cents an hour until 1945, Congress passed the legislation in mid-June 1938. President Roosevelt signed the landmark Fair Labor Standards Act (FLSA) on June 25. (A 25-cent hourly wage in 1938 would be equivalent to $4.13 today, and 40 cents in 1945 would be worth $5.18, using the Consumer Price Index to adjust for inflation.)[38]

In its final form, the FLSA covered only about one-fifth of the labor force: individuals working in manufacturing, mining, transportation and public utilities, if they produced goods or services that moved across state lines. The law exempted or excluded executives, supervisors and those who worked in agriculture, urban mass transit and retail. In all, only about 300,000 workers received a raise.[39]

As a result, "gendered state policies remained the only recourse for many low-paid workers, especially for many women workers," wrote scholar Vivien Hart in *Bound by Our Constitution: Women, Workers, and the Minimum Wage*.[40] Following the Supreme Court's 1937 decision, states and territories enacted new minimum wage laws, revived earlier laws and amended existing ones — but most applied only to women and teens. Within four years, 26 states, the District of Columbia, and the territories of Puerto Rico and Alaska (not yet a state) had minimum wage laws on the books. Only a handful, including the laws of New York, Rhode Island and Connecticut, applied to both sexes.[41]

## Postwar Years

Amendments to the FSLA over the next three decades extended the law's coverage to additional categories of employees and raised the minimum wage. "As a result, by the mid-1970s the minimum wage penetrated virtually every corner of the economy," wrote Waltman.[42]

The first decade following enactment of the FSLA saw enormous change in the United States. The country entered World War II, ramped up war production and expanded its manufacturing base and workforce.

However, war-induced inflation, which had seriously eroded the value of the 40 cents-per-hour minimum wage,

During the Great Depression, the U.S. Supreme Court upheld, 5-4, the constitutionality of Washington state's long-standing minimum wage law, which applied only to women. "The exploitation of a class of workers who are in an unequal position with respect to bargaining power, and are thus relatively defenseless against the denial of a living wage, is not only detrimental to their health and well-being but casts a direct burden for their support upon the community," Chief Justice Charles Evans Hughes (center, front row), wrote in March 1937.

coupled with the success of unions in raising wage levels for organized labor, "left the lowest-paid segment of the labor force further and further behind," wrote economist Willis Nordlund, author of *The Quest for a Living Wage: The History of the Federal Minimum Wage Program.* "Sixteen dollars per week could no longer buy the food, clothing, shelter and other necessities that Americans believed were necessary to share in the American dream."[43] Democratic President Harry S. Truman made raising the minimum wage a priority as he sought to reorient the post-war economy toward consumers, whose material desires had been put on hold during the war.

"The high prosperity which we seek in the postwar years will not be meaningful for all our people if any large proportion of our industrial wage earners receive wages as low as the minimum now sanctioned by the Fair Labor Standards Act," Truman told Congress on Sept. 6, 1945.[44]

It took four years to pass legislation to raise the minimum wage. Truman and his supporters had to compromise with Republicans and Southern Democrats, who, for the most part, opposed the minimum wage. Congress agreed to raise the wage floor from 40 cents to 75 cents an hour, but it would not extend coverage beyond workers already

subject to the federal minimum wage. In fact, supporters had to agree to shrink the number of workers covered by the law by 500,000.

The federal minimum wage was raised and its reach was expanded under Democratic presidents John F. Kennedy and Lyndon B. Johnson, despite business arguments that such changes would spur inflation, cause job losses and encourage businesses to substitute machines for human labor. By 1968, the federal minimum wage was $1.60 an hour. Coverage had been extended to include local transit, construction and service station employees as well as those working in laundries, dry cleaners, large retailers, hotels, motels, restaurants and farms. State and local government employees at hospitals, nursing homes and schools also were protected by the federal minimum wage.[45]

## Uneven Road

During the administrations of Republican President Richard M. Nixon in 1968 and again in 1972, Congress repeatedly blocked further hikes in the minimum wage. But in 1974, as Nixon and Republicans grappled with the fallout from the political scandal known as Watergate, Democrats reintroduced a bill to raise the minimum wage to $2.30 an hour over two years and cover an additional 6 million domestic and government employees. The bill passed 71-19 in the Senate and 345-50 in the House, making a presidential veto impossible.[46]

Democrats retook the White House when President Jimmy Carter took office in 1977. Carter soon sent a minimum wage bill to Congress calling for an increase to $2.65 per hour, and even more importantly, for future increases to be indexed so the minimum wage would remain at half of the nation's average manufacturing wage. The indexing proposal "triggered intense debate," wrote Waltman. "When the dust had settled, the indexing provision had foundered," and "a $3.35 minimum wage was to be realized in four steps."[47]

Ronald Reagan's electoral triumph in 1980 began a 12-year Republican hold on the White House. The new president had once said the minimum wage had "caused

# CHRONOLOGY

**1900s–1920s** *States establish minimum wages that apply only to women, but courts nullify the measures, arguing that women no longer need protection when entering work contracts.*

**1905** In *Lochner v. New York*, the U.S. Supreme Court voids a New York state law setting maximum working hours for male bakers.

**1908** In *Muller v. Oregon*, the U.S. Supreme Court upholds an Oregon law regulating women's working hours, setting the stage for minimum wage laws for women.

**1912** Massachusetts becomes the first state to enact a minimum wage for women.

**1923** By 1923, 14 other states, Puerto Rico and the District of Columbia have passed similar laws for women. . . . In *Adkins v. Children's Hospital*, the U.S. Supreme Court strikes down the District of Columbia's minimum wage law.

**1929** By now, minimum wage laws for women have been declared unconstitutional, repealed or barely enforced.

**1930s–1940s** *During the Great Depression and emergence of a more activist federal government, the Supreme Court upholds minimum wage for women; Congress and states follow with new laws covering more workers.*

**1937** Reversing *Adkins*, Supreme Court upholds constitutionality of Washington state's minimum wage law (*West Coast Hotel Co. v. Parrish*), which applied only to women.

**1938** Democratic President Franklin D. Roosevelt signs the landmark Fair Labor Standards Act, which establishes a minimum wage of 40 cents an hour by 1945 for both male and female workers but covers only about one-fifth of the labor force.

**1941** Twenty-six states, the District of Columbia, Puerto Rico and Alaska have minimum wage laws; most apply only to women and children.

**1949** In a compromise with pro-business legislators, Congress raises the minimum wage to 75 cents an hour while shrinking the number of workers covered.

**1950s–1970s** *Despite opposition from business, the minimum wage rises incrementally for three decades.*

**1955** Republican President Dwight D. Eisenhower recommends raising the minimum wage to $1 an hour; Congress complies.

**1961** Democratic President John F. Kennedy persuades Congress to raise the minimum wage to $1.25 an hour.

**1966** Democratic President Lyndon B. Johnson persuades Congress to raise the minimum to $1.60 and cover 9.1 million more workers.

**1974** During administration of Republican President Richard M. Nixon, a Democratically controlled Congress raises the minimum wage to $2.30 an hour.

**1977** Under Democratic President Jimmy Carter, Congress increases the minimum wage to $3.35 but rejects Carter's proposal to index it to the average manufacturing wage.

**1981-Present** *Federal minimum wage does not rise under two-term Republican President Ronald Reagan, then resumes sporadic increases.*

**1990** Republican President George H. W. Bush signs legislation to raise the minimum wage to $4.25 an hour.

**1996** Democratic President Bill Clinton signs law raising the hourly minimum wage to $5.15.

**2007** Thirty states and the District of Columbia have minimum wage levels above the $5.15 federal minimum. . . . Congress raises the minimum wage to $7.25 by July 2009 as part of a bill providing billions in small-business tax breaks.

**2013** Two Congressional Democrats introduce legislation to raise the minimum in three stages to $10.10.

**2014** As of Jan. 1, 21 states and the District of Columbia have wage floors above the federal minimum.

# Fast-Food Workers Seek Higher Hourly Wage

*"Expect more militant activities from fast-food workers."*

After two years working full time at a Wendy's in Kansas City, Mo., Latoia Caldwell still makes $7.35 an hour, Missouri's minimum wage. "These are starvation wages," said Caldwell in early December. "We're going to do whatever it takes to get this $15 wage and a union.[1]

Caldwell was one of thousands of protesters in 100 U.S. cities who demonstrated on Dec. 5 to demand the $15-per-hour wage — up from the sector's $9 median rate — and the right to unionize. It was the latest in a series of one-day strikes that began in November 2012, when roughly 200 fast-food workers walked off their jobs in New York City to protest low wages.

Business groups have charged that most of the strikers are labor organizers, not fast-food employees. "As far as these protests are concerned, you've got to call them for what they are," said John Holub, president of the New Jersey Retail Merchants Association. "It's a feeble attempt by unions to increase their membership rolls because they're obviously losing significant ground in the last few years."[2]

Fast-food companies have given no indication they will meet the wage demands, and most municipalities and states that have approved increases to their minimum wages in the past year haven't approached anywhere near $15 an hour. California's minimum wage is due to rise to $10 in 2016, which would be the highest among the states. Washington, D.C.'s minimum hourly wage will rise to $11.50 by 2016, one of the highest of any U.S. city.

Nevertheless, the fast-food workers' efforts this past year have had a "titanic" influence on the minimum wage debate, said Kendall Fells, organizing director of Fast Food Forward, a group of New York fast-food workers that helped plan the initial walkout. The campaign will continue this year, he says. "I think what people can expect is more and greater activity, bigger actions, more militant activities from fast-food workers across the country and continued growth."[3]

Mary Kay Henry, president of the Service Employees International Union, also expects the fast-food protests to grow. The union — with more than 2 million members working in health care, local and state government and the janitorial and security industries — has helped fund and organize the one-day strikes.

"I think we've totally changed the conversation about what these jobs are worth," Henry said. "These are no longer jobs being done by teenagers who need extra money. These are jobs being done by adults that can't find any other work."[4]

In reality, about 30 percent of fast-food workers are in their teens, and another 30 percent are between 20 and 24. The rest are 25 or older, according to an analysis of government survey data by the liberal-leaning Center for Economic and Policy Research, a Washington think tank. More than 80 percent of fast-food workers over 20 have at least a high school diploma.[5]

"What we're getting paid is not enough," said Benjamin Hunter, 43, a father of one who works at a Burger King in Wilmington, Del., and makes $7.25 an hour. His wife, he said, makes $9 an hour as a Burger King shift manager, and the family receives Medicaid and food stamps. "Who can actually live on what they [the fast-food restaurants] are paying?" Hunter asked.[6]

According to research funded by Fast Food Forward, half of the families of front-line fast-food workers employed for at least 27 weeks and at least 10 hours per week were receiving aid from one or more public-assistance programs — either Medicaid and the Children's Health Insurance Program; the Federal Earned Income Tax Credit (EITC) program; the Supplemental Nutrition Assistance Program, better known as food stamps; or Temporary Assistance for Needy Families, formerly known as welfare. The researchers say the public cost to support fast-food workers is $7 billion a year.[7]

The restaurant industry calls the report flawed and misleading. "I believe very strongly that they directed the research in a cherry-picked kind of manner," says Scott

DeFife, executive vice president of policy and government affairs at the Washington-based National Restaurant Association. Ten hours a week is a "random number," and the EITC is not a welfare program but a tax incentive to encourage people to work and should not have been included, he says.

"What is the public cost of folks not having any job?" asks DeFife. For some in the industry with low skills and a low educational level, "the restaurant industry may be one of the only industries where they can get a job, period," he says.

Stephen J. Caldeira, president of the Washington-based International Franchise Association, estimated that an increase to $15 an hour would lead to at least a 25 percent jump in fast-food prices. "Increasing the cost of labor would lead to higher prices for the consumer, lower foot traffic and sales for franchise owners and ultimately lost entry-level jobs," he said.[8]

Some economists said the potential consequences would be smaller. Ken Jacobs, chairman of the Center for Labor Research and Education at the University of California, Berkeley, estimated a 10 percent increase in fast-food prices, while Arindrajit Dube, an economics professor at the University of Massachusetts, Amherst, estimated a price increase of close to 20 percent.[9]

Dube's previous research has shown that modest increases in the minimum wage would have little impact on employment. But he says that research would not apply to the nearly 70 percent jump in wages demanded by fast-food workers, the effects of which haven't been studied.

"If you raise the minimum wage to $15 an hour, can we say that the evidence we have mustered will continue to suggest that there will be no job losses? No, you can't say that," says Dube.

— *Barbara Mantel*

Demonstrators at a McDonald's in New York City on Dec. 5, 2013, demand a $15-an-hour minimum wage as part of a nationwide protest by fast-food workers.

[1]Ned Resnikoff, "Fast food workers on strike in over 100 cities," MSNBC, Dec. 5, 2013, www.msnbc.com/all/the-biggest-fast-food-strike-yet.

[2]Linda Moss, "N.J. fast-food workers sit this strike out," *NorthJersey .Com*, Aug. 30, 2013, www.northjersey.com/news/221752261_N_J__still_in_debate_on_minimum_wage_increase.html.

[3]Ned Resnikoff, "Low-wage workers' movement looks to build on banner year," MSNBC, Jan. 3, 2014, www.msnbc.com/all/will-2014-be-the-year-unions-revived.

[4]Candice Choi, "Fast-food strikes and protests planned for 100 US cities," *The Christian Science Monitor*, Dec. 3, 2013, www.csmonitor.com/Business/Latest-News-Wires/2013/1203/Fast-food-strikes-and-protests-planned-for-100-US-cities.

[5]John Schmitt and Janelle Jones, "Slow Progress for Fast-Food Workers," Center for Economic and Policy Research, August 2013, www.cepr.net/documents/publications/fast-food-workers-2013-08.pdf.

[6]Michael A. Fletcher, "Fast-food workers plan a new wave of walkouts across the nation," *The Washington Post*, Dec. 3, 2013, www.washingtonpost.com/business/economy/fast-food-workers-plan-a-new-wave-of-walkouts-across-the-nation/2013/12/03/b64809e4-5b87-11e3-a49b-90a0e156254b_story.html.

[7]Sylvia Allegretto, *et al.*, "Fast Food, Poverty Wages: The Public Cost of Low-Wage Jobs in the Fast-Food Industry," Center for Labor Research and Education, University of California, Berkeley, Oct. 15, 2013, pp. 1, 4, http://laborcenter.berkeley.edu/publiccosts/fast_food_poverty_wages.pdf.

[8]Steven Greenhouse, "$15 Wage in Fast Food Stirs Debate on Effects," *The New York Times*, Dec. 4, 2013, www.nytimes.com/2013/12/05/business/15-wage-in-fast-food-stirs-debate-on-effects.html?_r=0.

[9]*Ibid.*

# Workers Reliant on Tips Hungry for a Higher Minimum

*"I made more 20 years ago than I do now, effectively."*

The federal minimum wage for workers who rely on tips — waiters, waitresses, bartenders, hairdressers, barbers and others — has been stuck at $2.13 an hour for 23 years. That's less than a third of the $7.25 federal minimum that applies to most other workers, its lowest share on record. In addition, two decades of inflation have substantially reduced what it can buy.

"As far as income goes, I made more 20 years ago than I do now, effectively," said Rebecca Williams, 50, who has waited tables, on and off, at upscale bistros in Atlanta, Ga., for 30 years. "My affluent friends, their jaws drop when I tell them."[1]

Three in four tipped workers are women, about half are 30 years old or older, and more than 60 percent are restaurant workers, mostly servers.[2] Their median hourly earnings, including tips, are $9 to $12 an hour, depending on occupation.[3]

"No one makes $2.13 an hour in the end," says Scott DeFife, the executive vice-president of policy and government affairs at the Washington-based National Restaurant Association. If an employee's tips combined with the tipped minimum wage don't add up to the regular federal minimum of $7.25 per hour federal law requires employers to cover the difference.

But this requirement is difficult to enforce, and even when workers file official complaints, employers have "rarely changed their practices," according to a University of California, Berkeley report.[4]

The tipped minimum wage hasn't always been flat. It remained at about half of the regular minimum wage as the two moved in tandem between 1966, when Congress first allowed employers to pay a lower minimum to tipped workers, and 1996. But in 1996, after lobbying by the National Restaurant Association, Congress severed the relationship and froze the tipped minimum.

Legislation introduced in Congress last year to raise the regular federal minimum in stages to $10.10 an hour would restore that relationship. The measure would raise the tipped minimum wage in annual increments of a little less than $1 until it reached 70 percent of the regular minimum. It then would continue to increase as needed to maintain that proportion.

The National Restaurant Association opposes the proposal, calling 70 percent "too radical and unworkable for the restaurant business model," in which "pre-tax profit margins for a typical restaurant range from 3 percent to 5 percent."[5]

Christopher Savvides, a past chair of the Virginia Restaurant Association, said he would struggle to pay a base wage higher than $2.13 an hour at his three Virginia restaurants, including the Black Angus Grille in Virginia Beach. Savvides said a higher wage would encourage him to "minimize the need for staff." Most of his staff makes $12 to $20 an hour, including tips, he said.[6]

But Jason Murphy, co-owner of Russell Street Deli in Detroit, starts his tipped workers at $5 an hour, higher than the $2.65 state minimum. "It gives the employees a sense of ownership and confidence," he said.[7]

Unlike the federal government, seven states do not allow employers to pay a subminimum wage to tipped workers. But the rest do, although most, like Michigan, have a tipped minimum wage that exceeds the federal minimum. Fourteen states have a tipped wage that matches the federal minimum.[8]

Still, DeFife says tipped employees in the restaurant industry are well paid, earning, including tips, far above the

more misery and unemployment than anything since the Great Depression."[48] During his time in office, House Democrats failed to bring a minimum wage bill to the floor for a vote, while their Senate counterparts could not overcome a Republican filibuster. The new president also ushered in an era of weakened unions after he fired nearly 11,500 federal air-traffic controllers who refused to return to work during an illegal strike. The action essentially broke the back of the Professional Air Traffic Controllers Organization.

Between 1990 and 1997, during the presidencies of Republican George H. W. Bush and Democrat Bill Clinton, the minimum wage rose twice, first to $4.25 per hour in two stages and then to $5.15 in another two-step process.

regular federal hourly minimum. "The tipped employees are typically among the highest earners among hourly workers in the [restaurant] industry," says DeFife. "Our data shows that anywhere from $12 to $17 an hour is the national average for tipped workers."

But according to government survey data, the hourly earnings for waiters and waitresses, including tips, averages just under $10 an hour.[9] "For everybody who works in a fancy restaurant, there are 100 people working in a Waffle House where you're just not going to make a lot of money," says Gordon Lafer, a professor at the University of Oregon Labor Education and Research Center.

While the impact on jobs of raising the federal tipped minimum wage to 70 percent of the regular federal minimum is open to debate, automation is already underway at some restaurant chains. Applebee's plans to have computer tablets at every table by the end of this year for customers to place orders, play games and swipe credit cards for payment. Chili's has announced a similar plan.

Applebee's parent company DineEquity CEO Julia Stewart said it is not about saving labor, since food servers will still be available. "This is really about creating an opportunity to talk to our guest, have an interactive conversation with our guest, and give our guest a lot more opportunities," said Stewart on CNBC.[10] But opponents to a wage hike point to Chili's and Applebee's as examples of how restaurants can use technology to save labor costs in the future.

"This is going to dramatically to reduce their need for servers," says James Sherk, a senior policy analyst in labor economics at the Washington-based Heritage Foundation, a conservative think tank.

— *Barbara Mantel*

A waiter serves customers at the Old Pointe Tavern in Indianapolis. Under federal law, waiters who earn tips must be paid at least $2.13 an hour — a federal wage floor that hasn't changed in 23 years. Some states have higher hourly minimums.

[2]Sylvia A. Allegretto and Kai Filion, "Waiting for Change: The $2.13 Federal Subminimum Wage," Center on Wage and Employment Dynamics & Economic Policy Institute, Feb. 23, 2011, p. 6, www.epi.org/publication/waiting_for_change_the_213_federal_subminimum_wage.

[3]"May 2012 National Occupational Employment and Wage Estimates," Bureau of Labor Statistics, www.bls.gov/oes/current/oes_nat.htm#39-0000.

[4]Allegretto and Filion, *op. cit.*, p. 4.

[5]"Minimum Wage," National Restaurant Association, 2013, www.restaurant.org/Downloads/PDFs/News-Research/20131112_Min_Wage_Issue_Brief.

[6]Jeanna Smialek, "Waitresses Stuck at $2.13 Hourly Minimum for 22 Years," Bloomberg Personal Finance, April 25, 2013, www.bloomberg.com/news/2013-04-25/waitresses-stuck-at-2-13-hourly-minimum-for-22-years.html.

[7]*Ibid.*

[8]"Minimum Wages for Tipped Employees," U.S. Department of Labor, Jan. 1, 2014, www.dol.gov/whd/state/tipped.htm.

[9]"Waiters and Waitresses," "Occupational Employment and Wages," May 2012, Bureau of Labor Statistics, March 29, 2013, www.bls.gov/oes/current/oes353031.htm.

[10]Rick Aristotle Munarriz, "Welcome to Applebee's. My Name Is Tablet. May I Take Your Order?" *Daily Finance*, Dec. 12, 2013, www.dailyfinance.com/on/applebees-tablets-tables-customers-order-pay-automation.

[1]Dave Jamieson, "Minimum Wage For Restaurant Servers Remains Stagnant For 20 Years Under Industry Lobbying," *The Huffington Post*, June 2, 2012, www.huffingtonpost.com/2012/06/02/minimum-wage-restaurant-workers_n_1515916.html?view=print&comm_ref=false.

But for the next 10 years, a Republican-controlled Congress blocked increases.

During the decade of federal inaction, state governments took the lead. Many raised their minimum wages while others adopted minimum-wage bills for the first time. By this time, state laws were gender-neutral. "By January of 2007, 30 states and the District of Columbia had pushed their own minimum wage levels above what Congress required employers to pay," wrote Waltman.[49]

Then in 2007, Congress approved and Republican President George W. Bush signed an increase in the federal minimum wage as part of a bill that provided more money for the Iraq war and nearly $5 billion in tax breaks for small businesses. The measure raised the minimum wage in three stages over two years — to $7.25 an hour, where it remains today.[50]

## CURRENT SITUATION

### Federal Legislation

Like Democratic presidents before him, President Obama repeatedly has called for the minimum wage to be increased. In his State of the Union address on Feb. 12, 2013, for example, he recommended raising it to $9 an hour. He called for a raise again in early December, and his aides have indicated the president supports the $10.10 rate proposed by congressional Democrats.[51]

"Millions of Americans clean our offices, wait on customers in restaurants and stores, and provide care for our children, parents or grandparents. Yet, despite all they do to keep our economy running, minimum wage workers earn just $7.25 an hour — not enough to pay the bills, much less aspire to the American Dream," said Sen. Harkin, when he and Rep. Miller introduced the Fair Minimum Wage Act of 2013 in early March.[52]

The legislation would raise the minimum wage to $10.10 an hour in three increments of 95 cents each over the course of two years and three months. After that, it would be indexed to rise with inflation. The bill would

Job seekers fill out applications at a job fair for concession positions at Chicago's O'Hare International Airport on Jan. 13, 2014. Business groups say increasing the minimum wage would force employers to eliminate jobs for low-wage workers. Supporters of an increase say a raise would cause minimal job loss and would put money into hands of low-wage workers, who would spend it, boosting the economy.

> **Pressure is building on Congress to raise the federal minimum wage, which has remained at $7.25 an hour since 2009. Polls show a majority of Americans support the idea.**

also increase the minimum wage for tipped workers, which has been stalled at $2.13 an hour for 23 years.[53]

Last March, all 227 House Republicans, along with six Democrats, defeated an amendment to a job-training bill that would have raised the minimum wage to $10.10 an hour. With Washington preoccupied with the federal budget, the rollout of health insurance exchanges and immigration, there was little movement on the issue during the rest of the year.

Still, both Harkin and Miller stepped up their efforts in July, the fourth anniversary of the last minimum-wage increase. At that time, they cited a Hart Research poll, which found that 92 percent of Democrats, 80 percent of independents, and 62 percent of Republicans backed the Harkin-Miller proposal.[54] Nevertheless, both the House and the Senate versions of the bill remained stuck in committee.

The bills' supporters hope this year will be different, and Obama's December speech indicates he's ready to spend political capital to try and make it so.

### States Step In

Jack Temple, a policy analyst with the National Employment Law Project (NELP), says that during the past year a growing number of states have become frustrated with "congressional foot dragging over raising the minimum wage and anxious about problems posed by the rapid growth in low-wage jobs, such as weak consumer spending." As a result, he says, California and four Northeastern states — Connecticut, New Jersey, New York and Rhode Island — passed bills in 2013 to raise their own minimums.

In September, California adopted a measure that will raise the state's minimum wage by $2 over three years — to $10 an hour, making California's the highest state minimum wage unless another state surpasses it during the phase-in period. Phase one, which goes into

Getty Images/Bloomberg/Tim Boyle

**AT ISSUE**

# Would raising the minimum wage help the economy?

## YES
**Jared Bernstein**
*Senior Fellow, Center on Budget and Policy Priorities; Former Chief Economist to Vice President Joseph Biden*

Written for *CQ Researcher*, January 2014

Based on one well-established theory and two equally well-established facts, raising the minimum wage would help.

The first fact is that the American economy is made up of 70 percent consumer spending.

Economists widely agree that an extra dollar earned by a wealthy person is less likely to be spent than an extra dollar earned by a low-income person. The reasoning — as per the theory of different spending and saving patterns by income level: The rich person is not "income constrained." If there's something they want to buy, they needn't wait for that extra dollar. On the other hand, the low-income worker is much more likely to consume their extra dollar of earnings.

The second fact is that moderate increases in the minimum wage boost the earnings of most low-wage workers without leading to large employment losses. The increase favored by the president and congressional Democrats, which would take the federal minimum wage from $7.25 up to $10.10 in three annual increments, would place the real value of the wage floor back where it was in the late 1960s and would directly affect about 13 percent of the workforce. In terms of the share of affected workers, that's slightly higher than many past increases, but given our older, more productive low-wage workforce, it's fair to label this proposed increase as "moderate." So, the empirical history of the minimum-wage program would suggest that the vast majority of low-wage workers would benefit from the increase.

Summing up the facts: In an economy driven in no small measure by consumer spending, moderately boosting the pay of low-wage workers with relatively high propensities to spend their new earnings should produce slightly faster macroeconomic growth.

Now, in a $16.5 trillion economy, a minimum wage increase that directly raises the pay of a relatively small share of the workforce by a small amount is unlikely to be a big deal in terms of the larger growth picture. I would not argue that raising the minimum wage is first and foremost a growth strategy, though it will help a bit at the margin. Where it really makes a difference is in helping working families toiling at the low end of the service economy get a bit closer to making ends meet.

## NO
**Douglas Holtz-Eakin**
*President, American Action Forum; Former Commissioner, Financial Crisis Inquiry Commission*

Written for *CQ Researcher*, January 2014

Raising the federal minimum wage will neither reduce poverty nor boost growth. Increasing the minimum wage to $10, or even $15, would ensure that millions of Americans got raises — raises that they would presumably turn right around and spend. Isn't the former going to reduce poverty and the latter boost the economy?

That would happen if the money came out of thin air. Unfortunately, it has to come out of the wallet of another American. In the worst case, forcing up the minimum wage at, say, a fast-food restaurant would mean not hiring another poor American. If so, the minimum wage hike for one low-wage worker comes directly out of the pocket of another. Which part of that is anti-poverty and which part is stimulus?

Of course, not every dollar will come from not hiring low-wage workers. But every dollar will have to come from somewhere. A minimum wage hike means higher prices, lower raises for other workers or fewer dividends for seniors, IRA holders and pension funds. Low-wage workers may pay those higher prices, blue-collar workers are desperately clinging to their pensions, and seniors need their dividends to make ends meet. There is simply no guarantee that the resources are transferred from the well-to-do to the deserving. And the diminished resources of those harmed by hiking the minimum wage offset the spending of the beneficiaries.

The minimum wage is a poor tool to fight poverty because it does not target those in poverty. Only 2 percent of workers earn the minimum wage, and only 20 percent of those are in poverty. The reality is that the dividing line between being poor and being non-poor is having a job. Only 7 percent of those who have a job are in poverty, while more than 27.5 percent of those without jobs are poor.

Even worse, the minimum wage does not help anyone get a job. There is little evidence that past minimum-wage increases have led to layoffs, but recent research indicates that hiking the minimum wage would harm new hiring. That's not stimulus.

The idea of increasing the minimum wage has a seductive appeal. No one opposes the idea that working Americans should make a few more dollars. Unfortunately, the idea does not stand up to close scrutiny.

effect in July, is highly anticipated by Walmart worker Anthony Goytia in Duarte, Calif. "If I had a higher wage, we would be able to rent an apartment," said Goytia, who was living in a garage with his wife and two children. "[Right now] we're living in poverty. I have to live check to check."[55]

Minimum wage legislation passed easily in Democratic-controlled Connecticut, where the wage will rise from $8.25 to $9 over a year and a half. The same is true in New York, where the minimum increases from $7.25 to $9 in stages over three years and in Rhode Island, which approved a raise from $7.75 to $8 an hour.

But in New Jersey, the battle was intense. After Republican Gov. Chris Christie vetoed a bill a year ago to increase the minimum from $7.25 to $8.25 and index it to inflation, the legislature put the measure on the November ballot. In the intervening months, both the business community and unions spent heavily to sway voters on the issue. In the end, voters overwhelmingly approved both the measure and Christie's return to office.

After the vote, opponents and supporters squared off one last time. "New Jersey's voters should be thanked tonight for understanding that the state's low-wage workers need more than $7.25 an hour to survive in this high-cost state," said Gordon MacInnes, president of New Jersey Policy Perspective, a left-leaning think tank.[56]

But Laurie Ehlbeck, state director of the National Federation of Independent Business, accused the measure's supporters of misleading workers. Employers "are not going to hire someone. They will give an employee fewer hours [or] they may reduce benefits," she said.[57]

Not all businesses opposed the wage hike. "A higher minimum wage will actually help business owners by reducing absenteeism and worker turnover, which costs businesses way more than nickel and dime-ing on wages," said Mitch Cahn, president of Unionwear, a Newark clothing manufacturer with 120 employees.[58]

The higher minimum wages in Connecticut, New Jersey, New York and Rhode Island began to kick in on Jan. 1, along with small increases in nine other states that index the minimum wage to inflation: Arizona, Colorado, Florida, Missouri, Montana, Ohio, Oregon, Vermont and Washington.[59] Nevada's minimum wage adjusts to the cost of living every July.

As of the beginning of this year, 21 states and the District of Columbia have minimum wages above the federal minimum, according to the National Conference of State Legislatures. In 19 states plus Guam, Puerto Rico and the Virgin Islands the minimum is the same as the federal minimum. The federal minimum wage also applies in four states and American Samoa, which have minimum wages below the federal minimum, and in six states that have no minimum wage.[60]

## Municipalities

In November, voters in SeaTac, a small town south of Seattle and the home of Seattle-Tacoma International Airport, approved the highest city minimum wage in the country — $15 an hour — an increase of 63 percent from the state's $9.19 minimum wage and more than double the federal minimum wage. Union leaders said they hoped to use the results to bolster battles for higher wages in other cities, including Seattle. "We have seen a national change in the conversation about wages," David Rolf, president of a Seattle chapter of the Services Employees International Union, said in late November.[61]

The SeaTac law excludes airlines, retail stores with fewer than 10 workers, hotels with fewer than 30 workers and other businesses with fewer than 25 workers. But roughly 6,500 workers — hospitality and ramp workers at the airport, as well as workers on off-airport property, such as hotel and car rental employees — would get the $15 wage. While no other municipality has such a high minimum wage, a few other airports impose similar wage floors. Workers at Los Angeles International Airport, for example, make a minimum of $15.37 an hour.

But a late December court decision may jeopardize the SeaTac increase. The airlines and the restaurant industry backed a lawsuit challenging the city's jurisdiction over the airport, which is actually managed by another municipality, the Port of Seattle. The King County Superior Court agreed with the plaintiffs and said the wage hike could apply only to the 1,600 people who work outside of airport property. Supporters of the ballot measure have promised to appeal.[62]

Meanwhile, three other cities approved a hike in their minimum wages in 2013: San Francisco (to $10.74), San Jose, Calif. (to $10.15) and the District of Columbia (to $11.50 in stages).

DeFife of the National Restaurant Association said minimum wage activity at the municipal level is "a bit out of control," and predicted that employers might move to neighboring areas for cheaper labor.[63] But in what the National Employment Law Project (NELP) called "a rare example of regional cooperation," two of the District of Columbia's neighboring counties, Montgomery and Prince George's in Maryland, approved measures to raise their own minimum wages to match the district's new base wage.[64]

## Restricting Wages

New Hampshire has no minimum wage since the Republican-controlled legislature in 2011 overrode Democratic Gov. John Lynch's veto to repeal the state's minimum wage law. The consequences were small, since the wage floor in New Hampshire was the same as the federal minimum. But the repeal "sent a political message that New Hampshire is opposed to raising wages for workers," says Temple of NELP.

A few other states have restricted their minimum wage laws in recent years as a way for pro-business legislators to keep wages as low as possible. For instance, Indiana banned "any city or county from having a higher minimum wage than the state's," according to Gordon Lafer, a professor at the University of Oregon Labor Education and Research Center who surveyed the state landscape.[65] "South Dakota exempted its summer tourism industry, and Maine's new law allows employers, rather than the state, to decide when to classify workers as disabled and thus pay them a sub-minimum wage." Many states and the federal government have a lower minimum wage for the disabled.

## OUTLOOK

### Action Expected

Advocates for raising the minimum wage are hopeful for their prospects at the state level in 2014. Six states are considering raising the minimum wage, according to NELP's Temple: Delaware, Hawaii, Illinois, Maryland, Massachusetts and Minnesota.

"This list is not comprehensive, but these are the states where I believe it is most likely to pass," says Temple.

For example, the Minnesota House and Senate each passed minimum wage bills last year and plan to reconcile them this term; the House version would raise the minimum wage to $9.50 an hour in stages, $1.75 more

than the Senate version. In Massachusetts, the state Senate overwhelmingly passed a bill to raise the minimum wage from $8 to $11 an hour. If approved, it would become the highest state minimum in the nation. The legislation is pending in the House.

Voters, rather than legislators, may decide the issue in some states. Advocates are collecting signatures for ballot initiatives to raise state minimum wages in Arkansas (from $7.25 to $8.50), Alaska (by $2 to $9.75 an hour) and New Mexico (by $1 to $8.50).

"I think in a lot of these states, they will get on the ballots," says Temple. "For example, in Arkansas and Alaska, the threshold [for getting on the ballot] is fairly low," and a ballot initiative has already been certified in South Dakota that would raise the state minimum from $7.25 to $8.50.

Cooper of the Economic Policy Institute expects an increase in the federal minimum wage as well. "I'm optimistic that we'll see a federal increase in the next five years or so," says Cooper. "It's important to remember, however, that because inflation is always eating away at the wage's purchasing power, a $10 minimum wage five years from now would be worth the same as having $9 minimum wage today — or even less depending on inflation."

Even some opponents predict Congress will act. "Odds are that if it is raised, and I expect that it will be, it will also be indexed to inflation," says Dunkelberg of the National Federation of Independent Business. "If the president gets his way, we get to $10 for 2016, and then inflation raises it after that. With 2 percent inflation, the [Federal Reserve] target, that would leave you at $10.60 by 2018, more if inflation is higher."

Democratic leaders hope to use the minimum wage as a wedge issue in this year's mid-term elections. "It puts Republicans on the wrong side of an important issue when it comes to fairness," Daniel Pfeiffer, President Obama's senior adviser, told *The New York Times*. "You can make a very strong case that this will be a helpful issue for Democrats in 2014. But the goal here is to actually get it done."[66]

"The White House seems committed to making a big push on the minimum wage in 2014. It might not pay off in 2014, but likely will pay off before the 2016 elections," says Schmitt of the Center for Economic and Policy Research. "The minimum wage is very popular with voters, including Republican voters."

## NOTES

1. Allison Linn, " 'By the grace of God': How workers survive on $7.25 per hour," NBC News, March 6, 2013, http://inplainsight.nbcnews.com/_news/2013/03/06/17195815-by-the-grace-of-god-how-workers-survive-on-725-per-hour?lite.

2. "Characteristics of Minimum Wage Workers, 2012," Table 4, U.S. Bureau of Labor Statistics, www.bls.gov/cps/minwage2012tbls.htm#4.

3. "Joined By Business Leaders and Workers, Sen. Harkin, Rep. Miller Unveil Bill to Raise the Minimum Wage to $10.10," press release, Committee on Education & The Workforce, Democrats, House of Representatives, March 5, 2013, http://democrats.edworkforce.house.gov/press-release/joined-business-leaders-and-workers-sen-harkin-rep-miller-unveil-bill-raise-minimum.

4. Pamela M. Prah, "Next Wave of State Minimum Wage Proposals Would 'Index' To Inflation," Stateline, The Pew Charitable Trusts, March 15, 2013, www.pewstates.org/projects/stateline/headlines/next-wave-of-state-minimum-wage-proposals-would-index-to-inflation-85899459281.

5. "Characteristics of Minimum Wage Workers: 2012—Table 1" U.S. Bureau of Labor Statistics, Feb. 26, 2013, www.bls.gov/cps/minwage2012tbls.htm#1.

6. David Cooper, "Raising the Federal Minimum Wage to $10.10 Would Lift Wages for Millions and Provide a Modest Economic Boost," Economic Policy Institute, Dec. 19, 2013, p. 7, http://s4.epi.org/files/2013/Raising-the-federal-minimum-wage-to-1010-would-lift-wages-for-millions-and-provide-a-modest-economic-boost-12-19-2013.pdf.

7. *Ibid.*, pp. 8-9.

8. Michael A. Flether and Peyton M. Craighill, "Majority of Americans want minimum wage to be increased, poll finds," *The Washington Post*, Dec. 18, 2013, www.washingtonpost.com/business/economy/majority-of-americans-want-minimum-wage-to-be-increased-poll-finds/2013/12/17/b6724bb0-6743-11e3-ae56-22de072140a2_story.html.

9. Sylvia Allegretto, *et al.*, "Fast Food, Poverty Wages: The Public Cost of Low-Wage Jobs in the Fast-Food Industry," Center for Labor Research and Education, University of California, Berkeley, Oct. 15, 2013, p. 5, http://laborcenter.berkeley.edu/publiccosts/fast_food_poverty_wages.pdf.

10. *Ibid.*, p. 7.

11. Carl Bialik, "Is Fast Food Bad Value for the Public," *The Wall Street Journal*, Nov. 1, 2013, http://blogs.wsj.com/numbersguy/is-fast-food-bad-value-for-the-public-1289.

12. "Minimum Wage," IGM Forum, www.igmchicago.org/igm-economic-experts-panel/poll-results?SurveyID=SV_br0IEq5a9E77NMV.

13. *Ibid.*

14. For summary of this approach, see David Neumark and William Wascher, *Minimum Wages* (2010), The MIT Press.

15. David Card and Alan B. Krueger," "Minimum Wages and Employment: A Case Study of the Fast-Food Industry in New Jersey and Pennsylvania," *The American Economic Review*, September 1994, p. 772, http://davidcard.berkeley.edu/papers/njmin-aer.pdf.

16. Wes Barrett, "White House resets focus to 'income inequality,' amid ObamaCare problems," Fox News, Jan. 6, 2014, www.foxnews.com/politics/2014/01/06/white-house-resets-to-income-inequality-amid-obamacare-problems.

17. "Poverty — Highlights," U.S. Census Bureau, www.census.gov/hhes/www/poverty/about/overview/index.html.

18. David Neumark, "The Minimum Wage Ain't What It Used to Be," *The New York Times*, Dec. 9, 2013, economix.blogs.nytimes.com/2013/12/09/the-minimum-wage-aint-what-it-used-to-be/?_r=0.

19. "Employed persons by class of worker and part-time status," U.S. Bureau of Labor Statistics, www.bls.gov/webapps/legacy/cpsatab8.htm.

20. Neumark, *op. cit.*

21. "Income, Poverty and Health Insurance in the United States: 2012 —Tables & Figures," U.S. Census Bureau, www.census.gov/hhes/www/poverty/data/incpovhlth/2012/tables.html.

22. *Ibid.*

23. Arindrajit Dube, "Minimum Wages and the Distribution of Family Incomes," Dec. 30, 2013,

p. 34, https://dl.dropboxusercontent.com/u/15 038936/Dube_MinimumWagesFamilyIncomes .pdf.

24. "Joined By Business Leaders and Workers, Sen. Harkin, Rep. Miller Unveil Bill to Raise the Minimum Wage to $10.10," *op. cit.*

25. Flether and Craighill *op. cit.*

26. Text is available at www.law.cornell.edu/supreme court/text/198/45.

27. Jerold Waltman, *Minimum Wage Policy in Great Britain and the United States* (2008), pp. 53-54.

28. Text is available at www.law.cornell.edu/supreme-court/text/208/412.

29. Waltman, *op. cit.*, pp. 54-55.

30. *Ibid.*, p. 55.

31. Clifford F. Thies, "The First Minimum Wage Laws," *Cato Journal*, winter 1991, p. 717, http://object .cato.org/sites/cato.org/files/serials/files/cato-jour nal/1991/1/cj10n3-7.pdf.

32. Text is available at www.law.cornell.edu/supreme court/text/261/525.

33. Thies, *op. cit.*

34. Text is available at http://straylight.law.cornell.edu/ supct/html/historics/USSC_CR_0300_0379_ZO .html.

35. Thies, *op. cit.*, 720.

36. Waltman, *op. cit.*, p. 58.

37. Jonathan Grossman, "Fair Labor Standards Act of 1938: Maximum Struggle for a Minimum Wage," U.S. Department of Labor, p. 5, www.dol.gov/dol/ aboutdol/history/flsa1938.htm.

38. Consumer Price Index inflation calculator, http:// data.bls.gov/cgi-bin/cpicalc.pl.

39. Grossman, *op. cit.*, p. 1; also see Waltman, *op. cit.*, p. 61.

40. Vivien Hart, *Bound by Our Constitution: Women, Workers, and the Minimum Wage* (2001), p. 169.

41. *Handbook of Labor Statistics, Volumes 1-2* (1942), U.S. Bureau of Labor Statistics, pp. 401-402.

42. Waltman, *op, cit.*, p. 125.

43. Willis J. Nordlund, *The Quest for a Living Wage: The History of the Federal Minimum Wage Program* (1997), p. 71.

44. For background, see Peter Katel, "Minimum Wage," *CQ Researcher*, Dec. 16, 2005, pp. 1053-1076.

45. "Federal Minimum Wage Rates Under the Fair Labor Standards Act," U.S. Department of Labor, www.dol.gov/whd/minwage/chart.htm.

46. Nordland, *op. cit.*, p. 137.

47. Waltman, *op. cit.*, p. 131.

48. *Ibid.*

49. *Ibid.*, p. 147.

50. Stephen Labaton, "Congress Passes Increase in the Minimum Wage," *The New York Times*, May 25, 2007, www.nytimes.com/2007/05/25/washington/ 25wage.html.

51. Catherine Rampell and Steven Greenhouse, "$10 Minimum Wage Proposal Has Growing Support From White House," *The New York Times*, Nov. 7, 2013, www.nytimes.com/2013/11/08/business/ 10-minimum-wage-proposal-has-obamas-backing .html.

52. "Joined By Business Leaders and Workers, Sen. Harkin, Rep. Miller Unveil Bill to Raise the Minimum Wage to $10.10," *op. cit.*

53. Text of the bill is at http://thomas.loc.gov/cgi-bin/ query/z?c113:S.460:.

54. Rampell and Greenhouse, *op. cit.*

55. Robin Wilkey and Kathleen Miles, "California Minimum Wage Increase Signed Into Law, Set to Be Nation's Highest," *The Huffington Post*, Sept. 26, 2013, www.huffingtonpost.com/2013/09/25/cali fornia-minimum-wage-increase-law_n_3989397 .html.

56. Susan K. Livio, "N.J. voters approve constitutional amendment raising minimum wage," *nj.com*, Nov. 5, 2013, www.nj.com/politics/index.ssf/2013/11/ nj_voters_approve_constitutional_amendment_ raising_minimum_wage.html.

57. *Ibid.*

58. *Ibid.*

59. "13 States to Increase Minimum Wage on New Year's Day," National Employment Law Project, Dec. 18, 2013, www.nelp.org/page/-/Press%20Releases/2013/ PR-NELP-13-States-Increase-Minimum-Wage-New-Years-Day-2014.pdf?nocdn=1.

60. "State Minimum Wages," National Conference of State Legislatures, www.ncsl.org/research/labor-and-employment/state-minimum-wage-chart.aspx.

61. Kirk Johnson, "Voters in SeaTac, Wash., Back $15 Minimum Wage," *The New York Times*, Nov. 26, 2013, www.nytimes.com/2013/11/27/us/voters-in-seatac-wash-back-15-minimum-wage.html.

62. Lydia Depillis, "SeaTac's minimum wage workers might not get their raise after all," *The Washington Post*, Dec. 29, 2013, www.washingtonpost.com/blogs/wonkblog/wp/2013/12/29/seatacs-minimum-wage-workers-might-not-get-their-raise-after-all.

63. Don Lee, "Getting the job done on minimum wage," *Los Angeles Times*, Dec. 8, 2013, www.latimes.com/business/autos/la-fi-minimum-wage-20131209,0,7295277.story#axzz2pB63C3wD.

64. "13 States to Increase Minimum Wage on New Year's Day," *op. cit.*

65. Gordon Lafer, "The Legislative Attack on American Wages and Labor," Economic Policy Institute, Oct. 31, 2013, www.epi.org/publication/attack-on-american-labor-standards.

66. Jonathan Martin and Michael D. Shear, "Democrats Turn to Minimum Wage as 2014 Strategy," *The New York Times*, Dec. 29, 2013, www.nytimes.com/2013/12/30/us/politics/democrats-turn-to-minimum-wage-as-2014-strategy.html?_r=0.

# BIBLIOGRAPHY

## Selected Sources

## Books

**Neumark, David, and William Wascher, *Minimum Wages*, The MIT Press, 2010.**
Two economists discuss the effects of minimum wages on employment and hours, income distribution, prices and the overall economy and conclude that minimum wages do not achieve their stated goals.

**Nordlund, Willis J., *The Quest for a Living Wage: The History of the Federal Minimum Wage Program*, Greenwood Press, 1997.**
An economist traces the history of the federal minimum wage, beginning with its origins in state laws in the early 20th century.

**Waltman, Jerold, *Minimum Wage Policy in Great Britain and the United States*, Algora, 2008.**
A political scientist examines the evolution of the minimum wage from its roots in progressive movements in the U.K. and the United States.

## Articles

**Lee, Don, "Getting the job done on minimum wage: Frustrated by lack of federal action, states and municipalities approve measures that raise workers' pay level," *Los Angeles Times*, Dec. 8, 2013, www.latimes.com/business/autos/la-fi-minimum-wage-20131209,0,7295277.story#axzz2pB63C3wD.**
Five states and four localities approved raises to their minimum wages in 2013 above the national rate of $7.25 an hour.

**Livio, Susan K., "N.J. voters approve constitutional amendment raising minimum wage," *nj.com*, Nov. 5, 2013, www.nj.com/politics/index.ssf/2013/11/nj_voters_approve_constitutional_amendment_raising_minimum_wage.html.**
New Jersey voters approve an increase to the state minimum wage, while reelecting Gov. Chris Christie, a vocal opponent of the measure.

**Needleman, Sarah E., and Daniel Lippman, "Businesses Stung by $15-an-Hour Pay," *The Wall Street Journal*, Dec. 11, 2013, http://online.wsj.com/news/articles/SB10001424052702304202204579252413945322426.**
Companies in SeaTac, Wash., a 10-square-mile Seattle suburb that includes the airport, complain that the city's new minimum wage of $15 an hour will hurt business.

**Rampell, Catherine, and Steven Greenhouse, "$10 Minimum Wage Proposal Has Growing Support From White House," *The New York Times*, Nov. 7, 2013, www.nytimes.com/2013/11/08/business/10-minimum-wage-proposal-has-obamas-backing.html.**
After proposing a federal minimum hourly wage of $9 early in 2013, President Obama now backs a congressional bill to raise it to $10.10 an hour.

**Smialek, Jeanna, "Waitresses Stuck at $2.13 Hourly Minimum for 22 Years," *Bloomberg Personal Finance*, April 25, 2013, www.bloomberg.com/news/**

2013-04-25/waitresses-stuck-at-2-13-hourly-mini mum-for-22-years.html.

Restaurant servers who rely on tips face a federal sub-minimum wage of $2.13 an hour, frozen at that level for 23 years.

**Wilkey, Robin, and Kathleen Miles, "California Minimum Wage Increase Signed Into Law, Set to Be Nation's Highest,"** *The Huffington Post*, **Sept. 26, 2013, www.huffingtonpost.com/2013/09/25/califor nia-minimum-wage-increase-law_n_3989397.html.**

California's minimum wage will rise from $8 to $10 an hour by January 2016, making it the nation's highest state wage unless other states surpass it.

## Reports and Studies

**"Going Nowhere Fast: Limited Occupational Mobility in the Fast Food Industry," National Employment Law Project, July 2013, www.nelp.org/ page/-/rtmw/uploads/NELP-Fast-Food-Mobility-Report-Going-Nowhere-Fast.pdf?nocdn=1.**

A legal-advocacy organization examines the limited mobility of fast-food workers.

**Allegretto, Sylvia,** *et al.***, "Fast Food, Poverty Wages: The Public Cost of Low-Wage Jobs in the Fast-Food Industry," UC Berkeley Center for Labor Research and Education, Oct. 15, 2013, http://laborcenter.berkeley .edu/publiccosts/fast_food_poverty_wages.pdf.**

Researchers estimate the cost to taxpayers of low-wage workers' reliance on four public-aid programs.

**Cooper, David, "Raising the Federal Minimum Wage to $10.10 Would Lift Wages for Millions and Provide a Modest Economic Boost," Economic Policy Institute, Dec. 19, 2013, http://s4.epi.org/files/2013/ Raising-the-federal-minimum-wage-to-1010-would-lift-wages-for-millions-and-provide-a-modest-eco nomic-boost-12-19-2013.pdf.**

A liberal think tank estimates that a $10.10 minimum wage would boost the incomes of nearly 28 million workers and add billions to the economy.

**Sherk, James, and John L. Ligon, "Unprecedented Minimum-Wage Hike Would Hurt Jobs and the Economy," Issue Brief, The Heritage Foundation, www.heritage.org/research/reports/2013/12/unprec edented-minimum-wage-hike-would-hurt-jobs-and-the-economy.**

Two conservative policy analysts conclude that increasing the federal minimum wage would damage jobs and the economy.

# For More Information

**American Action Forum**, 1747 Pennsylvania Ave., N.W., 5th Floor, Washington, DC 20006; 202-559-6420; http://americanactionforum.org. Research institute promoting free-market policies and smaller government.

**Center for Economic and Policy Research**, 1611 Connecticut Ave., N.W., Suite 400, Washington, DC 20009; 202-293-5380; www.cepr.net. Liberal think tank focusing on economic policy.

**Center on Budget and Policy Priorities**, 820 First St., N.E., Suite 510, Washington, DC 20002; 202-408-1080; www.cbpp.org. Liberal think tank that focuses on fiscal policy and programs affecting low- and moderate-income families and individuals.

**Economic Policy Institute**, 1333 H St., N.W., Suite 300, East Tower, Washington, DC 20005; 202-775-8810; www.epi.org. Liberal think tank focusing on the economic status of working America.

**Fast Food Forward**, www.fastfoodforward.org. Represents New York City fast-food workers seeking to raise wages and gain rights at work.

**The Heritage Foundation**, 214 Massachusetts Ave, N.E., Washington DC 20002; 202-546-4400; www.heritage.org. Conservative think tank that promotes principals of free enterprise, limited government and individual freedom.

**National Employment Law Project**, 75 Maiden Lane, Suite 601, New York, NY 10038; 212-285-3025; www.nelp.org. Legal-advocacy organization promoting workers' rights.

**National Federation of Independent Business**, 53 Century Blvd., Nashville, TN 37214; 615-872-5800; www.nfib.com. Trade group representing 350,000 small and independent business owners.

**National Restaurant Association**, 2055 L St., N.W., Suite 700, Washington, DC 20036; 202-331-5900; www.restaurant.org. World's largest food service trade association, representing nearly 500,000 restaurants.

**Service Employees International Union**, 1800 Massachusetts Ave., N.W., Washington, DC 20036; www.seiu.org. Represents 2.1 million workers in healthcare, public services and property services in the U.S. and Canada.

**U.S. Chamber of Commerce**, 1615 H St., N.W., Washington, DC 20062; 202-659-6000; www.uschamber.org. Represents more than 3 million businesses of all sizes, sectors and regions.

# 12

# Assessing the New Health Care Law

Marcia Clemmitt

Cancer patient Gail O'Brien greets President Obama during a backyard discussion of his administration's proposed health care reform law in Falls Church, Va., on Sept. 22, 2010. The Supreme Court on June 28, 2012, upheld the law's requirement that uninsured people buy medical insurance or pay a penalty. Conservative justices objected to forcing healthy young people to buy insurance they may not need.

From *CQ Researcher*,
September 21, 2012.

C aleb Medley, a 23-year-old aspiring stand-up comic, was at a midnight showing of "The Dark Knight Rises" in Aurora, Colo., on July 20, when a gunman entered the theater and shot 70 people, killing 12. Shot in the eye, Medley remained in a medically induced coma for more than a month. He has endured multiple brain surgeries, but is slowly improving, according to his family.[1] On Sept. 12, Medley was transferred from the hospital to a long-term-care facility.[2] Meanwhile, his wife, Katie, gave birth to the couple's first child a few days after the shootings.

The Medleys have no health insurance. To help with what doctors said could amount to $2 million in medical bills, Michael West, a longtime family friend, is soliciting donations through a website he set up. "Caleb . . . needs to get better because he needs to be a dad," said West.[3]

Stories of uninsured people who unexpectedly incur high medical bills have figured heavily in debates over the Obama administration's controversial health care law, the 2010 Patient Protection and Affordable Care Act (ACA). Ideological arguments over the legislation came into sharp focus June 28, when the U.S. Supreme Court upheld most of the ACA, whose main provisions take effect in 2014, but said states could opt out of a key provision aimed at expanding Medicaid coverage for the poor.[4]

The court rendered its decision in two parts:

- In a 5-4 ruling dominated by court liberals, with Chief Justice John G. Roberts unexpectedly providing the swing vote, the

## Biggest States Have High Rates of Uninsured

The Affordable Care Act and any other attempt to overhaul the health care system to increase insurance coverage will face daunting challenges. Not least is the fact that three of the nation's four most populous states — California, Texas and Florida — have among the highest rates of uninsured residents. Texas leads the pack with one in four residents uninsured.

### Percentage of Population Without Health Insurance
(2009-2010)

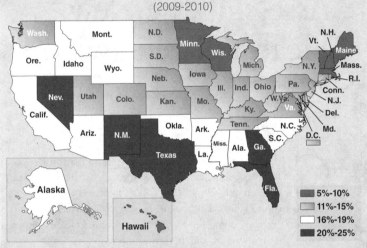

5%-10%
11%-15%
16%-19%
20%-25%

*Source:* "Health Insurance Coverage of the Total Population, States (2009-2010), U.S. (2010)," Henry J. Kaiser Family Foundation, 2012, www.statehealthfacts.org/comparetable.jsp?ind=125&cat=3&sub=39&yr=252&typ=2&rgnhl=1

over the measure since its enactment in March 2010.

In their dissenting opinion, the court's four conservative justices, who voted to strike down the entire law, asserted that Congress exceeded its constitutional authority by requiring every American to purchase health insurance or pay a penalty. Moreover, they wrote that healthy young people "may decide that purchasing health insurance is not an economically sound decision" — especially, they said, because the ACA allows them to purchase it in later years at the same cost, even if they have developed a pre-existing medical condition by then.[6]

But Justice Ruth Bader Ginsburg, a liberal who voted to uphold the ACA in its entirety, argued that getting everyone — even healthy young people — to buy insurance is the only way to ensure that there is enough money to pay for every American's care. "A victim of an accident or unforeseen illness will consume extensive medical care immediately, though scarcely expecting to do so," Ginsburg wrote. If that person hasn't bought coverage, others have to pick up the tab, she argued.[7]

Ultimately, the ACA's impact on health care costs and insurance coverage remains unclear. With implementation of the law's major provisions more than a year away, much of the debate is still driven by theories rather than data. But the ACA's supporters and detractors have long given voice to the issues raised by the Supreme Court.

President Obama said the court's affirmation of the law is a boon for average Americans. "Insurance companies no longer have unchecked power to cancel your policy, deny you coverage or charge women more than men," he said. Furthermore, "soon, no American will ever again be denied care or charged more due to a pre-existing condition, like cancer or even asthma."[8]

justices upheld the ACA's requirement that uninsured people buy medical insurance or pay a penalty — a stipulation in the law known as an "individual mandate." Conservative justices objected that it is unfair to force healthy young people to buy insurance they may not need.

• In a 7-2 vote dominated by court conservatives, plus two liberal justices, the court greatly narrowed the ACA's requirement that states either accept new federal grants to pay for expanded Medicaid coverage or risk losing all the money they receive from Washington for their Medicaid programs. The court said states can refuse the expansion grants without giving up their existing Medicaid funding.[5]

The Supreme Court's philosophical and legal differences over the health care law reflected a broad national divide

But GOP presidential nominee Mitt Romney, who derides the new law as "Obamacare," has vowed to repeal it if he is elected president in November. He has said he would replace it with another plan that relies more on the private sector to deal with many of the same problems the ACA addresses.[9] "Obamacare puts the federal government between you and your doctor," potentially limiting a physician's options for treating patients, Romney has said.[10] As governor of Massachusetts in 2006, Romney worked with Democrats to enact a plan similar to the ACA, but he has since said health care should be left to the states.[11]

Supporters say the ACA is structured in a way that will make the American health care system more effective and efficient and eventually save hundreds of millions of dollars annually in unnecessary or misdirected care. To keep insurance premiums for older, sicker people from becoming unaffordable, the ACA will subsidize them by raising premiums somewhat for young, healthy people.

And in an attempt to ensure that health coverage is worth its costs, the law also will require that all insurance plans cover a basic but comprehensive slate of benefits, essentially eliminating some bare-bones, low-cost plans available today. Beginning in 2014, four tiers of coverage will be available to individual purchasers, ranging from low-cost plans providing only basic benefits to comprehensive coverage, but at higher premiums.[12]

The ACA represents "tremendous progress towards reshaping our health system into one that saves the lives of at least 44,000 people who die annually simply because they do not have health insurance that could keep them healthy," said Georges Benjamin, executive director of the American Public Health Association.[13]

But many ACA opponents argue that it forces people to buy insurance they don't want and may not need. "Never before has the federal government coerced its citizens to purchase a personal commodity for private use," said Brooks Wicker, a Kentucky Republican running for a

## Medical Expenses Worry Younger Adults

The inability to pay medical bills or afford necessary health care services is of greatest concern to adults under age 65, when Medicare eligibility begins. About one in three adults 18-64 has delayed a medical procedure or doctor's visit because of financial concerns.

### Health Care Problems and Worries by Age, 2012

| Problem or worry | Age 18-29 | Age 30-49 | Age 50-64 | Age 65+ |
|---|---|---|---|---|
| Problems with paying medical bills in past 12 months | 29% | 30% | 26% | 17% |
| Put off or postponed necessary health care | 30% | 34% | 32% | 15% |
| Worried about not being able to afford health care services you think you need | 25% | 30% | 26% | 15% |

Source: "Health Security Watch," Henry J. Kaiser Family Foundation, June 2012, p. 7, www.kff.org/healthpollreport/CurrentEdition/security/upload/8322.pdf

U.S. House seat. "I'll work to repeal the mandate through legislation and to return [to] the American people the full measure of freedom taken from them."[14]

Meanwhile, some young adults complain that they are being required to buy a minimum level of coverage and, in their view, overpay for it to help hold down premiums for older, sicker people.

The law is biased against young people, who will be forced "to shoulder the burden of the entire health system," complained Ryan Fazio, a columnist for Northwestern University's *Daily Northwestern*, in Evanston, Ill.[15] Richard Cooper, a 26-year-old lawyer in Miami, said requiring all health plans to include basic coverage for such services as mental health treatment and maternity care is "one of the things I'm sort of leery about. I'm going to be paying for things I don't need."[16]

But both young and old will get far more comprehensive coverage from even the cheapest plans than many people find in the insurance they can buy today, said Paul Ginsburg, president of the Center for Studying Health System Change, a nonpartisan research group in Washington. "That's worth something."[17]

While much of the controversy over the ACA has centered on the individual mandate, the law's Medicaid provision has been equally contentious.

## Views on the Affordable Care Act

Roughly the same percentages of people oppose the individual mandate requiring Americans to obtain health coverage or pay a penalty whether it is described as a fine or a tax. The act's plan to expand Medicaid is favored by two-thirds of Americans and opposed by fewer than a third. Overall, slightly more Americans have unfavorable views of the act than favorable, and almost the same percentages favor repeal or keeping the law.

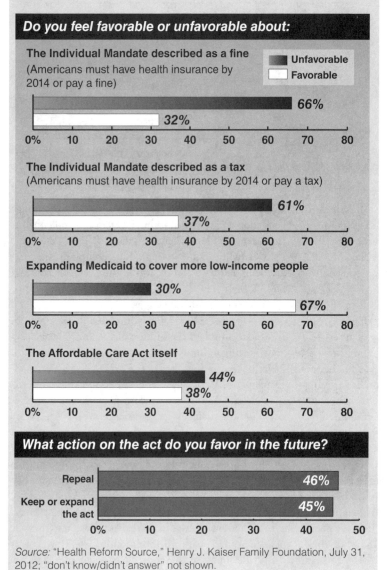

### Do you feel favorable or unfavorable about:

**The Individual Mandate described as a fine**
(Americans must have health insurance by 2014 or pay a fine)

- Unfavorable
- Favorable

Unfavorable: 66%
Favorable: 32%

**The Individual Mandate described as a tax**
(Americans must have health insurance by 2014 or pay a tax)

Unfavorable: 61%
Favorable: 37%

**Expanding Medicaid to cover more low-income people**

Unfavorable: 30%
Favorable: 67%

**The Affordable Care Act itself**

Unfavorable: 44%
Favorable: 38%

### What action on the act do you favor in the future?

Repeal: 46%
Keep or expand the act: 45%

*Source:* "Health Reform Source," Henry J. Kaiser Family Foundation, July 31, 2012; "don't know/didn't answer" not shown.

Medicaid is a program financed jointly by the states and the federal government that covers health care, including nursing home care, for some groups of poor people — children, their custodial parents, pregnant women and the blind, disabled and elderly. The ACA expansion provision was designed to broaden coverage to include some 17 million poor, able-bodied, childless adults.

States leery about expanding their Medicaid rolls worry that doing so will bust their budgets, despite the fact that under the law most costs will be covered by federal grants.[18]

But Stan Dorn, a senior fellow at the Urban Institute, a nonpartisan think tank in Washington that studies poverty and health care, says the ACA's Medicaid provision would help states save money and improve health care efficiency. Today states reimburse hospitals for care they provide to uninsured people and for mental-health care provided to low-income adults. The federally funded Medicaid expansion would pay for that care up front, at least as efficiently as today's fragmented programs do, he says.

"It's mind-boggling to see the opposition," given the way the law is structured, says Dorn. "There are lots of ways that states can actually save money on the expansion."

As lawmakers, health care providers and the public ponder the ACA's impact, here are some of the questions being asked:

### Should the health care law be repealed?

The ACA's opponents in Washington argue that nothing short of repeal will stop the law from damaging free-market economics and the American health care system. Central to their criticism is the law's individual-mandate provision requiring every American to buy health insurance or pay a financial penalty.[19]

But the law's supporters argue that it is that very mandate that holds the key to the law's success. By requiring universal coverage, they contend, the law prevents insured people from having to shoulder the cost of treating the uninsured, often through costly emergency room visits.

Senate Minority Leader Mitch McConnell, R-Ken., has said that if Republicans gain control of the Senate in November, he will schedule a vote to erase the ACA from the books. Ultimately, that may not work, he acknowledges, unless Republicans also win the White House and control of the House. Still, McConnell says most Americans agree with him that the law should go. "I'm confident they're going to give us the votes to repeal it," he said.[20]

Michael D. Tanner, director of health and welfare studies at the Cato Institute, a think tank in Washington that promotes a philosophy of individual liberty and limited government, said the "individual mandate crosses an important line" because it enshrines in law the principle "that it is the government's responsibility to ensure that every American has health insurance. It opens the door to widespread regulation of the health care industry and political interference in personal health care decisions. The result will be a slow but steady spiral downward toward a government-run national health care system."[21]

Others argue that the ACA usurps responsibilities that rightly belong to the states.

"States shouldn't be forced by the federal government to adopt a one-size-fits-all health care plan," said Sen. Scott Brown, R-Mass., whose home state, under Romney, adopted a health care system similar to the ACA in 2006. "Each state's health care needs are different."[22]

Thomas Miller, a resident fellow at the American Enterprise Institute (AEI), a conservative think tank in Washington that opposes the health care law, instead wants legislation that facilitates development of a nationwide market offering a wide variety of private medical plans for purchase.

Miller says the ACA will undermine the development of free-market dynamics in the health insurance field and force states to accede to federal dictates. At first, he says, states may be able to shape their own insurance exchanges through which people purchase health coverage. But that is simply because Washington made certain "concessions" to the states to induce them to back the law, he says. Once the new health regime is deeply rooted, he predicts, "the long-term dynamics will very much have Washington in control rather than having open markets."

But ACA supporters say the individual mandate — and the fact that the law is national, not limited to some states — ensure that health care will be available to as many people as possible. Furthermore, they say, states will have flexibility to shape their own insurance markets under the law.

Most states aren't willing or able to resolve the problem of the uninsured on their own because states rightly fear bankrupting themselves if they offer universal coverage and other states don't, Justice Ginsburg wrote. She quoted an earlier court ruling that described a universal state coverage program as a potential "bait to the needy and dependent elsewhere, encouraging them to migrate and seek a haven of repose." States that took the lead in offering universal coverage would be "placing themselves in a position of economic disadvantage as compared with neighbors or competitors," she wrote.[23]

The ACA does not create the one-size-fits-all nightmare for states that critics fear, says the Urban Institute's Dorn. The Obama administration's implementation rules for the law permit "a huge amount" of flexibility in the kind of insurance exchanges — markets — states may set up, thus accommodating "hugely different visions," both liberal and conservative, of how the health care market should operate.

"You can have a tightly managed exchange and allow only three health plans to come in and sell only a particular set of benefits" or "simply say that any company can come in" and give consumers a wide choice of health plans, Dorn says.

The ACA's supporters also say that the new law will relieve some of the pressure on workers' compensation and other parts of the health care system that have been strained in recent decades by the lack of universal insurance coverage.

Republican presidential nominee Mitt Romney has vowed to repeal the new health care law if he is elected president in November. He has said he would replace it with a plan that relies more on the private sector to deal with many of the same problems the law addresses. "Obamacare puts the federal government between you and your doctor," potentially limiting a physician's options for treating patients, Romney contends.

Workers' compensation insurance — mostly state-based programs that pay for injuries workers suffer on the job — will function better under the law, according to Joseph Paduda, a Connecticut-based consultant on managed care and workers' compensation insurance. Because so many people lack regular health insurance, workers' comp often ends up paying for care that has nothing to do with on-the-job injuries, he wrote.

In states such as Texas and Florida with high percentages of residents without insurance, a person who tears a rotator cuff on the job, for example, may also need treatment for unrelated maladies, such as diabetes or high blood pressure, before having rotator cuff surgery. The ACA's widespread insurance coverage will cut costs and red tape for the workers' comp system, he said.[24]

### Will Americans be better off because of the health care law?

With the ACA still in early stages of implementation, researchers have been unable to collect much data that either prove or refute claims of the law's success. Supporters point to millions of additional Americans who will gain insurance coverage. Opponents argue that new taxes and regulations will cripple innovation by medical firms such as health insurers and pharmaceutical companies.

Regardless of the ACA's merits, the changes it brings will cause some problems in the early going, even the law's supporters acknowledge. For example, expanded coverage and the emphasis on preventive care mean "there will (very) likely be an access problem over the near term as primary care providers are inundated with new patients, and over the medium term for specialists as folks who've long avoided care because they could not afford it now get those problems resolved — knee replacements, etc.," wrote insurance consultant Paduda.[25]

Meanwhile, supporters tout an ACA provision requiring insurers to spend a minimum percentage of premium payments on patient care or refund the money to employers and consumers. But many conservatives say this so-called Medical Loss Ratio rule will run insurance companies out of business. Sen. Charles Grassley, R-Iowa, said one insurer, the American Enterprise Group, left the business in Iowa and Nebraska last year, dropping thousands from its rolls and laying off 110 employees, and the "culprit is the new Medical Loss Ratio regulation."[26]

That's because selling health insurance to individuals and very small businesses is an economically tricky enterprise that works much differently than selling insurance to large-employer groups, Grassley said. The medical needs of an individual or employees at a small business are much harder for insurers to estimate than those of workers at a large employer, where the group's health status tends to mirror that of the general population. As a result, individual and small-group insurers must set each year's premiums high enough to ensure coverage of hard-to-predict costs, said Grassley. The Medical Loss Ratio rule, which penalizes insurers in any year the government deems their premiums are too high compared to spending on patient care, simply makes the risks of the insurance business "too great," he said.[27]

Opponents of the ACA point to what they see as other ill effects of the law. To help pay for expanded coverage, the ACA imposes new taxes that threaten research-and-development budgets and medical innovation, said Sally Pipes, president of the San Francisco-based Pacific Research Institute, a think tank that promotes a limited-government philosophy. "Excise taxes on drug-company sales are already in effect," Pipes wrote. "In 2013, there will be a new 2.3 percent excise tax on medical-device companies." As a result, she said, some firms have announced workforce cuts. "These industries are job creators and will no longer be unless the Affordable Care Act is repealed and replaced."[28]

John Goodman, a conservative analyst who heads the National Center for Policy Analysis, in Dallas, has found particular fault with efforts to expand Medicaid, the ACA's main means of insuring the poor. Medicaid, he argued, provides such low-quality care that "the Supreme Court has done a lot of families a big favor" by ruling that states can't be penalized for failing to expand coverage. As an example of what he sees as Medicaid's failings, he said 16 states cap the number of prescriptions Medicaid patients can get, with Mississippi limiting patients to two brand-name drugs and Arkansas limiting adult enrollees to six medications a month.[29]

Supporters of the law are just as vocal as opponents in their views about the ACA's impact on consumers.

Ron Pollack, founding executive director of the national consumer-advocacy group Families USA, says many people will be better off under the law and that some already are. "Right now, a significant but still clear minority of the benefits are already in effect," he says, and "we're hearing from people who've already gotten significant help."

Among those who have benefited are enrollees in Medicare, which provides health insurance for people age 65 and older, Pollack says. Under the ACA, they now receive additional government help with prescription-drug expenses, he says. Young adults also have benefited, Pollack notes. They now can remain on their parents' insurance plans until age 26.

And Pollack cites a host of other benefits: When insurers spend too little premium revenue on health care, they must provide rebates; children with pre-existing illnesses must be offered health coverage; preventive services such as diabetes and cervical-cancer screening are available without deductibles or copayments; and small businesses receive tax credits for providing worker coverage.

## Coverage of Young Adults Rises

A provision of the Affordable Care Act that took effect in 2010 allows adult children under age 26 to obtain health care coverage through their parents' policies. Experts credit the provision with increasing the share of young adults covered by medical insurance in 2011.

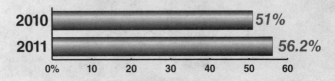

**Percentage of Adults Ages 19 Through 25 With Private Insurance Coverage, 2010-2011**

| | |
|---|---|
| 2010 | 51% |
| 2011 | 56.2% |

0%  10  20  30  40  50  60

Source: Matt Broaddus, "The Census Bureau's Upcoming Report on Health Insurance Coverage in 2011: What to Watch For," Center on Budget and Policy Priorities, September 2012, www.cbpp.org/cms/index.cfm?fa=view&id =3830

A study published in July in the *New England Journal of Medicine* concludes that previous Medicaid expansions similar to what the ACA calls for have resulted in decreased death rates. Researchers from the Harvard School of Public Health examined mortality data from three states — New York, Maine and Arizona — that added low-income, nondisabled adults with no children to their Medicaid programs in the past decade and found that the death rate for people age 20 to 64 decreased in the five years following the expansion.[30]

While the study included all deaths in the states, not just those among low-income people, the mortality rate dropped most for nonwhites and people living in poor counties, suggesting a Medicaid connection. Meanwhile, death rates rose in four neighboring states that didn't expand Medicaid. The coverage expansions are associated with a 6.1 percent decrease in death rates, or about 2,840 fewer deaths per year for each additional 500,000 adults insured.[31]

Some analysts say the ACA will provide economic as well as health benefits. "If basic insurance is made universally available on the individual market," the country could see a substantial drop in so-called job-lock — "people staying in jobs that might not be the best for them" simply because those jobs are the only potential source of health insurance, said Jonathan Kolstad, a professor of health care management at the University of

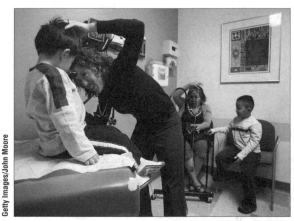

A youngster receives a check-up at a community health center in Lakewood, Colo., for low-income people. Passage of the new health care law will mean additional federal subsidies for such clinics as well as health care insurance coverage for as many as 30 million people.

Pennsylvania's Wharton School. Job-lock not only keeps workers from advancing in their careers but also hurts the economy by inhibiting innovation and productivity, he said.[32]

## Will the health care law cost too much?

ACA opponents say both the government and individuals will pay too much for health care under the new law. Supporters say expanded insurance coverage is worth its costs and that provisions aimed at creating a more efficient, prevention-focused system will eventually help to tame soaring medical expenses.

The ACA "virtually ignored the health care cost crisis facing this country and instead imposes billions of dollars in new mandates" — such as requiring insurers to devote a minimum amount of premium dollars to patient care — "and taxes that will increase the costs of coverage," said Robert Zirkelbach, a vice president of America's Health Insurance Plans, the main association representing health insurers in Washington.[33]

"Even accepting the law's assumptions about how the health care system should be reformed, actually putting all the pieces in place is exceptionally expensive," said Joseph Antos, who studies health and retirement policy at the free-market-oriented American Enterprise Institute in Washington. Furthermore, "the Supreme Court decision on Medicaid will . . . drive up federal spending"

even more because in states that decline to participate "the alternative is expanded enrollment in subsidized [private] insurance through the [state insurance] exchanges," and private insurance costs more than Medicaid, Antos said.[34]

Meanwhile, liberal ACA critics argue that by relying on private insurance companies, rather than making the government the single payer for all insured people, the law forgoes most cost savings it might have achieved. Insurance companies "only add cost and complexity" to the system without improving care, said Bill Mahan, a political activist and retiree in Lexington, Ky., who advocates a switch to a single-payer system.[35]

But ACA supporters point to analysis by the Congressional Budget Office, Congress' nonpartisan budget-analysis agency, which has repeatedly found that the law will actually lower government health care spending and pare federal deficits because cost-saving provisions will offset the price of expanded coverage. In 2011, the CBO estimated that the law's coverage expansion would cost the federal government $1.1 trillion between 2012 and 2021, but that the law as a whole would end up saving the government money. That's because the cost of the coverage expansion will be offset by ACA provisions aimed at trimming unnecessary and wasteful health-care spending. As a result, the ACA will lower federal deficits by about $210 billion in that period, CBO said.[36]

The fact that the law saves taxpayers some cash means that a Republican repeal of the ACA "would cause a net increase in federal budget deficits of $109 billion over the 2013-2022 period" — that is, repealing the law would cost money, not save it, as repeal supporters had hoped, the CBO wrote to House Speaker John Boehner, R-Ohio, in July.[37]

The law also invests heavily in studies designed to establish definitively which treatments are most successful. Many analysts believe that, eventually, the federal investment in such "comparative-effectiveness" research will discourage doctors from prescribing costly treatments that don't work. That's "good news indeed for [workers'] comp payers," for example, who are "saddled with back surgeries" that many experts now believe don't help but whose ineffectiveness hasn't yet been established by research, said insurance consultant Paduda.[38]

Few promise that cost savings will come easily, however. Besides comparative-effectiveness research, the law also will launch experiments on potential cost-control measures such as paying health care providers based on whether they keep people from getting sick rather than for rendering individual services. But because neither public nor private health care entities have yet seriously explored such techniques, "it will be at least 10 years" before it's known whether they work, says Robert Laszewski, an Alexandria, Va.-based insurance industry consultant.

## BACKGROUND

### The Mandate

In their bid to expand coverage to 30 million of the approximately 50 million uninsured Americans, the drafters of the Affordable Care Act (ACA) proposed two strategies:[39]

- Medicaid would be expanded, through a federal-state effort, to cover everyone in households earning less than 138 percent of the federal poverty level (FPL), or $26,344 for a family of three.
- The law would require everyone whose earnings exceed that threshold either to carry employer-sponsored insurance or to buy it from a new, federally subsidized government-regulated insurance market or else pay a financial penalty for not doing so.[40]

Both provisions are controversial. Opponents — largely Republicans — argue that states opting into the Medicaid expansion would be unreasonably burdened financially and that the individual mandate violates Americans' freedom by forcing them to buy a product — insurance — they may not want. Because the U.S. Supreme Court significantly altered the Medicaid provision, the CBO projects that about 3 million fewer people will be covered by the ACA than originally estimated.[41]

The individual mandate is a practical necessity to create a working insurance system, its defenders say. At any given time, only relatively few have high medical costs, and different people experience high costs in different years, wrote David Cole, a professor at Georgetown University Law Center in Washington. Because predicting when and whom serious accident or illness will strike is virtually impossible, it's crucial to bring everyone into the insurance pool so that

Opponents of possible cuts to government entitlement programs, including Medicaid, block a downtown Chicago intersection on Nov. 7, 2011. About 40 of several hundred protesters were arrested. The Affordable Care Act could increase the size of the Medicaid program to cover some 17 million poor, able-bodied, childless adults. But many state officials say they'll reject federal funds to expand health coverage in this way, saying it would strain their already tight budgets.

premiums paid by the currently healthiest can subsidize care for the currently sick and injured, said Cole.[42]

State experience proves that without a mandate, attempts to provide affordable coverage for all will collapse, Cole wrote. In 1994, for example, Kentucky enacted a law similar to the ACA, requiring insurers to cover people with pre-existing health conditions at affordable prices, "but without an individual mandate." Quickly, "costs rose so steeply that they became untenable," insurers left the market and Kentucky had to repeal its law, Cole said.[43]

Ironically, many conservatives have proposed health-system overhauls over the past quarter-century that included a mandate.

"In our scheme, every person would be required to obtain basic coverage, through either an individual or a family insurance plan," Mark Pauly, a professor of health care management at the University of Pennsylvania's Wharton School, wrote in 1991. Pauly, along with other conservative scholars, devised a plan they hoped President George H. W. Bush could use to expand coverage.[44]

"It is reasonable" to impose "a requirement on individuals to enroll themselves and their dependents in at least a basic health plan — one that at a minimum should protect the rest of society from large and unexpected medical costs incurred by the family," Stuart Butler, director of the

## CHRONOLOGY

**2006-2018** *Congress enacts legislation to expand health insurance coverage; controversies dog the law.*

**2006** Massachusetts, under Republican Gov. Mitt Romney, enacts mandatory, universal health coverage with bipartisan support, requiring residents to buy insurance in a state-regulated market.

**2007** As of July 1, all Massachusetts residents must purchase health insurance.

**2009** To control costs, Massachusetts officials consider paying doctors and hospitals flat, up-front fees to provide care. . . . In December, U.S. Senate passes the Affordable Care Act (ACA) 60-39, but with no Republicans voting in favor; House scheduled to take up the bill in spring 2010.

**2010** House passes Affordable Care Act (ACA) 219-212, with no Republican support. . . . President Obama signs the law March 23; it aims to expand coverage to 30 million people and trim costs while maintaining quality. . . . States and private groups challenge the ACA's constitutionality in court. . . . Federal government opens "high-risk" health plan, in which people with pre-existing health conditions can get affordable coverage; sign-up is slow because premiums remain costly. . . . Adults under 26 become eligible for coverage on their parents' health plans. . . . Health insurers must cover children with pre-existing illnesses.

**2011** Some Medicare enrollees get ACA rebates for prescription drug expenses. . . . Very small businesses become eligible for tax credits for insuring workers. . . . Newly elected House Republican majority repeatedly votes to repeal or defund the ACA, but Democrat-controlled Senate declines to consider the bills. . . . Federal appeals courts consider challenges to the ACA, upholding some but rejecting others; matter heads to the Supreme Court, which agrees to examine the ACA's "individual mandate" provision requiring people to buy insurance coverage or pay a penalty and the law's Medicaid-expansion provision. . . . Primary-care doctors treating Medicare patients get payment boost. . . . Copayments waived for some preventive-health services under Medicare. . . . High-income Medicare beneficiaries pay higher premiums. . . . States get grants to improve Medicaid care for chronic-disease patients. . . . Payments cut for private "Medicare Advantage" health plans. . . . Medicare Independent Payment Advisory Board (IPAB) established. Beginning in 2015, Medicare must implement cost-control measures recommended by IPAB, absent a two-thirds "no" vote by Congress.

**2012** Supreme Court declares ACA's individual mandate constitutional but makes Medicaid expansion optional for states. . . . Republican governors and state legislatures say they might not expand Medicaid to cover poor adults. . . . Health plans that spend too little on medical care must give cash rebates to enrollees. . . . With bipartisan support, Massachusetts clamps down on health care cost growth and adopts incentives to pay doctors and hospitals for "bundles" of high-quality care, rather than "fees for service." . . . GOP presidential nominee Mitt Romney and many congressional Republicans vow to repeal the ACA if they win November elections. . . . More than 2,000 hospitals lose some Medicare payments because of below-standard patient care. . . . Makers and importers of some brand-name drugs must pay new fees to help finance the law.

**2013** Primary-care doctors get Medicaid payment boost. . . . Taxpayers who itemize medical expenses must meet a higher threshold to claim a deduction. . . . Federal sales tax imposed on some medical devices. . . . Payroll tax on Medicare Part A, which pays for hospital services, rises. . . . With the ACA set to extend coverage to more uninsured people, special hospital reimbursements for providing free care to the uninsured are phased out.

**2014** ACA's Medicaid expansion and individual mandate slated to begin. . . . Individuals may buy federally subsidized insurance in state- or federally managed markets, called exchanges. . . . Insurers banned from imposing annual dollar limits on individuals' health spending. . . . Fees imposed on large employers who do not offer health coverage. . . . Insurers must sell coverage to people with pre-existing health conditions. . . . New fees imposed on health insurers.

**2018** Tax imposed on insurers offering employer-sponsored coverage costing more than $10,200 for individuals or $27,500 for families.

Center for Policy Innovation at the conservative Heritage Foundation, told a congressional panel in 2003.[45]

In 2004, Senate Majority Leader Bill Frist, R-Tenn., a transplant surgeon and heir to the founders of the large for-profit hospital chain Hospital Corp. of America, said "higher-income Americans today have a societal and a personal responsibility to cover in some way themselves and their children."[46]

Recently, though, most conservatives have turned against the mandate, arguing that requiring healthy people to buy insurance to subsidize the sick is an attack on individual freedom.

"The mandate's proponents call it an 'individual responsibility' requirement. But its real aim is to force young people to cover up for irresponsible government policies" — mainly government regulations on health care — "that make insurance too expensive," charged Avik Roy, a senior fellow at the conservative Manhattan Institute in New York.[47]

Mandate supporters, however, insist that buying insurance while healthy is essentially a prepayment plan for the unpredictable but inevitable day when illness or accident strikes. In rejecting mandates — as most Americans do in public-opinion polls — "Americans believe they have a moral right to critically needed health care, whether or not they can pay for it, but also believe that they should be free not to make financial provision for that event beforehand," wrote Princeton University economics professor Uwe Reinhardt.[48]

## The Poor

The ACA's other proposed coverage mechanism — Medicaid — also stirs controversy, mainly because many states worry about the program's rising costs and federal rules imposed on it.

Enacted in 1965, Medicaid replaced two federal grant programs that helped states provide medical care to the poor elderly and to people on welfare. Eventually, Medicaid used combined state and federal funds to provide health coverage for very poor families with children, long-term care and other services for low-income elderly and disabled people and, as a state option, coverage for other groups such as poor, childless adults.

States can choose whether or not to participate in Medicaid, and indeed not all states jumped on the Medicaid bandwagon at first. Arizona didn't start a Medicaid program

until the 1980s, for example. Today, every state provides Medicaid, although eligibility rules vary widely.[49] In Alabama and Louisiana, for example, parents with dependent children who make more than 11 percent of the federal poverty level — about $2,100 a year for a family of three — are ineligible for Medicaid, while in Minnesota the same family could earn more than $41,000 and receive benefits.[50]

Before the Supreme Court altered the ACA's Medicaid provision, the law essentially required states to help the federal government expand Medicaid coverage or risk losing the federal Medicaid funds they already received, a penalty intended to ensure that all states would participate.[51]

States provide a hefty share of the funding for traditional Medicaid. In fiscal 2010, for example, they spent a total of $126 billion, supplemented by $263 billion in federal funds.[52] The federal contribution to the ACA's Medicaid expansion is much bigger, with the government picking up 100 percent of costs from 2014 through 2016, then gradually shifting more costs to states until the federal share drops to 90 percent in 2020 and thereafter.[53]

About half of the people who were expected to gain coverage under the ACA were expected to gain it through the Medicaid program, said Alan Weil, executive director of the National Academy for State Health Policy, which helps states improve their health systems. "This is not a small change to Medicaid, and it's also not a small part of the Affordable Care Act."[54]

## The Court

As soon as the law was enacted, both the individual mandate and Medicaid-expansion mechanisms came under legal challenge. Twenty-six states eventually joined an anti-ACA lawsuit filed in Florida on March 23, 2010, the same day President Obama signed the act into law. In this and other suits, states and private groups charged that Congress had overstepped its constitutional authority by requiring individuals to buy health insurance or pay a penalty and by requiring states to expand Medicaid or lose federal Medicaid funding altogether.

Some of the first cases reached the U.S. Supreme Court in its 2011-2012 session, and the Court agreed to examine both the mandate and the Medicaid issues.[55]

# Caring for the Poorest and Sickest

*Expanding Medicaid challenges would-be reformers.*

Regardless of what happens to the Affordable Care Act (ACA) — whether it rolls out as planned over the next several years or is repealed under a new Republican administration — American health care still will face perhaps its biggest challenge: caring for the sickest and the poorest. Analysts from across the ideological spectrum agree on the urgency of the challenge, but solutions remain elusive.

Today, Medicaid, which is funded jointly by states and the federal government, provides care for poor families with children as well as many people with severe disabilities; it also provides long-term-care, mostly in nursing homes, for the low-income elderly. But as the costs of care have risen far faster than incomes, more Americans who fall outside these coverage categories continue to lose access to care. In 2010, 49.1 million Americans were uninsured.[1] (As of June 2011, 52.6 million people were covered by Medicaid.[2])

"You can be penniless" and yet receive no assistance in getting health coverage, says Ron Pollack, founding executive director of the national consumer-advocacy group Families USA. "We have 42 states that don't do anything for adults without children," making the Medicaid safety net "more holes than webbing," he says. But the ACA aims to remedy the problem by expanding Medicaid to low-income childless adults.

Some liberals have long predicted that such an expansion would not only provide much-needed access to care

but also save money. The savings would come from poor people getting preventive health care rather than ending up seeking expensive emergency room treatment after long-untreated medical conditions worsened. Some conservative commentators, on the other hand, scoff at the ACA expansion, arguing that Medicaid is such a skimpy program and pays doctors and hospitals so little that the new Medicaid enrollees will gain almost nothing of value.

"There's a lot of rhetoric on both sides" of the Medicaid-expansion question, says Katherine Baicker, a professor of health policy at the Harvard School of Public Health. She says new data she and other scholars collected show clearly that the most extreme claims of both proponents and detractors miss the mark.

The scholars, who also include Amy Finkelstein, a Massachusetts Institute of Technology economics professor, conducted the first-ever research on insurance coverage using the most rigorous standards of scientific evidence, says Baicker. In the study, nearly 90,000 very low-income Oregonians, ages 19 to 64, signed up for a lottery that randomly assigned them either to the Oregon Health Plan or left them uninsured.[3] The research, which is ongoing, ultimately will examine and compare the health care usage, health status and financial situations of both the group covered under the state health plan and those in the uninsured control group.

On June 28, the Court issued a mixed ruling that pleased ACA's defenders and left the law's critics with little to do but vow to try to repeal it.

The ACA's supporters and even some conservative legal commentators have argued that Congress has the power to require individuals to buy health insurance because the Constitution's Commerce Clause gives federal lawmakers the right to impose rules on business dealings that cross state boundaries. "The health industry is of course an interstate business; there is a continuous flow of health insurance payments, health insurance reimbursements, drugs, doctors, patients, donations to hospitals, research money, etc., across state boundaries,"

wrote Richard Posner, a conservative judge on the Seventh U.S. Circuit Court of Appeals and a lecturer at the University of Chicago Law School.[56]

But conservative justices, including Chief Justice Roberts, rejected that argument, maintaining that uninsured people to whom the mandate primarily would apply are not actually participants in the health care market and therefore may not be subjected to rules under the Commerce Clause.

Roberts, however, ultimately added his vote to those of the court's four liberal justices to uphold the mandate by a 5-4 majority, despite rejecting the idea that the Commerce Clause authorizes Congress to impose it. He

The data show that, after one year, those who gained Medicaid coverage gave their health status better marks than did their uninsured peers, and they also faced far fewer struggles with medical bills, says Baicker. The newly insured were more likely to describe their health as good and improving and themselves as happier than did the uninsured, she says.

In addition, the newly insured were 25 percent less likely to have had an unpaid medical bill sent to a collection agency and 40 percent less likely to have had to borrow money or leave other bills unpaid to pay their medical bills.

These findings prove that "expanding Medicaid has real benefits," not just for health but for people's financial status as well, says Baicker. The findings should effectively end speculation by Medicaid's critics that the program would be of no help to people if it were expanded, she says.

The data don't "tell you whether it's a good idea to expand Medicaid, but they do give you information about what the effects are," on individuals and on government budgets, Baicker says.

Nevertheless, the same data also dampens expectations by Medicaid-expansion supporters that hospital use might decline, along with expenses, if more people receive Medicaid coverage, says Baicker. Instead, she says, "we found a substantial increase [in hospital use], at least in the first year," she says. Still, she says, the increase came in scheduled hospital care such as non-emergency surgeries, not in pricey emergency-room visits that sometimes result from neglected preventive care.

Meanwhile, conservative economists who hope to see the ACA repealed and replaced with a less-regulated, more market-oriented system also acknowledge the importance — and trickiness — of serving the poorest and sickest people while allowing a free market to flourish in health care for the rest of the population.

"Sometimes there's a tendency to think only in dollar terms, but that's not the be-all and end-all," says Thomas Miller, a resident fellow at the free-market-oriented American Enterprise Institute. Miller says "you need a health care system that works for people" — both the poorest and sickest, who need more assistance than others, and the rest of the population, who are best served by having a health care market that offers them choices.

"You need first to acknowledge that the very poor or the very sick must get more" help to meet costs, Miller says. But at the same time, he adds, "you want to allow a wider variety of choices" for others so that savvy consumers can drive the market toward better quality and lower cost. Subsidies are required for the poor under any system, but the ACA's subsidies are too rich and reach people who earn too much, thereby undercutting the incentives for wiser spending, he says.

— *Marcia Clemmitt*

[1]"The Uninsured: A Primer," Kaiser Commission on Medicaid and the Uninsured, October 2011, p. 1, www.kff.org/uninsured/upload/7451-07.pdf.

[2]"Medicaid Enrollment: June 2011 Data Snapshot," Kaiser Commission on Medicaid and the Uninsured, June 2012, www.kff.org/medicaid/upload/8050-05.pdf.

[3]For background, see Amy Finkelstein, *et al.*, "The Oregon Health Insurance Experiment: Evidence from the First Year," National Bureau of Economic Research, 2011, www.rwjf.org/files/research/72577.5294.oregon.nber.pdf.

concluded instead that the ACA's financial penalty for failing to buy insurance falls under Congress' power to levy taxes.

The penalty raises revenue for the government — the distinguishing mark of a tax — even though it is "plainly designed to expand health insurance coverage," Roberts wrote. "But taxes that seek to influence conduct" — such as by heavily taxing alcoholic beverages or imported goods to dissuade people from buying them —"are nothing new" and are allowable, he said.[57]

But the court struck down the harsh penalty the ACA sought to impose on states unwilling to expand Medicaid, thus effectively transforming the provision from a requirement into a voluntary program. ACA opponents argued that the law's expansion plan as a whole should be struck down because the stiff penalty attached to it violated a basic constitutional principle — that the federal government can't compel states to either enact or administer any federal regulatory program.[58] The Obama administration, on the other hand, contended that the expansion plan falls under a provision in current law that requires states that participate in Medicaid to go along with any future changes Congress may make in the program or cease receiving federal Medicaid funds.

A seven-member court majority, led by Roberts, issued a split decision, allowing the Medicaid coverage proposal

# Trying to Trim the Waste From Health Care

*Conservatives and liberals both take "big picture" approach.*

In this campaign season of extreme political bickering, Democrats and Republicans agree on one thing: the pressing need to slow ever-rising health care costs. In 2010, U.S. spending, public and private, on health care totaled nearly $2.6 trillion, more than 10 times the cost in 1980.[1]

Moreover, conservative and liberal economists take essentially the same big-picture cost-cutting approach — setting annual budgets and giving them teeth by forcing an entity such as an insurance company or hospital-and-physician group to pick up the tab for cost overruns, says Michael Chernew, a professor of health care policy at Harvard Medical School.

In conservatives' preferred model — sometimes called a "voucher" or a "premium-support" system — the annual budget comes in the form of a capped payment that insurers receive in exchange for keeping an individual healthy for a year, says Chernew. (GOP vice presidential candidate Paul Ryan proposes such a plan as a new model for Medicare, for example.)

Under this kind of capped-payment plan, the government — or an employer — calculates what it deems fair for a year's worth of health care and hands each person a check to shop for an insurance plan at that price. Individuals must choose wisely, and insurers must provide adequate care at the set price, since extra spending won't be reimbursed, Chernew explains.

Chernew says left-leaning analysts favor a similar fixed-price approach, but with health-care providers, such as integrated hospital-physician practice groups, rather than insurers getting the cash. The Affordable Care Act (ACA) dubs such groups Accountable Care Organizations (ACOs). In this model, a group of providers, rather than an insurer, gets a "bundled" payment to provide all needed health services. The providers must provide adequate care at that price or else pick up the tab for additional services patients need.

Both models are intended to "change the nature of the good that's being bought" in the health care market from "specific services that are sold at certain fees" to "care overall" — a total package of care to keep people healthy, Chernew says.

The current system of buying one health service at a time encourages consumers to purchase unneeded, or even harmful, medical services, since health-care organizations profit by selling as many services as possible, says Robert Laszewski, an insurance consultant in Alexandria, Va. Both proposed capped-payment systems have promise and pitfalls, though, and which one a policymaker opts for is still largely a matter of ideology, since little evidence exists about either plan's effectiveness.

Chernew says he believes the conservative plan of offering insurers capped payments would encourage competition in the insurance industry. But many questions remain. For example, it is unclear how effective it would be to shape the health care system around consumers' ability to "shop around," Chernew says. Among other issues, such an approach makes it crucial for the government to prevent any insurers from gaining monopoly power, because only with a wide range of buying options can consumers run an overpriced or low-quality health plan out of business.

to stand, but only as a voluntary program that states could take or leave without penalty. Roberts concluded that the proposal was outside established Medicaid rules, meaning states' pledges to go along with all legislated changes in the program don't apply.

Medicaid "was designed to cover medical services for . . . particular categories of the needy: the disabled, the blind, the elderly, and needy families with dependent children," and previous Medicaid amendments "merely altered and expanded . . . these categories," Roberts wrote. The coverage expansion, by contrast, is not "a program to care for the neediest among us, but . . . an element of a comprehensive national plan to provide universal health insurance coverage."[59]

## CURRENT SITUATION

### Uncertain Future

The Supreme Court's June ruling has not ended the legal controversy surrounding the ACA. Church-run institutions are claiming in new lawsuits that a requirement in the

On the ACO side, too, "we know enough to be somewhat optimistic, but not enough to be sure," Chernew says.

Massachusetts, which enacted a universal health-coverage program similar to the ACA in 2006, has been experimenting with a version of ACOs — called Alternative Quality Contracts (AQCs). In an AQC, a hospital or physicians' group negotiates a set price from an insurer to cover the entire cost of care for all the insurer's patients whom the health care providers serve. If the provider group goes over budget, it must pay the difference. That gives it a financial stake in avoiding problems such as untreated chronic conditions that worsen until costly emergency care is needed.[2]

So far, evidence is mixed on AQCs. One study last year found no savings while another reported "modest" savings.[3] A 2012 study, however, concluded that the average AQC spent 1.9 percent less than control groups in the first year of operation and 3.3 percent less in the second year, while providing better chronic-disease and preventive-health care.[4]

Liberal proposals generally set strict rules to prevent an organization receiving a capped payment from skimping on care, while conservatives believe that a robust market will perform that function, says Laszewski. That difference gets to the heart of the debate over the competing models, says Laszewski. "Some people fear big business and prefer to be protected from it by the government, and others fear the government" and its potential to strangle choice and innovation with rules.

Whatever plan economists or lawmakers may propose to slow the growth in medical costs, consumers or the health care industry can undermine the effort. Consumers may balk at cost-cutting, fearing it deprives them of care. And providers, from medical-device manufacturers to individual physicians, have routinely pushed back against such efforts to avoid losing income. In Massachusetts, that dynamic is playing out with AQCs,

said Eric Beyer, president of Boston's Tufts Medical Center, which holds an AQC contract. Contrary to policymakers' hopes, "employers are not signing up for the [AQC] plans in droves — in fact, more of our population is moving toward products that have no requirement for paying providers for quality over quantity," Beyer said.[5]

Meanwhile, fearing they'll lose their clout as the government becomes more aggressive about demanding cost-efficient and high-quality care, doctors and hospitals are linking up into very large medical groups, says Stan Dorn, a senior fellow at the Urban Institute, an independent domestic-issues research group in Washington. Ideally, such arrangements could provide better integrated care, but "big systems can also extract high prices," Dorn says.

*— Marcia Clemmitt*

---

[1] "U.S. Healthcare Costs," Kaiser Family Foundation, www.kaiseredu.org/Issue-Modules/US-Health-Care-Costs/Background-Brief.aspx; for background, see Marcia Clemmitt, "Rising Health Costs," *CQ Researcher*, April 7, 2006, pp. 289-312.

[2] Dan Diamond, "To Gauge ObamaCare Impact, Ignore CBO and Focus on AQC," *California Healthline*, July 25, 2012, www.californiahealthline.org/road-to-reform/2012/to-gauge-obamacare-impact-ignore-cbo-and-focus-on-aqc.aspx.

[3] *Ibid.*

[4] Zirui Song, *et al.*, "The 'Alternative Quality Contract,' Based on a Global Budget, Lowered Medical Spending and Improved Quality," *Health Affairs*, July 2012, http://content.healthaffairs.org/content/early/2012/07/09/hlthaff.2012.0327.abstract.

[5] Eric Beyer, "State Needs to Take Stock Before Expanding Health Payment Methods Employers Are Rejecting," *The Boston Globe*, July 18, 2012, www.bostonglobe.com/opinion/2012/07/18/state-needs-take-stock-before-expanding-health-payment-methods-employers-methods-rejecting-state-needs-take-stock-before-expanding-health-payment/12nbA6ag2uUOCihzjFk7OI/story.html.

---

ACA that health plans provide contraception coverage violates the Constitution's guarantee of religious freedom.

The main ACA story of 2012, though, is uncertainty, as most of the law's provisions are a year or more from implementation and the Supreme Court ruling has made Medicaid expansion voluntary for states.

This year, several groups, including colleges run by the Roman Catholic Church and some conservative Protestant churches, as well as at least seven states and some for-profit businesses whose owners strongly oppose contraception out of religious conviction, have filed lawsuits seeking to

exempt employers from the contraception mandate.[60] (Churches, but not employers such as church-run hospitals and schools, already are exempt.)

"We're very clear on the sanctity of life, and this insurance mandate goes against our conscience," said Philip Graham Ryken, president of Wheaton College, an evangelical Protestant institution in Wheaton, Ill.[61]

The Obama administration announced a compromise plan last February. Women who work at nonprofit, church-affiliated entities can go directly to the insurance companies that administer their employer-based health plans

AFP/Getty Images/Timothy A. Clary

Demonstrators in New York City on March 23, 2012, protest a requirement of the health care law that most employers provide health insurance coverage for contraception. Several groups, including colleges run by the Roman Catholic Church, at least seven states and business owners who strongly oppose contraception out of religious conviction, have filed lawsuits seeking to exempt employers from the contraception mandate.

and get contraceptive coverage — free — so that employers can avoid acting as go-betweens. Under the ACA, insurers face stricter government rules than in the past on what coverage they offer and what they charge for it. In this case, the administration argues that insurers may not demand that women pay a higher premium to get contraceptive coverage because contraceptives are a preventive-health measure that reduces overall health spending.[62]

But opponents contend that the compromise still implicates employers in immoral activity.

"We have a president who, for the first time in American history, is directly assaulting the First Amendment and freedom of religion," said former Sen. Rick Santorum, R-Pa., in a campaign speech on behalf of Romney. President Obama, he said, is "forcing business people right now to do things that are against their conscience."[63]

## Court Fallout

Since the Supreme Court rendered its decision, numerous Republican governors and state lawmakers have expressed doubt about whether their states will undertake a Medicaid expansion. Officials in states including Mississippi, Nebraska, Missouri, Idaho, Texas, Wisconsin, Florida, Indiana, South Carolina, Iowa, Louisiana and Kansas have suggested they might reject the expansion funds, thus reducing by millions the number of people covered under the law.[64] About 1.8 million uninsured people who were expected to gain Medicaid coverage live in Texas alone, and nearly 1 million reside in Florida.[65]

Some officials have flatly announced that the expansion is a no-go. "I don't see any chance" of Missouri participating, said Ryan Silvey, a budget committee chairman in that state's Republican-dominated legislature.[66]

Opposition, by and large, is not about money, and that's why it will stick, argued Andrew Koppelman, a professor of law and political science at Northwestern University. Because the state funding share is so low — the federal government will pick up 100 percent of costs through 2016, gradually dropping to 90 percent in 2020 — the objections amount to "states refusing to spend federal money to help people that they do not want to help," he contends. "The temptation to trash Obamacare will be irresistible."[67]

However, many analysts expect states eventually to back away from their hardline resistance and adopt the program.

"I'm really excited about the ruling" because by freeing states to turn down the program altogether, it gives them leverage to bargain with the federal government for looser rules about how they structure it, says insurance consultant Laszewski. "I believe that states will implement the law, but [Louisiana's Republican Gov.] Bobby Jindal will do it in a different way than in New York" under Democratic Gov. Andrew Cuomo.

The result will be a variety of natural experiments carried out around the country that will test how different coverage models work, from single-payer systems to the most loosely regulated private markets, he says.

# Should the Affordable Care Act be repealed?

## YES
**Thomas Miller**
*Resident Fellow, American Enterprise Institute*

Written for *CQ Researcher*, September 2012

The Affordable Care Act (ACA) — also known as "Obamacare" — was unpopular, unwise and unsustainable when enacted in March 2010. Another two years of stumbling implementation and real-world analysis, amid fierce battles in the courts, on Capitol Hill and throughout the states, provided further evidence of the health law's flaws. The law is too costly to finance, too difficult to administer, too burdensome on health care practitioners and too disruptive of health care arrangements that many Americans prefer.

The ACA is not just too misguided to succeed. It's too dangerous to maintain and far too flawed to fix on a piecemeal basis. The law will jeopardize future economic growth, distort health care delivery and limit access to quality care. It doubles down on our already unsustainable entitlement spending for health care, transferring dedicated funds from one overcommitted program (Medicare) to expand another (Medicaid) and establish a new one — the subsidies the ACA provides consumers to buy insurance in government-run exchanges.

The ACA will further erode meaningful limits on the powers of the federal government. Its maze of current and future mandates, regulatory edicts and arbitrary bureaucracy undermines political accountability and the rule of law.

Obamacare was built on faulty premises, then disguised with accounting fictions and narrowly approved through cynical deal-making. Repealing it in whole is necessary to clear the way for the lasting reforms of health care we so desperately need.

The long overdue journey to health policy that drives sustainable health care improvement must be centered on better incentives, information, choices, competition, personal responsibilities and trust in the decisions of individuals and their families. It should not be guided by top-down mandates, arbitrary budgetary formulas and bureaucratic buck-passing. We won't improve our health until we move personal health care decisions out of politics and back into the hands of patients and physicians.

Repeal of the ACA is not enough by itself. But it opens the door to a more decentralized and market-based alternative that will work and improve the lives of Americans. The country needs a more competitive health care marketplace that encourages more entry and less command-and-control regulation, while retargeting our tax-funded resources on protecting the most vulnerable individuals and their families.

Rebalancing our resources, our values, our hopes and our fears is too important, complex and personal to leave in the hands of the many politicians, experts and entrenched interests that have failed us in the past.

## NO
**Ron Pollack**
*Founding Executive Director, Families USA*

Written for *CQ Researcher*, September 2012

In June, the Supreme Court upheld the constitutionality of the Affordable Care Act. Just last week, however, its theatrical opponents in the House of Representatives staged their 34th loud, divisive and utterly futile vote to repeal it. Afterward, nothing changed; it remains the law of our land. The benefits and protections it grants consumers are real, and many are already in place. Soon, even strident opponents will put aside their showmanship and recognize the positive impact and value of the law.

The law makes sure that insurance companies treat people fairly. Under the law, it will be illegal for insurers to discriminate against women by charging higher premiums simply because of their gender. Nobody — male or female — will be denied coverage or charged higher premiums because of a pre-existing condition, such as asthma or diabetes. No one will live in fear of their insurance being cancelled. People will no longer be subject to arbitrary lifetime or annual caps in what insurers pay out, thereby denying coverage when it is needed the most.

The act also comes with much-needed direct help for middle-class families. They will receive substantial subsidies to make health insurance premiums affordable. Seniors will no longer fall into the huge prescription drug coverage gap in Medicare euphemistically named the "doughnut hole." Comprehensive preventive care will be available at no cost for women, including mammograms and contraception.

A significant number of these benefits, and many others, already are being provided in whole or in part, such as the millions of young adults (under age 26) who are staying on their parents' policies. As more and more people feel the direct protections and benefits of the new law, repealing the Affordable Care Act will increasingly be considered an absurdity.

At its heart, the ACA is about keeping people healthy and giving Americans the peace of mind that health care will always be there when they need it. Irrespective of changes in any person's life circumstances — the desire to switch jobs or start a business, being laid off from work, changes in marital status or the sudden loss of income — the Affordable Care Act ensures the availability of quality, affordable health care.

Instead of playing politics with the act, it's time to fully implement it across the country. In fact, Democrats and Republicans should come together to build on the ACA so that additional steps can be taken to moderate health care costs for America's families and businesses.

Conducting such experiments has always been a good idea, "but the problem is that you need gobs of federal money" for states to do them, which the ACA now offers, he says.

"Virtually every state" will implement the expansion "after the rhetorical season" of the November election is over, says Pollack of Families USA. Some "very influential" health care sectors, such as hospitals, already are urging states to take the funding to help eliminate the unpaid medical bills they struggle with, he says.

"ACA provided a carrot and a stick" for the expansion, and "although the stick is gone, the very big carrot remains," he says.

### Only a Beginning

Because many aspects of health care are state responsibilities, such as setting and enforcing rules for health insurance sold to individuals and small businesses, the ACA puts additional burdens on state governments. However, the law allows the federal government to step in if states don't fulfill these responsibilities effectively and on time.

"A few states — including Massachusetts, California and Maryland — appear to be well along in their implementation activities" for the insurance exchanges through which individuals will buy health coverage using ACA subsidies, said Antos of the American Enterprise Institute. Nationwide, however, given the present rate of progress, both the states and the federal government are doomed to fall behind the aggressive schedule the law requires, he said.

For example, 37 states have not yet enacted enabling legislation or issued an executive order to establish an insurance exchange through which citizens can buy coverage, Antos noted. Citizens of those states risk becoming liable for the ACA's mandate-related tax penalty in January 2014 — before their states have managed to set up the exchanges through which affordable coverage is supposed to be available, he wrote. What's more, it's "doubtful that the federal government . . . will be capable of stepping in" to help states get their insurance exchanges up and running, he said. "The task is too large, the time is too short."[68]

But ACA supporter Pollack says the law's opponents are secretly rooting for the law to stumble hard out of the gate. He calls their predictions that lagging ACA implementation will harm citizens "wishful thinking." Even "a lot of governors who actually oppose the law and joined the lawsuit [against it] are still working quietly with folks to get ready" to implement it, he says. That's partly because many Republican governors hope to shape the exchanges according to their own ideas — not the Obama administration's — about how the insurance market should work he says. "It would put a conservative governor in an ironic situation — letting the federal government decide what goes on in the state."

Besides expanding insurance coverage, the ACA also is intended to reshape the way health care is delivered and paid for, with the goal to hold down cost increases while maintaining quality. The law includes a wide range of possible cost-control measures, such as establishment of an independent board empowered to make cost-saving changes to Medicare. It also offers financial incentives to induce physicians and hospitals to provide preventive care. But all these measures "have to be built" before it becomes clear whether they actually work, says insurance consultant Laszewski.

Furthermore, much more must be attempted on the cost-control front, Laszewski says. "This law didn't take a really serious shot at it" — not surprising, given the controversy that surrounds any attempt to reduce medical costs, he says. Massachusetts, which enacted a close-to-universal coverage system similar to the ACA in 2006, "just passed their cost-control bill this year," a full six years into the program's operation, Laszewski says.

## OUTLOOK

### Voting on Health

Parts of the ACA, if not the law as a whole, undoubtedly will have some impact in the November elections. The ACA provisions intended to trim some wasteful Medicare spending, for example, could undermine President Obama's popularity among older voters. Meanwhile, many congressional Republicans continue to say they'll cut implementation funding for the law and repeal it in January if they have the power.

On July 18, 127 members of the House GOP caucus — more than half its members — wrote House Speaker Boehner and House Majority Leader Eric Cantor, R-Va., expressing "outrage" over the Supreme Court's upholding of the health care law. They pledged to "continue efforts to repeal the law in its entirety this year, next year, and until we are successful."[69] Romney has repeatedly made the same vow in his campaign for the White House.

Still, says Robert Blendon, a professor of health policy and political analysis at the Harvard School of Public Health, the ACA may not be foremost on voters' minds this fall. "The polling is pretty clear," he says. "The economy and jobs are the main issues for voters, but if the election is within three or four points, then other issues matter." Health care counts high among those other issues, but in that category it is mainly Medicare that has voters concerned, Blendon says.

Ryan, the GOP vice presidential nominee, wants to provide future Medicare recipients with a fixed government payment and let them choose among private Medicare plans, Blendon notes. But the idea "has not done well in any poll," he says.

That doesn't mean the Medicare issue is friendly to Obama, however, Blendon says. The Romney campaign "is trying to do something quite politically sophisticated" by taking Medicare and reframing it in campaign ads, speeches and interviews to depict Obama as Medicare's chief foe, he says. Romney charged in an August TV ad and in an interview that in the ACA, Obama "cuts Medicare by $716 billion, takes that money out of the Medicare trust fund and uses it to pay for Obamacare."[70]

But the ACA's defenders argue that the cuts don't trim Medicare benefits but shift the payments in ways aimed at reducing wasteful spending. For example, the law trims payments to so-called Medicare Advantage private health plans that cost more than traditional Medicare. It also lowers payments to hospitals that discharge too many patients too quickly, only to readmit them to treat conditions that could have been prevented with better patient management. If those changes save money, as many expect they will, the savings will fund new Medicare benefits — such as free preventive care — as well as other ACA provisions, PolitiFact Florida, a fact-checking website run by the *Tampa Bay Times*, reported.[71]

Nevertheless, Republican ads and speeches condemning the cuts are successfully harming Obama's standing with senior voters, at least for now, says Blendon. "Just the one big number" — $716 billion — is enough "to make people very nervous," while details that could make the number sound less frightening "are awfully complex to explain to people." In states such as Florida and Ohio, where the presidential vote will be close, the Medicare ads could win the day for Republicans, he says.

In polls, most voters continue to say they dislike the ACA, despite expressing support for some of its provisions, such as its guarantee that people with pre-existing illnesses can buy insurance at a relatively affordable price. Public opposition stems in large part from people's lack of knowledge about what the law does, some analysts argue.

The Urban Institute's Dorn describes a conversation he had with a small-business owner who doesn't provide health insurance for his mainly low-wage workers and buys his personal coverage in the private market. "I said, 'Your own premiums will come down a lot" once the ACA kicks in in 2014, "and your low-wage workers will get subsidies" from the government to help them buy coverage, too. The man responded that he hadn't heard of these ACA features and wasn't sure he believed they existed, Dorn says.

Nevertheless, the ACA has set in motion some changes that will go forward, whatever the election results, says Dorn. For example, states are using ACA funds to automate and streamline their Medicaid administrative procedures, which may trim costs and make it easier for poor people to get access to all the state services they need. And some hospitals and doctors are shifting their focus to preventive care, in anticipation of ACA payment changes that will reward prevention.

"Even if Republicans sweep the table" in November, says Dorn, "they can't take all of those things away."

## NOTES

1. "Support Caleb," Facebook, www.facebook.com/supportcalebmedley.

2. Jeremy P. Meyer, "Caleb Medley, Last Shooting Victim at CU Hospital, Released," *Denver Post*, Sept. 13, 2012, www.denverpost.com/breakingnews/ci_21528421/caleb-medley-last-shooting-victim-at-cu-hospital.

3. Quoted in John Blackstone, "Aurora Shooting May Ruin One Victim's Finances," CBS News, July 23, 2012, www.cbsnews.com/8301-18563_162-57478303/aurora-shooting-may-ruin-one-victims-finances.

4. The decision is *National Federation of Independent Business v. Sebelius*, 567 U.S. 2— (June 28, 2012), www.supremecourt.gov/opinions/11pdf/11-393c3a2.pdf; For an account, see Kenneth Jost, "Health Care Law Upheld in Fractured Ruling," *CQ Researcher* Blog, June 28, 2012, http://cqresearcherblog.blogspot.com/2012_06_01_archive.html.

5. Phil Galewitz and Marilyn Werber Serafini, "Ruling Puts Pressure on States to Act," *Kaiser Health News*, June 28, 2012, www.kaiserhealthnews.org/stories/2012/june/28/pressure-on-states-to-act-after-supreme-court-ruling.aspx.

6. *NFIB v. Sebelius, op. cit.* (opinion of Scalia, Kennedy, Thomas, and Alito dissenting), p. 6.

7. *NFIB v. Sebelius, op. cit.*, (opinion of Ginsburg, J.), fn 5, p. 19.

8. Nancy-Ann DeParle, "Supreme Court Upholds President Obama's Health Care Reform," *The White House Blog*, June 28, 2012, www.whitehouse.gov/blog/2012/06/28/supreme-court-upholds-president-obamas-health-care-reform.

9. For background, see Julie Rovner, "Mitt Romney's Shifting Stance on Health Care," *Shots blog*, NPR, Sept. 10, 2012, www.npr.org/blogs/health/2012/09/10/160898409/mitt-romneys-shifting-stance-on-health-care.

10. Robin Abcarian and Maeve Reston, "Romney Uses Healthcare Ruling to Motivate Voters Against Obama," *Los Angeles Times*, June 28, 2012, http://articles.latimes.com/2012/jun/28/news/la-pn-romney-uses-healthcare-ruling-to-motivate-voters-against-obama-20120628.

11. For background, see Mitt Romney, "Romney: As First Act, Out With Obamacare," *USA Today*, May 11, 2011, www.usatoday.com/news/opinion/forum/2011-05-11-Romney-on-fixing-health-care_n.htm.

12. For background, see "Plan Levels/Standardization of Coverage," American Cancer Society, www.acscan.org/pdf/healthcare/implementation/background/PlanLevelsStandardizationofCoverage.pdf.

13. Quoted in Kim Krisberg, "Public Health Reacts to Supreme Court's ACA Ruling: 'Surprised and Then Ecstatic,'" *The Pump Handle blog*, June 28, 2012, http://scienceblogs.com/thepumphandle/2012/06/28/public-health-reacts-to-supreme-courts-aca-ruling-surprised-and-then-ecstatic.

14. "On ObamaCare," Wicker for Congress website, www.brookswicker.com/on-obamacare.

15. Ryan Fazio, "Health Care Reform Biased Against Youth," *The Daily Northwestern*, Feb. 13, 2012, www.dailynorthwestern.com/mobile/forum/fazio-health-care-reform-biased-against-youth-1.2700776.

16. Quoted in Jeffrey Young, "Health Care Reform Will Remake Health Insurance Market for Young Adults," *Huffington Post*, Aug. 1, 2012, www.huffingtonpost.com/2012/08/01/health-care-reform-young-adults_n_1711376.html.

17. Quoted in *ibid.*

18. For background, see Michael Cooper, "Many Governors Are Still Unsure About Medicaid Expansion," *The New York Times*, July 14, 2012, www.nytimes.com/2012/07/15/us/governors-face-hard-choices-over-medicaid-expansion.html?pagewanted=all.

19. For background, see "The Requirement to Buy Coverage Under the Affordable Care Act," *Health Reform Source*, Henry J. Kaiser Family Foundation, http://healthreform.kff.org/the-basics/Requirement-to-buy-coverage-flowchart.aspx.

20. "Mitch McConnell: Odds Are Against Health Law Repeal," The Associated Press/*Huffington Post*, July 2, 2012, www.huffingtonpost.com/2012/07/02/mitch-mcconnell-health-care-law_n_1644466.html.

21. Michael D. Tanner, "Individual Mandates for Health Insurance: Slippery Slope to National Health Care," *Policy Analysis No. 565*, Cato Institute, April 5, 2006, www.cato.org.

22. Quoted in Sarah Kliff, "Scott Brown, Ron Wyden Offering Health Care Revision," *Politico*, Nov. 17, 2010, www.politico.com/news/stories/1110/45316.html.

23. *NFIB v. Sebelius*, (opinion of Ginsburg, J.), *op. cit.*, p. 7.

24. Joseph Paduda, "Update — Health reform, the Supreme Court decision and workers comp," *Managed Care Matters*, June 29, 2012, www.joepaduda.com/archives/002363.html.

25. *Ibid.*

26. Quoted in Steve O'Keefe, "Loss Ratio Means Lost Care for Millions," *Health Care Compact Blog*, Nov. 14, 2011, http://healthcarecompact.org/blog/2011-11-14/loss-ratio-means-lost-care-millions.

27. *Ibid.*

28. Quoted in Kathryn Jean Lopez, "Post-Court Report: Sally Pipes on the Future of Health-Care Reform in America," *National Review Online*, March 29, 2012, www.nationalreview.com/critical-condition/294752/post-court-report-sally-pipes-future-health-care-reform-america-kathryn-je.

29. John Goodman, "The Supreme Court May Have Saved Lives," *The Health Care Blog*, July 30, 2012, http://thehealthcareblog.com/blog/2012/07/30/the-supreme-court-may-have-saved-lives.

30. Pam Belluck, "Medicaid Expansion May Lower Death Rates, Study Says," *The New York Times*, July 25, 2012, www.nytimes.com/2012/07/26/health/policy/medicaid-expansion-may-lower-death-rate-study-says.html?pagewanted=all; Benjamine D. Sommers, *et al.*, "Mortality and Access to Care Among Adults After State Medicaid Expansions," *The New England Journal of Medicine*, July 25, 2012, www.nejm.org/doi/full/10.1056/NEJMsa1202099.

31. Belluck, *op. cit.*

32. Quoted in "The Supreme Court Health Care Ruling: Now What?" *Knowledge at Wharton*, June 28, 2012, http://knowledge.wharton.upenn.edu/article.cfm?articleid=3038.

33. John Rossomando, "ObamaCare Forcing Americans out of Their Health Plans," *Human Events*, July 8, 2011, www.humanevents.com/2011/07/08/obamacare-forcing-americans-out-of-their-health-plans.

34. Joseph Antos, "After the Supreme Court, Higher Cost and Unrealistic Timeline Will Force Major Changes," *Health Affairs blog*, July 2, 2012, http://healthaffairs.org/blog/2012/07/02/after-the-supreme-court-higher-cost-and-unrealistic-timeline-will-force-major-changes.

35. Quoted in Tom Eblen, "Commentary: Medicare for Everyone," McClatchy/*Lexington Herald Leader* [KY], Aug. 7, 2012, www.mcclatchydc.com/2012/08/07/160417/commentary-medicare-for-everyone.html.

36. "Testimony on Last Year's Major Health Care Legislation," Congressional Budget Office, March 30, 2011, www.cbo.gov/publication/25155.

37. Douglas W. Elmendorf, letter to Rep. John Boehner, Congressional Budget Office, July 24, 2012, http://cbo.gov/sites/default/files/cbofiles/attachments/43471-hr6079.pdf.

38. Paduda, *op. cit.*

39. "Overview of the Uninsured in the United States: A Summary of the 2011 Population Survey," Assistant Secretary for Planning and Evaluation, U.S. Dept. of Health and Human Services, September 2011, http://aspe.hhs.gov/health/reports/2011/CPSHealthIns2011/ib.shtml.

40. For background, see Marcia Clemmitt, "Health-Care Reform," *CQ Researcher*, June 11, 2010 (updated May 24, 2011), pp. 505-528, and Marcia Clemmitt, "Health-Care Reform," *CQ Researcher*, Aug. 28, 2009, pp. 693-716.

41. "Estimates for the Insurance Coverage Provisions of the Affordable Care Act Updated for the Recent Supreme Court Decision," Congressional Budget Office, July 2012, p. 3, http://cbo.gov/sites/default/files/cbofiles/attachments/43472-07-24-2012-CoverageEstimates.pdf.

42. David Cole, "Is Health Care Reform Unconstitutional?" *The New York Review of Books*, Feb. 24, 2011, www.nybooks.com/articles/archives/2011/feb/24/health-care-reform-unconstitutional/?pagination=false.

43. *Ibid.*

44. Mark V. Pauly, Patricia Damon, Paul Feldstein and John Hoff, "A Plan for 'Responsible National Health Insurance,' " *Health Affairs*, Spring 1991, p. 10, http://hc.wharton.upenn.edu/danzon/html/CV%20pubs/1991_DanzonPaulyFesteinHoff_APlanForResponsibleNationalHealthInsurance_HA%20Spring%201991.pdf.

45. Stuart Butler, testimony before the Senate Special Committee on Aging, March 10, 2003, www.heritage.org/research/testimony/laying-the-groundwork-for-universal-health-care-coverage.

46. Quoted in Marcia Clemmitt, "Frist: Limit Tax Exclusion for Employer-Based Coverage," *Medicine and Health*, July 19, 2004.

47. Avik Roy, "Opposing View: Individual Mandate Masks and Ugly Deal," *USA Today*, March 28, 2012, www.usatoday.com/news/opinion/story/2012-03-27/supreme-court-individual-mandate/53815712/1.

48. Uwe E. Reinhardt, "The Supreme Court and the National Conversation on Health Care Reform," *Economix blogs*, *The New York Times*, March 30, 2012, http://economix.blogs.nytimes.com/2012/03/30/the-supreme-court-and-the-national-conversation-on-health-care-reform.

49. Galewitz and Serafini, *op. cit.*; for background, see Elicia J. Herz, "Medicaid: A Primer," Congressional Research Service, Jan. 11, 2011, www.ncsl.org/documents/health/MAPrimer.pdf.

50. "Eligibility Levels in Medicaid & CHIP for Children, Pregnant Women, Parents, and Childless Adults," Georgetown University Health Policy Institute, Center for Children and Families, January 2012, http://ccf.georgetown.edu/wp-content/uploads/2012/04/Eligibility-by-State.pdf.

51. "Who Benefits from the ACA Medicaid Expansion," The Kaiser Commission on Medicaid and the Uninsured, June 20, 2012, www.kff.org/medicaid/quicktake_aca_medicaid.cfm.

52. "Federal and State Share of Medicaid Spending FY2010," statehealthfacts.org, Kaiser Family Foundation, www.statehealthfacts.org/comparemaptable.jsp?ind=636&cat=4.

53. "Summary of New Health Reform Law," Kaiser Family Foundation, www.kff.org/healthreform/upload/8061.pdf.

54. Quoted in Julie Rovner, "Medicaid Expansion Goes Overlooked in Supreme Court Anticipation," *Shots blog*, NPR, June 27, 2012, www.npr.org/blogs/health/2012/06/27/155861308/medicaid-expansion-goes-overlooked-in-supreme-court-anticipation.

55. Galewitz and Serafini, *op. cit.*

56. Richard Posner, "Entry 17: The Commerce Clause Was Clearly Enough to Uphold the Affordable Care Act," *Supreme Court Year in Review, Slate*, June 28, 2012, www.slate.com/articles/news_and_politics/the_breakfast_table/features/2012/_supreme_court_year_in_review/affordable_care_act_upheld_why_the_commerce_clause_should_have_been_enough_.html.

57. *NFIB v. Sebelius*, (opinion of Roberts, C. J.), *op. cit.*, p. 36.

58. *Ibid.*, p. 45.

59. *Ibid.*, p. 53.

60. For background, see Robin Marty, "Hobby Lobby Files Suit Opposing Affordable Care Act Birth Control Benefit," *RH Reality Check*, Sept. 13, 2012, www.rhrealitycheck.org/article/2012/09/13/hobby-lobby-lawsuit-opens-new-realm-in-opposing-afforable-care-act.

61. Quoted in "Evangelical College Joins Suit Against ObamaCare Contraception Mandate," FoxNews.com, July 18, 2012, www.foxnews.com/politics/2012/07/18/evangelical-college-joins-suit-against-obamacare-contraception-mandate.

62. David Brown, "U.S. Bishops Blast Obama's Contraception Compromise," *The Washington Post*, Feb. 11, 2012, www.washingtonpost.com/national/health-science/us-bishops-blast-obamas-contraception-compromise/2012/02/11/gIQAlGVO7Q_story.html.

63. Quoted in Andrew Rafferty, "Santorum Says Government Forcing Catholics to Sin," First Read, NBCNews.com, Aug. 15, 2012, http://firstread.nbcnews.com/_news/2012/08/15/13303104-santorum-says-government-forcing-catholics-to-sin?lite.

64. Galewitz and Serafini, *op. cit.*; N.C. Aizenman and Sandhya Somashekhar, "More State Leaders Considering Opting Out of Medicaid Expansion," *The Washington Post*, July 3, www.washingtonpost.com/national/health-science/more-state-leaders-considering-opting-out-of-medicaid-expansion/2012/07/03/gJQADvMsLW_story.html. John Celock, "Health Care Reform Battles Taking Shape at State Level," *Huffington Post*, June 29, 2012, www.huffingtonpost.com/2012/06/28/health-care-reform-battle-states_n_1635545.html.

65. Galewitz and Serafini, *ibid.*

66. Quoted in *ibid.*

67. Andrew Koppelman, "Terrible Arguments Prevail!" *Salon*, June 28, 2012, www.salon.com/2012/06/28/terrible_arguments_prevail.

68. Antos, *op. cit.*

69. Letter to Reps. John Boehner and Eric Cantor, July 18, 2012, http://rsc.jordan.house.gov/UploadedFiles/Defund_ObamaCare_Letter_July_18.pdf.

70. Quoted in "Romney Says Obama 'Cuts' $716 Billion from Medicare to Pay for Obamacare," *PolitiFact Florida*, Aug. 20, 2012, www.politifact.com/florida/statements/2012/aug/20/mitt-romney/romney-says-obama-cuts-716-medicare-pay-obamacare.

71. *Ibid.*

## BIBLIOGRAPHY

### Selected Sources
### Books

**McDonough, John E., *Inside National Health Reform*, California/Milbank Books on Health and the Public, 2011.**
A Harvard professor of public health who supports the 2010 Affordable Care Act explains its background and why he believes it will improve American health.

**Starr, Paul, *Remedy and Reaction: The Peculiar American Struggle over Health Care Reform*, Yale University Press, 2011.**
A Princeton professor of sociology and public affairs chronicles legislative attempts to overhaul the U.S. health-care system over the past three decades and the vested interests of health-care practitioners, insurers and the public that have made those attempts so difficult.

**Turner, Grace-Marie, James C. Capretta, Thomas P. Miller and Robert E. Moffit, *Why ObamaCare Is Wrong for America: How the New Health Care Law Drives Up Costs, Puts Government in Charge of Your Decisions, and Threatens Your Constitutional Rights*, Broadside Books, 2011.**
Analysts from the free-market-oriented think tanks Galen Institute (Turner) and American Enterprise Institute argue that the Affordable Care Act (ACA) relies on government regulation rather than market competition to address health-system problems and say alternative approaches would allow consumer choice to determine how the health care market develops.

### Articles

**Keck, Anthony, "South Carolina's View: The Affordable Care Act's Medicaid Expansion Is the Wrong Approach," *Health Affairs Blog*, Sept. 6, 2012, http://healthaffairs.org/blog/2012/09/06/south-carolinas-view-the-affordable-care-acts-medicaid-expansion-is-the-wrong-approach.**
The director of South Carolina's Medicaid program argues that eliminating waste in the medical system and changing how health care providers are reimbursed can help his state provide care to more poor people than by accepting federal funds under the ACA to expand Medicaid.

**Rau, Jordan, "Medicare to Penalize 2,211 Hospitals for Excess Readmissions," *Kaiser Health News*, Aug. 13, 2012, www.kaiserhealthnews.org/Stories/2012/August/13/medicare-hospitals-readmissions-penalties.aspx.**
As ACA provisions aimed at trimming ineffective health care spending and improving care quality take effect, more than 2,000 hospitals will lose some Medicare payments because too many of their elderly patients were readmitted for conditions that could have been prevented during their hospital stay. ACA supporters argue that such penalties prevent hospitals from profiting from readmissions and protect patients from ineffective care. But hospitals that serve low-income neighborhoods contend they're being unfairly penalized because their patient populations tend to need more care than do wealthier people.

**Reinhardt, Uwe E., "Health Care: Solidarity vs. Rugged Individualism," *Economix blogs*, The New York Times, June 29, 2012, http://economix.blogs.nytimes.com/2012/06/29/health-care-solidarity-vs-rugged-individualism.**
A Princeton University professor of economics describes the differences between what he calls the European "social-solidarity" approach to health care and the American "libertarian" approach and why he considers the European view more practical.

## Reports and Studies

"The Affordable Care Act: A Brief Summary," *National Conference of State Legislatures*, March 2011, www.ncsl.org/portals/1/documents/health/HRACA.pdf.

A nonpartisan group that provides information to and about state governments offers a plain-language summary of the 2010 health-care law.

Hahn, Jim, and Christopher M. Davis, "The Independent Payment Advisory Board," Congressional Research Service, March 12, 2012, http://assets.opencrs.com/rpts/R41511_20120312.pdf.

Analysts from Congress' nonpartisan research office explain the workings of the ACA's highly controversial expert board that will develop payment and care-delivery changes to trim Medicare costs.

Lunder, Erika K., and Jennifer Staman, "NFIB v. Sebelius: Constitutionality of the Individual Mandate," Congressional Research Service, Sept. 3, 2012, www.fas.org/sgp/crs/misc/R42698.pdf.

Lawyers at Congress' nonpartisan research arm explain the Supreme Court's ruling upholding the 2010 Affordable Care Act's requirement that individuals buy health insurance.

Smith, Mark, Robert Saunders, Leigh Stuckhardt and J. Michael McGinnis, eds., "Best Care at Lower Cost: The Path to Continuously Learning Health Care in America," Institute of Medicine, September 2012, www.nap.edu/catalog.php?record_id=13444.

Experts on improving health care quality say 30 cents of every dollar in health care spending is wasted on useless services. To stem soaring medical costs, the United States should pay medical practitioners based on health outcomes rather than "per service rendered," they contend. Quick adoption of information technology also would help keep doctors up to date on which treatments are supported by science and on patients' medical histories, they also say.

# For More Information

**ACA Litigation Blog**, http://acalitigationblog.blogspot.com. Blog of Bradley Joondeph, a professor of law at the Santa Clara University School of Law in northern California, that chronicles legal challenges to the Affordable Care Act (ACA).

**Alliance for Health Reform**, 1444 Eye St., N.W., Suite 910, Washington, DC 20005; 202-789-2300; www.allhealth.org. Nonpartisan group that calls on health care experts representing a wide range of opinions to provide information about the ACA and other issues.

**American Enterprise Institute**, 1150 17th St., N.W., Washington, DC 20036; 202-862-5800; www.aei.org/issue/health/healthcare-reform/beyond-repeal-and-replace-series. Conservative think tank providing information and analysis on developing a more market-oriented health care system.

**Center on Budget and Policy Priorities**, 820 First St., N.E., Suite 510, Washington, DC 20002; 202-408-1080; www.cbpp.org. Liberal think tank that analyzes how economic policies, including the ACA, affect individuals and state and federal budgets.

**Families USA**, 1201 New York Ave., N.W., Suite 1100, Washington, DC 20005; 202-628-3030; www.familiesusa.org. Liberal consumer-advocacy group that is tracking the progress and effects of the ACA's rollout.

**Health Affairs Blog**, http://healthaffairs.org/blog. Blog run by an academic journal covering health policy that presents a range of opinion on the ACA.

**Healthcare.gov**, U.S. Department of Health and Human Services, 200 Independence Ave., S.W., Washington, DC 20201; www.healthcare.gov/law/index.html. Federal government website providing summaries and information about how the ACA is being implemented.

**Henry J. Kaiser Family Foundation**, Health Reform Source, http://healthreform.kff.org. Website of a nonpartisan foundation that provides information about U.S. health care and the ACA, including a law summary.

# 13

# Aging Population

Alan Greenblatt

Activists on Capitol Hill urge lawmakers on April 15 not to cut Medicare, the federal government's health insurance program for the elderly and disabled. The same day, however, the majority-Republican House approved a budget plan that would rein in Medicare costs. Democrats oppose the plan and intend to use it as a campaign issue in 2012. Economists say entitlement programs must be scaled back to control the country's deficit.

From *CQ Researcher*,
July 15, 2011.

J ames Kempthorne is running out of money. "He saved, or thought he was saving, for retirement," says his son, Dirk, a former Republican governor of Idaho. "He thought he would be okay, even if he lived to be 90."

But on the 4th of July, the senior Kempthorne turned 96. "His savings are gone, and his only source of income is Social Security — Social Security and a couple of sons," Dirk Kempthorne says.

As the proud patriarch of a successful family, James Kempthorne isn't happy about having to rely on his children for help. But he's not alone. Nearly 10 million adult children over age 50 in the United States provide care or financial help to their aging parents.[1]

Such numbers are only going to grow. The oldest members of the baby boom generation — 78 million Americans born between 1946 and 1964 — are turning 65 this year. The sheer number of them means that one will turn 65 every 8 seconds until 2030.[2]

But the population of the "old old" — those over age 85 — is growing, proportionately, faster. America has the largest number of centenarians in the world, at 72,000 — a total that has doubled over the past 20 years and will at least double again by 2020, according to the Census Bureau.[3]

That's the result of good news: increased life expectancy that stems from improved medicine and nutrition and a drastic decline over recent decades in infant mortality.

"I assume that most people would like to live a long, full life, and that's increasingly possible," says John Rother, policy director at AARP, the major advocacy group for seniors, formerly known as the American Association of Retired Persons. "Advances in health care make that more likely for people."

**309**

## More Americans Expect to Delay Retirement

One-fifth of American workers say they expect to retire later than planned — a lower percentage than in 2009 and 2010, but higher than when the economy was stronger in 2002.

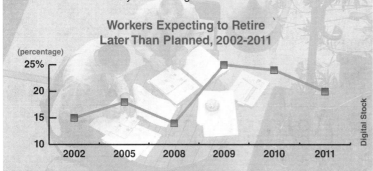

**Workers Expecting to Retire Later Than Planned, 2002-2011**

(percentage)

Source: Ruth Helman, *et al.*, "The 2011 Retirement Confidence Survey: Confidence Drops to Record Lows, Reflecting 'the New Normal,' " Employee Benefit Research Institute, March 2011, www.ebri.org/pdf/surveys/rcs/2011/ebri_03-2011_no355_rcs-11.pdf.

Still, Rother acknowledges that a good deal of concern exists about the challenges posed by the aging population. The rapid growth in the number of seniors — which will be much higher than population growth among young and working-age Americans — will lead to changes across society, including pressures on the workforce and federal budget.[4]

That's despite the fact that the United States is aging less rapidly than other developed nations, such as Germany, Italy, Spain and Japan. By 2015, the population of working-age people — typically defined as those between ages 15 and 64 — will begin to decline throughout the developed world, with the United States as the sole major exception.

"The demographics are obviously more favorable than just about anywhere else in the rich world," says Richard Jackson, who directs the Global Aging Initiative at the Center for Strategic and International Studies, a think tank in Washington. "We have an aging population, but at the end of the day, when the last of the boomers have passed on to that great Woodstock in the sky, we'll be about as old as Japan and Italy are today. And we'll have a growing population and not a stagnant or a declining one."

But the United States has a major problem those other countries don't have. Spending on health care is far greater here than in other developed countries and will only rise with the aging of the population.[5]

"We look as though our problem is very affordable, relative to other countries," says Neil Howe, president of LifeCourse Associates, a demographics consulting firm in Great Falls, Va., and author of several books about demographics. "The big factor that pushes hugely in the other direction is health care. We are anomalous in that we have a system in which health care costs are growing uncontrollably even before the age wave."

Total enrollment in Medicare, the federal government's health insurance program for the elderly, is expected to rise from 47 million today to just over 80 million by 2030.[6] Richard Foster, Medicare's chief actuary, predicts the program's trust fund could be depleted by 2024.[7]

The growing number of aging Americans also will put enormous strains on Social Security and Medicaid, the state-federal health insurance program for the poor and disabled, which pays for more than 40 percent of nursing home care in the United States.

"What were long-term problems are now at our doorstep," says Maya MacGuineas, director of the Fiscal Policy Program at the New America Foundation and president of the nonpartisan Committee for a Responsible Federal Budget, which advocates greater fiscal discipline.

On April 15, the U.S. House of Representatives approved a budget plan that would attempt to rein in Medicare costs by converting it from an insurance program to a limited subsidy for seniors buying private insurance. The plan is unpopular with the public, according to polls, and Democrats not only oppose it but plan to use it as a campaign issue in 2012.[8]

"We will never allow any effort to dismantle the program and force benefit cuts upon seniors under the guise of deficit reduction," five Democratic senators wrote June 6 to Vice President Joseph Biden, who had been leading negotiations with members of Congress on debt reduction. "Our nation's seniors are not responsible for the fiscal challenges we face, and they should not be responsible for shouldering the burden of reducing our deficits."

But many policy analysts insist some changes to entitlements benefiting seniors, particularly Medicare, will be necessary to bring down the federal deficit.

On average, says Richard W. Johnson, director of the retirement policy program at the Urban Institute, a centrist think tank in Washington, Americans are healthier than 30 years ago. But there's been an increase since the late 1990s in the number of Americans in their late 40s or 50s who are disabled or suffer ailments that make it harder for them to work.

"We're seeing increases in the number of handicapped people in late middle age, mostly because of obesity and sedentary lifestyles," says demographer Phillip Longman of the New America Foundation, a liberal think tank in Washington. "Here we have this generation that's physically unfit and has no savings and whose health care we can't afford at current prices."

Such health challenges are going to make it difficult for many Americans to work longer, which economists argue will be necessary to shore up not only Social Security but also personal retirement savings.

Rother, the AARP policy director, stirred up a great deal of controversy with remarks quoted in *The Wall Street Journal* that suggested the seniors' lobbying group, which had helped torpedo a plan to partially privatize Social Security in 2005, might be willing to accept benefit cuts in the program.[9] The group immediately sought to downplay Rother's comments.

Still, the open debate about cutting entitlement programs, combined with losses in the stock market and the collapse of the housing bubble, have left elder Americans nervous about their financial futures.[10] A "retirement confidence" survey by the Employee Benefit Research Institute found that the percentage of workers "not at all" confident they will be able to afford a comfortable retirement rose from 22 percent last year to 27 percent this year, the highest level in the 21 years the group has conducted the survey.[11]

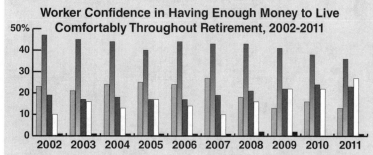

## Workers Gloomy About Retirement Prospects

More than one-fourth of American workers are "not at all" confident that they will have enough money to last through retirement. That's nearly a three-fold increase from nine years earlier. Fewer than one in eight workers is "very confident" about a comfortable retirement.

### Worker Confidence in Having Enough Money to Live Comfortably Throughout Retirement, 2002-2011

*Source:* Ruth Helman, *et al.*, "The 2011 Retirement Confidence Survey: Confidence Drops to Record Lows, Reflecting 'the New Normal,'" Employee Benefit Research Institute, March 2011, www.ebri.org/pdf/surveys/rcs/2011/ebri_03-2011_no355_rcs-11.pdf.

- Very confident
- Somewhat confident
- Not too confident
- Not at all confident
- Don't know/ refused to answer

And it's going to be harder for younger Americans to support the swelling population of seniors. Dowell Myers, a demographer at the University of Southern California, says the ratio of those over 65 to those between 25 and 64 has been constant for 40 years, with 24 seniors for every 100 working-age Americans. But that "dependency ratio" will spike by two-thirds over the next 20 years, to 38 seniors per 100 working-age adults, he says.

"When we come out of this recession, we're going to have fewer new workers and more boomers retiring," Myers says. "That's when we'll feel the changes."

As Americans contemplate the consequences of an aging population, here are some of the questions they're debating:

### Should Americans work longer?

In March, the Centers for Disease Control and Prevention announced that the U.S. death rate had hit a new low while life expectancy had once again ticked up. A male born in 2009 could expect to live 75.7 years, while a female could expect to live to 80.6.[12]

Those numbers are a vast improvement over life expectancy in 1935, when Social Security was created. Life expectancy at birth then was just 58 for men and 62 for women.[13]

# Cities Struggle to Meet Growing Needs of Elderly

*"We have a country that's aging everywhere."*

Rockford's not doing well. The Illinois city, about 90 miles northwest of Chicago, was once a leading furniture-making center, but those jobs are mostly gone. As a result, Rockford's unemployment rate was among the highest among U.S. cities during the recent recession.

Most jobs that remain are snatched up by workers 55 and older — about all that's left of Rockford's working-age population. Rockford Mayor Larry Morrissey, who is in his 40s, was elected on a platform of promising economic revitalization that would help bring young people — including natives who've left — back to town.

Without strong cultural amenities or a major university, it's been a tough sell. Lack of jobs presents the biggest obstacle. Even entry-level jobs paying just above minimum wage that once would have gone to teenagers or people in their 20s are now largely held by workers in their 50s. "We have an aging population, and it's getting poorer," said James Ryan, Rockford's city administrator.[1]

Rockford may be an extreme case, but it's not unique. Many former industrial cities in the Northeast and Midwest are growing both older and less affluent. Among the nation's 100 largest metropolitan areas, the ones that have had the highest percentage growth of seniors are struggling places such as Scranton, Pa., Buffalo, N.Y., and Youngstown, Ohio.[2]

"They have higher concentrations of seniors," says William Frey, a demographer at the Brookings Institution think tank who has analyzed 2010 census data on the location of seniors. "The younger people have left."

There are metropolitan areas in Florida that have a high density of people over age 65. But the number of seniors and aging baby boomers who pick up and move to warmer climes in Florida and Arizona is relatively small. Most people retire in their own homes, or at least their own counties.

"You can certainly find lots of upper-middle-class baby boomers who are coping quite well, moving into college towns where there are good social services available and good medical services," says demographer Phillip Longman, a senior research fellow at the New America Foundation. "The vast majority of baby boomers, however, are often stuck underwater in postwar tract housing and more recent exurban construction. They can't get out if they wanted to."

Frey says it's important for communities, particularly in the suburbs that were planned with younger populations in mind, to learn to adapt to aging ones. Every metropolitan area, he says, is seeing marked growth in its senior population — and will see more as boomers age. "The baby boom python keeps rolling along," he says.

In recent years, many local governments and nonprofit groups have tried to come up with programs, such as increased transit, that will help address the needs of populations that are "aging in place."

About 40 localities, including Atlanta, Iowa City, Iowa, and Pima County, Ariz., have passed ordinances mapping out voluntary or mandatory design requirements for new-home construction that would accommodate the needs of seniors and the disabled, sparing more of them from moving to nursing homes. "We could save a lot of money if individuals could continue to live in their own homes and

Those averages were held down by much higher rates of infant mortality. Most people who lived to adulthood could expect to live past 65, even then.

Still, people are living longer — and spending more years in retirement. Those two facts are putting additional strain on both Social Security and Medicare finances. "The typical beneficiary is expecting to receive benefits for almost nine years longer than when the Social Security

program started," says Charles Blahous, a trustee of the Social Security program and research fellow at the conservative Hoover Institution at Stanford University.

Not only are people living longer, but they are retiring earlier. Most men worked, on average, just past 65 during the 1950s. Now, the average retirement age is 62, says Blahous, who was an economic aide to former President George W. Bush.

receive in-home nursing if they need it," says Rep. Jan Schakowsky, D-Ill., who has introduced "inclusive home design" legislation at the federal level.

Helping seniors cope with chronic disease is another way to keep them out of nursing homes. That's why Elder Services of Merrimack Valley in Lawrence, Mass., has been working with seniors and physicians to help coordinate management of prescription drug regimens and other treatments. "We're not a medical facility, but what we have is the ability to draw elders in and educate them on their health care," says Rosanne DiStefano, the facility's executive director.

DiStefano's program has been widely imitated in Massachusetts, as have a number of other innovations designed to help residents adjust to old age. But such programs are having trouble attracting funding in the present budget environment.

Many local governments are providing exercise classes and nutrition assistance for seniors, but a survey by the National Association of Area Agencies on Aging found that finance and funding problems are the biggest challenge localities face in adjusting to an aging population. Thirty percent of local governments say that their overall revenues are in decline.[3]

"If you go community by community, sure, some have developed programs that are better than others," says Robert H. Binstock, a professor of aging and public policy at Case Western Reserve University. "Overall, it's a tremendous problem."

It's not just the lack of programming help offered by governments that is a problem for aging communities, but also a decline in basic services and amenities, Binstock says.

"You've got lots of places that are aging, and the young people are moving out, particularly in rural areas," he says. "You're going to have communities that aren't even going to have grocery stores."

Some states have a youth population that is growing more rapidly than the older population, notably in the

Eighty-year-old Ada Noda, of St. Augustine, Fla., developed health problems and couldn't work, forcing her to declare bankruptcy. Aging trends are seen by many experts as a significant reason for the climb in health care costs. But health economists say medical costs are rising largely because of the increasing availability of expensive treatments.

Southwest, says Frey. But aging populations are growing in many parts of the country not accustomed to accommodating them.

The localities where older residents are starting to predominate, such as Rockford, "are the ones that are going to be most severely hit," says Frey. "We have a country that's aging everywhere, but it's only young in certain spots."

— *Alan Greenblatt*

[1] Ted C. Fishman, *Shock of Gray* (2010), p. 235.

[2] For background, see Thomas J. Billitteri, "Blighted Cities," *CQ Researcher*, Nov. 12, 2010, pp. 941-964.

[3] "The Maturing of America: Communities Moving Forward for an Aging Population," National Association of Area Agencies on Aging, June 2011, www.n4a.org/files/MOA_FINAL_Rpt.pdf, p. iii.

The age for retiring with full Social Security benefits is slowly rising to 67. Some politicians and economists believe it needs to be raised further. That was the recommendation of President Barack Obama's debt commission last year and is a policy direction lately followed in several European countries.

"What we really need to do is raise the early-entitlement age, which has always been 62 since it was introduced, in

1956 for women and in 1962 for men," says the Urban Institute's Johnson. "The problem with having the early retirement age relatively young is that it does send a signal that 62 is an appropriate time to retire. It's not good for society as a whole, and it's also not good for individuals."

Many people may not be able to retire early, regardless of the official retirement ages set by Social Security.

## U.S. Population Growing Grayer

A record 40 million Americans are age 65 or older, nearly double the total four decades ago. The number of seniors has risen every decade since 1880.

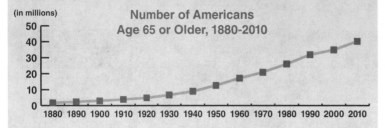

(in millions)

**Number of Americans Age 65 or Older, 1880-2010**

*Sources:* "Life Expectancy for Social Security," Social Security Administration, www.ssa.gov/history/lifeexpect.html; "Profile of General Population and Housing Characteristics: 2010," U.S. Census Bureau, 2010, factfinder2.census .gov/faces/tableservices/jsf/pages/productview.xhtml?pid=DEC_10_DP_DPD P1&prodType=table.

Americans do a bad job of saving in general, and retirement accounts, in particular, are not as full as they should be. Many people have yet to make up recent stock market losses, and a weak housing market has largely dashed hopes of turning homes into assets that can offer support in retirement.

Fewer private employers are offering guaranteed pension benefits, and pensions and other retirement benefits for government workers are under political pressure as well.[14] The result is that about half of U.S. households are at risk of not being able to maintain their living standards in retirement, according to the Center for Retirement Research at Boston College.[15]

More Americans might need to keep working, and market demand for them to do so may also rise, suggests MacGuineas, of the New America Foundation. "We're actually going to be having labor-market shortages as baby boomers move out of the workforce," she says.

A number of social scientists have speculated about whether boomers will keep working longer for that reason or perhaps out of a desire to keep mentally and socially active. Many have speculated that the next generation of older Americans will want to volunteer or work part time, if not stay in their same job past the normal retirement age. "There's not going to be a shrinking entry-level workforce, but it's not going to be growing" either, says Jackson of the Center for Strategic and International Studies. "There may be demand for older workers."

But not everyone is convinced that many more people will be able to keep working well into their 60s or even 70s. Robert H. Binstock, a professor of aging and public policy at Case Western Reserve University, notes that although people are living longer, they're also afflicted with chronic diseases for longer periods of time. "A lot of them can't do their jobs anymore," he says. "The whole notion that everybody is going to be able to keep doing their job until 70, it's silly."

Blahous, the former Bush administration official, dismisses such arguments. Social Security already makes provisions for disabilities, and people worked, on average, longer a half-century ago, he says. People take early retirement more often, Blahous says, "not because more people are physically breaking down. It's because it's financially beneficial."

But putting aside arguments about whether people are physically capable of working longer, there's also the question of whether they can find work. Alicia Munnell, director of the Boston College Center for Retirement Research, says employers will never say they wouldn't hire older people —"that's against the law" — but they are "very ho hum" about the prospect. Her center has conducted surveys that show employers are worried about issues such as older workers' stamina, ability to learn new skills and adaptability to changing technology.

Thus, although the economics of both entitlement programs and household finances would seem to dictate that more Americans will have to work longer, their chances of doing so might not be as good as they would wish.

"We see employers willing to keep older workers, but they are reluctant to hire [older] people who are new to the payroll," says the Urban Institute's Johnson. "We know that when older people lose their jobs, getting a new job is harder, and the periods of unemployment are longer."

### Will spending on health care for the elderly bankrupt the United States?

Health care costs already consume more than double the share of the economy that they did 30 years ago. They are expected to consume $2.8 trillion this year, or 17.9 percent of gross domestic product (GDP), according to the federal Centers on Medicare and Medicaid Services (CMS). That's up from 8.1 percent of the economy in 1975.[16]

Medicare and Medicaid spending have grown at a similar pace. The two programs, which provide coverage for seniors and the poor and disabled, respectively, are on course to grow from about 4 percent of GDP in 2008 to nearly 7 percent by 2035.[17]

The 2010 federal health-care law, known as the Affordable Care Act, was designed to cut Medicare costs by nearly $120 billion over the next five years.[18] But Medicare's actuaries worry that savings from the 2010 law can't all be relied upon. That's because Congress has frequently canceled plans to lower Medicare fees for hospitals and physicians.[19] As a result, the Medicare trust fund is on course to run out of money in 2024 — five years earlier than previously predicted — according to Richard Foster, the chief actuary at CMS.

Rising health care costs are a burden not just for the government but for individuals as well. "We're spending about $8,000 more annually for insurance for a family of four than we did in 2000," says Paul Hewitt, vice president of research at the Coalition for Affordable Health Coverage, an advocacy group in Washington.

Experts say aging trends are a significant reason for the climb in health care costs and an important source of pressure on the federal budget. "It's worth keeping in mind that a significant share of health care growth is demographically based," says Jackson of the Center for Strategic and International Studies. "You're looking at a steep rise in cost just because of the rise in the average age of the beneficiaries — the aging of the aged."

But health economists say aging trends are far from the whole story. Medical costs are rising largely because of the ever-increasing availability of expensive treatments in the health care system — a system that treats young and old alike. "The real problem is not the aging of the population, but the rise of health care costs," says Case

## Elderly a Growing Share of Electorate

The proportion of the American electorate age 65 and older has risen modestly over the past 20 years, from 17 percent in 1990 to 19 percent in 2010. But it is expected to grow sharply over the next 40 years, topping 30 percent by 2050.

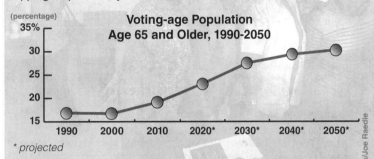

* projected

Sources: "United States 1990 Census of Population," U.S. Census Bureau, www .census.gov/prod/cen1990/cp1/cp-1-1.pdf; "United States 2000 Census of Population and Housing," U.S. Census Bureau, November 2010, www. census. gov/prod/ cen 2000/phc-1-1-pt1.pdf; "Projections of the Population by Selected Age Groups and Sex for the United States: 2010 to 2050," U.S. Census Bureau, 2008, www .census.gov/population/www/projections/files/nation/summary/ np2008-t2.xls.

Western's Binstock, a former president of the Gerontological Society of America. "We don't look at the elephant in the room here, which is the enormous profits of the medical-industrial complex."

Most experts agree that major alterations are in order. Some are discouraged that the two major parties seem worlds apart on health care issues. "Both parties have to recognize the need to compromise," says the Urban Institute's Johnson.

That does not appear imminent. Republicans have pledged to repeal the 2010 health care law, considered one of Obama's signature achievements, while Democrats intend to use the GOP's controversial plan to turn Medicare into something resembling a voucher program against them in the 2012 elections.

Even as congressional Republicans seek to slash Medicare and other entitlements, they oppose the Independent Payment Advisory Board, established by the 2010 health care law, which is meant to make recommendations for Medicare spending cuts when its growth exceeds GDP growth by more than 1 percent.

"Cutting providers eventually cuts benefits because they are less available," said Sen. Jon Kyl, R-Ariz., the minority whip. "You don't have as many physicians, for

Walter Breuning celebrates his 113th birthday at a retirement home in Great Falls, Mont., on Sept. 21, 2009. At his death in April 2011 at age 114, he was the last American man born in the 19th century and one of the world's oldest people. The oldest of the 78 million Americans born during the post-World War II baby boom are turning 65 this year, while the share of the population over 85 is growing even faster.

example, to take care of Medicare patients, so either people have to wait a lot longer or they never get to see the physician they'd like to."[20]

But if a political deal is not reached, the consequences could be dire, experts warn. The Congressional Budget Office (CBO) says health care costs, on their current course, could swallow all of GDP by 2082.[21]

The risk of bankruptcy from health costs in particular, says Hewitt, are exactly what bond rating agencies have warned about when they have threatened recently to downgrade U.S. debt — meaning the federal government may not be able to borrow money as cheaply because there's more risk that it won't be able to cover its interest payments.

"Three-quarters of the projected deficits over the next 10 years are new health care spending, according to CBO," Hewitt says. "If you could hold health costs at 2011 levels, you wouldn't have any deficit of note in 2021."

"There's no question that we're on course for health care costs to bankrupt the country," says the New America Foundation's MacGuineas. "You can't have anything growing faster than GDP forever, because it consumes more and more of the economy."

That may be the greatest danger. MacGuineas, like other budget experts, predicts that some sort of change will be made in health care spending, because present

trends are not sustainable. But the changes won't come without pain and political difficulty. In the meantime, rising health costs may continue to squeeze spending on other programs.

## Will the young and old fight over resources?

When he unveiled his budget in February, New York City Mayor Michael Bloomberg warned that the city faced tough choices because of a budget shortfall of nearly $5 billion. "Everybody expects you to do everything," the mayor said. "That's not the world we live in."[22]

Bloomberg felt he had no choice but to threaten layoffs of more than 4,000 school teachers. At the same time, however, his budget contained a new initiative: the construction of 10 "megacenters" for senior citizens.

Both ideas were ultimately rejected by the city council. Still, says the Urban Institute's Johnson, "That was striking. It seems to be the essence of the potential for intergenerational combat."

The idea that aging boomers will drain the nation's resources through entitlements such as Social Security and Medicare — and that younger generations are not just going to resent but protest it — has seeped into popular culture. It forms the premise, for example, of satirical novels such as Christopher Buckley's *Boomsday* and Albert Brooks' *2030*.

While older voters demand full funding for Social Security and Medicare, younger voters may worry that the growth of those expensive programs is crowding out spending on areas that benefit them more directly, such as education and transportation. Or the young might want to see entitlements cut in order to chop deficits that they'll eventually have to repay.

"I think it's amazing we've gotten this far without younger generations getting more agitated about constantly investing in seniors, with no similar promises made for productive investments for young people," says MacGuineas.

Voting schisms along generational lines have become apparent in some recent elections. "You had this overwhelming tilt of millennials to the Democrats and Obama in 2008," says Howe, co-author of *Millennials Rising*, about the generation born between 1982 and 2002. "Obama and McCain" — Sen. John McCain, Obama's GOP opponent —"were dead even among those 30 and over."

Older Americans voted disproportionately for GOP candidates in 2010. But Democrats won a special election in May in a traditionally Republican congressional district in upstate New York. The election was widely interpreted as a referendum on the House GOP's plan to turn Medicare into a form of voucher program, with seniors turning out in force to reject the idea and the Republican candidate.

"Over the years, until very recently, there's been very little evidence that older people vote on the basis of old-age benefits as a bloc," says Binstock at Case Western Reserve. "It's only in 2010 and the 26th District in New York that you begin to see some signs of this, particularly in relation to Medicare."

Howe and others say boomers, throughout their adult lives, have not voted as a predictable bloc. If they start to in old age, however, they would be formidable. As the population ages, the electorate — the group of people actually voting — is growing older at a disproportionate rate.

The percentage of the voting-age population that is over 65 is expected to climb by more than 10 percent over the next 25 years.[23] And, because older voters tend to go to the polls more regularly, their share of the electorate will climb even more, Binstock predicts.

Some political scientists are skeptical that there will be a young person's revolt, or even noticeable friction between the generations. "I don't buy the generational-conflict theory," says Alan Abramowitz, a political scientist at Emory University. "Programs that benefit the elderly, such as Social Security and Medicare, also benefit their children and grandchildren. If you cut benefits for the elderly, one consequence will be to shift costs onto their children and reduce income available to pay for, among other things, education for their children."

Others echo this point, noting that old-age entitlements keep seniors from being a financial burden on their children, while older voters will want to see young people succeed through education — in part, to help pay the taxes that fund their entitlements.

"Older people really do care about their grandchildren and obviously have a financial stake in having a productive workforce," says Rother, the AARP vice president. "Younger people need to look forward to a secure retirement, and they obviously can't vote to limit Medicare without having repercussions for them later."

Still, some observers say resentment among the young is only likely to grow as entitlements take up an increasingly large share of a strained federal budget. And some worry that the intergenerational compact may be frayed by the fact that the older Americans who receive entitlements are predominantly white, while the school and working-age populations will be increasingly made up of minorities, including Hispanics and Asians.

"Despite the rumblings, I think the population may come to appreciate that old-age benefits are actually things that benefit all generations," Binstock says. "However, I do think that the growing Latino population may very well come to resent paying taxes to support an older white generation."

# BACKGROUND

## Living Longer

For most of human history, journalist Ted C. Fishman points out in his book about global aging, *Shock of Gray*, people who lived past 45 had beaten the odds. Life expectancy barely budged from 25 years during the Roman Empire to 30 years at the dawn of the 20th century.[24]

Until the Industrial Revolution, people 65 or older never comprised more than 3 or 4 percent of the population. Today, they average 16 percent in the developed world — and their share is expected to rise to nearly 25 percent by 2030.[25] (The share of Americans over 65 will be nearly 20 percent by then.) Demographers call such shifts from historic norms the "demographic transition."

A confluence of factors has led to the current transition. Aging was once largely synonymous with death. Older people were both rarer and more vulnerable to sudden death due to such things as infectious diseases and poor sanitation. But even as modern medicine has conquered diseases that afflict the old, it has done even more to address infant mortality.

With fewer people dying young, life expectancy has increased. And healthier babies have coincided with other societal and economic factors to bring birthrates down. As prosperity grows, death rates fall. And the advent of pensions and other social-insurance programs has meant that parents no longer have as great a need for large families to support them as they age.

Meanwhile, women's roles have changed. Many now balance reproduction with concerns and responsibilities outside the home. Contraceptives are more widely available, while abortion has become legal and available.

Finally, as American society has urbanized, fewer families need to have multiple children to help work in the fields.

### "Fertility Splurge"

In the 1930s, demographers predicted that after a long period of decline in birthrates dating back to the Industrial Revolution, the U.S. population would stagnate and was unlikely to rise above 150 million by century's end. But birthrates shot up immediately after World War II, quickly rising to more than 4 million births per year.

All told, about 76 million children were born in the United States between 1946 and 1964, generally considered the period of the baby boom. (Several million have died, but immigrants have more than made up for those numbers, bringing the baby boom total to 78 million.) "Simply put, the baby boom was a 'disturbance' which emanated from a decade-and-a-half-long fertility splurge on the part of American couples," concluded the Population Reference Bureau in 1980.[26]

Childbearing long delayed — first by the Great Depression of the 1930s and then by war — was put off no longer. Women married younger and had their first babies at an earlier age than at any time in modern history.[27] The fertility rate, which refers to the average number of children born to women of child-bearing years, had averaged 2.1 children per woman during the 1930s but peaked at 3.7 in the late 1950s.[28]

The number of babies being born certainly surprised the General Electric Co. in January 1953. It promised five shares of stock to any employee who had a baby on Oct. 15, the company's 75th anniversary. GE expected maybe eight employees would qualify. Instead they had to hand over stock to 189 workers.[29]

The time was ripe, economically, for many more people to have children than had done so during the Depression. GDP expanded rapidly, from $227 billion in 1940 to $488 billion in 1960. Median family income and wages climbed steadily because of tight labor markets, while inflation remained low. The Servicemembers' Readjustment Act of 1944, commonly known as the GI Bill of Rights, helped more people in the middle class buy their first homes and get college educations,

significantly increasing their lifetime earnings. "Never had so many people, anywhere, been so well off," observed *U.S. News & World Report* in 1957.[30]

### The Baby Bust

Perhaps because of the advent of the birth control pill in 1960 and the fact that more women had careers, boomers were slower to become parents than their parents had been. Between 1965 and 1976 — the era of the so-called baby bust — fertility among whites dropped below replacement levels.[31]

After just two decades of a "fertility splurge," Americans went back to marrying later and producing fewer children. In 1990, only 32 percent of women 20-24 were married, compared to 70 percent in 1960. Social scientists began to posit that it was the baby boom that was exceptional in American history, not the subsequent bust.[32]

But the baby bust was followed by the uptick known as the "echo boom," when many boomers became parents, racking up 64 million live births between 1977 and 1993.[33]

Meanwhile, boomers continued to dominate many aspects of American life and culture. Some criticized them as frivolous, blaming their personal habits and quests for self-fulfillment for every social ill from divorce rates to teen drug use. Others defended them for fighting for greater rights for women and gays, among others. The debate about boomers' values became a recurring motif in politics — especially after Bill Clinton, who would become the first boomer president, emerged on the national stage in 1992. Political scientists have noted that boomers failed to coalesce behind a single political party, with many growing more fiscally conservative during the 1980s but remaining socially liberal, with views on race, AIDS, drugs and women's rights distinctly different from their parents' generation.

But the mere fact of their massive numbers made them hard to ignore — and created policy challenges as they aged. "This year, the first of about 78 million baby boomers turn 60, including two of my dad's favorite people, me and President Clinton," President George W. Bush said during his 2006 State of the Union address. "This milestone is more than a personal crisis. It is a national challenge. The retirement of the baby boom generation will put unprecedented strains on the federal government."[34]

# CHRONOLOGY

1940s-1960s *High postwar birth rates fuel suburban growth.*

**1946** First of the 78 million American baby boomers are born.

**1956** Women are allowed to collect early benefits under Social Security at age 62. The same deal is offered to men in 1962.

**1959** More than 50 million Americans are under age 14, representing 30 percent of the population.

**1960** Sun City opens in Arizona, pioneering the retirement community idea.

**1960** Seventy percent of women ages 20-24 are married.

**1965** Forty-one percent of Americans are under age 20. . . . Medicare and Medicaid, the main government health programs for the elderly, poor and disabled, are created.

1980s-1990s *Boomers set aside youthful rebellion to take a leading role in wealth creation and politics.*

**1983** Congress approves a gradual increase in the age at which Americans can collect full Social Security benefits, from 65 to 67.

**1986** The Age Discrimination Employment Act is amended to eliminate mandatory retirement ages.

**1990** Proportion of married women ages 20-24 drops to 32 percent.

**1992** Bill Clinton elected as the first boomer president.

2000s *Oldest boomers, enter their 60s, raising concerns about the cost of their retirements.*

**2000** For every American 65 or older, there are 3.4 workers contributing payroll taxes to Social Security — a ratio that will shrink to 2.0 by 2030.

**2003** Congress passes an expansion of Medicare that offers a prescription drug benefit to seniors. . . . Pima County, Ariz., becomes the first local government to require all new homes to be designed to accommodate seniors and the disabled.

**2005** The pregnancy rate of 103.2 per 1,000 women aged 15 to 44 years old is 11 percent below the 1990 peak of 115.8.

**2006** President George W. Bush, one of the oldest boomers, turns 60. . . . The Pension Protection Act allows workers to dip into their pensions while working past 62.

**2007** Federal Reserve Chairman Ben S. Bernanke predicts Social Security and Medicare will swallow 15 percent of annual economic output by 2030. . . . The Federal Aviation Administration proposes increasing the retirement age for pilots from 60 to 65. . . . The nation's earliest-born boomer, Kathleen Casey-Kirschling, applies for Social Security benefits.

2010s *The number of older Americans continues to rise, but the U.S. enjoys more growth among school and working-age populations than other rich nations.*

**2010** The number of workers 55 and over hits 26 million, which is a 46 percent increase since 2000. Congress enacts the Affordable Care Act, designed to expand health coverage, including a doubling of the eligible population under Medicaid.

**2011** March 16: The Centers for Disease Control and Prevention announces that life expectancy for Americans at birth increased in 2009 to 78.2 years. . . . April 15: The House passes a budget that would convert Medicare into a voucher program for those now under 55. . . . May 24: Democrats win a special election in a traditionally Republican district in upstate New York; the race is seen as a referendum on the House GOP Medicare proposal.

**2015** Working-age populations are projected to start declining in the developed world, with the United States as the major exception.

**2025** Population growth is expected to stall in every developed country except the United States, which is also expected to be the only developed nation with more children under age 20 than elderly over age 65.

# Minority Youths Are Rising Demographic Force

*Trend has major implications for aging whites.*

White America is aging, while its young people are increasingly dominated by members of ethnic and racial minorities. As a result, the days when the United States will no longer be a white-majority nation are coming sooner than demographers had long expected.

That could lead to a political struggle over resources, some social scientists contend. There could be a generational battle over governmental priorities — one with racial or ethnic overtones.

Younger members of minority groups may not want to fund entitlement programs that chiefly benefit a mostly white cohort of older Americans. Conversely, the elderly — who hold disproportionate political power thanks to higher rates of voter turnout — may seek to protect such programs at the expense of investments in government programs that chiefly benefit the young.

"Over time, the major focus in this struggle is likely to be between an aging white population that appears increasingly resistant to taxes and dubious of public spending, and a minority population that overwhelmingly views government education, health and social-welfare programs as the best ladder of opportunity for its children," political journalist Ronald Brownstein wrote in the *National Journal* last year.[1]

In a number of places, minorities already outnumber whites — at least among schoolchildren. The population of white children declined by 4.3 million from 2000 to 2010,

while that of Hispanic children rose by 5.5 million, according to the 2010 decennial census.

Indeed, the number of white children decreased in 46 states between 2000 and 2010. Whites now make up a minority among those younger than 18 in 10 states and 35 large metropolitan areas, including Atlanta, Dallas and Orlando. In Texas, 95 percent of the growth of the youth population occurred among Hispanics.

"What a lot of older people don't understand is that, to the extent we have a growing youth population, it's entirely due to minorities," says William Frey, a demographer at the Brookings Institution who has analyzed the 2010 census data on children. Twenty-three states have seen a decline in the total number of children. "In the baby boom generation, about 20 percent never had children, which is about double the rate of the previous generation of elders," says Phillip Longman, a policy researcher at the New America Foundation think tank in Washington.

"Now, you're talking about this aging population that doesn't have any family support and doesn't have any biological relations," he says. "It's not so much that they're white as they forgot to have children."

This opens one of the big questions regarding the differences between an older, white population and a younger population made up more from minorities. In his 2007 book *Immigrants and Boomers*, demographer Dowell Myers worried that there is little kinship — or sense of shared identification — between the groups.

Combined spending for Social Security, Medicare and Medicaid will consume 60 percent of the federal budget by 2030, Bush said, presenting future Congresses with "impossible choices — staggering tax increases, immense deficits or deep cuts in every category of spending."

Bush had spent a good chunk of 2005 touting a plan to revamp Social Security, meant to be the signature domestic achievement of his second term. But the

plan — which would have allowed workers born after 1950 to put part of their payroll taxes into private investment accounts in exchange for cuts in traditional benefits — went nowhere. A *Washington Post*/ABC News Poll found that 58 percent of those surveyed said the more they heard about Bush's plan, the less they liked it.[35]

More recent attempts to overhaul the major entitlement plans benefiting seniors have proved no more popular. A House Republican plan to convert Medicare from

But Longman says such concerns may be overstated. "Thirty years ago, I predicted that would be a big thing, the conflict between generations made even worse by the fact that it has an ethnic and racial component to it as well," he says.

Longman argues now, however, that racial lines are getting blurrier. Just as the definition of who was "white" expanded in the first half of the 20th century to include groups such as the Irish and Italians, Hispanics will increasingly be seen as "white," Longman says. "I just think the melting pot continues," he says.

Polls indicate that younger Americans are readier to embrace racial diversity than their elders, while more describe themselves as multiracial. Still, racial animosities and differences persist, and they may become exacerbated as the white population ages and the minority population grows larger.

The public-school system is one place where tensions could rise. Gaps on average reading and math test scores posted by Hispanics and non-Hispanic whites have been narrowing, but remain wide. "Despite the closing white-Hispanic gaps on civics performance, the fact is we're still seeing gaps in the double digits," said Leticia Van de Putte, a Texas state senator who sits on the board that oversees National Assessment of Educational Progress testing.[2]

Because school funding relies partly on property tax assessments in most places, such disparities may be perpetuated by racial segregation. Although the 2010 census showed a decline in residential segregation, black and Hispanic children are more likely to live in a segregated neighborhood than black and Hispanic adults, according to Frey.

"White parents with children may be more likely to locate in select neighborhoods and communities, perhaps those with better schools, or superior public amenities related to childrearing," he writes.[3]

It will be in the interest of the aging white population to see that young people, including Hispanics and other minorities, fulfill their educational potential, says Myers.

Minorities are fueling the nation's growing youth population. Above, black and Hispanic students at the Harlem Success Academy, a New York charter school.

Otherwise, they will be caught short as the working-age population, which pays the bulk of the taxes that support programs that benefit seniors, is made up largely of minorities. "The person you educated 20 years ago, that's who is going to buy your house," he says.

*— Alan Greenblatt*

[1] Ronald Brownstein, "The Gray and The Brown: The Generational Mismatch," *National Journal*, July 24, 2010, www.nationaljournal.com/magazine/the-gray-and-the-brown-the-generational-mismatch-20100724.

[2] "State Senators React to Hispanic Achievement Gains," *Hispanic Tips*, May 5, 2011, www.hispanictips.com/2011/05/05/state-senators-react-to-hispanic-achievement-gains-on-latest-naep-civics-report-card-that-showed-substantial-gains-in-the-performance-of-hispanic-students-at-grades-four-eight-and-12/

[3] William Frey, "America's Diverse Future," The Brookings Institution, April 2011, p. 10, www.brookings.edu/~/media/Files/rc/papers/2011/0406_census_diversity_frey/0406_census_diversity_frey.pdf.

an insurance program into a credit that would help seniors buy private insurance is an example. A survey conducted in May by the Pew Research Center for the People & the Press found opposition to the plan was especially high among "people who say they have heard a lot about this proposal — fully 56 percent are opposed, while 33 percent are in favor."[36]

"The politics of this is, the baby boom is a generation that's always been pretty willing to vote themselves good

fiscal deals," says MacGuineas of the New America Foundation.

## "Sandwich" Generation

Boomers will add to the rising number of seniors — but their parents, in many cases, will still be around. Those 85 and over now make up the fastest-growing segment of the U.S. population, according to the National Institute on Aging. That means that even as boomers enter what

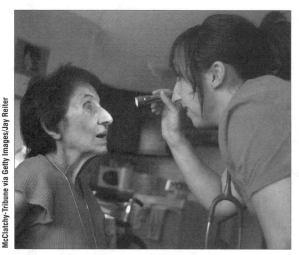

A nurse examines stroke victim Elvira Tesarek at her home in Warren, R.I., in May 2011. Nearly 1,300 elderly and disabled adults in the state have been able to return home under a pilot program designed to cut spending on Medicare.

has traditionally been considered old age, they are "sandwiched" between still-living parents and their own children and grandchildren.

The percentage of adults who are providing personal or financial care to a parent has tripled since 1994, according to the MetLife Mature Market Institute. "Nearly 10 million adult children over the age of 50 care for their aging parents," said Sandra Timmermann, the institute's director. "Assessing the long-term financial impact of caregiving for aging parents on caregivers themselves, especially those who must curtail their working careers to do so, is especially important, since it can jeopardize their future financial security."[37]

"Boomers are quite different from earlier generations as they're approaching this age," says William H. Frey, a demographer at the Brookings Institution, a centrist think tank in Washington. For example, boomer women "are much more likely to have lived independent lives, been head of households and worked."

But there's a great deal of economic inequality within the baby boom generation, he notes, which means many retirees will have a hard time making ends meet.[38] In addition, Frey says, boomers didn't have as many children as their parents' generation, so they "can't rely on them for support."

Not everyone views the aging of America as bad news. An aging population, says Eric Kingson, a professor of social work at Syracuse University, is a sign that society has successfully fostered an economy that helps people lead long, prosperous lives. "Population aging is not just about the old," he says. "It's about how all of our institutions are going to change."

## CURRENT SITUATION

### Financial Insecurity

Even as federal officials debate the affordability of Social Security and Medicare as the population ages, individual Americans are increasingly concerned about their own ability to support themselves during retirement.

Even before the financial crisis of 2008, income and wealth inequality was growing among seniors. "Back in 2004, the top 5 percent of the baby boomers controlled more than half of the assets," says Diane Oakley, executive director of the National Institute on Retirement Security in Washington. "The bottom half had less than 3 percent of the assets."

She hopes lower-income Americans have been able to save more for retirement since then, but stock market losses and the collapse of the housing bubble make that unlikely.

In a recent poll, "78 percent say they can't save enough on their own to be secure in retirement," says Brian Perlman, president and CEO of Mathew Greenwald & Associates, a market research firm in Washington. "People's beliefs are that it's harder and harder to do that."

The risk for retirement has shifted more onto individuals, Oakley says. From 1980 to 2008, she says, the percentage of private-sector workers covered by defined-benefit pension plans — which offer a guaranteed income throughout retirement — dropped from 38 percent to 20 percent.

Meanwhile, defined-contribution plans, such as 401(k) plans, have grown. These plans, which shift the burden for retirement savings onto individuals, have certain tax advantages, but like any personal savings account, they can be drained dry. Unlike defined-benefit plans, the money is gone once 401(k) assets are depleted.

Americans are not contributing enough to 401(k)s to build up sufficient retirement nest eggs. According to Towers Watson, a human-resources consulting firm, only 57.3 percent of Americans have enough in their retirement accounts to replace one year's worth of working salary. Only 10.9 percent had more than four times their current salary saved up.[39]

Because most people are going to be retired more than a few years, that presents a problem. For most, Social Security will represent the bulk of their retirement income, but benefits average only about $14,000 per year.

"Only about half of workers are in any kind of retirement plan through their employers," says the Urban Institute's Johnson. "People don't make the most of their 401(k) plans — they don't contribute the maximum, or at all."

## Automatic Enrollment

Most workers have to sign up for 401(k) plans, but Johnson favors automatic enrollment. Automatic enrollment plans would allow employers to deduct part of each paycheck and put the money toward employees' retirement, unless a worker made the express decision to opt out.

"We've run some simulations," Johnson says. "If most people behave as we expect they would, based on past experience, automatic enrollment would increase retirement incomes for low- and moderate-income people by about 20 percent."

The Obama administration supports the idea of automatic enrollment. The administration would like employers, even if they don't offer 401(k) accounts of their own, to enroll their workers in some kind of retirement account.

"The basic idea is that an employer would simply do payroll deduction," says J. Mark Iwry, senior adviser to Treasury Secretary Timothy Geithner. "When we do automatic enrollment in 401(k)s, the [participation] rate goes up from two-thirds or three-quarters to more than 90 percent."

But the idea of enrolling workers automatically into retirement savings accounts may run into opposition in Congress because of budget concerns. Obama's deficit commission last year recommended lowering the cap on annual contributions allowed to such retirement savings accounts.[40]

Aside from putting more money aside for retirement, individuals will also come to rely more on income earned later in life — whether by staying in their old job longer or finding a new one after "retiring," many economists believe.

"If people want to have a secure retirement, they really should work longer," says Alicia Munnell, director of the Center for Retirement Research at Boston College. "There's an enormous benefit in terms of what your Social Security benefits and 401(k) accounts will be. And then, you have [fewer] years over which to spread your savings. All we're talking about, basically, is three to four more years. We're not talking about into your 90s."

## Government Cutbacks

Most government workers can count on a relatively comfortable retirement. In contrast to private-sector employees, about 90 percent of state and local government workers are enrolled in defined-benefit programs.

But the disparity between the plans offered to government workers and those at private companies, along with severe budget problems confronting state and local government workers, is increasing pressure on retirement benefits in the public sector, too.

The gap between what states had promised to pay out in pensions and retirement health benefits and the assets they have to pay them had grown to more than $1.26 trillion by the end of the 2009 budget year, according to the Pew Center on the States.[41] Some economists say the gap is even larger.

About a dozen states have altered their pension systems over the past couple of years, according to the National Conference of State Legislatures. Most have made moves such as putting new employees into 401(k)-style accounts, rather than enrolling them in defined-benefit plans.

## Math and Politics

But some governors and lawmakers have sought changes in retirement coverage for current workers as well. The battle over retirement benefits has turned political, most notably in Wisconsin, where legislation to strip most public employees of collective bargaining rights led to weeks of large-scale protests at the capital.

State and local retirement accounts might be more than $1 trillion in the red, but union leaders say it's unfair to blame government workers because legislatures

> **"We are draining money out of services and pouring them into retirement benefits. However you define unsustainable, it's unsustainable."**
>
> — *Mayor Chuck Reed*
> *San Jose, Calif.*

failed to make scheduled payments to pension funds over the years.

Better to blame Wall Street, they say, for racking up record profits even as large-scale investment losses have blown a hole through pension accounts. "They've blamed public employees for problems they've never caused in the first place," says Randi Weingarten, president of the American Federation of Teachers.

Patrick O'Connor, an alderman in Chicago, agrees that unions have a point when they accuse government officials of not properly funding promised benefits. Still, he argues, cities and states have no choice but to cut back on benefits that are no longer affordable.

"Government can't blame the unions in total," O'Connor says. "Government is what put the benefits in place. But I don't think anybody who looks at pension plans thinks they can be funded at the levels they're at."

In San Jose, Calif., Mayor Chuck Reed declared a state of "fiscal emergency" in May, hoping he can persuade voters to give him additional powers that would allow him to change retirement-benefit formulas.[42]

Reed warns that he will have to lay off two-thirds of the city's work force if he can't achieve significant savings in retirement-benefit costs. What consumed $65 million of the city's budget a decade ago already accounts for $250 million and half the city's current budget shortfall. Retirement costs could rise to as much as $650 million annually over the next few years, Reed says.

In Reed's mind, it's simply a math problem. "We are draining money out of services and pouring them into retirement benefits," Reed says. "However you define unsustainable, it's unsustainable."

Public-employee unions concede that Reed's complaints are borne out of real problems with San Jose's finances. They don't agree that his approach is the best way to address those problems, however. And union leaders in San Jose, like their colleagues elsewhere, think stripping public employees of promised benefits will undermine one of the few pockets of retirement security.

"It's perfectly understandable that workers in the private sector are worried about their retirement security," says John Liu, New York City's comptroller. "But to scapegoat public employees will fuel a race to the bottom in our country."

Yet, further cutbacks appear inevitable, even for government workers who have long counted on benefits that would allow them to retire free of financial anxiety. State officials appear to have lost some of their initial enthusiasm for moving to 401(k)-style plans, however, because of the enormous upfront costs in switching from traditional pensions. In Kentucky, increased costs are estimated at $8 billion over 15 years. Nevada would run through $1.2 billion in just two years.[43]

Even the well-funded Pentagon is worried about whether it can afford to fund retirement benefits, including health care, at the levels soldiers and sailors have come to expect.

Retiree pay will cost the Department of Defense about $50 billion next year, according to the Obama administration's proposed fiscal 2012 budget. Military health costs, which have doubled over the past decade, will run even more, with a fair share going to coverage of military retirees.

"We in the Department of Defense are on the same path that General Motors found itself on," retired Marine Maj. Gen. Arnold Punaro, who advises the Pentagon on financial operations, told NPR. "General Motors did not start out to be a health care company that occasionally built an automobile. Today, we're on the path in the Department of Defense to turn it into a benefits company that may occasionally kill a terrorist."[44]

Robert Gates, who stepped down as Defense Secretary June 30, said the military may have to consider moving to a 401(k)-style plan. Financial problems make some sort of change to the Pentagon's pension and retirement health formulas inevitable, he told *Defense News*. "We are way behind the private sector in this."[45]

# Should the retirement age be raised?

## YES    Andrew G. Biggs
*Resident Scholar, American
Enterprise Institute*

Written for *CQ Researcher*, July 2011

## NO    Nancy Altman and Eric Kingson
*Co-chairs, Strengthen Social
Security Campaign*

Written for *CQ Researcher*, July 2011

Social Security's retirement age should not be increased for anyone on the verge of retirement, but there's a good case for doing so over coming decades, as the Baby Boomers retire and the population ages.

In 1950, the average retiree claimed Social Security benefits at age 68.5 and lived to around 76. Today, a typical retiree claims benefits at 63 and will live an additional two decades. Americans today live almost one-third of their adult lives in retirement, supported by an increasing tax burden on their kids and grandkids. This isn't simply unfair to future generations. It is also a waste of human talent.

Are there some people who can't work longer? Of course. And for them, early retirement or disability benefits remain an option. But it would be strange in today's service economy if Americans, who work mostly in offices, could not work as long as prior generations who toiled in mines, mills and farms.

Indeed, our longer lives are also healthier lives. According to the National Center for Health Statistics, among individuals ages 65-74 the share describing themselves as in fair or poor health dropped from 25.1 percent in 1983 to 18.5 percent in 2007. Overall, 75 percent of individuals over 65 report being in good, very good or excellent health.

It's easy to scare people — for instance, President Obama's Commission on Fiscal Responsibility and Reform would increase the retirement age to 69. But this would apply only to people who haven't even been born yet and at retirement would live on average to age 88 — almost 10 years longer than they did when Social Security started in the 1930s.

It is true that life expectancies have risen faster for high-earners than for low-income Americans. This is why almost every reform plan that raises the retirement age also makes Social Security more progressive, by boosting benefits for low-earners while trimming them for the rich.

One option is to let the retirement age rise to 67 as scheduled, then increase it in future years as life spans rise. If life expectancies increase quickly, then the retirement age will follow; if life spans stay constant, the retirement age won't need to increase further. By itself, this would fix nearly one-quarter of Social Security's deficit.

Mathematically, we can't fix the entire entitlement deficit by raising taxes. And Medicare is far more likely to require tax increases than Social Security. So it only makes sense to reduce costs where we can. Increasing the retirement age is a reasonable response to longer lives.

To reduce unemployment during the 1961 recession, and in recognition that many Americans were unable to work until age 65, Congress allowed men to claim reduced Social Security benefits at age 62, just as it had for women in 1956. Speaking in support, Democratic Ohio Rep. Charles Vanik said that "if 2 million male workers eventually retire under this program, 2 million job opportunities will be created."

Ironically, with unemployment topping 9 percent, many in Congress today favor increasing Social Security's full retirement age. This is the wrong policy today, would have been wrong in 1961 and will be wrong in the future.

A retirement age increase is mathematically indistinguishable from a benefit cut, and ill-advised because benefits are too low. Congress has already increased the retirement age from 65 to 67, a 13 percent cut for people born after 1960. A further increase, from 67 to 69, would be another 13 percent cut for retired workers, no matter whether they claim benefits at age 62, age 70, or any age in between, and translates into lower benefits for many spouses and widow(er)s. Benefits are modest, averaging about $14,000, and the retirement prospects for persons in their 40s and early 50s are already dimmed by diminishing pension protections, shrinking 401(k) and IRA retirement savings, unemployment and declining home values.

Retirement-age increases especially burden lower-wage and minority workers, who often have no choice but to retire early. It is well-known that many workers must stop work because of serious health and physical challenges; still others face age discrimination and job loss. Sixty-two percent of Latino males and 53 percent of older black male workers are in physically demanding or difficult jobs, compared with 42 percent of their white male counterparts. By retiring early, they claim permanently reduced benefits. A hardship exemption for these categories of workers has never been found to be politically feasible or workable.

Lower-wage workers, on average, have seen little or no increase in life expectancy. Over the past quarter-century, the life expectancy of upper-income men increased by five years while life expectancy among lower-income men increased by only one year and that of lower-income women actually declined.

For all these reasons, Congress should follow the will of the American people, who reject increasing the retirement age. Congress should consider eliminating Social Security's projected shortfall by scrapping the cap on earnings subject to Social Security's FICA contributions, as the American people strongly favor.

# OUTLOOK

## Political Prospects

Given the costs associated with aging — particularly those involving medical care — some economists are growing pessimistic about the country's long-term budget health. By the time the last of the boomers have turned 65, in 2029, there will be nearly twice as many people enrolled in Medicare as there are today, according to AARP.

"Social Security has pretty much anticipated the aging population and built up a very large trust fund," says Rother, AARP's policy director. "Medicare is the place where the stress shows."

Health care costs are bound to be driven higher by an older population. Some worry Congress won't be able to agree on ways to significantly reduce growth in entitlement programs and thereby reduce the federal deficit.

"I just think the two parties are kind of locked in cement on this stuff," says Hewitt of the Coalition for Affordable Health Care.

The question of whether Congress will change entitlements really depends on the attitudes of the voting public, he says. "I frankly don't think that fiscal conservatives are going to be able to hold the line, because baby boomers in the end are going to decide they don't want to defund their retirement," Hewitt says.

Myers, the USC demographer, says politicians will need to appeal to older voters to make big policy changes. Older Americans may love their entitlements, but they'll have to be convinced that younger, working-age people need money left over for productive investments in areas such as education and infrastructure — and shouldn't be saddled with crippling debt, Myers says.

"The only winning political strategy is not to fight [older voters] but persuade them it's in their interest," Myers says. "I believe they control the electorate for the next 20 years, and we don't have 20 years to wait."

Budget realities will force changes to entitlement programs in the next decade, says MacGuineas of the New American Foundation. And, she says, waiting until financial markets force fiscal changes, as has been happening in European countries such as Greece, won't be pleasant.

"There's no question that by 2020, changes will have been made," she says. "What I'm worried about is that changes may have been forced upon us — changes made because of markets will be much more painful."

Not everyone thinks some kind of fiscal crisis is inevitable. Blahous, the Hoover Institution fellow and Social Security trustee, says he's pessimistic, but not because he worries the country will face "economic Armageddon."

Instead, Blahous worries that continuing unbridled growth in major entitlement programs will mean "we'll have more expensive government than we've ever had before," he says. "People's after-tax income will not have the growth we've seen in the past."

There are some positive predictions. The Urban Institute's Johnson says widowhood is becoming less common. "Men are living longer, and the differences between men and women's mortality is lessening. Widowhood is still associated with poverty."

Still, Johnson expects income inequality among the aged to continue to grow and more older Americans will need to work longer. Others say policy changes to health coverage are inevitable, despite the political opposition engendered both by President Obama's 2010 health care-expansion law and the House GOP's current effort to limit Medicare growth.

"We're going to be moving more and more toward managed care," says Binstock, the Case Western Reserve health policy professor, "in the sense that there'll be a fixed budget in terms of care for older people." Older people will be hurt as a result, Binstock contends.

But the New America Foundation's Longman isn't convinced. A move toward some form of managed care will lead to better health outcomes than the current U.S. health system, which is prone to ill-informed treatment and mistakes, he says.

"I would hope in 10 years, we have turned the corner on the health care thing," Longman says. "The idea that we're going to let people go get any care they want from anybody they want, that's not going to work."

Longman says the outlook is "gloomy" but that it won't be impossible to turn things around. As long as health care is restructured and "as long as today's young people don't forget to have children," the U.S. should be able to care for its growing senior population, he says.

But fewer people are having children — and certainly fewer are having multiple children, notes Fishman, the author of *Shock of Gray*. "We're about a generation away from children having no brothers and sisters, no aunts and uncles, no cousins," he says. "People may be looking continuously for more family supports, but the family just won't be there."

The prospect of fewer children and longer life expectancy means the median age will continue to rise. No matter the difficulties posed by the aging of the baby boom generation, they won't be solved by that generation's passing.

"The boomers may seem like a large cohort of older people," Fishman says, "but the median age is increasing and that won't turn around."

## NOTES

1. "Double Jeopardy For Baby Boomers Proving Care For Their Parents," MetLife Mature Market Institute, June 2001, p. 2, www.metlife.com/assets/cao/mmi/publications/studies/2011/mmi-caregiving-costs-working-caregivers.pdf.

2. For background, see Thomas J. Billitteri, "Rethinking Retirement," *CQ Researcher*, June 19, 2009, pp. 549-572.

3. Matt Sedensky, "Number of 100-Year-Olds is Booming in U.S.," The Associated Press, April 26, 2011, http://news.yahoo.com/s/ap/20110426/ap_on_re_us/us_centenarian_boom.

4. For background, see Marcia Clemmitt, "National Debt," *CQ Researcher*, March 18, 2011, pp. 241-264.

5. For background, see the following *CQ Researcher* reports: Marcia Clemmitt, "Health-Care Reform," June 11, 2010, pp. 505-528, updated May 24, 2011; Beth Baker, "Treating Alzheimer's," March 4, 2011, pp. 193-216; Alan Greenblatt, "Aging Baby Boomers," Oct. 19, 2007, pp. 865-888; and Marcia Clemmitt, "Caring for the Elderly," Oct. 13, 2006, pp. 841-864.

6. Richard Wolf, "Medicare to Swell With Boomer Onslaught," *USA Today*, Jan 1. 2011, http://abcnews.go.com/Politics/medicare-swell-baby-boomer-onslaught/story?id=12504388.

7. From remarks at "The 2011 Medicare Trustees Report: The Baby Boomer Tsunami," American Enterprise Institute, May 16, 2011.

8. See, for instance, "CNN Poll: Majority Gives Thumbs Down to Ryan Medicare Plan," CNN.org, June 1, 2011, http://politicalticker.blogs.cnn.com/2011/06/01/cnn-poll-majority-gives-thumbs-down-to-ryan-plan/.

9. Laura Meckler, "Key Seniors Association Pivots on Benefit Cut," *The Wall Street Journal*, June 17, 2011, http://online.wsj.com/article/SB10001424052702304186404576389760955403414.html.

10. For background, see Thomas J. Billitteri, "Middle-Class Squeeze," *CQ Researcher*, March 6, 2009, pp. 201-224.

11. Employee Benefit Research Institute, "The 2011 Retirement Confidence Survey: Confidence Drops to Record Lows, Reflecting 'the New Normal,' " March 2011, www.ebri.org/pdf/surveys/rcs/2011/EBRI_03-2011_No355_RCS-11.pdf.

12. "U.S. Death Rate Falls for 10th Straight Year," Centers for Disease Control, March 16, 2011, www.cdc.gov/media/releases/2011/p0316_deathrate.html.

13. "Life Expectancy for Social Security," Social Security Administration, www.ssa.gov/history/lifeexpect.html.

14. For background, see Kenneth Jost, "Public-Employee Unions," *CQ Researcher*, April 8, 2011, pp. 313-336; and Alan Greenblatt, "Pension Crisis," *CQ Researcher*, Feb. 17, 2006, pp. 145-168.

15. For background, see the center's Web page on its "National Retirement Risk Index" publications at http://crr.bc.edu/special_projects/national_retirement_risk_index.html.

16. See Annual Report of the Medicare Trustees, Center for Medicare and Medicaid Services, May 13, 2011, www.cms.gov/ReportsTrustFunds/downloads/tr2011.pdf.

17. "Choosing The Nation's Fiscal Future," National Academies Press (2010), p. 79, available at www.ourfiscalfuture.org/wp-content/uploads/fiscalfuture_full_report.pdf.

18. "Strengthening Medicare: Better Health, Better Care, Lower Costs," Centers for Medicare and Medicaid Services, www.cms.gov/apps/files/medicare-savings-report.pdf.

19. Matthew DoBias, "Medicare's Actuary Paints a Darker Picture Than Trustees," *NationalJournal.com*, May 23, 2011, www.nationaljournal.com/health care/medicare-s-actuary-paints-a-darker-picture-than-trustees-20110523.

20. Emily Ethridge, "Republicans Decry Medicare Cost-Control Panel While Seeking Broad Cuts," *CQ HealthBeat*, June 8, 2011.

21. "CBO'S 2011 Long-Term Budget Outlook," Congressional Budget Office, www.cbo.gov/doc.cfm?index=12212.

22. Jonathan Lemire and Erin Einhorn, "Mayor Bloomberg Unveils $65.6 Billion Budget," *New York Daily News*, Feb. 17, 2011, http://articles.nydailynews.com/2011-02-17/local/28628742_1_president-michael-mulgrew-mayor-bloomberg-teacher-layoffs.

23. "As Boomers Wrinkle," *The Economist*, Dec. 29, 2010, www.economist.com/node/17800237?story_id=17800237.

24. Ted C. Fishman, *Shock of Gray* (2011), p. 13.

25. Richard Jackson and Neil Howe, *The Graying of the Great Powers* (2008), p. 7.

26. Paul C. Light, *Baby Boomers* (1988), p. 10.

27. Herbert S. Klein, "The U.S. Baby Bust in Historical Perspective," in Fred R. Harris., ed., *The Baby Bust: Who Will Do the Work? Who Will Pay the Taxes?* (2006), p. 115.

28. Light, *op. cit.*, p. 23.

29. Steve Gillon, *Boomer Nation: The Largest and Richest Generation Ever and How It Changed America* (2004), p. 1.

30. *Ibid.*, p. 6.

31. Klein., *op. cit.*, p. 173.

32. Jeremy Greenwood, Ananth Seshadri and Guillaume Vandenbroucke, "The Baby Boom and Baby Bust." *American Economic Review*, 2005, p. 183.

33. William Sterling and Stephen Waite, *Boomernomics: The Future of Money in the Upcoming Generational Warfare* (1998), p. 3.

34. President George W. Bush, State of the Union address, Jan. 31, 2006, www.washingtonpost.com/wp-dyn/content/article/2006/01/31/AR2006013101468.html.

35. Jonathan Weisman, "Skepticism of Bush's Social Security Plan Is Growing," *The Washington Post*, March 15, 2005, p. A1, www.washingtonpost.com/wp-dyn/articles/A35231-2005Mar14.html.

36. "Opposition to Ryan Plan Among Older, Attentive Americans," Pew Research Center, June 6, 2011, http://people-press.org/2011/06/06/opposition-to-ryan-medicare-plan-from-older-attentive-americans/.

37. Sheryl Nance-Nash, "Caring for Aging Parents Will Cost Boomers $3 Trillion," *AOL DailyFinance*, June 15, 2011, www.dailyfinance.com/2011/06/15/caring-for-aging-parents-will-cost-boomers-3-trillion/.

38. For background, see Marcia Clemmitt, "Income Inequality," *CQ Researcher*, Dec. 3, 2010, pp. 989-1012.

39. See, "Retirement Attitudes," Towers Watson, September 2010, www.towerswatson.com/assets/pdf/2717/TowersWatson-Retirement-Attitudes_NA-2010-17683.pdf.

40. "Will Congress Slash Your 401(k) Tax Break," Reuters Wealth, June 16, 2011, http://blogs.reuters.com/reuters-wealth/2011/06/16/will-congress-slash-your-401k-tax-break/.

41. William Selway, "U.S. States Pension Fund Deficits Widen by 26%, Pew Center Study Says," Bloomberg, April 25, 2011, www.bloomberg.com/news/2011-04-26/u-s-states-pension-fund-deficits-widen-by-26-pew-center-study-says.html.

42. Elizabeth Lesly Stevens, "San Jose Mayor Declares State of 'Fiscal Emergency,' " *The Bay Citizen*, May 21, 2011, www.nytimes.com/2011/05/22/us/22bcstevens.html.

43. Stephen C. Fehn, "States Overhaul Pensions But Pass On 401(k)-Style Plans," *Stateline*, June 21, 2011, www.stateline.org/live/details/story?contentId=582585.

44. Tamara Keith, "Health Care Costs New Threat to U.S. Military," NPR, June 7, 2011, www.npr.org/2011/06/07/137009416/u-s-military-has-new-threat-health-care-costs.

45. Vago Muradian, "Q&A: Robert Gates, U.S. Defense Secretary," *Defense News*, June 13, 2011, p. 32, www.defensenews.com/story.php?i=6792060&c=FEA&s=INT.

# BIBLIOGRAPHY

## Selected Sources

### Books

**Fishman, Ted C., *Shock of Gray*, Scribner, 2010.**
The author, a former financial trader, uses statistics and sketches of representative individuals to portray how aging is presenting fiscal, health and economic challenges to countries including Japan, China and the United States.

Gillon, Steve, *Boomer Nation: The Largest and Richest Generation Ever and How It Changed America*, Free Press, 2004.
The History Channel's Gillon writes a sympathetic history of the boomers, whose birth, he says, is the "single greatest demographic event in American history."

Pearce, Fred, *The Coming Population Crash and Our Planet's Surprising Future*, Beacon Press, 2010.
A former New Scientist news editor traces the history of population changes, looking at past state-sponsored efforts at population control and the implications for possible population decline in decades to come.

## Articles

"As Boomers Wrinkle," *The Economist*, Dec. 29, 2010, www.economist.com/node/17800237?story_id=17800237.
Aging baby boomers will resist any cuts to their entitlements.

Brownstein, Ronald, "The Gray and the Brown: The Generational Mismatch," *National Journal*, July 24, 2010; www.nationaljournal.com/magazine/the-gray-and-the-brown-the-generational-mismatch-20100724.
The United States is seeing a divergence in attitudes and priorities between a heavily nonwhite population of younger people and an overwhelmingly white cohort of older people.

Fehr, Stephen C., "States Overhaul Pensions But Pass on 401(k)-Style Plans," *Stateline*, June 21, 2011, www.stateline.org/live/details/story?contentId=582585.
Pensions for state government workers are badly underfunded, but officials are still wary of switching employees to retirement savings accounts.

Hare, Kristin, "Older Americans Are Working Longer," *St. Louis Beacon*, April 24, 2011, www.stlbeacon.org/issues-politics/172-Economy/109733-retiring-retirement-americans-are-working-longer-.
Ten years ago, 4 million people age 65 and older were working or looking for jobs. By March, that number had increased to 7 million.

Johnson, Kirk, "Between Young and Old, A Political Collision," *The New York Times*, June 3, 2011, www.nytimes.com/2011/06/04/us/politics/04elders.html.
Is there such a thing as a Medicare voting bloc? Some political scientists suggest there increasingly could be pitched political battles between generations over government resources.

Ludden, Jennifer, "Boomers Take the 'Retire' Out of Retirement," NPR.org, Jan. 1, 2011, www.npr.org/2011/01/01/132490242/boomers-take-the-retire-out-of-retirement.
As baby boomers reach age 65, many are optimistic, but a bit more than half may not be able to maintain current living standards in retirement.

Rucker, Philip, "NY Race Is Referendum on GOP Medicare Plan," *The Washington Post*, May 15, 2011, www.washingtonpost.com/politics/ny-special-election-becomes-referendum-on-gop-medicare-plan/2011/05/15/AFnoVR4G_story.html?hpid=z3.
Democrats successfully test a strategy they intend to use in 2012, castigating Republicans for looking to overhaul Medicare.

## Studies and Reports

Arno, Peter S., and Deborah Viola, "Double Jeopardy for Baby Boomers Caring for Their Parents," MetLife Mature Market Institute, June 2011, www.metlife.com/assets/cao/mmi/publications/studies/2011/mmi-caregiving-costs-working-caregivers.pdf.
Nearly 10 million adult children over age 50 care for their aging parents.

Cohn, D'Vera, and Paul Taylor, "Baby Boomers Approach 65 — Glumly," Pew Research Center, December 2010, http://pewsocialtrends.org/files/2010/12/Boomer-Summary-Report-FINAL.pdf.
As they approach 65, boomers continue to be accepting of changes in social trends and aren't ready to concede they have reached old age.

Frey, William, "America's Diverse Future," Brookings Institution, April 2011, p. 10, www.brookings.edu/~/media/Files/rc/papers/2011/0406_census_diversity_frey/0406_census_diversity_frey.pdf.
The 2010 census showed that the number of white and black children shrank, while there was significant growth among Hispanics and Asians younger than 18.

Jackson, Richard, and Neil Howe with Rebecca Strauss and Keisuke Nakashima, "The Graying of the Great Powers: Demography and Geopolitics in the 21st Century," Center for Strategic and International Studies, 2008, www.agingsociety.org/agingsociety/publications/public_policy/CSISmajor_findings.pdf.
The report offers a comprehensive survey of aging trends in the developed and developing world.

# For More Information

**AARP**, 601 E St., N.W., Washington, DC 20049; (888) 687-2277; www.aarp.org. The largest advocacy organization for older Americans.

**American Society on Aging**, 71 Stevenson St., Suite 1450, San Francisco, CA 94105; (415) 974-9600; www.asaging .org. Founded as the Western Gerontological Society; offers programs and online learning for professionals in health care, social services, government and other fields who seek to improve the quality of life for older adults.

**Boston College**, Center for Retirement Research, Hovey House, 140 Commonwealth Ave., Chestnut Hill, MA 02467; (617) 552-1762; crr.bc.edu. Conducts research on issues related to retirement, particularly finance and health.

**Center for Strategic and International Studies**, Global Aging Initiative, 1800 K St., N.W., Washington, DC 20006; (202) 887-0200; csis.org/program/global-aging-initiative. Conducts research and education programs on long-term economic, social and geopolitical implications of demographic change in the United States and abroad.

**Employee Benefit Research Institute**, 1100 13th St., N.W., Suite 878, Washington, DC 20005; (202) 659-0670; www .ebri.org. Conducts research on employee benefits, including pensions and defined-contribution plans such as 401(k)s.

**National Association of Area Agencies on Aging**, 1730 Rhode Island Ave., N.W., 4th Floor, Washington, DC 20036; (202) 872-0888; www.n4a.org. Umbrella organization for local area aging agencies.

**National Institute on Aging**, Building 31, Room 5C27, 31 Center Dr., MSC 2292, Bethesda, MD 20892; (301) 496-1752; www.nia.nih.gov. Leads the federal government's scientific effort to study the nature of aging.

**National Institute on Retirement Security**, 1730 Rhode Island Ave., N.W., Suite 207, Washington, DC 20036; (202) 457-8190; www.nirsonline.org. Studies retirement-income issues such as pensions.

**Urban Institute**, Program on Retirement Policy, 2100 M St., N.W., Washington, DC 20037; (202) 833-7200; www .retirementpolicy.org. Conducts research on issues relevant to retirement, such as Social Security, long-term care and unemployment rates among older Americans.

**UCLA**, Center for Policy Research on Aging, 3250 Public Policy Building, Box 951656, Los Angeles, CA 90095; (310) 794-5908; www.spa.ucla.edu. Studies major policy and political issues surrounding aging; devotes particular attention to issues relating to ethnic populations.

# 14

# Gun Control

Barbara Mantel

Colorado supporters of gun ownership, including Theresa White of Estes Park, demonstrate at the state Capitol in Denver on Jan. 9, 2013. The nation's state lawmakers are divided on new gun legislation. Many favor tougher background checks, but others oppose limits on assault weapons and high-capacity magazines. The public strongly favors expanding background checks to private gun sales, but reinstating a federal ban on assault weapons seems unlikely.

From *CQ Researcher*,
March 8, 2013.

T he debate over gun control has been inescapable since last December, when Adam Lanza used a so-called assault rifle* to kill 20 first-graders and six adults at Sandy Hook Elementary School in Newtown, Conn., before taking his own life in one of the most horrific mass shootings in the nation's history.

The fallout from the massacre has been widespread and relentless: marches and protests, fiery advertisements, celebrity endorsements, contentious congressional and state hearings, proposed federal and state legislation and a tough, new gun-control law in New York state.

But whether the shooting will spur Congress to pass stricter nationwide controls remains a toss-up — some support exists, even among conservatives, for expanding background checks to include private firearm sales, but a federal ban on assault weapons seems to be a nonstarter. Meanwhile, more than 1,000 firearm-related bills have been introduced in state legislatures, but only New York has passed one to date.

In late January, more than 2,000 people descended on Connecticut's statehouse in Hartford for a packed public hearing that ran more than 17 hours. In a visual symbol of the revived and often rancorous discussion of gun violence, gun-rights advocates sported round yellow stickers reading "Another Responsible Gun

---

*Federal and state laws banning semiautomatic weapons with detachable magazines and military-style features use the term "assault weapon" to describe such firearms. But gun-rights advocates say only fully automatic firearms, such as machine guns, are true assault weapons.

## Concealed-Carry Laws Sweep Nation

Forty-nine states now allow gun owners to carry concealed firearms, compared with 31 in 1981. Thirty-five states — up from two in 1981 — have adopted "shall issue" laws, which require concealed-carry permits to be granted to gun owners who meet minimum qualifications. Meanwhile, the number of states with "may issue" laws, which allow officials to deny concealed-carry permits at their discretion, has declined by more than half.

### Concealed-Weapon Laws by State, 1981 and 2013*

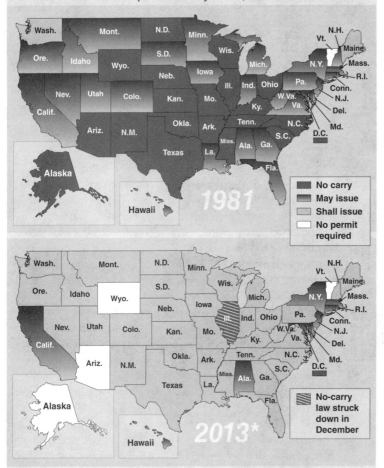

*\* As of March 6, 2013*

*Sources:* "Guns in Public Places: The Increasing Threat of Hidden Guns in America," Law Center to Prevent Gun Violence, August 2011, smartgunlaws.org/guns-in-public-places-the-increasing-threat-of-hidden-guns-in-america/; "State Concealed Weapons Permitting," Law Center to Prevent Gun Violence, January 2012, smartgunlaws.org/category/state-concealed-weapons-permitting/

Owner," while gun-control supporters wore green ribbons in remembrance of Newtown.[1]

Advocacy groups on both sides testified, along with gun industry representatives, gun-violence victims and private citizens. Parents of children killed at Sandy Hook, though joined in mourning, were not always united in their testimony.

"I believe in a few simple gun laws. I think we have more than enough on the books," said Mark Mattioli, whose son James, 6, was killed.

"That wasn't just a killing. That was a massacre," said Neil Heslin, who lost his 6-year-old son, Jesse Lewis. Heslin told lawmakers that private citizens have no need for assault weapons like the one Lanza used to kill his son.[2]

But an impassioned Henson Ong, a Waterbury, Conn., resident, said that if Korean shop owners had not armed themselves with semiautomatic weapons with large-capacity magazines during the 1992 riots in Los Angeles, many of their stores would have been burned to the ground. "Their's stood because they stood their ground," said Ong, who told lawmakers he was an immigrant and an American by choice.[3]

Fresh memories of the Newtown shootings formed the backdrop for the public hearing. Lanza, a withdrawn 20-year-old, shot his way into the school wearing combat gear and armed with two semiautomatic pistols, a Bushmaster AR-15 semiautomatic rifle and numerous large-capacity ammunition magazines, each holding 30 rounds. Lanza used the rifle to shoot his victims, all of them multiple times, in under 10 minutes. The guns were legally owned by his mother, Nancy, whom Lanza had shot dead earlier in the day.

"We're going to have to come together and take meaningful action to prevent more tragedies like this, regardless of the politics," President Obama said that afternoon.[4]

After a week-long silence, Wayne LaPierre, executive vice president of the National Rifle Association of America (NRA), the country's leading gun-rights organization, headquartered in Fairfax, Va., blamed "vicious, violent video games" and lax law enforcement for violent crime.[5]

"The only thing that stops a bad guy with a gun is a good guy with a gun," said LaPierre. He called for placing armed security officers — whether police or trained volunteers — at every public school in the nation.[6] But according to the Justice Department, nearly half of the nation's public schools already had assigned police officers even before the Newtown massacre. Few reliable studies have been done on their effectiveness.[7]

Unlike other recent mass shootings, which spurred outrage but no federal legislation, Newtown is different, say gun-control advocates. "People are really feeling like they have had enough of this violence and these deaths," says Laura Cutilletta, a senior staff attorney with the San Francisco-based advocacy group Law Center to Prevent Gun Violence.

Several members of Congress with "A" ratings from the NRA have re-evaluated their positions on gun control. Sen. Joe Manchin, D-W.Va., told a radio host that "everything is on the table."[8] Sen. Mark Warner, D-Va., said, "there's got to be a way that we can do a bit more."[9]

Meanwhile, the NRA continues to oppose all gun-control proposals. The debate has gotten only more heated since mid-January, when Obama unveiled sweeping recommendations from a gun-violence working group

## Anatomy of an AR-15 Rifle

Gun-control advocates say firearms such as the Rock River Arms AR-15 rifle in this photo illustration have features that make them "assault weapons." Such features can include a threaded barrel for mounting a silencer or flash suppressor, which reduces the visible flash that emanates from the muzzle when the gun is fired; a pistol grip that gives the shooter added control, and a detatchable magazine. This rifle is similar in style to the Bushmaster AR-15 used by Adam Lanza in his deadly attack on schoolchildren at Sandy Hook Elementary School in Newtown, Conn., on Dec. 14, 2012. However, assault-style weapons account for only a small fraction of gun crimes, experts say.

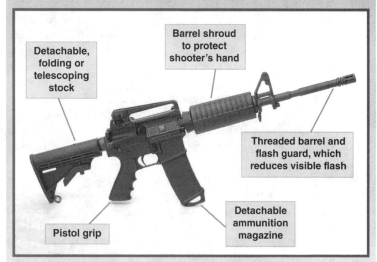

Detachable, folding or telescoping stock

Barrel shroud to protect shooter's hand

Threaded barrel and flash guard, which reduces visible flash

Pistol grip

Detachable ammunition magazine

*Source:* Photo illustration by Getty Images/Joe Raedle

headed by Vice President Joseph Biden. Obama called on Congress to mandate universal background checks, ban the sale of assault weapons and large-capacity magazines and stiffen penalties for gun trafficking. Obama also announced 23 more modest executive actions, including launching a national safe and responsible gun ownership campaign and improving mental-health care.[10]

Gun-control advocates uniformly praised Obama's proposals. "It's really unprecedented in its scope and complexity," said Matt Bennett, co-founder of Third Way, a centrist think tank in Washington.[11] But many Republicans were highly critical of the proposals, including Senate Minority Leader Mitch McConnell, R-Ky., who sent a recorded message to gun owners across his state: "Their efforts to restrict your rights, invading your personal privacy and overstepping their bounds with executive orders, is just plain wrong."[12] The NRA sponsored attack advertisements against the administration's proposals, including one warning of a middle class left defenseless against "madmen, drug cartels and home-invading killers."

Meanwhile, the Senate Judiciary Committee is preparing gun-control legislation, and lawmakers in several states have introduced bills to toughen gun laws. At the same time, legislators in two dozen Western and Midwestern states have introduced bills to block enforcement of any forthcoming federal gun control within their borders.

Mass shootings such as Newtown garner national headlines but account for a small fraction of gun violence, much of which is concentrated among inner-city minorities. "In 2012, for the first time, there will probably be more firearm-related homicides and suicides than motor vehicle traffic fatalities," said Garen Wintemute, director of the Violence Prevention Research Program at the University of California Davis Medical Center.[13]

Nevertheless, the homicide rate in America, while dramatically higher than in many other Western democracies, is falling.[14] "We are at a 45-year historic low in terms of our murder rate," says political scientist Patrick Egan of New York University. Since reaching a peak of 10.2 reported murders per 100,000 people in 1980, the rate steadily declined during the next 20 years, plateaued through 2007, then dropped to 4.7 in 2011.[15]

About two-thirds of murders are committed with firearms — mostly handguns — and the gun-related homicide rate has dropped as well. Researchers say possible reasons include violence-prevention programs, a decline in the crack-cocaine market, the nation's aging population and the use of community policing, among others. Suicides by gun account for more than half of firearm-related deaths, and that rate also has fallen.[16]

In addition, individual gun ownership is at or near all-time lows, says Egan. "Back in the 1970s, about one in two households kept a gun, and these days it's more like one in three," he says, citing data from the University of Chicago's General Social Survey (GSS). Egan attributes the trend to increasing urbanization; an increase in households headed by single women, who are less likely to own guns than men; and a resulting decline in the number of children who inherit the habit of gun ownership from parents.

While fewer individuals own guns today, more guns are in circulation, a trend that accelerated after Newtown, as gun buyers flocked to retailers and gun shows in expectation of future restrictions. "Our best guess is that fewer people are owning more guns," says Egan.

Americans own about 300 million guns today, up from just under 200 million 20 years ago, according to the Bureau of Alcohol, Tobacco, Firearms and Explosives (ATF).[17]

Data on gun violence, ownership and sales have been used to marshal arguments on all sides of the debate. However, such data are often "unreliable" and "inadequate," and the lack of dependable information severely hampers research, according to a National Academy of Sciences report.[18]

For instance, how many U.S. households own guns? While the GSS says about one-third, other surveys put it higher. How many guns are in circulation? Because no national gun registry exists, the ATF's 300 million number is only an estimate.

How about the number of stolen guns? "We really don't know," says economist David Hemenway, director of the Boston-based Harvard Injury Control Research Center. If the aggregate figure is unknown, researchers certainly can't know "the who, what, when, where and how," he says. Since 2004, Congress has restricted the ATF from releasing information from its Firearms Tracing System database. The restriction is known as the "Tiahrt Amendment," after its principal sponsor, former Rep. Todd Tiahrt, R-Kan.

Even FBI crime data can be incomplete because local, county, state, tribal and federal law enforcement agencies provide it voluntarily.

The lack of extensive gun-violence research dates to the early 1990s. After two studies funded by the Centers for Disease Control and Prevention (CDC) showed that a gun in the home is associated with increased risks of homicide and suicide in the home, the NRA pressed a Republican-controlled Congress in 1996 to strip the CDC of the $2.6 million funding for such research. It then succeeded in casting the CDC's gun research as motivated by support for gun restrictions, getting the following sentence into 1997 legislation: "None of the funds made available for injury prevention and control at the Centers for Disease Control and Prevention may be used to advocate or promote gun control."[19]

The CDC stopped funding research on gun violence, and other sources have not picked up the slack. As one of his executive actions, Obama has directed the CDC to resume research into causes and prevention of gun violence, saying it is not "advocacy," and has asked Congress for $10 million in funding.

Against this backdrop, here are some of the questions researchers, gun-rights and gun-control advocates, elected officials and law enforcement are asking:

## Would a ban on assault weapons reduce gun violence?

The semiautomatic rifle that Lanza used is one of the most popular rifles in America. But the gun — a civilian version of the military's fully automatic M-16 rifle — also has been the weapon of choice in several other recent rampages. Jacob Tyler Roberts, 22, used one to kill two people and wound another before taking his own life in an Oregon shopping mall in December.[20] James Holmes, 24, is accused of using one, along with a 12-gauge shotgun, to open fire in a Colorado movie theater last July, killing 12 and wounding 58.[21]

So-called long guns — shotguns and rifles — are not the only firearms used in mass shootings, defined by the FBI as incidents in which four or more victims are killed. Forty-year-old Wade Michael Page, for example, used a semiautomatic handgun equipped with a 19-round magazine last August to kill six people and wound three at a Sikh temple in Wisconsin.[22]

In January, Sen. Dianne Feinstein, D-Calif., introduced a ban on assault weapons and large-capacity magazines that hold more than 10 rounds of ammunition.

"If 20 dead children in Newtown wasn't a wakeup call that these weapons of war don't belong on our streets, I don't know what is," she said. A press release from her office claimed that a previous ban, the Federal Assault Weapons Ban of 1994 in effect until 2004, "was effective

## Types of Firearms

**Semiautomatic:** *Each pull of the trigger results in a complete firing cycle, from discharge through reloading. Most guns sold in the United States, including handguns, are semiautomatic.*

**Automatic:** *Loads, discharges and reloads as long as the trigger remains depressed. Machine guns, for example, are automatic.*

**Assault weapon:** *Gun-rights advocates say only automatic firearms are assault weapons. Others say the definition also includes semiautomatic firearms with detachable magazines and at least one military-style feature, such as a bayonet mount or threaded barrel for attaching a silencer.*

AFP/Getty Images/Joe Klamar

at reducing crime and getting these military-style weapons off our streets."[23]

The NRA's LaPierre has called Feinstein's proposal "a phony piece of legislation" that is "built on lies" and said the previous ban had no impact on lowering crime.[24]

Both Feinstein and LaPierre were selectively quoting from a Department of Justice analysis of the 1994 law, which banned the manufacture, transfer and possession of 18 specific models by name and all other semiautomatic firearms that fell under its general definition of assault weapons: those that could accept a detachable magazine and had at least two specified military-style features, such as a bayonet mount, folding rifle stock and a threaded barrel for attaching silencers.[25]

While the ban was in effect, "the percentage of crime guns that were assault weapons went down by a third or more," says Christopher Koper, the report's principal investigator and a professor of criminology at George Mason University in Fairfax, Va. However, prior to the ban assault weapons had been used in only a small fraction of gun crimes — about 2 percent — his study showed.

The law also prohibited large-capacity magazines holding more than 10 rounds of ammunition. Many non-banned semiautomatics accept such magazines, and such guns represented up to 26 percent of crime guns prior to the ban.

A newspaper's analysis of Virginia data found a reduction in the number of large-capacity magazines seized by police during the ban.[26] But more generally, "we found that it was inconclusive whether the use of large-capacity magazines declined in any real way," says Koper. "That,

## Public Backs Most Gun-Control Proposals

A majority of Americans support requiring background checks for gun-show and private gun sales, establishing a federal database to track gun sales, barring people who are mentally ill from purchasing guns and putting police in more schools. However, most oppose arming more teachers.

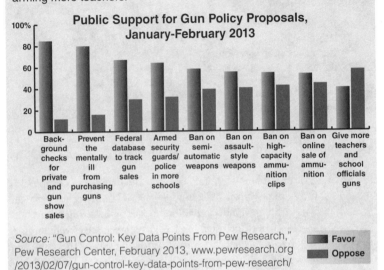

**Public Support for Gun Policy Proposals, January-February 2013**

*Source:* "Gun Control: Key Data Points From Pew Research," Pew Research Center, February 2013, www.pewresearch.org /2013/02/07/gun-control-key-data-points-from-pew-research/

Favor
Oppose

weaknesses. It would ban 157 specific weapons by name. And it would reduce the number of military-style features that define a semiautomatic weapon as an assault weapon from two to one, making it more difficult for gun manufacturers to make cosmetic changes to elude the ban, as they did under the expired law. As before, large-capacity magazines holding more than 10 rounds of ammunition would be prohibited.

While the law would exempt assault weapons lawfully possessed at the date of enactment, it would require purchasers of such weapons to undergo a background check, and it would prohibit the sale or transfer of grandfathered large-capacity magazines. In addition, the law would not automatically expire.[28]

"We are very supportive of the bill," says Cutilletta of the Law Center to Prevent Gun Violence. "The hope is that even the grandfathered weapons and magazines will at least be regulated and their potential damage will be curtailed."

But gun-rights groups say Feinstein's bill wouldn't reduce gun violence. "There would be instant weapon substitution," says Alan Gottlieb, executive vice president of the Second Amendment Foundation, a legal-action group in Bellevue, Wash., that promotes gun rights. "A shotgun can do as much damage as a so-called assault weapon."

Gottlieb says the ban on large-capacity magazines wouldn't reduce gun violence either because someone intent on inflicting mass damage could use many smaller magazines. "It takes a whopping three seconds to change a magazine," says Gottlieb.

Koper offers this assessment. "In the long run, the bill, if passed, would probably not affect the overall rate of gun crime. But it could result in a small reduction in shootings because you are forcing offenders to substitute less-lethal weapons and magazines. By small, I don't mean trivial."

The Johns Hopkins Center for Gun Policy and Research also warned of the need to be realistic about the

of course, has to be linked to the grandfathering provision in the law."

Indeed, the law had a huge loophole. Any banned magazine or assault weapon manufactured before the law took effect remained legal to own or sell. There were nearly 1.5 million assault weapons privately owned in the United States at the time, along with nearly 25 million guns equipped with large-capacity magazines.[27]

Did the ban reduce gun crime? "We didn't really expect to see a reduction in the rate of gun crime overall," Koper says. "People could substitute other guns for the ones that were banned. But by forcing that substitution, we thought it could reduce the number of gunshots and the number of victims."

But, there was no evidence that it did, Koper says. "However, if the law had been in place longer and we had had a drop in the use of large-capacity magazines, would you then see more of an impact on gun deaths and gun injuries?" he asks.

Feinstein's proposed legislation tries to correct what gun-control advocates believe were the expired law's

likely impact of any ban, pointing to a study in Jersey City, N.J., that found 10 or more rounds were fired in fewer than 5 percent of gun incidents. Still, the center said, "We have decided to regulate the design of numerous consumer products, such as cribs and small, high-powered magnets, in order to prevent far fewer deaths than could be prevented with a ban of [large-capacity magazines]."[29]

But gun-rights advocates say Feinstein's law would contradict a 2008 ruling by the U.S. Supreme Court in *District of Columbia v. Heller*, in which the court struck down the District's handgun ban.[30] "The *Heller* case said that guns that are in common use by law-abiding people are protected by the Second Amendment," says Virginia attorney Stephen Halbrook, who has successfully argued gun-rights cases before the court. "And the kinds of guns that are being banned are very much in common use."

"That's a reasonable interpretation of the *Heller* case," says Adam Winkler, a constitutional law professor at UCLA School of Law, "yet I think the counterargument is that the Supreme Court might interpret the common-use requirement to only apply when needed for self-defense." The firearms banned under Feinstein's bill are not self-defense weapons, says Winkler.

### Would mandatory background checks of all gun buyers keep guns away from criminals and other dangerous people?

Federal law prohibits possession of firearms by — among others — felons, fugitives, certain categories of domestic-violence offenders, drug addicts and those found mentally incompetent or a danger to themselves or others because of mental illness or who have been involuntarily committed to a mental institution. The 1994 Brady Handgun Violence Prevention Act requires gun buyers to submit to background checks — usually taking just a few minutes — but only if purchasing through a federally licensed gun dealer. Private sales — at gun shows, online or person-to-person — are exempt, yet they may account for 30 to 40 percent of firearms sales, according to 1994 survey data, the most recent available.[31]

The proposal to expand background checks to include private firearms sales — a less controversial idea than banning assault weapons or large-capacity magazines — is gathering bipartisan momentum, at least in the Senate. Judiciary Committee Chairman Patrick Leahy, D-Vt., is a strong supporter, and a diverse group of four senators — including Democratic Sen. Charles Schumer of New York, a liberal, Republican Sen. Tom Coburn of Oklahoma, an NRA member and strong conservative, and moderate GOP Sen. Mark Kirk of Illinois — has been meeting privately to work out a compromise. "We'll get something, I hope. I'm praying for it," said Sen. Manchin of West Virginia, one of the participants.[32] Sen. Coburn's resistance to requiring private sellers to keep a record of transactions is apparently holding up the compromise.

"Until you close this loophole, you're giving people with a propensity for violence an opportunity to buy guns without any background check," says Ladd Everitt, director of communications for the Washington-based advocacy group Coalition to Stop Gun Violence. "It makes no sense."

A survey of state prison inmates convicted of crimes committed with a handgun found that nearly 80 percent said they got their guns from private sources — either friends or families or from street or black-market suppliers. Another 10 percent said they stole their gun; one in 10 said they purchased a gun from a licensed dealer.[33]

The NRA is opposed to expanding background checks. "Let's be honest, background checks will never be 'universal' because criminals will never submit to them," said LaPierre.[34]

Everitt calls that response the anarchy argument: "They say that criminals don't obey laws, so why should we have laws?" But that misses the point, he says. "There still would be ways for criminals to get around background checks, but the people who sold them the gun would be held accountable. Now they are not."

The NRA argument also assumes that criminals are smart, determined and informed, says Philip Cook, a professor of economics and sociology at Duke University in Durham, N.C. "A large percentage of criminals are youthful, not very well educated and very impatient, and even if you put small obstacles in their path that might discourage them from getting guns, it would help."

Gun-control advocates say the Brady Act, even with the private-sales exemption, has been effective. "By blocking 2 million attempts to purchase [since 1994], we have placed a barrier," says Becca Knox, director of research at the Washington-based Brady Campaign to Prevent Gun Violence. "The estimate is that half of those denials are to felons."

But a study of the law's first five years, conducted by Cook and Jens Ludwig, director of the University of Chicago Crime Lab, a research institute, found "no evidence of a reduction in the homicide rate that could be attributed to Brady." The researchers compared homicide rates in 32 states directly affected by the Brady Act with the 18 states that already had their own similar laws on the books.

Homicide rates were dropping nationwide before the act was passed, due in part, experts say, to the end of the crack cocaine epidemic, changes in policing and increased imprisonment rates. The trends were remarkably similar in both groups of states, and the researchers found the trends in homicide rates remained remarkably similar after the Brady Act was passed.[35]

So how do the researchers reconcile the Brady Act's lack of a detectable impact on homicide rates with the millions of people denied handguns through background checks since the act became law? "We did some back-of-the-envelope calculations using what we know about the people who attempt to buy a gun from a dealer even though they are disqualified — how likely they are to go commit homicide," says Cook. Using data from California and extrapolating nationwide, he estimates that the 60,000 annual denials in the five years he studied would have prevented roughly 40 homicides — or about eight per year.

Cook blames "the private-sale loophole" primarily for the Brady Act's lack of detectable impact on homicide rates. "And we can close that," he says. In addition, a majority of adults who end up committing a crime with a gun did not fall into any of the categories that would have disqualified them from buying the gun, says Cook. "In Cook County [Ill.] data, only 40 percent of defendants in murder cases were disqualified by having a felony conviction."

That's why many criminologists want Congress to expand the list of people ineligible to possess a gun to include those convicted of violent misdemeanors, such as misdemeanor assault and battery, which are generally punishable with jail time of up to one year. "The Brady Campaign is in favor of that expansion," says Knox.

The gap in records that states voluntarily submit to the FBI's National Instant Criminal Background Check System, particularly mental health records, also prevents the Brady Act from having a more measurable impact on homicide rates. As a result of that gap, buyers who should be disqualified slip through the system, people on all sides of the gun debate agree.

California, Rhode Island and New York have completely closed the background-check loophole, requiring such checks for every gun purchase. (New York just did so in January). Yet Cook says researchers don't know how effective those laws been in stemming gun violence. "There is no money for these evaluations," says Cook.

In any case, it's not easy to conduct such evaluations because guns flow from states with lax laws to states with strict laws. At gun shows in Reno, Nev., "a third of the cars in the parking lot are from California," said gun violence expert Wintemute.[36]

### Do state laws allowing citizens to carry concealed weapons make communities safer?

More than 76,000 Ohio residents received licenses to carry concealed weapons last year, the highest number since the state began licensing in 2004, according to Ohio Attorney General Mike DeWine. Six out of seven were new licenses and the rest renewals. "As a strong supporter of the Second Amendment, I am pleased to see more Ohioans than ever before are exercising their rights under Ohio's concealed carry law," DeWine said.[37]

Over the past 30 years, states have drastically loosened their "right-to-carry" laws, which allow citizens who can legally own firearms to carry concealed weapons in public, often except in parks, schools, government offices, bars and places of worship. For example:

- Nineteen states prohibited concealed carry in 1981; today none do. (Washington, D.C. does ban it.) In December, the Seventh U.S. Circuit Court of Appeals in Chicago told Illinois its ban was unconstitutional and gave it until early June to draft a concealed-carry law.
- In 1981, 28 states had "may-issue" permit laws, which allow officials to grant or deny a concealed-carry permit; today 10 states have such laws.
- In 1981, two states had "shall-issue" permit legislation, which require officials to issue a concealed-carry permit to anyone meeting minimum qualifications; today, 35 states have such laws.
- In 1981, only Vermont did not require a gun owner to have a permit to carry a concealed firearm; today Alaska, Arizona, Vermont and Wyoming require no permit.[38]

Gun-rights advocates say right-to-carry laws, especially "shall-issue" laws, reduce crime. "The presence of a gun in the hands of good person makes us all safer. It's true. History proves it," said the NRA's LaPierre.[39] He and others argue that not only can gun-carrying individuals ward off attackers, but criminals are deterred because they don't know who does or does not carry a concealed weapon. In most states, the percentage of adults with active concealed-carry permits is in the single digits. For example, in Ohio the figure is 3.2 percent.[40]

Gun-control advocates could not disagree more. "Carrying guns in public puts American families and communities at risk of more gun deaths and injuries, as opposed to providing greater protection," says Knox of the Brady Campaign, which opposes shall-issue permit laws.

It's a fierce debate that was turbocharged in 1997, when economist John Lott concluded, based on his analysis of nationwide county data, that right-to-carry laws deter violent crime. The NRA and state legislatures have used Lott's research to justify right-to-carry legislation.

Lott's work triggered a tremendous number of followup studies. "There have been more than two dozen, each claiming to be somewhat superior to the others," says Harvard's Hemenway. Some researchers lined up with Lott while many others found serious problems with the data and analysis. The National Academy of Sciences' 2004 report found "no credible evidence that the passage of right-to-carry laws decreases or increases violent crime."[41]

One persistent Lott critic, John Donohue of Stanford Law School, revisited the issue in 2010 and concluded, again, that right-to-carry laws do not deter crime. In fact, he said, "aggravated assault rises when [such] laws are adopted."[42]

"Screening is very weak, and you have people getting these permits who have some type of criminal record, who have mental health history, a history of drug abuse or a history of domestic violence," says Everitt of the Coalition to Stop Gun Violence. In addition, "The presence of a gun can turn something that should have been a fistfight into something far more lethal."

Donohue and fellow researcher Ian Ayres of Yale Law School have said that arming citizens could encourage an "arms race" in which criminals "respond to shall-issue laws by packing more heat and shooting quicker." And with as many as one million or more guns stolen each year, "putting more guns in the hands of the law-abiding population necessarily means that more guns will end up in the hands of criminals," they wrote.[43]

The majority of shall-issue states recognize permits from other states, but most states with may-issue permit laws do not.[44] The U.S. House of Representatives passed a bill in 2011 that would create reciprocity in every state that gives citizens the right to carry concealed weapons.

"It's something that we absolutely oppose," says Knox. "This would be a race to the bottom. The state with the loosest regulations would be driving who could carry."

## BACKGROUND

### Early Gun Culture

Gun-control and gun-rights regulations share a long history in the United States. Adult white men in the American colonies had the right to own firearms for hunting and self-defense and, in fact, were required to use them in the service of local militias, often in battles with Native Americans. But the colonies also placed restrictions on gun ownership.

In 1637 about 100 Massachusetts Bay colonists were ordered to surrender their "guns, pistols, swords, powder, shot & match" on suspicion of being heretics, wrote journalist Craig Whitney.[45] Maryland barred Roman Catholics from possessing firearms, and Pennsylvania disarmed Loyalists during the Revolutionary War. These were not "criminals or traitors who took up arms on behalf of the British" but "ordinary citizens exercising their fundamental right to freedom of conscience," wrote UCLA's Winkler.[46]

Colonies also forbade slaves, free blacks and people of mixed race — who in some states far outnumbered whites — from owning firearms, fearing they might revolt. Combine their numbers with the up to 40 percent of the population who were Loyalists, and the colonies "were perfectly willing to confiscate weapons from anyone deemed untrustworthy — a category so broadly defined that it included a majority of the people," wrote Winkler.[47]

After the Revolution, the Founding Fathers addressed gun rights in the Second Amendment, part of the Bill of

# CHRONOLOGY

## 1920s-1930s *States and Congress pass gun-control legislation.*

**1926** American Bar Association commission, with National Rifle Association (NRA) support, adopts model state legislation regulating the concealed carry and sale of handguns; Pennsylvania is among the first to adopt it.

**1934** National Firearms Act of 1934 — first federal gun-control law — levies $200 tax on the manufacture or sale of machine guns and "sawed-off" shotguns; owners must register them with the U.S. Treasury Department.

**1938** National Firearms Act of 1938 requires interstate gun dealers to be licensed and to record sales; prohibits gun sales to convicted felons. . . . Carrying concealed handguns is either prohibited or permitted only with a license in every state but two.

## 1960s-1990s *Democratic administrations sign major gun-control legislation into law. Republican President Ronald Reagan promotes gun rights.*

**1968** After the assassinations of President John F. Kennedy, Democratic presidential candidate Sen. Robert F. Kennedy and the Rev. Martin Luther King Jr, President Lyndon B. Johnson signs the Gun Control Act of 1968; it prohibits convicted felons, drug users and the seriously mentally ill from buying guns, raises the age to purchase guns from a federally licensed dealer to 21 and expands dealer licensing requirements.

**1986** Reagan signs Firearm Owners' Protection Act limiting the Bureau of Alcohol, Tobacco and Firearms from inspecting licensed gun dealers more than once a year and forbidding the government from creating a national registry of gun owners.

**1990** Gun-Free School Zones Act makes it a federal crime to knowingly bring a gun within 1,000 feet of a school or fire a gun within that zone. In 1995 the U.S. Supreme Court rules that punishment of gun possession or use near schools is a state matter.

**1993** President Bill Clinton signs Brady Handgun Violence Act requiring licensed gun dealers to conduct background checks of buyers; unlicensed private sellers are exempt.

**1994** Violent Crime Control and Law Enforcement Act of 1994 (often called the "assault weapons ban") prohibits the manufacture and sale of semiautomatic assault weapons for 10 years; it also bans ammunition magazines holding more than 10 rounds.

## 2000s *Gun-control advocates face defeats in Congress and Supreme Court, but massacre of 20 children in Newtown, Conn., in December reignites gun-control debate.*

**2003** Congress passes Tiahrt Amendment prohibiting law enforcement from releasing data showing where criminals bought their firearms.

**2004** "Assault weapons" ban expires.

**2005** President George W. Bush signs Protection of Lawful Commerce in Arms Act granting gun manufacturers immunity from civil lawsuits involving crimes committed with guns.

**2008** Supreme Court holds that Americans have an individual right under the Second Amendment to posses firearms for self-defense within the home.

**2012** Federal appeals court rules that Illinois' ban on concealed carry of firearms is unconstitutional and gives the state until early June to draft a concealed carry law (Dec. 11). . . . Adam Lanza kills 20 children and six adults at Sandy Hook Elementary in Newtown, Conn., sparking national outrage and renewing gun-control debate (Dec. 14).

**2013** President Obama proposes sweeping gun-control legislation. . . . Congress begins gun-control hearings. . . . Sen. Dianne Feinstein, D-Calif., introduces legislation to ban assault weapons and large-capacity ammunition magazines. . . . New York legislature passes one of the nation's strictest gun-control laws. Thirty-four of 62 New York counties pass resolutions demanding that lawmakers repeal the act; a state court has agreed to review whether the new law was rushed through the legislature in violation of the state constitution.

Rights attached to the U.S. Constitution in 1791. The amendment reads: "A well regulated Militia being necessary to the security of a free State, the right of the people to keep and bear Arms shall not be infringed." Various states drafted constitutions with similar provisions. Their intended meaning became the subject of debate in the early 19th century as states enacted "the first comprehensive laws prohibiting handguns and other concealed weapons," according to historian Saul Cornell.[48]

In 1813, Kentucky and Louisiana became the first states to ban the carrying of concealed weapons. Indiana did so in 1820, followed over the next two decades by Georgia, Tennessee, Virginia and Alabama.[49] The Southern states were responding to the extraordinary violence in the region, where an honor culture meant "that insults could not be safely ignored," wrote historian Clayton Cramer. "If someone insulted you publicly, or cast doubts about your honor, you challenged them to a duel" or pulled out a gun or Bowie knife to "settle the matter right on the spot."[50]

These early gun-control laws spawned legal challenges asserting constitutional rights to bear arms for individual self-defense. Most courts disagreed and upheld the laws, interpreting the right to bear arms as a community duty and not an individual right. However, "a few courts embraced the new ideology of gun rights," wrote Cornell.[51]

While some states were tightening gun regulations, "others, such as Mississippi and Connecticut, were writing into their constitutions more robust statements affirming the right of individuals to have weapons for self-defense," he wrote. At the same time, "Other states rejected the new language and reaffirmed the traditional civic model of the right to bear arms." For example, Maine's constitution, adopted in 1820, declared that "every citizen has a right to keep and bear arms for the common defense."[52]

## Federal Gun Control

The NRA was not initially a gun-rights organization. "Dismayed by the lack of marksmanship shown by their troops [during the Civil War], Union veterans Col. William C. Church and Gen. George Wingate formed the National Rifle Association in 1871," reads the NRA website. Its primary goal would be to "promote and encourage rifle shooting on a scientific basis," according to Church.[53]

The NRA held target-shooting competitions and sponsored gun clubs and shooting ranges. Membership swelled between World War I (1914-1918) and World War II (1939-1945), when the U.S. military gave more than 200,000 surplus rifles to NRA members for free or at government cost.

The NRA also helped write model state gun-control legislation containing some provisions similar to those vehemently opposed by the association today. The Uniform Firearms Act, produced by an American Bar Association commission in 1926, applied mostly to handguns. It recommended that states require individuals to apply for a license to carry a concealed gun in public and that states issue such licenses with discretion. Handgun sellers had to be licensed, keep sales records and forward them to law enforcement officials and refrain from selling guns to those convicted of violent crimes.[54]

The NRA promoted this model legislation nationwide, and numerous states adopted it in whole or in part. In fact, a 1938 scholarly article concluded: "Today the carrying of concealed pistols is either prohibited absolutely or permitted only with a license in every state but two."[55]

Congress came later to gun control. The federal government's first major attempt occurred in the 1930s as Prohibition-era gangsters with compact machine guns outgunned city police, and notorious criminals such as John Dillinger, Bonnie Parker and Clyde Barrow, George "Machine Gun" Kelly, Charles "Pretty Boy" Floyd and Kate "Ma" Barker used guns and cars for crime sprees across state lines.

The National Firearms Act of 1934, signed into law by President Franklin D. Roosevelt, imposed a $200 tax on the manufacture, sale or transfer of machine guns and "sawed-off" shotguns and rifles with barrels less than 18 inches long. Anyone possessing such guns had to register them with the U.S. Treasury Department. While no one expected criminals to comply, their failure to do so meant that if caught with such a gun, a criminal could be jailed for tax evasion or non-registration, and "the government wouldn't have to prove that the person had killed anyone," wrote Winkler.[56]

The Roosevelt administration initially wanted to include handguns in the law, a provision the NRA opposed because it said it would make it difficult for ordinary citizens to defend themselves against criminals. After a massive

# Background-Check System Has Serious Gaps

*Crucial mental-health and drug-abuse records are not included in the database.*

The nation's system for checking the background of gun buyers is supposed to help keep firearms out of the hands of felons, fugitives, drug abusers, people legally determined to be dangerous or incompetent to manage their affairs due to mental illness or those who have been committed to a mental institution, among others. Licensed firearms dealers call or email the National Instant Criminal Background Check System (NICS) and usually receive an immediate answer about whether to deny or allow a sale.

But the NICS database has serious gaps. Crucial mental-health and drug-abuse records are missing because states are not required to share them with NICS. They do so voluntarily. "Unfortunately, as long as these gaps remain, they are going to be fatal," says John Feinblatt, chairman of New York-based Mayors Against Illegal Guns, a coalition of 800 mayors that issued a recent report on gaps in the background system.

The report points to two mass killers who eluded the background check system:

- Seung Hui Cho passed several background checks to purchase the guns he used to kill 32 people and himself at Virginia Tech University in 2007, despite a judge's earlier determination that he was mentally ill. Virginia had never entered his mental-health records in the NCIS system.
- Jared Loughner had a history of drug abuse, according to media accounts, that was never reported to NCIS before he passed background checks to purchase guns he used to kill six people and critically wound 13 others — including Rep. Gabrielle Giffords, D-Ariz., in Tucson in 2011.[1]

Before the Virginia Tech shootings, only Alabama, Colorado, Connecticut and Georgia required agencies to share relevant mental-health records with NCIS. After the shootings, 19 additional states — including Virginia — adopted such laws.[2]

The federal government also increased funding to help states with record keeping and reporting after the Virginia Tech shootings.

Since then, the gap has narrowed. From 2004 to 2011, states increased the number of mental-health records available to NICS for background checks by 500 percent. However, according to the Government Accountability Office (GAO), a federal watchdog agency, "this progress largely reflects the efforts of 12 states." Most states, the GAO said, "have made little or no progress in providing these records."[3]

"Many states are still performing poorly," says Feinblatt. For instance, 23 have reported fewer than 100 mental-health records to the federal background-check database since its creation in 1999, and 44 states have submitted fewer than 10 records about drug abuse. As a result, Mayors Against Illegal Guns has concluded that millions of records identifying drug abusers and people with serious mental illness are absent from the system.[4]

But even if the background check system worked perfectly, it would have only a marginal impact on gun violence, says Jeffrey Swanson, a professor of psychiatry at Duke University and a leading expert in the causes and control of violence. "It would probably reduce overall gun violence against others by 4 or 5 percent," says Swanson, because the mentally ill account for a very small fraction of violent crime.

NRA-organized letter writing campaign, Congress dropped the handgun provision.

The NRA supported the law because it was an "indirect" approach to controlling gun violence. "I think that under the Constitution the United States has no jurisdiction to legislate in a police sense with respect to firearms," NRA president Karl T. Frederick testified at a 1934 congressional hearing before the law was passed. "I think that is exclusively a matter for state regulation, and I think that the only possible way in which the United States can legislate is through

its taxing power, which is an indirect method of approach, through its control over interstate commerce, which was perfectly proper, and through control over importations."[57]

Four years later, Congress expanded the federal government's reach, requiring gun sellers to obtain a license from the Internal Revenue Service and prohibiting the sale of guns and ammunition to felons — provisions the NRA supported.

"After this flurry of activity, Congress and the NRA went back to their respective corners and more or less left

While the mentally ill are responsible for close to 20 percent of mass shootings, said Michael Stone, a New York forensic psychiatrist, "most mass murders are done by working-class men who've been jilted, fired or otherwise humiliated — and who then undergo a crisis of rage and get out one of the 300 million guns in our country and do their thing."[5]

In an article earlier this year, Swanson and his colleagues detailed other flaws in assumptions underlying the background-check system.[6] For example, the small fraction of the mentally ill who are dangerous often don't seek treatment before doing something harmful, so they would not show up in a background-check database. And even when they do seek help, doctors often can't identify them as dangerous, according to studies. "Psychiatrists are just not very good at predicting who is going to be violent or not," says Swanson. "It's not much better than chance."

Despite that record, New York's newest gun-control law requires a doctor, psychologist, registered nurse or licensed clinical social worker who determines that a patient is a danger to himself or others to report that patient to the government. The government may then decide to prevent the person from possessing a firearm or revoke an existing license.[7] Under current professional guidelines, only involuntary hospitalizations and direct threats made by patients are required to be reported to state authorities, who then share the information with the federal background-check database, according to *The New York Times*.[8]

Many mental-health professionals oppose this new provision, fearing that people will avoid treatment or not reveal their true thoughts in therapy. "If people with suicidal or homicidal impulses avoid treatment for fear of being reported in this way, they may be more likely to act on those impulses," said Paul Appelbaum, director of law, ethics and psychiatry at New York's Columbia University Medical Center.[9]

Some experts say it's debatable whether mental-health professionals will take the reporting requirement seriously, because the law does not hold them liable if the decision to report or not to report a patient to authorities is made — in the statute's wording — "reasonably and in good faith."[10]

*— Barbara Mantel*

[1]"Fatal Gaps," Mayors Against Illegal Guns, November 2011, p. 2, www.mayorsagainstillegalguns.org/downloads/pdf/maig_mimeo_revb.pdf.

[2]*Ibid.*, p. 14.

[3]"Sharing Promising Practices and Assessing Incentives Could Better Position Justice to Assist States in Providing Records for Background Checks," Government Accountability Office, July 2012, p. 9, www.gao.gov/assets/600/592452.pdf.

[4]"Fatal Gaps," *op. cit.*, p. 3.

[5]Benedict Carey and Anemona Hartocollis, "Warning Signs of Violent Acts Often Unclear," *The New York Times*, Jan. 15, 2013, www.nytimes.com/2013/01/16/health/breaking-link-of-violence-and-mental-illness.html?_r=0.

[6]Jeffrey W. Swanson, *et al.*, "Preventing Gun Violence Involving People with Serious Mental Illness," *Reducing Gun Violence in America: Informing Policy with Evidence and Analysis* (2013), p. 36.

[7]"Program Bill #1," New York Legislative Bill Drafting Commission, pp. 19-20, www.governor.ny.gov/assets/documents/GPB_1_GUNS_BILL_LBD_12007_03_3.pdf.

[8]Carey and Hartocollis, *op. cit.*

[9]"Experts: Tougher N.Y. gun control law may discourage therapy," The Associated Press, Jan. 16, 2013, www.usatoday.com/story/news/nation/2013/01/15/ny-gun-law-therapy/1836323.

[10]"Program Bill #1," *op. cit.*, p. 20.

each other alone," wrote journalist Osha Gray Davidson. The NRA's "lobbying wing remained incidental to the organization's primary mission of serving hunters and target shooters."[58]

## Gun Debate

That changed dramatically three decades later. "The 1960s were the turning point for the cultural war over guns as we know it," wrote Whitney. Rising crime, racial tensions and a loss of public confidence in the police "led millions of Americans to buy weapons for personal protection," he wrote.

Despite more guns and more homicides, Congress was "reluctant to pass gun laws that would be taken as a threat to the lawful use of weapons by ordinary Americans," said Whitney.[59]

Congress took no action on guns after the assassination of President John F. Kennedy in Dallas in 1963. But public opinion shifted a few years later, as race riots engulfed the nation's cities and members of the revolutionary Black

Wayne LaPierre, the executive vice president of the National Rifle Association (NRA), has criticized proposed gun-control legislation, although a January Pew Research Center poll shows 85 percent of gun owners support making private gun sales subject to background checks. Only 43 percent of gun owners, however, said they support a ban on assault-style weapons.

Panther Party openly — and legally — displayed their guns in public to attract media attention. And after the assassinations of civil rights leader Dr. Martin Luther King Jr. and Democratic senator and presidential candidate Robert F. Kennedy two months apart in 1968, President Lyndon B. Johnson pleaded with Congress to pass gun-control legislation "in the name of sanity, in the name of safety and in the name of an aroused nation."[60] In October, he signed into law the Gun Control Act of 1968.

The statute requires all persons manufacturing, importing or selling firearms as a business to be federally licensed; prohibits the interstate sale of firearms through the mail; bans all interstate sales of handguns; lists categories of people to whom firearms may not be sold, including convicted felons and the seriously mentally ill; and requires dealers to maintain records of gun sales.

Franklin Orth, NRA executive vice president — the seat of power at the organization — testified before Congress in favor of the law. "We do not think any sane American, who calls himself an American, can object to placing into this bill the instrument which killed the president of the United States," he said.

But a growing number of NRA members were furious at Orth. "Their objections didn't so much stem from opposition to any specific sections of the legislation; it was the concept of gun control itself that they disliked, even hated," wrote Davidson.[61]

The 1968 dispute was "the opening volley in what was to become an all-out war, one that would split the gun group wide open over the next decade," wrote Davidson. The division pitted mostly older members who believed the NRA should focus on teaching gun safety and organizing shooting competitions and hunting clinics against younger members who wanted the NRA to focus on blocking any and all gun-control measures as violations of the Second Amendment. At the organization's 1976 annual meeting in Cincinnati, the young "hard-liners" took control, using parliamentary procedure to shift power from officials to the membership, which then voted out the old guard and voted in the new.

"The Cincinnati Revolt (as the episode became known) changed forever the face of the NRA," according to Davidson. It "became more than a rifle club. It became the Gun Lobby."[62]

In 1986, the NRA scored a victory when President Ronald Reagan signed into law the Firearm Owners' Protection Act. It prohibits civilian transfer or possession of machine guns but legalizes shipments of ammunition through the mail; allows gun owners to transport firearms through states where they are banned; prohibits the federal government from maintaining a registry of guns and their owners; and mandates that the Bureau of Alcohol, Tobacco and Firearms (ATF) inspect licensed gun dealers for compliance with the 1968 law no more than once a year. The NRA had complained that ATF agents had been harassing dealers.

The pendulum swung the other way under President Bill Clinton. In December 1993 he signed the Brady Handgun Violence Prevention Act instituting background checks for gun purchases through licensed dealers. The law was named after Reagan Press Secretary James Brady, who was seriously wounded in an assassination attempt on Reagan in 1981. And in 1994 Clinton signed a measure banning what it defined as assault weapons and large-capacity ammunition magazines. The NRA vehemently opposed both laws. After the Brady Act was passed, the NRA told its members that rogue government agents will start to "go house to house, kicking in the law-abiding gun owners' doors."[63]

Congress has passed no major gun-control legislation since then. In 2008, the Supreme Court surprised gun-control advocates in its *District of Columbia v. Heller* ruling, which nullified Washington, D.C.'s ban on handgun ownership by declaring that individuals have a Second Amendment right to possess firearms "for traditionally lawful purposes, such as self-defense within the home." But the court made it clear that its opinion did not "cast doubt" on a wide variety of gun-control laws that regulated who could possess firearms, where they could be carried and how they could be sold. The court also recognized limitations on "dangerous and unusual" weapons but did not define them.[64]

"The court went out of its way to make clear that the right to bear arms can co-exist with gun control," says Winkler.

## CURRENT SITUATION

### New York Is First

New York has become the first — and so far only — state to pass gun-control legislation since the Newtown shootings. "I'm proud to be a New Yorker because New York is doing something — because we are fighting back," Democratic Gov. Andrew M. Cuomo said in mid-January as he signed the New York Secure Ammunition and Firearms Enforcement Act, or SAFE Act, into law.[65]

The act makes the state's already-strict gun regulations some of the nation's toughest. It broadens the definition of banned assault weapons; requires owners of existing assault weapons, grandfathered under the law, to register them with the New York State Police; reduces the limit on magazine capacity from 10 rounds of ammunition to seven; requires background checks of not only gun purchasers but also ammunition buyers; expands background checks to private sales, except between immediate family members; and establishes tougher penalties for the use of illegal guns.

The legislation won praise from gun-control advocates, including New York City Mayor Michael R. Bloomberg,

who said it "protects the Second Amendment rights of people, and at the same time it makes all New Yorkers safer."[66]

But 34 of 62 New York counties have passed resolutions demanding that lawmakers repeal the act.[67] And a state court has agreed to review whether the new law was rushed through the legislature in violation of the state constitution. "To have Cuomo dictate to the honest gun owners of New York because of the few criminals is criminal in itself," says Harold "Budd" Schroeder, chairman of the Shooters Committee on Political Education (SCOPE), a volunteer gun-rights organization with 12 chapters across the state.

In addition, "the law is unworkable," says Schroeder. While Feinstein dropped from her proposed federal assault-weapons ban a requirement that owners of grandfathered weapons register their guns, New York state's law kept a registration provision. "If you don't require registration, someone could say that they had the gun when the ban went into effect, and there is no way to prove that they didn't. It's an enforcement tool," says Cutilletta of the Law Center to Prevent Violence.

Schroeder, like the NRA, calls registration the first step toward firearms confiscation. However, seven states and Washington, D.C., require registration of some or all firearms and "no guns have been confiscated," says Cutilletta. "It's either paranoia or it's a political argument to try to scare people."

Nevertheless, a civil disobedience movement is brewing. "The sense I get from all the gun owners I have been talking to is that the [New York] law says register your long guns — and that is not going to happen," says Schroeder. According to the *New York Post*, gun-club leaders, gun dealers and Second Amendment advocacy groups are organizing a registration boycott. While the boycott's size won't be known until the registration deadline of April 15, 2014, the state expects "widespread violations," an unnamed Cuomo-administration source told the newspaper. "Many of these assault-rifle owners aren't going to register; we realize that," the source said. Failing to register is a class-A misdemeanor, punishable by up to a year in prison.[68]

### More State Action

Currently, few states have strict gun-control measures on the books. Six states and Washington, D.C., require

## State Gun Laws Vary Widely

Since the massacre at Sandy Hook Elementary School, state legislatures have been debating various proposals for changing gun laws, but so far only New York's has acted. It joins California, Rhode Island and the District of Columbia in adopting some of the nation's toughest gun measures, including requiring "universal" background checks on all gun purchases, some of which are now exempt under the federal Brady Act.

| Key State Gun Laws* |
| --- |

### Universal Background Checks
(Checks required for sales by both licensed dealers and private sellers)

- California, New York, Rhode Island and Washington, D.C., require universal background checks on sales of all classes of firearms.
- Maryland requires universal background checks on purchases of handguns and assault weapons.
- Connecticut and Pennsylvania require universal background checks on all handgun sales.

### Licenses and Permits

- Anyone buying or owning a gun in Hawaii, Illinois, Massachusetts or New Jersey must get a license or permit.
- California, Connecticut, Iowa, Michigan, New York, North Carolina and Rhode Island require a license or permit for handguns only.

### Safety Training and Exams

- Massachusetts requires gun buyers to take a firearms safety course before buying a gun.
- California, Connecticut, Hawaii, Michigan and Rhode Island also require gun-safety training, but only for handgun purchasers or owners.

### Assault Weapons

- Although the definitions of "assault weapon" vary, the following states ban sales of assault weapons: California, Connecticut, Massachusetts, New Jersey, New York and the District of Columbia.
- Hawaii and Maryland ban assault pistols.
- Maryland, Minnesota and Virginia regulate the sale and use of assault weapons.

### Large-Capacity Ammunition Magazines

- New York has banned magazines holding more than seven rounds.
- California, Hawaii, Massachusetts and the District of Columbia ban magazines holding more than 10 rounds. New Jersey bans magazines holding more than 15 rounds.
- Maryland bans magazines holding more than 20 rounds.

*\* includes the District of Columbia*

*Source:* "Search Gun Laws By Policy," Law Center to Prevent Gun Violence, 2013, smartgunlaws.org/search-gun-law-by-gun-policy/

universal background checks — for private firearm sales and sales through licensed dealers — but in some states the requirements don't apply to all types of guns. Four states require licenses for anyone buying or owning any firearm, while seven states require only handgun buyers and owners to be licensed. Seven states and Washington, D.C., ban variously defined assault weapons, while six of those states also ban large-capacity ammunition magazines.[69]

But by the first week of March, 1,159 firearms-related bills had been introduced in state legislatures, 308 more than during the same period in 2012, according to Cutilletta. Slightly more than half of this year's proposals would expand gun controls. Some would for the first time ban assault weapons or limit magazine size, such as proposals in Vermont, South Carolina and Virginia; others would tighten existing bans, as New York did. Several would require background checks on private firearms sales, such as a measure introduced in New Mexico.

"Regulating ammunition sales is also popular," says Cutilletta, "like banning Internet sales or mail-order sales of ammunition or requiring a background check before buying ammunition — that's been introduced in California." Gun safety also is being addressed; laws that would regulate the way guns are stored have been introduced in Montana, Nebraska, California, Missouri and South Carolina.

Perhaps no state is being watched more closely by both sides of the gun debate than Colorado, a historically pro-gun state and home to two of the nation's most notorious mass shootings: the 1999 Columbine High School massacre and last year's killing spree at an Aurora movie theater.[70] In late

February, the state's Democratic-controlled House approved a package of bills that would require background checks for all gun transactions, paid for by the purchaser; ban ammunition magazines with more than 15 rounds; and allow colleges to ban concealed weapons on campus. No Republicans voted for the bills, and several Democrats crossed party lines to vote against them.

"This is part of our heritage," Democratic Rep. Ed Vigil said during the debate, explaining why he opposed the measures. "This is part of what it took to settle this land. I cannot turn my back on that." The bills have moved to the state Senate, where Democratic control is much slimmer.[71]

Meanwhile, pressure is building on Connecticut's elected officials to strengthen the state's gun-control laws in the wake of the Newtown shootings. A bipartisan legislative task force has missed a self-imposed deadline to recommend consensus gun-control measures, and a separate task force appointed by Democratic Gov. Dannel P. Malloy is not expected to produce its recommendation until later this month.

"The public is demanding they act," said Scott McLean, an analyst with the Quinnipiac University Polling Institute in Hamden, Conn. In mid-February, 5,500 people rallied for gun control at the statehouse. Soon after, Malloy announced his own proposals — expanded background checks, lower magazine limits and a broader definition of assault weapons — and vowed to push his plan through the legislature. "I think it's time to lay it out on the table and get it done," Malloy said.[72]

## Nullification

Just under half of the firearm-related measures introduced in states this year would loosen gun controls. Some would allow guns to be carried in public schools, and others attempt to nullify new, and in some cases existing, federal gun-control laws. For instance, Alaska Republican state Rep. Michael Kelly has proposed the Alaska Firearm Freedom Act, which would make it illegal for federal agents to enforce new gun-control legislation on Alaskan soil. Similar legislation has been introduced in 23 other states. In two — Montana and Wyoming — such bills have passed the House, and a nullification measure has passed the Senate in Kentucky.[73]

These bills are being promoted by a national states'-rights group called the Tenth Amendment Center, which argues that states do not have to enforce laws they believe

are unconstitutional.* But the U.S. Supreme Court has repeatedly rejected state nullification laws. "The states can't simply choose to defy and override a valid federal law," said Allen Rostron, a professor of constitutional law at the University of Missouri-Kansas City. The U.S. Constitution deems federal statutes "the supreme law of the land," he said.[74]

### Liability Insurance

In at least six states legislators have proposed bills requiring gun owners to purchase liability insurance. Backers hope insurers would reward safe behavior — such as having a trigger lock — with lower premiums, according to *The New York Times.* "I believe that if we get the private sector and insurance companies involved in gun safety, we can help prevent a number of gun tragedies every year," said David P. Linsky, a Democratic state representative in Massachusetts. "Insurance companies are very good at evaluating risk factors and setting their premiums appropriately."

However, the insurance industry is wary of such proposals, according to the paper, especially if they require coverage for damages resulting not just from negligence but also from "willful acts," such as shooting an intruder, which are generally not covered.[75]

"Insurance will cover you if your home burns down in an electrical fire, but it will not cover you if you burn down your own house, and you cannot insure yourself for arson," said Robert P. Hartwig, president of the New York-based Insurance Information Institute.[76]

## OUTLOOK
### Political Reality

Broad public support exists for certain gun-control measures, and a sharp partisan divide separates the public on others, according to a Pew Research Center poll. Eighty-three percent of Americans support background checks for private and gun-show sales, a position for which there is bipartisan agreement. But only slightly more than half of Americans support proposals to ban

---

*The 10th Amendment to the Constitution states: "The powers not delegated to the United States by the Constitution, nor prohibited by it to the States, are reserved to the States respectively, or to the people."

**AT ISSUE**

# Should all gun sales be registered in a national database?

## YES
**Garen Wintemute**
*Baker-Teret Chair in Violence Prevention, University of California, Davis*

Written for *CQ Researcher*, March 2013

An estimated 478,422 firearm-related violent crimes occurred in 2011, including 11,101 homicides. To help prevent such violence, federal statute prohibits felons and certain others from acquiring or possessing firearms. People who acquire firearms from licensed gun dealers and pawnbrokers must provide identification and undergo a background check to verify they can legally own them. The retailer keeps a permanent record of the transaction.

Our current system is plagued by two major shortcomings. First, perhaps 40 percent of all firearm acquisitions, and at least 80 percent of those made with criminal intent, are made from private parties. No identification need be shown, no background check conducted, no record kept.

Second, licensed retailers keep their records to themselves. If a firearm is used in a crime and an effort is made to trace its chain of ownership, the trace ordinarily ends with the first retail purchaser. Yet 85 percent of the time, the criminal who used the firearm is someone else. Without an archive of transactions, the firearm cannot be traced beyond its first purchaser.

Background checks and purchase denials are very effective, reducing by approximately 25 percent the risk of the buyer committing new firearm-related or violent crimes. Six states already require all firearm transfers to be routed through licensed retailers, so background checks are completed and records are kept.

In California, handgun transaction records are archived by the state's Department of Justice; records for rifles and shotguns will be added in January 2014. Comprehensive background-check policies interfere with the criminal acquisition of firearms and disrupt firearm trafficking. In California, traces of a firearm used in a crime end with the most recent purchaser, not the first. Cold cases become hot cases.

The United States should set a single, simple, equitable standard for firearm transfers. It should require all transfers (with certain exceptions for those within a family) to include a background check and a permanent record. The policy should not be limited to acquisitions at gun shows, which account for only a small proportion of private-party firearm transfers. To make it easier for law enforcement to trace firearms used in crimes, retailers should report to the FBI the make, model, caliber and serial number of the firearms they sell; they shouldn't have to report the purchasers, except for the first. Law enforcement can then trace a firearm used in a crime to its most recent transaction and obtain more information from the retailer.

## NO
**Stephen P. Halbrook**
*Attorney; Author, The Founders' Second Amendment*

Written for *CQ Researcher*, March 2013

"your papers are not in order!" It's five years in prison for not registering to exercise a constitutional right. Unthinkable for any other right, but not the "right" to keep and bear arms — just ignore the "shall not be infringed" part of the Second Amendment.

Attorney General Eric Holder proposed that punishment for not registering a firearm in the District of Columbia when he was U.S. attorney there. Sen. Dianne Feinstein demands the registration of millions of "assault weapons," which means anything she wants it to mean. Right now, in the Southern Border States, anyone buying more than one semiautomatic rifle per week is reported to the Bureau of Alcohol, Tobacco, Firearms and Explosives.

New York City required registration of hunting rifles and other "long guns" in the 1960s. It later declared them "assault weapons" and sent the police to confiscate them. New York state just passed a law saying countless ordinary rifles have "assault" traits needing registration. California even records purchases of duck-hunting guns and single-shot rifles.

Criminals don't register guns. That's why, even where registration is required, the police don't check registration records before responding to crime scenes. Canada just abolished its billion-dollar gun-registration system because it never solved a single crime.

Germany just implemented a central database of all lawful firearms, a European Union diktat. The German interior minister promised very high security for handling the data, while a skeptic said "everything that is registered can be taken away by the government." Sound familiar? A year before the Nazis seized power, Germany decreed gun registration, and the Interior Minister warned at the time: "Precautions must be taken that these lists not . . . fall into the hands of radical elements." Hitler then used them first to disarm democratic "enemies of the state" and then, in 1938, the Jews during the violent pogrom known as Kristallnacht.

In France, Prime Minister Pierre Laval decreed gun registration. After France fell to Germany in 1940, Laval guided the French police to collaborate with the Nazis, who executed anyone failing to surrender firearms in 24 hours.

Americans were well aware of these events. Just before Pearl Harbor, Congress forbade registration of guns used for sport or self-defense. It did the same in the Firearms Owners' Protection Act of 1986 and Brady Act of 1993.

The purpose of registration is confiscation. Until then, the records are fodder for exploitation by hackers and burglars.

assault weapons and high-capacity ammunition magazines, and those opinions break along party lines.[77]

Similar thinking is reflected in the Democratic-controlled U.S. Senate, where the gun-control debate is currently centered. "I'm very optimistic about legislation on universal background checks, [because] you see even conservative politicians coming forward and supporting it," says Everitt of the Coalition to Stop Gun Violence. In fact, Republican Sen. John McCain of Arizona told NBC's "Meet the Press" on Feb. 17, "I think most of us will be able to support" bipartisan gun-control legislation whose centerpiece is an expansion of background checks.[78]

Support also is growing in the Senate for increased penalties for illegal gun trafficking and "straw purchases," in which an individual buys a gun through a licensed dealer and then passes the gun to someone who typically would not pass a background check. The Senate Judiciary Committee was scheduled to consider bills addressing those issues — plus school-safety measures, universal background checks and an assault-weapons ban — on March 7.

But the chances of Congress banning assault weapons are close to zero, says Gottlieb of the Second Amendment Foundation. "This is not going to go anywhere," he says. Many political analysts agree chances are slim and doubt that the controversial ban would become part of any gun-control legislation emerging from the Senate Judiciary Committee.

As an alternative, Feinstein could offer her legislation banning assault weapons and limiting large-capacity magazines on the floor of the Senate as an amendment. However, "If it's just offered as a floor amendment it's likely to fail, because it's a stand-alone provision and Republicans will filibuster and it will be almost impossible for Democrats to get 60 votes," said Darrell West, director of governance studies at the Washington-based Brookings Institution.[79] (A filibuster is a procedure to delay or block a vote by one or more senators speaking on any topic for as long as they wish. It takes 60 Senators to agree to end a filibuster.)

While Everitt favors a ban on assault weapons, his highest priority is a requirement for universal background checks. "Universal background checks are a staple of any civilized country's gun laws, and one that we've never had on the books and should have been done decades ago in this country," he says.

Meanwhile, the Republican-controlled House is waiting to see what the Senate does before it takes up the issue of gun violence. "They feel if we're able to do something, there might be a chance," said Senate Judiciary Committee Chairman Leahy." "If we're unable, frankly, they're not going to try anything at all. I think that's a political reality."[80]

## NOTES

1. Ray Rivera and Peter Applebome, "Sandy Hook Parents' Testimony to Legislature Reflects Divide on Guns," *The New York Times*, Jan. 28, 2013, www.nytimes.com/2013/01/29/nyregion/connecticut-legislature-hearing-on-gun-violence.html.

2. Mattioli and Heslin quotes are from *ibid.*

3. "Gun Violence Prevention Testimony — Henson," YouTube, Feb. 27, 2013, www.youtube.com/watch?v=sJt-yrXKYG4&feature=endscreen.

4. "President Obama Makes a Statement on the Shooting in Newtown, Connecticut," The White House, Dec. 14, 2012, www.whitehouse.gov/photos-and-video/video/2012/12/14/president-obama-makes-statement-shooting-newtown-connecticut.

5. For background, see Sarah Glazer, "Video Games," *CQ Researcher*, Nov. 10, 2006, pp. 937-960; updated, Sept. 23, 2011. For background on gun debates, see the following *CQ Researchers*: Kenneth Jost, "Gun Violence," May 25, 2007, pp. 457-480; Bob Adams, "Gun Control Debate," Nov. 12, 2004, pp. 949-972.

6. National Rifle Association press conference, Dec. 21, 2012, www.washingtonpost.com/blogs/post-politics/wp/2012/12/21/nras-wayne-lapierre-put-armed-police-officers-in-every-school/.

7. Barbara Raymond, "Assigning Police Officers to School," U.S. Department of Justice, April 2010, pp. 1, 7, www.cops.usdoj.gov/Publications/e041028272-assign-officers-to-schools.pdf.

8. "The Andrea Tantaros Show," Jan. 14, 2013, www.trn1.com/tantaros-audio.

9. "Gun Rights Supporter Sen. Mark Warner Says Tighter Firearms Laws Needed," "Newshour," PBS,

Dec. 18, 2012, www.pbs.org/newshour/bb/politics/july-dec12/warner_12-18.html.

10. "Now is the Time: Gun Violence Reduction Executive Actions," The White House, Jan. 26, 2013, www.whitehouse.gov/sites/default/files/docs/wh_now_is_the_time_actions.pdf.

11. Ruby Cramer, "Gun Control Advocates: Obama's Proposals 'Unprecedented,'" *Buzzfeed*, Jan. 16, 2013, www.buzzfeed.com/rubycramer/gun-control-advocates-obamas-proposals-unpreced.

12. Joseph Gerth, "Mitch McConnell vows to block President Obama's gun control initiatives," *The Courier-Journal*, Jan. 20, 2013, www.courier-journal.com/article/20130119/NEWS010605/301190088/Mitch-McConnell-vows-block-President-Obama-s-gun-control-initiatives?nclick_check=1.

13. Garen J. Wintemute, "Tragedy's Legacy," *The New England Journal of Medicine*, Jan. 31, 2013, p. 397, www.nejm.org/doi/full/10.1056/NEJMp1215491.

14. Letter, The University of Chicago Crime Lab, Jan. 10, 2013, p. 1, http://crimelab.uchicago.edu/sites/crimelab.uchicago.edu/files/uploads/Biden%20Commission%20letter_20130110_final.pdf.

15. "Crime in the United States 2011," Table 1, FBI, www.fbi.gov/about-us/cjis/ucr/crime-in-the-u.s/2011/crime-in-the-u.s.-2011/tables/table-1; "Uniform Crime Reporting Statistics Data Building Tool," FBI, www.ucrdatatool.gov/Search/Crime/State/TrendsInOneVar.cfm.

16. "WISQARS Injury Mortality Reports, 1981-1991," Centers for Disease Control and Prevention, http://webappa.cdc.gov/sasweb/ncipc/mortrate9.html; "WISQARS Injury Mortality Reports, National and Regional, 1999-2010," Centers for Disease Control and Prevention, http://webappa.cdc.gov/sasweb/ncipc/mortrate10_us.html.

17. William Krouse, "Gun Control Legislation: Executive Summary," Congressional Research Service, Nov. 14, 2012, p. 8, www.fas.org/sgp/crs/misc/RL32842.pdf.

18. "Firearms and Violence: A Critical Review," National Research Council of the National Academies, December 2004, p. 3, www.nap.edu/openbook.php?record_id=10881&page=2.

19. Zachary Roth, "Blackout: How the NRA suppressed gun violence research," MSNBC, Jan. 14, 2013, http://tv.msnbc.com/2013/01/14/blackout-how-the-nra-suppressed-gun-violence-research.

20. Jordan Yerman, "Jacob Tyler Roberts IDed as Oregon mall shooter: Photos," examiner.com, Dec. 12, 2012, www.examiner.com/article/jacob-tyler-roberts-ided-as-oregon-mall-shooter-photos.

21. "Mass Shooting Incidents in America (1984-2012)," Citizens Crime Commission of New York City, www.nycrimecommission.org/initiative1-shootings.php.

22. *Ibid.*

23. "Feinstein Introduces Bill on Assault Weapons, High-Capacity Magazines," The Office of Senator Dianne Feinstein, U.S. Senate, Jan. 24, 2013, www.feinstein.senate.gov/public/index.cfm/press-releases?ID=5dffbf07-d8e5-42aa-9f22-0743368dd754.

24. Eric Lichtblau, "N.R.A. Leaders Stand Firm Against Gun Restrictions," *The New York Times*, Dec. 23, 2012, http://thecaucus.blogs.nytimes.com/2012/12/23/n-r-a-leaders-defiant-in-television-appearances; "Wayne LaPierre Testimony Before the U.S. Senate Committee," National Rifle Association, Jan. 31, 2013, http://home.nra.org/classic.aspx/blog/350.

25. Christopher S. Koper, "An Updated Assessment of the Federal Assault Weapons Ban: Impacts on Gun Markets and Gun Violence, 1994-2003," U.S. Department of Justice, June 2004, p. 1, www.sas.upenn.edu/jerrylee/research/aw_final2004.pdf.

26. David S. Fallis and James V. Grimaldi, "In Virginia, high-yield clip seizures rise," *The Washington Post*, Jan. 23, 2011, www.washingtonpost.com/wp-dyn/content/article/2011/01/22/AR2011012204046.html.

27. Koper, *op. cit.*

28. "Assault Weapons Ban of 2013," The Office of Senator Dianne Feinstein, U.S. Senate, Jan. 24, 2013, www.feinstein.senate.gov/public/index.cfm/assault-weapons-ban-summary.

29. Daniel W. Webster, *et al.*, "The Case for Gun Policy Reforms in America," Johns Hopkins Center for Gun Policy and Research, October 2012, p. 10, www.jhsph.edu/research/centers-and-institutes/

johns-hopkins-center-for-gun-policy-and-research/ publications/WhitePaper102512_CGPR.pdf.

30. For background see Kenneth Jost, "Gun Rights Debates," *CQ Researcher*, Oct. 31, 2008, pp. 889-912; updated July 22, 2010.

31. Philip J. Cook and Jens Ludwig, "Guns in America: Results of a Comprehensive National Survey on Firearms Ownership and Use," Police Foundation, 1996, p. 27, www.policefoundation.org/content/ guns-america.

32. "Keystone of Obama gun control plan gains steam as Dem, GOP senators seek background check pact," The Associated Press (*The Washington Post*), Feb. 8, 2013.

33. Daniel W. Webster, *et al.*, "Preventing the Diversion of Guns to Criminals through Effective Firearm Sales Laws," *Reducing Gun Violence in America: Informing Policy with Evidence and Analysis* (2013), p. 110.

34. "Wayne LaPierre Testimony Before the U.S. Senate Committee," *op. cit.*

35. Philip J. Cook and Jens Ludwig, "The Limited Impact of the Brady Act: Evaluation and Implications," *Reducing Gun Violence in America: Informing Policy with Evidence and Analysis* (2013), pp. 22-25.

36. Wintemute, *op. cit.*, p. 398.

37. "Attorney General's Concealed Carry Report Shows Record Number of Licenses Issued in 2012," press release, Office of Ohio Attorney General, Feb. 27, 2013, www.ohioattorneygeneral.gov/Media/News-Releases/February-2013/Attorney-General's-Concealed-Carry-Report-Shows-Re.

38. "Guns in Public Places: The Increasing Threat of Hidden Guns in America," Law Center to Prevent Gun Violence," July 1, 2011, http://smartgunlaws. org/guns-in-public-places-the-increasing-threat-of-hidden-guns-in-america.

39. "NRA EVP and CEO Wayne LaPierre — Speech to CPAC 2011," YouTube, Feb. 10, 2011, www.you tube.com/watch?v=Bg_uy9_2a1U.

40. "Gun Control: States' Laws and Requirements for Concealed Carry Permits Vary across the Nation," U.S. Government Accountability Office, July 2012, pp. 75-76, www.gao.gov/assets/600/592552.pdf.

41. "Firearms and Violence: A Critical Review," *op. cit.*

42. Abhay Aneja, John J. Donohue III and Alexandria Zhang, "The Impact of Right-To-Carry Laws and the NRC Report: Lessons for the Empirical Evaluation of Law and Policy," Social Sciences Research Network, June 29, 2010, http://papers .ssrn.com/sol3/papers.cfm?abstract_id=1632599.

43. Ian Ayres and John J. Donohue III, "Shooting Down the 'More Guns, Less Crime' Hypothesis," *Stanford Law Review*, April 2003, pp. 1204-1205, http://islandia.law .yale.edu/ayers/Ayres_Donohue_article.pdf.

44. "Gun Control: States' Laws and Requirements for Concealed Carry Permits Vary across the Nation," *op. cit.*, p. 19.

45. Craig R. Whitney, *Living with Guns: A Liberal's Case for the Second Amendment* (2012), pp. 45-47.

46. Adam Winkler, *Gun Fight: The Battle Over the Right to Bear Arms in America* (2011), p. 116.

47. *Ibid.*

48. Saul Cornell, *A Well Regulated Militia: The Founding Fathers and the Origins of Gun Control in America* (2006), p. 4.

49. Clayton E. Cramer, *Concealed Weapon Laws of the Early Republic: Dueling, Southern Violence, and Moral Reform* (1999), pp. 2-3.

50. *Ibid.*, pp. 6-7.

51. Cornell, *op. cit.*, p. 4.

52. *Ibid.*, pp. 142-143.

53. "A Brief History of the NRA," www.nrahq.org/ history.asp.

54. Winkler, *op. cit.*, pp. 208-209.

55. Sam B. Warner, "The Uniform Pistol Act," *Journal of Criminal Law and Criminology*, November-December 1938, p. 530.

56. Winkler, *op. cit.*, pp. 203-204.

57. "Hearings Before the Committee on Ways and Means," House of Representatives, Seventy-third Congress, on H.R. 9066, April and May 1934, p. 53, www.keepandbeararms.com/nra/nfa.htm#KarlT.

58. Osha Gray Davidson, *Under Fire: the NRA & the Battle for Gun Control* (1993), p. 29.

59. Whitney, *op. cit.*, p. 3.

60. *Ibid.*, pp. 5-6.

61. Davidson, *op. cit.*, p. 30.

62. *Ibid.*, pp. 30-31, 36.

63. Winkler, *op. cit.*, pp. 71-72.

64. "Personal Guns and the Second Amendment," *The New York Times*, Dec. 17, 2012, www.nytimes.com/2012/12/18/opinion/the-gun-challenge-second-amendment.html.

65. Thomas Kaplan, "Sweeping Limits on Guns Become Law in New York," *The New York Times*, Jan. 15, 2013, www.nytimes.com/2013/01/16/nyregion/tougher-gun-law-in-new-york.html.

66. *Ibid.*

67. "Documenting County and Town resolutions on the NY SAFE act," NY SAFE Resolutions, www.nysaferesolutions.com.

68. Fredric U. Dicker, "Hit us with your best shot, Andy!" *New York Post*, Jan. 21, 2013, www.nypost.com/p/news/local/hit_us_with_your_best_shot_andy_5rxZg0gYBJJhkLBtiTPMfJ.

69. "Private Sales Policy Summary," Law Center to Prevent Gun Violence, http://smartgunlaws.org/private-sales-policy-summary; "Licensing of Gun Owners and Purchasers Policy Summary," Law Center to Prevent Gun Violence, http://smartgunlaws.org/licensing-of-gun-owners-purchasers-policy-summary; "Summary of State Assault Weapon Laws," Law Center to Prevent Gun Violence, http://smartgunlaws.org/assault-weapons-policy-summary; "Large Capacity Ammunition Magazines Policy Summary," Law Center to Prevent Gun Violence, http://smartgunlaws.org/large-capacity-ammunition-magazines-policy-summary.

70. For background, see Kathy Koch, "Zero Tolerance," *CQ Researcher*, March 10, 2000, pp. 185-208. Also see Kathy Koch, "School Violence," *CQ Researcher*, Oct. 9, 1998, pp. 881-904.

71. Amanda Paulson, "Gun-control bills pass Colorado House: Was Aurora a tipping point?" *The Christian Science Monitor*, Feb. 20, 2013, www.csmonitor.com/USA/2013/0220/Gun-control-bills-pass-Colorado-House-Was-Aurora-a-tipping-point-video.

72. Laura Nahmias, "Malloy Charts New Course on Gun Laws," *The Wall Street Journal*, Feb. 21, 2013, http://online.wsj.com/article/SB10001424127887324048904578316573460812236.html.

73. "2nd Amendment Preservation Act: 2013 Legislation," Tenth Amendment Center, http://tracking.tenthamendmentcenter.com/2ndamendment.

74. John Hancock and Brad Cooper, "Legislators in Missouri, Kansas and elsewhere look to nullify federal laws," *The Kansas City Star*, Jan. 23, 2013, http://midwestdemocracy.com/articles/states-looking-to-nullify-the-feds.

75. Michael Cooper and Mary Williams Walsh, "Buying a Gun? States Consider Insurance Rule," *The New York Times*, Feb. 21, 2013, www.nytimes.com/2013/02/22/us/in-gun-debate-a-bigger-role-seen-for-insurers.html.

76. *Ibid.*

77. "Gun Control: Key Data Points from Pew Research," Pew Research Center, Feb. 7, 2013, www.pewresearch.org/2013/02/07/gun-control-key-data-points-from-pew-research.

78. Peter Grier, "Which gun control measures are gaining momentum in Congress?" *The Christian Science Monitor*, Feb. 19, 2013, www.csmonitor.com/USA/DC-Decoder/Decoder-Wire/2013/0219/Which-gun-control-measures-are-gaining-momentum-in-Congress-video.

79. Alexander Bolton, "Senate Dems face gun-control dilemma," *The Hill*, Feb. 6, 2013, http://thehill.com/homenews/senate/281343-senate-democrats-face-gun-dilemma.

80. Grier, *op. cit.*

# BIBLIOGRAPHY

## Selected Sources

### Books

**Cornell, Saul, *A Well Regulated Militia: The Founding Fathers and the Origins of Gun Control in America*, Oxford University Press, 2006.**
A constitutional historian examines the origins of the Second Amendment and the ensuing constitutional debate.

Webster, Daniel W., and Jon S. Vernick, eds., *Reducing Gun Violence in America: Informing Policy with Evidence and Analysis*, The Johns Hopkins University Press, *2013*.
Leading experts summarize relevant research and recommend policies to reduce gun violence, including expanding background checks to private firearms sales and prohibiting more categories of criminals from possessing firearms.

Whitney, Craig R., *Living with Guns: A Liberal's Case for the Second Amendment*, PublicAffairs, *2012*.
A journalist explores the history behind today's polarized debate about guns and concludes that both more guns and more gun control would help reduce violence.

Winkler, Adam, *Gun Fight: The Battle Over the Right to Bear Arms in America*, W.W. Norton & Co., Inc., *2011*.
An expert in constitutional law examines America's four-century political battle over gun control and the right to bear arms.

## Articles

Dicker, Fredric U., "Hit us with your best shot, Andy!" *New York Post*, Jan. 21, 2013, www.nypost.com/p/news/local/hit_us_with_your_best_shot_andy_5rxZg0gYBJJhkLBtiTPMfJ.
Gun-rights advocates and gun dealers are organizing a boycott of New York's new gun-control law.

Gerth, Joseph, "Mitch McConnell vows to block President Obama's gun control initiatives," *The Courier-Journal*, Jan. 20, 2013, www.courier-journal.com/article/20130119/NEWS010605/301190088/Mitch-McConnell-vows-block-President-Obama-s-gun-control-initiatives?nclick_check=1.
In a taped call to Kentucky gun owners, the Senate minority leader promises to block the president's gun-control proposals.

Grier, Peter, "Which gun control measures are gaining momentum in Congress?" *The Christian Science Monitor*, Feb. 19, 2013, www.csmonitor.com/USA/DC-Decoder/Decoder-Wire/2013/0219/Which-gun-control-measures-are-gaining-momentum-in-Congress-video.

Support in the Senate is growing for expanded background checks, but backing for the more controversial ban on assault weapons is slim.

Redden, Molly, "Meet John Lott, the Man Who Wants to Arm America's Teachers," *The New Republic*, Dec. 19, 2012, p. 1, www.newrepublic.com/blog/plank/111263/meet-john-lott-the-man-who-wants-to-teach ers-carry-guns.
Economist John Lott argues that carrying concealed weapons makes communities safer.

Roth, Zachary, "Blackout: How the NRA suppressed gun violence research," MSNBC, Jan. 14, 2013, http://tv.msnbc.com/2013/01/14/blackout-how-the-nra-suppressed-gun-violence-research.
In the 1990s, the National Rifle Association helped insert language into federal legislation restricting government-sponsored research on gun violence.

## Reports & Studies

"Firearms and Violence: A Critical Review," National Research Council of the National Academies, December 2004, www.nap.edu/openbook.php?record_id=10881&page=2.
A prominent research council finds that reliable data and research on gun violence and gun control are lacking.

"Gun Control: States' Laws and Requirements for Concealed Carry Permits Vary Across the Nation," U.S. Government Accountability Office, July 2012, pp. 75-76, www.gao.gov/assets/600/592552.pdf.
An independent congressional agency evaluates states' concealed-carry laws.

"Guns in Public Places: The Increasing Threat of Hidden Guns in America," Law Center to Prevent Gun Violence, July 1, 2011, http://smartgunlaws.org/guns-in-public-places-the-increasing-threat-of-hidden-guns-in-america.
A gun-control advocacy group analyzes states' concealed-carry laws and concludes they lead to increased violence.

Koper, Christopher S., "An Updated Assessment of the Federal Assault Weapons Ban: Impacts on Gun Markets and Gun Violence, 1994-2003," U.S. Department of Justice, June 2004, www.sas.upenn.edu/jerrylee/research/aw_final2004.pdf.

A criminology professor finds that the federal ban on assault weapons had a negligible impact on crime.

**Webster, Daniel W., et al., "The Case for Gun Policy Reforms in America," Johns Hopkins Center for Gun Policy and Research, October 2012, p. 10, www.jhsph** .edu/research/centers-and-institutes/johns-hopkins-center-for-gun-policy-and-research/publications/WhitePaper102512_CGPR.pdf.

A group of academic researchers argues for gun-control legislation.

---

# For More Information

**Brady Campaign to Prevent Gun Violence**, 1225 Eye St., N.W., Suite 1100, Washington, DC 20005; 202-289-7319; www.bradycampaign.org. Education and advocacy group that works to pass federal and state laws to reduce gun violence.

**Gun Owners of America**, 800 Forbes Pl., Suite 102, Springfield, VA 22151; 703-321-8585; http://gunowners.org. Lobbying organization that works to preserve Second Amendment rights of gun owners.

**Harvard Injury Control Research Center**, 677 Huntington Ave., Boston, MA 02115; 617-432-8080; www.hsph.harvard.edu/hicrc. Academic research center that studies the causes of injury, as well as intervention strategies and policies.

**Johns Hopkins Center for Gun Policy and Research**, Bloomberg School of Public Health, 615 N. Wolfe St., Baltimore, MD 21205; 410-955-6878; www.jhsph.edu/research/centers-and-institutes/johns-hopkins-center-for-gun-policy-and-research. Academic research center that works to reduce gun-related injuries and deaths.

**Law Center to Prevent Gun Violence**, 268 Bush St., #555, San Francisco, CA 94104; 415-433-2062; http://smartgunlaws.org. National law center that promotes gun-control legislation and policies.

**Mayors Against Illegal Guns**, Mayor of New York City, City Hall, 260 Broadway, New York, NY 10007; 212-788-2958; www.mayorsagainstillegalguns.org. Coalition of 800 mayors supporting policies and laws to keep guns away from criminals.

**National Rifle Association of America**, 11250 Waples Mill Rd., Fairfax, VA 22030; 800-672-3888; http://nra.org. Membership organization that promotes gun ownership rights and trains firearm users.

**National Shooting Sports Foundation**, 11 Mile Hill Rd., Newtown, CT 06470; 203-426-1320; www.nssf.org. Trade association whose members include firearms manufacturers, distributors, retailers, shooting ranges, clubs and publishers.

**Second Amendment Foundation**, 12500 N.E. 10th Pl., Bellevue, WA 98005; 425-454-7012; www.saf.org. Advocacy group that promotes gun ownership rights through education and legal action.

**Tenth Amendment Center**; www.tenthamendmentcenter.com. Think tank advocating states' rights and the decentralization of federal government power.

**Violence Policy Center**, 1730 Rhode Island Ave., N.W., Suite 1014, Washington, DC 20036; 202-822-8200; www.vpc.org. Advocacy and research organization working to reduce gun violence.

# 15

# Mental Health Policy

Barbara Mantel

Janett Massolo of Reno, Nev., holds a photo of her daughter Shannon on March 22, 2013. Using her father's handgun, Shannon committed suicide when she was 15 years old. Nine out of 10 people who take their own lives have a diagnosable mental illness, most often depression or a substance-abuse disorder. More than 38,000 people committed suicide in 2010, nearly half with guns.

From *CQ Researcher*,
May 10, 2013.

Four months after the massacre of six adults and 20 first-graders in Newtown, Conn., Senate Majority Leader Harry Reid, D-Nev., took to the floor of the chamber in early April to make a deeply personal plea for gun control legislation.

"Sometimes people in a fit of passion will purchase a handgun to do bad things with it . . . even as my dad did — killed himself," said Reid.[1]

More than 38,000 people committed suicide in 2010, the latest year of available data, nearly half with guns. Nine in 10 who take their lives have a diagnosable mental illness, most often depression or a substance abuse disorder, according to the National Institute of Mental Health (NIMH), a government research institute in Bethesda, Md.[2]

After Newtown, Congress swiftly held hearings on gun control and on mental health care, despite the fact that the mentally ill account for a tiny fraction of gun crimes. While mental health advocates, researchers and scientists were wary about tying discussions about the fragmented mental health care system to the gun control debate, they welcomed the chance to advocate for better access to diagnosis, treatment and support services.

"The burden of mental illness is enormous," Thomas Insel, director of the NIMH, told lawmakers a month after Newtown. An estimated 58 million American adults, or one in four, suffer from a diagnosable mental disorder in any given year, and it takes a decade, on average, for them to make contact with a mental health professional, said Insel. More than 11 million of those adults suffer from serious mental illness, including schizophrenia, bipolar

## Government Funds Most Mental Health Treatment

Mental health spending in 2005, the latest year for which data are available, totaled $113 billion, about 60 percent of it paid by Medicaid, Medicare or other government sources. Private insurers paid nearly 30 percent. Mental health accounted for about 6 percent of total health spending.

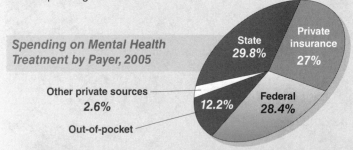

*Spending on Mental Health Treatment by Payer, 2005*

State 29.8%

Private insurance 27%

Other private sources 2.6%

Out-of-pocket

12.2%

Federal 28.4%

*Source:* "National Expenditures for Mental Health Services and Substance Abuse Treatment, 1986-2005," Substance Abuse and Mental Health Services Administration, Tables 74 & 75, pp. 201-202, http://hcfgkc.org/sites/default/files/documents/MHUS_2010_part3_508.pdf

disorder and major depression, and for them the average delay in treatment is five years. "That is five years of increased risk for using potentially life-threatening, self-administered treatments, such as legal or illicit substances, and even death," said Insel.[3]

Experts disagree on how to fix the country's broken mental health system. Proposed legislation to improve access by pumping more federal Medicaid money into community mental health centers, which treat more than 8 million low-income people a year, has some bipartisan support in Congress. But calls by families for states to make it easier to force the mentally ill into treatment are generating spirited opposition from civil liberties groups. Meanwhile critics complain that the American Psychiatric Association's latest manual of psychiatric disorders, released this month, will do nothing to stop over-diagnosis of mental illness.

The bipartisan Excellence in Mental Health Act would set new standards of care at community mental health centers. It includes a list of mandated services and requires better integration of treatment for mental illness and substance abuse; provides more Medicaid dollars for centers meeting those standards and funds the modernization of existing centers and construction of new ones.

Sen. Debbie Stabenow, D-Mich., author of the Senate version of the bill, estimated that it would allow community mental health centers to treat an additional 1.5 million people each year.[4]

"As we've listened to people on all sides of the gun debate, they've all talked about the fact that we need to address mental health treatment, and that's what this does," Stabenow said in mid-April as the Senate prepared to vote on the bill as an amendment to gun control legislation.[5] But gun control legislation failed, and the vote on the Excellence in Mental Health Act was shelved.

"Today, our nation's community mental health centers are simply stretched too thin and struggling to provide essential services," said Linda Rosenberg, president and CEO of the Washington-based National Council for Community Behavioral Healthcare, a nonprofit association of 2,000 providers that supports the bill.

But Rosenberg criticized President Obama, whose fiscal 2014 budget, submitted to Congress in April, did not include funding for the proposed legislation. "I am extremely disappointed that the White House has not embraced the Excellence Act, which would increase access and early intervention in communities around the country," said Rosenberg.[6]

The White House budget does call for $130 million in funding for other mental health proposals, including $55 million to train teachers and other adults to recognize the signs of mental illness in students and to help them refer students, when necessary, for services. The proposed budget also includes $50 million in tuition support to help train an additional 5,000 social workers, counselors and other mental health professionals to address critical shortages in many parts of the country.[7]

Some professional groups said the money was welcome but far too little. "While we applaud President Obama's budget proposal, it doesn't come close to restoring the drastic cuts in funds for mental health services that have been imposed over the last several years," said

Robert Cabaj, chair of the Council on Advocacy and Government Relations at the American Psychiatric Association, a medical society in Arlington, Va.[8]

Spending on mental health care totaled $113 billion in 2005, before adjustment for inflation, according to the latest available data, about twice the amount spent a dozen years earlier. The money went mostly toward prescription drugs and outpatient treatment. Nevertheless mental health spending as a share of total health care outlays has been slipping; it was 6.1 percent in 2005, down from 7.2 percent in 1986.

Private insurance has picked up an increasing portion of mental health expenditures, accounting for 27 percent in 2005, up about 6 percentage points from a dozen years earlier. Patients' out-of-pocket expenditures remained at roughly 12 percent, and the federal government's share was not much changed either, at about 28 percent. States' share of mental health spending, however, dropped from 35 percent in 1993 to 30 percent in 2005 and is likely to have dipped further since.[9]

The deep recession that officially began in December 2007 and ended in June 2009 took a huge toll on state finances, and states cut approximately $5 billion in public mental health spending from 2009 through 2013, according to the National Association of State Mental Health Program Directors in Alexandria, Va. Over the same period, demand for publicly financed inpatient and outpatient mental health services rose 10 percent.

"Those cuts have had a devastating impact on access to services for people," says Ronald Honberg, national director for policy and legal affairs at the National Alliance on Mental Illness (NAMI), an advocacy group in Arlington, Va. "It's helped to further precipitate a system that is responding to emergencies rather than doing ongoing care and prevention."

The number of state psychiatric hospital beds fell by about 4,500 — 9 percent of total capacity — between 2009 and 2012. Outpatient services have suffered as well. "In my own state of Arizona, virtually all state-only funded behavioral health services* have been dramatically reduced or eliminated over the last few years," Laura Nelson, chief medical officer of the Arizona Department

of Health, told Congress last year. "Over 4,600 children have lost behavioral health services. Nearly 6,300 adults lost access to substance abuse treatment services.[10]

"Due to mental health cuts, we are simply increasing emergency department costs, increasing acute care costs and adding to the caseloads in our criminal and juvenile justice systems and correction systems," said Nelson. For example, in a survey of more than 6,000 hospital emergency departments, 70 percent reported boarding psychiatric patients for hours or days, and 10 percent reported boarding such patients for weeks while staff looked for psychiatric beds.[11] And according to a recent report, the percentage of inmates in New York City jails with mental health problems rose from 24 percent in 2005 to 33 percent in 2011.[12]

Sheriff Brian Gootkin, who supervises 48 deputies in Gallatin County, Mont. — an area twice the size of Rhode Island — blamed reductions in community mental health funding for a significant jump in psychiatric emergencies that his force must handle. "Every deputy that is diverted to the Montana State Hospital or even to a local hospital is not on patrol maintaining public order and deterring crime," Gootkin complained.[13]

The 2010 Patient Protection and Affordable Care Act — the sweeping health care system overhaul championed by Obama — will add to the demand for mental health services as it extends health coverage to more than 30 million Americans, including an estimated 6 million to 10 million with mental illness.

Against that backdrop, here are some of the issues that lawmakers, advocates, mental health professionals and people with mental illness and their families are debating:

### Should states make it easier to force the mentally ill into treatment?

On March 19, 2005, Roger Scanlan of Allentown, Pa., diagnosed with schizophrenia and off his medications, killed his parents with a knife and then took his own life by cutting his throat. Five years later, his brother, Michael, testified on behalf of proposed legislation in Pennsylvania to make it easier for courts to order outpatient treatment of the mentally ill.

"I always knew when he wasn't taking his meds," Scanlan said of his brother. "He would become very passionate about government, religion, and then he would

---

*Behavioral health services refers to mental health as well as substance abuse services.

believe that he was the second coming of Christ or Moses or some other biblical figure."

"Everyone from crisis, the Allentown Police Department, his doctors, they all knew the pattern. We, as a family, we couldn't intervene to help him. We couldn't get him off the street. We were told that Roger had rights," said Scanlan. "What rights did my mother and father have?"[14]

The legislation died in committee in 2010. But since the Newtown massacre, families and a prominent advocacy group favoring easing rules for court-ordered treatment have renewed their campaign, testifying before Congress and at state forums. Civil liberties groups and other mental health advocates are strongly opposed, saying patients should not be forced into treatment.

Forty-four states allow courts to order outpatient treatment of mentally ill people who have a history of not complying with treatment, which is sometimes referred to as assisted outpatient treatment or AOT. Most states require the person to be an imminent danger to self or others. For example, in Pennsylvania, a court can't order treatment unless the person committed or tried to commit serious harm to self or others within the past 30 days.[15]

But 10 states have less stringent criteria. For example, New York's Kendra's Law, named for a young woman pushed to her death in front of a subway train in 1999 by a schizophrenic man off his medications, does not require evidence of recent harm. A New York court can order outpatient treatment for someone who is not complying with mental health treatment if non-compliance led to hospitalization or confinement in a mental health unit in a jail or prison at least twice in the last three years or to serious or attempted serious violent behavior in the past four years.[16]

Doris Fuller, executive director of the Treatment Advocacy Center, a nonprofit based in Arlington, Va., wants states to model their laws on New York's. Making it easier for courts to order outpatient treatment would help the small subset of people known in the mental health world as "frequent flyers," says Fuller. "Many of them don't acknowledge that they are ill or they don't know that they are ill," she says. Court-ordered treatment, which is monitored and carries penalties for failing to take required medication, is needed to stabilize people until they voluntarily comply with treatment, she says.

Many states rarely use their court-ordered outpatient treatment laws, and Fuller wants that to change as well. "California has a law similar to Kendra's Law, but there are 58 counties in California and at this point, only one county has opted in and another has a pilot program," says Fuller. The same is true in Texas, she says, where courts in Dallas County have started using the state's outpatient treatment law more frequently. "But then you have other counties that aren't using it for whatever reason," she continues. "The local mental health officials haven't gotten on board, [and] there are concerns about what it will cost."

Patient-rights groups strongly object to looser criteria for or greater use of court-ordered outpatient treatment. "These laws [such as New York's Kendra's Law] are based on speculation," says Debbie Plotnick, senior director of state policy at Mental Health America, a national advocacy group for people with mental illness based in Alexandria, Va. Mental health disorders are episodic, she says. "People could have been in the hospital within the past three years and doing very well now in the community. You cannot say they are likely to be a danger to self or others."

The problem is not that the seriously mentally ill are refusing treatment, say Plotnick and others. "We have interventions that are effective for the people that the Treatment Advocacy Center claims cannot be reached. The problem is that those interventions are not available for those who need them," because of a lack of insurance and funding, says Ira Burnim, legal director at the Washington-based Judge David L. Bazelon Center for Mental Health Law.

These interventions include support provided by trained peers (people living successfully with mental illness); supported housing staffed by mental health workers; and so-called assertive community treatment or ACT, in which a team consisting of a psychiatrist, nurse, social worker, employment counselor and a case worker provides highly individualized services to an individual at home.

"Another missing element of community care that is sorely lacking around the country is the presence of a crisis center that can take people in for brief periods of time, arrange hospitalization if needed and is available 24/7," says Michael Hogan, New York state's commissioner of mental health until retiring late last year.

But Fuller says making treatment and support services more widely available is not enough if people in crisis refuse to use them. "You could literally park people who are actively psychotic on the front door of the best service center in the country, and if they don't think they are sick, they are not going to [voluntarily] walk through that door and access those services."

Plotnick rejects that argument. "I'm saying we should give people services upstream before they reach a crisis. We have to help them before they are in that stage," she says.

The largest and latest study of the impact of Kendra's Law was published four years ago. It compared people's experience under court-ordered outpatient treatment with their prior experience, controlling for other factors.[17]

"Overall, under assisted outpatient treatment, people were less likely to get hospitalized, more likely to receive appropriate medications for their condition, less likely to be arrested, and generally functioned better, with no apparent effect of feeling coerced," as long as individuals were under court order for at least six months, says Marvin Swartz, a psychiatry professor at Duke University and the study's principal investigator. The study found that these improvements were sustained once the court order expired.

"It makes sense because a Kendra's Law order pushes you to the top of the line," says Burnim. "They got better because they got access to much better services, not because of the court order."

In fact, unlike other states with assisted outpatient treatment, New York created a new stream of funding to administer Kendra's Law and also plowed money into expanding services for those who have a serious mental illness.

But Swartz says his study showed that the court order itself conferred benefits. In one analysis, the researchers looked at people who were receiving intensive treatment from a team of professionals without a court order and with a court order. "We found that people under court order did better," says Swartz.

Hogan says there could be another explanation. Under court-ordered outpatient treatment, government watchers monitor the professional team delivering services, and, as a result, the quality of the treatment may have simply been better, he says.

AP Photo/Charlie Riedel

Caseworker Cheryl Boone talks to a client during a therapy session at the Johnson County Mental Health Center in Shawnee, Kan., on Jan. 23, 2013. Proposed legislation to improve access to mental health treatment calls for pumping more federal Medicaid money into community mental health centers.

## Does the medical profession define mental illness too broadly?

No laboratory tests exist to help mental health professionals diagnose and treat mental illness. That absence is a huge disadvantage for psychiatry, according to Allen Frances, former chair of the psychiatry department at Duke University, and "it means that all of our diagnoses are now based on subjective judgments that are inherently fallible and prey to capricious change."[18] As a result, the psychiatric profession has cast the net too broadly, capturing both those with mental disorders and those without, he says.

Frances is an outspoken critic of the forthcoming fifth edition of the *Diagnostic and Statistical Manual of Mental Disorders* (*DSM*), to be published this month by the American Psychiatric Association (APA). First published in 1952, the *DSM* classifies mental disorders,

## Cost Deters Many From Treatment

About 11 million adults age 18 or older said in 2011 they did not receive treatment for a mental health problem. Many said treatment was unaffordable or that their insurance was inadequate. Nearly 30 percent said they could handle their problems without treatment.

**Reasons for Not Receiving Mental Health Treatment, 2011**

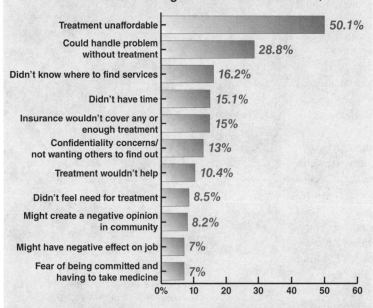

*Source:* "Results From the 2011 National Survey on Drug Use and Health: Mental Health Findings," Substance Abuse and Mental Health Services Administration, 2012, www.samhsa.gov/data/NSDUH/ 2k11MH_Findingsand DetTables/2K11MHFR/NSDUH mhfr2011.htm

influence has grown. It "shapes who will receive what treatment," said Mark Olfson, a Columbia University psychiatry professor not involved in the revision. "Even seemingly subtle changes to the criteria can have substantial effects on patterns of care."[20] There have been plenty of not-so-subtle changes over the years, including an expansion of the number of diagnoses from 106 in the first edition to 297 in *DSM-4*.[21]

Critics of the version due to be published this month come from outside and inside the profession. Frances, in fact, was the chair of the task force for *DSM-4*, published in 1994. He points to a new diagnosis included in the *DSM-5* as just one example of what he says is wrong.

It's called Disruptive Mood Disregulation Disorder (DMDD), and it's an attempt to reduce the number of young children who increasingly are diagnosed with bipolar disorder and medicated with powerful antipsychotic drugs. DMDD is a diagnosis for irritable children who have been having "severe recurrent temper outbursts that are grossly out of proportion in intensity or duration to the situation."[22]

describing their symptoms and listing the number and duration of symptoms needed to make a diagnosis. The task force overseeing the newest iteration, the *DSM-5*, "gave their experts great freedom, and the experts have used that freedom to do what experts always do, which is try to expand their area of interest," says Frances.

But the manual's supporters reject that view. "We developed *DSM-5* by utilizing the best experts in the field and extensive reviews of the scientific literature and original research, and we have produced a manual that best represents the current science and will be useful to clinicians and the patients they serve," said Dilip Jeste, APA president and chief of geriatric psychiatry at the University of California, San Diego.[19]

The diagnostic manual has drawn criticism since its origin and has become increasingly controversial as its

"The threshold for DMDD is high and children must meet several diagnostic criteria," David Kupfer, chair of the *DSM-5* task force and head of the psychiatry department at the University of Pittsburgh, says in an email. The outbursts must occur three times a week on average and have been present for at least a year.

But "in real life, it will be kids with temper tantrums who will get the diagnosis," says Frances. "So instead of reducing the risk of excessive medication, I think this greatly increases it. If you want to attack the excessive diagnosis of bipolar disorder in children, you should have big warnings in the bipolar section that this is being terribly over-diagnosed in kids, explain why and explain what should be done."

Several other changes to the diagnostic manual also are raising hackles. In the *DSM-4*, an individual grieving the loss of a loved one could not be diagnosed with major depressive disorder (MDD) unless symptoms persist for at least two months. For all other individuals, the threshold for a diagnosis of MDD is lower. Symptoms, such as sadness, loss of interest, loss of appetite, trouble sleeping and reduced energy, need last only two weeks before a diagnosis can be made.

The *DSM-5* removes the exclusion for bereavement. Its elimination "shows that psychiatry has no idea how to define what's normal, what's abnormal and how to differentiate between them," said Allan Horowitz, author of *The Loss of Sadness* and a sociology professor at Rutgers University in New Jersey. "One of the essential ways we show our humanity is to grieve after the death of an intimate. Amazingly, psychiatry now sees this as a mental disorder."[23]

Psychiatrist Ronald Pies said such concern is misplaced. "Grieving persons are not immune to major depressive disorder, and, indeed, bereavement is a common trigger" for it, said Pies, a professor at Tufts University School of Medicine in Boston. Many mood disorder specialists think "the risk of overlooking MDD, with its high potential for suicide, far outweighs the less serious risk of 'over-calling' MDD," said Pies. Besides, most experienced clinicians can tell the difference between grief and major depression, he added.[24]

But often, primary care physicians and pediatricians are making the diagnosis, not specialists with years of training in mental illness, who are in short supply. "Primary care physicians look at the *DSM* with confusion," says Peter Jensen, a child psychiatrist at the Mayo Clinic in Rochester, Minn. "If they use the *DSM* carefully, it will help them not treat someone as having Attention Deficit Disorder when they might actually have anxiety or depression.[25] But if they're rushed, they can't do that, and that's why we see over-diagnosis and over-treatment."

The *DSM* is not the problem, he says. "The scientists who come up with the criteria have really struggled to make them as tight as possible," Jensen says.

## Do insurers treat mental and physical health equally?

When Congress passed the Mental Health Parity and Addiction Equity Act in 2008, it required group insurance plans sponsored by employers with 50 or more workers to put coverage of mental illness and substance abuse on an equal footing with physical health.

But the Obama administration has yet to release the final rules implementing the law. "It took 12 years to pass that parity act, and four years later we still have no rules and therefore no enforcement," said James Ramstad, a former Republican congressman from Minnesota and supporter of the bill. "It's unconscionable."[26]

"A law without rules isn't worth the paper it's written on, and what that means is that insurance companies can continue to do business as usual," said Patrick Kennedy, a former Democratic congressman from Rhode Island and another of the law's champions.[27]

At a congressional budget hearing in April, U.S. Department of Health and Human Services (HHS) Secretary Kathleen Sebelius had only this to say: "We are committed to finalizing the rule this year and are in the process of doing just that."[28]

"Insurance plans have been working hard on implementation," based on an interim final rule the administration released in 2010, says Susan Pisano, spokeswoman for the Washington-based America's Health Insurance Plans, the industry trade association. The industry supported the parity law, she says.

The law is supposed to ensure that insurance plans don't impose financial requirements — deductibles, copayments, out-of-pocket payments and co-insurance — for mental health care and substance abuse treatment that are more restrictive than for physical health benefits. Parity also applies to treatment limitations.[29] For example, if an insurance plan doesn't limit the number of hospital days or out-patient visits for most physical care, it can't place such limits on mental health care.

Mental health advocates say insurers have done a pretty good job of getting those numerical limits in line but are falling down when it comes to scope of services. "We still continue to see wholesale exclusion of benefits on the behavioral health side that we don't see on the medical/surgical side," says Andrew Sperling, director of legislative advocacy for the National Alliance on Mental Illness. For example, plans will cover rehabilitation after a hospital stay for a stroke, but many won't cover intensive day-therapy after hospitalization for substance abuse, he says.

"We believe this violates the spirit of the law," Sperling says. The Obama administration interim final rule mentions parity for scope of services but has no binding requirements. Sperling hopes the final rule will make such requirements clear.

The interim rule also states that insurance plans must manage utilization of benefits evenly across mental health and physical health care. For example, if a plan does not require prior authorization for medical and surgical admissions, then it can't require prior authorization for mental health admissions, advocates say.

The New York State Psychiatric Association, along with three individuals, filed a class action lawsuit in March against UnitedHealth Group, one of the country's largest health insurers, charging that the company "improperly processed and discouraged claims for mental health and substance abuse," says New York attorney Brian Hufford, the lead lawyer in the case. At its heart is a charge that the insurer requires pre-authorization for psychotherapy sessions but not for most outpatient medical care.

"The only explanation I've seen is that for certain ancillary services, like physical therapy, they require pre-authorization, and so they say they can do it for mental health care," says Hufford. But mental health is not an ancillary service like physical therapy, he says.

"We are committed to helping people with mental health issues reach long-term recovery," UnitedHealth Group said in a statement. "We have received the complaint and are currently reviewing it."[30]

Comparing utilization review criteria across mental and physical health sounds straightforward, but it's not as simple as comparing copays, says Pamela Greenberg, president and CEO of the Washington-based Association for Behavioral Health and Wellness, the trade association for the specialized companies that insurers often hire — or own — to manage mental health benefits. "It's a little bit like comparing apples and oranges," she says.

In addition, her members often cannot get the information they need from insurance plans to make these comparisons, says Greenberg. "We're being asked to find out when does the medical plan require prior authorization and under what circumstances, but there is no requirement [in the parity law] that [insurers] share it with us."

That lack of information also makes it difficult for consumers to know if their insurer is treating mental health benefits equitably. "The consumer is at a complete loss," said Julie Clements, deputy director of regulatory affairs at the American Psychiatric Association.[31]

Advocates hope the final rule better clarifies what information insurers must share. "The delay really does reflect the complexity of these issues and the need to get extensive input. People really had a lot to say about this," says Gary Blau, chief of the Child, Adolescent and Family Branch of the federal Substance Abuse and Mental Health Services Administration.

# BACKGROUND

## Rise of State Hospitals

Before 1800, mentally ill people in America were cared for at home or in their communities though charity. But after 1800, rapid population growth, immigration, urbanization and growing geographic mobility upset those traditions, and an increasing number ended up in jail, in poorhouses, or in the few existing — and often overcrowded — mental hospitals, inspiring one woman's crusade for better care.

Dorothea Dix, a retired Boston teacher, visited a jail in 1841 to teach women prisoners and was horrified by the number of mentally ill and the conditions in which they were kept. Galvanized by the experience, she visited jails and poor houses across Massachusetts and addressed the legislature in 1843, denouncing "the present state of Insane Persons confined within this Commonwealth, in cages, closets, cellars, stalls, pens! Chained, naked, beaten with rods, and lashed into obedience!"[32]

Dix helped convince lawmakers to expand the Worcester State Lunatic Asylum and, in the 1850s, build two new mental hospitals. Dix's success in Massachusetts "launched her on a lifetime career as an apostle for asylums," wrote psychiatrist E. Fuller Torrey and his research assistant Judy Miller in *The Invisible Plague*.[33]

During the 1840s and '50s, a total of 23 public mental hospitals were built in 19 states, almost three times more than had been built in the previous 20 years. Public officials and legislators supported the expansion of public mental hospitals in part because proponents promised the institutions "could cure insane individuals and therefore would ultimately save money," wrote Torrey and Miller.[34]

But most mental hospitals had more patients than they could handle effectively, making it difficult to pursue time-consuming individualistic therapy. By the early 1900s, "public facilities persisted as large and impersonal institutions characterized by a custodial attitude, meager allowances for active psychiatric treatment, limited professional staff, and a dependence on untrained and unskilled personnel," according to health policy experts David Mechanic, Donna McAlpine and David Rochefort in *Mental Health and Social Policy*.[35]

### Shift to Community Care

During the 1940s, several journalists published exposés of conditions in state mental hospitals. *Life* magazine published the lengthy article "Bedlam 1946" accompanied by "dramatic and horrifying photographs" that "only added to its emotional impact," wrote historians Gerald Grob and Howard Goldman in *The Dilemma of Federal Mental Health Policy*.

At the same time, demoralized psychiatrists were abandoning mental institutions for private or community practice, replaced by "foreign medical graduates with little or no training in psychiatry."[36] Advocates for the mentally ill as well as lawmakers looking for cost savings began to embrace the idea of treating the seriously mentally ill as outpatients in their communities. In the 1950s, New York and California passed laws establishing community mental health clinics.

"The advent of the first generation of antipsychotic drugs was one of several factors contributing to the release of patients from state mental hospitals," wrote health economists Richard Frank and Sherry Glied in *Better But Not Well*. "Chlorpromazine was the first medication to take the psychiatric world by storm, heralding the modern era of biological psychiatry." It was first marketed in the United States in 1954 under the brand name Thorazine as a treatment for schizophrenia. Considered widely effective, it came, however, with serious neurologic side effects, including rigidity and tremors.[37]

In 1963, President John F. Kennedy signed into law the Mental Retardation Facilities and Community Mental

## Mental Health Prescriptions Soar

More than 260 million prescriptions were filled in 2008 for mental health and substance-abuse medications for adults, more than twice the number in 1996. Antidepressants were the most prescribed drug. Other prevalent medications were for anxiety, psychosis and manic illnesses.

**Prescriptions Filled for Mental Health and Substance-Abuse Conditions Among Adults, 1996-2008**

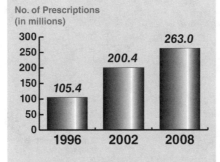

Source: "Mental Health, United States, 2010," Substance Abuse and Mental Health Services Administration, 2010

Health Centers Construction Act. States could apply for federal grants to establish a system of community mental health centers. The new centers were required to provide five essential services: inpatient hospitalization; partial hospitalization (in which patients live at home but come to the center up to seven days a week); outpatient care; round-the-clock emergency care; and education and consultation services.

The resident population in state and county mental hospitals fell from more than 500,000 in the 1950s to fewer than 40,000 by 2005.[38] Many patients were released back to families, group homes or single-occupancy residences to receive treatment locally, but others were simply shifted to nursing homes or general hospitals.

"Federal programs offered an irresistible bargain to state administrators," wrote Mechanic and colleagues. Medicare, created in 1965, covered mental health treatment for enrollees who entered general hospitals and private psychiatric hospitals; Medicaid, created at the same time to provide health care for the poor, paid a large share of mental health treatment costs for enrollees in general hospitals and nursing homes.

"By directing patients away from public mental hospitals, then, the state could capture huge budgetary savings," Mechanic and colleagues said. The result was a vast expansion in private nursing homes and private mental hospitals and a boom in specialized psychiatric and substance abuse units in general hospitals, they noted. "Over time, such facilities became the main entry point for acute inpatient behavioral health care."[39]

Meanwhile, the creation and construction of community mental health centers (CMHCs) proceeded slowly. A shortage of mental health professionals was one problem. Another was the Vietnam War's diversion of funding. A total of 2,000 mental health centers were supposed to be built by 1980, but the actual number was 754.

## CHRONOLOGY

**1840s-1950s** *States build public mental hospitals; drugs for mental illness are developed.*

**1843** Activist Dorothea Dix denounces condition of the mentally ill confined in jails and poorhouses.

**1860** Twenty-three public mental hospitals are built between 1840-1860.

**1946** *Life* magazine publishes an exposé of deplorable conditions in many state mental hospitals.

**1950s** New York state and California pass laws establishing community mental health clinics as alternatives to hospitalization.

**1954** Thorazine is marketed in U.S. to treat schizophrenia, heralding the modern era of biological psychiatry; considered widely effective, thorazine has serious neurologic side effects.

**1956** The first tricyclic antidepressant to treat clinical depression is introduced. . . . More than 500,000 people reside in state and county mental hospitals.

**1960s-1980s** *Federal laws empty public mental hospitals, as new drugs revolutionize treatment.*

**1963** Congress provides federal grants to states to establish community mental health centers to serve the deinstitutionalized mentally ill.

**1965** Newly created Medicare and Medicaid pay for treating acutely mentally ill in general hospitals, private psychiatric hospitals and nursing homes; states shift many patients out of public mental hospitals into these facilities instead of into communities.

**1968** Congress expands role of community mental health centers to serve children and the elderly.

**1980** Only 754 community mental health centers have been built since 1963, far short of the projected 2,000. . . . Congress passes the Mental Health Systems Act.

**1981** At President Ronald Reagan's urging, Congress repeals the Mental Health Systems Act and reduces federal funding to states for mental health care.

**1983** Reagan administration purges 500,000 people from federal disability rolls, a disproportionate number mentally ill.

**1984** The Disability Benefits Reform Act prevents the government from terminating an individual's disability benefits unless there is enough medical improvement to allow gainful employment.

**1988** Prozac, the first selective serotonin reuptake inhibitor, or SSRI, is introduced for depression treatment.

**1989** The first so-called atypical antipsychotic medication is introduced, followed by three more such drugs in the 1990s.

**1990s-Present** *Insurance plans shift to managed care; government requires parity.*

**1990s** Managed care plans adopted in effort to control rising health care costs.

**1996** Mental Health Parity Act restricts large group health insurance plans from placing lower dollar caps on mental health benefits than on physical care.

**2005** Resident population of state and county mental hospitals has fallen to 40,000.

**2008** The Paul Wellstone and Pete Domenici Mental Health Parity and Addiction Equity Act significantly extends parity to insurance coverage of mental health and coverage of physical health in large group plans.

**2010** Patient Protection and Affordable Care Act extends parity to individual and small group plans purchased through newly created state insurance exchanges.

**April 2013** Mental health legislation tied to gun control dies in the Senate when gun control bills fail to muster enough votes for passage; sponsors say they hope to reintroduce mental health legislation later in the year.

"By then it had become abundantly clear that . . . CMHCs were not serving as replacements for traditional public mental hospitals," according to Grob and Goldman.[40]

In 1968 Congress expanded the role of the centers to serve substance abusers, children and older people. Grappling with a broader mission and tight resources, centers "chose to serve a great number of less impaired and lower-cost people rather than disproportionately allocating their budget to high-cost severely ill people," wrote Frank and Glied.[41] In addition, the centers did not, and were not required to, coordinate continuing treatment and support for thousands of individuals being discharged each year from mental hospitals.

By the end of the 1970s, the mental health system was a decentralized, uncoordinated and bewildering array of institutions and practices: public and private psychiatric hospitals; nursing homes; residential care facilities; community mental health centers, funded mostly by Medicaid but also by county, state and federal programs, Medicare and private insurance; outpatient and inpatient units in general hospitals; group homes; and client-run services.[42]

## Changing Federal Policy

In 1980, Congress passed the Mental Health Systems Act. The federal government would continue to issue grants to states, but now there would be performance contracts to ensure accountability. The role of community mental health centers was reaffirmed, with an emphasis on caring for the seriously mentally ill, and states could apply for grants to coordinate state and federal services.

But upon taking office in 1981, President Ronald Reagan reversed course and successfully persuaded Congress to repeal the act. Next, Congress significantly cut funding and then bundled the federal grants for community mental health centers and other federal funding for mental health into a single lump sum given to each state annually with few strings attached. Finally, in response to a drastic expansion in the number of people receiving federal disability payments, the Reagan administration began extensive in-person reviews in 1983 to weed from the rolls those it decided were not permanently disabled.

About 500,000 people lost their disability payments, a disproportionate number of whom were mentally ill. The purge led to a public outcry, and in response Congress passed the 1984 Disability Benefits Reform Act: The government could terminate benefits only if an individual's medical condition improved enough to allow the person to return to gainful employment. The disability rolls have been increasing ever since, with the mentally ill the fastest growing group.[43]

The late 1980s and '90s also saw the development of new drugs to treat mental illness. A new generation of so-called atypical antipsychotic medications — including clozapine, olanzapine, quetiapine and risperidone — have been shown in studies to be as effective as the older antipsychotic drugs in treating schizophrenia but with a reduction in the tremors and rigidity that made many people reluctant to stick with their drug regimen. However, the new drugs are more costly and have been associated with weight gain and diabetes.

Tricyclic antidepressants were introduced in the 1950s and '60s to treat major depression, but they had a long list of side effects, including drowsiness, dizziness, constipation, weight gain, headache and increased heart rate. The development of selective serotonin reuptake inhibitors, or SSRIs, beginning with Prozac in 1988, "transformed the treatment of depression," according to Frank and Glied. SSRIs are of equal efficacy as tricyclic antidepressants but are safer, better tolerated by patients and pose less danger from overdose, according to researchers. "These drugs entered both the medical mainstream, through their widespread use by primary care providers, and the popular culture, with Peter Kramer's best-selling book in 1993, *Listening to Prozac*," wrote Frank and Glied.[44]

## Equal Treatment

As the cost of health care rose due to an aging population, expensive new drugs and costly technological advances, such as the development of sophisticated imaging machines, managed care emerged in the 1990s as a way to try to subdue the rising costs.

Previously, an employer signed a contract with a single health insurance company to provide employees with a traditional indemnity plan — also known as a fee-for-service plan — that allowed individuals to use any doctor they chose and submit their bills to the insurer for partial reimbursement, typically 80 percent. Under managed care, employers often give employees a choice of plans. A health maintenance organization, or HMO, the oldest form of managed care, puts doctors on staff or signs contracts with medical practices to provide care for enrollees, who must use the physicians in the plan. A preferred provider organization (PPO), another form of managed care, is closer to a traditional fee-for-service plan. But enrollees are reimbursed at a lower rate if they use doctors outside of the PPO network. In-network doctors have agreed to provide medical care at a discount.

# Shortage of Mental Health Professionals Cited

*"It's a huge problem, starting with the child mental health system."*

Tens of millions of Americans are living with mental illness, but many are going without care, in part because of a shortage of qualified mental health professionals.

The 2010 Affordable Care Act — the sweeping health care law championed by President Obama — will extend health coverage to an estimated six to 10 million individuals living with mental illness.[1] But experts cite a shortage of psychiatrists, clinical psychologists, psychiatric nurses and specialized social workers to handle current demand, let alone any expansion.

"It's a huge problem, starting with the child mental health system," says Ronald Honberg, national director for policy and legal affairs at the National Alliance on Mental Illness (NAMI), an advocacy group in Arlington, Va. "There is a severe shortage of child psychologists and psychiatrists around the country, especially in rural areas." (Child psychiatrists are medical doctors with special training in treating psychiatric problems in children and adolescents.)

Dividing the number of children estimated to be suffering from serious emotional disturbance by the hours worked by practicing child psychiatrists yields, on average, one hour a year of attention per child. "You can't even do an evaluation in an hour," says Peter Jensen, a child psychiatrist at the Mayo Clinic in Rochester, Minn. "You can't manage complex medications. You can't do followup."

"The largest factor behind the shortage is the longer period of education [required] to be a child psychiatrist," says Kristin Kroeger Ptakowski, director of government affairs and clinical practice at the American Academy of Child & Adolescent Psychiatry, a professional medical association in Washington, D.C. (It takes six years of training after medical school to become a licensed child psychiatrist.)

Moreover, practitioners say that once they are out of training, the hours are long and the pay is relatively modest compared to other specialties. To accommodate children's schedules, child psychiatrists often work afternoons and evenings, says Harold Koplewicz, himself a child psychiatrist and president of the Child Mind Institute in New York, which conducts research and offers clinical services. "And if you are accepting insurance, you are paid for seeing the child. You are not paid for talking to school teachers or for counseling parents," says Koplewicz.

Students finishing a Ph.D. in psychology face their own hurdles. "There is a shortage of internship positions," which is the capstone of clinical training and a requirement for a degree, says Cynthia Belar, executive director for education at the Washington-based American Psychological Association. Nearly 800 students out of roughly 4,500 could not find an internship in 2013, according the Association of Psychology Postdoctoral and Internship Centers.[2]

The Obama administration has proposed spending $50 million in fiscal 2014 to help train 5,000 new social workers, counselors, psychologists and peer professionals (individuals with mental illness who have successfully navigated the mental health system and can advise others). "It's a step in the right direction," says Honberg.

But some experts expressed concern when they learned that the money would be spent to train only master's degree-level psychologists, social workers and counselors and not doctorate-level psychologists or psychiatrists as well. An administration official told *The Washington Post* that the aim is to help alleviate the current demand for services. "We can't take 12 years training doctors and postdocs to meet the need in 2014," the official said.[3]

But Kroeger Ptakowski says the administration's strategy is short-sighted. "It's unfortunate that it doesn't include all

From the beginning, employers and general health plans chose to carve out coverage of mental health care and assign it to specialized behavioral health care companies. These companies saved money by limiting the number of days allowed for inpatient care, reducing prices paid to their network of mental health providers, limiting the number of outpatient visits and requiring preauthorization

for treatment. The reliance on behavioral health care companies eventually spread from the private sector to Medicaid.

Mental health advocates argued that the behavioral health care companies' cost controls were discriminatory because they were stricter than those for physical care. They lobbied Congress for parity, or equal treatment.

mental health professionals," she says. "If these funds were available now, I'm sure there would be many medical students who would be interested in going into child psychiatry."

Adds Belar: "An investment in one year of training [for psychology internships] for already-prepared doctoral students would seem as practical as supporting three-year programs."

Koplewicz advocates increased spending to encourage pediatricians and family physicians to pursue advanced education in mental health because they do most of the diagnosing and treating of children with mental illness. "They must be better trained," he says.

Koplewicz proposes that primary care physicians who take an approved course in diagnosing and treating ADHD, adolescent depression, anxiety disorders and autism receive higher reimbursement from Medicaid and possibly from private insurance as well.

Jensen founded the 5-year-old Reach Institute in New York, which trains pediatricians and family doctors around the country in child mental health during an intensive three-day interactive program followed by six months of consultations with national experts.

"We teach them pediatric psychopharmacology, but a little more than 50 percent focuses on assessment, diagnosis, forming a relationship with the family and how they can do this in 15 minutes every week or every other week until the family is stabilized," says Jensen. "And we teach them when they should refer to a specialist," mostly if they see signs of bipolar disorder or schizophrenia.

Physicians also learn about cognitive behavioral therapy and other so-called evidence-based psychotherapy techniques so they can knowledgeably refer patients to counselors or psychologists.[4]

Experts say better mental health care often requires a collaborative approach in which a primary-care practice hires a social worker, counselor or psychologist on staff or as a consultant or contracts with a mental health group to treat adults or children.

But there are barriers to making collaborative care work. One is financial. "The time that a pediatrician spends on the phone with a child psychiatrist discussing a case is not necessarily time that can be reimbursed by insurance," says Darcy Gruttadaro, director of the child and adolescent action center at NAMI. Massachusetts legislators are working on a state law that would require insurers to pay for that time, she says.

In addition, "The primary care physician may have a contract with one insurer and the mental health provider with another," says Wayne Lindstrom, president and CEO of Mental Health America, an advocacy group in Alexandria, Va. Another barrier may be something as mundane as office space. "It may not be available, and the primary care practice may be bound by a long-term lease" that would prevent the practice from moving into joint space with the mental health professionals, says Lindstrom.

Some of these challenges may be eased as the 2010 Affordable Care Act is phased in. Through a variety of pilot programs and other enticements, the law encourages collaborative care and will experiment with paying integrated group practices a lump sum for bundled services or for the annual care of each patient. However, many programs and incentives sanctioned under the new law have not been funded because of federal budget problems.

— *Barbara Mantel*

---

[1] For background, see the following *CQ Researchers* by Marcia Clemmitt, "Assessing the New Health Care Law," Sept. 21, 2012, pp. 789-812; "Health Care Reform," June 11, 2010, pp. 505-528, updated May 24, 2011; and "Treating ADHD," Aug. 3, 2012, pp. 669-692.

[2] "2013 APPIC Match Statistics Combined Results: Phase I and Phase II," Association of Psychology Postdoctoral and Internship Centers, March 25, 2013, www.appic.org/Match/MatchStatistics/MatchStatistics2013Combined.aspx.

[3] Sarah Kliff, "Obama's proposed budget to seek $235 million for new mental health programs," *The Washington Post*, April 9, 2013, http://articles.washingtonpost.com/2013-04-09/national/38403598_1_mental-health-services-gun-violence-health-insurance-coverage.

[4] For background, see Sarah Glazer, "Treating Anxiety," *CQ Researcher*, Feb. 8, 2002, pp. 97-120.

Congress passed the Mental Health Parity Act of 1996, but its scope was limited. The act restricted the ability of group health insurance plans to place lower annual or lifetime dollar caps on mental health benefits than on medical and surgical benefits. But the act did not stop group plans from having higher copayments for mental health care or from limiting the number of inpatient days or outpatient visits even when no such limits existed for medical or surgical care. The act also did not prevent group plans from dropping mental health coverage. It applied only to health plans sponsored by employers with 51 or more workers, and it did not apply to health insurance coverage purchased by individuals. It also did not apply to treatment for substance abuse.[45]

# Police Trained to Deal With the Mentally Ill

*More than 2,700 crisis teams exist nationwide.*

When the U.S. Justice Department cited the Portland, Ore., police department last September for a history of excessive force against the mentally ill, city officials agreed to join a nationwide movement aimed at helping police better deal with people experiencing psychiatric problems.[1]

As part of a settlement with the Justice Department, Portland formed a crisis intervention team within its police department to train law-enforcement personnel in how to respond to calls involving the mentally ill. "We all agree we can do better as a police bureau and as a community," said Portland Police Chief Mike Reese. "This agreement will provide us a road map as we move forward."[2]

The first 50 police officers were selected for the specialized training in April.

More than 2,700 crisis intervention teams exist within law enforcement departments nationwide. The program originated in Memphis, Tenn., in 1988 and has spread to every state except Alabama, Arkansas and West Virginia.[3]

"At least 10 percent of all police encounters involve someone with a serious mental illness," says psychiatrist Michael Compton, a professor of prevention and community health at George Washington University in Washington, D.C. The vast majority of these interactions don't involve a high risk to public safety, he says. "They are minor infractions and misdemeanors, like loitering, subway fare evasions, things like that."

Crisis intervention teams are dispatched when police encounter mentally ill individuals experiencing a psychiatric crisis. The teams aim to defuse the situation, prevent injury to the individual or police officers and decide whether the best course is arrest or mental health care.

Police officers volunteer for the training. "A significant percentage volunteer because someone they know and love suffers from mental illness," says Jeffry Murphy, a 37-year veteran of the Chicago Police Department who supervised the creation of Chicago's training program for crisis intervention teams, which the city launched in 2004. Murphy has a son living with mental illness.

During the 40-hour course, officers receive intensive instruction on how to de-escalate a crisis situation, visit mental health facilities, speak with mental health professionals, interact with individuals with mental illness, role-play and ride along with experienced team officers. Police dispatchers also receive special training.

---

The percentage of workers with dollar caps on mental health coverage fell substantially as a result of the law, according to researchers. But, contrary to advocates' hopes, restrictions on inpatient days and outpatient visits for mental health care increased.[46]

In 1999, President Bill Clinton's surgeon general, David Satcher, issued *Mental Health — A Report of the Surgeon General*, a landmark analysis of the mental health field. It emphasized the need to understand mental illnesses as real, often disabling, health conditions and identified a range of effective treatments backed by research that often had not been put into practice.

In 2002, President George W. Bush formed the New Freedom Commission on Mental Health to study the nation's mental health system and recommend improvements that would not increase spending. After a year of study, the commission found that "recovery from mental illness is now a real possibility," but that the mental health care system was a "patchwork relic — the result of disjointed reforms and policies."[47]

The report, though not a blueprint for action, defined several goals for transformation, including integration of mental and physical health care; empowerment of consumers and families; increased early screening, assessment and referral; research-guided treatment; and improved access to and coordination of care.[48]

When Bush announced the formation of the commission, he identified three barriers to mental health care: stigma, the fragmented delivery system and private health insurance plans' often unfair treatment limitations and financial requirements on mental health benefits. Insurance companies "must treat serious mental illness like any other disease," the president said.[49]

At the time, however, many congressional Republicans were opposed to so-called "mental health parity" for fear that it would drive up health care costs and discourage

Police departments also are encouraged to forge relationships with mental health providers and advocacy groups in the community.

Studies have shown that crisis intervention teams have a noticeable impact on police officers. They are less inclined to stigmatize people with mental illness, know more about mental illness, display better de-escalation skills and are better able to refer people to mental health services, says Compton, who has studied crisis intervention teams. "And we know that these improvements last beyond the training period."

But the ultimate goal of the teams is to reduce arrests and find help for those suffering from mental illness. Here the research is much thinner. "There have only been a couple of studies that I know of pertaining to arrest and referral decisions," says Compton. "In my own study, we did find evidence that [crisis intervention team] officers were less likely to make an arrest."

But training is only one of several factors driving arrest decisions, says Compton, "the big ones being the level of resistance of the subject and the level of violence potential."

No completed studies have examined the longer-term outcomes for individuals with mental health problems who encounter the intervention teams. Do most get appropriate care or end up in jail? Can they successfully live in the community, or do they have repeat encounters with police? A large, five-year study in Chicago designed to answer these questions is underway.

Much depends on the availability and quality of mental health care providers and their relationships with the crisis intervention teams. Key, say researchers, is having a mental health facility nearby with a no-refusal policy. But a study of intervention teams across the country found that few programs had access to such a site and only about a third held "any type of formal agreement with mental health receiving facilities."[4]

State and city budget cuts have put pressure on crisis intervention teams. For example, Chicago has closed six of its 12 community mental health clinics, promising that access to services wouldn't be affected. But Murphy says that hasn't happened.

"We're responding to more crisis calls because we have more people not linked to services," he says.

— *Barbara Mantel*

[1] For background, see Kenneth Jost, "Police Misconduct," *CQ Researcher*, April 6, 2012, pp. 301-324.

[2] Maxine Bernstein, "Portland mayor, chief, and Oregon U.S. Attorney announce settlement on Portland police reforms," *The Oregonian*, Oct. 26, 2012, www.oregonlive.com/portland/index.ssf/2012/10/portland_mayor_chief_and_orego.html.

[3] CIT Center, The University of Memphis, http://cit.memphis.edu.

[4] Michael T. Compton, *et al.*, "The Crisis Intervention Team (CIT) Model of Collaboration Between Law Enforcement and Mental Health," *Advances in Sociology Research*, Volume 9, 2011.

employers from offering coverage. But in 2008, after Democrats gained control of both houses of Congress, lawmakers passed the Paul Wellstone and Pete Domenici Mental Health Parity and Addiction Equity Act.

Like the 1996 law, it applied only to group plans, exempted plans sponsored by small employers and allowed plans to drop mental health coverage. But it was far more ambitious than the previous law. It expanded parity by including deductibles, copayments, out-of-pocket expenses, co-insurance, covered hospital days and covered outpatient visits. It also expanded parity to substance abuse treatment.

The 2010 Patient Protection and Affordable Care Act will eventually expand parity. Starting at the end of this year, individuals and employers with fewer than 100 employees — 50 or fewer in some states — can purchase health insurance through online exchanges operating in every state. Insurance plans offered through the exchanges must provide mental health coverage and abide by federal parity rules. However, most Americans will continue to get health insurance through employer-sponsored plans that are not purchased through the exchanges.[50]

The health law also expands Medicaid to anyone who earns less than 133 percent of the federal poverty level (about $31,320 for a family of four), with the federal government footing most of the bill.[51] That could potentially extend health insurance coverage to up to 10 million people with mental illness. However, as of early May, 12 states were leaning toward opting out of Medicaid expansion and another 13 were undecided.[52]

## CURRENT SITUATION

### Integrating Care

A number of Democrats and Republicans in Congress are backing legislation they say will address the problems plaguing the nation's mental health system. The Excellence in Mental Health Act would:

- Increase funding for qualified community mental health centers;
- Increase access to an array of treatments and services that research has shown to be effective, including peer support, cognitive behavioral therapy, supported employment and supported housing;
- Require community mental health centers to screen for physical health problems and collaborate with primary care providers to give people with mental and addiction disorders medical treatment and preventive care.

"Integrating care is critically important," says Honberg of the National Alliance on Mental Illness. "We've had these two systems — mental health care and physical health care — operating far apart without talking to each other, and there have been huge consequences."

Honberg is referring to a 2006 report from the National Association of State Mental Health Program Directors that shocked many of those working in mental health care at the time. Analyzing state data, researchers found that people with serious mental illness die, on average, 25 years earlier than the general population.

While suicide and injury accounted for about one-third of those premature deaths, most were due to what the report called preventable medical conditions, such as cardiovascular, pulmonary and infectious diseases as well as diabetes. Higher rates of smoking, alcohol and intravenous drug use and poor nutrition put those with serious mental illness at greater risk for developing those diseases than the general population. Homelessness, unemployment, poverty, incarceration and social isolation

## Serious Mental Illness in Adults Most Prevalent in Young

Nearly 8 percent of adults ages 18 to 25 had a serious mental illness in 2011, compared with 6 percent of those 26 to 49 and 3 percent of those 50 and older (top). More than 6 percent of women had a serious mental illness, compared with about 3 percent of men (bottom).

### Adults With a Serious Mental Illness, by Age and Gender, 2011

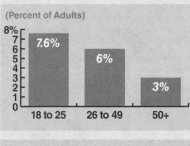

(Percent of Adults)

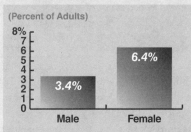

(Percent of Adults)

*Source:* "Results From the 2011 National Survey on Drug Use and Health: Mental Health Findings," Substance Abuse and Mental Health Services Administration, 2012

also contribute to poor physical health.

The new generation of antipsychotic drugs also plays a significant role. While they have far fewer neurologic side effects than older drugs, they are highly associated with weight gain, diabetes, insulin resistance and other metabolic disorders.

But equally important is the lack of access to primary care.[53] In response, four years ago the Substance Abuse and Mental Health Services Administration (SAMHSA) began issuing grants to communities that wanted to add primary care to services available at community mental health centers. SAMHSA currently funds 93 such projects.

"Just from being on medication for mental illness, I gained about 60 pounds," said Gary Ward, who participates in a Washington County, Maine, program that provides primary and mental health care in one location. In two years, Ward has lost 38 pounds. "It's given me my life back, it really has."[54]

Integrating care seems like a simple idea, but Kathleen Reynolds, vice president for health integration and wellness promotion at the National Council for Community Behavioral Healthcare, says there are several challenges.

"One is financing," says Reynolds. Complicated Medicaid and Medicare billing rules don't make it easy to bill for both primary and mental health care from one location. Another challenge is confidentiality. Federal and state confidentiality rules and regulations can make it difficult for a mental health provider and a primary care provider working together onsite to share information if they are

# Will the new mental-disorders manual lead to over-diagnosis?

## YES

**Dr. Allen Frances**
*Professor Emeritus of Psychiatry,*
*Duke University School of Medicine;*
*Former Chair of the* DSM-4 *Task Force;*
*Author of* Saving Normal

Written for *CQ Researcher,* May 2013

We already are in the midst of a troublesome diagnostic inflation, and the revised edition of the *Diagnostic and Statistical Manual of Mental Disorders* (*DSM-5*) threatens to expand it into an even more harmful hyperinflation.

The numbers are startling and scary. In any given year, 25 percent of the general population qualifies for a mental disorder; 50 percent will over their lifetime; and 20 percent take a psychotropic medicine. More people now die from overdoses caused by medicines prescribed by doctors than by street drugs sold by the cartels. In the last 20 years, rates of adult bipolar disorder have doubled, attention deficit disorder (ADD) has tripled, and autism and childhood bipolar disorder have grown a remarkable 40-fold.

People don't change quickly, but labels do. Small changes in how disorders are defined can result in large changes in who gets labeled. Diagnostic fashions are heavily influenced by drug-company marketing, which in the United States is fueled by enormous budgets and conducted with unprecedented freedom from regulation. The ubiquitous advertising has successfully sold the misleading message that expectable problems of living are mental disorders that are caused by a chemical imbalance and require a pill solution. Illegal drug company marketing has led to multiple billion-dollar fines that are not much of a deterrent given the enormous revenues generated by artificially created demand.

The other major driver of diagnostic inflation is the fact that DSM diagnosis has become too important in decisions that determine eligibility for mental health care, school services and disability benefits.

Except for autism, all the changes in *DSM-5* will increase the rates of diagnosis — either by adding new disorders or reducing thresholds for existing ones. Expectable grief becomes major depressive disorder; the normal forgetting of old age is mild neurocognitive disorder; worrying about a medical illness is somatic symptom disorder; overeating is binge eating disorder; temper tantrums are disruptive mood dysregulation disorder; and adult ADD will be so easy to diagnose that the already large illegal market of diverted stimulant drugs will be even harder to control.

We should be tightening diagnostic standards, not loosening them. When we increase the resources devoted to the worried well who don't need them, we deprive the really sick who desperately do.

## NO

**Dr. Michael B. First**
*Professor of Clinical Psychiatry,*
*Columbia University*

Written for *CQ Researcher,* May 2013

No one can say for sure what impact the new revision of the American Psychiatric Association's *Diagnostic and Statistical Manual* (*DSM-5*) will have on diagnosis — the book isn't out until this month, and its impact will slowly unfold over months, if not years. But it probably won't lead to over-diagnosis. Anomalous rises in diagnostic rates are, frankly, much more likely to be rooted in factors other than the diagnostic system. These include external pressures on clinicians to make diagnoses in a limited period of time; pressure from patients and families for quick fixes to complex problems, and pharmaceutical marketing influences.

Psychiatric diagnosis is a complex process in which a trained clinician interacts with a patient to collect a psychiatric history, gathers corroborating information from family members, reviews medical records and laboratory findings and then determines the diagnosis by synthesizing this information and applying clinical judgment to the technical rules laid out in the American Psychiatric Association's classification of mental disorders. When shortcuts are taken by not conducting a thorough evaluation or by ignoring the manual's diagnostic rules, over-diagnosis and misdiagnosis, with its consequent overtreatment and mistreatment, can occur.

The marked rise in the attention-deficit/hyperactivity disorder (ADHD) diagnosis over the past 20 years and the consequent escalation in stimulant prescriptions is a perfect illustration of the complex nature of this phenomenon. Under pressure from some parents, school systems and patients for a quick fix to improve attention and concentration or to get an edge over the competition, combined with heavy promotion by the pharmaceutical industry of new drug formulations, many clinicians applied the ADHD label inappropriately. They did so to justify their decision to write a prescription for stimulants without having conducted a proper symptomatic or functional assessment or having determined that the requirements for the diagnosis, as laid out in the *DSM*, were met. For example, there should be clear evidence of clinically significant impairment in social, academic or occupational functioning.

The best hope to combat misdiagnosis of any kind would be an intensive educational campaign promoting comprehensive diagnostic evaluation using accepted scientific methods. Suggesting that the *DSM* classification itself is the main reason for over-diagnosis ignores the fact that psychiatric diagnoses do not simply exist in the abstract. They are tools used by clinicians to foster communication and to improve clinical care. Diagnoses are only as good as the people making them.

University of Maryland junior Grace Freund studies to become a volunteer at the school's student-run Help Center, which works with students dealing with mental health crises. Of the estimated 58 million American adults with a diagnosable mental disorder, more than 11 million have a serious mental illness, such as schizophrenia, bipolar disorder or major depression.

from different agencies. "Yes, you can do it by getting every person to sign a release, but it is a burden to make sure those releases are up to date and cover all the information," says Reynolds.

Yet another challenge is cultural and organizational, she says. Mental health professionals typically spend long periods with individuals and get paid to do so. Primary care providers get paid per encounter, no matter how long the visit, so "the pace of the work in primary care is much faster," says Reynolds. Combining the two types of care in one visit can be a challenge. "You don't want

to have a person come in and spend two or three hours," says Reynolds. "In most cases, it's the behavioral health side that modifies its practices, coming up with shorter interventions."

## Mental Health in Schools

President Obama has called for spending $55 million in fiscal 2014 to reach 750,000 young people through programs to identify mental illness in schools and refer them to treatment when needed. "If you think about adult mental illness, about 50 percent of all those illnesses can be traced and manifest by the age of 14, and three-quarters manifest by the age of 24," says Blau of SAMHSA, which would fund the effort if it survives congressional budget negotiations. "That's why we need to emphasize prevention in early childhood."

But schools do not have enough qualified staff members to work as part of mental health teams, according to groups representing such professionals. Jill Cook, assistant director of the Alexandria, Va.-based American School Counselor Association, says there currently are 471 students per school counselor nationwide — far too many. "Even though there has been improvement over the past several decades, our association's recommendation is one school counselor for every 250 students," she says.

In addition, many states don't require school nurses. As a result, the coverage varies widely, from a high of 4,411 students per school nurse in Michigan in 2011 to a low of 396 in Vermont.[55] "In the Northeast the ratios are more realistic and safe for kids, but as you go further South and West, there often is no requirement for school nursing, and the ratios get larger," says Linda Davis-Alldritt, president of the National Association of School Nurses, based in Silver Spring, Md.

Obama's plan calls for bringing a program called Mental Health First Aid into schools to train teachers, school security officers and even front-desk personnel to recognize the signs of mental illness in youngsters.

Introduced in the United States in 2008 and modeled after a program in Australia, Mental Health First Aid is a 12-hour interactive training course designed to help the public identify, understand and respond appropriately to signs of mental illness and substance use disorders. More than 120,000 people have been trained since its inception in the United States.

"It has the potential to normalize mental illness in the public eye, not unlike physical illness," says Wayne Lindstrom, president and CEO of Mental Health America.

Mental Health First Aid recently modified its program for use in schools, reducing it to eight hours and altering the content to better reflect signs and symptoms in young people. Two school districts — in McAllen, Texas, and Tulare County, Calif. — have signed on so far. "We don't teach people how to diagnose or treat mental illness," says Bryan Gibb, director of public education at the National Council for Community Behavioral Healthcare, which helps run the program. Nor do Mental Health First Aid instructors simply give teachers a list of warning signs with instructions: "If you see these, pick up the phone," says Gibb. "There would be so many false alarms."

Instead, instructors show teachers how to de-escalate a crisis, such as when someone threatens suicide or hallucinates. But instructors spend the most time teaching adults how to have a nonjudgmental conversation with students and "refer them to professional help if necessary," says Gibb.

That referral doesn't happen without permission from a parent or guardian, he adds.

Gibb says the organizers also recognize the risk that teachers might see signs and symptoms of mental disorders, such as depression, anxiety or an eating disorder, where there are none. "We tell teachers . . . we really want you to be aware of that bias," says Gibb.

So far, there have been no studies of Mental Health First Aid's effectiveness in schools, but Gibb says studies are planned. SAMHSA says it will monitor the program's impact on teachers and students if Congress authorizes funding.

## OUTLOOK

### Legislation in Limbo

Senators sponsoring mental health legislation planned to piggy-back on the gun control bill that was up for a vote in the Senate last month, offering their proposals as amendments. During two days of tense voting on the gun bill, the Senate overwhelmingly passed the Mental Health Awareness and Improvement Act, which would reauthorize several federal programs, such as suicide prevention, and fund a new initiative to bring Mental Health First Aid into schools. But when the gun bill died, so did the Mental Health Awareness law, at least for now.

The gun bill's death in the Senate also has left the more heavily lobbied Excellence in Mental Health Act in limbo. It never even came up for a vote as an amendment. Now its Senate sponsors and mental health advocates must adjust their strategy.

"We're pushing for co-sponsors, and the more co-sponsors we get the more likely it is that Senate Majority Leader Harry Reid will give us a vote," says Sperling of the National Alliance on Mental Illness. Sperling says NAMI is preparing for two possibilities: that the Senate gets a second crack at voting on gun legislation or that the mental health act's sponsors will offer it as amendment to some other bill. "We have our members and affiliates calling senators, writing in, emailing, you name it," he says.

The lead sponsors of the Excellence in Mental Health Act will decide the ultimate strategy. "I think there's a really good opportunity we can still get this done. It should not be dependent on gun legislation," Sen. Roy Blunt, R-Mo., told *Politico* after the gun bill was pulled from the Senate floor. "I feel very confident we will get a vote at some point," added Michigan Democrat Debbie Stabenow.[56]

Without a federal law, action on mental health is left to the states. Some states — such as Pennsylvania and Wisconsin — are considering restoring some of the money cut from mental health budgets. But Joel Miller, senior director of policy and healthcare reform at the National Association of State Mental Health Program Directors, says he doesn't think most states will restore mental health money. "There are Midwestern industrial states like Illinois and Michigan that have not funded their public pensions properly, so they're going to take it out on the health care side."

The most important action states can take right now, says Miller, is to sign on to the Affordable Care Act's Medicaid expansion program, which could extend health care coverage to as many as 10 million additional people living with mental illness. "That will bring new federal monies into state budgets for treating people with mental illness," he says. In the first three years of the expansion, beginning in 2014, the federal government will cover 100 percent of the costs for expanded enrollees and then 90 percent after that. But as of early May, only 20 states had committed to Medicaid expansion, with another six leaning toward it.[57]

Several Republican governors have spoken out against expanding Medicaid, including Gov. Rick Perry of Texas. "Texas will not be held hostage by the Obama administration's attempt to force us into the fool's errand of adding more than a million Texans to a broken system," Perry said in early April.[58] The Southern-most states from Texas to North Carolina, with the exception of Florida, are leaning toward opting out of Medicaid expansion. So are Idaho, Missouri, Oklahoma, Montana and Alaska.[59]

Advocates are working hard to convince legislatures and governors in those states to change their minds. "There are so many people who have no access whatsoever to health care and who have extreme needs," says Plotnick of Mental Health America. "The Medicaid expansion would reach those folks who have nothing."

## NOTES

1. Ginger Gibson, "Harry Reid cites father's suicide in gun debate," *Politico*, April 9, 2013, www.politico.com/story/2013/04/harry-reid-gun-debate-father-suicide-89805.html.

2. "Web-based Injury Statistics Query and Reporting System," Centers for Disease Control and Prevention, www.cdc.gov/ncipc/wisqars; "The Numbers Count: Mental Disorders in America," The National Institute of Mental Health, www.nimh.nih.gov/health/publications/the-numbers-count-mental-disorders-in-america/index.shtml.

3. Thomas Insel, testimony before the Committee on Health, Education, Labor, and Pensions, U.S. Senate, Jan. 24, 3013, pp. 2, 4, www.help.senate.gov/imo/media/doc/Insel.pdf; "The Numbers Count: Mental Disorders in America," *op. cit.*

4. Debbie Stabenow, "Strengthening Mental Health Services," www.stabenow.senate.gov/?p=issue&id=80.

5. Jeremy W. Peters, "In Gun Debate, No Rift on Better Care for Mentally Ill," *The New York Times*, April 12, 2013, www.nytimes.com/2013/04/13/us/

politics/senators-make-bipartisan-push-for-mental-health-care.html?pagewanted=all&_r=0.

6. "Crucial Mental Health Legislation to be Considered Next Week," National Council for Community Behavioral Healthcare, April 11, 2013, www.thenationalcouncil.org/cs/press_releases/crucial_mental_health_legislation_to_be_considered_next_week.

7. "Fiscal Year 2014, Budget in Brief," Department of Health and Human Services, p. 41, www.hhs.gov/budget/fy2014/fy-2014-budget-in-brief.pdf.

8. "Obama Includes Mental Health Funding Increase in Budget Proposal," *Psychiatric News Alert*, April 10, 2013, http://alert.psychiatricnews.org/2013/04/obama-includes-mental-health-funding.html.

9. "National Expenditures for Mental Health Services and Substance Abuse Treatment, 1986-2005," Substance Abuse and Mental Health Services Administration, Tables 74 & 75, pp. 201-202, http://hcfgkc.org/sites/default/files/documents/MHUS_2010_part3_508.pdf.

10. Laura Nelson, "Opening Presentation: Impact of the State Budget Crisis and Treatment Gap on the Public Substance Abuse and Mental Health System," National Association of State Mental Health Program Directors, March 22, 2012, pp. 6-7.

11. *Ibid.*, pp. 4, 7.

12. "Improving Outcomes for People with Mental Illnesses Involved with New York City's Criminal Court and Correction Systems," Justice Center of the Council of State Governments, December 2012, p. 1, http://consensusproject.org/jc_publications/improving-outcomes-nyc-criminal-justice-mental-health/FINAL_NYC_Report_12_22_2012.pdf.

13. "Proceedings on the State Budget Crisis and the Behavioral Health Treatment Gap: The Impact on Public Substance Abuse and Mental Health Treatment Systems," National Association of State Mental Health Program Directors, March 22, 2012, p. 14, www.nasmhpd.org/docs/Summary-Congressional%20Briefing_March%2022_Website.pdf.

14. Public Hearing re: House Bill 2186, Health and Human Services Committee, Pennsylvania House of Representatives, April 8, 2010, pp. 66-68,

www.legis.state.pa.us/cfdocs/legis/tr/transcripts/2010_0082T.pdf.

15. "State Standards for Assisted Treatment: Civil Commitment Criteria for Inpatient or Outpatient Psychiatric Treatment," Treatment Advocacy Center, January 2013, pp. 65-66, www.treatmentadvocacy center.org/storage/documents/Standards_-_The_Text-_June_2011.pdf.

16. *Ibid.*, p. 56.

17. Marvin S. Swartz, *et al.*, "New York State Assisted Outpatient Treatment: Program Evaluation," New York State Office of Mental Health, June 30, 2009, www.omh.ny.gov/omhweb/resources/publications/aot_program_evaluation/report.pdf.

18. Allen Frances, *Saving Normal: an insider's revolt against out-of-control psychiatric diagnosis, DSM-5, big pharma, and the medicalization of ordinary life* (2013), p. 27.

19. "Asperger's syndrome dropped from American Psychiatric Association manual," CBSNews.com, Dec. 3, 2012, www.cbsnews.com/8301-204_162-57556754/aspergers-syndrome-dropped-from-american-psychiatric-association-manual.

20. *Ibid.*

21. David Mechanic, Donna McAlpine, and David Rochefort, *Mental Health and Social Policy: Beyond Managed Care* (2014), p. 25.

22. "Proposed criteria for DSM-5: Disruptive Mood Dysregulation Disorder," University of Colorado at Boulder, Department of Psychology, http://psych.colorado.edu/~willcutt/pdfs/dsm5_disrupt_mood.pdf.

23. "James Coyne, "Bereavement dropped as an exclusion in diagnosis of depression: protecting reimbursement, but hurting science," *PLAS Blogs*, Jan. 10, 2013, http://blogs.plos.org/mindthebrain/2013/01/10/bereavement-dropped-as-an-exclusion-in-diagnosis-of-depression-protecting-reimbursement-but-hurting-science.

24. Ronald W. Pies, "Bereavement Does Not Immunize Against Major Depression," *Medscape*, Jan. 24, 2013, www.medscape.com/viewarticle/777960.

25. For background, see Marcia Clemmitt, "Treating ADHD," *CQ Researcher*, Aug. 3, 2012, pp. 669-692.

26. Michael Ollove, "Parity for Behavioral Health Coverage Delayed by Lack of Federal Rules," *Stateline*, Dec. 2, 2012, www.kaiserhealthnews.org/stories/2012/december/03/stateline-behavioral-health-coverage.aspx.

27. *Ibid.*

28. "Rep. Joe Pitts Holds a Hearing on the Department of Health and Human Services F.Y. 2014 Budget," *Political Transcript Wire*, April 19, 2013.

29. Fact Sheet: The Mental Health Parity and Addiction Equity Act of 2008, U.S. Department of Labor, www.dol.gov/ebsa/newsroom/fsmhpaea.html.

30. Jim Spencer, "Suit against UnitedHealth tests mental health coverage rules," *Minneapolis Star Tribune*, April 6, 2013, www.startribune.com/business/201677791.html?refer=y.

31. Noam N. Levey, "Obama intends to fix holes in mental health coverage," *Los Angeles Times*, Jan. 19, 2013, http://articles.latimes.com/2013/jan/19/nation/la-na-mental-health-20130119.

32. E. Fuller Torrey and Judy Miller, *The Invisible Plague: The Rise of Mental Illness from 1750 to the Present* (2002), p. 219.

33. *Ibid.*, p. 220.

34. *Ibid.*, p. 226.

35. Mechanic, *et al.*, *op. cit.*, pp. 47, 62.

36. Gerald N. Grob and Howard H. Goldman, *The Dilemma of Federal Mental Health Policy: Radical Reform or Incremental Change?* (2006), p. 17.

37. Richard G. Frank and Sherry A. Glied, *Better But Not Well: Mental Health Policy in the United States since 1950* (2006), pp. 28-29.

38. Mechanic, *et al.*, *op. cit.*, p. 61.

39. *Ibid.*, p. 62.

40. Grob and Goldman, *op. cit.*, p. 45.

41. Frank and Glied, *op. cit.*, p. 60.

42. Grob and Goldman, *op. cit.*, p. 52.

43. Frank and Glied, *op. cit.*, p. 63.

44. *Ibid.*, p. 35.

45. "Mental Health Parity," *Advocacy On Call*, www.advocacyoncall.org/health/mental_health_parity.

46. Mechanic, *et al.*, *op. cit.*, p. 62.

47. "Achieving the Promise: Transforming Mental Health Care in America," New Freedom Commission on Mental Health, July 22, 2003, cover letter, http://store.samhsa.gov/shin/content//SMA03-3831/SMA03-3831.pdf.

48. *Ibid.*, pp. 24-25.

49. "Bush endorses 'mental health parity,' " CNN.com, April 29, 2002, http://archives.cnn.com/2002/ALLPOLITICS/04/29/bush.mental.illness.

50. Julie Appleby, "A Guide To Health Insurance Exchanges," *Kaiser Health News*, Jan. 10, 2013, www.kaiserhealthnews.org/stories/2011/march/30/exchange-faq.aspx.

51. "2013 Poverty Guidelines," U.S. Department of Health and Human Services, http://aspe.hhs.gov/poverty/13poverty.cfm#thresholds.

52. *Health Reform's Medicaid Expansion*, Center on Budget and Policy Priorities, www.cbpp.org/cms/index.cfm?fa=view&id=3819.

53. "Morbidity and Mortality in People with Serious Mental Illness," National Association of State Mental Health Program Directors, October 2006, pp. 5-6, www.nasmhpd.org/docs/publications/MDCdocs/Mortality%20and%20Morbidity%20Final%20Report%208.18.08.pdf.

54. Morgan Small, "Community Members Visit New Integrated Medical and Mental Health Facility in Bangor," WABI TV5, March 28, 2013, www.wabi.tv/news/38847/community-members-visit-new-intergrated-medical-and-mental-health-facility-in-bangor.

55. "Healthy Children Learn Better! School Nurses Make a Difference," National Association of School Nurses, www.nasn.org/Portals/0/about/press_room_faq.pdf.

56. Joanne Kenen and Paige Winfield Cunningham, "Mental health advocacy hits reset," *Politico*, April 21, 2013, www.politico.com/story/2013/04/guns-mental-health-advocacy-sandy-hook-90407.html.

57. Paige Winfield, "Health Reform's Medicaid Expansion," Center on Budget and Policy Priorities, www.cbpp.org/cms/index.cfm?fa=view&id=3819.

58. Corrie MacLaggan, "Texas governor reiterates Medicaid expansion opposition," Reuters, April 1, 2013, www.reuters.com/article/2013/04/01/us-usa-texas-medicaid-idUSBRE9300FN20130401.

59. *Health Reform's Medicaid Expansion*, op. cit.

# BIBLIOGRAPHY

## Selected Sources

### Books

Frances, Allen, *Saving Normal: An Insider's Revolt Against Out-of-Control Psychiatric Diagnosis, DSM-5, Big Pharma, and the Medicalization of Ordinary Life*, William Morrow, 2013.
A prominent psychiatrist analyzes the factors behind what he says is the casting of normal behavior as mental illness.

Grob, Gerald N., and Howard H. Goldman, *The Dilemma of Federal Mental Health Policy: Radical Reform or Incremental Change?*, Rutgers University Press, 2006.
A historian of psychiatry (Grob) and a mental health policy expert trace changes in government mental health policy since the 19th century.

Mechanic, David, *et al.*, *Mental Health and Social Policy: Beyond Managed Care*, Pearson Education, 2013.
Health policy experts examine current social policy debates in mental health care.

### Articles

Appleby, Julie, "A Guide To Health Insurance Exchanges," *Kaiser Health News*, Jan. 10, 2013, www.kaiserhealthnews.org/stories/2011/march/30/exchange-faq.aspx.
State insurance exchanges will allow individuals and small businesses to purchase health insurance, which must cover mental health care.

Kliff, Sarah, "Obama's proposed budget to seek $235 million for new mental health programs," *The Washington Post*, April 9, 2013, http://articles.washingtonpost.com/2013-04-09/national/

38403598_1_mental-health-services-gun-violence-health-insurance-coverage.

President Obama includes more money for mental health programs in his proposed fiscal 2014 budget; advocates call it a small step.

Goodman, Brenda, "Study: Newer Antipsychotic Drugs Are Overused," *WebMD*, Jan. 7, 2011, www.webmd.com/mental-health/news/20110107/study-newer-antipsychotic-drugs-are-overused.

Researchers have found that doctors are overprescribing the latest generation of antipsychotic drugs.

Levey, Noam N., "A hole in mental health system; Obama orders the completion of regulations that will direct insurers to cover more services," *Los Angeles Times*, Jan. 19, 2013, http://articles.latimes.com/2013/jan/19/nation/la-na-mental-health-20130119.

The president directed the secretary of Health and Human Services to complete regulations directing insurers to cover mental health services more fairly.

Peters, Jeremy W., "In Gun Debate, No Rift on Better Care for Mentally Ill," *The New York Times*, April 12, 2013, www.nytimes.com/2013/04/13/us/politics/senators-make-bipartisan-push-for-mental-health-care.html?pagewanted=all&_r=0.

Both Democrats and Republicans in Congress support legislation to fund mental health care, but tying it to gun control is a risky political move.

Pies, Ronald W., "Bereavement Does Not Immunize Against Major Depression," *Medscape News*, Jan. 24, 2013, www.medscape.com/viewarticle/777960.

A psychiatrist argues that ordinary grief from the death of a loved one can be distinguished from depression.

Spencer, Jim, "Suit against UnitedHealth tests mental health coverage rules," *Minneapolis Star Tribune*, April 6, 2013, www.startribune.com/business/201677791.html?refer=y.

A class-action lawsuit alleges that a large insurer violated federal law forbidding treating mental health claims differently from medical and surgical claims.

## Reports and Studies

"Improving Outcomes for People with Mental Illnesses Involved with New York City's Criminal Court and Correction Systems," Justice Center of the Council of State Governments, December 2012, p. 1, http://consensusproject.org/jc_publications/improving-outcomes-nyc-criminal-justice-mental-health/FINAL_NYC_Report_12_22_2012.pdf.

A criminal justice research organization examines the intersection of mental illness and incarceration in New York City and finds the percentage of inmates with mental illness is increasing.

"Proceedings on the State Budget Crisis and the Behavioral Health Treatment Gap: The Impact on Public Substance Abuse and Mental Health Treatment Systems," National Association of State Mental Health Program Directors, March 22, 2012, www.nasmhpd.org/docs/Summary-Congressional%20Briefing_March%2022_Website.pdf.

State mental health officials describe the detrimental impact of budget cuts on mental health and substance abuse treatment services.

Swartz, Marvin S., *et al.*, "New York State Assisted Outpatient Treatment: Program Evaluation," New York State Office of Mental Health, June 30, 2009, www.omh.ny.gov/omhweb/resources/publications/aot_program_evaluation/report.pdf.

Academic researchers evaluate the impact of court-ordered outpatient treatment in New York state on patients and find fewer hospitalizations and better medication management.

# For More Information

**American Psychiatric Association**, 1000 Wilson Blvd., Suite 1825, Arlington, VA 22209; 703-907-7300; www .psych.org. Medical society representing more than 33,000 psychiatric physicians from the United States and around the world.

**American Psychology Association**, 750 First St., N.E., Washington, DC 20002; 800-374-2721; www.apa.org. National association of psychologists representing more than 134,000 researchers, educators, clinicians, consultants and students.

**Judge David L. Bazelon Center for Mental Health Law**, 1101 15th St., N.W., Suite 1212, Washington, DC 20005; 202-467-5730; www.bazelon.org. National legal-advocacy organization representing people with mental disabilities.

**Mental Health America**, 2000 N. Beauregard St., 6th Floor, Alexandria, VA 22311; 703-684-7722; www.mental healthamerica.net. Advocacy organization with 240 affiliates in 41 states working to prevent mental illness and substance abuse conditions.

**National Alliance on Mental Illness**, 3803 N. Fairfax Dr., Suite 100, Arlington, VA 22203; 703-524-7600; www.nami .org. Grassroots organization with local affiliates nationwide advocating for access to mental health services, treatment, support and research.

**National Association of State Mental Health Program Directors**, 66 Canal Center Plaza, Suite 302, Alexandria, VA 22314; 703-739-9333; www.nasmhpd.org. National organization representing state mental health commissioners/ directors and their agencies.

**National Council for Community Behavioral Healthcare**, 1701 K St., N.W., Suite 400, Washington, DC 20006; 202-684-7457; www.thenationalcouncil.org. National advocacy group representing more than 2,000 community behavioral health organizations.

**National Institute for Mental Health**, 6001 Executive Blvd., Rockville, MD 20852; 301-443-4513; www.nimh.nih.gov. Federal institute conducting and funding basic and clinical research to improve the understanding and treatment of mental illness.

**Substance Abuse and Mental Health Services Administra-tion**, 1 Choke Cherry Rd., Rockville, MD 20857; 877-726-4727; www.samhsa.gov. Federal agency that administers grants to states and collects data on mental health disorders and substance abuse.

**Treatment Advocacy Center**, 200 N. Glebe Rd., Suite 730, Arlington, VA 22203; 703-294-6001; www.treatmentadvo cacycenter.org. National nonprofit working for timely and effective treatment of severe mental illness.

# 16

# Domestic Violence

Barbara Mantel

Demonstrators at the Capitol rally last year for renewal of the Violence Against Women Act, which Congress renewed in February 2013. The White House and lawmakers who supported renewal credit the act with reducing domestic violence. Some victim advocates believe, however, that VAWA should devote more funds to primary prevention steps rather than criminal justice.

From *CQ Researcher*, November 15, 2013.

fter separating from her husband in June, North Carolina school teacher Laurrissa Armstrong twice asked judges for protective orders, once in late July and again in early August. Both times she was denied. The 62-year-old Armstrong wrote the court that she feared her husband, who she said had hit her and recently slashed her tires.

"His behavior was escalating," she wrote. Bruce Ray Armstrong, 61, denied his wife's charges, although he admitted hitting and grabbing her decades earlier. "I am not a violent person," he wrote the court.[1]

Laurrissa Armstrong died on Sept. 7, a little more than a week after police say her estranged husband shot her in the parking lot outside her Greensboro apartment. A few hours after the shooting, police found his body in a parked car a few miles away, although officials would not confirm a suicide.[2]

Despite such tragedies, domestic violence has been falling for decades, according to Justice Department crime statistics. The number of homicides by an intimate partner fell from 2,080 in 1993 to 1,341 in 2008, the latest year for which data are available.* And about 811,000 people age 12 or older are estimated to have been victims of non-fatal intimate-partner violence in 2012 — down from a little more than 2 million in 1993.[3] The department defines intimate-partner violence as victimization by a current or

---

*Data are from FBI Supplementary Homicide Reports, which rely on state reporting and are incomplete.

## Quarter of Women Suffer Severe Violence

One in four women and one in seven men in the United States have experienced severe physical violence by an intimate partner in their lifetime, while nearly a third of women and a fourth of men have been slapped, pushed or shoved. Almost 10 percent of women and 1 percent of men have experienced a partner trying to choke or suffocate them.

### Percentage of Women and Men Who Have Experienced Violence by an Intimate Partner Over Their Lifetime

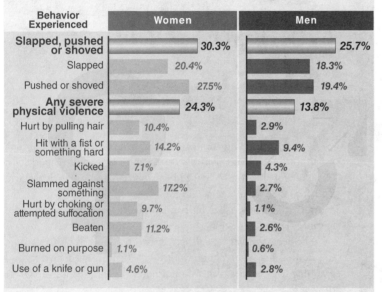

| Behavior Experienced | Women | Men |
|---|---|---|
| **Slapped, pushed or shoved** | **30.3%** | **25.7%** |
| Slapped | 20.4% | 18.3% |
| Pushed or shoved | 27.5% | 19.4% |
| **Any severe physical violence** | **24.3%** | **13.8%** |
| Hurt by pulling hair | 10.4% | 2.9% |
| Hit with a fist or something hard | 14.2% | 9.4% |
| Kicked | 7.1% | 4.3% |
| Slammed against something | 17.2% | 2.7% |
| Hurt by choking or attempted suffocation | 9.7% | 1.1% |
| Beaten | 11.2% | 2.6% |
| Burned on purpose | 1.1% | 0.6% |
| Use of a knife or gun | 4.6% | 2.8% |

*Source:* "The National Intimate Partner and Sexual Violence Survey: 2010 Summary Report," Centers for Disease Control and Prevention, www.cdc.gov/violenceprevention/pdf/nisvs_report2010-a.pdf

former spouse, boyfriend or girlfriend. Some advocates and lawmakers attribute the falling rates to the growth of women's shelters, campaigns to convince police and prosecutors to intervene in what traditionally had been considered a private matter and federal laws such as the 1994 Violence Against Women Act (VAWA), which have poured billions of dollars into shelters, social services and training programs.

Yet others point out that since all types of personal violence — between strangers, casual acquaintances and relatives other than spouses — have been declining equally fast, it is difficult to determine exactly why reported cases of domestic violence are down so much.[4] As a result, advocates, researchers, police and prosecutors

are left to wrestle with the best way to continue to address the problem. They struggle over how much to rely on arrest and prosecution, whether courts should order abusers into behavior modification programs and how to enable health care providers to identify and counsel victims and help to ultimately reduce partner violence.

Further complicating the picture is the fact that the Justice Department figures contradict what advocates are seeing in the field.

The number of domestic violence victims remains "distressingly high," says Anne Menard, chief executive officer of the Harrisburg, Pa.-based National Resource Center on Domestic Violence, a nonprofit that supports the work of domestic violence programs. "We have reports from domestic violence programs and the National Domestic Violence Hotline that more victims than ever are reaching out for assistance."

Part of the explanation, Menard says, could be that "we are much better at informing victims, their families, their friends and employers that there is help available."

Some experts have another explanation. They say the Justice Department figures, which are based on an annual survey of about 90,000 households, underestimate the yearly toll because it asks about crimes, such as burglaries and car theft. "A lot of people don't see domestic violence in the home as a crime," says John Hamel, a licensed clinical social worker and editor of the journal *Partner Abuse.* "So they tend to downplay it."

To better understand the true scope of domestic violence, the Centers for Disease Control and Prevention (CDC) has devised its own ongoing survey. Questioners identify it as a survey about health — not crime — which research shows leads people to be more forthcoming. And it focuses exclusively on intimate-partner violence, asking more detailed questions about such incidents than crime surveys. The CDC's first survey, conducted in 2010, found much higher numbers than the Justice Department's survey: An estimated 12.7 million people age 18 or older suffered rape, physical violence and/or stalking by an intimate partner in the prior 12 months.[5]

Adding to the confusion, the CDC found a much smaller difference in the rates of domestic abuse by gender. While the Justice Department found that about one-sixth of the victims are male, the CDC found the sexes more evenly split: About 55 percent of the victims (6,982,000) were female and 45 percent were male (5,691,000).

However, the sexes experienced different patterns of intimate-partner violence. Female victims faced all forms — rape, physical violence and stalking — while male victims mostly suffered physical violence. In fact, more men experienced physical violence than women in the 12 months prior to the survey.

From this data and other studies, Hamel concludes that "men and women perpetrate acts of violence at close to the same rate," and takes issue with advocacy groups' emphasis on women victims and their male abusers.

But others point out that the CDC survey did not ask about context, motive and meaning. "It's totally incorrect to assume that men and women are equally violent," says Walter DeKeseredy, a sociology professor at West Virginia University in Morgantown. He says his research shows that most women who engage in domestic violence hit their male partners in self defense, often while fighting off sexual assault, strangulation and assault related to separation or divorce.

Hamel says studies he has compiled show that men and women in intimate relationships hit in self-defense at about the same rates, but DeKeseredy calls those studies "crude."

In any case, there is agreement that women suffer the most severe forms of physical violence. Nearly one in

## Many Victims Face Lack of Emergency Housing

Sixty-five percent of unmet requests for services from domestic violence victims were for emergency shelter or transitional housing, according to an annual nationwide census of local domestic violence programs during a typical 24-hour period.

### Domestic Violence Services Provided on Sept. 12, 2012

**64,324 victims served** — More than 35,000 found emergency shelter or transitional housing, and 29,000 received nonresidential help and services, such as counseling, legal advocacy and aid from children's support groups.

**20,821 hotline calls answered** (more than 14 per minute)

**25,182 individuals trained in violence prevention**

**10,471 unmet requests for services** — 65 percent were for emergency shelter or transitional housing

### Reasons services not met:
- Insufficient funding — 42 percent of programs
- Insufficient staff — 30 percent of programs
- Lack of beds or funds for hotel rooms — 26 percent of programs
- Insufficient specialized services — 23 percent of programs
- Limited funding for translators, bilingual staff or accessible equipment — 10 percent of programs

*Source:* "Domestic Violence Counts: 2012 National Summary," National Network to End Domestic Violence, http://nnedv.org/downloads/Census/DVCounts 2012/DV Counts12_NatlSummary_Color.pdf

three women and one in four men have been slapped, pushed or shoved by an intimate partner in their lifetime, according to the CDC. Meanwhile, a fourth of women and one in seven men have been hit with a fist, slammed against a wall, choked, beaten, burned or attacked with a knife or gun.[6]

The ultimate impact of intimate-partner violence also falls most heavily on women. More than three times as many women as men told the CDC of living in fear; being injured; requiring medical attention; suffering symptoms of post-traumatic stress disorder; needing advocacy, legal or housing services, and missing work or school.[7] "If you are interested in the individual and community costs of what is going on, then you have to look at impact," says Menard.

The impact extends beyond intimate partners, whose experience of this kind of abuse most often begins

Vice President Joe Biden embraces domestic violence advocate Janet Blackburn, of Ellicott City, Md., after speaking in Rockville, Md., on March 13, 2013, about the need to reduce domestic homicides. Blackburn lost her sister, niece and two nephews to domestic violence. As a U.S. senator in 1994, Biden sponsored the Violence Against Women Act. Attorney General Eric Holder is at left.

before age 25.[8] Children exposed to domestic violence also suffer.

"Children in homes with domestic violence have a very high risk of being physically abused," says Jeffrey Edleson, dean of the School of Social Welfare at the University of California, Berkeley. "And even if they are not being physically abused, they are at higher risk of developmental problems." Boys typically become more aggressive and antisocial, while girls exhibit depression and sleep disorders, he says.

But some children are resilient, and some have "buffers," such as a protective battered mother, older sibling, aunt, uncle, grandparent or teacher, Edleson says. The presence or absence of other risk factors, such as alcohol abuse, guns in the home and mental illness among caregivers, helps to determine the impact of domestic violence on children. The services they receive also play a role.

Meanwhile, the programs that provide services to victims are facing budget cuts. New Beginnings, a nonprofit that provides housing and support to women and children fleeing abuse in San Juan County, N.M., is facing a

funding crisis after charitable contributions shrank drastically over the past four years because of the weak economy. "We are now only able to serve half the number of women and children we did before," said Executive Director Susan Kimbler.[9]

New Beginnings also receives some state and federal funds, but the automatic federal budget cuts that went into effect this past spring, known as sequestration, are hitting such programs hard. Tens of thousands of victims across the country may lose access to shelters, hotlines, legal help and other services that rely on grants administered by the departments of Justice and Health and Human Services.[10]

"I think lots of programs are living hand to mouth," says Joyce Grover, executive director of the Topeka-based Kansas Coalition Against Sexual and Domestic Violence. With the future of state, federal and private funding so uncertain, Grover wonders how communities can add needed programs, such as those that focus on abuse among teenage dating couples or that coordinate the work of police and advocates. "That's not something you can do one year and be gone the next," she says.

Against this backdrop, here are some of the questions about how to further reduce domestic violence that experts and advocates are debating:

### Should violent partners be arrested and prosecuted against a victim's wishes?

The Violence Against Women Act, which applies to victims of both genders, ties its grants to evidence that states are aggressively pursuing domestic violence crimes. As a result, state laws mandating or strongly encouraging arrest of alleged abusers have flourished. Yet, while domestic violence advocates at first supported such laws, some now see them as problematic.

"I am not a fan," says Leigh Goodmark, a visiting law professor at the University of Maryland and codirector of the Center on Applied Feminism at the University of Baltimore School of Law, who has worked with hundreds of abused women over the past 20 years. Victims want the violence to stop, but many do not want their abuser arrested, says Goodmark, who believes the decision should rest with them —"the person it affects the most" — and not with the state.

At least 24 states have some form of mandatory arrest law, according to the American Bar Association. In

Colorado, for example, police *shall* arrest if the officer on the scene has probable cause to believe a crime involving domestic violence, from simple assault to assault with a weapon, was committed. Other states, such as Arkansas, have pro-arrest laws: Where probable cause exists, arrest is the *preferred* action. And some states, such as Idaho and Georgia, leave it to police discretion: An officer *may* arrest if there is probable cause to believe domestic assault or battery has occurred.[11]

"If there is evidence that a crime has been committed, the police should arrest the offender even if the victim at that moment requests that he not be taken into custody," says Cheryl Hanna, a former prosecutor and professor of law at Vermont Law School in South Royalton. Mandatory arrest "ensures the victim's safety at that moment. It communicates to the offender that he is accountable for his behavior, and it communicates more broadly on a social level that violence against women is not going to be tolerated," she says.

"My concern is if you do away with mandatory arrest, you're going to go back to a time where the police considered it a private matter and they didn't do anything about it," says Michelle Kaminsky, deputy chief of the Domestic Violence Bureau in the Brooklyn District Attorney's Office in New York City. "The majority of the police on the street are very young, and if they're not told arrest is the policy, then they won't do it."

But Goodmark says mandatory arrest laws disregard the practical reality of many victims' lives and the many reasons someone might not want a partner arrested and possibly jailed. "Your partner may be the primary breadwinner, so not having him there may mean not having a roof over your head, not having food in your mouth and not having somebody to coparent with you," she says. Arrest can lead to the loss of housing subsidies, which are denied people with an arrest record. And it can lead to deportation if the abuser is an undocumented immigrant, she adds.

Beth Richie, director of the Institute for Research on Race and Public Policy at the University of Illinois at Chicago, has studied how law enforcement affects communities of color and says economic empowerment might do far more to reduce domestic violence in poor black neighborhoods than get-tough policing and prosecution. "When it becomes the only thing we do and it takes so much lobbying and research attention, it does harm other strategies," said Richie.[12]

Hanna says all those concerns are legitimate. That's why mandatory arrest must be coupled with community support services for victims, such as counseling, legal aid and support in navigating government services "so that the victim is in a position where she can really make autonomous decisions," says Hanna.

But Goodmark says that line of reasoning assumes victims of domestic abuse are isolated and need official help. "Some people have families and religious groups and communities that they are a part of and don't need the state intervening in their lives," she says. In addition, if worries about finances are keeping someone in an abusive relationship, social services can't provide the victim with a living wage, she says. "Similarly, social services can't replace an arrested coparent, if that's what you need," says Goodmark.

Opponents of mandatory arrest also say that too often, police arrest both partners, failing to distinguish the primary aggressor. Many states require police on the scene to make that determination, but the ability to do so in a volatile, heated situation requires extensive training.

Mark Wynn helped to create the domestic violence division at the Nashville Metropolitan Police Department, where he served for 21 years. He now trains police across the country and spends a big part of each session on how to determine the aggressor. Once a victim is wrongly arrested, "horrible things can happen," says Wynn. "It affects employment, you can't get public housing, you can't get public assistance, you could lose custody of your kids."

Still, even in states with laws requiring police to identify the primary aggressor, such as New York, the police sometimes leave it to prosecutors to figure things out. "If both parties are screaming and things are moving quickly, the police can't always assess who is the primary aggressor," says Kaminsky. "And there are safety concerns for the officer, too."

Multiple studies have failed to show that arrest does much to deter future acts of domestic violence, except perhaps for first-time abusers with steady jobs and strong stakes in the community.[13] But Hanna says those studies are flawed because they did not look at what happens after arrest. Is there significant jail time? Is the abuser ordered into treatment? Does the victim get any counseling and advocacy services? "If you arrest someone and they spend the night in jail and then go free and there's no community followup [and] nothing else happens," she says, "then of course the arrest policy isn't going to affect recidivism" — that is, whether the abuser will commit a violent act again.

Prosecution, even of cases with strong evidence, does not always follow arrest. Some district attorneys have so-called hard "no-drop" policies. If there's strong evidence, such as witnesses and police testimony, they'll pursue a case of domestic violence even without the victim's cooperation. Both Hanna and Kaminsky, while in favor of mandatory arrest laws, favor a more nuanced approach when it comes to prosecution: Prosecutors can pursue a case against a victim's wishes, but only after careful consideration of the victim's concerns.

If the crime is not severe, if there is no history of violence and no clear signs of risk for worse abuse in the future, such as prior weapons charges, alcoholism or recent separation, "why not listen to what the woman wants?" says Kaminsky, whose cases most often involve female victims. "It is better to establish a relationship of trust with the woman so that she knows if things change, she has a place to go."

## Do batterer intervention programs work?

Most people arrested and prosecuted for domestic violence face misdemeanor charges and little or no jail time. But judges often order them into so-called batterer intervention programs as a condition of probation. Yet the programs are controversial, with some research showing modest results at reducing violence and other studies showing no impact at all.

"There are some men who have slapped their girlfriend one time and got arrested, and there are some who have a pattern of abuse," Juan Rodriguez says of the men in the state-certified batterers intervention program he coordinates at People's Place, a nonprofit social services provider in Milford, Del. The men attend weekly two-hour group sessions for 25 weeks.

Men are screened for mental health or substance abuse problems and referred to programs to address those issues before being allowed into Rodriguez's program. Rodriguez and his colleagues use a curriculum that is common across the country, based on the notion that some men are socialized in childhood and young adulthood to use force to resolve perceived conflicts and to control their partners.

"Domestic violence is not about anger. . . . It's not the reason he is slapping her," says Rodriguez. "We don't spend a lot of time talking about anger in the group; we spend more time trying to impact their beliefs," such as the belief that the man should make all the decisions. The men also discuss ways to change their behavior and step back from tactics they may be using to control their partners, such as intimidation, emotional abuse and manipulation.

"It can be pretty intense," says Rodriguez, and about a third of the men drop out after a few weeks, despite being reported to their probation officers. In fact, nationwide, dropout rates can be more than 50 percent. Rodriguez believes that some of those who stay do change. "But I think there are a lot who don't change, and some are sent back [to the program] by the courts after a year or two."

Psychologist Donald Dutton, a professor at the University of British Columbia in Vancouver and a long-time critic of standard batterer intervention programs, says they don't work, and they can't work. Dutton calls the talk in the sessions about men's socialized need for power and control "brainwashing" and says the programs "demand public adherence to a set of sociopolitical beliefs which, for the most part, are not true."

Instead, Dutton says, domestic violence is rooted in individual psychological issues, including inappropriate emotional reactions, the failure to form normal attachments to caregivers in childhood, inappropriate anger and overreaction to perceived abandonment. These, he says, should be the focus of behavioral therapy.

As evidence that the standard approach is not working, Dutton points to a handful of experimental studies that randomly assigned some abusers to a batterer intervention program and other abusers to a control group. These studies have found little or no impact on recidivism.[14]

But sociologist Edward Gondolf, a researcher at the Mid-Atlantic Addiction Research and Training Institute at Indiana University of Pennsylvania, says those studies were seriously flawed. Many men assigned to treatment programs didn't complete them, so the programs' true impact was not measured, he says. The studies didn't examine whether men who left treatment early faced fines or jail time or other penalties, and they followed up with the men at a single point in time rather than at intervals, says Gondolf.

Gondolf conducted a multistate study that followed men enrolled in batterer intervention programs. No one was randomly assigned to treatment or a control group. He found that men who completed at least three months of batterer intervention were 50 percent less likely to physically assault their partner in a 15-month follow-up period than men of similar age and background who dropped out.

"We found a de-escalation over time not only in the physical assaults but also in psychological and verbal abuse and controlling behaviors," says Gondolf, who says batterer intervention programs can clearly make a difference.

Edleson, of the University of California, who has reviewed batterer intervention studies, agrees, but says the research doesn't shed light on why these programs may work for some abusers. It's unclear, he says, whether the key ingredient is the emphasis on changing beliefs about men's roles in relationships or the emphasis on changing controlling behavior or whether some men may behave better simply because they have to show up once a week and be accountable while they're on probation, he says.

"Many people find this lack of knowledge about what works very frustrating," says Edleson.

Even without this data, many states have rules specifying the length, content and format of batterer intervention programs and don't allow other kinds of therapy, such as couples counseling, as an alternative. Many in the field think couples counseling is, at a minimum, ineffective, and at worst, dangerous.

"Many times a woman is not going to talk about the violence in front of her partner, because if she does, they'll go home afterwards and he'll knock her head off," says Rodriguez.

But those who offer couples counseling say that concern is overblown, especially with proper screening. "We

## Coercion and Intimidation Are Signs of Abuse

Domestic violence can take many forms, from emotional abuse and coercion to physical violence. Here are some of the troubling behaviors to watch out for in a relationship:

**Emotional Abuse**
Telling you that you can never do anything right
Shaming or putting you down
Calling you a bad parent or threatening to harm or take away your children

**Isolation**
Controlling whom you see, where you go or what you do
Discouraging or keeping you from seeing friends or family
Preventing you from working or attending school

**Control**
Taking your money or refusing to give you money for expenses
Controlling every household expenditure
Preventing you from making your own decisions

**Coercion**
Pressuring you to have sex when you don't want to or doing things sexually you're uncomfortable with
Pressuring you to use drugs or alcohol

**Threats of Aggression or Violence**
Looking or acting in ways that scare you
Destroying your property or threatening to hurt or kill your pets
Intimidating you with guns, knives or other weapons

*Source:* "Warning Signs and Red Flags," The National Domestic Violence Hotline, www.thehotline.org/is-this-abuse/abuse-defined/

don't take every Tom, Dick or Harry into the program," says Daniel O'Leary, a professor of psychology at Stony Brook University in Stony Brook, N.Y., who runs a counseling program for couples involved in domestic abuse.

O'Leary says traditional batterer programs assume that one size fits all. But they are not appropriate for men who have pushed, shoved or slapped their partners but do not repeatedly batter or instill fear in their partners, he says. That's because power and control may not be the issue, he says, and because less aggressive men may feel out of place.

Some dropouts from these programs have sought out his services. "They'll say, 'I'm with a bunch of guys who

San Francisco Sheriff Ross Mirkarimi was sentenced to three years' probation in March 2012, after grabbing his wife during an argument and injuring her arm. Mirkarimi was suspended by Mayor Edwin F. Lee, who pressed for his removal. But liberal members of the city's Board of Supervisors voted to retain Mirkarimi, who previously served seven years as a liberal member of the board.

are really beating up their spouses and maybe have alcohol and drug abuse, and I don't see myself like that,'" says O'Leary.

O'Leary works individually for three or four sessions with each partner in a couple, screening to make sure that they will be able to contain their verbal aggression during subsequent couple's counseling, which can last 15 weekly sessions or more. The focus is on trying to make communication more positive.

Unlike O'Leary, however, many clinicians who conduct counseling for couples with a history of domestic violence are not trained in domestic violence, says Lonna Davis, director of the Children & Youth Program at San Francisco-based Futures Without Violence, an advocacy organization. Yet some victims want such counseling. Instead of denouncing couples counseling, "It would be better if advocates could engage in a conversation about what would need to be in place for safe couples counseling to happen for women [victims] who want it," says Davis.

## Can health care practitioners effectively screen and counsel victims of domestic violence?

Victims of intimate-partner violence often fail to report it to police, hotline counselors or domestic violence programs in their communities. But most everyone eventually seeks medical care, not necessarily because of abuse but for other medical problems. For that reason, several professional organizations, such as the American Congress of Obstetricians and Gynecologists, have long recommended that health care practitioners routinely ask patients about violence in the home.

But until recently, insurers did not have to pay for preventive care, including domestic violence screening. That changed after President Obama signed the Affordable Care Act (ACA) in March 2010.

Insurance plans created after the ACA became law must cover screening and brief counseling for intimate-partner violence for enrolled women and adolescent girls at no additional cost to the patient. Beginning next year, insurance plans sold in the new health insurance marketplaces will be required to do the same. Such screening and counseling can be part of an annual wellness checkup or can occur during visits for other medical or mental health concerns.[15]

"Providers are knocking on our door and asking, 'Given this, how do I do it?'" says Lisa James, director of health at Futures Without Violence.

But the health care law doesn't require doctors to actually provide the screening. "Some providers might think that domestic violence is more of a social issue rather than a health issue, although I think that this is changing," says James. Research shows that battered women are at risk not only for injury but for gastrointestinal disorders, pelvic pain, depression, panic attacks, sleep disturbances and other medical problems.[16]

In addition, doctors and other providers are telling James they often don't know how to broach the subject with patients and where to send them for help. Her organization runs the government-subsidized National Health Resource Center on Domestic Violence, which has developed in-person and online training for health care practitioners and brochures to guide them through patient screening and counseling.

Many local medical associations have done the same. Since 2004, the Pennsylvania Medical Society has given health care practitioners tens of thousands of cards with screening instructions on one side and a list of the state's domestic violence programs on the other. The cards are designed to help providers overcome reluctance they may have in broaching such a personal issue.

"The patient could be mortified and embarrassed and not feel like they can come back," says Mary Ellen Corum, the society's director of practice economics and payer relations. "You have to be very, very careful and sensitive to that."

But possibly the biggest barrier for physicians and others is time. "Implementing routine screening and making sure there is follow-through with services is just so hard," says recently retired internist Gwendolyn Poles, former supervisor of the internal medicine residency program at Pinnacle Health System in Harrisburg, Pa. Nevertheless, she favors routine screening for domestic violence.

Routine screening can add to an already jam-packed schedule. "The list is enormous of what a physician must already discuss in an exam" including the chief complaint, a history of the present illness, a review of other bodily systems, a review of medications and a family history, says Poles.

However, James says screening and referring patients to domestic violence services should add just about three minutes. "The vast majority of people are not in crisis at that moment," she says.

But Poles says, in practice, it can add as much as 10 precious minutes to the total encounter.

"For some patients, it will take about five minutes. They may say, 'Yes, I'm feeling unsafe, but I'm not ready to do much about it right now.' So you give them information" and the card from the medical society, says Poles. "But if you have a person you suspect of being a victim of domestic abuse who is reluctant to talk, that can be very time consuming to draw them out. And for the patient who is experiencing abuse and wants to escape, you don't just give them a card and say, 'call.'"

James agrees. "We recommend if that does happen that the provider acknowledge and thank the patient for disclosing, and say something like, 'I'm not an expert in this issue but may I put you on the phone with someone who is?'" says James, and allow the patient to use the office phone right then and there.

But Poles says it's not that simple. "I feel compelled to do a slower, softer transition to someone else, so that, metaphorically speaking, the patient doesn't feel like, 'Hey, you've taken all my clothes off and now you're going to bring in someone else to see me naked?'"

Time is also a critical barrier in emergency rooms. Research shows that emergency departments could be doing a much better job of identifying victims of domestic abuse and referring them to services, despite a 22-year-old requirement by the Joint Commission on Accreditation of Hospitals that all emergency room personnel be trained to identify victims of domestic violence.[17]

In a recent study of a semirural Midwestern county, researchers looked through police reports to find female victims of intimate-partner violence. Their study found that the vast majority were using emergency departments for health care but were unlikely to be identified as victims of abuse by emergency personnel.

"What is so depressing is what happened after they were identified," says physician Karin Rhodes, director of the University of Pennsylvania Health System's Division of Emergency Care Policy Research and the study's lead researcher. Only a fraction of victims were referred to a hospital social worker, assessed for safety or referred to what Rhodes says are the county's outstanding victim services.

"That's why I don't think screening should be left up to busy nurses and doctors," says Rhodes.

Instead, Rhodes would like to see emergency department patients, once they are stabilized, privately fill out a computerized health risk assessment that would include questions about partner violence. If they answer positively, information about local resources would automatically come up on the screen. "And then a light should go off in the social workers' office, and a social worker would come by and ask, 'Are you willing to talk about this?'" says Rhodes. If the answer is "yes," the social worker could help the patient make a call to a domestic violence program or even to the police from the hospital. Right now, such computerized screening tools are used primarily for research.

Even if the patient, frequently a woman, is not ready to get help, "At least she knows she is not alone, she doesn't deserve this, and if she needs help, we are here for her," says Rhodes.

## BACKGROUND

### Family Patriarchy

The first law against spousal abuse in the Western world was passed in the Puritan colony of Massachusetts Bay.

"Every married woman shall be free from bodily correction or stripes by her husband, unless it be in his own

# CHRONOLOGY

## 1600s-1800s *Early colonists pass domestic violence laws.*

**1641** Puritans of the Massachusetts Bay Colony adopt the first law in the Western world prohibiting spousal abuse.

**1672** Pilgrims of nearby Plymouth, Mass., enact similar law.

**1824** Mississippi Supreme Court upholds English common law principle that a husband may beat his wife with a rod no thicker than his thumb.

**1868** North Carolina Supreme Court rules a husband cannot be prosecuted for assault and battery if his wife's injuries are not permanent.

**1871** Alabama Supreme Court is first appellate court to rescind a husband's common law right to beat his wife.

**1880s** Maryland, Delaware and Oregon make wife beating a crime, punishable by whipping, but the laws are rarely enforced.

## 1910-1990s *Specialized family courts emerge; women's rights activists successfully press for legal changes.*

**1910** Buffalo, N.Y., establishes the first specialized family court to handle domestic violence complaints; judges emphasize keeping couples together.

**1974** A St. Paul, Minn., women's consciousness-raising group establishes one of the earliest shelters for battered women.

**1981** The Domestic Abuse Intervention Project in Duluth, Minn., is created to coordinate domestic violence services and provide batterer intervention programs. It becomes a national model.

**1984** Congress passes the Family Violence Prevention and Services Act and the Victims of Crime Act, providing states for the first time with federal funds to support battered-women shelters.

**1985** U.S. surgeon general identifies domestic violence as a major public health problem.

**1991** Joint Commission on Accreditation of Hospitals requires emergency room staff to be trained to identify victims of domestic violence.

**1992** American Medical Association suggests all women patients be screened for domestic abuse.

**1994** After eight-month trial, football legend O. J. Simpson is acquitted of charges that he murdered his ex-wife. . . . Congress passes the Violence Against Women Act (VAWA), which encourages mandatory arrest for domestic violence, funds shelters, makes crossing state lines to stalk or injure an intimate partner a federal crime and creates the National Domestic Violence Hotline.

## 2000-Present *Congress reauthorizes key domestic violence laws; government focuses on prevention.*

**2000** Congress extends VAWA for five years and includes grants to train police, prosecutors and judges.

**2001** Coaching Boys Into Men is launched in partnership with the Advertising Council to create a comprehensive violence prevention curriculum for coaches and athletes.

**2002** Centers for Disease Control and Prevention (CDC) creates the DELTA program, which funds local efforts to prevent first-time intimate partner violence.

**2005** U.S. Supreme Court rules a domestic violence victim cannot sue a police department for failing to enforce a restraining order. . . . Congress reauthorizes VAWA and includes provisions on teen dating, stalking and violence prevention.

**2010** CDC launches the National Intimate Partner and Sexual Violence Survey (NIPSVS). . . . Congress reauthorizes the Family Violence Prevention and Services Act.

**2011** The first NIPSVS results show that intimate partner violence affects more than 12 million each year.

**2013** Congress renews VAWA for five years and adds protections for college students, immigrant women, tribal women and members of the LGBT community.

defense upon her assault," the 1641 colonial laws, *Body of Liberties*, stated.

A few years later, the colony outlawed husband beating by wives. The Puritans wished to prevent the family from becoming "a sanctuary for cruelty and violence," wrote historian Elizabeth Pleck, a professor emerita at the University of Illinois at Urbana-Champaign, because the family formed the foundation of the colony, which hoped to set an example of religious devotion for the rest of the world.[18] In 1672 the Pilgrims of nearby Plymouth, Mass., enacted a similar law.

Yet the Puritan-era courts intervened in only the most severe instances of abuse and "invariably chose to preserve the male-dominated family," said Pleck. They were "reluctant to separate wives from husbands, and infrequently granted divorce, attempting instead to reconcile unhappy and quarrelsome couples." Courts appeared to believe that wives provoked their husbands into beating them and sometimes ordered runaway wives to return to their abusive spouses.[19]

The colonial laws in Massachusetts against spousal abuse, then, were largely a symbolic guide to the communities' religious principles, according to Pleck. As New England became more pluralistic and less religious in the late 1600s and early 1700s, she wrote, "the campaign to eradicate wicked behavior yielded to tolerance and indifference."[20]

These early laws never migrated beyond New England. Researchers have found no specialized state legislation to control domestic violence during the late 1700s through the 1850s. In fact, during this period, when husbands were infrequently charged with assault, judges commonly dismissed the criminal charges.

For example, in 1824 the Mississippi Supreme Court upheld in *Bradley v. State* the English common law principle that a husband may beat his wife "with a rod no thicker than his thumb." In 1868, the North Carolina Supreme Court ruled in *State v. Rhodes* that a husband could not be prosecuted for assault and battery as long as his wife's injuries were not permanent. It is better to "shut out the public gaze, and leave the parties to forget and forgive," said the court.[21]

However, the public's indifference to domestic violence began to fade after the Civil War, as emerging professional and middle classes became frightened by what they perceived as uncontrollable crime among working-class immigrants.[22] In addition, upper-class women activists from the suffragist and temperance movements began to agitate for laws punishing wife beating. They pointed to poverty and drunkenness as the principal causes of domestic violence, but "shied away from political action that related men's violence to gender inequality," said feminist writer Elizabeth Felter.[23]

In 1871, the Alabama Supreme Court became the first U.S. appellate court to rescind the common law rights of a husband to beat his wife. In the 1880s, Maryland, Delaware and Oregon passed laws making wife beating a crime, punishable at the whipping post. "Although these statutes demonstrated a new level of societal concern, we believe that they were rarely officially enforced," wrote criminal justice experts Eve and Carl Buzawa and Evan Stark. After a series of financial panics in the late 1800s and early 1900s, middle-class Americans focused on economic rather than social concerns, and female activists shifted efforts to their primary goals of suffrage and temperance.[24]

Meanwhile, specialized family courts, which handled complaints such as domestic assault and nonpayment of child support, began to emerge, with the first established in Buffalo, N.Y., in 1910. By the 1920s, most large cities had followed Buffalo's lead. "Family court judges believed they were helping to decriminalize family violence," wrote Pleck, and their official policy was to discourage divorce and urge reconciliation whenever possible in the belief that each partner was equally at fault. As a result, women would return home, where they might be beaten for having filed a complaint.[25]

It took the women's movement of the 1970s to fundamentally change the nation's attitude toward domestic violence.

## Mounting Pressure

One of the earliest shelters for battered women in the United States was founded by a consciousness-raising group in St. Paul, Minn., in 1974. Early leaders in the women's liberation movement believed that "disadvantages women faced in marriage, work and family life directly contributed to their abuse," wrote Felter. Social-service organizations, such as the Salvation Army, also created shelters and "were better able than shelter-movement

# Abusers Use Technology to Control and Harass

*"Document, document, document. The victim has to take control."*

Technology is making it easier for abusers to control, threaten and intimidate their intimate partners. But it also is leaving a digital trail that can help police and prosecutors bring domestic violence perpetrators to justice.

Kerry Gregg had a history of domestic violence, according to his estranged wife, Shawna. The 40-year-old Helena, Okla., resident physically assaulted her and threatened her with a gun, Shawna Gregg charged in July. Despite a protective order aimed at keeping her husband away, she says the abuse continued: He followed her, hacked into her cell phone account and turned on its GPS system, allowing him to track her movements; he sent her dozens of threatening text messages and emails, one telling her the threats would stop if she were gone, she told the county sheriff's office in August.

Gregg was arrested and charged with stalking in violation of a court order — a felony. In the evidence file are the text and email messages he had sent, printed out by Shawna Gregg.[1]

"Years ago an abuser would check the odometer on the car. Now they can hide a GPS device on the car or install location-tracking software on a phone without the victim's knowledge," says Cindy Southworth, founder of the Safety Net Technology Project at the National Network to End Domestic Violence in Washington, D.C., which trains victim advocates, police, prosecutors and judges on technology safety issues that concern domestic abuse victims.

In addition, "Abusers are doing everything from physically looking at phone calls, messages and Web browsing history to surreptitiously installing spyware," says Southworth. Spyware can record calls, save text messages and emails, log visits to websites, monitor contacts and even turn on the microphone when the phone is off. All the information is sent to the installer's account. Installing such software on another's phone or computer without the person's consent may violate local, state and federal laws, the spyware companies warn on their websites.

But abusers aren't just surreptitiously watching their victims online. Many barrage their partners with threatening emails and text messages — as Kerry Gregg is accused of doing — and some humiliate their partners on social media.

feminists to compete for scarce funding." These organizations typically held the more traditional view at the time that family pathology and psychology were the root causes of domestic violence.[26]

In 1984, Congress passed the Family Violence Prevention and Services Act as well as the Victims of Crime Act. For the first time, states could apply for federal grants to help support women's shelters. By 1989, 1,200 battered women's programs existed across the country, sheltering 300,000 women and children per year. But need far exceeded supply, and many shelters received little federal or state funding, relying heavily on charitable contributions. Still, shelters provided counseling, support groups, hotlines, transportation, legal advice and temporary shelter. However, they were not as effective at providing employment training and safe housing, which would allow a woman to materially change her life, wrote Felter.[27]

During this period, public pressure was mounting to change the classic police response to domestic violence, in which officers called to a home would typically make no arrest. Instead, they often would urge the abuser to walk around the block to cool off and possibly refer the family to family court or social services agencies for counseling. Most states required an officer to witness a misdemeanor assault and battery before making an arrest without a warrant.

Beginning in the mid-1980s, states began to allow warrantless arrests for domestic violence without requiring an officer to witness the crime. By 1992, 47 states and the District of Columbia had enacted such statutes. Today, they exist in every state. In addition, nearly half the states have laws that mandate arrest when a police officer has

Nancy Duong couldn't explain at first why strange men began making lewd calls to her house. But the San Jose, Calif., college student soon discovered that her ex-boyfriend, who punched her when she broke up with him, had electronically pasted her face onto a picture of a nude woman and posted it, along with her contact information, on an escort service's website.[2] Impersonating someone online is illegal under California law.

Southworth says the solution is not for victims of domestic violence to shun technology. Domestic violence victims can use technology to learn about their legal rights, find advocates and shelters, reconnect with friends and relatives cut off by their abusers and link to websites where victims share stories, she says.

"The last thing we want to do is isolate a victim further by telling her to get rid of technology that would allow her to connect with her support system," Southworth says. "Her abuser has already tried to isolate her."

Southworth's organization has created tip sheets on how to safely use computers, cell phones and social media by locking settings, creating effective passwords, monitoring applications, turning off a phone's GPS function and searching for hidden cameras.[3]

The flip side of an abuser's use of technology is that it can provide solid evidence of a crime. In fact, the federal government, every state, the District of Columbia and the U.S. territory of Guam have laws against cyberstalking, or electronically following or harassing someone in a way intended to create fear.

"Document, document, document," said investigator Sherry Bush of the Rochester, Minn., police department at a local event for Domestic Violence Awareness Month in October. The "victim has to take control of the situation" and save every threatening Facebook post, email and text message, said Bush. Law enforcement officials can then use the evidence to prove an abuser has, for example, violated an order of protection.

Southworth recommends that victims who believe they are being monitored or threatened through the misuse of technology contact a trained advocate. The Safety Net Technology Project, which is expanding across the country, has trained more than 60,000 practitioners — including victim advocates, police, prosecutors and judges — on how to use technology safely and hold offenders accountable.

"Physically striking someone is often a misdemeanor assault, while, ironically, computer fraud or wiretapping can be a felony with greater penalties," says Southworth.

*— Barbara Mantel*

---

[1]Marione Martin, "Helena man charged with stalking," *Alva Review-Courier* (Oklahoma), Aug. 14, 2013.

[2]Tracey Kaplan, "San Jose assemblywoman authors bills to protect victims from domestic abuse," *San Jose Mercury News*, June 30, 3013, www.mercurynews.com/ci_23572155/sj-assemblywoman-authors-bills-protect-victims-from-domestic.

[3]"Technology Safety," Safety Net Technology Project, www.nnedv.org/resources/safetynetdocs.html.

probable cause to believe a crime of domestic violence has been committed, and many others encourage arrest. And all states now allow victims of domestic abuse to go to court to seek a civil protective order to limit contact between the victim and abuser and have made it a crime to violate such orders.

As states slowly made these reforms, media coverage of celebrity domestic violence captured the public's attention. In 1994, actor and football legend O. J. Simpson was arrested — following a televised two-hour car chase along the freeways of Southern California — and charged with murdering his ex-wife, Nicole Brown Simpson, and her friend, Ronald Goldman. Citing 911 calls and testimony from friends and relatives, prosecutors alleged that Simpson had repeatedly hit, degraded and stalked Simpson. The eight-month trial, which ended in Simpson's acquittal in 1995, gripped the nation and focused attention on the issue of domestic violence. Calls to domestic violence hotlines, shelters and the police increased sharply.

## Congressional Action

Through the 1980s, conservative members of Congress had kept federal funding for shelters and domestic violence research to a minimum. For example, in 1980, Sen. Jesse Helms, R-N.C., critiqued domestic violence shelters as a challenge to the husband's place as the "head of the family."[28] But by the 1990s, enough members of Congress supported increased federal support to overcome the mostly Republican opposition.

In 1994, Congress passed the Violence Against Women Act (VAWA), sponsored by then-Sen. Joseph Biden, D-Del., which "dramatically affected the federal government's role"

# New Tools Aim to Prevent Domestic Homicides

*"We contain the offender, so the victim doesn't have to be contained."*

In early August, 28-year-old Jessie Cavett of Gresham, Ore., told a court that her husband had beaten her multiple times and threatened to tie her to a chair and "peel my skin off layer by layer and light me on fire alive."[1]

Two months later, despite having obtained a restraining order against her estranged husband, Cavett was dead from a single gunshot wound to the head. Nine hours after the shooting, police arrested Joshua Cavett, 36, found with a loaded gun and the couple's 2-year-old daughter. He pleaded not guilty to killing his wife and kidnapping the child.

In cases where law enforcement can determine the relationship between killer and victim, nearly half of female murder victims are killed by an intimate partner. About 5 percent of male murder victims are killed by a spouse, ex-spouse, girlfriend or, in the case of same-sex relationships, boyfriend.[2]

Studies suggest that such homicides are largely predictable. "We are learning about who is facing what level of physical danger," says Jill Davies, deputy director at Greater Hartford Legal Aid and author of *Advocacy Beyond Leaving*, a guide for advocates with clients who remain in contact with current or former partners. "The violence that folks are experiencing is not all the same," she says. "And every bit of violence that gets called domestic violence is not battering, is not extreme or life threatening."

Researchers have developed danger-assessment tools and tested them for their predictive power. In 2005 the Maryland Network Against Domestic Violence — an advocacy, training and educational organization in Lanham, Md. — began using an evidence-based, 11-question screening tool and referral protocol called the Lethality Assessment Program. The U.S. Department of Justice has said it is one of two "promising practices" in intimate partner homicide prevention, and it has become a national model.

"We now have 100 percent of our law enforcement agencies [in Maryland] using our screening tool," says Michaele Cohen, executive director of the network. Hospitals, social workers, faith-based organizations and a Head Start program in the state also are using it. "The idea is to identify people who might not have picked up the phone and called the police," says Cohen. In a 12-city study, half of women who were killed or almost killed did not perceive their intimate partners as highly dangerous or tended to underestimate their level of danger.[3]

The goal is to connect people at high risk of serious injury or homicide with domestic violence programs that can provide hotline, shelter and advocacy services such as safety planning and help getting a protective order. "Research has shown that people who go in for domestic violence services are less likely to be killed or seriously injured, and research shows that the majority of people killed or seriously injured had never gone in for services," says Cohen.

in reducing domestic violence, wrote Eve Buzawa and colleagues. Key provisions provided funding to state and local governments and Native American tribes to implement mandatory arrest policies; increase coordination among police, prosecutors and judges; strengthen legal advocacy and service programs for victims; and educate judges about domestic violence.

The law also created the National Domestic Violence Hotline, which began operating in 1996. It now has a database of more than 5,000 shelters and agencies across the country and is available 24 hours a day, seven days a week in 170 languages. Last year, it received 265,000 calls from victims, survivors, their families and friends, service providers and abusers.[29]

VAWA also made it a federal crime to travel across state lines to injure or stalk an intimate partner and required state courts to enforce protection orders issued in other states.

Conservatives attacked the law as an unnecessary intrusion into states' rights and the family domain, while some fathers' rights groups argued that it ignored the needs of male victims of domestic abuse, despite the fact that VAWA

A police officer responding to a domestic violence call or a health care practitioner, social worker, teacher or other trained community professional who suspects abuse conducts the screening. The first three questions are the most important:

- Has she/he ever used a weapon against you or threatened you with a weapon?
- Has he/she threatened to kill you or your children?
- Do you think he/she might try to kill you?

"A 'yes' to any one of those automatically triggers the high-risk referral," says Cohen. The screener then will call trained staff at a local domestic violence hotline and ask if the victim wants to get on the line. The victim can consent or decline the service.

Even if the domestic violence victim answers "no" to all of the first three questions, a "yes" answer to at least four of the remaining eight questions also will trigger a high-risk referral. These questions ask about gun possession, unemployment, choking, threatening messages and more.

Research is under way to determine the program's effectiveness at reducing serious injury and homicide. "We don't know how many people were not killed because they got services," says Cohen. "At this point in time, we cannot say, 'This is the cause, and this is the effect,'" although she says intimate partner homicides in Maryland have dropped by a third since reaching a high in 2007. Jurisdictions in 31 other states have been trained to use the lethality assessment.

The same year Cohen's organization began using its homicide prevention program, the Jeanne Geiger Crisis Center in Amesbury, Mass., created the Domestic Violence High Risk Team, the other program the Justice Department finds promising. It also uses a screening tool to identify victims of domestic violence at high risk of homicide or serious injury, but it goes a step further by coordinating the efforts of advocates, probation officers, police, prosecutors, hospitals, legal services and batterer intervention programs. High-risk cases are assigned to a multidisciplinary team that maps out a response. The goal is to provide services to the victim and to contain and track the offender, so the victim can remain in the community, preferably at home.

The team can help with free legal assistance, transitional housing and safety planning in case of an emergency. The police can make home visits and extra drive-bys. Federal law allows them to confiscate the gun of an abuser who is subject to a restraining order. An offender who has violated a restraining order can be made to wear a GPS device to track his or her location.

"We contain the offender, so the victim doesn't have to be contained," said Kelly Dunne, the center's chief operating officer. [4] Since the program began eight years ago, no domestic violence homicides have occurred in the nine communities, including Amesbury, that it serves. Massachusetts now has 22 High Risk Teams, and the approach is being replicated across the country.

— *Barbara Mantel*

[1] Sara Roth, "Gresham murder suspect had history of violence," KGW.com, Oct. 14, 2013, www.kgw.com/home/Estranged-husband-told-police-he-killed-somebody--227740951.html.

[2] Alexia Cooper and Erica L. Smith, "Homicide Trends in the United States, 1980-2008," *Patterns & Trends*, Bureau of Justice Statistics, November 2011, p. 18, www.bjs.gov/content/pub/pdf/htus8008.pdf.

[3] "What is LAP?" Maryland Network Against Domestic Violence, http://mnadv.org/lethality/what-is-lap.

[4] Rachel Louise Snyder, "A Raised Hand: Can a new approach curb domestic homicide?" *The New Yorker*, July 22, 2013, p. 40, www.newyorker.com/reporting/2013/07/22/130722fa_fact_snyder.

is officially gender neutral and applies to both male and female victims of domestic abuse. And some civil libertarians worried that mandatory arrest could potentially violate a person's constitutional right to due process.

In 2000, Congress extended VAWA for another five years and significantly increased community funding for shelters; training programs for police, prosecutors and judges; and legal assistance to help women obtain civil protective orders. Much smaller amounts were targeted for transitional housing for victims of domestic abuse and their families. The law also established special visas for immigrants, both legal and illegal, who experience domestic violence, sexual assault, dating violence or stalking. Previously, immigrant victims could be deported if they left their abusers, who often were their sponsors for residency and U.S. citizenship.

In 2005, Congress renewed the law for another five years, strengthening provisions to protect immigrant victims of domestic violence and addressing violence against teenagers. In addition, for the first time, funding became available to develop strategies to prevent domestic violence before it occurred.

Ciara Taylor and Justin Clayton are among the students from Southwind High School, in Memphis, Tenn., who gathered on Feb. 17, 2012, to remember classmate Janette Corria, who was killed by domestic violence. The memorial was held in conjunction with National Teen Dating Violence Awareness & Prevention Week and hosted by Southwind's Students Against Dangerous Decisions (S.A.D.D.) organization.

In February 2013, after months of debate, Congress renewed the law for another five years. The renewal had been delayed by conservative House Republicans, who opposed provisions extending specific protections to Native Americans and gay, bisexual and transgender victims of domestic abuse.

The law gives tribal courts jurisdiction over non-Native Americans who assault Native American women on tribal land. Previously, those cases could be heard only in state and federal courts.[30] Advocates for the change said it takes too long for state and federal prosecutors to get to a crime scene on remote Indian reservations. At that point, "your witnesses are not there. Your victim may or may not be there," said Lisalyn Jacobs of New York-based Legal Momentum, a legal advocacy organization.[31]

*The New York Times* reported that more than 1,300 women's and human rights groups had signed a letter supporting the legislation.[32]

## CURRENT SITUATION

### Workplace Protections

In October, Democratic California Gov. Jerry Brown signed legislation aimed at protecting victims of domestic violence from losing their jobs or being discriminated against at work. The measure was sought by former second-grade teacher Carie Charlesworth, who had warned officials at Holy Trinity School in El Cajon that she had obtained a temporary restraining order against her husband after years of emotional and verbal abuse. When her husband appeared on the campus in January, the Catholic school put Charlesworth on leave and then fired her in April.

The director of the diocese's Office for Schools wrote parents and parishioners of Charlesworth's termination, saying, "We couldn't possibly jeopardize innocent children to justify her return." But Charlesworth, now divorced, said the school treated her like a criminal. "I felt victimized all over again," she said.[33]

State Sen. Hannah-Beth Jackson, D-Santa Barbara, sponsored the measure, saying it will prevent victims from staying silent out of fear of being fired. "I strongly believe that an unknown threat to a workplace is much more dangerous than a known threat," she said.[34]

Also in October, the New Jersey Security and Financial Empowerment Act took effect. The law requires employers with 25 or more workers to provide up to 20 days of unpaid leave during a 12-month period to employees dealing with domestic violence or sexual assault issues.[35]

Both laws are part of a growing trend to mandate employment protections for victims of domestic violence. The protections fall into three broad policy areas: unpaid leave; anti-discrimination and workplace awareness and safety.

At least 11 states, including New Jersey, permit victims to request leave for medical care or other services related to domestic violence. Oregon is unique in that it exempts only the very smallest employers, those with five or fewer employees. Forty-nine states have laws that bar threatening or penalizing a victim of domestic violence, that ensure victim rights to unemployment benefits or provide victims with legal services to encourage employers to cooperate with the criminal justice system. And three states — New York, Illinois and Oklahoma — require employers to educate workers and train supervisors about domestic violence and relevant state laws.[36]

But Jennifer Swanberg, a professor of social work at the University of Maryland in Baltimore, and colleagues report in a study that the penalties for violating these laws are so low — generally ranging from $250 to $500 — that "even small-sized employers can afford" to pay them.

# Are mental health issues the main cause of domestic violence?

## YES  John Hamel

*Editor-in-Chief, Partner Abuse;*
*Author, Gender-Inclusive Treatment of*
Intimate Partner Abuse, 2nd Edition:
Evidence-based Approaches

Written for *CQ Researcher*, November 2013

Partner violence, also known as domestic violence, is a major public health problem affecting millions in the United States. Partner violence has been defined as a gender issue for two reasons: The most severe types more often involve female victims, and advocacy efforts on behalf of battered women have been directed largely by feminists concerned about women's broader social, economic and political rights. Yet, while gender certainly does play a role in the root causes and dynamics of partner violence, social science research suggests that other factors, including an individual's mental health, play a much larger role.

The most empirically sound, reliable national surveys have, since the 1970s, found that women physically assault men as often as men assault women. Current research also indicates that women and men strike the first blow in comparable numbers and are motivated for similar reasons — for example, control, retaliation, anger or, less often, self-defense. Except for rape and physical stalking, women perpetrate nonphysical emotional abuse and attempt to dominate their partners at rates equal to men. And men who harbor sexist attitudes toward women are no more likely to perpetrate partner violence than men who see women as equals.

Furthermore, there is only mixed evidence, in even the most highly patriarchal countries, for correlations between women's lack of empowerment and rates of male-perpetrated partner violence. Far more important than societal attitudes or individual gender hostility is the desire to dominate one's intimate partner.

Indeed, the most relevant causes of partner violence are low socioeconomic status, the degree of conflict in a relationship and whether the perpetrator of domestic violence experienced family dysfunction in childhood, such as abuse, neglect or witnessing of violence between parents. A main risk factor for the perpetration of partner violence, particularly battering, are mental health issues of post-traumatic stress disorder, depression and substance abuse and such personality traits as impulsivity, aggressive tendencies, pro-violent attitudes, a need to control, emotional dependency and an insecurity-driven attachment to others. Such mental health factors predict violence by both male and female batterers.

This research can be found in the Partner Abuse State of Knowledge Project, a comprehensive database on partner violence research that can be accessed at www.domesticviolence research.org.

## NO  Walter S. DeKeseredy

*Anna Deane Carlson Endowed Chair of*
*Social Sciences and Professor of Sociology,*
*West Virginia University*

Written for *CQ Researcher*, November 2013

Why do men physically assault the women they love? The most common answer people give is that these men must be "sick" or mentally disturbed. How could a "normal" person punch, kick, stab or shoot someone he loves and depends on? Certainly, the media contribute to the myth that male-to-female violence is only and always committed by pathological individuals.

Unfortunately, abuse of women is deeply entrenched in our society. At least 11 percent of North American women in marital or cohabiting relationships are physically abused by their male partners annually. In addition, approximately 25 percent of North American college students experience some type of sexual assault every year, and most of the perpetrators are intimate partners or acquaintances. Statistics such as these and others in leading scientific journals suggest that if violence is a function of mental illness, then close to a third, if not more, of the men in our society are sick. Of course, some abusive men have clinical pathologies, but the vast majority do not.

If violent husbands, cohabiting or estranged partners and boyfriends are in fact mentally ill, why do they beat only their current or former female partners and not their bosses, friends or neighbors? Admittedly, many men do attack these others, but those who abuse women in intimate relationships generally have not been convicted of violence outside private places, such as their homes. If we are dealing with men who have terrible problems with self-control, how do they manage to keep from hitting people until they are at home with their partners? How do they manage to exercise self-control until they are in a situation where they can generally get away with beating someone up? If they are "out of control," why do they mostly only beat their partners instead of killing them? Psychological theories cannot answer these questions nor do they address the unequal distribution of power between men and women in North American society and in domestic contexts.

Of course, not all men abuse their female partners, but the ones who do are more likely to consume pornography and have sexist male peers and sexist attitudes and beliefs. Obviously, other factors contribute to violence against women, such as poverty and unemployment. Nevertheless, it is important to recognize that violence against women is deeply rooted in our society and not limited to only a few people. Indeed, prison, counseling and other individualistic approaches will never solve this society-wide problem.

In any case, they said, states don't seem to have any mechanisms to monitor compliance.[37]

Employers may be willing to accommodate top-performing employees, but less-valued employees may be at risk, the researchers said. "Will the employer use the domestic violence disclosure as an opportunity to terminate her employment?" they asked.[38]

## Nuisance Property Laws

Meanwhile, localities are passing ordinances to try to reduce 911 calls. These so-called nuisance property ordinances shift the burden of dealing with noise, brawling, drug dealing and domestic violence to landlords, forcing them to pay a fine when "nuisance" calls to 911 from their properties get too numerous. The laws have caused many domestic violence victims to be evicted from their homes and are raising concerns that some, to avoid that fate, will stop calling for help.

"Nuisance property ordinances hold landlords accountable for their tenants' behavior," says Harvard University sociologist Matthew Desmond. For example, in Miami, two "nuisance" 911 calls from a property in a six-month period can trigger a letter from the police to the landlord, threatening the property owner with fines and jail time if the calls don't cease. In Milwaukee, police can notify a landlord after three or more "nuisance" calls from a property in a 30-day period.

Desmond published a study last year analyzing every nuisance property citation issued by the Milwaukee police in 2008 and 2009. The study found the catchall category "trouble with subjects" was the most common nuisance category, followed by noise violations. The third most common nuisance activity was domestic violence, far above drugs, trespassing or property damage.[39]

The police letter instructs landlords to respond within 10 days with a written course of action and concludes by saying property owners may be subject to a fine as high as $5,000 or imprisonment for nonpayment if the nuisance activities continue.

"We're not talking about a parking ticket. We're talking about excessive fines that are designed to snap landlords into actions," says Desmond. While the ordinances do not suggest eviction as an abatement strategy, Desmond found that Milwaukee property owners frequently relied on eviction or the threat of eviction to respond to police citations. "In over 70 percent of cases landlords would evict the

household in a nuisance complaint, and with domestic violence, it was even higher, at 80 percent," says Desmond.

"I evict them," one landlord told researchers as he explained how he deals with citations for domestic violence in his properties. The police "want the problem eliminated. Not gradually fixed, but totally eliminated. A five-day [eviction] notice is exactly what the police want," he said.[40]

But, says Desmond, "These ordinances force victims of domestic violence to choose between calling the police and risking eviction or not calling the police and risking more abuse."

His study found that in white neighborhoods, one in 41 properties that could have received a citation did. In Hispanic neighborhoods, that proportion was one in 54 properties. But in black neighborhoods, one in 16 eligible properties received a police citation.[41]

Milwaukee police chief Edward Flynn defended the city's nuisance property ordinance. "Nuisance abatement is a tool in the toolkit. It is a problem-solving technique to abate an ongoing condition," said Flynn. "The overarching goal is not, 'Can we get out of work?' It is, 'Can we solve the problem?'"[42]

Nevertheless, Milwaukee changed its ordinance in 2011 to explicitly exempt stalking, domestic violence and sexual assault or harassment from police citation. Some other cities around the country have done the same.

The American Civil Liberties Union has brought a test case challenging the constitutionality of a nuisance ordinance in Norristown, Pa., after 34-year-old nursing assistant Lakisha Briggs let her abusive ex-boyfriend move in rather than insist he leave and risk a fight and a call to 911. She feared eviction. But after he assaulted her with a broken ashtray, a neighbor called 911 anyway. Police arrested her boyfriend, and Briggs' landlord moved to evict her. In their defense, Norristown officials said Briggs had failed to comply with an instruction to obtain an order of protection.[43] The case could go to trial early next year.

## GPS Tracking

Across the country, criminal justice systems are experimenting with programs to require people subject to protective orders, which can last from one to several years, to wear GPS tracking devices.

"All too often I hear about victims who have been given court-issued orders of protection, and those orders are then violated by the defendant," said Staten Island, N.Y., district attorney Daniel Donovan in discussing his county's pilot program that began in September. Donovan said the devices would also protect offenders from false accusations.[44]

Participants will pay a $10-a-day fee, and once fitted with the ankle device, be given a map of exclusion zones they are forbidden to enter. That's usually a half mile around a victim's home, job or school. Beyond that is a half mile buffer zone. If the offender enters the buffer zone, the victim receives an automatic cell phone notification. If the offender then enters the exclusion zone, an operator will call and instruct the victim to call 911. County officials will evaluate the program in February to determine if it should continue.[45]

A similar but larger pilot program in Connecticut is already proving a success, say its proponents. The program has placed GPS ankle bracelets on 168 offenders in the Hartford, Bridgeport and Danielson areas. It targets offenders who have previously violated protective orders and are considered high risks.

"I think the preliminary results are fabulous," said state Sen. John Kissel, R-Enfield, who wants to expand the program statewide. No victims in the test areas have been injured or killed since the pilot program began.[46]

Unlike in Staten Island, offenders in Connecticut do not pay a fee because the state determined that many of the offenders were indigent. If the program were expanded statewide, it could ultimately cost close to $2 million a year.

Vermont, Massachusetts, Illinois and Washington, D.C., have similar, but smaller, test programs. The key to any GPS program's success, say advocates, is prompt police response and tight coordination among courts, police and social services agencies.

"I like it if it is done well, but what if there is no police who respond?" says Cindy Southworth, vice president of development and innovation at the National Network to End Domestic Violence, an advocacy organization in Washington. "If there is no budget behind it, it doesn't work."

## OUTLOOK

### Shrinking Resources

State and federal budget cuts have led to the shutdown or scaling back of social services that provide victims of domestic violence with temporary shelter, legal aid,

counseling and safety planning. "Other services that may be part of a victim's recovery plan, such as mental health services, affordable housing, employment supports and affordable childcare have also been cut back," says Menard of the National Resource Center on Domestic Violence.

On just one day last year — even before the sequestration budget cuts — more than 10,000 requests for emergency shelter, housing, transportation, childcare and legal representation went unmet because domestic violence programs did not have the needed resources.[47]

That leaves little room for innovation in the future. James of Futures Without Violence hopes to see thousands more health care practitioners begin screening patients for domestic violence and referring them to community-based programs. "But how can these programs meet this demand if they are literally closing their doors because of the sequestration cuts?" she asks.

Budget constraints also threaten clinical social worker Hamel's vision of more services for male victims of domestic abuse. "I know of one shelter that has beds for men in Southern California," he says, "but I don't know many more." And while an increasing number of programs make an effort to work with male victims and provide them with counseling and legal services, more needs to be done, he says.

Police consultant Wynn would like to see more communities build programs like the Enhanced Police Intervention Collaboration in Cumberland County, Maine. "It takes services directly to the victim," says Wynn. Staff members from Portland-based nonprofit Family Crisis Services are paired with police during patrols. When the police respond to a domestic violence call, the staff can tell the victim about the community and government support that is available.

Law professor Goodmark, on the other hand, would like to see funding go in a different direction. "I would be more hopeful if we started to redirect some of the resources that we pour into police and prosecution into primary prevention, figuring out how we stop people from being abusive in the first place," says Goodmark. "But we don't."

In fiscal 2012, the CDC spent about $5.4 million to fund primary prevention efforts of state-level domestic violence coalitions, a tiny fraction of the nearly $600 million the government spent on other domestic violence programs.[48]

"Primary prevention means looking at how do we change our attitudes and beliefs and our culture," says Grover of the Kansas Coalition Against Sexual and Domestic Violence, a grant recipient. "It's doing primary prevention work in schools, in communities, engaging men and boys, encouraging bystander intervention, creating peer pressure so that kids say something if they see something."

This kind of work has just gotten started in the past 10 years. "It is the work of the future," says Grover.

## NOTES

1. Scott Gustin, *et al.*, "Teacher shot, husband dead after apparent domestic incident," Fox 8 WGHP, Aug. 30, 2013, http://myfox8.com/2013/08/29/person-shot-at-adams-farm-apartment-complex.

2. Sarah Newell Williamson, "Greensboro law firm pursues stronger domestic violence law," *News & Record*, Sept. 10, 2013, www.news-record.com/news/article_a4638cbc-1a37-11e3-bd0d-0019bb30f31a.html.

3. "NCVS Victimization Analysis Tool: Custom Tables," Bureau of Justice Statistics, Department of Justice, www.bjs.gov/index.cfm?ty=nvat.

4. *Ibid.*

5. "The National Intimate Partner and Sexual Violence Survey: 2010 Summary Report," Centers for Disease Control and Prevention, November 2011, p. 38, www.cdc.gov/violenceprevention/pdf/nisvs_report2010-a.pdf.

6. *Ibid.*, pp. 43-44.

7. *Ibid.*, p. 38.

8. *Ibid.*, p. 2.

9. Leigh Black Irvin, "New Beginnings domestic violence shelter in Farmington faces financial crisis," *The Daily Times*, Sept. 28, 2013, www.daily-times.com/four_corners-news/ci_24198845/new-beginnings-domestic-violence-shelter-farmington-faces-financial.

10. Tim Murphy, "Congress Helps Air Travelers, Ignores Victims of Rape and Domestic Violence," *Mother Jones*, May 6, 2013, www.motherjones.com/politics/2013/05/sequestration-next-targets-domestic-violence-victims.

11. "Domestic Violence Arrest Policies by State," American Bar Association Commission on Domestic Violence, June 2011, www.americanbar.org/content/dam/aba/multimedia/domestic_violence/Resources/statutorysummarycharts/Domestic%20Violence%20Arrest%20Policies%20by%20State%202011%20(complete).authcheckdam.pdf.

12. Kate Pickert, "What's Wrong with the Violence Against Women Act?" *Time*, Feb. 27, 2013, http://nation.time.com/2013/02/27/whats-wrong-with-the-violence-against-women-act.

13. Eve S. Buzawa, Carl G. Buzawa and Evan Stark, *Responding to Domestic Violence: The Integration of Criminal Justice and Human Services* (2012), pp. 151-162.

14. "What Works To Reduce Recidivism By Domestic Violence Offenders?" Washington State Institute for Public Policy, January 2013, pp. 1-5, www.wsipp.wa.gov/rptfiles/13-01-1201.pdf.

15. "FAQ: Implementation of ACA Screening and Brief Counseling Recommendations for Domestic Violence and Intimate Partner Violence," Futures Without Violence, September 2013, www.futureswithoutviolence.org/userfiles/file/HealthCare/FAQs%20Implementation%20of%20IPV%20Screening%20and%20Counseling%20Guidelines.pdf.

16. Buzawa, *et al.*, *op. cit.*, pp. 377-378.

17. Karin V. Rhodes, *et al.*, "Intimate Partner Violence Identification and Response: Time for a Change in Strategy," *Journal of General Internal Medicine*, March 15, 2011, www.ncbi.nlm.nih.gov/pubmed/21404130.

18. Elizabeth Pleck, *Domestic Tyranny: The Making of American Social Policy against Family Violence from Colonial Times to the Present* (2004), pp. 17, 21-22.

19. *Ibid.*, pp. 18, 23-24.

20. *Ibid.*, p. 33.

21. Buzawa, *et al.*, *op. cit.*, pp. 57-59.

22. *Ibid.*, p. 58.

23. Cynthia R. Daniels, ed., *Feminists Negotiate the State: The Politics of Domestic Violence* (1997), p. 10.

24. Buzawa, *et al.*, *op. cit.*, pp. 58-60.

25. Pleck, *op. cit.*, pp. 136-137.

26. Daniels, *op. cit.*, p. 14.

27. *Ibid.*, pp. 17-18.

28. Material on VAWA is drawn from Buzawa, *et al.*, *op. cit.*, pp. 234-239.

29. The National Domestic Violence Hotline, www.thehotline.org.

30. Ashley Parker, "House Renews Violence Against Women Measure," *The New York Times*, Feb. 28, 2013, www.nytimes.com/2013/03/01/us/politics/congress-passes-reauthorization-of-violence-against-women-act.html.

31. Alisa Chang, "House Passes Expansion of Violence Against Women Act," NPR, Feb. 28, 2013, www.npr.org/2013/02/28/173181449/house-passes-expansion-of-violence-against-women-act.

32. Parker, *op. cit.*

33. Michael Gardner, "Law bans firing domestic violence victims," *U-T San Diego*, Oct. 12, 2013, www.utsandiego.com/news/2013/Oct/12/new-law-bans-firing-of-domestic-violence-victims.

34. *Ibid.*

35. John McDonald, "Domestic Violence and Sexual Assault, NJ Becomes the Latest to Provide Leave for Victimized Employees," *Forbes*, Sept. 26, 2013, www.forbes.com/sites/theemploymentbeat/2013/09/26/domestic-violence-and-sexual-assault-nj-becomes-the-latest-to-provide-leave-for-victimized-employees.

36. Jennifer E. Swanberg, *et al.*, "State Employment Protection Statutes for Victims of Domestic Violence: Public Policy's Response to Domestic Violence as an Employment Matter," *Journal of Interpersonal Violence*, December 2011, pp. 601, 604, 607, http://jiv.sagepub.com/content/27/3/587.abstract.

37. *Ibid.*, p. 611.

38. *Ibid.*

39. Mathew Desmond and Nicol Valdez, "Unpolicing the Urban Poor: Consequences of Third-Party Policing for Inner-City Women," *American Sociological Review*, Dec. 20, 2012, p. 131, http://scholar.harvard.edu/files/mdesmond/files/desmond.valdez.unpolicing.asr__0.pdf.

40. *Ibid.*

41. *Ibid.*, p. 125.

42. John Deidrich, "Abuse victims faced eviction for 911 calls: City rule has changed, but problems persist, advocates say," *Milwaukee Journal Sentinel*, Aug. 18, 2013, www.jsonline.com/news/milwaukee/domestic-violence-victims-in-milwaukee-faced-eviction-for-calling-police-study-finds-b9976751z1-220111761.html.

43. Erik Eckholm, "Victim's Dilemma: 911 Calls Can Bring Eviction," *The New York Times*, Aug. 16, 2013, www.nytimes.com/2013/08/17/us/victims-dilemma-911-calls-can-bring-eviction.html.

44. Thomas Tracy, "Staten Island domestic violence perpetrators to get ankle bracelets to monitor movements in pilot study," *NY Daily News*, Sept. 2, 2013, www.nydailynews.com/new-york/exclusive-staten-island-program-ankle-monitors-track-domestic-batterers-article-1.1443152.

45. *Ibid.*

46. Grace Merritt, "GPS ankle bracelets reduce domestic violence injuries in Connecticut," *The CT Mirror*, Sept. 2, 2013, www.ctmirror.org/story/2013/09/02/gps-ankle-bracelets-reduce-domestic-violence-injuries-connecticut.

47. "Domestic Violence Counts 2012: A 24-Hour Census of Domestic Violence Shelters and Services," National Network to End Domestic Violence, March 25, 2013, p. 1, http://nnedv.org/downloads/Census/DVCounts2012/DVCounts12_NatlReport_Color.pdf.

48. "FY 2013 Appropriations Briefing Book," Campaign for Funding to End Domestic and Sexual Violence, March, 2012, pp. 6-7, http://nnedv.org/downloads/Policy/FY_13_Briefing_Book.pdf.

## BIBLIOGRAPHY

### Selected Sources
### Books

Buzawa, Eve S., Carl G. Buzawa and Evan Stark, *Responding to Domestic Violence: The Integration of Criminal Justice and Human Services*, 2012.

Two academic researchers and an attorney (Carl Buzawa) explore how the criminal justice system, social service agencies and health care practitioners respond to domestic violence.

**Daniels, Cynthia R., ed., *Feminists Negotiate the State: The Politics of Domestic Violence*, 1997.**
Seven feminists examine how the women's movement helped change policies on domestic violence.

**Kaminsky, Michelle, *Reflections of a Domestic Violence Prosecutor: Suggestions for Reform*, 2012.**
An assistant district attorney in Brooklyn, N.Y., explores how the criminal justice system treats victims of domestic violence.

**Pleck, Elizabeth, *Domestic Tyranny: The Making of American Social Policy against Family Violence from Colonial Times to the Present*, 2004.**
A historian traces official reaction to family violence from colonial times.

## Articles

**Eckholm, Erik, "Victims' Dilemma: 911 Calls Can Bring Eviction," *The New York Times*, Aug. 16, 2013, www.nytimes.com/2013/08/17/us/victims-dilemma-911-calls-can-bring-eviction.html?_r=0.**
Holding landlords responsible for reducing nuisance 911 calls can lead to the eviction of domestic violence victims.

**Gardner, Michael, "Law bans firing domestic violence victims," *U-T San Diego*, Oct. 12, 2013, www.utsandiego.com/news/2013/Oct/12/new-law-bans-firing-of-domestic-violence-victims.**
California passes legislation to protect victims of domestic violence from workplace discrimination.

**Murphy, Tim, "Congress Helps Air Travelers, Ignores Victims of Rape and Domestic Violence," *Mother Jones*, May 6, 2013, www.motherjones.com/politics/2013/05/sequestration-next-targets-domestic-violence-victims.**
The automatic federal budget cuts known as sequestration take a toll on domestic violence programs.

**Parker, Ashley, "House Renews Violence Against Women Measure," *The New York Times*, Feb. 28,** 2013, www.nytimes.com/2013/03/01/us/politics/congress-passes-reauthorization-of-violence-against-women-act.html.
Congress renews the Violence Against Women Act, including new protections for college students, immigrant women, tribal women and members of the lesbian, gay, bisexual, transgender (LGBT) community.

**Pickert, Kate, "What's Wrong with the Violence Against Women Act?" *Time*, Feb. 27, 2013, http://nation.time.com/2013/02/27/whats-wrong-with-the-violence-against-women-act.**
Some advocates argue that the Violence Against Women Act's emphasis on criminal justice undercuts the autonomy of victims who may not want their abusers arrested.

## Reports and Studies

**"Domestic Violence Arrest Policies by State," American Bar Association Commission on Domestic Violence, June 2011, www.americanbar.org/content/dam/aba/multimedia/domestic_violence/Resources/statutorysummarycharts/Domestic%20Violence%20Arrest%20Policies%20by%20State%202011%20(complete).authcheckdam.pdf.**
A national association of lawyers details the domestic violence arrest policies of each state.

**"Domestic Violence Counts 2012: A 24-Hour Census of Domestic Violence Shelters and Services," National Network to End Domestic Violence, March 25, 2013, http://nnedv.org/downloads/Census/DVCounts2012/DVCounts12_NatlReport_Color.pdf.**
A national advocacy organization tracks the use of shelters and services and documents the thousands of calls for help that go unmet because of tight resources.

**"The National Intimate Partner and Sexual Violence Survey: 2010 Summary Report," Centers for Disease Control and Prevention, November 2011, www.cdc.gov/violenceprevention/pdf/nisvs_report2010-a.pdf.**
In its 2010 survey of intimate partner and sexual violence, the CDC finds a higher incidence than Justice Department crime surveys.

Rhodes, Karin V., *et al.*, "Intimate Partner Violence Identification and Response: Time for a Change in Strategy," *Journal of General Internal Medicine*, March 15, 2011, www.ncbi.nlm.nih.gov/pubmed/21404130. University of Pennsylvania researchers document the poor performance of hospital emergency departments in identifying domestic violence victims and referring them to services.

Swanberg, Jennifer E., *et al.*, "State Employment Protection Statutes for Victims of Domestic Violence: Public Policy's Response to Domestic Violence as an Employment Matter," *Journal of Interpersonal Violence*, December 2011, www.ncbi.nlm.nih.gov/pubmed/22203636. Researchers examine workplace protection laws for victims of domestic violence across the country.

# For More Information

**Futures Without Violence**, 100 Montgomery St., The Presidio, San Francisco, CA 94129; 415-678-5500; www.futureswithoutviolence.org. Trains professionals working to end violence against women, children and families and develops relevant national policies.

**Kansas Coalition Against Sexual and Domestic Violence**, 634 S.W. Harrison, Topeka, KS 66603; 785-232-9784; www.kcsdv.org. Trains domestic violence advocates, creates public awareness programs and supports local crisis centers.

**Lethality Assessment Program**, Maryland Network Against Domestic Violence, 4601 Presidents Dr., Suite 370, Lanham, MD 20706; 301-429-3601; http://mnadv.org/lethality. Identifies victims of domestic violence at risk of being seriously injured or killed by intimate partners and connects them to local services.

**Mid-Atlantic Addiction Research and Training Institute**, Indiana University of Pennsylvania, Stright Hall, 210 South 10th St., Indiana, PA 15705; 724-357-4405; www.iup.edu/marti. Trains professionals and coordinates research in the fields of chemical dependency and related problems, such as domestic violence.

**National Center for Injury Prevention and Control**, Centers for Disease Control and Prevention, 4770 Buford Hwy., NE, MS F-63, Atlanta, GA 30341; 800-232-4636; www.cdc.gov/violenceprevention. Federal agency that conducts research and surveys on injuries and violence, including domestic violence.

**National Network to End Domestic Violence**, 1400 16th St., N.W., Suite 330, Washington, DC 20036; 202-543-5566; www.nnedv.org. Membership and advocacy organization of state domestic violence coalitions and allied groups.

**National Resource Center on Domestic Violence**, 3605 Vartan Way, Suite 101, Harrisburg, PA 17110; 800-537-2238; www.nrcdv.org. Supports organizations, communities and individuals addressing domestic violence.

**Office on Violence Against Women**, Department of Justice, 145 N St., N.E., Suite 10W.121, Washington, DC 20530; 202-307-6026; www.ovw.usdoj.gov. Administers financial and technical assistance to communities developing programs, policies and practices to end domestic violence, dating violence, sexual assault and stalking.

**Partner Abuse State of Knowledge Project**, University of New Hampshire Family Research Center, Murkland Hall, Durham, NH 03824; 603-862-2062; www.domesticviolenceresearch.org. Repository of research papers supporting a gender-neutral view of domestic violence.

# 17

# Border Security

Reed Karaim

Hundreds of motorists from Mexico wait to enter the United States at the Nogales, Ariz., border crossing. Many are Mexicans who work in the United States or are visiting relatives there. Such scenes have been common along the 1,933-mile U.S.-Mexican border — and to a lesser extent along the 4,000-mile Canadian border — since the United States began intensifying security, especially after the Sept. 11, 2001, terrorist attacks.

From *CQ Researcher*, September 27, 2013.

L ess than 30 yards from the U.S.-Mexican border outside Nogales, Ariz., new, 80-foot concrete poles rise into the desert air. They will soon be topped with the latest in surveillance hardware, including infrared and radar-directed cameras that can be controlled remotely from the U.S. Border Patrol station in Nogales, the nation's biggest.

"It's going to make a tremendous difference," says Leslie Lawson, chief of the Nogales station, standing beneath one of the surveillance towers. "It's going to extend our view several more miles, and it's going to be stuffed with the newest technology."

Already running along the border is a new 18-foot-tall fence made with concrete-filled posts that extend six to eight feet underground.[1]

In addition, agents have an array of sophisticated personal surveillance gear, including Recon, a $135,000 portable device that looks like a giant pair of binoculars but features infrared and thermal vision. It can read heat signatures of people and objects and then bounce a laser off the target to get an exact reading of its location.

Back in the station's windowless control room in Nogales, agents monitor 30 screens linked to cameras, along with alarms connected to ground sensors along the border. Also watching the border from above are tethered radar blimps, surveillance aircraft and unarmed Predator drones.[2] About 25 miles farther into the United States, a Border Patrol checkpoint on the major highway in the area provides another layer of security.

"We've built a new road or had a new piece of technology installed every month, or so it seems," says Lawson, who credits the new infrastructure and technology with helping her agents effectively patrol more than 1,000 square miles of country.

## Illegal Crossings Fall to Record Low

The number of people apprehended after crossing the U.S.-Mexican border illegally hit a 30-year low in 2012, with most apprehensions occurring near Tucson, Ariz. After the United States began beefing up security along the border in 1980, apprehensions rose sharply, reaching 1.6 million in 1986 — the year Congress enacted landmark immigration reform. Subsequently, apprehensions fell and rose unevenly, hitting 1.5 million in 1996, when Congress passed another immigration law. Apprehensions reached a record 1.6 million in 2000 before falling well below 400,000 in 2011 and 2012, in part because of poor job prospects in the U.S.

*Illegal Crossings on the Southwest Border, by Sectors, FY1980-2012*

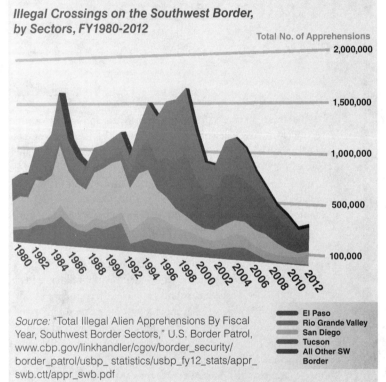

Total No. of Apprehensions

Legend:
- El Paso
- Rio Grande Valley
- San Diego
- Tucson
- All Other SW Border

*Source:* "Total Illegal Alien Apprehensions By Fiscal Year, Southwest Border Sectors," U.S. Border Patrol, www.cbp.gov/linkhandler/cgov/border_security/ border_patrol/usbp_ statistics/usbp_fy12_stats/appr_ swb.ctt/appr_swb.pdf

2,500 in the early 1980s to more than 21,000, doubling in just the last eight years.[3] Since 1986, the United States has spent more than $219 billion in today's dollars on border and immigration enforcement, building some 650 miles of fencing along the Southern border while beefing up high-tech surveillance along both borders and at so-called ports of entry, including authorized land crossings, seaports and airports.[4]

The buildup began in response to concerns about rising illegal immigration from Mexico but accelerated after the Sept. 11, 2001, terrorist attacks, which created a new sense of urgency concerning national security and led to a new surge in spending along both borders.

The reaction to 9/11 "provided a stimulus package for border control," says Peter Andreas, a professor of political science and international studies at Brown University. Border Patrol agents now "were supposed to be the front line in the war on terror. They never really had that job before, and it was added to their mission — not just added, but put up front."

In addition to beefing up the Border Patrol, "about 5,000 ICE [Immigration and Customs Enforcement] agents are deployed to [the] U.S. border, along with numerous other federal law enforcement agents . . . and various state and local law enforcement agents," Marc R. Rosenblum, an immigration policy specialist with the Congressional Research Service, told a House committee this year.[5]

The situation in Nogales is representative of a vastly intensified security effort along the 1,933-mile U.S.-Mexican border, and to a lesser degree along the 4,000-mile U.S.-Canadian border. Since the mid-1980s, the United States has poured more personnel and resources into policing its borders than at any other time in history.

Since the buildup began, the number of Border Patrol agents on the Mexican border has jumped from less than

Nevertheless, political debate continues to rage about the effectiveness and focus of the nation's border security programs. Some analysts question the need for the buildup and how resources have been allocated, while others believe it still falls far short of what is needed to completely secure America's borders.

Other observers claim the federal government is still too concerned about the rights of undocumented border crossers, is not prosecuting enough to deter illegal crossing and unnecessarily restricts Border Patrol operations in environmentally sensitive areas and on Native American lands.

"The effort, the additional agents, that's all been tempered by the fact that the administration — the current one or the prior one — would not allow the agents out in the field to go out and do their job," says Jeffery L. Everly, vice chairman of the National Association of Former Border Patrol Officers. "We say one thing, but we have policies and procedures that water it down."

But others say the border buildup is eroding civil rights. "It's been called a Constitution-lite, or even a Constitution-free zone, [because] agencies have greater rights to stop and question people than they do elsewhere in the country," says Brian Erickson, a policy advocate at the American Civil Liberties Union (ACLU) Regional Center for Border Rights in Las Cruces, N.M.

The Constitution's Fourth Amendment prohibits "unreasonable" searches and seizures of American citizens, but within 100 miles of the border the U.S. Supreme Court's longstanding "border search exception" rule gives authorities the right to stop and search individuals or vehicles without probable cause or a warrant.[6]

That's only one way federal authority is exercised to a greater degree close to the border. In 2005, for example, the Real ID Act gave the Department of Homeland Security the power to sweep aside environmental regulations and other legal impediments to speed the building of the border security fence.[7]

Some human-rights activists blame the fence and personnel buildup for a 27 percent jump in deaths among migrants since last year, even as the number of border crossings fell.[8] Activists say border crossers are diverting to more remote and dangerous terrain, making them more dependent on violent smugglers.

There also have been more charges of harassment or brutality by the swelling force of Border Patrol agents.

## One-third of Mexican Border Is Fenced

The United States has built 636 miles of fencing along the nation's 1,933-mile Southwestern border since 1996, when only 14 miles were fenced. Much of the expansion was financed by the Secure Fencing Act of 2006, which initially required construction of about 800 miles of fencing. A subsequent law reduced the requirement, but the recently passed Senate immigration reform bill would mandate another 50 miles of fence, bringing the total to 700 miles.

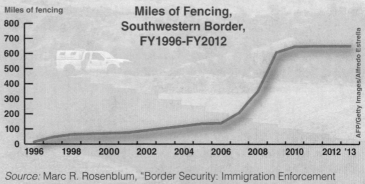

Miles of fencing

**Miles of Fencing, Southwestern Border, FY1996-FY2012**

AFP/Getty Images/Alfredo Estrella

*Source:* Marc R. Rosenblum, "Border Security: Immigration Enforcement Between Ports of Entry," Congressional Research Service, May 3, 2013.

The Department of Homeland Security has received hundreds of complaints of rights violations, and at least 15 people have been killed by Border Patrol agents in the last three years.[9]

The debate over border security has become entangled in the larger controversy over immigration policy.[10] In June the Senate passed an immigration reform package that would provide a path to citizenship for many of the estimated 11.7 million unauthorized immigrants in the United States in 2012.[11] To broaden support for the bill, provisions were added that would further boost border security, including the addition of another 20,000 Border Patrol agents, essentially doubling the number of agents. House Republicans strongly oppose the Senate measure, however, arguing the bill does not clearly establish measurable standards for securing the border from further illegal immigration.

Although blocking terrorists now tops Border Patrol agents' agenda, Andreas says, "in practice, the day-to-day activity is the same old same old: drug smuggling, customs work and illegal immigration."

As a reflection of that reality, the vast majority of Border Patrol agents and most resources remain concentrated on the U.S. border with Mexico.[12] But some security experts believe America's coastlines and its main Canadian border, which is nearly twice as long at about 4,000 miles and more lightly patrolled than the Mexican border, pose the greater threats of terrorist incursion.*

President Obama and administration officials often cite a sharp decline in the number of people crossing the U.S.-Mexico border illegally as proof that the border buildup is working. "We put more boots on the ground on the Southern border than at any time in our history," Obama said in a speech on immigration this year in Las Vegas. "And today, illegal crossings are down nearly 80 percent from their peak in 2000."[13]

But critics of the administration's efforts say proof of success is still lacking. "Every day, everything from humans to illicit drugs are smuggled across our borders," Rep. Michael McCaul, R-Texas, chairman of the House Homeland Security Committee, said shortly after Obama's speech. "While the administration claims it has spent more funds to secure the border than ever before, the fact remains that the Department of Homeland Security still does not have a comprehensive plan to secure the border that includes a reasonable definition of operational control we can measure."[14]

As the debate continues on nearly all aspects of border security, here are some of the questions being discussed:

### Has the border security buildup made the United States more secure?

Analysts point out that the effort to secure America's borders is a reaction to three challenges: international terrorism, drug smuggling and illegal immigration.

Most border security analysts say there is little evidence the buildup has significantly reduced the availability of illegal narcotics in the United States. The U.S. Drug Enforcement Administration (DEA) has cited reduced use of some drugs, especially cocaine, as proof the buildup is working. But other drugs have grown in popularity, and smugglers have proved adept at shifting their methods and locations in response to interdiction efforts.[15] "I don't think the U.S. has gotten fundamentally better at stopping drugs," says Brown

University's Andreas. "I don't think there's anybody who argues otherwise."

The debate over the effectiveness of border security centers on terrorism and illegal immigration. Although much public attention has focused on immigration, counterterrorism is the focus of many security analysts, some of whom believe the bolstered security on the border has made the United States safer.

"The U.S. has tripled the size of the Border Patrol, so there's a higher probability of detection of anybody coming across the border illegally, whether they're a terrorist or anybody. So in that sense, yes, we've reduced the likelihood of terrorists coming across the border," says Seth M. M. Stodder, who served as director of policy and planning at U.S. Customs and Border Protection during the George W. Bush administration.

But Stodder, a senior associate with the Center for Strategic and International Studies, adds that effectively fighting international terrorism requires a layered approach that includes working closely with other nations. Land borders, he says, should be seen as "the last line of defense in regard to terrorism."

However, other experts say the U.S.-Mexico border has never been a likely avenue for terrorists. "Mexico is not a hotbed of international terrorism, and to say it is is just not to understand the facts," says Erik Lee, executive director of the North American Research Partnership, a think tank in San Diego that focuses on the relationship between the United States, Mexico and Canada.

Lee thinks the border is an illogical route for terrorists from outside Mexico to choose. "People who want to do harm to the United States will choose the paths of least resistance, and the ports of entry will be among those paths," he says. "Crossing the U.S.-Mexico border is much more logistically difficult. These are remote areas, dangerous and hard to cross."

Even more dismissive is Scott Nicol, a member of the No Border Wall Coalition, a grassroots group opposed to the construction of the fence separating the United States and Mexico. The idea of terrorists crossing the Mexican border is "a total red herring. A terrorist has never come across the Southern border," says Nicol, who lives near the border in McAllen, Texas. "There may be some people who really believe it's a threat. But I think a lot of it is, when you're going to militarize something so heavily, you have to have a big excuse for it."

---

*The Canadian border with the Lower 48 states is about 4,000 miles long. The border with Alaska is about 1,500 miles long, but that border is nearly all wilderness and has not been a focus of security concerns.

But Paul Rosenzweig, who served as deputy assistant secretary for policy in the Department of Homeland Security in the George W. Bush administration, says, "The best evidence we have is that there haven't been seizures of terrorists on the Southern border. On the other hand, we did have at least one case of a seizure on the Northern border." However, terrorists might have been seized on the Southern border without the government disclosing it, he says. "It could be classified."

The Northern border case occurred before 9/11, when a U.S. customs agent in December 1999 stopped Ahmed Ressam, an Algerian who had received training from al Qaeda, trying to enter the United States from Canada in Port Angeles, Wash., with a rental car full of explosives. Ressam, dubbed the "Millennium Bomber," had planned to detonate a bomb at Los Angeles International Airport on New Year's Eve.

Rosenzweig, now a visiting fellow with the Heritage Foundation, a conservative think tank in Washington, says any potential terrorist today faces more challenges on both borders. "If the question is, have we done a better job of preventing terrorist incidents in the United States through a ramp-up in border security, I think the answer is clearly yes," he says.

Whether the border buildup is curbing illegal immigration is also a subject of strong debate. Speaking this August, outgoing Homeland Security Secretary Janet Napolitano said the effort is having a significant impact. "Over the past four-and-a-half years, we have invested historic resources to prevent illegal cross-border activity," Napolitano said. "And because of these investments in manpower, and technology, and infrastructure, our borders are now better staffed and better protected than any time in our nation's history, and illegal crossings have dropped to near 40-year lows."[16]

The claim that illegal crossings have fallen is based largely on the sharp decline in the number of apprehensions along the Mexican border in recent years — from more than 1.6 million in 1986 to about 357,000 last year.[17] But some analysts believe the decline says more about the slowdown in the U.S. economy than increased

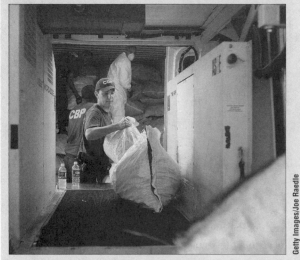

*Getty Images/John Moore*

*Getty Images/Joe Raedle*

***Methods of Detection***

U.S. Border Patrol cameras along the Niagara River monitor the U.S.-Canadian border in Grand Island, N.Y. (top). Customs agents in Miami X-ray incoming bags of charcoal to prevent undeclared goods, including drugs, from entering the country (bottom). Controversy over immigration policy has complicated the debate over border security. In June the Senate passed an immigration reform package that would provide a path to citizenship for the estimated 11.7 million unauthorized immigrants in the United States. The bill also would add 20,000 Border Patrol agents.

border protection: Fewer available jobs draw fewer undocumented workers.

Wayne Cornelius, director emeritus of the Center for Comparative Immigration Studies at the University of California, San Diego, says the security buildup may have had some effect on illegal migration levels, primarily by

## Border Patrol Concentrated in Southwest

Far more U.S. Border Patrol agents guard the Mexican border than monitor coastal ports or the Canadian border. The number of agents patrolling the Southwestern border rose fivefold between 1993 and 2012, to 18,546. The Canadian border has only about one-eighth the Border Patrol force as the Mexican border but saw a more than sevenfold rise in the number of agents — from 310 to 2,206.

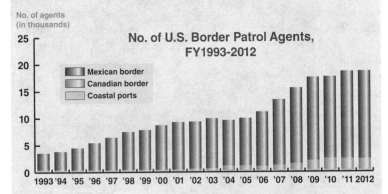

**No. of U.S. Border Patrol Agents, FY1993-2012**

No. of agents (in thousands)

Legend:
- Mexican border
- Canadian border
- Coastal ports

*Source:* "Border Patrol Agent Staffing By Fiscal Year," U.S. Border Patrol, www.cbp. gov/linkhandler/cgov/border_security/border_patrol/ usbp_ statistics/usbp_fy12_stats/staffing_1993_2012.ctt/staffing_1993_2012.pdf

secure. "The Mexican drug war and the U.S. border security crackdown have given rise to a new wave of criminality at the border in the form of highly armed bandits who seize drug loads and rob immigrants and their guides," wrote policy analyst Tom Barry in his book *Border Wars.* "In other words, thanks in part to U.S. government attempts to secure the border . . . the border has grown more violent."[19]

But federal statistics indicate that U.S. communities along the Southern border have some of the lowest crime rates in the nation. And Lawson says her 19 years of experience in the Border Patrol, including in Nogales, which was once besieged by unauthorized migrants, leave her no doubt that the agency is making a positive difference.

"We've come a long way," she says. "You talk to anybody in this Nogales area, and there aren't aliens running through their back yards anymore."

### Is it possible to "seal" the U.S. borders?

Calls to secure or even "seal" the nation's borders have become a rallying cry among some conservative politicians and members of the public who feel the nation is being overwhelmed by undocumented immigrants.

Defining what a secure border would look like remains a subject of debate, however. "It's a very subjective, highly politicized question," says Mike Slaven, a policy analyst for the Morrison Institute Latino Public Policy Center at Arizona State University, Tempe, and the author of a new report, "Defining Border Security in Immigration Reform."[20]

"Most experts agree that preventing 100 percent of unlawful entries across U.S. borders is an impossible task," Rosenblum, the Congressional Research Service policy analyst, concluded.[21]

Other analysts also say it's an unrealistic expectation. "Sure, if you want to stop all trade and set up minefields, make it like the DMZ between North and South Korea, yeah, you could stop it. But I don't think that's what

driving up smugglers' fees. But the center's interviews with unauthorized border crossers indicate that 85 percent still eventually make it into the country. "It has yet to be proven that it's an effective way of keeping people out of the country," Cornelius says.

Others doubt the reported falloff in attempted border crossings. Janice Kephart, research fellow at the Center for Immigration Studies, a Washington think tank that favors low immigration, says her analysis and observations by citizens' groups along the Southern border indicate the opposite, especially since President Obama issued a policy directive last year allowing young immigrants who had arrived illegally — many brought by their parents — and who were of "good moral character" and doing well in school to avoid deportation.

"At least over the central Arizona border, there has been a tremendous surge in the amount of illegal border crossing activity from August to December of last year," Kephart, a former counsel to the 9/11 Commission that investigated the 2001 terrorist attacks, said in Senate testimony last April.[18]

Some experts, in fact, believe that the "militarization" of the border, as they refer to it, has made the border less

most Americans want," says Rey Koslowski, a political science professor who directs the Program on Border Control and Homeland Security at the University at Albany, part of the State University of New York system. "That kind of absolutism — that if we don't stop everybody, it's not good enough — isn't really useful."

The more realistic question, say border experts, is whether security at the legal land border crossing points and airports and seaports can be built up to the point that almost all migrants wishing to cross illegally are either caught or deterred from trying. Some analysts believe that is possible. "Given the right resources, it's realistic to think about stopping the vast majority of people attempting to cross," says Koslowski.

However, experts estimate that around 40 percent of the undocumented workers already in the United States entered the country legally through ports of entry and then overstayed their visas.[22] Thus, Koslowski says, halting illegal immigration would also require a system that not only tracks the entry of visitors into the United States but also accurately records the exit of every visitor. Currently, the United States does not have such a system at all its ports of entry.[23]

But Koslowski says the experience of Australia, where such as system exists, indicates it can be a powerful tool to identify those overstaying their visas.

Another crucial part of the effort, he adds, would be to impose stiff penalties for businesses that hire undocumented workers. "There are a lot of businesses whose business model is to employ undocumented workers," he says. "And until that changes there's going to be people coming through."

But Tony Payan, a political science professor at the University of Texas, El Paso, who has done extensive cross-border research, says the sheer volume of legal traffic along the border and the economic significance of that traffic for both countries means it is unrealistic to try to halt all illegal traffic.

"Every year you have 400 million trips across the [Southern] border at the ports of entry. Say, at the peak, there were about 1 million people who crossed without legal papers or overstayed," Payan says. "In the end, illegality on the border is a very small part of border crossing. . . . People who say [you can stop it] have never lived on the border."

However, Everly, of the Association of Former Border Patrol Officers, believes the primary problem has been

the refusal of the government to give those policing the border the resources, authority and backing they need to succeed. Government policies that make it easy for those who arrived illegally to escape prosecution or remain in the United States, he says, encourage illegal migration, making it difficult to stem the flow of undocumented border crossers.

"It's never going to be possible to stop all of it, but having an effective process where we can go down there and enforce the laws, using the right technology with the right intel, I think it can be really reduced," Everly says. With those changes, he says, illegal crossings could be diminished so much that most Americans would feel the border was secure.

But Brown University's Andreas argues that porous borders are a part of American and world history. "Sealing the border is a complete utopian fantasy because sealing the border wasn't actually achieved with the Iron Curtain or the Berlin Wall," he says. "Even there, even then, there was leakage. I can guarantee you there will always be a leaky border. The question is how many leaks? Where is it flowing? . . . You can imagine a lot more tunnels; you can imagine a lot more people coming through the ports of entry. It's going to be leaky; it's just a question of where."

## Is the United States paying enough attention to security at its ports of entry, Canadian border and coasts?

With the debate about border security focused primarily on America's boundary with Mexico, the Southern border has received most of the resources and personnel committed to building up security along the nation's perimeter.

As of January 2013, a total of 18,462 Border Patrol agents were posted at the Southwestern border compared with only 2,212 on the Northern border with Canada, according to the Congressional Research Service.[24] Most federal spending on border security also has gone to the Southwestern border.

Some experts believe the focus on the vast open spaces in the Southwest has led the country to neglect other parts of its border infrastructure. "Much more attention needs to be placed on what is happening at the ports of entry," says the North American Research Partnership's Lee.

Failure to upgrade and expand the infrastructure at ports of entry — which include authorized land crossing points, seaports and airports — not only increases the security risk, it exacts an economic toll by slowing down legal crossings between nations that are economically interdependent, notes Lee.

The resources the United States has dedicated to its ports of entry have expanded, but not as dramatically as for the rest of the border, according to the Migration Policy Institute, a Washington think tank that studies the movement of people worldwide. "Border Patrol resources have doubled since 2005, while port-of-entry increases have grown about 45 percent," the institute concluded.[25]

But former Homeland Security official Stodder thinks security gains at the ports of entry have been among the most significant, particularly when it comes to thwarting potential terrorist incursions. He cited deployment of radiation detectors and other equipment to improve cargo inspections, better training of personnel and greater collaboration between the Border Patrol and other law enforcement agencies. "A big part of the buildup is actually at the ports of entry," says Stodder.

In addition to concerns about the ports of entry, some political leaders and security analysts say the United States needs to devote more resources to protecting the Canadian border and coastlines.

Rosenzweig, the former Homeland Security assistant secretary, says the Coast Guard is in "desperate need" of more money for modernizing and upgrading its fleet. "One of the key reasons to recapitalize the Coast Guard is precisely because we have three borders — a Northern, a Southern and a maritime border," he says. "A speedboat can get to the U.S. from the Bahamas in 60 to 90 minutes. I tell you truthfully, if I had a nuclear device I wanted to sneak into the United States, I wouldn't try to drive it into the U.S. because we've got the land borders pretty locked up. I would bring it on a boat."

But in testimony before a House subcommittee, Coast Guard Rear Adm. William Lee said the Coast Guard is working closely with other U.S. security entities and nations to position its ships to protect the United States. "The Coast Guard's mix of cutters, aircraft and boats — all operated by highly proficient personnel — allows the Coast Guard to exercise layered and effective security through the entire maritime domain," he said.[26]

The Obama administration has made $93 million available this year through the Port Security Grant Program to help the nation's ocean ports improve their security.[27] However, in its 2014 budget request the administration called for $909 million more to modernize the Coast Guard fleet.[28]

Everly, of the Association of Former Border Patrol Officers, believes the United States could use more personnel for both the Northern and maritime borders. "The Canadian border, there are not a lot of folks assigned up there," he says. "We have them at the ports of entry, but there's so many places you can cross up there, and with the geography, it's so hard to get at some of the spots. It's the same with the coastline. We've got marine and air units, but it's not uncommon for a boatload of people to go from Tijuana beyond detection and then come inshore down the California coast."

The number of Border Patrol agents on the Northern border increased by nearly 550 percent, from 340 in 2001 to more than 2,200 in 2013, or roughly one agent for every two miles of border.[29] But that's still far fewer than the nearly 10 agents per mile along the U.S.-Mexican border.

Stodder, however, says that disparity simply reflects the difference between the two borders. "There's a reason why we haven't put tons and tons of border patrol agents on the Northern border," he says, "Number one is that they would be really, really bored."

The issue along the Northern border, Stodder says, isn't mass illegal migration but the possibility that terrorists would come through Canada to the United States. Stodder argues that good intelligence and police work are more effective in countering that threat. "The Royal Canadian Mounted Police plus the Canadian intelligence service are really quite good," he says.

Other analysts note the high level of cooperation between Canadian and U.S. border agents, intelligence agencies and immigration officials. "There are a lot of good things that have been happening along the Northern border in terms of cooperation, with [joint patrolling] teams and a few other things," including more sharing of information about travelers and potential threats, says the University at Albany's Koslowski. "I think it's addressed the most glaring kinds of holes."

# CHRONOLOGY

**1980s** *U.S. grants amnesty to some undocumented immigrants; Border Patrol, a small agency since its creation in 1924, begins to expand.*

**1980** U.S. Border Patrol has 2,268 agents, 1,975 of them assigned to the Southern border.

**1986** Nearly 1.7 million illegal aliens are apprehended nationwide, the highest one-year total on record. . . . Immigration Reform and Control Act of 1986 grants amnesty under certain conditions to illegal immigrants who have been in the United States since 1982.

**1987** The first of six helium-filled balloons with radar capability is deployed along the Southwestern border to track illegal crossers.

**1990s** *United States turns to fences and other barriers along the U.S.-Mexico border, while continuing to expand the number of Border Patrol agents.*

**1990** Border Patrol begins erecting 14-mile fence to deter illegal entries and drug smuggling in the San Diego sector.

**1994** After the fence proves ineffective, the Border Patrol launches Operation Gatekeeper, which greatly increases the number of border agents.

**1995** The number of Border Patrol agents reaches 5,000.

**1996** Illegal Immigration Reform and Immigrant Responsibility Act gives the U.S. attorney general broad authority to construct border barriers.

**2000s** *Terrorist attacks heighten U.S. concerns about openness of its borders.*

**Sept. 11, 2001** Terrorist attacks on the World Trade Center, Pentagon and United Airlines Flight 93 kill nearly 3,000 people. All 19 airline hijackers entered the U.S. legally.

**October 2001** USA Patriot Act gives more law enforcement authority to Immigration and Naturalization Service and provides $50 million for expanded security on the U.S.-Canadian border.

**2002** The number of Border Patrol agents tops 10,000.

**2003** New Department of Homeland Security takes over functions of Immigration and Naturalization Service.

**2004** Intelligence Reform and Terrorism Prevention Act of 2004 requires U.S., Mexican and Canadian citizens to have a passport or other accepted document to enter United States.

**2005** REAL ID Act authorizes Homeland Security secretary to expedite the construction of border barriers.

**2006** Secure Fence Act of 2006 directs Homeland Security to construct 850 miles of additional fencing along border.

**2007** Consolidated Appropriations Act gives Homeland Security secretary greater freedom to build the border fence and changes the requirement to not less than 700 miles of fencing along the Southern border.

**2007** Illegal immigration begins to plummet as worst economic downturn since the Great Depression hits United States.

**2010** Gov. Jan Brewer, R-Ariz., signs hardline immigration enforcement law (SB1070) designed to catch illegal border crossers (April). Other states adopt similar measures.

**2011** Apprehension of illegal aliens nationwide falls to below 350,000, the lowest one-year total since 1971.

**2012** U.S. Supreme Court rules parts of Arizona SB1070 illegal, but says police can investigate the immigration status of a person they have stopped if they have reasonable cause for suspicion. . . . Pew Hispanic Center estimates the United States may be seeing a net outflow of undocumented migrants because they can't find jobs.

**2013** Border Patrol has 21,370 agents, with 18,462 posted at the Southwest border and 2,212 on the Northern border. The number of agents has more than doubled since 2001. . . . Senate passes immigration reform bill in June that calls for hiring 20,000 more border agents, completing 700 miles of border fence and spending $40 billion over 10 years on border security. Many Republicans denounce the bill as inadequate.

# BACKGROUND

## Two-Way Street

For most of U.S. history, the nation's land borders have been relatively unguarded, reflecting the country's sense of security about its relationships with its neighbors to the north and south and its tradition of being an open society where people are largely free to come and go as they please.

Although mounted patrols were conducted sporadically along the borders earlier, the U.S. Border Patrol wasn't created until 1924. It began with 450 officers responsible for patrolling 6,000 miles of U.S. borders.[30] The patrol was created in conjunction with the Immigration Act of 1924, which stiffened requirements for entering the United States and established quotas for immigration from different countries.

More than half a century later, in 1980, the number of agents had increased to 2,268, or about one agent for every three miles of border.[31] Informal crossings remained common on both borders, but security was almost non-existent along the 4,000-mile boundary with Canada, which was often referred to as the "world's longest undefended border."[32]

Illegal trade also has moved across the Canadian border over time. During Prohibition it was the favorite route of illegal alcohol shipments into the United States.[33] In more recent years, Canadians have worried about illegal gun trafficking into Canada from the United States, says Emily Gilbert, director of the Canadian Studies Program at the University of Toronto.

Historically, the U.S.-Mexican border was even more lawless and wide open. The remoteness of much of the region made it a popular place for people — or smugglers — to slip from one country to the other undetected. "The popular notion that the U.S.-Mexico border is out of control falsely assumes that there was once a time when it was truly under control," Brown University's Andreas writes in *Border Games: Policing the U.S.-Mexico Divide.*[34]

Today's illegal border activities are "part of an old and diverse border smuggling economy that thrived long before drugs and migrants were being smuggled," Andreas notes.[35] In the 19th century, he writes, much of the smuggling was from the United States into Mexico, to avoid Mexico's high tariffs.

Illegal immigration, too, initially followed a north-to-south route, as Americans moved without authorization into Mexico's northern regions in the early 1800s. "The so-called Mexican Decree of 3 April 1830 had prohibited immigration from the United States, and Mexico deployed garrisons to try to enforce the law," Andreas writes.[36]

## Changing Attitudes

The flow of illegal border traffic began to shift the other way in the early 20th century, as migrant workers traveled north to U.S. agricultural fields. Attitudes toward the workers swung back and forth, with Americans welcoming them when labor was short and rounding them up and shipping them home when they weren't needed.

Facing a labor shortage during World War I, the United States temporarily admitted 77,000 "guest" workers from Mexico. But when the Great Depression led to a steep rise in joblessness, thousands of Mexican immigrants were deported. With the U.S. entry into World War II in December 1941, the country again found itself short of workers and created the Bracero Program — bracero being Spanish for laborers — which eventually brought more than 400,000 Mexicans into the United States for jobs.[37]

The program was controversial, with many unions, religious groups and other critics citing cases of abuses of workers by employers. The initial effort ended in 1947, but it continued under various laws for agricultural workers until 1964.[38]

By the 1950s, illegal immigration was accelerating as more Mexicans sought to take advantage of America's postwar boom. In 1954, the U.S. Immigration and Naturalization Service (INS) initiated "Operation Wetback," choosing a name that had become a derogatory way to refer to migrants, who often swam or wadded across the Rio Grande River to reach the United States. Immigration officers swept through Mexican *barrios* (neighborhoods) in U.S. cities looking for immigrants living in the United States illegally. At least 1 million people were deported in 1954 alone.[39]

Although American attitudes toward Mexican labor have shifted back and forth, depending on whether U.S. companies needed workers, the Southern border remained relatively unguarded. Even in the late 1990s, in many remote parts of Arizona, New Mexico and Texas the border was protected by only a waist-high wire fence, with occasional stone markers denoting the international line.[40]

In cross-border communities such as Nogales, which straddles Arizona and Mexico, and El Paso (Texas) and Cuidad Juarez (Mexico), many families had members on both sides of the line and crossed back and forth casually. "People don't understand how a border community works. In my case, I live in Mexico. I cross every day to the United States to go to work, and then I go back again," says Astrid Dominguez, advocacy coordinator for the American Civil Liberties Union of Texas. "It's not just them and us — you have friends and relatives on both sides."

Dominguez lives in Matamoros, Mexico, and works across the border in Brownsville, Texas. She says she has heard stories from her parents and grandparents about how much easier it used to be to cross and how much casual interaction existed between the two communities. Now, she says, "Every time I go across the border I get questioned by Border Patrol agents."

The American Civil Liberties Union and other groups have criticized U.S. border and customs enforcement personnel for using excessive force, both with migrants in custody and in the field. Since 2010, at least eight people have been killed by the Border Patrol while throwing rocks at agents, including six who were on the Mexican side of the border.[41]

In one of the most publicized cases, agents shot and killed José Antonio Elena Rodriguez, a 16-year-old Mexican, in October 2012, just across the border from Nogales, Ariz. Agents said a group of men were throwing rocks at them while others tried to bring drugs across the border. But a witness in Mexico said Rodriguez was simply walking down the street and not involved in the confrontation. An autopsy found he had been shot multiple times, with five of the shots hitting his back at an angle that indicated he was already lying on the ground.[42] While not responding directly to this case, Border Patrol officials have noted that agents frequently come under dangerous assault from people throwing rocks from Mexico.[43]

On the Canadian border, too, in sister cities such as Detroit and Windsor, Ontario, social and economic exchanges between Canada and the United States were casual. Before the 9/11 terrorist attacks led to changes, half the crossings between Canada and the United States were unguarded at night, with traffic cones simply set out to close the roads.[44] "The level of openness that existed was unbelievable, if you think about it," says the University at Albany's Koslowski, given how heavily guarded many international borders are around the world.

But security has tightened. In an article earlier this year in *Mother Jones*, Americans of Arab descent reported being subjected to lengthy interrogations and even handcuffed by the U.S. Border Patrol when crossing into the United States from Canada.[45] "Previously, there was this sense of community there," says the University of Toronto's Gilbert, speaking of the cross-border culture. "Even though there was a border, there was a sense of generosity across it. Now, it's one of belligerence."

## Security Buildup

Through most of the 1960s, the Border Patrol apprehended fewer than 50,000 undocumented immigrants a year. The total began to climb in the late 1960s as more Mexicans turned to the prospering U.S. economy for work. The pace quickened further in the 1970s, and by 1983 apprehensions topped 1.1 million for the first time since 1954, during Operation Wetback.[46]

Still a relatively small agency with fewer than 3,000 agents, the Border Patrol by the early 1980s found itself overwhelmed at the most popular crossings, mostly in border cities.[47] In March 1986 alone, more migrants were caught crossing illegally in San Diego than had been caught there in three years in the mid-1960s. Alan E. Eliason, the chief Border Patrol agent in the area at the time, said that on a Sunday night, agents could see as many as 4,000 people gathering on the Mexican side, preparing to rush across the border.[48]

By then, public impatience with the immigrant surge was growing.[49] At the same time, protecting the border was given new urgency by the Reagan administration. It supported anti-Communist insurgencies in Central America, most notably an effort by so-called Contra rebels to overthrow the ruling Sandinista government in Nicaragua. Tying border security to national security, President Ronald Reagan said in 1986 that failure to overthrow the Sandinistas would leave "terrorists and subversives just two days' driving time from Harlingen, Texas."[50]

# Robots May Soon Help Guard the Border

*"We can get more reliability and cut down on the manpower needed."*

The U.S. border agent has brushed-back hair, sculpted cheekbones and a somewhat distant gaze. Politely but persistently he questions you. "Have you ever used any other names? Do you live at the address you listed on your application? Have you visited any foreign countries in the last five years?"

It's a fairly routine interview aimed at checking whether you qualify for a preferred-traveler program that will allow you easier entry into the United States. Routine, that is, except for one thing. The agent isn't really an agent at all but a human face on a kiosk screen, and this virtual agent is watching you more closely than any human ever could to determine the truthfulness of your responses.

The Automated Virtual Agent for Truth Assessment in Real Time, or AVATAR, is one of several projects at the National Center for Border Security and Immigration at the University of Arizona, Tucson. The center is part of BORDERS, a consortium of 18 research institutions, primarily universities, working on innovative technologies and procedures to protect the nation's borders.[1] Taken together, the projects are a snapshot of the next wave of border security.

For example, AVATAR's cameras, microphone and sensors quietly measure a variety of stress indicators as a person speaks to it: how your body is shifting, how much and where your eyes move, the changing timbre of your voice.

The data are run through computer algorithms that combine the different responses to develop a risk assessment for every person interviewed.

In limited field tests last year, AVATAR has been accurate between 70 percent and 100 percent of the time, better than human screeners, who are generally about as reliable as flipping a coin, says Nathan Twyman, the project's lead researcher.

Twyman stresses that human agents will always be needed to follow up on cases identified as high risk. But an average of 1.1 million people are processed at the nation's borders daily.[2] By automating the first level of screening, Twyman says, "We can get a lot more reliability . . . and cut down on the manpower needed at the border."

BORDERS also is working on a project at the University of Washington, Seattle, designed to locate people hiding behind boulders or other objects by triangulating radio waves and other signals. Another project is aimed at determining what combination of fingerprints, retina scans and other biometric data provides the fastest and most accurate way to identify an individual.

BORDERS also has looked at the role of dogs used at many border ports of entry to sniff for illegal drugs and people hidden in trucks or other vehicles. "We had a project that was a favorite of mine — developing an [electronic] sniffer that could do what a dog does," says Jay Nunamaker Jr.,

Congress addressed the border security issue with the 1986 Immigration Reform and Control Act. For the first time, the law made it illegal to recruit or hire undocumented workers, while also allowing approximately 3 million unauthorized immigrants who had arrived before 1982 and who met certain other conditions to remain legally in the United States.[51] Lawmakers hoped the combination would sharply reduce illegal border crossings.[52]

The number of apprehensions along the border did fall — by more than 700,000 from 1986 to 1988 — but then resumed an uneven climb. The Border Patrol responded with a series of targeted efforts, such as Operation Hold the Line in El Paso, Texas, and Operation Gatekeeper in San Diego, to shut down illegal crossings in the worst areas.[53]

But the flow of migrants tended to shift quickly from one spot to another. In California, for example, the Border Patrol built a fence that ran from the Pacific Ocean to the port of entry in San Ysidro, Calif., a land-border crossing between Tijuana, Mexico, and San Diego. The Border Patrol also greatly increased the number of agents behind the fence. But illegal migration shifted to San Ysidro itself, with illegal crossers making "bonzai runs," racing through traffic at the border in an effort to escape into the community.

director and principal researcher at the center. "But we had an awful time getting the drugs to test the sniffer with." The project was finally shelved, he says.

In addition, Twyman says the center has experimented with even more advanced ways to measure human reaction, including a laser that measures the carotid artery for an increased heart rate. Researchers found, however, that beards interfere with the process.

In the future, thermal cameras could detect the opening of the pores on a person's face, providing information similar to how a lie detector measures sweat to detect stress, Twyman says. The idea, he says, is "a polygraph that works without having to hook people up."

Another part of BORDERS research involves developing the best procedures and training for agents operating at the border. For example, researchers have examined the process by which agents record where they find migrants crossing illegally and have noted a high degree of error, probably caused by manual entry at the end of work shifts. Creating a digital data-entry system, which BORDERS is working on, and training agents to use it properly could result in a more accurate picture of crossing patterns, which should help agents operate more effectively.

While it's not as eye-catching as the technology under development, researcher Jeff Proudfoot says it's as important. "Just buying gadgets isn't going to make any difference," he says. "They have to be used properly."

— *Reed Karaim*

AVATAR, an innovative screening device developed by the National Center for Border Security and Immigration, allows for speedier border-security checks.

*BORDERS/University of Arizona*

---

[1] A list of the participating institutions, along with more information about research projects, is at www.borders.arizona.edu.

[2] Rey Koslowski, "The Evolution of Border Controls as a Mechanism to Prevent Illegal Immigration," Migration Policy Institute, February 2011, p. 1 www.migrationpolicy.org/pubs/bordercontrols-koslowski.pdf.

Through the 1990s, both the Clinton and George W. Bush administrations responded to public concern about unauthorized immigration by further increasing border personnel, equipment and barriers. The 1996 Illegal Immigration Reform and Immigration Responsibility Act included provisions for more border security but also increased interior enforcement of immigration laws and barred deportees from returning for from three to 10 years, depending on the length of their illegal stay.[54]

The security buildup and other measures had an impact on the routes chosen by border crossers. As it became more difficult to cross in urban areas, illegal immigration moved into remote areas, such as the Arizona desert, where it formerly had been less of a problem.

Migrant deaths in the desert and other remote areas rose steeply. But apprehensions indicated that as many, or more, people were still trying to cross. In 2000, the Border Patrol apprehended 1.68 million illegal crossers — close to the 1.69 million apprehended during the previous peak in 1986.[55]

Experts generally agree that the Sept. 11, 2001, terrorist attacks placed border security in a different light. Even though all the 9/11 terrorists had entered the United States legally, the nation's land borders were seen as potential routes for further terrorist incursions. Border security "used

# Senate Considers Mandatory E-Verify System

*Backers see workplace as a key to border security; critics say the system hurts businesses.*

The United States has deployed thousands of Border Patrol agents along its border with Mexico and spent billions of dollars in an effort to halt illegal immigration. But some policy analysts believe the focus on the border has led government to neglect one of the most effective places to curb illegal immigration: the American workplace.

Surveys of immigrants who arrived illegally by the Center for Comparative Immigration Studies at the University of California, San Diego, and others have found that most undocumented border crossers come to the United States for work. Yet, while it has been illegal to hire an unauthorized immigrant since passage of the Immigration and Control Act in 1986, many businesses have ignored the law.

The act, which requires employers to attest to their employees' residency status and fines employers who hire undocumented workers, "has never been enforced to the letter of the law," says Mike Slaven, a policy analyst with the Morrison Institute Latino Public Policy Center at Arizona State University, Tempe.

In 1996, Congress attempted to make it easier for businesses to abide by the law by creating E-Verify, a Web-based system that allows employers voluntarily to check the immigration status of newly hired employees. The program has grown steadily and was being used by 424,000 employers nationwide at the start of 2013.[1] But a comprehensive immigration reform act, which passed the Senate in June and is awaiting action in the House, would make E-Verify mandatory for almost all businesses within five years.[2]

Some analysts see it as a key to ending unauthorized border crossings. "Effective employer verification must be the linchpin of comprehensive immigration reform legislation if new policies are to succeed in preventing future illegal immigration," concluded immigration policy experts Marc R. Rosenblum and Doris Meissner, a former commissioner of the Immigration and Naturalization Service, in an early study of the E-Verify system.[3]

But other analysts are skeptical E-Verify alone can solve the problem of illegal immigration. E-Verify "could be very effective when it comes to formal employment, but I think it partially loses sight of the big problem, which is that there are labor demands by U.S. businesses that have to be met by immigrants," says Slaven. Effective immigration reform must include a way for those workers to enter the United States legally, he contends.

to be a labor-enforcement issue," says Payan, the University of Texas professor. "Now it becomes a national security issue," a view that echoed the earlier Reagan administration attempt to tie the border to international threats. In the years since 9/11, Payan adds, "It's been transformed and swallowed by the national security agenda."

The post-9/11 change was dramatic. Besides the growth of the Border Patrol, which doubled from 2002 to 2012, the United States assigned thousands of National Guard troops to the U.S.-Mexico border, along with officers from a variety of other agencies.[56]

U.S. Customs and Border Protection became part of the newly created Department of Homeland Security, which was given broad authority to secure the border.

In 2006, the Secure Fencing Act required construction of about 800 miles of fencing along the Southern border. Subsequent legislation modified the length required, but by 2012 the United States had some 650 miles of fencing along the border with Mexico.

Some projects were failures. An initial effort to create a "virtual fence" along the border using a coordinated system of sensors, radar, cameras and other technology was plagued with enough problems when installed in a 53-mile section along the border in Arizona that the government did not deploy it more widely.[57]

But the government has proceeded with a wide range of roads, surveillance towers, lights and other security measures, according to the Congressional Research Service, including, as of December 2012:

- 35 permanent interior checkpoints and 173 tactical checkpoints;
- 12 forward-operating bases in remote areas to house personnel in close proximity to illegal-crossing routes;

Rey Koslowski, a political science professor at the University at Albany (SUNY), New York, points out that many unauthorized migrants work in the cash-based shadow economy. "As long as there's a way for someone to come to the United States and go to work cutting people's lawns for 10 bucks an hour cash, I'm sorry, but young guys will try to do it," he says, "and they'll take the risk to do it."

Some conservative commentators have argued that E-Verify will expand into a national identification system that could be used more broadly by government.[4] In addition, some business groups believe it will unfairly hamper their ability to hire qualified workers.

Todd McCracken, president and CEO of the National Small Business Association, writing in *The Washington Post*, said results from E-Verify, so far, indicate that as many as 420,000 legal job hunters a year could receive an initial non-approval from the database, requiring them to file an appeal if they wish to keep working. "Those authorized, perfectly legal workers will then be forced — along with their employers — to navigate a bureaucratic morass," McCracken wrote. "It currently takes several months, on average, to resolve database mistakes, leaving both the employer and employee in legal and business limbo."[5]

But Rep. Lamar Smith, R-Texas, author of House legislation to expand E-Verify, said it has proved to be quick and effective while confirming 99.7 percent of employees checked by the system. Nationwide use of E-Verify, he said, will reduce illegal immigration "by shutting off the jobs magnet that draws millions of illegal workers to the U.S."[6]

*— Reed Karaim*

[1] "E-Verify Celebrates 2012!" *The Beacon*, the Official Blog of USCIS, March 28, 2013, http://blog.uscis.gov/2013/03/e-verify-celebrates-2012.html.

[2] "A Guide to S.744: Understanding the 2013 Senate Immigration Bill," Immigration Policy Center, July 20, 2013, www.immigrationpolicy.org/special-reports/guide-s744-understanding-2013-senate-immigration-bill.

[3] Doris Meissner and Marc R. Rosenblum, "The Next Generation of E-Verify: Getting Employment Verification Right," Migration Policy Institute, July 2009, p. i, www.migrationpolicy.org/pubs/verification_paper-071709.pdf.

[4] Jim Harper, "E-Verify Wrong for America," CATO Institute, May 23, 2013, www.cato.org/publications/commentary/e-verify-wrong-america.

[5] Todd McCracken, "Verification for job applicants is needed, but mandating E-Verify is not the answer," *The Washington Post*, May 13, 2012, www.washingtonpost.com/blogs/on-small-business/post/verification-for-job-applicants-is-needed-but-mandating-e-verify-is-not-the-answer/2012/05/11/gIQAD3KwMU_blog.html.

[6] "Smith Bill to Expand E-Verify Approved by Committee," press release, office of Rep. Lamar Smith, June 26, 2013, http://lamarsmith.house.gov/media-center/press-releases/smith-bill-to-expand-e-verify-approved-by-committee.

- 337 remote video surveillance systems (up from 269 in 2006);
- 198 short and medium range mobile vehicle surveillance systems; 41 long-range mobile surveillance systems (up from zero in 2005);
- 15 portable medium range surveillance systems (up from zero in 2005);
- 15 fixed towers with surveillance gear;
- 13,406 unattended ground sensors (up from about 11,200 in 2005); and
- 10 unmanned aerial vehicle systems (drones), up from zero in 2006.[58]

Since 9/11 the government "has built a formidable immigration enforcement machinery," said a Migration Policy Institute report.[59]

## CURRENT SITUATION

### Deep Divisions

Congress faces sharp divisions over immigration reform and border security.

A Senate immigration reform bill that passed with bipartisan support on June 27 offers a path to citizenship for some unauthorized immigrants. The bill also would bolster border security even further, most notably by adding 20,000 Border Patrol agents. It also would require completing 700 miles of new fence along the U.S.-Mexico line and deploying $3.2 billion in additional security technology.[60]

The Department of Homeland Security would have to certify that these provisions were in place before laws providing a path to citizenship for undocumented immigrants went into effect.

Pedestrians wait to enter the United States at the San Ysidro, Calif., immigration station, across the border from Tijuana, Mexico. Although blocking terrorists from entering the country is now considered the Border Patrol's top priority, agents continue to focus on drug smuggling, customs work and illegal immigration.

The border security measures were stiffened in a late amendment by Sens. Bob Corker, R-Tenn., and John Hoeven, R-N.D., in an effort to garner more Republican support and allay concerns about the measure among immigration hardliners.[61]

Nevertheless, House Republicans remain opposed to the legislation, particularly in the Tea Party caucus. The primary objection centers on allowing unauthorized immigrants a path to citizenship, which opponents have denounced as "amnesty." But several Republicans also have called for placing border security front and center, ahead of immigration concerns. "The first step right now is to secure the border," said Rep. Pete Olson, R-Texas.[62]

Yet, several experts question the bill's increased border security provisions. "All of this becomes less a matter of a thorough planning process and much more driven by symbolic politics," says the University at Albany's Koslowski.

The proposal to add 20,000 more Border Patrol agents draws particular skepticism. A comprehensive study examining conditions along the border concluded that current staff levels are already "at or past a point of diminishing returns."[63] "We absolutely stand by that analysis," says the North American Research Partnership's Lee, the study's principal author. He cites the El Paso sector as an example. "If you do the math there, we're talking about not quite three apprehensions per agent per year," he says. "El Paso is a clear case of overstaffing."

Whether either comprehensive immigration reform legislation or a narrower bill targeting border security will

make it out of the House remained an open question as lawmakers returned in September. President Obama had originally called on Congress to pass immigration reform by the end of the summer.[64] But many observers believe it's unlikely the House will deal with comprehensive legislation this fall, and the final timetable for any vote on a bill remains unclear.[65]

## State Efforts

Policing the borders is generally recognized as a federal responsibility, but in recent years frustration with what some state leaders considered the U.S. government's failure to halt illegal crossings has led to aggressive action in some border states, particularly Texas and Arizona.

The most highly publicized legislative effort was a 2010 Arizona law, SB1070, allowing police to ask anyone they stopped to produce proof they were in the United States legally if the police suspected otherwise. The law also contained provisions designed to deter unauthorized migrants from entering Arizona.

Defending the law, Arizona Republican Gov. Jan Brewer painted a picture of a violent border. "Our law enforcement agencies have found bodies in the desert, either buried or just lying out there, that have been beheaded," Brewer told a local television station.[66] Brewer recanted her claim after local law enforcement officials said they had no cases of beheadings in the desert.[67] The U.S. Supreme Court eventually declared much of SB1070 unconstitutional, but not before five states had passed similar laws.[68]

Arizona recently has concentrated on cooperative efforts with authorities in the Mexican state of Sonora, directly to the south, to increase border security, according to the governor's office.

Texas has taken a more aggressive approach. "The Texas legislature, with the support of state leaders, has dedicated substantial funding over the last several years, and the DPS [Department of Public Safety] has dedicated a significant amount of resources, technology, equipment and personnel for border security," Texas Department of Public Safety Director Steven McCraw stated in an email interview. Staff for a state legislative board estimated total spending on border security at $452 million from 2008-2013.[69]

Texas has sent Ranger Reconnaissance Teams to gather intelligence, conduct interdictions and disrupt drug cartel criminal activity in remote border areas where conventional law enforcement cannot operate, according to the DPS.

# Should the United States tighten its border security?

## YES
**Janice Kephart**
*Special Counsel, Senate Judiciary Committee, During Consideration of Immigration Reform in 2013; Former Border Counsel, 9/11 Commission*

Written for *CQ Researcher,* September 2013

Do we need more border security? Yes. Specifically, we need more efficient and cost-effective measures that identify those who seek to do us harm and keep them out or apprehend them. This can be achieved by defining a secure border, creating a secure border system and adopting measures to determine success.

A "secure border" should be capable of blocking those who pose a threat or attempt illegal entry via visas, ports-of-entry or immigration-benefit processing. That's in addition to the interdiction work of our 20,000 Border Patrol agents. It is essential to verify visitors' identities and ensure they abide by the terms of their entry. Creating secure borders requires Congress to support a balance of resources, law and policy so that we can:

- Maintain and expand visa investigations to prevent those with nefarious intentions from entering.
- Install, where feasible, fencing across the Southern border that can't be stepped over, cut, tunneled under or ramped over.
- Use technology to achieve 100 percent detection and safer, more efficient operations without increasing Border Patrol staff.
- Deploy cost-effective, feasible biometrics at airports and seaports of entry to ensure that holders of expired visas depart on time.
- Empower states and localities to support federal immigration enforcement and enable local agents to retain certain powers that the Obama administration has severely curtailed by invoking "prosecutorial discretion."
- Discourage inadequate review of immigration-benefit applications and reward proper vetting.
- Expand E-Verify, the worker authorization program.

Congress must exercise its authority in measuring success. A Senate immigration bill allows the Department of Homeland Security to exercise discretion or grant waivers in more than 200 types of immigration cases, enabling the department — not Congress — to measure success.

Nearly all of the 550,000 individuals on the terrorist watch list are foreign-born, and up to 20,000 of them are U.S. residents. In addition, every major U.S. city is infiltrated by violent drug cartels. Illegal-entry numbers for the January-April period increased substantially between 2012 and 2013, after the administration recommended immunity from deportation for young illegal immigrants brought here as children. So yes, we need more border security. But mostly, we need better border security.

## NO
**Wayne A. Cornelius**
*Director, Mexican Migration Field Research and Training Program, Division of Global Public Health, University of California-San Diego; Co-Author, Budgeting for Immigration Enforcement*

Written for *CQ Researcher,* September 2013

Spending taxpayer dollars on more border security has reached the point of diminishing returns. With attempts at illegal entry down to 1971 levels, no appreciable additional deterrence can be wrung from more investments in Border Patrol agents, fencing, drones and high-tech surveillance systems.

The key statistic for measuring the effectiveness of border enforcement is migrants' "eventual success rate." In other words, on a given attempt to cross the border, what percentage of unauthorized migrants, even if apprehended initially, can get through if they keep trying? Each year since 2005, my research team has interviewed hundreds of undetected and returned migrants on both sides of the border. In every study we have found that nine out of 10 people apprehended on the first try were able to re-enter undetected on the second or third try — impressive testimony to the near impossibility of stopping migrants determined to feed their families or reunite with relatives in the United States.

The recent decline in attempted entries is driven by weak U.S. labor demand and recession-related declines in wages. Among migrants who returned from the United States since 2008, four of five of those interviewed this year said their U.S. wages had declined — on average, by $428 per week — during the period before they returned to Mexico. Diminished economic returns, coupled with greater physical risks of border crossings and drug-related violence in border areas, have strongly discouraged new migrations.

Spending up to another $46 billion on border enforcement, as the Senate-approved immigration reform bill would authorize, will only enable people-smugglers to charge more for their services, increase the death toll among migrants crossing in ever-more dangerous areas and induce more permanent settlement among those already here.

If Congress were serious about reducing future growth of the nation's undocumented population, it would direct more resources to screening people passing through our legal ports of entry — where a third of unauthorized entries occur — and at U.S. embassies and consulates, which issue tourist and other short-term visas. That would be far more cost-effective than spending more to fortify remote stretches of the Southwestern border.

We should declare victory at that border and move on to the hard work of ensuring that future flows of migrants will be predominantly legal and creating a meaningful path to legalization for undocumented immigrants already here.

Texas also has created a Tactical Marine Unit that uses special shallow-water interceptor boats to patrol the state's intracoastal waterways and the Rio Grande River.

In a collaboration called Operation Drawbridge, the DPS, U.S. Border Patrol and border-county sheriffs have installed motion detectors and surveillance cameras along the border. Since its launch in January 2012, the operation has resulted in the apprehension of more than 16,000 individuals and seizure of 35 tons of narcotics, according to DPS. Texas also has increased collaborative efforts with Mexican authorities in communities across the border.

McCraw says the state had to take action. "Due to the increasingly confrontational nature of ruthless and powerful Mexican cartels and transnational gangs and the lack of sufficient federal resources on the Texas border, the Texas-Mexico border remains unsecure," he says.

But some Texas border residents disagree with that characterization. "I live in McAllen," says border activist Nicol, "and McAllen is one of the quietest places I've ever lived in my life. I think the hysteria that comes out of the 'border wars' view of the borders is absolutely misplaced."

The vision of the border as a lawless zone also does not square with government crime statistics, at least for urban areas. "As measured by Federal Bureau of Investigation crime statistics, U.S. border cities rank among the safest in the United States," according to "The State of the Border Report" published earlier this year by the Wilson Center, a Washington think tank that fosters dialogue in the social sciences.[70]

El Paso, which sits across the border from Cuidad Juarez, the scene of much drug cartel violence, has been rated the safest large city in America for the last three years by CQ Press's *City Crime Rankings*.[71] Still, the report notes there is a split in perceptions between urban and rural areas, with many rural residents who live near the border in Texas, New Mexico and Arizona concerned about illegal crossings.

Earlier this year, Gary Thrasher, a veterinarian and rancher in southern Arizona, told NBC News he feels the border is now more dangerous because there are more armed smugglers. "The border statistically is securer than ever. That means nothing," Thrasher said. "That's like saying we fixed this whole bucket, except for this hole down here."[72]

## Cooperative Efforts

Little noticed amid the border security buildup and the immigration debate has been the level of increased cooperation between U.S. officials and those in Mexico and Canada in the post 9/11 era.

During a visit to Brownsville, Texas, last July, Homeland Security Secretary Napolitano announced an agreement with Mexico on a border communications network that would include increased sharing of intelligence on drug smuggling and other illegal activities.[73] She also announced the start of coordinated patrols by the Mexican Federal Police and the U.S. Border Patrol.

"The United States and Mexico have taken unprecedented steps in recent years to deepen our cooperation along our shared border," Napolitano said.[74]

Cooperation may be even closer with Canada. Besides sharing intelligence and traveler watch lists, the two nations already operate Integrated Border Enforcement Teams (IBET) on land and station officers on each other's vessels through the Shiprider Program, effectively strengthening the border security efforts of both nations.

In addition, since 9/11 Canada has tightened its visa and immigration system, which previously was more open than the U.S. system to refugees and foreign travelers, bringing it closer in line with U.S. requirements.

In December 2011, the United States and Canada announced the Beyond the Border Action Plan, which pursues "a perimeter approach to security" in which the nations share more intelligence and work in greater collaboration along the border.[75] "I think that's the most effective thing we've done since 9/11 — sharing more information," say Stodder, the former Homeland Security official, adding the effort has made the United States and its borders less vulnerable.

But the effort to harmonize Canada's immigration and border security policies with those of the United States has been controversial in some Canadian circles, according to the University of Toronto's Gilbert. She says Canadians have questioned the necessity for the changes and wondered whether the country is surrendering too much sovereignty as it tries to accommodate concerns. "I think the amount of money we're putting toward border security isn't really justified," she says.

# OUTLOOK

### 'Drone Recycling'

The United States has been building up security along its Southern border for more than 25 years. For analysts, the question is whether the trend will continue into the next quarter-century or is nearing its end.

"I don't anticipate a rollback or de-escalation. Very rarely do you have buildups of this kind that are dismantled," says Brown University's Andreas. "The real question is, at what point does it sort of plateau? How militarized does it become?"

He adds that the recent end of the war in Iraq and the winding down of the war in Afghanistan could lead to an expanded use of military technology on the border.[76] "All these drones are going to come home from Iraq and Afghanistan looking for work," he says. "Homeland Security would like to beef up its fleet of drones. To what extent does the border become a drone recycling center?"

Gilbert, the director of the Canadian studies program at the University of Toronto, believes a fundamental change has occurred along the U.S.-Canadian border. "The Canadian government keeps pushing this idea that the more we work with the U.S. the more we'll get back. Canadians keep saying we can return to that mythical moment where we have this open border between us," Gilbert says. "But I don't see the border between Canada and the U.S. ever going back to that moment."

Slaven, the Morrison Institute policy analyst, believes the future of security on the U.S.-Mexican border depends on the ability of the United States to adopt effective immigration reform that provides a legal avenue for immigrants to fill U.S. labor needs. "It's a matter of whether the political will is going to be there to do it," he says.

But in the longer term, the University of Texas' Payan says, demographic shifts in Mexico and Latin America could change the situation drastically. He notes that the Mexican population is aging, and since most unauthorized migrants are young men, that should reduce the pressure on the border. Fertility rates in Mexico and El Salvador, another source of unauthorized border crossers, are also forecast to drop significantly.[77]

"I suspect that the great wave of Mexican migration is over," says Payan, "and I suspect that the great wave of Central American migration is not going to come in the numbers that some predicted."

If the United States does not change its immigration policies, Payan says, it could eventually face a labor shortage. "If they don't pass the immigration reform they're considering now," he says, "they're going to have to pass another immigration reform 10 or 15 years down the road. They're going to have to pass a law that says: 'Please come.'"

# NOTES

1. For background, see Reed Karaim, "America's Border Fence," *CQ Researcher*, Sept. 19, 2008, pp. 745-768.

2. Bob Ortega, "Border technology remains flawed," *The Arizona Republic*, June 3, 2013, www.azcentral .com/news/politics/articles/20130524border-tech nology-flawed.html.

3. Marc R. Rosenblum, "Border Security: Immigration Enforcement Between Ports of Entry," Congressional Research Service, May 3, 2013, p. 13, http://fpc .state.gov/documents/organization/180681.pdf.

4. Doris Meissner, *et al.*, "Immigration Enforcement in the United States: The Rise of a Formidable Machinery," Migration Policy Institute, January 2013, p. 9, www.migrationpolicy.org/pubs/enforce mentpillars.pdf.

5. Customs agents generally work at official ports of entry while immigration agents deal with immigrants already in the country illegally, not just along the border. See in addition, Marc R. Rosenblum, "What Would a Secure Border Look Like?" Congressional Research Service, Feb. 26, 2013, p. 8, http://docs .house.gov/meetings/HM/HM11/20130226/1003 00/HHRG-113-HM11-Wstate-RosenblumM-20130226.pdf.

6. "Fact Sheet on U.S. 'Constitution Free Zone,'" American Civil Liberties Union, Oct. 22, 2008, www.aclu.org/technology-and-liberty/fact-sheet-us-constitution-free-zone. For background, see Chuck McCutcheon, "Government Surveillance," *CQ Researcher*, Aug. 30, 2013, pp. 717-740.

7. "Emergency Supplemental Appropriation Act for Defense, the Global War on Terror, and Tsunami

Relief of 2005 (Pub. L. No. 109-13)," House Committee on Oversight and Government Reform, http://oversight-archive.waxman.house.gov/bills.asp?ID=36.

8. Alan Gomez, "Big surge in border-crossing deaths reported," *USA Today*, March 18, 2013, www.usatoday.com/story/news/nation/2013/03/18/immigrant-border-deaths/1997379/.

9. Todd Miller, "War on the Border," *The New York Times*, April 17, 2013, www.nytimes.com/2013/08/18/opinion/sunday/war-on-the-border.html?pagewanted=all&_r=0.

10. For background, see Reed Karaim, "Immigration," "Hot Topic," *CQ Researcher*, June 15, 2013; and Kenneth Jost, "Immigration Conflict," *CQ Researcher*, March 9, 2012, pp. 229-252.

11. Jeffrey S. Passel, D'Vera Cohn and Ana Gonzalez-Barrera, "Population Decline of Unauthorized Immigrants Stalls, May Have Reversed," Pew Research Hispanic Trends Project, Sept. 23, 2013, www.pewhispanic.org/2013/09/23/population-decline-of-unauthorized-immigrants-stalls-may-have-reversed/.

12. About 18,000 of the Border Patrol's 21,000 agents are assigned along the Southern border, according to Rosenblum, "What Would a Secure Border Look Like?" *op. cit.*, p. 8.

13. "Remarks by the President on Comprehensive Immigration Reform," The White House, Jan. 29, 2013, www.whitehouse.gov/the-press-office/2013/01/29/remarks-president-comprehensive-immigration-reform.

14. "DHS Cmte: McCaul: Border Security Must Come First," website of Rep. Michael McCaul, U.S. House of Representatives, Feb. 2, 2013, http://mccaul.house.gov/press-releases/dhs-cmte-mccaul-border-security-must-come-first/. For background, see Martin Kady II, "Homeland Security," *CQ Researcher*, Sept. 12, 2003, pp. 749-772.

15. Claire O'Neill McCleskey, "Will Meth Overtake Cocaine on the Southwest Border?" *inSight Crime*, April 3, 2013, www.insightcrime.org/news-analysis/meth-cocaine-trafficking-mexico-us-southwest-border.

16. "Remarks by Secretary of Homeland Security Janet Napolitano at the National Press Club," Department of Homeland Security, Aug. 27, 2013, www.dhs.gov/news/2013/08/27/remarks-secretary-homeland-security-janet-napolitano-national-press-club.

17. "Southwest Border Sectors, Total Illegal Alien Apprehensions by Fiscal Year," U.S. Border Patrol, www.cbp.gov/linkhandler/cgov/border_security/border_patrol/usbp_statistics/usbp_fy12_stats/appr_swb.ctt/appr_swb.pdf.

18. Janice L. Kephart, "The Border Security, Economic Opportunity, and Immigration Modernization Act, S.744," testimony before the Senate Committee on the Judiciary, April 22, 2013.

19. Tom Barry, "Border Wars," Kindle Edition (Locations 35-37) (2011). For background, see Peter Katel, "Mexico's Drug War," *CQ Researcher*, Dec. 12, 2008, pp. 1009-1032.

20. Mike Slaven, "Defining Border Security in Immigration Reform," ASU Morrison Institute, July 2013, http://morrisoninstitute.asu.edu/publications-reports/2013-defining-border-security-in-immigration-reform.

21. Rosenblum, "Border Security: Immigration Enforcement Between Ports of Entry," *op. cit.*, p. 29.

22. Sara Murray, "Many in U.S. illegally overstayed their visas," *The Wall Street Journal*, April 7, 2013, http://online.wsj.com/article/SB10001424127887323916304578404960101110032.html.

23. For background, see Pamela M. Prah, "Port Security," *CQ Researcher*, April 21, 2006, pp. 337-360.

24. Rosenblum, "Border Security: Immigration Enforcement Between Ports of Entry," *op. cit.*, p. 13.

25. Meissner, *et al.*, *op. cit.*, p. 18.

26. "Written testimony of U.S. Coast Guard Deputy for Operations Policy and Capabilities Rear Admiral William Lee," House Committee on Homeland Security Subcommittee on Border and Maritime Security, Department of Homeland Security, June 18, 2012, www.dhs.gov/news/2012/06/18/written-testimony-us-coast-guard-house-homeland-security-subcommittee-border-and.

27. "DHS Announces Grant Allocation for Fiscal Year (FY) 2013 Preparedness Grants," Department of

Homeland Security, Aug. 23, 2013, www.dhs.gov/news/2013/08/23/dhs-announces-grant-allocation-fiscal-year-fy-2013-preparedness-grants.

28. "Fact Sheet, Fiscal Year 2014 President's Budget," U.S. Coast Guard, April 10, 2013, www.uscg.mil/posturestatement/docs/fact_sheet.pdf.

29. Chad Haddal, "Border Security: The Role of the U.S. Border Patrol," Congressional Research Service, Aug. 11, 2010, p. 25, www.fas.org/sgp/crs/homesec/RL32562.pdf. For the 2012 figures, see Rosenblum, "What Would a Secure Border Look Like?" *op. cit.*, p. 14.

30. "Border Patrol History," CBP.gov, Jan. 5, 2010, www.cbp.gov/xp/cgov/border_security/border_patrol/border_patrol_ohs/history.xml.

31. Rosenblum, "Border Security: Immigration Enforcement Between Ports of Entry," *op. cit.*, p. 13.

32. "Legacy of 9/11: the world's longest undefended border is now defended," *The Globe and Mail*, Sept. 9, 2011, www.theglobeandmail.com/commentary/editorials/legacy-of-911-the-worlds-longest-undefended-border-is-now-defended/article593884/.

33. Peter Andreas, *Smuggler Nation: How Illicit Trade Made America* (2013), p. 243.

34. Peter Andreas, *Border Games: Policing the U.S. Mexico Divide*, Second Ed. (2009), p. 29.

35. *Ibid.*

36. *Ibid.*, p. 32.

37. Karaim, "America's Border Fence," *op. cit.*

38. For background, see William Triplett, "Migrant Farmworkers," *CQ Researcher*, Oct. 8, 2004, pp. 829-852.

39. *Ibid.*

40. Reed Karaim, "The Mexican Border: Crossing a Cultural Divide," *American Scholar*, summer 2011, http://theamericanscholar.org/the-mexican-border-crossing-a-cultural-divide/#.UiOTuOArzww.

41. Ted Robbins, "Border Killings Prompt Scrutiny Over Use Of Force," NPR, Nov. 24, 2012, www.npr.org/2012/11/24/165822846/border-killings-prompt-scrutiny-over-use-of-force.

42. Bob Ortega, "New details in Mexico teenager's death," *The Arizona Republic*, April 11, 2013, www.azcentral.com/news/arizona/articles/20130410border-patrol-new-details-mexico-teens-death.html.

43. "Border Patrol under scrutiny for deadly force," *USA Today*, Nov. 14, 2012, www.usatoday.com/story/news/nation/2012/11/14/border-patrol-probe/1705737/.

44. *Ibid.*

45. Todd Miller, "U.S. Quietly Ramps Up Security Along the Canadian Border," *Mother Jones*, Feb. 7, 2013, www.motherjones.com/politics/2013/02/US-canada-border-constitution-free-zone.

46. "Nationwide Illegal Alien Apprehensions Fiscal Years 1925-2012," *op. cit.*

47. Figure 3, "U.S. Border Patrol Agents, Total and by Region, FY 1980-FY2013," in Rosenblum, "Border Security: Immigration Enforcement Between Ports of Entry," *op. cit.*, p. 14.

48. Robert Lindsey, "The Talk of San Diego: as flow of illegal aliens grows, complaints mount in the West," *The New York Times*, April 27, 1986, www.nytimes.com/1986/04/27/us/talk-san-diego-flow-illegal-aliens-grows-complaints-mount-west.html.

49. *Ibid.*

50. Eleanor Clift, "With Rebel Leaders at his Side, Reagan Presses for Contra Aid," *Los Angeles Times*, March 4, 1986, http://articles.latimes.com/1986-03-04/news/mn-15033_1_contra-aid.

51. "Immigration Reform and Control Act of 1986," U.S. Citizenship and Immigration Services, www.uscis.gov/portal/site/uscis/menuitem.5af9bb95919f35e66f614176543f6d1a/?vgnextchannel=b328194d3e88d010VgnVCM10000048f3d6a1RCRD&vgnextoid=04a295c4f635f010VgnVCM1000000ecd190aRCRD.

52. "A Reagan Legacy: Amnesty For Illegal Immigrants," NPR, July 10, 2010, www.npr.org/templates/story/story.php?storyId=128303672.

53. "Southwest Border Security Operations," National Immigration Forum, December 2010, www.immigrationforum.org/images/uploads/SouthwestBorderSecurityOperations.pdf.

54. "Illegal Immigration Reform and Immigration Responsibility Act," Legal Information Institute,

Cornell University Law School, www.law.cornell .edu/wex/illegal_immigration_reform_and_immi gration_responsibility_act.

55. "Nationwide Illegal Alien Apprehensions Fiscal Years 1925-2012," *op. cit.*

56. Rosenblum, "Border Security: Immigration Enforcement Between Ports of Entry," *op. cit.*, p. 14.

57. "After SBINet: DHS' New Border Control Strategy," FCW: The Business of Federal Technology, Jan. 14, 2011, http://fcw.com/articles/2011/01/14/dhs-can cels-rest-of-sbinet-and-plans-mix-of-new-technolo gies-at-border.aspx; and, Rey Koslowski, "The Evolution of Border Controls as a Mechanism to Prevent Illegal Immigration," Migration Policy Institute, February 2011, www.migrationpolicy.org/ pubs/bordercontrols-koslowski.pdf.

58. Rosenblum, "What Would a Secure Border Look Like?" *op. cit.*, p. 9.

59. Meissner, *op. cit.*

60. Alan Silverleib, "Senate passes sweeping immigration bill," CNN, June 28, 2013, www.cnn .com/2013/06/27/politics/immigration.

61. Ashley Parker and Jonathan Martin, "Senate, 68 to 32, Passes Overhaul for Immigration," *The New York Times*, June 27, 2013, www.nytimes.com/2013/06/28/ us/politics/immigration-bill-clears-final-hurdle-to-senate-approval.html?pagewanted=all&_r=0.

62. Todd J. Gillman, "House Republicans dig in on demand for border security fix before citizenship in immigration bill," *The Dallas Morning News*, July 10, 2013, www.dallasnews.com/news/politics/ headlines/20130710-house-republicans-dig-in-on-demand-for-border-security-fix-before-citizenship-in-immigration-bill.ece.

63. Erik Lee, "The State of the Border Report: A comprehensive analysis of the U.S.-Mexico border," Wilson Center, May 2013, www.wilsoncenter.org/ publication/the-state-the-border-report.

64. Steven T. Dennis, "Obama Urges Congress to Pass Immigration Bill by End of Summer," *Roll Call*, June 11, 2013, www.rollcall.com/news/obama_ urges_congress_to_pass_immigration_bill_by_end_ of_summer-225504-1.html.

65. Matt Canham, "House GOP to take it slow on immigration," *The Salt Lake Tribune*, July 10, 2013, www.sltrib.com/sltrib/politics/56579284-90/ bishop-chaffetz-citizenship-immigrants.html.csp.

66. "Brewer says she was wrong about beheadings in the desert," Fox News, Sept. 3, 2010, www.foxnews .com/politics/2010/09/03/brewer-says-wrong-be headings-arizona/.

67. *Ibid.*

68. The five states were Alabama, Georgia, Indiana, South Carolina and Utah. The case is *Arizona v. United States*, 11-182. Background and legal filings compiled on SCOTUSblog, www.scotusblog.com/_ case-files/_cases/_arizona-v-united-states/_?wpmp_ switcher=desktop.- For background see Kenneth Jost, "Immigration Conflict," *CQ Researcher*, March 9, 2012, pp. 229-252.

69. "Texas Border Security Funding Overview," Legislative Board Budget Staff, April 2013, www .lbb.state.tx.us/Issue_Briefs/420_Texas_Border_ Security_Funding_Overview.pdf.

70. Lee, *et al.*, *op. cit.*, p. 90.

71. *CQ Press City Crime Rankings*, 2012-2013, 2011-2012, and 2010-2011, www.cqpress.com/pages/ cc1213. See also, Daniel Borunda, "El Paso ranked safest large city in America for third straight year," *The El Paso Times*, Feb. 6, 2013, www.elpasotimes. com/tablehome/ci_22523903/el-paso-ranked-safest-large-city-u-s.

72. Mark Potter, "Despite safer border cities, undocumented immigrants flow through rural areas," NBC News, May 2, 2013, http://dailynightly.nbcnews .com/_news/2013/05/02/17708115-despite-safer-border-cities-undocumented-immigrants-flow-through-rural-areas?lite.

73. "Readout of Secretary Napolitano's Trip to Mexico and Texas," Department of Homeland Security, July 23, 2013, www.dhs.gov/news/2013/07/23/readout-secretary-napolitano's-trip-mexico-and-texas.

74. *Ibid.*

75. "United States-Canada Beyond the Border: A shared vision for perimeter security and economic competitiveness," The White House, December 2011,

www.whitehouse.gov/sites/default/files/us-canada_
btb_action_plan3.pdf.

76. For background, see Thomas J. Billitteri, "Drone
Warfare," *CQ Researcher*, Aug. 6, 2010, pp. 653-676.

77. "The U.S.-Mexico Border: Secure enough," *The
Economist*, June 22, 2013, www.economist.com/
news/united-states/21579828-spending-billions-
more-fences-and-drones-will-do-more-harm-good-
secure-enough.

# BIBLIOGRAPHY

## Selected Sources

## Books

**Andreas, Peter, *Smuggler Nation: How Illicit Trade
Made America*, Oxford University Press, 2013.**
A political science professor at Brown University argues
that the current battles over border security are part of a
historic tradition of smuggling and federal attempts to
control it.

**Barry, Tom, *Border Wars*, MIT Press, 2011.**
The director of the TransBorder Project at the Center for
International Policy concludes that federal and state border security policies have made U.S. borders more dangerous, rather than safer.

**Brewer, Jan, *Scorpions for Breakfast: My Fight Against
Special Interests, Liberal Media, And Cynical Politicos
To Secure America's Border*, Broadside Books, 2011.**
Arizona's governor explains the threat she sees to the
country and her state posed by unauthorized border
crossers and the need for Arizona's law allowing police to
ask people to produce papers showing legal residency.

**Payan, Tony, *The Three U.S.-Mexico Border Wars*,
ABC-Clio, 2006.**
A political science professor at the University of Texas, El
Paso, looks at the social and economic costs of America's
three border "wars" on terrorism, drug smuggling and
undocumented migration.

## Articles

**"Secure Enough: spending billions more on fences
and drones will do more harm than good," *The***

*Economist*, **June 22, 2013, www.economist.com/
news/united-states/21579828-spending-billions-
more-fences-and-drones-will-do-more-harm-good-
secure-enough.**
Increasing security along the U.S.-Mexico border in
Arizona could lead undocumented crossers to take more
desperate risks, leading to more deaths, the British news-
weekly concludes.

**"US border security data not reliable, government
reports show," FOXNews.com, Aug. 16, 2013, www
.foxnews.com/politics/2013/08/16/us-border-secu
rity-data-not-reliable-government-watchdog-groups-say.**
The Obama administration says a steep decline in apprehensions along the U.S.-Mexican border shows the border is more secure, but Fox News cites analyses by
independent government agencies concluding apprehensions alone are a flawed measure of border security.

**Castillo, Mariano, "For those living on border, secu-
rity is complicated subject," CNN, July 21, 2013,
www.cnn.com/2013/07/21/us/immigration-border-
security.**
CNN examines the various, sometimes contradictory,
reactions to increased border security.

**Miller, Todd, "US Quietly Ramps Up Security Along
the Canadian Border," *Mother Jones*, Feb. 7, 2013,
www.motherjones.com/politics/2013/02/US-canada-
border-constitution-free-zone.**
The 4,000-mile U.S.-Canadian border was once largely
unpatrolled, and citizens could pass freely between the
two countries, but that has changed since the 9/11
attacks, particularly for Muslims.

**Ortega, Bob, "Border Technology Remains Flawed,"
*The Arizona Republic*, June 3, 2013, www.azcentral
.com/news/politics/articles/20130524border-tech
nology-flawed.html.**
Despite $106 billion spent on militarizing U.S. borders
over the past five years, much of the surveillance technology used in catching migrants crossing illegally is unreliable, Ortega writes.

## Reports and Studies

**Martin, Jack, "Ten Years Later: We Will Not Forget,"
Federation for American Immigration Reform**

**(FAIR), September 2011, www.fairus.org/publica tions/ten-years-later-we-will-not-forget-2011.**
The director of special projects for a group supporting increased border security and lower immigration levels surveys U.S. policies a decade after the 9/11 terrorist attacks and concludes the nation has failed to secure its borders and ports.

**Meissner, Doris, *et al.*, "Immigration Enforcement in the United States: The Rise of a Formidable Machinery," Migration Policy Institute, January 2013, www.migra tionpolicy.org/pubs/enforcementpillars.pdf.**
A former commissioner of the U.S. Immigration and Naturalization Service and now a senior fellow at a Washington think tank focused on international migration says the main challenge of the massive increases in U.S. border security resources is determining how they can be used most effectively.

**Rosenblum, Marc R., *et al.*, "Border Security: Understanding Threats at U.S. Borders," Congressional Research Service, Feb. 21, 2013, www.fas.org/ sgp/crs/homesec/R42969.pdf.**
An analysis prepared for members of Congress reviews the threats along U.S. borders, including terrorists, drug smugglers and undocumented border crossers.

**Slaven, Mike, "Defining Border Security in Immigration Reform," Arizona State University, Morrison Institute, Latino Public Policy Center, July 2013, http://morrisoninstitute.asu.edu/publications-reports/2013-defining-border-security-in-immigra tion-reform.**
A university researcher looks at the twin difficulties of defining what constitutes a secure border and measuring how effective various security measures are in the current, polarized political environment.

# For More Information

**American Immigration Council**, 1331 G St., N.W., Suite 200, Washington, DC 20005-3141; 202-507-7500; www .americanimmigrationcouncil.org. Supports a path to citizenship for immigrants who arrived illegally and de-emphasizes "enforcement first" as an approach.

**Center for Comparative Immigration Studies**, University of California, San Diego, 9500 Gilman Dr., Mail Code 0548, La Jolla, CA 92093-0548; 858-822-4447; http://ccis .ucsd.edu. Studies worldwide migration. Conducts extensive field interviews with migrants crossing the border illegally into the United States.

**Migration Policy Institute**, 1400 16th St., N.W., Suite 300, Washington, DC 20036; 202-266-1940; www.migrationpol icy.org. An independent, nonpartisan think tank that analyzes the movement of people worldwide. Publishes *The Migration Information Source*, an online resource providing current migration and refugee data and analysis.

**National Center for Border Security and Immigration**, University of Arizona, McClelland Hall, Room 427, P.O. Box 210108, Tucson, AZ 85721-0108; 520-621-7515; http://

borders.arizona.edu/cms/. A consortium of 18 institutions dedicated to the development of technologies, processes and policies designed to protect the nation's borders, foster international trade and enhance understanding of immigration.

**The National Immigration Forum**, 50 F St., N.W., Suite 300, Washington, DC 20001; 202-347-0040; www.immi grationforum.org. Promotes "responsible and humane" federal immigration policies that address the nation's economic and security needs while "respecting the rights of workers and employers, families and communities."

**NumbersUSA**, 1601 N. Kent St., Suite 1100, Arlington, VA 22209; https://www.numbersusa.com/content/. Advocates for significantly lower immigration levels and stepped-up enforcement of immigration laws.

**U.S. Customs and Border Protection**, 1300 Pennsylvania Ave., N.W., Washington, DC 20229; 877-227-5511; www .cbp.gov. Section of the Department of Homeland Security that is charged with securing the border, enforcing drug and immigration laws and facilitating legal international trade and travel.

# 18

# Assisted Suicide

Reed Karaim

Opponents of a measure that would have legalized physician-assisted suicide for the terminally ill in Massachusetts celebrate the measure's narrow defeat on Nov. 6, 2012. Religious, medical and disability groups said the measure was open to manipulation and relied on diagnoses that could be wrong.

From *CQ Researcher*, May 17, 2013.

Lee Johnson, a retired federal worker in Portland, Ore., had started a second career as a furniture maker. When he developed terminal brain cancer, he opted for radiation treatments and chemotherapy to extend his life, even though the disease "was undeniably going to kill him," says his daughter, Heather Clish.

But as his condition deteriorated and he became bedridden, with blurred vision, sores and pain, Johnson didn't want to go on, she says. In March 2011, Johnson took advantage of Oregon's Death with Dignity Act and swallowed a lethal dose of pills prescribed by a doctor.* He was 66.

Before he ended his life, Clish says, Johnson and his family talked a lot about his values. "The essence of his being was that he was a deeply independent person who really came to believe in living by choice," she says. "What he ended up doing was very consciously going about dying with dignity and grace. If this was what he needed to have as an option to be the person he is, we understood. That was okay."

---

*The fatal prescription is most often a lethal dose of barbiturates, usually Seconal or Pentobarbital.

## Physician-Assisted Suicides Rise in Oregon Law

Oregon enacted the Death With Dignity Act in 1994, allowing terminally ill adults to self-administer lethal doses of medication prescribed by physicians. Last year 115 people received prescriptions, compared to 24 in 1998. The number of deaths involving use of the prescriptions has risen steadily since the law took effect in 1998, to 77 last year.

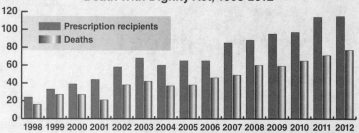

**Prescription Recipients and Deaths Under Oregon Death With Dignity Act, 1998-2012**

Source: "Oregon's Death With Dignity Act — 2012," Public Health Division, State of Oregon, January 2013, p. 1, public.health.oregon.gov/Provider Partner Resources/EvaluationResearch/DeathwithDignityAct/Documents/year15.pdf

Clish felt so strongly about her father's decision that when Massachusetts, where she lives, voted on an assisted-suicide** law modeled on Oregon's in a ballot initiative last November, she volunteered her family's story in support.

But Clish was not the only person who felt strongly about the issue. In a written statement, John Norton, a retired bus driver from Florence, Mass., offered his own life as evidence — in opposition to the measure.

When he was 18, Norton said, he noticed a twitching in his right hand. Doctors at the University of Iowa Medical School diagnosed Norton with the usually fatal

---

** Supporters prefer the term "death with dignity" or "aid in dying," arguing that because the terminally ill already are dying, "assisted suicide" mischaracterizes their choice. Opponents, who view the procedure as suicide, note that the Oregon, Washington and likely to be enacted Vermont laws require only a physician's diagnosis that a patient is going to die within six months. That is too far out to know when the end will occur, and thus those who take lethal doses of medicine are choosing to end their lives prematurely, the opponents contend. Physician-assisted suicide is the term most used by the media.

amyotrophic lateral sclerosis (ALS), commonly known as Lou Gehrig's disease. "I was told I would get progressively worse, be paralyzed and die in three to five years," he wrote.

The Mayo Clinic in Rochester, Minn., confirmed Norton's diagnosis, and for awhile his condition worsened. Twitching began in his right hand and both got weaker. Then the disease's progression stopped. That was in 1960. Today Norton is 75 with a wife and family. He enjoys singing in an amateur choir and still volunteers occasionally as a bus driver.

None of that would have happened, he wrote, if assisted suicide had been available when he was initially told he had the disease. "If, when I was diagnosed with ALS, I had been given an easy way out with a doctor's prescription and support, I would have taken that opportunity," he said. "I would have missed the bulk of my life."

Johnson's and Norton's cases are not identical. Johnson was almost certainly in the final days of his life, whereas Norton's ALS stopped progressing before he reached that stage. But their stories testify to the deeply personal nature of the public debate surrounding physician-assisted suicide, currently legal in just three states: Oregon, Washington, Montana and soon likely in Vermont, when Gov. Peter Shumlin signs a bill enacted on May 13.

In 1997 the U.S. Supreme Court declined to recognize the right to assisted suicide but invited the states to address the issue. In his majority opinion, the late Chief Justice William Rehnquist concluded, "Americans are engaged in an earnest and profound debate about the morality, legality and practicality of physician-assisted suicide. Our holding permits this debate to continue, as it should in a democratic society."[1]

The debate is still going strong. Supporters cast the issue as one of individual choice, believing the terminally ill have a right to decide whether to obtain prescriptions that allow them to avoid final days stricken with pain or other debilitating conditions and choose the manner in which they meet an inevitable death. Opponents see the practice as a threat to some of the most vulnerable Americans, including the elderly and disabled, fearing some could be coerced or manipulated into making the decision to end their lives. They believe physician-assisted suicide devalues life, encourages a premature halt to medical treatment and could open the door to cutting off medical care for other patients who aren't terminally ill but may be severely disabled or incapacitated.

The Roman Catholic Church has been a leading, politically active opponent of assisted suicide. But several disability-rights groups also actively oppose it. The American Medical Association has adopted a position against the practice but does not actively lobby against it. Two public-interest groups are the leading voices supporting legalization: the Denver-based Compassion & Choices, and the Portland-based Death with Dignity National Center, which originally organized to work for the Oregon law. Some smaller religious denominations such as Unitarian Universalism also support the right of terminally ill individuals to choose assisted suicide.

Despite the passion surrounding the issue, physician-assisted suicide remains rare, even in the states where it is legal. Oregon, which passed its Death with Dignity Act through a voter referendum in 1994 and began allowing the practice in 1998, has the longest track record. The number of Oregonians who choose physician-assisted suicide has been slowly climbing; 673 cases were recorded between 1998 and 2012. In 2012, the 77 cases reported to the Public Health Division amounted to about 0.2

## Americans Slightly Divided on Assisted Suicide

Slightly more Americans say physician-assisted suicide is morally wrong than acceptable. However, in another poll, when the question about assisted suicide was worded differently — "Do you think people have the right to end their own lives?" — a strong majority approved.

### Percentage Who Say Assisted Suicide is Morally Acceptable, 2011, by Age, Political Party

| Overall | |
|---|---|
| Morally acceptable | 45% |
| Morally wrong | 48% |
| **By Party** | |
| Democrats | 51% |
| Republicans | 32% |
| Independents | 50% |
| **By Age Group** | |
| 18 to 34 | 46% |
| 35 to 54 | 45% |
| 55+ | 43% |

*Source:* Lydia Saad, "Doctor-Assisted Suicide Is Moral Issue Dividing Americans Most," Gallup, May 2011, www.gallup.com /poll/147842/doctor-assisted-suicide- moral-issue-dividing-americans.aspx

percent of the total deaths recorded in the state.[2] In Washington, where the law — also passed by referendum — has been in effect only since 2009, 70 people took lethal doses of prescription medicine in 2011.[3]

The number of individuals requesting the prescriptions is higher in both states, but in Oregon a little more than a third haven't used the drugs after obtaining them. "I think it's a peace-of-mind thing," says Peg Sandeen, executive director of the Death with Dignity National Center. "You're terminally ill and you're facing the possibility of some pretty tremendous suffering, and just the idea that you have this [prescription] and tomorrow you can take it if it gets really bad provides some comfort."

Montana does not spell out as clearly the requirements for assisted suicide to occur legally. The state's Supreme Court ruled in 2009 that a physician helping a terminally ill patient die was protected by existing state law.[4] But the state has not passed a specific law regulating the practice, and it is unknown how many people have died with the assistance of their doctor.[5]

Supporters of assisted suicide point to national opinion polls and the fact that Oregon's and Washington's laws were passed by referendum in arguing that the public backs their cause.[6] "I think it's fairly clear the public believes this is a right they have," says Sandeen.

But similar laws have been defeated by referendum or failed to advance through legislatures in roughly half the states, including Massachusetts, where a ballot measure was defeated last November, 51 to 49 percent, despite leading in early polls. "It doesn't gather a lot of attention, but there's been a lot of rejection of physician-assisted suicide," says Marilyn Golden, a policy analyst with the

Berkeley, Calif.-based Disability Rights Education and Defense Fund, one of several disability groups opposing assisted suicide. "Once the problems are brought out on legalization, it's very common for public opinion to shift."

However, on May 13 the Vermont House gave final approval to a bill that would make Vermont the first state to legalize physician-assisted suicide by legislation. Democratic Gov. Peter Shumlin, a supporter of the measure, is expected to sign it into law.

As advocates, physicians and the general public debate the question of whether assisted suicide should be legal, here are some of the questions they are discussing:

### Do the terminally ill have a right to choose when to end their lives?

Supporters of what they call aid in dying align their cause with American values of individual liberty and freedom of choice. Barbara Coombs Lee, Compassion & Choices president, says the organization believes individuals should have options as they near the end of their lives, including expanded hospice and palliative care, which focus on relieving patients' pain and discomfort.

"We don't promote just one choice (in end-of-life decisions). We think people deserve an entire spectrum of choices," says Coombs Lee. "But people who are mentally alert and who are making a rational decision to choose — not life or death, because that decision has already been made — but when and how they will meet death, those people deserve a peaceful and gentle option in the dying process."

But Golden with the Disability Rights Education and Defense Fund believes considering the issue simply as a matter of individual rights ignores the implications for society as a whole. "Public policy is about weighing benefits and harms," she says. "Proponents of assisted suicide would want you to believe there [are] only benefits and no harms. . . . But if you look at everything, I think the risk of harms vastly overwhelm the benefits."

By supporting the idea that there is a class of people whom doctors can legally help die and by legitimizing one form of suicide, Golden and other opponents say, physician-assisted suicide potentially harms many more people than it helps both because it makes suicide more culturally acceptable and because it involves doctors in the process of ending lives, which ends a prohibition that

could eventually make other forms of assisted-death acceptable, such as euthanasia.

Supporters, however, say the relatively small number of people who choose physician-assisted suicide where it is legal shows the procedure does not threaten the larger population. "Modern medicine, palliative care, pain release, hospice care can provide relief for most people," Sandeen says. "But not all people, and the Death with Dignity Act can provide relief for them."

Sandeen, who was a social worker before joining Death with Dignity, says her experience was that too many "people die badly in this country. The way modern medicine works is that they can keep people alive for a very long time past what any natural death would be, and people die badly." Individuals should have a right to escape a bad — in other words painful or lingering, debilitating — death, she says.

But opponents believe advances in palliative care including at the end of life, means a "bad death" need no longer be the case. "It is a national and international scandal that so many people do not get adequate pain control," writes Rita Marker, the founder of the Patients Rights Council, a nonprofit group in Steubenville, Ohio, that opposes assisted suicide. "But killing is not the answer to that scandal. The solution is to mandate better education of health care professionals."[7]

Some opponents say that in the most extreme cases, palliative sedation, in which a patient is drugged into unconsciousness to escape pain until he dies, provides a legal alternative. But David Mayo, a bioethicist and professor of philosophy emeritus at the University of Minnesota, Duluth, who is on the Death with Dignity board, believes such an intervention amounts to assisted dying. "The practice of terminal [palliative] sedation — which is, 'now I can't give you the drugs to kill yourself, but we can put you in a coma while you starve to death' — the idea that's somehow better is just crazy," Mayo says.

In their statement on the issue, the United States Conference of Catholic Bishops rejects the idea that assisted suicide represents an expression of freedom. "The assisted-suicide agenda promotes a narrow and distorted notion of freedom, by creating an expectation that certain people, unlike others, will be served by being helped to choose death," the statement declares. "One cannot uphold human freedom and dignity by devaluing human life. A choice to take one's life is a supreme contradiction of freedom, a choice to eliminate all choices."[8]

Orthodox Judaism, Islam and most major Protestant denominations also oppose physician-assisted suicide, although they generally have not been as active politically as the Catholic Church on the issue. Some Christian denominations, however, have not taken a position, or they support the practice as one end-of-life option.

The United Church of Christ, for instance, considers the right to choose aid in dying a legitimate decision under certain circumstances. The Unitarian Universalist Association adopted a resolution in 1988 stating, "Unitarian Universalists advocate the right to self-determination in dying, and the release from civil or criminal penalties of those who, under proper safeguards, act to honor the right of terminally ill patients to select the time of their own deaths."[9]

The Oregon and Washington laws do not require the participation of a doctor or pharmacist who, for religious or any other reason, objects to physician-assisted suicide. "The underpinning of this law is the concept of self-determination," says Sandeen. "There is no way we would want someone who believes this is wrong to have to participate. My struggle with the religious-based opposition is that they want everybody else not to be able to participate because of their [own religious] beliefs."

## Does permitting assisted suicide lead to abuse?

Oregon's Death with Dignity Act and the Washington law that followed have safeguards that supporters believe clearly prevent abuses of the process. (Vermont's pending law has similar provisions.)

The laws require that a physician diagnose a terminally ill patient as having a life expectancy of six months or less. A second doctor must concur with the diagnosis. Patients must request the lethal prescription twice verbally and once in written form with a waiting period of at least two weeks between the first and last request, and the doctor who writes the prescription must believe the patient is mentally competent to make the decision. The law also requires that patients be able to take the pills on their own.

State health agencies are required to provide annual reports on how often physician-assisted suicide is used, and by whom. Outside researchers also have conducted

Australian physician Philip Nitschke, a supporter of voluntary euthanasia, displays a drug kit used in assisted suicides following a workshop he gave on May 5, 2009, in Bournemouth, England.

*Getty Images/Matt Cardy*

several studies on the laws' impact. "There has never been a medical treatment that has been so closely, comprehensively and continually studied as this one," says Coombs Lee of Compassion & Choices. In all that examination, she says, there have been no substantiated cases of abuse.

But opponents question the safeguards in the laws, saying compliance is self-reported, so there is no way to be sure what's really happening. "Do we have any evidence of abuse? No, but we have a lot of circumstances that show that abuse is very possible," says Golden of the Disability Rights Education and Defense Fund.

Opponents note the laws don't require an independent witness present when a person is taking the

## Cancer Most Prevalent Malady in Oregon Cases

Of the 77 people who died last year under Oregon's Death With Dignity Act, 75 percent suffered from cancer. The median age for all deaths under the law was 69. More than 90 percent said they were concerned about losing autonomy and finding life's activities no longer enjoyable.

### Characteristics of Deaths Under Oregon's Death With Dignity Act, 2012

| | |
|---|---|
| **Sex** | |
| Male | 50.6% |
| Female | 49.4% |
| **Age** | |
| 18-34 | 0% |
| 35-44 | 1.3% |
| 45-54 | 10.4% |
| 55-64 | 20.8% |
| 65-74 | 29.9% |
| 75-84 | 23.4% |
| 85+ | 14.3% |
| **Marital status** | |
| Married | 42.9% |
| Widowed | 29.9% |
| Never married | 7.8% |
| Divorced | 19.5% |
| **Underlying illness** | |
| Cancer | 75.3% |
| Amyotrophic lateral sclerosis | 6.5% |
| Chronic lower respiratory disease | 2.6% |
| Heart disease | 2.6% |
| HIV/AIDS | 1.3% |
| Other | 11.7% |
| **End-of-life concerns** | |
| Losing autonomy | 93.5% |
| Activities no longer enjoyable | 92.2% |
| Loss of dignity | 77.9% |
| Losing control of bodily functions | 35.1% |
| Burden on loved ones and caregivers | 57.1% |
| Inadequate pain control | 29.9% |
| Financial implications of treatment | 3.9% |

*Source:* "Oregon's Death With Dignity Act — 2012," Public Health Division, State of Oregon, January 2013, pp. 4-5, public.health.oregon.gov/Provider Partner Resources/EvaluationResearch/DeathwithDignityAct/Documents/year15.pdf

College and executive officer of Suicide Prevention Initiatives, a nonprofit group. "The weakness of the laws is that they don't enforce the practice of ordinary medical standards. They could insist on a palliative care [discussion with the patient as an alternative to assisted suicide]. They could insist on a psychiatric consult."

The idea that hundreds of people have received aid in dying without formal psychiatric evaluation or counseling undercuts the claim the law is being used solely by people making competent choices, Hendin says. "An awful lot of people who are physically ill are also depressed, and if you relieve their depression, they're no longer interested in ending their life early," he says.

But Dr. Marcia Angell, a senior lecturer in social medicine at Harvard Medical School, says the terminally ill are in a different situation from other seriously ill patients. "This is not a question of life versus death," she says. "It's often misconstrued that way. These people are going to die. Who are we to tell them they must soldier on?"

Critics, however, believe the laws' lax definition of terminally ill invites abuse of the intent to limit assistance to those in their last weeks of their lives. "Terminal illness is a meaningless term," says Dr. Rex Greene, a longtime oncologist now semi-retired in Elida, Ohio. "The law in Oregon says a six-month prognosis. There's no physician on Earth [who] can make a six-month prognosis. The best we can do is in the last weeks of life we can be pretty close."

The issue strikes a nerve with disability groups. "Anytime I'm doing training on this issue within the disability community, I ask, 'Who of you here were first diagnosed as terminally ill and are still going strong?'" says Golden, "and every time, hands go up."

prescription, so there is no way to be sure every dose is self-administered or taken by free will. Opponents also point out that the law does not require an outside psychological evaluation of patients who request the drugs.

"It's bad psychiatry and bad medicine," says Dr. Herbert Hendin, a professor of psychiatry at New York Medical

Advocates for the disabled are among the most vocal in arguing that the laws could encourage some people to end their lives to save loved ones trouble. Ben Matlin, an author born with a neuromuscular condition so debilitating that he has never been able to stand and now is unable to hold a pencil, explained his opposition to the laws. "I've lived so close to death for so long that I know how thin and porous the border between coercion and free choice is, how easy it is for someone to inadvertently influence you to feel devalued and hopeless — to pressure you ever so slightly but decidedly into being 'reasonable,' to unburdening others, to 'letting go,'" he wrote.[10]

Opponents also raise the possibility that the nature of the health care system could lead to abuse. "The frightening potential for profit-driven health care organizations to drive people toward assisted suicide for cost control is something we can't ignore," says Golden.

But supporters respond that all these concerns have proved unfounded through years of experience with the Oregon law. "When we talk about aid in dying, a tactic of those who oppose end-of-life choice is to raise unreasonable doubt, to cast aspersions on the situation in Oregon," says Coombs Lee of Compassion & Choices.

Supporters point to a study of cases published in the *Journal of Clinical Ethics* that found no unreported cases of physician-assisted suicide in Oregon. In addition, the researchers found that terminally ill people in Oregon were no more likely to consider assisted suicide than people in states where the procedure was illegal.[11]

Supporters also cite a study led by Margaret Battin, a distinguished professor of philosophy and an adjunct professor of internal medicine in the Division of Medical Ethics, at the University of Utah in Provo. The study found no evidence that physician-assisted suicide has had a disproportionate impact on patients in vulnerable groups, including the physically disabled, the poor, individuals with low educational status or racial minorities. "Those who received physician-assisted dying in the jurisdictions studied appeared to enjoy comparative social, economic, educational, professional and other privileges," Battin and her team concluded.[12]

### Does the Hippocratic Oath ethics code prevent doctors from helping patients die?

Physicians have been pledging themselves to the principles of the Hippocratic Oath, named after an ancient Greek physician, since the 4th century BC. The classical version of the oath includes this prohibition, "I will never give a deadly drug to anybody who asked for it, nor will I make a suggestion to this effect."[13]

Most graduating U.S. medical students still swear to some form of the oath, although the modern version used by most medical schools does not include that prohibition.[14]

The American Medical Association (AMA) code of ethics, however, rejects the idea of doctors providing deadly prescriptions. "Physician-assisted suicide is fundamentally incompatible with the physician's role as healer, would be difficult or impossible to control, and would pose serious societal risks," the code states.[15]

Some bioethicists, however, believe medical care must include recognizing when death is inevitable and respecting a patient's wishes at that time. "While doctors in general want and should work to extend life, suppose that's no longer possible?" says Angell of Harvard's medical school. "That's the case here, and if that's the case, then they must shift their objective to relieving suffering in accordance with the patients' wishes."

But many physicians believe assisting in death, even of a terminally ill patient, undermines their essential covenant with the public. "It's in the seminal code of medicine, that physicians are not to do anything to take the patient's life," says Greene, the retired oncologist, referring to the Hippocratic Oath. "One of the reasons medicine has endured all these centuries is that we have remained trustworthy in that regard. I personally don't see any way physicians can maintain that trust if they're involved [in] ending people's lives."

Greene is the current chairman of the AMA Council on Ethical and Judicial Affairs but emphasizes that he is expressing his personal opinion. He spent more than 30 years as an oncologist and now consults on palliative care.

The AMA, along with most opponents of assisted suicide, supports the removal of life-sustaining devices in the last stages of life, if patients have indicated such a preference. But Greene sees a crucial distinction between removing life-sustaining medical equipment and actively assisting patients in killing themselves.

By removing devices such as ventilators or respirators, in accordance with their wishes, a physician is allowing the patient to assume the natural risk of dying

**To Assist or Not to Assist**

Cathy Ludlum, a disabled-rights activist in Manchester, Conn., is concerned that physician-assisted suicide is being considered by her state's legislature. Lawmakers should focus more on "giving people a good life than giving people a good death," says Ludlum, who has spinal muscular atrophy (top). Opponents of the measure to permit assisted suicide in Connecticut succeeded in April in derailing the proposal. Supporters of Oregon's physician-assisted suicide law demonstrate in front of the U.S. Supreme Court (bottom) on Oct. 5, 2005, as the court heard Bush administration attorneys argue that the law violated the Controlled Substances Act. The court later ruled against the administration, allowing the law to stand.

that is part of their condition, he says. The physician is not taking action that has the specific intent of killing the patient, he says. "That's not the intent," Greene says. "If we take on the responsibility of deciding who lives and who dies, we have so overstepped the bounds of human experience."

Other physicians, however, believe fulfilling a patient's wish to end his or her suffering at the end of life is part of the responsibility a doctor assumes when caring for the person. Dr. Eric Kress, who practices family medicine and hospice care in Missoula, Mont., says an experience with one particular patient persuaded him of that.

The patient was terminally ill with ALS; he had lost 100 pounds, couldn't walk and was being fed through a tube. "He used to be a vigorous guy, but now he was wasting away, and there was no question where he was headed," Kress recalls. His patient, whom Kress considered of sound mind, felt very strongly that he did not want to wait a few more weeks for the disease to end his life. He requested lethal medication.

Kress told him he couldn't provide it. A few weeks later the patient had stockpiled enough pain medication to kill himself anyway. But before he died, Kress says, "He called me a coward and said, 'Who are you treating here? Are you treating yourself or are you treating me?' And he got me thinking, what kind of doctor am I? Am I going to do what I want or what my patients needs?"

Kress became one of the few doctors to speak openly about providing lethal prescriptions when testifying before the Montana state legislature. He says several patients have raised the possibility of assisted suicide with him, but he has ended up providing medication to only three patients. In each case, Kress says, he obtained a written second opinion from another doctor that the patient's condition was terminal and would result in death "in a few months or less." He also says he met with the patients several times over extended periods to make sure they understood what they were doing. Moreover, he says, he sought to make sure they could self-administer the drugs.

Kress says he checked with attorneys to make sure he was in accordance with Montana law, but he says his primary concern was fulfilling his obligation to care for his patients. "This is really an issue about aiding people in the dying process. It's not about letting people commit suicide," Kress says. "One of the questions I asked everyone was, 'If you didn't have this [terminal] disease, would you want to die, and they all universally said no.'"

Even with all such steps, some bioethicists believe legalizing physician-assisted suicide places too much power in the hands of doctors. Daniel Callahan, president emeritus of the Hastings Center, a leading bioethics research institution in Garrison, N.Y., says he become opposed to physician-assisted suicide after studying the situation in the Netherlands, where it is legal.

An anonymous survey of doctors there revealed abuses, he says, including the euthanasia of patients without their permission. "I don't like the idea of empowering physicians to do this sort of thing," Callahan says. "They're too good at it."

## BACKGROUND

### 'Robes of the Executioner'

Assisted suicide has been part of human culture since antiquity, and so have prohibitions against it, as Hippocrates' oath shows. A forerunner of Compassion & Choices was the Hemlock Society, named after the poison the ancient Greek philosopher Socrates drank to fulfill his death sentence.

In 1870, schoolteacher Samuel D. Williams was one of the first U.S. proponents of using an overdose of morphine, then a new pain-relieving drug, to assist death "in all cases of hopeless and painful illness."[16] Williams's euthanasia proposal was reprinted in newspapers and magazines over the years, creating enough of a stir that in 1885 the *Journal of the American Medical Association* attacked the idea, saying it made "the physician don the robes of the executioner."

The contemporary movement in support of assisted suicide can be traced to Derek Humphry, a British journalist, who in 1978 wrote the bestselling memoir, *Jean's*

Physician-assisted suicide supporter Jack Kevorkian talks to college students about prison reform at Detroit's Wayne State University on Nov. 29, 2007, not long after his release from prison. Nicknamed Dr. Death, the controversial pathologist spent eight years in prison following his conviction in 1999 for second-degree murder for helping in an assisted suicide. He died in 2011, at age 83, of natural causes.

*Way*, about assisting the suicide of his cancer-stricken wife. In 1991, Humphry published *Final Exit*, a how-to guide on assisted suicide that became a bestseller and has been translated into 12 languages.

Humphry, now 83, remains controversial. Critics charged that *Final Exit* could be used by anyone to commit suicide, not just the terminally ill. Humphry responded that many commonly known means of suicide existed and there was no evidence that the book had raised the suicide rate. The suicide of Humphry's second wife, Ann, after a bitter divorce in which she denounced him and the assisted-suicide movement she had previously supported, led to further controversy.[17]

Humphry believes assisted suicide should be available to more than just those with advanced terminal illnesses, but also for those with what he terms "hopeless illness," meaning debilitating and without cure, but not necessarily terminal. He acknowledges his position puts him on "the radical left" of the movement.[18] Many of the leading organizations, now focused on physician-assisted suicide for the terminally ill, have distanced themselves from his views.

Still, Humphry, who co-founded the Hemlock Society and is a past president of the World Federation of Right to Die Societies, continues to promote assisted suicide publicly and through the Final Exit Network,

## CHRONOLOGY

**1960s** *As medicine advances, the question of how long and under what circumstances life should be sustained by medical means gains new urgency.*

**1967** After watching a friend die a slow, painful death, human-rights attorney Luis Kutner writes the first "living will," specifying under what conditions a patient should be taken off life-sustaining devices. . . . A right-to-die bill fails in Florida.

**1969** The Hastings Center is founded in New York to study ethical problems in biology and medicine, including end-of-life decisions.

**1970s** *The idea that patients have a right to refuse treatment gains acceptance. In England, a best-selling memoir starts a debate about assisted suicide.*

**1973** American Hospital Association recognizes the right of patients to refuse treatment.

**1976** California Gov. Jerry Brown signs nation's first law giving terminally ill people the right to authorize withdrawal of life-sustaining medical treatment when death is imminent. Eight other states pass similar laws within a year.

**1978** British journalist Derek Humphry writes a best-seller, *Jean's Way*, a memoir about helping his terminally ill wife commit suicide, kicking off international debate.

**1980s** *Right-to-die movement gains strength; Catholic Church issues objections.*

**1980** Humphry helps form the Hemlock Society to support assisted suicide. . . . Pope John Paul II opposes "willful suicide," but supports the use of pain-relieving medicines and the right to refuse extraordinary means to sustain life.

**1988** Unitarian Universalist Association becomes first religious body to support a right to die and call for those who assist in that act to be free from criminal or civil penalties.

**1990s** *The first state approves physician-assisted suicide; Detroit physician Jack Kevorkian further spurs debate over the procedure.*

**1990** Kevorkian helps Alzheimer's patient Janet Adkins commit suicide; he will help more than 130 others die before being convicted of murder in 1999.

**1991** Washington state voters reject physician-assisted suicide.

**1992** California voters defeat a similar measure.

**1994** American Medical Association opposes physician-assisted suicide. . . . Oregon voters approve nation's first law permitting terminally ill patients to obtain a prescription to end their life; challenged in court, the law doesn't go into effect for four years.

**1997** U.S. Supreme Court rules there is no constitutional right to die, but invites states to continue debating the issue.

**2000-Present** *Three more states join Oregon in allowing physician-assisted suicide, but opponents win in Massachusetts.*

**2005** Terri Schiavo, a Florida woman who doctors say is in a persistent vegetative state, dies after her feeding tube is removed, ending a controversial seven-year battle between her husband and parents that generates international debate on end-of-life decisions.

**2008** Washington voters make the state the second to allow physician-assisted suicide.

**2009** Montana Supreme Court effectively allows physicians to provide lethal prescriptions to terminally ill patients who request it.

**2012** Massachusetts voters reject physician-assisted suicide.

**2013** Vermont House and Senate pass differing version of a physician-assisted suicide measure (April); governor indicates willingness to sign a final bill modeled on Oregon's law. . . . Vermont House approves bill legalizing physician-assisted suicide (May 13). Democratic Gov. Peter Shumlin is expected to sign the measure into law.

which provides counseling and support to individuals considering assisted suicide.[19]

If Humphry was the movement's inspiration, Dr. Jack Kevorkian was its first American celebrity. Kevorkian, a pathologist dubbed "Dr. Death," attracted national attention in the 1990s when he built devices that allowed the patient to self-administer lethal injections. At least 130 people used the devices, which allowed people to kill themselves by pulling a trigger that sent either a lethal dose of drugs or carbon monoxide into their blood. Early on, Kevorkian tried to advertise in Detroit newspapers for volunteers. Janet Adkins, who had been a college instructor, was the first. Adkins decided to kill herself on the day she was diagnosed with Alzheimer's disease and later did so in Dr. Kevorkian's van.[20] She was 54.

Kevorkian was brought to trial four times on various cases, but was acquitted three times and the fourth case was declared a mistrial. Eventually, he was found guilty of second-degree murder in a case in which he was shown on CBS' "60 Minutes" administering a lethal injection to a patient himself, after he had lost his license to practice medicine.[21] He served eight years in prison, and the conditions of his parole prevented him from participating in other assisted suicides. Kevorkian died of natural causes in 2011 at age 83.[22]

After-the-fact examinations of Kevorkian's patients found that many did not have terminal diseases, and five did not have any diseases at all.[23] His actions are cited by opponents of physician-assisted suicide as an example of the dangers of allowing the practice to spread. "He was just, in my opinion, a serial killer with an M.D.," says Greene, the retired oncologist, who participated in a review of Kevorkian's cases.

The next highly public battle over the life and death of a critically ill patient did not involve direct physician assistance, but it galvanized Americans about end-of-life decisions. Terri Schiavo, a young woman from St. Petersburg, Fla., originally suffered extensive brain damage in 1990 and doctors had diagnosed her condition as a "persistent vegetative state" by the time her husband sought to have her feeding tube removed in 1998.[24]

Her parents objected, believing her condition was not beyond hope, and went to court to have the feeding tube reinserted. The ensuing legal and political battle lasted seven more years and eventually involved several court rulings, the Florida legislature, the U.S. Congress and President George W. Bush, who flew back to Washington from a vacation to sign a law giving Schiavo's parents one last attempt to appeal their case.[25]

Schiavo's feeding tube was removed, then reinserted on a judge's order, removed again on another judge's order, then reinserted once again after the Florida Legislature passed "Terri's Law," which gave Gov. Jeb Bush authority to order the tube reinserted. The tube was removed a final time when the U.S. Supreme Court decided not to hear a final appeal of the case.[26] She died on March 31, 2005, but by then the battle had become a touchstone both for right-to-life and right-to-die advocates around the world.[27]

Coombs Lee of Compassion & Choices believes it also had an impact on the public view of physician-assisted suicide. "We were all privy to the very difficult battle that family was going through and how our politicians reacted, how completely tone-deaf they were to the real views and concerns of the public," she says. "And I think the public learned from that as well that this type of decision shouldn't be political; it's personal."

## Battle in the States

Before the Schiavo case became public, Oregon voters had made their state the nation's first to allow physician-assisted suicide. In 1993, Oregonians organized Oregon Right to Die to lobby for an assisted-suicide law, led by Portland attorney Eli Stutsman, whom Sandeen and others cite as its principal author.

The state's Death with Dignity Act was adopted after voters approved a referendum on the issue by a 51 to 49 percent margin in 1994. Because of legal challenges, however, it did not go into effect until 1998.

In 1997, opponents placed another initiative on the ballot — one that would overturn the measure — but it failed 60 percent to 40 percent. There have been no serious repeal efforts since.

In 2001 U.S. Attorney General John Ashcroft attempted to block the law by declaring that he had the authority to prevent doctors from prescribing lethal drugs through the Controlled Substances Act. But in 2006 the U.S. Supreme Court ruled against Ashcroft's claim, allowing the Oregon law to continue.[28]

Oregon's initiative, however, was not the first attempt by supporters of physician-assisted suicide to get voters

# Researchers Seek Advances in Pain Management

*"Death isn't a medical condition."*

Medicine is making advances in pain management and end-of-life care that some say may eliminate one of the reasons patients may choose assisted suicide.

Advances in the relatively new discipline of pain management known as palliative care can go a long way toward relieving unbearable pain and making people more comfortable in their last days, according to researchers.

"When we talk about palliative care, we're talking about relief of suffering," says Nancy Berlinger, who teaches ethics at the Yale School of Nursing and is co-author of *The Hastings Center Guidelines for Decisions on Life-Sustaining Treatment and Care Near the End of Life.* "The field of palliative care and hospice care has greatly taken off in the last 20 years. There are now specialized palliative care units in children's hospitals and adults' hospitals. It's still a work in progress, but it's growing."

The Center to Advance Palliative Care, based in New York City, reports that more than 1,500 hospitals now have palliative care teams — twice as many as six years ago.[1] A palliative care team includes doctors, nurses and other specialists who provide relief from the symptoms, pain and stress of serious illness.

A 2010 *New England Journal of Medicine* study found palliative care can make a significant difference in the life of patients. The study found that patients receiving early palliative care experienced less depression and survived an average of 2.7 months longer than those who did not receive the same kind of care.[2] Medical researchers also have been exploring new approaches to pain management that go beyond the typically prescribed drugs such as Oxycontin, Vicodin or morphine. Researchers at the University of Colorado in Boulder are studying the glial cells, which wrap around the neurons that transmit pain sensations and are thought to amplify chronic pain. Scientists are working on drugs that could block that effect.[3]

At Stanford University and other institutions, researchers are exploring the use of magnetic fields to cause electrical changes in the brain. The process, called "transcranial magnetic stimulation," involves putting an eight-inch electrical coil around the head. Originally developed to treat severe depression, the procedure can also reduce pain, most

to back a law. Similar efforts in Washington and California failed in 1991 and 1992, respectively. The Hemlock Society of Oregon also backed a bill in the state legislature in 1990 that failed to get out of committee. Bills introduced in several other states also failed to gain sufficient support throughout the 1990s.

In Oregon, a key figure in helping to overcome resistance to the referendum was Dr. Peter Goodwin, a physician who spoke up on behalf of the idea at a meeting of the Oregon Medical Association.

Goodwin argued in part that doctors already were taking actions to help terminally ill patients die but were acting "often without the family knowing enough, without the patient knowing enough because it's all illegal," he told ABC News. "I wanted the patient in control, not the doctor."[29]

Goodwin later recalled that after he spoke, the medical association's incoming president met his eyes as he returned to his chair. The president-to-be then took the podium and suggested to the association that they "let the people of Oregon tell us what they want." Goodwin said, "What happened then was that the Oregon Medical Association was neutral throughout the campaign, and I think that had a huge influence on the outcome."[30]

The argument that assisted-suicide laws merely illuminate what has been going on in the shadows all along has continued to be an important one for supporters. But despite their success in Oregon, proponents of similar laws did not win in another state until Washington residents approved a law based on Oregon's in November 2008.

probably by disrupting the pain signals traveling along the neurons in the brain, early results indicate.[4]

Less intrusive pain management techniques being studied focus on mental activity and biofeedback. A project at Stanford allows patients to see on a screen when the part of the brain that handles pain is activated. "They then use this information to learn to control their brain activation in a specific region associated with the processing and perception of pain," according to an article on a Stanford website.[5]

Dr. Ray Barfield, a pediatric oncologist who directs the Pediatric Quality of Life/Palliative Care Program at Duke University's Medical Center, says many new approaches being studied have great potential, especially those involving techniques to mentally manage one's own pain. "Some of the advances that we're making in hypnosis, biofeedback and medication that some people scoff at are tremendously effective," he says.

A major problem in managing pain, says Barfield, is the reluctance many doctors feel about prescribing pain drugs for fear of potential negative effects or of the patient becoming addicted. And patients often resist taking drugs they feel will dull their senses.

"One of the biggest advances that we need is not coming up with new medicines; we need to get people educated about the stuff we already have," Barfield says. "We have some good pain medicines and good experiences with them, and we still can't get people to use them the right way."

Barfield is a leading advocate for an end-of-life approach that focuses on medical interventions, pain management and careful attention to the physical and mental journey the patient is taking — the questions they need answered and the help they need facing what is happening to them.

Doctors, he believes, can get too focused on treatment as an end in itself and lose track of the larger needs of patients and their families. "Death isn't a medical condition," Barfield says. "Death is experiential. Your last day is still a day meaningful things can happen."

Combining careful attention to a patient and family's larger needs with proper palliative care and pain management, Barfield says, can "go a long way to reducing the need for [physician-assisted suicide] as an option." If palliative medicine continues to advance, he believes, that's where end-of-life care is headed.

*— Reed Karaim*

[1]"Palliative Care FACTS AND STATS," Center to Advance Palliative Care, www.capc.org/news-and-events/press-kit/.

[2]Jennifer S. Temel, *et al.,* "Early Palliative Care for Patients with Metastatic Non-Small-Cell Lung Cancer," *The New England Journal of Medicine,* 2010, www.nejm.org/doi/pdf/10.1056/NEJMoa1000678.

[3]Michelle Andrews, "Advances Against Chronic Pain," *U.S. News & World Report,* Sept. 5, 2012, http://health.usnews.com/health-news/articles/2012/09/05/advances-against-chronic-pain.

[4]*Ibid.*

[5]Sean Mackey, "The Strain in Pain Lies Mainly in the Brain," Stanford Systems Neuroscience and Pain Lab, http://med.stanford.edu/snapl/research/.

Supporters were optimistic that Massachusetts would provide a similar victory in 2012, and pre-election polls showed majority support for an assisted-suicide measure. After its defeat, supporters blamed heavy outspending by opponents. "I think it was four to one or even six to one," says Steve Crawford, who was a spokesman for the Massachusetts Death with Dignity Coalition during the campaign.

Public campaign-finance records indicate Catholic dioceses and organizations from around the country contributed heavily to opposition efforts, and supporters of the proposed law say they believe Catholic opposition made a crucial difference. "It's a very Catholic state," Crawford says. "I'm Roman Catholic myself, and I knew early on, based on some of the reaction we were getting from the Church, that they saw this as a red line [that could not be crossed] and they were going to put everything they could into defeating this question."

But opponents, especially disability-rights activists, believe Massachusetts voters changed their minds as they came to understand the lack of safeguards in the law. "The ballot question was defeated last year in large part by the antidiscrimination and social justice arguments of progressives in the disability community," says Denise Karuth, a spokesperson for Second Thoughts, a group that opposed the measure. "We described — with examples from our personal experience — how misdiagnosis, inaccurate terminal diagnoses and coercion could cause people to lose years of their lives," says Karuth, a peer counselor for people with disabilities who is, herself, a blind wheelchair user. "We were adamant that no one should ever have to die to have dignity."

Getty Images

The case of Terri Schiavo, a severely brain damaged young woman in Florida, galvanized Americans about end-of-life decisions. After doctors said she was in a persistent vegetative state, her husband sought to have her feeding tube removed in 1998. Her parents went to court to have the tube reinserted, and during a seven-year court battle Florida's legislature enacted Terri's Law, which gave Florida Gov. Jeb Bush authority to have the tube reinserted. Ultimately, the state Supreme Court ruled the law unconstitutional, and the U.S. Supreme Court declined to hear a final appeal of the case. Schiavo died on March 31, 2005.

## Global Measures

The Netherlands, Switzerland, Belgium and Luxembourg all allow assisted suicide. In all but Luxembourg, people who are not terminally ill are eligible for an assisted death if doctors agree their suffering is lasting and unbearable.

In Belgium and the Netherlands, euthanasia, in which a doctor puts a patient who requests it to death by directly administering drugs, is legal under certain conditions.[31]

The request must be made voluntarily by a patient once again suffering from a condition considered lasting and unbearable. In the Netherlands, acceptable conditions include an incurable disease or "hopeless psychological problems," according to the Radio Netherlands website.[32] A second doctor must concur in a written opinion that the patient meets the criteria.

The Netherlands law is generally considered the most liberal. U.S. opponents of assisted suicide often cite it as an example of how allowing doctors to assist in suicide can lead to more and more conditions being considered acceptable for requesting death.

The Netherlands has a series of guidelines intended to ensure that euthanasia meets the wishes and is in the best

interest of patients.[33] But Callahan, the Hastings Center president emeritus, says a survey that provided doctors anonymity found the rules were widely ignored and that "somewhere near a thousand people had been euthanized without their permission."

Hendin, of Suicide Prevention Initiatives, also spent time in the Netherlands studying its system. "The more I was there, the more I saw that end-of-life care was abysmal . . . there was no interest in end-of-life care," he says. Netherlands doctors, he says, had come to see assisted suicide and euthanasia as "a quick solution" when dealing with the dying.

U.S. supporters of physician-assisted suicide respond that the situations are not comparable. "The Netherlands is a completely different culture," says Sandeen. "The 15 years of stability with Oregon's Death with Dignity Act is what we need to look at. The law has stood the test of time. It works as written."

Political leaders in several other Western nations do not seem to share the same concerns about the record in the Netherlands or other countries where assisted suicide is legal. A recent poll in the United Kingdom found strong support for legalization, and a member of Parliament is expected to introduce such a bill later in the year.[34] Other nations, including New Zealand, along with parts of Australia, are contemplating similar measures.[35]

Cultural and religious prohibitions against assisted suicide remain strong in predominantly Islamic and Catholic countries, however, and physician-assisted suicide or euthanasia remain against the law in most of the world.[36]

## CURRENT SITUATION

### Landmark Legislation

Vermont is set to become the first state to approve physician-assisted suicide by legislation, following action by the state House on May 13. Democratic Gov. Peter Shumlin, who supported the measure, has pledged to sign it.

"I am grateful that the legislature had such a thoughtful, respectful debate on this deeply personal issue," Shumlin said. "We will now offer Vermonters who face terminal illness at the end of life a choice to control their destiny and avoid unnecessary suffering. I believe this is the right thing to do."[37]

Vermont is set to become the first state to approve physician-assisted suicide by legislation. Bills modeled after Oregon's law also have been introduced this year in Connecticut, Hawaii, Kansas, Montana, Massachussetts and New Jersey.

Several safeguards are built into the measure. Two doctors, the patient's primary physician and a second doctor, must agree the patient has a terminal illness and is able to request death-inducing drugs. The law also requires two requests for the drugs by the patient, with 15 days separating the first and second requests.

The patient must have less than six months to live, and must self-administer the drugs.

Furthermore, drugs would have to be prescribed by doctors in Vermont for state residents only, and the patient's request for drugs would have to be witnessed by two disinterested people who are not relatives or potential heirs, employees of health care facilities where the patient is being treated, nor the patient's doctor.

The Roman Catholic Diocese of Burlington fought the legislation and urged residents to press lawmakers to defeat it. "Physician-assisted suicide will forever transform the role of physician from one who preserves life to one who takes life," the diocese said in a statement earlier this year.[38]

Vermont's action would represent a landmark in the battle over physician-assisted suicide. No such law has made it through any other state legislature since the effort to legalize assisted suicide in the United States began. Vermont, however, is considered one of the nation's most liberal states, and Shumlin pledged to sign the law after it is reviewed.

Bills modeled after Oregon's law also have been introduced this year in Connecticut, Hawaii, Kansas, Montana, Massachussetts and New Jersey. Similar bills have been introduced many times in other states in the past, however, and prospects differ widely. Massachussetts lawmakers, for example, would be unlikely to pass legislation a year after a similar measure was rejected in a referendum.

After the Vermont House voted on May 13, Coombs Lee of Compassion & Choices said "this historic legislative victory proves that the aid-in-dying issue is

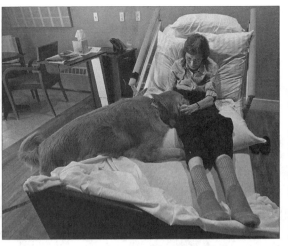

Patrick the hospice dog visits a resident on Sept. 12, 2012, at the Kaplan Family Hospice House, a 20-bed facility run by the Hospice of the North Shore & Greater Boston. The facility provides end-of-life care, along with grief resources, for terminally ill patients and their families.

no longer the third rail of politics. In fact, it's a winning issue on which Gov. Shumlin campaigned."

## In the Courts

Lawyers for Compassion & Choices served as co-counsel in the case that finally led the Montana Supreme Court to declare physician-assisted suicide legal under certain conditions in the state. The organization is pursuing a case in New Mexico that could similarly result in legalization. "This is a case brought by two physicians and a terminally ill patient that asks the court to clarify that an old criminal statute [applying to suicide] does not have application to the conduct of a physician providing aid in dying," says Kathryn Tucker, Compassion & Choices director of legal affairs. "The argument of the case is that the choice of a dying patient for a peaceful death is no kind of suicide." The New Mexico case is expected to get a hearing in December.

In Hawaii, the state chapter of Compassion & Choices is arguing the state's existing laws on patient rights and advance medical directives, along with the privacy clause in the state constitution, effectively mean that physician-assisted suicide already is legal in the state.[39] "We contend in Hawaii that patients can choose aid in dying there," says Tucker.

# Should the terminally ill have the right to assisted suicide?

## YES

**David J. Mayo, PhD.**
*Professor of Philosophy Emeritus,*
*University of Minnesota, Duluth;*
*Board Member, Death with Dignity*

Written for *CQ Researcher*, May 2013

My father, 93 and dying of colon cancer, remarked to the nurse enrolling him in hospice care that "the sooner this is over with, the better." At that point, his final life-projects were closing down. His only remaining fundamental interest and concern were the time and circumstances of his death. In Oregon or Washington state — and probably soon in Vermont — he could have ended his life peacefully, with dignity and on his own terms. As it was, he quit eating. Self-starvation struck him as his least-worst option.

Two arguments for death with dignity leap from this experience. The most intuitive derives from compassion: What possible good is served by denying escape from those final weeks of slow decline and suffering? And what horrible fear haunts many more terminal patients, not brave or determined enough to starve themselves but terrified of how their final days might play out as circumstances strip them of every shred of control? This suggests the second argument: The supreme value we place on self-determination in matters that are both private and also of fundamental concern to the individual.

Critics argue that embracing death with dignity would be a risky departure from the value we in general, and medicine in particular, place on prolonging human life — that allowing death with dignity would invite horrible abuses. But consider:

- Current law and medical practice already recognize the right of competent adults to refuse life-prolonging therapies, however trivial (for example, an antibiotic to end a life-threatening pneumonia), and even feeding tubes and hydration via IV.
- The law also recognizes a terminal patient's right to adequate palliative care, even if this requires doses of powerful analgesics high enough to hasten death by suppressing respiration. The fundamental proviso is that the earlier death must not be intended, but merely foreseen by the physician. In practice this often means the line between "optimal palliative care" and culpable homicide is drawn in terms of the invisible intentions of the physician (on which even he may not be clear). Few patients or family are informed (or ask) whether lethal doses are administered. If ever there was a situation ripe for abuse, surely this is it.
- The question of risk is always an empirical one. It's our good fortune that Oregon's 15-year experience with legalized death with dignity provides such conclusive data: The threatened abuses simply have not materialized.

As these considerations become more widely understood I expect death with dignity to gain wider acceptance.

## NO

**Daniel Callahan**
*President emeritus, The Hastings Center;*
*Co-director, Yale-Hastings Program in Ethics*
*and Health Policy; Author, The Troubled Dream*
*of Life: In Search of a Peaceful Death*

Written for *CQ Researcher*, May 2013

Few of us want to die, and no one wants to die a poor death, one marked by pain and suffering. But modern medicine has brought us to a difficult place: We now live longer than earlier generations, but there are ever more clever technological ways to prolong our dying, well beyond what we may desire. One solution to that kind of end is physician-assisted suicide, giving us the power to end our life on our own terms. And it has a common-sense attraction: "It's my body, isn't it?"

I believe it is a bad solution to an unnecessary problem. We now have good home and hospital palliative care programs, effectively able to eliminate or greatly reduce pain and suffering. Making good use of those medical skills is the hospice program, now helping more than a million persons a year receive sensitive care in dying. Physician-assisted suicide is thus rarely needed, as the citizens of Oregon and Washington state, where it is legal, have demonstrated. They make use of it in exceedingly small numbers.

But what of that minority who believe they can't be helped and who even reject hospice care? By and large, research shows, they are those mainly drawn to physician-assisted suicide by a loss of autonomy and self-control in their dying — that is, not by a medical problem but by a set of values about what they consider a life worth living. Doctors should not be empowered to provide that kind of relief, which never was and is still not a valid goal of medicine. Nor is the implicit message of physician-assisted suicide one our society needs: that suicide is a good way to deal with the suffering life can bring.

We all die. Death is not an indignity. It is simply our human fate. With the help of advance directives or the appointment of a surrogate — and a final enrollment in hospice care — the odds of dying in a really bad way have been extraordinarily reduced, even if not to the vanishing point. The most important need is to greatly reduce the present aggressive medical war against death. Greater prognostic candor on the part of doctors is needed with those clearly on the way to death even if not yet clearly dying. The good doctor is one who balances the goal of saving life and seeking a patient's peaceful death.

In 2011, Hawaii Attorney General David M. Louie issued an opinion to the contrary, saying that physicians who wrote lethal prescriptions with the intention of assisting in death could be charged with manslaughter. In 2012, however, several physicians in the state indicated their willingness to offer assisted suicide to patients to test the ruling.[40]

Compassion & Choices' emphasis on fighting in court to establish the legality of assisted suicide in states where the group believes existing laws make it possible reflects a different strategy than that of the Death with Dignity National Center.

Death with Dignity supports replicating the Oregon law in other states, including provisions that spell out the steps doctors must take before participating in an assisted suicide. Mayo, the Death with Dignity board member, says the organization believes this is the best way to make sure the procedure has adequate safeguards.

But Tucker says, "I don't think the provisions in the Oregon statute are a Holy Grail in any sense." The ruling in Montana established "three bright lines" that must be legally respected, she says. "The patient must be mentally competent and also terminally ill, and physician involvement is limited to providing a prescription."

But within these lines, Compassion & Choices argues that doctors should be able to work out the parameters of physician-assisted suicide within their professional standards, as they would any other procedure.

"Medicine is not typically governed by statute," says Tucker. "I think what is happening in Montana is reflecting the normalization of aid in dying, and that's the direction it's appropriate to go at this point in time. Will Montana doctors incorporate all the procedures there are in Oregon and Washington state? Probably not. There will be some organic evolution."

That evolution is one of the things that most worry opponents, who fear it will become too easy for people to receive medical assistance in killing themselves, even crossing the line to allow non-terminal cases to request and receive such help.

## Health Care Costs

Opponents of physician-assisted suicide argue that pressure to cut costs could make assisted-suicide more attractive to health care providers. In the Massachusetts debate, "We said, 'If private insurance companies and

Demonstrators in Paris lie in simulated body bags on Jan. 25, 2011, to protest a bill that would legalize euthanasia in France. The protest in front of the Luxembourg Gardens was organized by the Right to Life Alliance. The French Senate defeated the bill the next day, 170-142.

[health-maintenance organizations] have a choice between expensive care or a cheap lethal prescription, what do you think they will be tempted to choose?" says Karuth of Second Thoughts.

But supporters counter that there is no evidence medical costs have played a role in encouraging assisted suicide in either Oregon or Washington. "In 15 years there's not been one incidence of coercion," says Sandeen of the Death with Dignity National Center, "for the disabled or any other vulnerable population." She adds that doctors who participated in such lobbying pressure would risk losing their license.

Analysts differ over whether cost savings would be significant enough to encourage the practice. In a 2011 study, the New York State Department of Health concluded, "Under any new system of health care delivery, as at present, it will be far less costly to give a lethal injection than to care for a patient throughout the dying process."[41]

However, in a 1998 article published in *The New England Journal of Medicine*, Ezekiel Emanuel, chair of the Department of Clinical Bioethics at the Warren G. Magnuson Clinical Center, National Institutes of Health, and the University of Utah's Battin concluded, "Physician-assisted suicide is not likely to save substantial amounts of money in absolute or relative terms, either for particular institutions or for the nation as a whole."[42]

## OUTLOOK

### Young Movement

Coombs Lee of Compassion & Choices thinks the aging of the baby boom generation is likely to boost support for physician-assisted suicide in coming years. As the generation has watched its parents struggle at the end of their lives, "too many of us have witnessed really horrific deaths, and from those experiences comes a vow that this will not be how I'm meeting my death," she says. "I think there's sort of a determination to make it different for ourselves."

In 10 or 15 years, Coombs Lee contends, "There will be a growing acknowledgement that this is a medical treatment, just like disconnecting feeding tubes or providing palliative sedation."

But Callahan, the Hastings Center president emeritus, notes that resistance to assisted suicide based on religious beliefs remains strong in much of the United States, and he doesn't see that changing. "It's certainly not going anywhere very fast," he says. "If it has trouble in places like Massachusetts, it's not going to fly in places like Louisiana or Mississippi down in the Religious Belt."

However, Sandeen of Death with Dignity contends the effort to legalize assisted suicide nationwide is just getting started: "We are a very young social movement," she says. "We can really trace our roots back to 1990, and if you look at movements surrounding things like gay marriage or abortion, they go back way farther than that. . . . We look like we haven't had as many accomplishments, but give us 20 years, and we'll be there."

Karuth of Second Thoughts says people close to her and close to those she has counseled have asked, "If you really are this sick, why don't you just kill yourself and get it over with?" If assisted suicide becomes more widely available in coming years, Karuth says, more people who are seriously ill or living with disabilities will face those kinds of questions.

Hendin of Suicide Prevention Initiatives believes the future of the assisted-suicide movement depends on whether the nation makes further advances in pain management and palliative care. "If end-of-life care improves, I think the issue [of assisted suicide] is going to become irrelevant," he says. "If you had proper palliative care, I'm persuaded at least half of [the patients who have chosen physician-assisted suicide] would not have dreamed of going that way."

Although she found the narrow defeat in Massachusetts disappointing, Clish, the Massachusetts woman whose father chose assisted suicide in Oregon, thinks that because the referendum focused attention on the issue it will benefit the cause in the coming years. "People had to go and mark a box for something that most people don't even want to talk about," Clish says. "It definitely opened up a conversation, and I believe more will come of that conversation, now that we're finally talking about it."

## NOTES

1. "Washington v. Glucksberg," 521 U.S. 702 (1997), Legal Information Institute, Cornell University School of Law, www.law.cornell.edu/supct/html/96-110.ZO.html.

2. "Oregon's Death with Dignity Act — 2012," Oregon Public Health Division, January 2013, http://public.health.oregon.gov/ProviderPartner Resources/Evaluationresearch/deathwithdignityact/Pages/index.aspx.

3. "Washington State Department of Health 2011 Death with Dignity Act Report, Executive Summary," Washington State Department of Health, February 2012, www.doh.wa.gov/portals/1/Documents/5300/DWDA2011.pdf.

4. Some lawyers disagree that the Montana Supreme Court decision made physician-assisted suicide legal in the state. Most prominent is Margaret Dore, an attorney in Washington state who heads Choice is an Illusion, an organization opposed to physician-assisted suicide. However, many legal analysts have characterized the ruling as allowing the practice.

5. Kirk Johnson, "Montana Ruling Bolsters Doctor-Assisted Suicide," *The New York Times*, Dec. 31, 2009, www.nytimes.com/2010/01/01/us/01suicide.html.

6. "Large Majorities Support Doctor Assisted Suicide for Terminally Ill Patients in Great Pain," Harris Interactive, Jan. 25, 2011, www.harrisinteractive.com/NewsRoom/HarrisPolls/tabid/447/mid/1508/articleId/677/ctl/ReadCustom%20Default/Default.aspx.

7. Rita L. Marker and Kathi Hamlon, "Isn't euthanasia or assisted suicide sometimes the only way to relieve excruciating pain?" Euthanasia and Assisted Suicide: Frequently Asked questions, the Patients Rights Council, www.patientsrightscouncil.org/site/frequently-asked-questions/.

8. "To Live Each Day with Dignity: A Statement on Physician-Assisted Suicide," United States Conference of Catholic Bishops, adopted June 16, 2011, www.usccb.org/issues-and-action/human-life-and-dignity/assisted-suicide/to-live-each-day/upload/bishops-statement-physician-assisted-suicide-to-live-each-day.pdf.

9. "The Right to Die with Dignity, 1988 General Resolution," Unitarian Universalist Association, www.uua.org/statements/statements/14486.shtml.

10. Ben Matlin, "Suicide by Choice? Not So fast," *The New York Times*, Oct. 31, 2012, www.nytimes.com/2012/11/01/opinion/suicide-by-choice-not-so-fast.html.

11. Susan W. Tolle, *et al.*, "Characteristics and Proportions of Dying Oregonians Who Personally Consider Physician Assisted Suicide," *The Journal of Clinical Ethics*, Summer 2004, www.ncbi.nlm.nih.gov/pubmed/15481162.

12. Margaret P. Battin, *et al.*, "Legal physician-assisted dying in Oregon and the Netherlands: evidence concerning the impact on patients in 'vulnerable' groups," *Journal of Medical Ethics*, October 2007, www.ncbi.nlm.nih.gov/pubmed/17906058.

13. Peter Tyson, "The Hippocratic Oath Today," "Nova," March 27, 2001, www.pbs.org/wgbh/nova/body/hippocratic-oath-today.html.

14. *Ibid.*

15. "Opinion 2.211 — Physician-Assisted Suicide," American Medical Association Code of Ethics, www.ama-assn.org/ama/pub/physician-resources/medical-ethics/code-medical-ethics/opinion2211.page.

16. Ezekiel J. Emanuel, "Whose Right to Die?" *The Atlantic*, March 1997, www.theatlantic.com/magazine/archive/1997/03/whose-right-to-die/304641/.

17. Trip Gabriel, "A Fight to the Death," *The New York Times Magazine*, Dec. 8, 1991, www.nytimes.com/1991/12/08/magazine/a-fight-to-the-death.html?pagewanted=all&src=pm.

18. Biography page, Derek Humphry, www.derekhumphry.com/derek_humphry_biography.html.

19. "Our Mission," Final Exit Network, www.finalexitnetwork.org/.

20. "Jack Kevorkian," *The Economist*, June 9, 2011, www.economist.com/node/18802492.

21. Joe Swickard, Patricia Anstett and L. L. Brasier, "Jack Kevorkian sparked a debate on death," *The Detroit Free Press*, June 4, 2011, www.freep.com/article/20110604/NEWS05/106040427/Jack-Kevorkian-sparked-debate-death. Also see "Nov. 22, 1998: Kevorkian," "60 Minutes," CBS News, www.cbsnews.com/video/watch/?id=4462047n.

22. *Ibid.*

23. "Jack Kevorkian," *op. cit.*

24. Abby Goodnough, "Schiavo Dies, Ending Bitter Case Over Feeding Tube," *The New York Times*, April 1, 2005, www.nytimes.com/2005/04/01/national/01schiavo.html.

25. *Ibid.*

26. "A Timeline in the Terri Schiavo Case," *The New York Times*, April 1, 2005, www.nytimes.com/imagepages/2005/04/01/national/20050401schiavo_graphic.html.

27. "Terri Schiavo dies, but battle continues," NBCnews.com, March 31, 2005, www.nbcnews.com/id/7293186/ns/us_news/t/terri-schiavo-dies-battle-continues/#.UYNHzHArzww.

28. "The Assisted Suicide Decision," *The New York Times*, Jan. 19, 2006, www.nytimes.com/2006/01/19/opinion/19thu1.html?_r=1&hp&oref=slogin.

29. Susan Donaldson James, "Dr. Peter Goodwin, Father of Oregon Suicide Law, Takes Own Life," ABC News, March 13, 2012, (interview in video link), http://abcnews.go.com/blogs/health/2012/03/13/dr-peter-goodwin-father-of-oregon-suicide-law-takes-own-life/.

30. *Ibid.* Years later, when he was terminally ill, Goodwin took advantage of the state's assisted suicide law.

31. "Assisted suicide: Over my dead body," *The Economist*, Oct. 20, 2012, www.economist.com/ news/international/21564830-helping-terminally-ill-die-once-taboo-gaining-acceptance.

32. Belinda van Steijn, "Nine myths about euthanasia in the Netherlands," Radio Netherlands Worldwide, Feb. 29, 2012, www.rnw.nl/english/article/nine-myths-about-euthanasia-netherlands.

33. "FAQ — Euthanasia in the Netherlands," Radio Netherlands Worldwide, Sept. 29, 2009, www.rnw .nl/english/article/faq-—-euthanasia-netherlands.

34. Ruth Gledhill and Francis Gibb, "Christians back change in assisted suicide law, poll finds," *The Times* (U.K.), May 1, 2013, www.thetimes.co.uk/tto/ faith/article3752991.ece.

35. "Assisted Suicide: Over my dead body," *op. cit.*

36. "The legality of assisted suicide around the world," The Associated Press (*The Detroit Free Press*), June 4, 2011, www.freep.com/article/20110604/ NEWS07/110604004/The-legality-assisted-suicide-around-world.

37. "Vermont Legislature Approves Assisted-Suicide Bill," NPR, May 14, 2013, www.npr.org/2013/05/ 14/183896062/vermont-legislature-approves-assisted-suicide-bill?sc=nd.

38. Jacob Gershman, "Vermont Lawmakers Approve Assisted Suicide Bill," *The Wall Street Journal*, Law Blog, May 14, 2013, http://blogs.wsj.com/ law/2013/05/14/vermont-lawmakers-approve-assisted-suicide-bill.

39. Kevin B. O'Reilly, "5 Hawaii doctors offer assisted suicide to terminally ill patients," *American Medical News*, April 17, 2012, www.amednews.com/arti cle/20120417/profession/304179996/8/.

40. *Ibid.*

41. "When Death is Sought," The New York State Department of Health, April 2011, http://euthana sia.procon.org/view.answers.php?questionID=00 0207.

42. Ezekiel Emanuel and Margaret P. Battin, "What Are the Potential Cost Savings from Legalizing Physician-Assisted Suicide?" *The New England Journal of Medicine*, July 16, 1998, www.scribd .com/doc/18428440/What-Are-the-Potential-Cost-Savings-From-Legalizing-Physician-Assisted-Suicide.

# BIBLIOGRAPHY
## Selected Sources
## Books

**Ball, Howard, *At Liberty to Die: The Battle for Death with Dignity in America*, NYU Press, 2012.**
A professor of political history and law considers whether it is appropriate, legally and ethically, for a competent individual to have the liberty to decide how and when to die when faced with a terminal illness.

**Berlinger, Nancy, Bruce Jennings and Susan M. Wolf, *The Hastings Center Guidelines for Decisions on Life-Sustaining Treatment and Care Near the End of Life, Revised and Expanded Second Edition*, Oxford University Press, 2013.**
Three scholars connected to the Hasting Center, a bio-ethics institution in Garrison, N.Y., update a guide intended to help health care professionals navigate the ethical and medical decisions they might face in treating terminally ill patients.

**Hendin, Herbert, *Seduced by Death: Doctors, Patients, and Assisted Suicide*, W. W. Norton & Co., 1998.**
A psychologist and expert on suicide shares his experiences studying assisted suicide in the Netherlands and argues against legalizing the practice in the United States.

**Rollin, Betty, *Last Wish*, Public Affairs, August 1998.**
A veteran television correspondent writes about her struggle to come to terms with her terminally ill mother's wish to die and how she finally helped fulfill her wish.

**Smith, Wesley J., *Forced Exit: Euthanasia, Assisted Suicide and the New Duty to Die*, Encounter Books, 2006.**
A prolific author and journalist who writes about bioethics argues against assisted suicide and euthanasia as denigrations of the value of human life.

Wazner, Sidney, and Joseph Glenmullen, *To Die Well: Your Right to Comfort, Calm and Choice in the Last Days of Life*, De Capo Press, 2008.

The former director of Harvard Law School health services reviews the options available for making a patient's final days as comfortable as possible and defends physician-assisted suicide as one of those options.

## Articles

**"Over my dead body: Helping the terminally ill to die, once taboo, is gaining acceptance,"** *The Economist*, Oct. 20, 2012, www.economist.com/news/inter national/21564830-helping-terminally-ill-die-once-taboo-gaining-acceptance.

The British business magazine examines the international right-to-die movement and the effort to spread acceptance.

**"Why Do Americans Balk at Euthanasia Laws?"** *The New York Times*, April 10, 2012, www.nytimes.com/ roomfordebate/2012/04/10/why-do-americans-balk-at-euthanasia-laws.

In a series of short opinion pieces, supporters and opponents of physician-assisted suicide and euthanasia examine why it is more controversial in the United States than in Europe.

**Hafner, Katie, "In Ill Doctor, a Surprise Reflection of Who Picks Assisted Suicide,"** *The New York Times*, Aug. 11, 2012, www.nytimes.com/2012/08/12/ health/policy/in-ill-doctor-a-surprise-reflection-of-who-picks-assisted-suicide.html?pagewanted=all.

Opponents of right-to-die laws suggest they might be used to pressure poorer people to kill themselves to save money, but a review of patients who have used the laws finds they overwhelmingly were well educated and financially comfortable.

**Lloyd, Janice, "Support grows in Vermont for end-of-life bill,"** *USA Today*, March 22, 2013, www.usato day.com/story/news/nation/2013/03/21/death-with-dignity-vermont-laws/2003365/.

A reporter examines the efforts of supporters of physician-assisted suicide to get a bill through the Vermont legislature.

**Pickert, Kate, "A Brief History of Assisted Suicide,"** *Time*, March 3, 2009, www.time.com/time/nation/ article/0,8599,1882684,00.html.

The writer provides an overview of some of the most significant moments in the debate over assisted suicide, including the actions of Dr. Jack Kevorkian and the decision to remove Florida's Terri Schiavo from life support.

**Swickard, Joe, Patricia Anstett and L. L. Brasier, "Jack Kevorkian sparked a debate on death,"** *The Detroit Free Press*, June 4, 2011, www.freep.com/article/ 20110604/NEWS05/106040427/Jack-Kevorkian-sparked-debate-death.

The controversial life of Kevorkian, known as "Dr. Death," is reviewed by his hometown newspaper upon his death.

## Reports and Studies

**"Oregon's Death With Dignity Act — 2012,"** **Oregon Public Health Division, January 2013,** http://public .health.oregon.gov/ProviderPartnerResources/Evalu ationResearch/DeathwithDignityAct/Documents/ year15.pdf.

The Oregon law requires the state to release an annual report on patients who have requested lethal medication and on how many have subsequently used the pills.

**"Washington State Department of Health 2011 Death with Dignity Act Report,"** **Washington State Department of Health, Feb. 29, 2012,** www.doh.wa .gov/portals/1/Documents/5300/DWDA2011.pdf.

Washington provides an executive summary of its latest report on the state's Death with Dignity Act.

# For More Information

**Center to Advance Palliative Care**, 1255 Fifth Ave., Suite C-2, New York, NY 10029; 212-201-2670; www.capc.org. Works to increase the availability of quality palliative care services for people facing serious, complex illness. Website includes information for health care professionals and the general public.

**Compassion & Choices**, P.O. Box 101810, Denver, CO 80250; 800-247-7421; www.compassionandchoices.org. Advocates legalization of "assisted dying" and other end-of-life options; has 60 chapters nationwide.

**Death with Dignity National Center**, 520 S.W. Sixth Ave., Suite 1220, Portland, OR 97204; 503-228-4415; www .deathwithdignity.org/. Leads the defense of Oregon's Death with Dignity Act; promotes education about the law and supports passage and implementation of similar laws in other states.

**Disability Rights Education and Defense Fund**, 3075 Adeline St., Suite 210, Berkeley, CA 94703; 510-644-2555; http://dredf.org. Disability-rights group opposed to legalizing physician-assisted suicide.

**The Hastings Center**, 21 Malcolm Gordon Rd., Garrison, NY 10524; 845-424-4040; www.thehastingscenter.org. Nonpartisan research center that studies ethical issues in health, medicine and the environment.

**Patient Rights Council**, P.O. Box 760, Steubenville, OH 43952; 740-282-3810; www.patientsrightscouncil.org/site/. Provides information on end-of-life decisions and works with other groups to oppose physician-assisted suicide.

# ⑤SAGE research**methods**

The essential online tool for researchers from the world's leading methods publisher

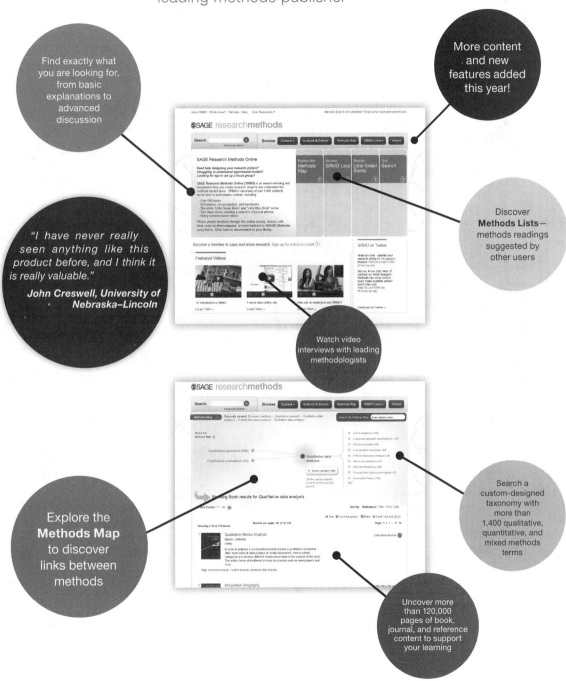

Find exactly what you are looking for, from basic explanations to advanced discussion

More content and new features added this year!

*"I have never really seen anything like this product before, and I think it is really valuable."*

**John Creswell, University of Nebraska–Lincoln**

Discover **Methods Lists**— methods readings suggested by other users

Watch video interviews with leading methodologists

Explore the **Methods Map** to discover links between methods

Search a custom-designed taxonomy with more than 1,400 qualitative, quantitative, and mixed methods terms

Uncover more than 120,000 pages of book, journal, and reference content to support your learning

# Find out more at
# www.sageresearchmethods.com